DATE DUE

MY 28 '92			

DEMCO 38-296

Minds of the New South

ROBERT F. MARTIN
Howard Kester and the Struggle for Social Justice
in the South, 1904–77

JANIS P. STOUT
Katherine Anne Porter: A Sense of the Times

WAYNE MIXON
The People's Writer: Erskine Caldwell and the South

MARK ROYDEN WINCHELL
Cleanth Brooks and the Rise
of Modern Criticism

Cleanth Brooks and the Rise of Modern Criticism

Mark Royden Winchell

University Press of Virginia

Charlottesville & London

ty Winchell

THE UNIVERSITY PRESS OF VIRGINIA
Copyright © 1996 by the Rector and Visitors
of the University of Virginia

First published 1996

∞The paper used in this publication meets the minimum requirements of
the American National Standard for Information Sciences—Permanence
of Paper for Printed Library Materials, ANSI Z39.48-1984.

Library of Congress Cataloging-in-Publication Data

Winchell, Mark Royden, 1948–
    Cleanth Brooks and the rise of modern criticism / Mark Royden
    Winchell.
        p.. cm.—(Minds of the new South)
    Includes bibliographical references and index.
    ISBN 0-8139-1647-X (alk. paper)
        1. Brooks, Cleanth, 1906–   . 2. American literature—
    History and criticism—Theory, etc.   3. English literature—History
    and criticism—Theory, etc.   4. Criticism—United States—Intel-
    lectual life—1865–   6. New Criticism.   I. Title.   II. Series.
    PS39.B74W56   1996
    809—dc20   95-46642
                                                                CIP

Printed in the United States of America

Labour is blossoming or dancing where
The body is not bruised to pleasure soul, . . .
O body swayed to music, O brightening glance
How can we know the dancer from the dance?

    —William Butler Yeats
    "Among School Children"

CONTENTS

13   A Connecticut Yankee   239

14   The Backlash   263

15   The Squire of Northford   284

16   A Postage Stamp of Soil   307

Part Five: A Moveable Feast (1964–85)

17   Albion Revisited   329

18   The Attack on Tory Formalism   347

19   A Place to Come To   368

20   Claiming Criticism   395

Part Six: Toward Sunset (1985–94)

21   Ogden Street   425

22   April Is the Cruellest Month   446

      Notes   463

      Works Cited   477

      Index   489

ILLUSTRATIONS

Frontispiece: Cleanth Brooks, 1946

Following Page 150
Brooks's maternal grandfather
Brooks's maternal grandmother
Brooks's father
Brooks's mother
Brooks and his brother, ca. 1912
Tinkum as a child
Tinkum's mother
Brooks, ca. 1928
Brooks and fellow students at Oxford, 1931
Brooks at Kenyon, 1948
Brooks, Lady Astor, and Burgess Meredith at the Library
　of Congress
Honorary Consultants in American Literature, 1958

Following Page 326
Fugitives' reunion, 1956
Brooks as cultural attaché, mid-1960s
Brooks as cultural attaché, 1965
Brooks with Evangeline Bruce and George Ballanchine,
　1965
Brooks at Allen Tate's seventy-fifth birthday party
Brooks at the U.S. Air Force Academy, 1978
Brooks, 1979
Brooks and his wife
Brooks at the fiftieth anniversary celebration of the
　Southern Review
Robert Penn Warren and Brooks at the fiftieth anniversary
　celebration of the *Southern Review*
Brooks and Warren, 1985

PREFACE

Cleanth Brooks (1906–94) was probably the most important literary critic to come to prominence during the second third of the twentieth century. In the generation before him, such pioneers as T. S. Eliot, I. A. Richards, and John Crowe Ransom helped fashion a criticism sophisticated enough to explain the radical innovations being wrought in poetry and fiction. (This approach to literary interpretation came to be called the "new criticism" simply because Ransom had given that innocuous title to a book he published in 1941.) Brooks applied the methods of this new criticism, not only to the modernist texts for which they were created, but to the entire canon of English poetry from John Donne to William Butler Yeats. In his many critical works, especially *The Well Wrought Urn* and the textbooks he edited with Robert Penn Warren and others, Brooks taught several generations of students how to read literature without prejudice or preconception. In addition to these achievements, Brooks helped invent the modern literary quarterly and wrote the best book yet on the works of William Faulkner.

Given the amount of attention that has been devoted to lesser literary figures, it is remarkable that only one full-length book—Lewis P. Simpson's *The Possibilities of Order* (1976)—has been published on Cleanth Brooks. (I am not counting a tendentious little monograph that appeared in India some years ago, but which is virtually unavailable in the Western world.) Simpson's book is a collection of biographical and critical essays by various hands. However valuable it may be, it cannot hope to serve as an extended critical biography. That is what this book attempts to be.

Because it is impossible to understand modern literary criticism apart from Cleanth Brooks or Cleanth Brooks apart from modern literary criticism, I have tried to supply an intellectual context, which sometimes veers far from the circumstances of Brooks's life. Nevertheless, that life is interesting in its own right. When Thomas Daniel Young undertook a biography of John Crowe Ransom, Robert Penn Warren told him that it was impossible to write a good book about a good man. If I had believed that myself, I would have abandoned this project long ago. Cleanth Brooks was a good man as well as a great one. For those interested in the life of the mind, he was also a profoundly interesting man.

This book would not have been possible without the assistance of many generous people. They include Ann Phillips of the Memphis Conference Archives in Jackson, Tennessee, and the reference librarians at the Special Collections of the Jean and Alexander Heard Library at Vanderbilt University, the Special Collections of the Hill Memorial Library at Louisiana State University, and the Beinecke Rare Book and Manuscript Library at Yale University. The late Mel Bradford introduced me to the University Press of Virginia and the Minds of the New South series; Jack Roper brought my proposal for this book to the attention of the press; and Richard Holway and Gerald Trett shepherded the book through production. Jeffrey H. Lockridge provided expert copyediting, while Michael Waters and Guilford Walpole rendered important editorial assistance. I am also grateful for financial assistance from the National Endowment for the Humanities and from the late Russell Kirk and his colleagues at the Marguerite Eyer Wilbur Foundation.

The following individuals consented to interviews or supplied information through letters: Randy Anderson, Carver Blanchard, Paul Blanchard, Reid Buckley, Frances Neel Cheney, George Core, Robert Drake, George and Judith Farr, George Garrett, Wade Hall, Robert B. Heilman, Hugh Kenner, Jane Ann Klock, Jonathan Leff, Andrew Lytle, Maynard Mack, Harold McSween, Louis Martz, Mrs. Merrill Moore, Harriet Owsley, John Palmer, Claude Rawson, Louis D. Rubin, Jr., Joseph M. Richardson, Lewis P. Simpson, Monroe and Betty Spears, Walter and Jane Sullivan, Alphonse Vinh, David Totman, Eugene Waith, John Michael Walsh, Rosanna Warren, René Wellek, and C. Vann Woodward.

In addition, Paul and Carver Blanchard, John Michael Walsh, and Maynard Mack all read this book in manuscript and offered valuable corrections and suggestions. Throughout this project Carver and Paul Blanchard were immensely helpful in providing information, encouragement, and generous hospitality to their uncle's biographer. On very short notice, Carver assembled the pictures in this volume, which appear with the permission of the Brooks estate.

I am also grateful beyond measure to my wife, Donna, and my sons, Jonathan and Matthew, for putting up with me during my work on this book. Donna's proofreading and her many editorial suggestions have made this a better book.

Finally, my most substantial debt is to Cleanth Brooks himself: for living such a remarkable life, for consenting to many hours of tedious tape-recorded interviews, for being a generous host, and for reading and commenting on drafts of this book even as he was dying. He combined a kind heart and a tough mind more successfully than anyone else I have ever known.

PART ONE

To Nashville and Beyond (1906-32)

CHAPTER ONE

The Road to Nashville

For seventy-five years or more after the Civil War, the rural towns of west Tennessee resembled the cultural desert H. L. Mencken described in "The Sahara of the Bozart."[1] The effects of Reconstruction were still being felt, and high culture remained a largely unattainable luxury for people who had a hard enough time putting food on their tables and clothes on their backs. Although a few fortunate families could listen to music on the Victrola, they could not hear a symphony orchestra. They had no legitimate theater, either—only popular melodramas and, much later, Saturday matinees at the local movie house. Lending libraries were few and their holdings sparse. Public schools were rudimentary and underfunded, while the private academies served only those gifted few with intellectual aspirations. It was in such an environment that the Reverend George Brooks spent almost his entire adult life.

George Kirkby Brooks, the second child of John and Susan Brooks, was born in White Pitts, Swaby Parish, Lincolnshire, England, on July 29, 1837. The son of devout Methodists, he was himself converted some time in early youth at a six o'clock prayer service and joined the church later that day. He was licensed to preach at age sixteen and, the following year, accompanied the Reverend Amos Kendell to America. He arrived in New York in 1854, traveled directly to Memphis, Tennessee, and settled soon thereafter in Hernando, Mississippi. In short order, he became a naturalized American citizen, a Methodist deacon, and finally an elder of the church. In 1860, while he was pastor of the First Church in Jackson, Tennessee, Brooks was responsible for 150 conversions. He seemed destined for a remarkable ministerial career when the Civil War broke out.

Casting his lot with the Confederacy, George Brooks helped to establish a hospital for soldiers. He was stricken with typhoid fever while in

Aberdeen, Mississippi. Despite this potentially fatal illness, he continued his service between Corinth, Mississippi, and Memphis. According to his biography in the conference records of the Methodist Church, George Brooks took two leaves of absence during his ministry. One was to recuperate in England from his illness, and the other was to fulfill an unspecified trust imposed upon him by his father-in-law, General J. J. Brooks (who was no blood relation). The conference records note that "on each return, [George] received an appointment that ranked lower than he left" (*Memphis Conference Yearbook* 1919, 105). The records also indicate that, like so many Methodist clergy of his day, George Brooks was moved by his church every year or two until, at the end of a career that spanned over forty years, he was "superannuated" on November 20, 1899, in Brownsville, Tennessee.

Apparently, George Kirkby Brooks was sustained in his difficult life by deep piety and a stoicism that often made him seem cold and aloof. What sustained his wife is less clear. The helpmeets of Methodist ministers were expected to share the hardships of their husbands' calling, while trying to raise a family in communities they would soon leave and in homes they would never own. It is no wonder that so many of these women died young. George Brooks married his first wife, Lizzie H. Brooks, in Jackson, Tennessee, in 1866 and buried her in Fulton, Kentucky, in 1894. The third of their six children was born on January 11, 1873, in Denmark, Tennessee. At the suggestion of Lizzie's mother, Mrs. J. J. Brooks, the child was named Cleanth. Despite the cultural deprivation of the region, this woman evidently knew of the ancient Athenian poet and philosopher Cleanthes or of Molière's character Clèante. At the age of twenty-one, and in the same year that his mother died, Cleanth Brooks followed his father into the Methodist ministry.

                                    I

The institution served so faithfully by George Kirkby Brooks and his son Cleanth traced its roots back to the Wesleyan reform movement in the Church of England. As has often been remarked, John Wesley lived and died an Anglican. He believed in the apostolic succession as it had been preserved within the Anglican Communion and had no intention of forming a separate church. Nevertheless, Anglican worship had become so moribund by the first half of the eighteenth century that some form of revival was necessary. Moreover, the established church was not ministering effectively to the needs of the people. The Industrial Revolution was driving too many of the peasantry away from their local parishes and into developing cities such as Leeds, Birmingham, and Liverpool, where they found themselves without a church. In large part, the Methodist movement was a pastoral response to the needs of such people.

In 1783, Wesley took the fateful step of establishing an American episcopacy when he ordained Francis Asbury and Thomas Coke as joint superintendents of the American Methodist Church. Wesley defended this break with apostolic tradition—which held that only bishops can ordain priests, much less consecrate other bishops—by consulting Scripture. As there was no legal Anglican establishment in America at the time, Wesley undoubtedly believed that the only way his movement could be preserved in the new republic was through a denominational structure all its own. (In the wake of the Revolution, most American Methodists probably saw the Church of England as a Tory institution anyway.) As High Church as Wesley may have been in many of his personal beliefs, the movement he spawned in America was Protestant, evangelical, and fiercely independent.

The southern branch of the Methodist Church took its role as moral teacher quite literally and became a major force in both theological and secular education. In 1854, for example, its quadrennial conference called for a convention of leading Methodist educators. This group, which met in Nashville in April 1856, formed the Educational Institute of the Methodist Episcopal Church, South—a group that met annually to improve textbooks, raise larger college endowments, and provide special training for teachers. It was within this group, according to Paul K. Conkin, that the "dream of a great Methodist university in Nashville" first matured (Conkin, *Ivy*, 3).

As the location of both the publishing house and the missionary board of the Southern Methodist Church, Nashville was the logical site for the denomination's central university—an institution "capable of providing advanced training for the graduates of the thirty or so struggling colleges supported by the annual conferences of the church" (Conkin, *Ivy*, 3). Although this dream was deferred by the Civil War, it finally became a reality when, in 1873, Methodist bishop Holland N. McTyeire persuaded Commodore Cornelius Vanderbilt to endow the university that would bear his name. (Vanderbilt was neither a southerner nor a Methodist, but his second wife—a distant relative of McTyeire—was both.) The presence of Vanderbilt University in Nashville would continue to shape the educational ethos of the state and region for years to come. In no small part, the gospel of a Vanderbilt education was spread by its alumni, a group that included the Reverend Cleanth Brooks, who attended the university from 1891 to 1894, when its distinction and piety were both beyond question.

II

After leaving Vanderbilt in 1894 (he would not actually complete the requirements for his degree until 1903), Cleanth Brooks was admitted on trial as a minister of the Memphis Conference of the Methodist Episcopal Church, South. The region encompassed by this conference (which is the jurisdictional equivalent of a diocese in the Roman Catholic or Episcopal Church) covered west Tennessee and southern Kentucky. In a pattern that would be repeated often during the thirty years he served in the conference, Brooks was appointed to the Buena Vista Mission in Carroll County, Tennessee, in 1894 and transferred the following year to the Station Church in Columbus, Kentucky. After serving what amounted to a two-year apprenticeship, Brooks was admitted into "full connection" with the Memphis Conference at its annual meeting held in Jackson, Tennessee, on November 18–23, 1896.

While serving in Columbus, Kentucky, Cleanth Brooks married May Browder, a native of Fulton, Kentucky, on June 12, 1895. (May's distant relative Earl Browder would run for president on the Communist Party ticket in 1948.) The bride was over two months shy of her twentieth birthday. The newlyweds remained one more year in Columbus before being transferred south to the Gleason Circuit in Tennessee in 1897. The following year found them in the First Church of Bolivar, Tennessee, and the year after that, nineteen miles farther south in Grand Junction, near the Mississippi border. After another year in Grand Junction, the Brookses moved forty-four miles north to Henderson, in 1901. Two years later, they were transferred seventeen miles east to the Campbell Street Church in Jackson. Although none of the moves in Tennessee was over a great distance, all involved leaving newly made friends and setting up house in a new environment. During the nine years of their marriage, the Brookses produced four children—Elizabeth, John Kirkby, Mary, and Ruth.

On December 8, 1904, May Brooks died in the Campbell Street parsonage. Her obituary in the Memphis Conference minutes for 1905 does not indicate the cause of death, but it does mention "the devotion of friends and tenderest nursing and most skillful medical treatment and earnest prayers." In addition to her family responsibilities, she had assumed the burdens of a preacher's wife, working in the Sunday school, the Epworth League, and the various women's societies of the church. Her funeral, which was conducted by the Reverend J. W. Blackard, drew an overflow throng of mourners. Approximately two weeks before Christmas 1904, May Browder Brooks was buried in the Hollywood Cemetery in Jackson.

One can imagine the grief of a young husband who had to watch an even younger wife die, but such experiences were not uncommon in that age and in that region. Moreover, Cleanth Brooks's duties as both pastor and father left little time for the luxury of mourning. The following year brought him a new ministerial assignment, in Murray, Kentucky, and a new wife in Bessie Lee Witherspoon. Like her husband, the new Mrs. Brooks was a native of Madison County, Tennessee. She had been born on August 5, 1882, the daughter of William and Elizabeth Weir Witherspoon. Like her predecessor, Bessie Lee Witherspoon Brooks accepted the peripatetic life of a Methodist minister's wife. She was apparently a devoted and loving stepmother. She was also the sort of housekeeper who would leave a parsonage cleaner than she had found it. But she was her own woman, as well. Church work was not suited to her, and she resisted becoming an extension of her husband's vocation.

As west Tennesseans, the Brookses lived in a region quite different from the rest of their state. Opening up to the Mississippi River, it was the threshold of the American frontier and part of what used to be called the "Old Southwest." It is significant that when one of America's most legendary folk heroes, Davy Crockett, first became a national figure it was as a politician from west Tennessee. While serving in the state legislature, Crockett had been ridiculed by a lawmaker from east Tennessee because of his backwoods dress and uncouth manner. Seizing the political advantage, Crockett parlayed his rustic image into a seat in Congress and a ghostwritten autobiography. Following martyrdom at the Alamo and apotheosis in song, tall tale, and celluloid myth, this bumpkin from west Tennessee became better known and more revered than all but a handful of American presidents.

At the dawn of our own century, another west Tennessean joined the ranks of the immortals. With Frederick Jackson Turner's announcement of the close of the frontier in 1893, the nation looked for legends more suitable to the modern technological age. They found one in a railroad engineer from Jackson, named John Luther "Casey" Jones. On the evening of April 29, 1900, Jones pulled his northbound train into Memphis for what should have been the end of his shift. But when the engineer who was supposed to make the southbound run to New Orleans turned up sick, Casey not only volunteered to take the man's place but vowed to make up for lost time. Thundering into Vaughn, Mississippi, at the incredible speed of seventy miles per hour, he spotted some unexpected railroad cars in his path; by staying with his engine to reduce its speed, Jones averted what might have been an even worse disaster. When his body was found, one hand was clutching the throttle and the other the air-brake control. A few years later, Jones's heroism was celebrated in what has become one of our greatest folk songs. For decades thereafter, his widow continued to live in Jackson, Tennessee, which now houses a railroad museum bearing his name.

Davy Crockett and Casey Jones are both figures who loom larger in legend than they ever did in life. Their popularity reflects an American fascination with two seemingly contradictory character traits—an iconoclastic sense of personal independence and an unswerving fidelity to duty. It is also worth noting that Crockett and Jones are better remembered for how they died than for anything they had done earlier in life. An American society that presumably worships success has always found room in its pantheon of heroes for a few magnificent losers. This is particularly true of the South, where the morale of an entire region has been sustained by the myth of a glorious and undeserved defeat. Certainly, southerners would agree with T. S. Eliot that there are no lost causes because there are no gained ones. That philosophy is borne out in the life of a west Tennessean considerably less famous than either Davy Crockett or Casey Jones— Bessie Lee Brooks's father, Confederate Lieutenant William Witherspoon.

III

Bill Witherspoon was twenty-one years old when the state of South Carolina fired on Fort Sumter. Enlisting in a Madison County company that joined the Seventh Tennessee Cavalry, Witherspoon fought for the autonomy of his home region under the command of General Nathan Bedford Forrest. Himself a native of Madison County, which was then part of the west Tennessee backwoods, Forrest was a unique figure in the Confederate army. Unlike Lee, Stuart, and others, he was neither a patrician nor a professional soldier. Forrest was the eldest son of eleven children and, after his father's death when Nathan was sixteen, the sole support of his mother and siblings. The family lived on a rented farm and subsisted on hard manual labor. Forrest acquired his skill with arms not at West Point but "in what Napoleon termed the best of military schools—that of poverty" (Wolseley, 27). Forrest achieved a modicum of economic comfort through horse dealing and slave trading and had become a man of standing in his own community when the War of Secession broke out. Barely literate, he knew no grand military strategy but led by fearless example. His intuition and courage brought him victories denied to more learned and cautious officers.

Bill Witherspoon fought with Forrest at the Battle of Tishomingo Creek (better known as the Battle of Bryce's Cross Roads) in 1864 and published his reminiscences forty-two years later in an attempt to earn enough money to attend Confederate reunions. Although scholarly accounts of that battle have been published before and since, Witherspoon's perspective is that of the ordinary soldier. Through his eyes, we see Forrest ordering his men to throw burning beds off wagons the Yankees have set on fire. When one lieutenant fails to respond on the grounds that he is an officer, Forrest rides at him with his sabre drawn, yelling, "I'll officer you!" (Witherspoon, 127). Employing brilliant guerilla tactics, Forrest's men carry the day against a much better armed enemy force over four times as large.

In another Civil War memoir, this one published in 1910, Witherspoon recalls that in 1861 he volunteered for a spy mission to Madison County, which was then occupied by Federal troops. After eating dinner at his own home, he and a companion, Allen Shaw, were apprehended by a company of the Second Illinois Cavalry. Knowing that he would be hanged if he were judged a spy, Witherspoon outsmarted his captors with a fiendishly clever job of acting. Playing upon certain Northern stereotypes of the South, he pretended to be an ignorant country boy who had been conscripted into fighting by wealthy slave owners. He claimed that when captured he was fetching a doctor (his companion Shaw) for a sick old woman called "Granny." He asked that he simply be allowed to return home to Pa and Ma with his faithful farm horse Charley. Not only did Witherspoon gain his own release and the return of his horse, but before leaving enemy custody, he even engaged his captors in a card game to win back his pistols. One need not doubt the veracity of this memoir to note how much it reads like humor of the Old Southwest. Once again, the supposed country hayseed has hoodwinked the Northern sophisticate.

If Witherspoon's spy narrative recalls an older tradition in southern literature, one striking passage in it seems to anticipate the later Southern

Renascence. Pondering the use to which he would now put guns that for-
merly had killed squirrels and rabbits, Witherspoon writes:

> Now it was for different game, a two-legged biped, who had come down in
> our Southland, regarding us as barbarians, one type removed from the
> wild horde of Aborigines that once roamed our country, teaching what
> constituted a higher civilization, by entering our homes, abusing and in-
> sulting those we had left at home, unable by the decree of nature, unable
> on account of sex and age (our mothers, daughters, sisters, and sweet-
> hearts, our fathers decrepid [sic] with age and boys too young) to shoulder
> the musket to defend what is dear and first in the heart of every true citi-
> zen, his home. (Witherspoon, 88)

In theme and syntax that sentence could very easily have been spoken by
Faulkner's Colonel Sartoris.

Witherspoon concludes his Civil War reminiscences with a comparison
between himself and his grandfather John Witherspoon, who served under
Francis Marion, the great cavalry leader of the Revolutionary War. Like
his grandfather, Bill Witherspoon fought to defend his home against what
he regarded as aggression from a central government. Like his grandfather, he furnished his own horse and squirrel gun. "My grandfather was
proud of the term 'Rebel,'" the later Witherspoon writes. "I may have the
love for the term 'Rebel' by inheritance, yet I love it and will so teach my
children. I simply look at it that my grandfather in 1776 and myself in
1861 were standing in the same shoes" (136). William Witherspoon continued standing in those shoes until his death on November 10, 1923. Well
into the twentieth century, this gaunt old man with a bushy white beard
could be found at his home in Jackson, Tennessee, telling stories of past
glory and playing seemingly endless games of chess.

                    IV

On October 16, 1906, Cleanth and Bessie Lee Brooks became the parents
of a son they named Cleanth, Jr. Although the place of his birth was Murray, Kentucky, the family moved eight more times during his childhood
and early adolescence. Over eighty years later, Cleanth, Jr., would recall
"a life of genteel poverty in a Methodist parsonage . . . ; the necessary
counting of pennies; the worry when mid-autumn arrived and the pastoral appointments were read out and our family found out that we
would stay on at least one more year in the town in which we were then

living and would not have to move a hundred miles away, with new friends to make and a new school to attend" (Brooks, *Community*, 146–47). Cleanth, Jr.'s, later reverence for a sense of place in both literature and life is at least in part a function of the rootlessness of his childhood.

The one constant factor during these childhood years was the family unit itself. In addition to his father and mother, there were three half-siblings (Ruth, a daughter from Cleanth, Sr.'s, first marriage, had died in a fire before Cleanth, Jr., was born) and a brother named William, who was born in February 1908. Although the communities in which the family lived were the sort that H. L. Mencken disdained, the Brooks family itself was well-read by anyone's measure. Brother Brooks (as Cleanth, Sr., was known to his parishioners) loved books and delivered extraordinarily literate sermons. His son remembers that by the time he was five his father was reading to him from such tales as *Robinson Crusoe, The Swiss Family Robinson*, and *The Iliad*. In fact, the first book he ever owned was a prose translation of *The Iliad*.

If Cleanth, Jr.'s, love of literature came early, his critical sensibility was a later acquisition. As a child reading, he looked not for paradox, irony, and metaphor but for plot, excitement, and adventure in his reading. His boyhood favorites included tales of military valor from King Arthur to the Civil War. (He enjoyed visiting Grandfather Witherspoon in Jackson and hearing the old man recall the battles he had fought with Forrest.) Although there was plenty of poetry in his father's library, young Cleanth found it dry and dull. When he tried his own hand at creative writing, he produced a story set in England. Upon proudly showing it to his Grandfather Brooks, the lad was informed that some of the terms he used gave him away as not being British. This was Cleanth Brooks's first encounter with literary criticism.

One of young Cleanth's favorite childhood books was Alfred Ollivant's classic *Bob, Son of Battle*. Ollivant was a British soldier who had been thrown by his horse in 1893 and so badly injured that he remained a cripple for many years. During his long and painful convalescence, he turned to writing, drawing on childhood memories of the sheep land of north England. *Bob, Son of Battle* is the story of two sheepmen, each with a famous collie. Adam M'Adam is an arrogant and scheming little Scotsman, whose dog Red Wull is called "Tailless Tyke" because its tail has been cut off. James Moore of Kenmuir owns Owd Bob, a collie of very distinguished ancestry. When sheep are killed throughout the region ex-

cept on land owned by M'Adam and Moore, suspicion begins to settle on
Bob and Tyke. As one might imagine, Bob weathers the false accusations
and eventually helps to expose the actual rogue dog.

Although Cleanth, Jr., was too young to remember Murray, Kentucky,
or Milan, Tennessee (where the family lived in 1907 and 1908), he does
recall spending 1909 and 1910 in Collierville, Tennessee. In 1911 his father became pastor of the Mississippi Boulevard Church in Memphis,
where young Cleanth saw streetcars for the first time. The following year
brought the family to Lexington, Tennessee, where Cleanth, Sr., was
presiding elder of the district. Cleanth, Jr., remembers returning with
his brother William and their father one afternoon to their home in Lexington. Although they could sense their father's apprehension and his
eagerness to see his wife and house, they did not realize at the time that
a tornado had done considerable damage on the other side of town.
Brother Brooks was visibly relieved to find his wife safe and his parsonage
unharmed.

In many respects, Mayfield, Kentucky, was the first real home that
Cleanth, Jr., knew. He was seven when his family first moved there in
1913, and they remained there for three years. Mayfield was where the
family acquired its first car (a Dodge) and where young Cleanth learned
how to play baseball and football. (As he later told me, a boy with thick
glasses and a name such as Cleanth had to play sports just to avoid merciless teasing.) The childhood games would sometimes include boys of
both races. Although blacks were viewed as social inferiors, there was no
racial hatred in the Brooks household. Blacks were called "niggruhs" (not
"neegrows," as in the North) instead of "niggers," and the Brooks children were taught to treat them with paternalistic regard. Cleanth, Jr., recalls his father's belief that in the black race America had been blessed
with the best peasantry of any land.

The virtues of religious tolerance were also taught in the Brooks household. Cleanth, Sr., was firm enough in his own faith not to need to reinforce it by condemning those who believed differently. In fact, in 1913, he
headed a committee in the Memphis Conference that vigorously censured
the persecution of Jews in Russia. In its report, the committee declared
"that as men and Christians we are indignant that any government in this
humanitarian age, or any church which claims the name of Jesus, Son of
Mary, and Son of God, should abase itself by giving support to such a race
bitterness and persecution especially against that great family from which,

in His earthly lineage, came Jesus, our Lord" (*Memphis Conference Minutes* 1913, 68).

Cleanth, Jr., was over two months shy of his eighth birthday and bedridden with diphtheria when world war broke out in Europe. Because of his youth and the remoteness of rural Tennessee from the European front, he was largely unaffected by the conflict. He remembers only that his father was staunchly pro-British and opposed to the prolonged neutrality of the Wilson administration. Because of his illness, young Cleanth had considerable time to follow the war (including the "Rape of Belgium") in the local newspapers. It was not until years later, when he would read revisionist accounts of the conflict, that he would begin to question his youthful jingoism. By then, he had abandoned his childhood desire to become a soldier like Grandfather Witherspoon.

The Brookses returned to Collierville, Tennessee, in 1917. Some of the boys from Memphis, only fourteen miles away, regarded the people of Collierville as little more than hicks. This big city condescension proved somewhat embarrassing when the Boy Scouts held a competition that included troops from Memphis and the outlying regions. The skills being judged included flag signaling, knot tying, and other scouting lore. When the points were totaled, the boys from Collierville had a higher overall score than any of the troops from Memphis. Their cause was aided by Cleanth Brooks, Jr., who had spent weeks learning how to tie every knot in the Boy Scout manual. He was chided, however, for being too bashful to shout out his name when he finished tying a knot and for almost having his efforts overlooked.

In 1914, while still living in Mayfield, Kentucky, Brother Brooks was appointed Secretary of Education for the Memphis Conference. During the next five years, he held no pastorate but traveled the conference in an effort to advance the cause of education. Because of his scholarly predilections, he was well suited for the job. At the same time, he couldn't help being concerned about the quality of education his own children were receiving. Because conference assignments were made in November of each year, he had seen his children continually uprooted from public schools they had just entered in September. Under the circumstances, it was remarkable that Cleanth, Jr., did as well as he did. By the time the boy was thirteen, his father was encouraging him to think about eventually applying for a Rhodes Scholarship. In order to compete for such an honor, however, young Cleanth would need better training than he could get in the

public high schools. Consequently, in the fall of 1920, he was sent to the
McTyeire School in McKenzie, Tennessee.

V

The institution that would become the McTyeire School began as Caledonia College in 1858. Established in the town of Caledonia in Henry
County, Tennessee, it was chartered in 1860 but soon closed when its faculty and students went to war. With its buildings burned during the war,
the school was moved in 1867 to McKenzie, a railroad crossing in Carroll
County. There it was supported by the local Methodist church and was
known for the next twelve years as McKenzie College. In 1879 its president, Edwin B. Chappell, persuaded the school's board of trustees to stop
awarding "college" degrees, to make the school preparatory to Vanderbilt
and similar universities, and to change its name to McTyeire Institute.

In 1899 James A. Robins and R. Grier Peoples (both of whom were
graduates of Vanderbilt) assumed the joint principalship of the institute—
now called "McTyeire School." After the departure of Peoples in 1902,
Robins became sole principal, a position he held until the school closed in
1931. According to William O. Batts: "At the close of the First World War,
when Robins returned after a year's absence with the YMCA in France,
he found an aroused constituency with plans for equipping a new
McTyeire on a more permanent basis. A more widely distributed board of
trustees, composed largely of alumni of the school, was duly elected; and
plans were made for ample grounds and buildings beautifully located on
the outskirts of the town" (Batts, 40–41).

In addition to intellectual attainments, schools such as McTyeire
stressed the development of character. This was effected not only through
a strict code of discipline but through the example of teachers who took
the doctrine of in loco parentis very much to heart. The dominant presence at the McTyeire School during the years of Cleanth Brooks's attendance (and, indeed, for the last thirty years of the school's existence) was
James Robins—known to generations of students simply as "Mr. Jim." In
a brief sketch published more than fifty years after his own graduation
from McTyeire, former Vanderbilt football coach Ray Morrison recalled
some of Mr. Jim's methods of discipline. If a boy were late for school without a sound excuse, he would be required to be at Robins's home each
morning for up to a week to accompany the headmaster to class and
everywhere else he went (Morrison, 20–22).

The schedule of classes at McTyeire was determined not by the ringing of Pavlovian bells but by the eccentric rhythms of Mr. Jim's own day. He simply kept his boys until he was done with them. Class might end at three o'clock in the afternoon, but if the assignment was difficult, or Mr. Jim had been delayed by sighting a species of warbler not often seen in Tennessee, it could drag on until six in the evening. As Cleanth reminisced seven decades later:

> The members of the senior class of the McTyeire School would be sitting—if it was a mild October—out in the open in our split bottom chairs, perhaps discussing a difficult passage in the Virgil assignment, or more likely, speculating on how we were going to come out of the football game with our old rival, McFerrin, next Saturday. Then someone would sight Mr. "Jim" walking up the hill, his bird glasses in hand, a little late today, but not hurrying to take charge of our Latin class: the headmaster never hurried. Someone would sing out, "Fourth year Latin is up; Fourth year Latin's up." ("McTyeire School," 1)

Robins believed in the character building power of athletics and required every boy to take part in some team sport. During the later years of his life, he made his home on the Vanderbilt campus (where years before he had been an undergraduate at the same time as Cleanth Brooks, Sr.) and became something of a fixture at campus athletic events. He sat on the bench at home football games, often accompanied the team to away games, and rarely missed a practice. Ray Morrison recalls that "one day in the football dressing room at the stadium a player remarked that he was having trouble understanding his college algebra. 'Mr. Jim' heard him and took him in the coaches' room and there on the blackboard instructed him for half an hour. The boy later told the coach he learned more algebra in that thirty minutes than he had in the fall term" (Morrison, 21).

In addition to being a learned man, Mr. Jim was the sort of mild eccentric who is most easily tolerated in a regional culture. Along with bird watching and athletics, he was fascinated by the lore of calendars. At one time or another, his charges learned everything there was to know "about the Roman calendar and its connection with our own." Mr. Jim took great delight in telling his students on February 22, 1922, that they "should all write letters home with a date composed of the same digit five times repeated: thus, 2/22/22" ("McTyeire School," 8). This would be the last time in the century that they could do so, as March had only thirty-one days, not thirty-three.

Beneath the mirth and eccentricity, there was a Victorian earnestness about Mr. Jim's approach to life and learning. Cleanth was not at all surprised that "Rugby Chapel," Matthew Arnold's tribute to his father, Thomas, was the headmaster's favorite poem, because Mr. Jim's character was so much like that of Thomas Arnold. Matthew may have made a religion of poetry, but his father remained a staunch defender of the Protestant faith. By the same token, Jim Robins was a quiet but committed Methodist, whose belief was too deep to require evangelical histrionics. "I see him now as a saint," Cleanth writes, "one of that not inconceivable band of provincial saints that the South produced around the turn of the last century, the kind that often impress only a small group of people in a small community and who are soon forgotten, because they left no permanent work. They did not publish a book nor build a building. They worked in a more fragile and impermanent material, for they worked to build men" ("McTyeire School," 10–11).

Cleanth later discovered that the instruction he received at McTyeire had been comparable to what he would have had in a British "public school." The curriculum consisted of four years each of English, mathematics, and Latin, three of Greek, and one of United States history. (Because there were no laboratories, there was no instruction in science, and the study of modern languages was still a thing of the future.) In a typical language class, the seats made up a numbered row (the numbers were drawn from a bowl). The students were then called upon to translate passages. Those who did so successfully moved up in the hierarchy; those who did not fell back. The object was to see how many "firsts" one could accumulate during the course of a term. This meant moving literally to the head of the class. If one could remain at the head during an entire class session, he would earn a "distinction" next to his name. He would begin at the foot of the class the next day and try to work his way to the top again. In less than thirty years, that tiny rural school produced three Rhodes Scholars. Many colleges using more "advanced" pedagogical methods have not done nearly so well.

Ironically, the subject that Cleanth recalls as being the most poorly taught at McTyeire was English. The native speaking writers generally paled in comparison to the noble pagans read in Greek and Latin class. The British and American scribes favored by Mr. Jim and company were mostly Victorians taught for moral instruction. But there were some surprising exceptions. Cleanth and his classmates "listened to 'The Fall of the House of Usher,' but . . . also heard such amusing skits as John Kendrick Bangs's 'Houseboat on the Styx' or Thomas Bailey Aldrich's 'Marjorie

Daw'" ("McTyeire School," 9). They also read verse by the black poet
Paul Laurence Dunbar.

During Cleanth's years at McTyeire the school had between fifty and
sixty students. Most of these were boys, and about half were boarders. As
one of the boarders, Cleanth was living away from home for the first time
(returning home during the school year only for the Christmas holidays).
The adjustment proved difficult. When his father visited him after he had
been at the school for only a few weeks, he appeared so dejected and
homesick that the elder Brooks offered to take him home. Tempted as he
might have been to accept his father's offer, young Cleanth persevered,
even though he was not yet committed to the life of the mind. Perhaps in
part because of the popularity of debate at McTyeire, he thought that he
probably would become a lawyer.

Where he would go to pursue his education after prep school was still
an open question. Although he had family and regional ties to Vanderbilt,
Emory and Trinity (which would later become Duke) were also excellent
southern universities with a Methodist tradition. What finally caused
Cleanth to choose his father's alma mater was the visit of a deputation
team of Vanderbilt undergraduates recruiting able secondary school students who had not yet made their college choice. One member of this
team, a junior named Saville Clark, who would later become a career
Marine officer stationed for a time at Hiroshima, so impressed Cleanth
that he decided not only to go to Vanderbilt but to room with Clark his
freshman year.

As studious as he was, Cleanth Brooks maintained normal interests
outside the classroom during his years at McTyeire. In addition to debate,
his favorite extracurricular activity was football. Although the boys were
incredibly light by today's standards, they played hard and were devoted
students of the game. During Cleanth's junior year the most experienced
player was not the quarterback but the left tackle. So, the coach con-
founded the opposition by having the tackle call every play from the line
of scrimmage. During a game against Grove High School of Paris, Tennessee, the McTyeire coach sent his team out with four set plays. They were
to run these four plays in succession (the huddle had yet to be invented),
provided they continued to gain yardage. This strategy so unnerved Grove
High that McTyeire won the game, 92-0.

McTyeire's football coach, "Puss" Puryear, was also a Latin teacher.
As committed as he was to victory on the playing field, Puryear was even
more demanding in the classroom (a sort of combination Bear Bryant and

Mr. Chips). When he discovered that his third-year Latin class couldn't handle its assignments very well, he lengthened the morning class. When that didn't work, Puryear kept them in late in the afternoon—day after day. Cleanth recalls that the rest of the team would be out on the field, passing and punting, waiting for their coach and remaining teammates to show up. "But when 45 minutes had passed and still no coach and no junior players, we fell back on our own resources. We ran signals and formations with what of the squad were present. Even if next Saturday's game loomed up, the coach was adamant. No practice for the delinquents until they could do their assignment" ("McTyeire School," 12).

Although he weighed only 135–140 pounds and suffered from poor eyesight, Cleanth was an important member of the football squad. He was a substitute as a sophomore, a starter as a junior, and captain of the team his senior year. As this was before the two-platoon system, he played left end on defense and fullback on offense. Despite being primarily a blocking back, he scored three touchdowns in his career—one after catching a forward pass. To the end of his days, Cleanth kept the letter he earned in football among his most prized possessions. Joseph Epstein has written that "in the neighborhoods in which I grew up, being a good athlete was the crowning achievement; not being good at sports was permitted, though not caring at all about sports, for a boy, was a certain road to unpopularity" (Epstein, 143). Although Epstein is talking about Chicago, what he says is equally true of the South, where football has long run a close race with evangelical Christianity as the dominant religion of the region.

During the 1920s, Vanderbilt University was an ideal environment for any southern boy who cared about football. Under coach Dan McGugin, Vanderbilt had had the most formidable team in the South from 1904 to 1913 and, after a few years of mediocrity, was again achieving regional dominance. In comparison to the gridiron excitement and general party atmosphere on campus, the after-hours literary activity of a few young English professors and students must have paled to insignificance. Cleanth Brooks recalls that when he left prep school for college in 1924, Vanderbilt seemed one of the least intellectual places imaginable.

CHAPTER TWO

The Campfire Still Glowing

The year 1924 was a boom time in America. Four years earlier, the voters had endorsed a "return to normalcy" by electing Warren G. Harding and Calvin Coolidge president and vice president over James M. Cox and Franklin D. Roosevelt. Apparently believing that you can't get too much of a good thing, they made Coolidge president in his own right in 1924. That was also the year that an Illinois halfback named Red Grange became the first superstar in college football by scoring four touchdowns in twelve minutes. For this feat, he was dubbed the "Galloping Ghost" by the legendary sportswriter Grantland Rice, who was himself a Vanderbilt alumnus. The Pulitzer Prize in Poetry went to Robert Frost's *New Hampshire*. Margaret Wilson's *The Able McLaughlins* won the award in fiction. A young resident of Oxford, Mississippi, named William Faulkner published his first book, a volume of verse called *The Marble Faun*. And approximately 130 miles southeast of Nashville, a biology teacher named John T. Scopes began what would prove to be an eventful school year in Dayton, Tennessee.

The dominant force in the Vanderbilt English department in 1924 was its head Edwin Mims. A social progressive, a theological liberal, and a humanist of the Matthew Arnold school, Mims was one of the most prominent figures in what Michael O'Brien calls the "middle years" of southern intellectual history—the decades between Appomattox and the modern Southern Renascence. "Born when Grant was in the White House, he died worrying whether John Kennedy was too young to run for the presidency" (O'Brien, "Middle Years," 133). Next to William P. Trent, Mims was probably the most significant literary critic teaching in a southern university from the turn of the century until World War I. His theatrical presence in the classroom instilled a love of literature in generations of undergraduates, one of whom endowed a chair in his name nearly three decades after his death.

As a child of the Victorian era, Edwin Mims was very much a man of his time. Although he shunned the old-line philology, he was not ready to embrace the new aestheticism. Believing in social progress and moral uplift, he stressed those values in the poetry of Browning and Tennyson (neither of whom died until Mims was an undergraduate) and required his students to memorize a thousand lines or more of verse. Like Henry Adams, Mims had been greatly impressed by the 1893 World's Fair in Chicago and its vision of a technologically advanced future. But unlike Adams, Mims did not retreat into a romantic medievalism. Although he had little understanding of technology, he was convinced that it would pave the way to a more prosperous world from which even literary folk might benefit. In a letter to his future wife, Mims wrote: "When we have absorbed all the good results from material advancement, when science has done its work, then the old world will seek a new and larger life in some things that science and materialism have kept down in this age" (see O'Brien, "Middle Years," 139).

I

Like so many progressive department heads, Edwin Mims brought in brilliant young professors who eventually outshone him. By far the most prominent of these was a Vanderbilt alumnus and Rhodes Scholar named John Crowe Ransom. Because Ransom would later become such a fixture in the literary history of the twentieth century, it is difficult not to think of him as having been born at around age sixty. In point of fact, Ransom was something of a child prodigy. The son of a Methodist parson in Pulaski, Tennessee, he was tutored at home until he was ten. After attending public school for one year, he matriculated at the Boman prep school in Nashville, where he completed a curriculum in the classics that enabled him to enter Vanderbilt when only fifteen.

During Ransom's undergraduate years, the typical candidate for a Vanderbilt B.A. took half his courses in English, philosophy, and the classical and modern languages. (Students were required to have had some Greek and Latin simply to be admitted.) Despite a brief period of distinction in the 1890s, Vanderbilt was in decline during Ransom's undergraduate years. (This was particularly true of the English department, which was then languishing in mediocrity.) Nevertheless, Ransom picked up enough classical training to earn a B.A. at Oxford while spending half his time playing golf, tennis, chess, and various card games. On a 3–2 vote of his examiners, he missed being awarded the first-class honors he might have won through more disciplined study.

When Ransom returned to Vanderbilt as a young instructor in 1914, the university had just won a court case that led to its independence from the Methodist Church. Although finances and academic quality remained continuing problems, Vanderbilt possessed some imposing strengths. As at most times in the history of American higher education, the years before World War I constituted a buyer's market for universities wishing to hire first-rate teachers in the humanities. (It was not old-school ties so much as an inability to secure a position at a more prestigious northern institution that kept Ransom in Nashville.) Vanderbilt probably provided the best university education in the trans-Appalachian South. According to Paul Conkin, it attracted its student body from those academically gifted young people "who could not afford to enroll in northern universities or who were fearful of the challenges in an alien North. . . . This meant, at any one time, a pool of exceptionally able but homogeneous southern students . . . , [drawn mostly] from central and western Tennessee and Kentucky, from northern Georgia, Alabama, and Mississippi, and from parts of Arkansas and Texas" (Conkin, *Agrarians*, 4). One such student, who was enrolled in John Crowe Ransom's Shakespeare class in the fateful year of 1914, was a native of Campbellsville, Tennessee, named Donald Grady Davidson.

As the son of a middle Tennessee school teacher, Davidson had an even harder time financially than Ransom. Born in 1893, he entered Vanderbilt in 1909, the year Ransom graduated. Poverty forced him to drop out after a year, and only a part-time teaching job at a nearby academy enabled him to return in 1914. Not only was this the year that Vanderbilt was "divorced" from the Methodist Church and that Ransom joined the faculty, it was also the year that Ransom, Davidson, and several other young men began meeting for philosophical discussions at the home of Sidney Mttron Hirsch on Nashville's Twentieth Avenue.

Lacking a university degree, Hirsch was an eccentric autodidact. Three years older than Ransom, he had grown up in one of the most prominent Jewish business families in Nashville. As a photograph taken in 1956 shows, Hirsch was an imposing physical specimen even in his seventies. While in the Navy, he had won the heavyweight championship of the Pacific Fleet and had later served as a model for Rodin. During a tour in the

Far East, he developed a dilettantish interest in Buddhism, Rosicrucian-
ism, numerology, etymology, astrology, and Hebrew myth—all of which
must have seemed quite exotic to the young Tennessee Methodists at Vanderbilt. In addition to Rodin, Hirsch's Parisian acquaintances included
Gertrude Stein (another Jewish literary mentor, with whom Paul Conkin
has compared Hirsch) and the Irish poet A.E. Back in New York, Hirsch
became a model for the sculptress Gertrude Vanderbilt Whitney and a
close friend of Edwin Arlington Robinson. During this time, he also continued his study of the occult and wrote one-act plays. Prior to the Saturday evening seminars at his house, Hirsch's most notable contribution to
local culture came in 1913, when the Nashville Art Association and the
Board of Trade decided to promote a May Festival. According to Louis D.
Rubin, Jr., "Hirsch came forth with a pageant, 'The Fire Regained,' which
was produced with a cast of six hundred, complete with chariot races,
three hundred sheep, and one thousand pigeons" (Rubin, *Wary Fugitives*,
14). An aesthete and decadent in the fin de siècle mode, Hirsch would hold
court on Saturday nights while reclining on a chaise lounge. He was, by
all accounts, charming, vain, and crazy as a loon. However, the informal
discussions he held in his home would eventually change the course of
twentieth-century literature.

The informality of these off-campus gatherings was well suited to
Ransom's personality. Had student evaluations been in vogue back in
those days, Ransom would certainly have received low marks for his classroom presence. Rather than luxuriating in the beauties of great literature
in the manner of Mims, Ransom specialized in the close reading of specific
passages, usually in a flat, inflectionless voice. (Lewis Simpson remembers
him reading *Daisy Miller* in its entirety during one session of summer
school; see Sullivan, *Allen Tate*, 30.) He employed the Socratic method,
making tentative assertions and asking many questions of his students.
Those who were used to dynamic, elegantly constructed lectures must
have considered Ransom something of a dud. In fact, Mims was so doubtful of Ransom's ability to keep order in class that "for the first six weeks
he sat just inside the door of his office, which opened upon the room in
which Ransom was teaching. One day after Ransom had finished a class,
Mims motioned him into the office. 'I'm going to close my door and get
on with my work,' he said, 'for I'm satisfied you can keep order. But,
young man, I'm afraid you aren't a very good teacher' " (see T. D. Young,
Gentleman, 87–88).

Although Ransom was committed in a general way to the literary life by the time he returned from Oxford, his final decision to become a poet probably does not predate his departure for the Army during World War I. By the summer and fall of 1915, he had guided the weekly discussions of the Hirsch circle away from abstract philosophical issues toward the analysis of specific poems. At first, these were poems Ransom had assigned to his class. Then, as Donald Davidson recalled years later: "One day of days I remember well. My teacher, John Ransom, beckoned me aside and led me to a shady spot on the campus near the streetcar stop called 'Vanderbilt Stile'—though the stile had long since yielded to an open entrance. Ransom drew a sheet of paper from his pocket. Almost blushingly, he announced that he had written a poem. It was his very first, he said. He wanted to read it to me. He read it, and I listened—admiringly, you may be sure. The title of the poem was 'Sunset' " (Davidson, *Southern Writers*, 14). Ransom began publishing his poems in little magazines, and by the time he was ready to go to France to help make the world safe for democracy, he had left an entire manuscript of them with his old Oxford chum Christopher Morley to place with a publisher. The volume was eventually accepted by the firm of Henry Holt on the recommendation of its expert consultant, Robert Frost.

II

Even though Ransom had no advanced degree, Edwin Mims was eager to bring the young poet back to Vanderbilt after the war on a parity with Walter Clyde Curry, who was a more traditional scholar with more conventional credentials. But Ransom was not at all certain that he wanted to return to Nashville. If his years at Oxford had made him restless with the provincialism of Tennessee, being in France during the war had had much the same effect on him. As in 1914, he once again looked for newspaper and teaching jobs in the Northeast. Only when he visited Nashville and saw how his parents had aged did he abandon the job search and return to Vanderbilt as an assistant professor of English. By now, Sidney Hirsch had moved in with his brother-in-law James Frank at 3802 Whitland Avenue, and the returning veterans began gathering there on alternate Saturday nights. Among the newer members of the group was a junior from Kentucky named John Orley Allen Tate.

Tate added a new and volatile element to the Saturday night festivities. Unlike most of the other young men, who had come from stable Protestant families, Allen Tate was the product of a broken home and a rather sporadic Catholic education. He enjoyed shocking more conservative students by playing the role of campus atheist and radical. He also delighted in challenging stodgy old professors, none more so than Edwin Mims. Tate's cockiness was no doubt a mixture of intellectual arrogance and psychological defense. In any event, the meetings at the Frank house were never the same after he began showing up. Ransom remained the respected patriarch and Hirsch the crazy uncle, but young Tate was the precocious and bratty kid. He knew more than any of the others about the avant garde literature that was calling itself "modernism," and he championed T. S. Eliot. By now the group was producing enough provocative talk and first-rate poetry that Hirsch thought it was time to go public.

In April 1922 the Hirsch circle published the first issue of *The Fugitive: A Journal of Poetry*. With intermittent backing from the business community in Nashville and what little they could raise in subscriptions, the group continued publishing the magazine through 1925, always skirting the brink of financial disaster. The name "Fugitive" was suggested by Sidney Hirsch, although its precise meaning always remained enigmatic. (Conkin suspects that Hirsch was making a veiled allusion to "the diaspora of the Jews"; Conkin, *Agrarians*, 16.) In "Ego," the opening poem of the first issue (written by Ransom under the pseudonym "Roger Prim"), the penultimate stanza closes with the lines: "I have run further, matching your heat and speed, / And tracked the Wary Fugitive with you" (*Fugitive* 1:4). More to the point, the editorial foreword to that issue declares: "Official exception having been taken by the sovereign people to the mint julep, a literary phase known rather euphemistically as Southern Literature has expired, like any other stream whose source is stopped up. The demise was not untimely: among other advantages, THE FUGITIVE is enabled to come to birth in Nashville, Tennessee, under a star not entirely unsympathetic. THE FUGITIVE flees from nothing faster than the highcaste Brahmins of the Old South" (1:2).

When word got out that the Whitland Avenue poets were getting ready to publish a magazine, Edwin Mims asked them to lunch and tried to talk them out of it. As Tate would recall years later, Mims's main argument was "that if we were any good we would be published in the Eastern journals" (see Cowan, 47). Coming from a supposed partisan of southern culture, that contention seemed more than a trifle disingenuous. In any event, it didn't work. So rather than try to block the venture, Mims gritted his teeth and hoped for the best. When the *Fugitive* turned out to be a great critical success, he praised it so heartily that one would have thought that the magazine had been Mims's idea from the outset. In his 1926 book *The Advancing South*, Mims lauded Davidson's lyricism and said that "Ransom may never be popular; but for a combination of intellectual subtlety, refined sentiment, originality, boldness of poetic diction, and withal a certain whimsical imagination, his poetry is destined to increasing recognition" (Mims, 201). When his two employees had received favorable mention in a leading literary magazine three years earlier, Mims had written to Davidson: "I rejoice in this recognition. It confirms my judgment with regard to your promise (you have the makings of the poet) and Ransom's critical achievement" (see O'Brien, "Edwin Mims," 908).

Mims was not being entirely hypocritical in praising Ransom and Davidson. They might not have been his kind of poets, but Mims did nothing to undercut their work, and he was shrewd enough to know that their prominence in the literary world brought credit to his department. A lesser man might have been envious and vindictive toward them. Unfortunately, in his dealings with some of the younger Fugitives, particularly Allen Tate, Mims was that lesser man. Given the personalities involved, that hardly seems surprising. Virtually everyone who knew Tate found him irritating at times. (Brainard Cheney, who was one of Tate's oldest and dearest friends, said of him while pounding on his own dinner table: "He's a monster! God damn it, he's a monster! But I love him"; see Sullivan, *Allen Tate*, 1.) And among the Fugitives, Tate was the primary Mims baiter.

Young Tate was a combative gadfly who bruised the egos of some of the less talented Fugitives (notably his hosts Hirsch and Frank), while maintaining the respect of all for the high level of intellectual energy he brought to the gatherings. When he took that same manner to Mims's classroom, it was like waving a red flag in front of the old man's face. In his youthful brashness, Tate did not realize that Mims regarded him not as a younger colleague in the profession of letters but as an obnoxious troublemaker. When he confidently solicited Mims for a recommendation to graduate school, Tate was shocked to learn that the price of that recommendation would be "some sort of apology for past irreverences" (see O'Brien, "Middle Years," 149). When he got a graduate fellowship to Yale without Mims's endorsement, Tate could not resist the impulse to flaunt that fact before his nemesis. In revenge, Mims used his academic influence to have Tate's fellowship revoked. As a result, Tate found it much more difficult to survive while trying to make it as a writer and critic. "If Allen had had an advanced degree, he might have got work teaching," his first wife, Caroline Gordon, pointed out to Walter Sullivan. "As it was, we went hungry part of the time" (see Sullivan, *Allen Tate*, 19).

The youngest and most precocious member of the Fugitives was born in Guthrie, Kentucky, in 1905 and entered Vanderbilt in 1921, at the age of sixteen. At that time—Allen Tate would later recall—Robert Penn Warren "was tall and thin, and when he walked across the room he made a sliding shuffle, as if his bones didn't belong to one another. He had a long quivering nose, large brown eyes, and a long chin—all topped by curly red hair" (see Bohner, 16). Falling under the influence of his roommates, Allen Tate and Ridley Wills, Warren submitted a poem to a *Fugitive* contest in 1923. By February 1924, the magazine listed him as one of the Fugitives, and he had given up all ambitions of becoming a chemical engineer.

By all accounts, Red Warren was an overly sensitive and awkward young man—obsessively afraid of going blind because of an injury to his left eye and even more afraid of admitting his problem to anyone, including himself. During those years of undergraduate torment he lived for literature, drawing pictures from *The Waste Land* on his dormitory wall and sustenance from the fellowship of Fugitives. When he attempted suicide by covering his face with a chloroform-soaked towel in the spring of 1924, his cryptic and disingenuous note said that he no longer wanted to live because he could never be a poet. (The real reason seems to be that he was falling behind schedule in his academic work and suffering romantic disappointment, as well.) Later that year, Warren made an acquaintance that meant little to him at the time, but which would later do much to shape the course of twentieth-century criticism.

The story of that first meeting has been told so many times that it has become part of the folklore of modern southern literature. One day, during the fall of 1924, Red Warren and Lyle Lanier stopped by Kissam Hall to visit their friend and classmate Saville Clark. With Clark was his new roommate, a freshman named Cleanth Brooks, Jr. Remembering that day nearly fifty years later, Brooks recalls Warren as "a tall, lanky red-haired youth of nineteen, full of a wonderful energy and endowed with obvious genius" ("Brooks on Warren," 19). Although only a year and a half older than Brooks, the precocious Warren was already a senior and an important figure on campus. At the time, Brooks knew of the Fugitive movement only as a campfire in the distance.[1] What would surely have impressed him more was the fact that Warren was a leading candidate for the Founder's Medal, the highest academic honor that can be bestowed on a Vanderbilt undergraduate. Despite his eminence, Red Warren took enough of an interest in his new acquaintance to look at one of Cleanth's freshman themes and to compliment him on his "natural style." As Humphrey Bogart said to Claude Rains at the end of *Casablanca*, it was the start of a beautiful friendship.

For several reasons, that friendship did not really flourish at Vanderbilt. Not only was Cleanth less advanced in intellect and less committed to the literary life, he also possessed a very different temperament from Red. At age eighteen, Cleanth Brooks was a preacher's kid who had experienced no real adolescent rebellion. The years at McTyeire had been spent in an environment morally consistent with everything he had learned in his father's home. Although not sinful in themselves, dancing and card games were considered dangerously frivolous. Frowned upon at any time, drinking was strictly forbidden now that Prohibition was the law of the land. Courtship was permitted but sexual liberties were not. The boys at McTyeire even had to take an oath not to leave campus after dark. Had Cleanth chafed under any of these restrictions, the more open atmosphere at Vanderbilt would have been an invitation to bacchanalian revels. In fact, he neither participated in such revels nor condemned them. He simply seemed interested in other things.

In contrast, Red Warren was a creature of the Jazz Age, whose nocturnal exploits read like something out of a Scott Fitzgerald story about life on a small southern campus. Warren's frequent companion in these exploits was a student of French named Bill Bandy. As Warren recalls, Bandy "had the only Stutz Bearcat on the campus. About three o'clock one morning, with several of us as passengers, he undertook to climb the great story-high stone flight of entrance steps to Wesley Hall in the Bearcat. He succeeded, and then made a hair-raising descent, bouncing back step by step in reverse as astonished theological heads popped out of the upper windows of the building. Bandy leveled off at the bottom and sped away. The culprits were never identified" (Warren, "Reminiscence," 208). On another night Red Warren, so drunk on bootleg liquor he could not make it back to his own lodging, appeared at Kissam Hall and collapsed in bed with Cleanth Brooks.

III

Another student enrolled in Vanderbilt in 1924 was a native of Newberry, South Carolina, named Frances Neel. Although a bit too provincial to be a southern flapper in the Zelda Fitzgerald mold, Fannie (as she was known to all) was one of the few women on campus to smoke cigarettes and drink bootleg liquor (the favored brew was white lightning, colored and flavored with cherry juice, until a graduate student in chemistry began distilling peach and apricot brandy in his laboratory). Her active social life did not prevent Fannie from earning a degree in sociology in 1928 and going on to a distinguished career as a librarian, first at Vanderbilt and later at George Peabody College. (When Allen Tate held the Chair of Poetry at the Library of Congress in 1943, he made Fannie his special assistant, and together they published the landmark bibliography *Sixty American Poets, 1896–1944.*) With her husband, Brainard Cheney (called "Lon" after the silent movie star), she entertained the Fugitives and their brethren whenever they returned to middle Tennessee, and eventually came to know most of the major figures of twentieth-century southern literature, as well as such non-southerners as Robert Lowell and Ford Madox Ford. In the fall of 1924, however, Fannie's main concern was finding someone to tutor her in Latin. The person who assumed that responsibility was her classmate Cleanth Brooks, a studious minister's son who had arrived on campus with his left arm in an airplane brace.

The injury to Cleanth's arm had been incurred in an automobile accident the previous summer. He had been driving on a country road with several other young people when a bee flew in the car. Distracted by the bee, Cleanth had swerved to one side of the road and then back too sharply to the other side. Although the top of the family car was wrecked, no one else was seriously hurt. (Knowing his son to be a generally prudent driver, Cleanth, Sr., took the accident in stride.) Because Cleanth was right-handed and the damage was to a nerve in his left arm, he could still write. Of even more immediate concern, his ability to make much-needed money through tutoring was unimpaired. (Later, he helped pay his bills by delivering the afternoon edition of a local newspaper.) Not only did classmates such as Fannie Neel need assistance with their Latin, but a few Divinity School students found this undergraduate from McTyeire an able teacher of Greek.

After the brace came off, Cleanth resumed an even more industrious life. As with so many young men at Vanderbilt, much of his time outside the classroom was devoted to the activities of his fraternity. (By the mid-twenties, seventy percent of the men in the College of Arts and Sciences and the School of Engineering belonged to fraternities.) Like his father,

Cleanth belonged to Alpha Tau Omega (ATO), and in his sophomore year he moved from Kissam Hall into the fraternity house. Although he maintained his abstemious ways, his friendly nature and enthusiastic involvement in campus affairs made him popular among his fraternity cohorts. One of these was Donald Davidson's younger brother Bill.

During part of the time that he lived at the ATO house, Cleanth roomed with Bill Davidson and got to know him much earlier than he did Bill's brother Don. Like Don, Bill was committed to writing poetry and to studying literature. Intensely loyal to his brother, Bill became somewhat bitter in later years that Ransom, Tate, and Warren were so much more highly regarded than Donald Davidson. Although he had little use for Mims as either person or teacher, Bill Davidson's critical views were closer to those of the old Victorian autocrat than to the advanced theories of the new critics. He believed that students did not need close textual analysis to understand and appreciate poetry; they needed only an anthology that printed the right kind of poems. When Bill edited such an anthology himself, it was a dismal failure in comparison to the more popular textbooks of his friends Brooks and Warren. For many years an English professor at the University of Georgia, the younger Davidson lived a quiet life at home only to turn into an out-of-town Dionysus at professional conventions. His romance with the muse did not outlast early adulthood, and for much of his professional life his poetic output consisted of faintly bawdy limericks passed through the oral tradition.[2]

Although too light to consider intercollegiate football, Cleanth did play in the intramural program. He was also an avid spectator at varsity games and even joined the marching band his senior year. Apparently, Cleanth's musical ability was marginal. He was not a trained musician like Allen Tate, nor did he possess the natural talent of a Donald Davidson; his efforts were those of the eager amateur. He learned to play the clarinet passably well and enjoyed being part of the athletic scene at a time when Vanderbilt was still a regional powerhouse (during the 1920s, it was the dominant team in the South). The experience also enabled him to travel. Despite being constantly uprooted as a child, his world had been the circumscribed region of the Memphis Conference. Playing in the band took him as far east as Knoxville, where the Commodores tied the University of Tennessee, and as far west as Dallas, where they lost to the University of Texas.

In contrast to the athletic and social scene, religious life at Vanderbilt was in decline. During the first two decades of the century, one of the most prominent organizations on campus had been the Young Men's Christian Association. In an effort to counter the licentious morality of some of the fraternities, the YMCA had become a force for clean living and religious faith. The emphases of the organization included both evangelism and an advanced version of the social gospel. Ironically, it was when the university cut itself loose from the Methodist Church that religious fervor was greatest on campus.

Within a year of the court verdict that separated the school and the church, the YMCA conducted a hugely successful revival on campus. (Edwin Mims eagerly solicited decisions for Christ and promised to do follow-up work among the newly converted.) By the mid-1920s, however, the Y had generally lost the interest of the students; neither its religious campaigns nor its extracurricular Bible courses attracted much attention. Even visiting speakers, such as the young Reinhold Niebuhr, went largely unnoticed. Still, the organization continued to send out deputation teams to high schools and prep schools in an effort to attract the right sort of student to Vanderbilt. Cleanth Brooks went on several of these deputation visits during his junior year, when he was a member of the YMCA cabinet.

Another of Cleanth's continuing interests as an undergraduate was in public speaking. At Vanderbilt, this activity was almost as old as the university itself. In the 1880s, the only sanctioned extracurricular organizations were the two literary societies—the Philosophic and the Dialectic. According to Paul Conkin, these groups "met after classes ended at eleven o'clock on Saturday morning." With the encouragement of the administration, "the boys were to debate weighty issues, learn how to run a meeting, develop speaking ability, and bend their hopes and energies toward the one authorized competitive challenge at the early Vanderbilt—winning the right to give an oration at commencement" (Conkin, *Ivy*, 57). Although lacking the influence they had possessed forty years earlier, these organizations still existed in the 1920s. (In 1929, they held a debate over the role of women at Vanderbilt.) Cleanth belonged not only to the Philosophic Society, but to the Forensic Council and the debating team, as well. But the oratorical fire of his prep school years was gone. Increasingly, an interest in literature had become the focus of his academic life.

In addition to such informal off-campus groups as the Fugitives, Vanderbilt students could write and talk about literature in several officially recognized campus organizations. Although Cleanth never worked on the student newspaper or the yearbook, he did spend part of his time during his sophomore and junior years on the staff of the *Masquerader*, a campus humor magazine. By the standards of the *Harvard Lampoon* or even of earlier Vanderbilt publications, this periodical was fairly tame (one of its recent predecessors, the *Jade*, had been suspended and its editors denied their degrees when a "woman's issue" of the magazine featured a picture of a girl in a bathing suit with a broken shoulder strap and too much exposed breast). The *Masquerader*'s pages contained mild double entendres, caricatures of such campus icons as Eddie Mims (saying after his first lecture to each freshman class: "I'm sure this has been the most important hour in all your lives"), and the sort of "darky jokes" that no one seemed to find offensive in that politically incorrect age.[3] The only contribution Cleanth Brooks can remember making to this enterprise was a poem about a halfback who improved his running game by dancing the Charleston. In general, however, Cleanth did not take the business of humor very seriously. The same could not be said of his involvement in another literary organization—the Blue Pencil Club.

Blue Pencil was an organization for freshmen and sophomores interested in creative writing and contemporary literature. It was an offshoot of the Calumet Club, a similar group founded for upperclassmen in 1907. Although the official purpose of the Calumet Club was merely to improve the quality of writing in campus publications, it accomplished far more than that. Among the prominent professional writers who had passed through its ranks were John Crowe Ransom and Donald Davidson. Speaking of Calumet and Blue Pencil, Red Warren observed half a century later, "A peculiar feature about the little university that was the Vanderbilt of the 1920s was an active and spontaneous interest in literature and writing among a good many students" (Warren, "Reminiscence," 207). One of these students, Warren later learned, was "an all-Southern football player [who] wrote . . . little poems like A. E. Housman—but never read them aloud in the locker room" (211). Cleanth recalls the members of Blue Pencil discussing, among others, the venerable Conrad and the upstart Hemingway. It was a far cry from memorizing a thousand lines of Browning or Tennyson, as they had done for Edwin Mims.

What is lost in any mere recitation of activities and accomplishments, however, is a sense of the young Cleanth Brooks as a person. With so many of his contemporaries gone from the scene, it is next to impossible to know the undergraduate of seventy years ago. Nevertheless, we have glimpses of this person in a few letters he wrote to Fannie Neel in the summer between their freshman and sophomore years at Vanderbilt.[4] By this time, Cleanth, Sr., had moved, at his own request, to the Louisiana

Conference of the Southern Methodist Church, and the family was living in the central Louisiana town of Alexandria.

In a letter mailed to Fannie on July 3, 1926, Cleanth describes his new hometown as follows: "Everything is flat here, hardly a hill. If you like water oaks and Spanish moss and water lilies and wild roses and lazy little bayous, you'd love it down here—and if you don't, you'd probably go crazy." He also thanks Fannie for putting him on to a popular novel of the day, Donn Byrne's *Hangman's House*. The only other specifically literary reference is in a letter mailed on July 20, where, Cleanth writes: "I've just finished reading one of the books that I wanted to read years ago and never did—Blasco Ibañez's 'Mare Nostrum.' I'm not very fond of Ibañez but I think that it is one of the most intense things that I have ever read."

Throughout these four surviving letters to Fannie one finds the ingenuous spirit of a young romantic who seems to have discovered love for the first time. (That feeling mellowed into a friendship that would last the rest of Cleanth's life.) In the first letter, written "somewhere near Jackson" on the train heading south from Nashville to Alexandria, Cleanth writes: "I was hoping that today or rather tonight now that I would be able to express the things that I want to say. But I am tired, or the train rocks too much, or the moon is not up—something—and I cannot say them." He does implore Fannie to write him but is careful to emphasize that the letters be addressed to "*Junior*," apparently not wanting Cleanth, Sr., to open these intimate communications by mistake.

One recurring motif in the letters is Cleanth's continuing struggle to write. On July 20 he says: "I've been frittering away too much time on what to write instead of actually writing. I'm sending you a couple anyway. One I'm sure you will think is too soft and mawkish—I'm afraid it is. The other is simply an experiment that I knocked off on the typewriter while I was resting this morning. (Don't worry, I won't repeat the experiment again.) I am going to write something worthwhile, though, soon. (This isn't prediction—it's hope.)" He sounds a similar note on August 7. After thanking Fannie for liking "some of the stuff that I sent," he confesses: "I'm writing most of the time or getting ready to write, but I'm far from sure of myself yet,—at all."

IV

During his sophomore year at Vanderbilt, Cleanth enrolled in John Crowe Ransom's course in modern literature. A Hollywood script writer would have had him mesmerized by Ransom's presence and committing himself on the spot to the vocation of letters. In actual fact, Cleanth was intimidated by the difficulty of the work and soon dropped the class. In his junior year, he did take Ransom's course in advanced composition, but that too was less than a life-altering experience. "I must have learned something," he recalls, "but except for various remarks that I remember having heard him make, only a few of which had anything to do with the writing process, I am not conscious now of having carried anything away from his instruction" (Brooks, *Community*, 147). Apparently, Ransom was most effective not as a platform orator but as a mentor to those students who had enough intellect and initiative to establish a personal relationship with him (Red Warren was a classic example of such a student). As an undergraduate, Cleanth possessed the intellect but not the initiative.

Ransom's extreme courtliness could be easily misinterpreted as aloofness or even arrogance. When he met his future wife, Robb Reavill, during her ten-day visit with Chancellor Kirkland's daughter, Elizabeth, in January 1920, the poet sent her a series of unsigned sonnets on her breakfast tray. (She responded by sending him such gifts as a stalk of bananas and a live duck.) Walter Sullivan remarks that "I never met another poet who seemed to me so perfectly the person to have written his work as Mr. Ransom. The turns of phrase in his conversation mimicked the patterns of his verse; the juxtapositions of ideas, the vocabulary were common to his informal utterance and to his art" (Sullivan, *Allen Tate*, 28). Sullivan's wife, Jane, knew Ransom much better than Walter did and had even been maid of honor at the wedding of Ransom's daughter, Helen, to Duane Forman in 1945. Because Forman was in the military and did not know when he would get leave, the wedding party had to be on call for an entire week. During the week at the Ransom house in Gambier, Ohio, a severe thunderstorm knocked the electricity out. Jane recalls dining by candlelight, with Mr. Ransom announcing when dinner was served. She cannot remember his being without a coat and tie the entire week.[5]

If Ransom's poetry was well suited to his personality, his critical writing and his life were also a perfect match. His manners were an expression of his belief in ritual (which he clung to tenaciously after he was no longer able to believe in dogma). So, too, was his passion for games. His love letters to Robb during their courtship were filled with references to golf, at which Robb was usually able to beat him, and to football games, which he often attended with "Betsy" Kirkland in Robb's absence. After the Ransoms moved to Ohio, they became avid fans of both the Cleveland

Browns and the Cleveland Indians. Red Warren recalls that during their
years in Nashville, "my wife and I often disastrously played bridge with
the Ransoms on Saturday night. I remember one marathon performance
that began early one Saturday afternoon and continued until Sunday
night, with only short breaks for necessary food and drink and a little
sleep. It seemed scarcely less than natural that the Ransoms rented a bank-
rupt country club for a year before they settled in the country and invited
friends to share their tennis courts and billiard tables" (Warren, "Reminiscence," 216).

Although it would be years before Cleanth enjoyed such terms of familiarity, the very presence of Ransom and other practicing poets on the
Vanderbilt campus served as a vicarious inspiration to a young man who
aspired to follow in their footsteps. The only problem was that Ransom
neither looked nor wrote like Percy Shelley, who was Cleanth's idea of
a poet. Then, in Cleanth's senior year, an important transformation
occurred:

> It happened easily and suddenly. I was in a friend's dormitory room one
> evening, rather idly chatting when I opened a volume of Ransom's poetry
> lying there on the table before me and started reading—really reading, for
> I had gone over the poems many times before. Suddenly the scales fell from
> my eyes. The code was broken, the poems became "readable." I do not
> mean that they became magically transparent. I continue to find fresh
> meanings in them and depths I had not noticed before. But a serious block-
> age had suddenly disappeared. I was now a true convert.
> (Community, 149)

A similar epiphany in Cleanth's understanding of literary criticism was
produced by an unlikely source—Donald Davidson. The conventional
wisdom is that Davidson was a southern romantic who spent his career
writing old-fashioned verse and refighting the Civil War, while his more
sophisticated cohorts were defining southern modernism in poetry and
inventing the new criticism. This view represents at best a gross caricature
of Davidson as poet and social polemicist and is just plain wrong in ignoring his contributions to literary criticism. Between February 1924 and
November 1930 (surely among the most significant half a dozen years in
American literary history), Davidson edited the book page of the Nashville Tennessean. In this capacity, he introduced some of the most important contemporary writers to the general public. He also provided a forum
for the ablest critics of the region, among them Cleanth Brooks and
Robert Penn Warren.

Although his own creative writing consisted almost exclusively of verse, Davidson's most astute criticism was of the techniques of fiction (Brooks and Warren would dedicate their textbook *Understanding Fiction* to him). One day, in a literature class, Cleanth Brooks heard a graduate student, whose name he has since forgotten, read an essay that Davidson had written on a short story by Rudyard Kipling. It was at that moment that Cleanth fully realized the value of close reading as a critical technique. No doubt he was already used to thinking of poetry in technical terms, but to discuss fiction as craft suggested that aesthetic formalism was a critical method that could illuminate all of literature. Davidson performed this same service for several generations of Vanderbilt students. Even though Cleanth never had Davidson for a class, the cogency of that one essay was sufficient to start him thinking about literature in a new way.

As far as I can determine, Davidson left no published criticism of Kipling.[6] We can only imagine what he might have said in that essay that so impressed Cleanth. For a contemporaneous example of Davidson's critical method, one could turn to his essay "Joseph Conrad's Directed Indirections," published in the *Sewanee Review* in the spring of Cleanth's freshman year (1925). Taken from his M.A. thesis on Conrad, which he had completed under Ransom's supervision in May 1922, Davidson's essay is a broad discussion of inversive narration in Conrad's fiction.

Whether Cleanth eventually would have become an active member of the Fugitives had the magazine continued to appear and the group continued to meet is impossible to say. With Tate and Warren and so many of the younger Fugitives gone through graduation, the collective phase of the movement was over. But the interest in literature it had generated continued, largely on its own momentum. Despite his friendship with Bill Davidson and his admiration for Donald's criticism, there was still a distance between student and professor that Cleanth could not easily have bridged. This would have been even more true with the Olympian Ransom. A few years earlier the Fugitives—both students and faculty—were simply young men beginning to discover poetry together. As always happens at a school, the students had seemed to stay the same age while the faculty had gotten older. As published poets with growing reputations, Ransom and Davidson were more like distant uncles than older brothers to Cleanth and his classmates. When the members of the Calumet Club decided to publish their own volume of verse in 1928, it was with the blessing but not the participation of John Crowe Ransom and Donald Davidson.

V

If the publication of the *Fugitive* in the early 1920s is considered a land-mark in the literary history of this century, the appearance of *Facets: An Anthology of Verse* in 1928 was not even a footnote in the literary history of Vanderbilt. (It is not mentioned by either Mims or Conkin in their re-spective histories of the university.) However, taken on its own terms, this publication of the Calumet Club was an impressive achievement. Among the contributors were Henry Blue Kline, who would write an essay for *I'll Take My Stand* in 1930, and Richmond Beatty, who would become one of the premier scholars of American and southern literature during a dis-tinguished career at Vanderbilt. Bill Davidson wrote three poems for the volume, as did Edwin Mims's son, Puryear. But the two best represented poets were the driving forces behind the book—a varsity football player named Hugh Cecil, with seven poems, and Cleanth Brooks with six.

Not only did the students provide the contents for the book, they also arranged for its production and distribution. At one point, Cleanth and some friends made the ninety-mile drive southeast to Sewanee to discuss their project with William Knickerbocker, who was then editor of the *Sewanee Review*. Although Knickerbocker received the young poets, it was clear that he did not take their efforts seriously. (What Cleanth did not know at the time was that very few people in the literary world took Knickerbocker very seriously; his personal eccentricities finally prompted his removal from the editorship of the review in 1944.) Knickerbocker seemed less interested in helping these novices than in scrutinizing their verse to detect the influence of Ransom, whom he envied. The young poets eventually contracted with a Nashville press to print the book and sold it by subscription. If nothing else, his contributions to the volume demon-strate the early eclecticism of Cleanth Brooks's poetic sensibility.

Wit, fancy, and a fiendishly clever sense of humor are the most ob-vious qualities of Brooks's English sonnet "Abner Gardner, Tired Business Man." The probable influence here is Edwin Arlington Robinson. One can easily imagine Gardner in Robinson's Tilbury Town (modeled, after all, on Gardiner, Maine), except that the setting of Brooks's poem is not New England but a classical version of Hell. Rather than be altered by his exotic surroundings, Gardner seems by his very dim-witted presence to make those surroundings more commonplace. Nothing is actually as-serted about the setting; it is described provisionally in a whole string of subjunctive clauses that lead to a main clause in the concluding couplet.

That main clause, which is the only definite assertion in the poem, concerns Gardner directly. The irony of the poem owes a good deal to its being framed as a single periodic sentence:

> If Lethe stream (as Grecian bards have said)
> Does really flow through drowsy plains in Hell,
> Meand'ring slowly for the weary dead
> Who come with pale hands clutching asphodel—
>
> If Lethe stream is calm and pure and deep—
> Its waters never roiled by Charon's boat—
> With bubbles never bursting from their sleep
> When once by trailing willows set afloat—
>
> And most of all, if Lethe stream has fish
> (And surely in its pools some fish must hide!)
> With silver scales and rising to a wish—
> If in the Lethe stream bright fishes glide,
>
> Then Abner Gardner still may have his wish:
> To loll upon a bank and smoke and fish. (*Facets*, 51)

That Gardner is a businessman may be meant as a criticism of the commercial ethic. Abner has not been consigned to some Dantesque inferno because of rapacious capitalistic greed; he is simply a dense and inattentive character, who seems to fit in quite naturally by Lethe stream. Because he almost certainly has read no Greek mythology, he cannot be expected to recognize his surroundings. He probably realizes that he is in some sort of afterlife; because he has been granted his mundane wish to smoke (a pun?) and fish, he may even think that he is in Heaven. As Kierkegaard observed, "the specific character of despair is precisely this: it is unaware of being despair." Abner Gardner is the inauthentic man.

As interesting and well constructed as his other poems might have been, none was as special as "Birth of Aphrodite," the first of Cleanth's selections in *Facets*. At first glance, this poem seems to reflect the influence of the aesthetes and decadents of the British fin de siècle. One of the persistent motifs in the literature of that group was the superiority of art to nature. In his poem Cleanth begins in the imperative mood (recalling the "Come" poems of Marvell, Donne, and Jonson), urging unnamed workers to help him build a statue of the Greek goddess. The intention from the outset is not to celebrate this mythological figure but to surpass the original. (Note that they are building a stone representation of a goddess who was originally created from sea foam.) The designers will begin with blueprints, use alabaster stone, and "take a calipers and test / Its contours, that it may conform / Nicely to our chosen norm." By the time we finish the first, eighteen-line, stanza, we suspect that the perfection that has been created is that of a stone-cold mathematical symmetry. Even the colors (calling our attention back to the blueprints) suggest this. The speaker says of the statue: "Let her be the perfect fair, / With *hard* blue beryls for her eyes, / And blue-veined marble for her thighs" (emphasis added). The irony becomes even more pointed in the concluding, six-line stanza:

> Surely, wrought so carefully,
> Will not our Aphrodite be,
> Fairer, fairer far than she,
> Born upon the restless tide,
> And with no pattern for a guide
> Except the careless sea? (*Facets*, 9)

The boy who had dropped John Ransom's class in modern literature three years earlier had himself become a fledgling modern poet. Now, in his last semester at Vanderbilt, he was confident enough of "Birth of Aphrodite" to read it aloud before what must have been one of the last meetings of the Fugitive group.

VI

Because of his involvement with the Calumet Club and his obvious dedication to his art, Cleanth was selected class poet for the commencement of 1928. For the occasion, he produced a suitably ceremonial ode. Much longer than any of the contributions to *Facets*, the "1928 Class Poem" runs to eighty-five lines. (All but one of its fourteen stanzas are six lines long and exhibit rhyme and meter that suggest the sestina of an Italian sonnet.) The emotions it expresses are the expected ones of school spirit and loyalty to alma mater. What makes the poem eerie, however, is a tone of nostalgia that seems decidedly premature for one who hadn't yet celebrated his twenty-second birthday.

Using the first person plural, the speaker of the poem imagines a time when he and his classmates will be far removed from Vanderbilt in both time and space. The years will then create a haze every bit as palpable as the one that used to shadow the campus in the early mornings of their youth. The attempt to maintain tangible memories is thwarted by their brains themselves being in a constant state of flux. Thus, when the speaker asks, "For what sure alchemy can serve to bind / This present to a present yet to be," he realizes that it would be "As well to paint a picture on the wind / Or fabricate a statue of the rain" ("1928 Class Poem").

It is easy to condescend to such emotions, but there is a real sense in which the Vanderbilt of 1928 was the closest thing to a permanent home that Cleanth had ever known. He had lived there longer than in any of the houses of his childhood. He had come of age as an adolescent at McTyeire, but Vanderbilt was where he became an adult. It was there that he formed friendships that would last for fifty, sixty, even seventy years. If McTyeire was in some ways an extension of the Methodist parsonage, Vanderbilt was a more cosmopolitan world. Although Cleanth lost neither his faith nor his moral rectitude, he at least saw another way of life. He also experienced a calling that, in its own way, was just as real as the calling of his father and his grandfather to preach the word of God. When Cleanth Brooks left Vanderbilt for graduate school, he was committed to the vocation of literature.

If Cleanth was different in 1928 from the freshman who had arrived in Nashville with an airplane brace on his arm, the nation itself was different as well. Calvin Coolidge had declined to run for reelection, but his secretary of commerce, Herbert Hoover, was carrying the standard of the Republican Party with the promise of "a chicken in every pot and a car in every garage." His opponent, Al Smith, the Roman Catholic governor of New York, was forcing the solidly Protestant and solidly Democratic South to choose between its most deep-seated religious and political loyalties. In 1928 T. S. Eliot published *For Lancelot Andrewes*, a book in which he declared himself "an Anglo-Catholic in religion, a classicist in literature, and a royalist in politics." Also, that year the Pulitzer Prize in fiction went to Thornton Wilder's *The Bridge of San Luis Rey*, while the award in poetry was given to Edwin Arlington Robinson's *Tristram*. And back in Louisiana, a public service commissioner named Huey P. Long was making his second race for governor.

CHAPTER THREE

Tinkum

The Reverend Cleanth Brooks was fifty-one years old when he transferred to the Louisiana Conference of the Methodist Episcopal Church, South. He had devoted thirty years to the ministry of the Memphis Conference, serving in both large and small pastorates. Although he had had the consolations of family life to sustain him, his vocation was one of poverty and obedience—and it had taken its emotional toll. As a Protestant minister, he may have lacked the power of absolution, but he heard more than his share of confessions. He was expected to be not only a stirring orator, a crack administrator, and a paragon of virtue, but an amateur psychiatrist as well. He knew the frustrations that people kept hidden from the rest of the world and saw enough of the seamy side of life to confirm the doctrine of Original Sin. (He was particularly shaken when a man he knew and respected was found to have embezzled a large sum of money from the bank where he worked.) Moving from assignment to assignment, he was constantly sowing seeds that other men would reap. For all of this, he would sometimes find that the resources of his church were not adequate to pay his meager salary. Under such circumstances, he would simply remit the difference as a donation. The move to Louisiana offered a change of scenery along with the hope of greater professional advancement and more financial security.

Although all of Brother Brooks's biological offspring were grown by this time, the family's monetary and emotional resources were strained by the adoption of one of Bessie Lee's nephews when the child's mother died shortly after his birth. (The boy's father, who was Mrs. Brooks's brother, was either unable or unwilling to care for his son and turned him over to his sister with little protest.) As was the custom in those days, the Brookses allowed young Murray, who was always called "Tookie," to believe himself the natural-born son of the family. It was not until he was forced to obtain a birth certificate upon entering the military that he discovered his true parentage.

When the Brookses moved to Alexandria, Louisiana, the church faithful were asked to supply furniture for the parsonage. One woman, Jeannette Foote, contributed an unusual item that she had bought on time around 1908. It was "a chair, which on releasing a hook on the back folded forward and became a table—or vice versa, it was a table that became a chair." Shortly thereafter, Mrs. Foote paid a courtesy call on Bessie Lee Brooks. As Mrs. Foote's daughter recalls the story:

> Apparently they became very congenial, for after they had visited for a while, Mrs. Brooks in a very forthright manner which my mother greatly admired, began telling of the trials of a minister's life; the moving, the expectations various congregations had, and the restrictions on their lives. The very worst ordeal, she said, was having to live with other people's cast offs, the most remarkable of which she had just encountered on her move to Alexandria. She then described this strange piece of furniture in the parsonage, which was neither a comfortable chair nor an adequate table.[1]

Mrs. Foote did not have the heart to reveal the source of this white elephant.

During Cleanth, Sr.'s, four years as pastor, the First Church of Alexandria had between 1,000 and 1,200 members. (He brought in 362 of them himself.) His most notable accomplishment was the construction of a religious education building adjacent to the church. The August 10, 1927, edition of the Alexandria *Daily Town Talk* describes the structure as "approximately 85 x 95 feet in area for the main portion with a rear wing 42 by 30 feet, both portions being three stories in height or about forty-two feet." After giving a more detailed account of the facility and its various accessories, the newspaper goes on to declare that "the First Methodist Church will have a religious education center which will not, except in point of size, be excelled in the entire South" (*Daily Town Talk*, 1). The cornerstone for this building was laid on October 16, 1927. One year later, Cleanth, Sr., was transferred to the Noel Memorial Church in Shreveport.

I

Shortly after Cleanth, Jr., left Vanderbilt for the graduate program at Tulane University in New Orleans, the literary brethren back in Nashville began to develop a regional self-consciousness they had not known during their Fugitive days. The explanation that is often given for this transformation is that the Scopes trial in Dayton, Tennessee, was forcing all southern intellectuals to reexamine their relationship to the region in which they lived. Certainly, there is some truth to this notion. The ridicule to which Mencken and other Yankee commentators subjected the South as a result of the Monkey Trial tended to force intelligent southerners into one of two positions. They could accept the progressive secular values of the Darwinians and argue that the persecution of Scopes, not unlike an occasional lynching, was simply an aberration in the Modern South. Or they could mount a more intellectually cogent defense of cultural conservatism. This second possibility was the stance advocated by John Crowe Ransom.

There is reason to believe that Ransom would have gravitated to this position whether or not there had been a Scopes Trial. It seems that the farther he moved intellectually from the Methodist faith of his fathers the more he yearned for some controlling myth and system of ritual to give life coherence. He found such a myth in the culture of the antebellum South, complete with its literal Old Testament religion. He tried to get around the dilemma of practicing a faith in which he did not believe by arguing that religion exists for the sake of its ritual, not its dogma. But his attempt, as a purely secular exercise, to be a good, churchgoing Methodist was thwarted by an inability to affirm the Apostle's Creed while attending Sunday worship. He ended up defending the Old South and its old time religion for largely aesthetic reasons.

Donald Davidson experienced no similar crisis of faith. He was largely uninterested in theology and at least initially had no particular quarrel with the progressive New South. More than any of the other Fugitives, however, he was aware of the extent to which an artist is either nurtured or hampered by the material and social conditions of his existence. Among other things, this meant that the southern writer must come to terms with his southern heritage. Davidson believed that instead of doing this, many modern southern writers—the Fugitives included—had felt inhibited and self-conscious about their habitat.

If this was true of Davidson in Nashville, it was no less true of Allen Tate and Red Warren, who were pursuing careers outside the South. By the late 1920s, all three were trying to banish their sense of cultural inhibition by passionately embracing the myth of the Old South. In 1925 Tate wrote the first version of his poem "Ode to the Confederate Dead";

in 1927 he began touring Civil War battlefields and closing his letters to Davidson with "The Stars & Bars forever!"; and in 1928 he published a biography of Stonewall Jackson, followed in 1929 by one of Jefferson Davis.

After graduating from Vanderbilt in 1925, Warren had resolved to continue his studies wherever he was offered the largest scholarship. This led him to the University of California at Berkeley, where he earned an M.A. degree in 1927. What he encountered there simply reinforced his high opinion of the literary atmosphere at Vanderbilt. "He thought the literary men [at Berkeley] 'fifty years behind the times.' At Nashville the talk had been all Pound and Eliot, but at Berkeley the campus intellectuals discoursed interminably about Marx and Engels" (Bohner, 19). In the fall of 1927, Red entered Yale for further graduate work and, in the summer of 1928, visited Allen Tate and Caroline Gordon in New York. Tate introduced Warren to the literary agent Mavis McIntosh, who secured him a contract to write a biography of John Brown. If Tate and Warren had fled the legacy of the Old South while they were living in Nashville, they seemed to be closer than ever to it now that they were residing in the North.

Another one of the Vanderbilt fraternity who was keeping the faith while living in the Northeast was Andrew Nelson Lytle. Although Lytle attended meetings of the Fugitives during his senior year and published a poem in the March 1925 issue of the magazine, his primary literary interest was in drama. In 1926 he became a student in George Pierce Baker's playwriting class at Yale. He met Tate in New York in 1927 and, in 1929, secured a contract for a biography of Nathan Bedford Forrest. If Tate's biographical labors were suited to his patrician sympathies and Warren's to his interest in race, Lytle had found in General Forrest the sort of yeoman hero who he believed exemplified the South at its best.

By the spring of 1927, Ransom, Davidson, and Tate were discussing the possibility of a collection of essays on the South. Warren and Lytle were soon enlisted in the project, and quite a few southerners of already established prominence were solicited. (At one point, Davidson even suggested Mims as a possible contributor!) Among those who declined invitations were U. B. Phillips, William Yandell Elliott, Howard Mumford Jones, Gerald Johnson, and Stringfellow Barr. The final group of essayists turned out to be a mixed lot. In addition to Ransom, Tate, Davidson, Warren, and Lytle, there were two current Vanderbilt professors (John Donald Wade from English and Frank Lawrence Owsley from his-

tory), one former professor (Herman Clarence Nixon, who had moved on
to Tulane in 1928), a current graduate student (Henry Blue Kline), one
former student (Lyle Lanier), and two well-established southern writers
with no direct Vanderbilt connections (John Gould Fletcher and Stark
Young).

The book that resulted from this collaboration was edited rather
casually—by Davidson with some help from Ransom. Its contents varied
in both quality and ideology. Published in 1930, it was held together
loosely by a statement of principles Ransom composed after more than
half the essays were in, and its title—*I'll Take My Stand*—so infuriated
Tate that he stayed in the volume only on condition that he could attach a
disclaimer to his essay. (Believing that the sectional title would limit the
appeal of the book, he and Warren had wanted to call the collection *Tracts
against Communism*, thus arguing that collective state ownership of property was simply another form of industrialism rather than an alternative to
it.) "If one were trying to assure the failure of a project," Thomas Daniel
Young notes, "one could hardly improve on the procedure followed in
putting together *I'll Take My Stand*" (T. D. Young, *Waking*, 9).

II

In contrast to the intellectual excitement in Nashville, Cleanth found the
graduate program at Tulane to be tepid and uninspiring. Younger even
than Vanderbilt, the school was founded in 1884 by Paul Tulane, a
wealthy Franco-American merchant, who in 1882 had donated his local
real estate holdings (with an annual income of $38,000) to the city of New
Orleans. With this money, the board of administrators of the Tulane Educational Fund absorbed the debt-ridden University of Louisiana and established a more solvent and more distinguished private university. Unfortunately, it was a place where neither the new criticism nor the Old South
counted for very much.

During most of his year in New Orleans, Cleanth roomed near the Tulane campus in a big house owned by Mr. and Mrs. Gus Capdeville at
1459 Calhoun Street. Capdeville was the son of a former mayor, and his
wife had been Queen of Comus in the annual Mardi Gras parade. When
Cleanth moved in with them, they were still in grief over the recent death
of their son. The family doctor had suggested that Mrs. Capdeville might
best cope with her loss by boarding some students from Tulane. Cleanth
remembers accompanying her on several occasions to the race track and

speaking with her in French on long afternoon drives among the Creole houses on Esplanade Avenue.

Living with Cleanth at the Capdeville house was a fellow graduate student in English named William Hodding Carter II. A native of Hammond, Louisiana, Hodding Carter had graduated from Bowdoin College (alma mater of Nathaniel Hawthorne, Henry Wadsworth Longfellow, and Franklin Pierce) at the age of twenty. After studying journalism and English literature at Columbia for a year, he returned to Louisiana and entered graduate school at Tulane. Hodding's fiery temperament and extroverted demeanor contrasted with Cleanth's more laid-back and scholarly approach to the world, but the two became fast friends and remained on good terms for the balance of Carter's life. According to Carter's biographer, Ann Waldron, "The Capedevilles made no money from their boarders; it was impossible, the way the table groaned with the best of New Orleans cuisine. The house always smelled of coffee and garlic and bourbon and cigarette smoke" (Waldron, *Hodding Carter*, 30). During the time they lived together, Hodding made sport of the methodical way that Cleanth would sometimes take on projects that were beyond him— such as the time he blew out all the lights in the Capdeville house while trying to change a fuse.

One thing that bound Cleanth and Hodding together was their shared interest in writing poetry. In a letter to Donald Davidson dated February 24, 1929, Cleanth describes Hodding as "a brilliant sort of chap . . . who writes a very facile, and I think, a very good line."[2] The purpose of this letter was to ask Davidson to look at a volume of poems on which the roommates had collaborated. Although Davidson consented and did offer criticism that Cleanth found helpful, neither the poems nor Davidson's comments seem to have been preserved. As Cleanth recalls the project, he and Hodding and another student were to write poems about the human body—flesh, blood, and bones. This apparently proved too ambitious a project for graduate students who were both taking courses and teaching freshman composition (Cleanth also worked in the library). The only surviving poem that appears to have been part of that endeavor is "Portrait of an Intellectual," which was published in the September / October 1929 issue of *Midland*. This poem describes an individual whose "gray, lean-fingered, haggard nerves" invade the rest of his body until he is left with only "a groping tentacle of brain." The fantastic metaphor and grotesque imagery suggest a sensibility influenced by the conceit poetry of the Elizabethan era.

Probably Cleanth's most distinguished poetic publication was in the *New Republic*, which printed his sonnet "Geometry of Sunset" (picked up by the *Literary Digest* in November 1929). Although his theme (the impossibility of measuring beauty) is quite conventional, Cleanth brings it to life by imagining a mathematician trying to reduce the sunset to some geometrical equation. The sonnet thus makes an implicit statement about the difference between concrete poetic truth and the more abstract formulations of science. If a metaphor establishes imaginative equivalences, Cleanth's basic strategy in this poem is ingeniously antimetaphorical.

In addition to their love of poetry, Cleanth Brooks and Hodding Carter were also of one mind in their contempt for Louisiana's new governor, although the two roommates arrived at this position from slightly different perspectives. Despite not being involved in the plans for *I'll Take My Stand*, Cleanth was enough of an Agrarian (as the Vanderbilt movement called itself) to realize that Huey Long was no friend to the cause. Long may have given the industrialists unshirted hell, but that was not because he questioned the basic premises of industrialism. He just wanted to share the wealth of industry with more people. The road-building and other public works projects he instituted as governor made Louisiana one of the most industrialized states in the South during the Depression. Moreover, if a stable Agrarian society relied on the sanctity of class and property, Huey's radical egalitarianism promised widespread upheaval.

As a southern liberal, Hodding Carter found Long's means to be more objectionable than his ends. Long's defenders have always contended that their man simply did what had to be done in order to accomplish good for the common people of Louisiana. If it required ruthless measures to dislodge the entrenched oligarchy, that was an unfortunate necessity. Long was determined not to be just another populist demagogue who became part of the establishment as soon as he seized power. Or so the argument went. Whether he was a pragmatic idealist or a power-hungry dictator, Huey Long eventually became enamored with his own ability to get things done. (If conservatives regarded him as a near-Communist, liberals branded him a Fascist.) Years later, Red Warren would note that the only time Long's "presence was ever felt in my classroom was when, in my Shakespeare course, I gave my little annual lecture on the political background of *Julius Caesar*; and then, for the two weeks we spent on the play, backs grew straighter, eyes grew brighter, notes were taken, and the girls stopped knitting in class, or repairing their faces" (Warren, "*All King's Men*," 161).

Huey Long made his presence felt in Cleanth's temporary hometown of Alexandria through his relations with one of the town's most prominent citizens, the attorney and future U.S. Senator John Overton. (One summer, Cleanth took Overton's daughter, Katherine, on her first date.) Having established a thriving law practice during the lumber boom at the turn of the century, Overton could easily afford to allow visiting lawyers to use his office when they needed to do business in Alexandria. Among his frequent guests was Huey's brother, Julius Long. Then, one memorable evening in 1925, Huey himself descended upon Overton's office. John McSween, who was then a law clerk (later a partner) of Overton recalled the incident years later. According to McSween's son, Harold:

> Huey showed up at five in the afternoon asking for a toddy and somebody to type a plaintiff's petition. It would take only a few minutes, he informed Overton with a smile and twinkle that would win over the help late in the day. Overton joined Huey for a toddy, assigned McSween the chore of staying late with Huey, said goodbye, and walked the short distance home from the Commercial Bank Building overlooking Red River. My father never did get home that night. Huey made the bottle last until morning, when he rushed to a barber shop before filing his petition with a Clerk of Court somewhere on the last possible day before it would have been too late.

The reason this ordeal lasted all night was that Long was practicing law and planning his 1928 race for governor at the same time. "Huey dictated four allegations of the petition off the top of his head until he remembered that he needed to make telephone calls. . . . Between and during telephone conversations Huey would dictate additional allegations. His last call was to [his brother] Earl in New Orleans, although it had taken until after midnight to locate him. In the meanwhile Huey had finished the petition and turned to barking out a dozen or more letters."[3] It was this sort of personal drive and ability to command others that would lead Huey Pierce Long to victory in 1928 and permanently change the face of Louisiana politics.

Like Willie Stark in Robert Penn Warren's *All the King's Men*, Huey Long promoted himself as champion of the little man. He depicted his opponents as landed aristocrats and corporate robber barons who regarded the state as their personal fiefdom. What was left out of his populist demonology, however, was the class to which Huey himself belonged—those in the middle, who wore neither silk stockings nor wool hats. These individuals had little wealth to share but not much to gain from its forcible redistribution. One such man was a south Louisiana lumber merchant named Paul Adam Blanchard.

III

Paul Blanchard hailed from Madisonville, on the northwest shore of Lake Pontchartrain. He was a fun-loving, stocky man who told amusing stories with a slight French Louisiana accent. Although of Roman Catholic descent, he had long since drifted into the generic social Protestantism fashionable in small southern towns. Blanchard was prominent enough in the affairs of Madisonville that his name appears on the cornerstone of the old Faulknerian courthouse that still serves that small community. One day, in the Madisonville bank, he met Emily Price, a young teller whose forebears had lived in Wisconsin and fought for the Union during the Civil War. Despite differences in background and temperament, the two fell in love and were soon married.

If Paul Blanchard was an easygoing, affable southerner, his wife, Emily, approached the world with deadly seriousness, even as a bride not yet out of her teens. (Her grandson, Carver, believes she saw herself as a "cross between Eleanor Roosevelt and Queen Victoria.")[4] She was a committed Unitarian at a time when that church was virtually unknown in the South. What set her even more apart from the community was her political activism. She was a force in both the Madisonville PTA and a local group for improving scholarship in the public schools. (After the family moved to New Orleans, Emily created something of a minor scandal when she sought to forge closer ties with a group of blacks trying to achieve similar goals in their segregated schools.) In 1948 she helped run Henry Wallace's campaign for president in Louisiana. Emily Blanchard's one brush with notoriety came in the early sixties, when a friend in Dallas wrote to see if she could find a job for a Russian immigrant recently estranged from her husband. Shortly thereafter, the estranged husband—Lee Harvey Oswald—assassinated President John F. Kennedy. If any of his wife's assertive and unconventional behavior bothered Paul Blanchard, he never let on. In addition to all else, Emily was a faithful wife who looked after the house and cooked her husband a big southern breakfast at 4:30 every morning.

Paul and Emily's daughter, Edith Amy, was ten years old when the family moved across the lake to New Orleans in 1921. Well before that time, she had grown to loathe her given name. For reasons that made sense to her, if to no one else, she thought that her name didn't fit her personality. Because of her fussy ways, she acquired the childhood nickname of "Tinkum," after a local cartoon character named Tinkum Tidy. In 1928 Tinkum Blanchard was an attractive and petite ash blonde, who read her own imagist verse at gatherings of the New Orleans Poetry Society. It was at one of these meetings that she heard the young Tulane graduate student Cleanth Brooks talk about a school of poets both more recent and more southern than the Imagists—the Fugitives of Nashville, Tennessee. It wasn't long before the two young people became informally committed to each other.

During his years at Vanderbilt, Cleanth had never suffered for lack of female companionship. His personal charm, dapper appearance, and courtly manner assured his popularity. (Well into his eighties, a particular warmth and sensuality entered his voice whenever he spoke to women.) At the same time, he seems to have had only one serious romance as an undergraduate. The young woman in question was a town girl named Ann Leslie Nichol. Cleanth and Ann Leslie met in Latin class during the 1924–25 school year and saw each other frequently during that winter. Although she spent the next two winters at Smith College in Massachusetts, Ann Leslie and Cleanth shared several mutual friends, including her cousin, Andrew Lytle. Another cousin, Chink Nichol, helped inspire Red Warren's suicide attempt when she failed to reciprocate his youthful adoration. Both Nichol girls were also related to the Cheeks, a family of prominent Nashville merchants who presided over the Maxwell House coffee empire. Chink eventually married Lyle Lanier, the friend who had accompanied Warren to Kissam Hall the day he met Cleanth. Ann Leslie married Merrill Moore, a minor Fugitive who became a prominent Boston psychiatrist while writing many thousands of sonnets in his spare time. Shortly before their wedding in August 1930, Ann Leslie destroyed the poems Cleanth had given her, along with sentimental souvenirs from other boyfriends.[5]

Tinkum Blanchard had no coffee fortune in her family, but she proved a more kindred spirit to Cleanth. In addition to the love of literature that initially brought them together, the two shared interests in music, art, and ideas. Occasionally, Cleanth and Tinkum would go on double dates with Hodding Carter and his fiancée, attending dances in New Orleans and stopping afterwards for coffee and beignets in the French Market. At other times, the two couples would go "to the beach at Gulfport or Bay St. Louis, where friends had houses" (Waldron, *Hodding Carter*, 31). But the generic poverty of graduate student life meant that Cleanth and Tinkum often had to be content with nothing more than long walks and amusing conversations. These same economic constraints made an early marriage impractical. A young scholar who had neither a job nor the union card of a Ph.D. was in no position to support a wife and family. Still, an alternative career was out of the question. Cleanth's professional ambitions had been so shaped during his years at Vanderbilt that he needed a woman who shared those ambitions and wanted to be part of the life he had chosen for himself. For nearly sixty years Tinkum would be that sort of woman.

When she met Cleanth, however, it was something less than love at first sight. "You make me so angry at times," she wrote him on November 15, 1928. "Of course I'm going to give you a date if you ask for one! I refuse to be a partner in any such conspiracy designed to make two people miserable." Later in the same letter, she observes: "We do like each other a lot, you know we do. You're the first person I've enjoyed listening to in about two years (and before that I didn't have so much discrimination in what to listen to). You'd call me a little story teller if I told you we were soul-mates or any of that hooey, and I would be. I never expect to fall very much in love."[6]

The character of their relationship had changed radically by the following spring. Shortly after Cleanth received his M.A. degree, Tinkum wrote: "I love you in your cap and gown. When I marry you, I shall dress you up in it every once in a while, and look at you, and smile happily, tenderly, and kiss you many, many times." In a letter sent a few days later, she reveals her loneliness as she and Cleanth have just parted for the summer: "I feel awfully like a little girl tonight. . . . Please write me a soothing, rocking-me-to-sleep-in-your-arms letter."

Tinkum spent part of that summer at a camp that made her realize what a sedentary life she had lived in New Orleans. Reporting her experience to Cleanth, she writes, "I'm getting some fine training in living on a Tennessee hill with you some day. It's almost necessary to cut out smoking, cause you need your wind so much to climb these darn mountains." Later in the letter she writes teasingly: "Darling, darling, how I love you! You know it, don't you? And don't you feel sorry for me so far away from cokes and cigarettes and men? (No, I can see you licking your chops, you cruel wretch!)"

In another letter from camp, she writes to praise some sonnets he had sent her. (They may well have been a series of "Sonnets for Tinkum" that were found among Cleanth's personal papers after his death.) "I hardly know what to tell you about the sonnets," she writes, "—they're marvelous, Cleanth—they're perfect!" But as the letter continues, the praise modulates into apprehension. "I've read them over a hundred times today and each time I get a new thrill out of them. There's such bigness to them! I don't know how to praise them correctly, but they're as good as anything that was ever written—you know they are! I feel small and afraid when I read some of the lines—oh I wish you were here now to hold me and comfort me tenderly—tonight I'm so desperately afraid of losing you. . . . I couldn't bear to think of giving you up. Please don't hurt me. I love you so."

IV

If this special romance helped to sustain Cleanth's spirits, other aspects of his life were not going nearly so well. In moving from Alexandria to Shreveport, his father was encountering the same professional frustration he had experienced in the Memphis Conference. He could offer his son encouragement and inspiration but little else. Even more vexing to Cleanth was the paucity of literary stimulation he found in the supposedly exotic and cosmopolitan city of New Orleans. If he had arrived at Vanderbilt too late to sit at the Fugitive campfire, he had also missed by a year or two a minor Renaissance in the environs of Bourbon Street.

Although it would never produce a group of writers as exciting or innovative as the Fugitives, the New Orleans literary scene had been home— in the mid-twenties—to a community of bohemians, who came from more prosaic parts of the United States, and to the *Double Dealer*, one of the most remarkable little magazines of the twentieth century. By the time that Cleanth arrived in New Orleans in 1928, however, this great literary ferment had largely disappeared. Not only was the *Double Dealer* gone, but the most famous bohemians had departed as well. Sherwood Anderson had left to become a newspaper publisher in Marion, Virginia, and Hamilton Basso and Bill Faulkner were no longer playing drunken games of tag across the roofs of the French Quarter. Although Cleanth was still

writing poetry, he did not find the same kind of support at Tulane that
he had known in the Calumet Club. Perhaps for this reason, he maintained correspondence with his Calumet friends Hugh Cecil and Margaret
Moore (she would later become a physical therapist at Warm Springs,
Georgia, and include President Franklin Roosevelt among her patients),
as well as with Donald Davidson.

In an undated letter written shortly after he got settled, Cleanth
thanked Davidson for commenting on some poetry he had sent him and
for inviting him to contribute to the book page of the *Tennessean*. The
letter goes on to say: "The English Department at Tulane has been very
kind in every way, and I look forward to a good year. Just now, though, it
looks as if I will be too busy to do much writing." After mentioning a
couple of professors who did write poetry, he concludes, "for the most
part, New Orleans seems to be barren ground as far as literature is concerned. I hope we can stir up something down here."

From an intellectual standpoint, Cleanth's year at Tulane was also of
marginal benefit. Not among the elite institutions in the South, the university fell far short of the standards of the best northern schools. The courses
he took were competently taught, but none of his professors had the stature of Edwin Mims or Walter Clyde Curry, much less John Crowe Ransom
or Donald Davidson. For that matter, Vanderbilt itself had not offered a
notable advance over the education Cleanth obtained at McTyeire. His
intellectual maturation in both Nashville and New Orleans occurred outside the classroom and revealed the inadequacy of what he was experiencing in it.

Nearly fifty years later, Cleanth remembered the limitations of his
graduate training in the following terms:

> The question of whether a given poem was good or bad was either waived
> or never asked. You consulted a book to find out whether somebody had
> said it was a good poem. If you couldn't find anybody who had passed
> judgment on it, you were at sea. You had no equipment to make an aes-
> thetic judgment. I remember a pleasant, big, blonde girl who sometimes,
> when she had searched the library for some judgment on a poem, would
> bring it to me. If I said, "This is God-awful stuff," she would write down
> in her paper the academic equivalent of that. But otherwise, she didn't
> know, honestly didn't know. No one had ever taken the trouble to raise the
> question for her—how you thought about these things. (See Warren,
> "Conversation," 4–5)

The more he wrote poetry, the more Cleanth thought about these things himself. What he was not getting from the literary historians at Tulane was any sense of the interior life of the poem. Although this had been revealed for him by the distant glow of the Fugitive campfire, the relative darkness of graduate school was forcing him to see by his own light.

The years at Vanderbilt had provided Cleanth with several key moments of illumination—such as the time he first encountered Davidson's criticism or the evening he began to understand Ransom's poetry. No doubt, these experiences were shaping his critical sensibility long before he left Nashville. The earliest extant evidence we have of Brooks as critic, however, is in the M.A. thesis he wrote at Tulane in 1929. Entitled "Studies in Baroque: An Examination of the Conceit-Poetry of the Elizabethan Sonnet-Sequences," this thesis begins what would be a lifelong engagement with Renaissance verse, in addition to reflecting a view of poetry that was becoming increasingly evident in some of Cleanth's own work. Although the figures with whom he deals were of an earlier period than the metaphysical poets, whose stock was then rising in the literary world, his discussion of metaphor in the Elizabethan sonnets helps show the way that was later followed by Donne, Marvell, and company.

The phenomenon that Brooks examines is the curious appearance of sonnet sequences in British poetry during the last two decades of the sixteenth century, with the craze reaching its height between 1593 and 1597. Except for those by Shakespeare, the poems have been roundly condemned on two grounds. First, they are so derivative of French and Italian models that many of them skirt the borders of plagiarism. Second, and this is the issue with which Brooks is most concerned, they employ figures of speech so extravagant as to divert attention away from the subject of the poem. What critics have failed thus far to explain is why some of the finest poets of the age were guilty of such loose literary morals and such ostentatious craftsmanship.

The charge of plagiarism can be dismissed on the grounds that the Elizabethan age observed standards different from ours. Much that we might regard today as protected literary property would have been in the public domain in the sixteenth century. It is harder to explain why poets such as Spenser, Sidney, Drayton, and Daniel, who wrote so well otherwise, would succumb to artificial imagery and strained comparisons (what have been called "conceits") simply to ape a literary fad. Brooks suggests that Kathleen Lea may have been on to something when she questioned the very terms of this indictment:

> The conceit, she holds, is not artificial but wholly natural. The mind naturally in the creative moment catches at hints of similarity; it is the afterthought, the critical reflection, that judges and discriminates among these intuitive flashes and uses only those which are judged fit on sober reconsideration. In short, the imagination makes the conceit; reflection discards it, instead of vice versa. We might even say that the English Petrarchists (again excluding the obviously servile imitators) were hasty romanticists who had not learned what the later and more sober romanticists were to learn; namely, that "poetry is the spontaneous overflow of powerful emotions, *recollected in tranquillity.*" ("Studies in Baroque" 3 : 3 – 4; emphasis Brooks's)

If the Romantics expressed their emotions with original utterances from the heart, the courtly poets of the Elizabethan age were more given to "playful elaboration and comparison, provided it be, at the same time, graceful and dainty" ("Studies in Baroque" 5 : 18). This extended literary foreplay may not appeal to the taste of another age, and it may consign the Elizabethan sonnets to a rank in the literary pantheon lower than that of lyric poetry, but judged on their own terms, the imaginative conceits of the Elizabethans (like the logical ones of the later metaphysical poets) accomplished what they set out to do.

Although Brooks's thesis is obviously an apprentice effort, it shows an original mind at work. His discussions of Dante and Petrarch also prove that the young critic is solidly based in literary history; he also knows the relevant scholarship and prevailing opinions about his subject. But he has enough intellectual curiosity and self-confidence to push beyond the conventional wisdom. Brooks asks fundamental questions about the function of metaphor and, hence, about the nature of poetry itself. When the answers given by the experts fail to satisfy him, he comes up with his own explanations—even to the point of coining the term *vers de court*. Eight years earlier, Sir Herbert Grierson had published his influential anthology *Metaphysical Lyrics and Poems of the Seventeenth Century.* The reaction to this book (particularly T. S. Eliot's review of it) helped to focus the attention of critics and scholars on the importance of intellect and wit in poetry. As Brooks would demonstrate a decade later in *Modern Poetry and the Tradition* (1939), this is a lesson that the Fugitives and other modernists (Eliot included) were already learning on their own. One of the by-products of that lesson was a renewed appreciation for the substantial, if lesser, achievement of the Elizabethan court poets.

V

One of Cleanth's objectives in attending Tulane was to put himself in a more strategic position to compete for a Rhodes Scholarship from Louisiana. The Rhodes Scholarships had been instituted in 1903 from money left in the will of the British financier Cecil John Rhodes. A product of the Victorian age, Rhodes had spent most of his short life (he died at age fifty-five) bearing the "White Man's burden" in southern Africa. He amalgamated the diamond mines around Kimberley, South Africa, in 1888 and served as prime minister of the Cape Colony from 1890 to 1896. His most lasting legacy, however, is probably the scholarship program that bears his name. Because of his imperialistic confidence in the superiority of British culture, Rhodes believed that the Anglo-Saxon world would benefit if the best young men from abroad were allowed to study at Oxford University. Within the provisions of his will, thirty-two scholarships per year were allotted to the United States.

Vanderbilt University had done quite well during the first quarter century of the Rhodes Scholarship program. John Crowe Ransom had gone to Christ Church College, Oxford, from 1910 to 1913, and William Yandell Elliott had attended Balliol College from 1921 to 1923. Then, in 1928, Red Warren was accepted as a Rhodes Scholar at New College. To win a Rhodes Scholarship would not only put Cleanth among a distinguished group of Vanderbilt alumni, it would also be the realization of a dream he had cherished from the age of thirteen. But it was far from a foregone conclusion. Candidates were judged by local committees on the basis of scholarship, extracurricular activities (mainly sports), and moral stature. The list of those who failed to earn appointment contained many impressive names (in fact, Red himself had lost the first time he tried). The prospective competition from Louisiana included a young man from Centenary College, who had traveled in England and met several of the leading figures in the Labour Party, and Cleanth's own roommate, Hodding Carter.

The year at Tulane, however, had dampened Hodding's enthusiasm for the academic life. He had fallen in love with Betty Brunhilde Werlein and was not willing to delay marriage for the two or three years it would take to complete a degree program at Oxford. Hodding recalled those days in a letter he wrote to Cleanth on January 23, 1967:

> Do you still have that bathrobe which used to scrape your toenails when we lived at the Capdevilles? Sometimes it seems as if it were only yesterday that you would walk up to me with an earth moving notion, clad in that speckled monk's habit and punch me in the chest with a finger to prove a point. I also remember that arrogant confidence of yours when, upon my telling you I wasn't going to apply for a Rhodes Scholarship because I knew if I won it Betty wouldn't be here when I got back, you answered with Saxon simplicity, "If I get it, Tinkum will be here." [7]

In addition to his desire to marry and his disillusionment with academia, Hodding was also committed to the profession of journalism and was eager to start a newspaper from which he could launch a crusade against Huey Long. Not only did he withdraw from the competition for a Rhodes Scholarship, but he also put Cleanth up in his home in Hammond the night before he was to meet with the screening committee and drove him to Baton Rouge for the meeting the next day. The chairman of the screening committee was a professor of government at Louisiana State University and former Rhodes Scholar from Arkansas named Charles W. Pipkin.

The student from Centenary College lost out, and in 1929 Cleanth Brooks, Jr., became a Rhodes Scholar from Louisiana. Because the ship for England was leaving from New York, Cleanth asked Donald Davidson for an introduction to Allen Tate, the most cosmopolitan member of the Vanderbilt fraternity and an unofficial literary patron for his friends from the South. But other activities kept the young scholars busy the night before the ship left, allowing little time to visit New York or its residents. So Cleanth's first meeting with Tate would not occur until later that year.

From aboard the *Aquitania* on October 3, Cleanth wrote to Tinkum: "I have been able to keep off sea-sickness so far but my life has been made miserable by an abominable cold I caught in the New York drizzle, and standing on the wet deck in the rain as we left New York." Continuing the letter the next day, he writes: "I saw the wake of the Aquitania the other night, billowing white with all sorts of phosphorous fires twinkling in it— witch's fire, I suppose. It looks almost as if the Aquitania were a great lady with a gorgeous train, filled with sparkling sequins. At least, I thought so."

Elsewhere in the same letter, Cleanth mentions a friend named Billy who came down from Yale to see him in New York. "Florence Sawrie, a Nashville girl whom we both know was in town," he writes, "and while I had to go to the shore dinner Billy carried her to a show. We met at my hotel at 11, all set for a midnight show but Florence's shoes were wet so she took them off to dry and we all sat on my bed and talked—mostly about heart-broken love affairs until nearly 2."

Cleanth left for Europe at a time when American exiles of an earlier generation were beginning to return to the country of their birth. Back home, the Museum of Modern Art was being founded. The season's fiction included Hemingway's *A Farewell to Arms*, Faulkner's *The Sound and the Fury*, and Wolfe's *Look Homeward, Angel*. The very month the stock market crashed Cleanth's boat docked at Southampton. Too eager to wait even another night to claim his place in the community of scholars, he took the bus to Oxford and arrived at dusk. Returning to his rooms in Exeter College the next afternoon, he found a note from Red welcoming him to the university.

CHAPTER FOUR

A Reb at Oxford

As a Rhodes Scholar, Cleanth had essentially the same academic options as any other student at Oxford. For his first two years of residence, he pursued an Honours B.A. in English Language and Literature. As the British are always quick to point out, the Honours B.A. resembles an American baccalaureate degree in name only. Whereas graduates of the elite preparatory schools in England are presumed to be ready for Oxford, most American students require some postsecondary education, with solid training in Latin and Greek. The one difference is that a fair number of British students will take the B.A. program for a Pass degree. This is a general curriculum that more closely approximates the American B.A. It is assumed that Rhodes Scholars, who already have an American B.A., will seek the more rigorous and prestigious Honours degree.

The academic calendar for the B.A. program begins with two eight-week terms, each of which is followed by a six-week vacation. A third eight-week term is followed by a four-and-a-half-month vacation. The same sequence is repeated the second year, except that the climax of the third eight-week term is a weeklong series of written examinations. The course of study is far more specialized than that of a typical American baccalaureate (or the Pass B.A. at Oxford itself). To use the current jargon, the student is expected to gain a holistic and interdisciplinary understanding of his given field. For Cleanth, this meant an appreciation of British history and culture as well as a knowledge of imaginative literature.

The letters Cleanth sent to Tinkum during his first few weeks at Oxford describe his new life in England and a scholarly routine far different from anything he had known at Vanderbilt or Tulane. In his first letter, dated October 14, 1929, he writes: "I go to see my tutor again tonight. You'd like him: he's all Irish. Perhaps you'd even like his Pekinese. I haven't done any studying so far—but this can't last forever. I suppose I'll start soon." According to custom, tutors were assigned by the residential college to which a student belonged. Cleanth's tutor, Nevill Coghill, was a Chaucer specialist, who was descended from an English family that had settled in Ireland in the seventeenth century (Nevill had an aunt who wrote Irish stories that he enjoyed repeating). Although Coghill was no great scholar, Cleanth remembers him as a decent and competent fellow, who was always a bit aloof. During his career at Oxford, his students included Richard Burton and W. H. Auden.

In that first letter to Tinkum, Cleanth also reveals his excitement at meeting Red Warren: "The 'Fugitive' I told you was at Oxford looked me up last night. I wasn't in and he left a note. I saw him this morning and had a very nice chat with him. I guessed right: he is bringing out a life of John Brown next month and a volume of poems in the winter; and he stands in big with *The New Republic*. He is, I suppose, as I had hoped, the biggest man at Oxford in poetry." Within a week, Cleanth and a student named McMullan were trying to interest Red and his friend Dixon Wector in starting a literary review. In a letter dated October 20, Cleanth wonders if this is such a good idea: "According to Warren, the Oxford Poetry Society would make that of New Orleans look tame indeed. They all dress like young Shelleys or Oscar Wildes and writhe on the floor and meditate in sepulchral tones on what to 'react to in this complex modern age.'"

Less than two weeks later, Cleanth gave a breakfast for Wector, Warren, and McMullan. "Oxford breakfasts are nice things," he writes in a letter on November 1. "The guests leave by ones and twos to go to lectures and things. McMullan and Warren just left a little while ago. And I've been reading Chaucer—was reading it when the porter brought your letter." A few paragraphs later, he informs Tinkum that the first sonnet in the sequence he had written for her was to be published in the *Archive*, along with two of his other poems. "That's 6 magazines and 8 poems for the summer. I'll send it to you when it comes out; and I mean to finish the sequence someday. That stands whether I have you in deed or only as a beautiful dream."

Cleanth was not a complete scholar and aesthete, however. Within his first few weeks at Oxford, he had begun playing rugby and continued to do so regularly for the next two years. Although it is restricted to a cult following in the United States, rugby is an extremely popular game overseas. Combining the pace of soccer with the violence of American football, it is a physically demanding sport. Although Cleanth was no star, he did play on the second team (the equivalent of a junior varsity squad) for Exeter College. He and his cohorts would play against the second teams of other colleges—mostly within but some outside of Oxford. On occasion, Cleanth would even be called up to play for Exeter's first team. What most impressed the British were the solid tackling skills he had acquired from playing American football. He ended up at inside three-quarterback and acquitted himself well for as long as his stamina held up. He no longer exercised every day as he had at McTyeire. And his wind was affected by cigarette smoking, a habit he had taken up at Vanderbilt.

"I'm still sore from my first rugger match," Cleanth writes on October 25. "Tuesday I played wing three quarter or something like that on Exeter's second against Trinity's second. We got all gloriously beaten but I learned something about the game. I drew several penalties at first but after the first quarter I caught on to most of it. . . . I think you'd like the rugger outfit: foot-ball shoes, stockings, blue flannel shorts, and a red and black jersey. It feels as if you were playing football in basket-ball clothes. I miss the shoulder pads when I tackle, but it's not a bad game."

Less than a month later, on November 23, Cleanth tells Tinkum about a novel he has just read. "I finished Ernest Hemingway's 'A Farewell to Arms' last night. It is a terrible book—it flays you and leaves you bleeding. McMullan thinks so too. Perhaps it cut me so deep because Catherine reminds me of you. I don't know why she should, Tinkum, but she does— very much. Somehow I think that you would do what she does in the last chapters. For that reason, the book seems more real and terrible to me. At the end, I felt that I had seen you dead and told you goodbye forever."

I

If Red Warren had been a cordial acquaintance at Vanderbilt, his friendship with Cleanth matured both socially and intellectually at Oxford. Their academic work differed, as Red was pursuing a B.Litt. degree while Cleanth was enrolled in the Honours B.A. program, but they spent many an after-hours session either in Red's lodgings in Wellington Square or among mutual friends in Exeter College. Cleanth recalls a night in Exeter College when a group of young men (some Rebels, some Yankees, some British) began discussing the Civil War: "It was a matter of intense interest to Red and he promised to lay out before us then and there precisely what had gone on at the Battle of Gettysburg and particularly what had gone awry for the Confederate side. . . . Unfortunately, just before the batteries opened up on Cemetery Ridge in preparation for Pickett's Charge, the college bell began its hideous racket, warning that one had to be in his rooms before 12:15. So Pickett's Charge was over before it began, Red was out of the room in a trice, his scholar's gown fluttering behind him as he fled" ("Brooks on Warren," 20).

Another memorable occasion was a dinner party that Red gave for a friend at his digs in Wellington Square. The meal was to be served by Red's landlord, who claimed to be familiar with the dishes Red had ordered. When he saw the landlord carrying a punchbowl filled with sweet martini and a dozen raw oysters, "Red asked what in the world it was. The land-lord's reply was 'The gentleman asked for oyster cocktail, didn't he?'" ("Brooks on Warren," 20). Although Cleanth was not present that evening, he had been around Red enough to visualize the expression of controlled rage he knew was on his friend's face.

The B.Litt. program Red was finishing was for an advanced research degree similar to a Ph.D. in an American university. He was also writing poetry notably influenced by the extravagant and baroque imagery one finds in the plays of Shakespeare and his contemporaries. Unlike Donne, who was better known for the logical development of a controlling meta-phor, Warren sought psychological unity through an accumulation of striking, often violent, images rendered in archaic diction. (He had already developed an interest in Elizabethan drama, which would become one of his primary teaching areas during his later academic career.) At the same time, Red never got so absorbed in the literature of another age and an-other land that he lost his American roots. (On many an evening at Ox-ford, he enjoyed hearing Cleanth's angelic rendition of "Frankie and Johnny," an American folk song about a homicidal woman and the man "who done her wrong.") His year in England had also made Red more of a southerner than he had been back home in Kentucky and Tennessee. His book on John Brown came out in 1929, and his participation in *I'll Take My Stand* kept the fate of southern culture on his mind.

From the moment of its publication by Harper and Brothers in November 1930, the Agrarian manifesto was the focus of controversy throughout the South. Cleanth read the book not too long after its appearance and responded to it with a mixture of enthusiasm and thoughtful criticism. He displays plenty of both in a twelve-page handwritten letter from "The Moss, Great Warford, Alderley Edge, Cheshire," sent to Donald Davidson on March 18, 1931:[1]

Dear Donald—

I am spending a few days in the midlands resting up before I go back to hard work again, and I take this opportunity to write you a long delayed letter. As a matter of fact I read "I'll Take My Stand" some months ago, and in fact started you a long letter about it. The two tutors I had last term started in on me, however, and the letter was never finished. In the meantime I've done a great deal of re-reading and a great deal of talking it over with my friends—a great deal of it against intelligent opposition, which was fortunate, for me at least, since it gave me an opportunity to spot the weak points in the program and to find out which features could be defended—and most easily or tellingly defended. I am writing you a long letter about it therefore, not so much to advise (I have a thoroughly sincere humility about that, as I think you know) as to congratulate, and state for the benefit of myself my own attitude.

In the first place, I think that the book is strongest where it attacks the American plutocracy, and weakest where it dismisses socialism with a too casual gesture. I do not mean at all that there is no case against socialism—if one means by it a sort of white-tiled, antiseptic, efficient scientific Garden of Eden. At the same time this case needs to be made. Socialism needs to be accused of being preoccupied with economics—it also needs to have the question put squarely: What is life for, anyway? And if it gives you the answer (which many socialists will give) which defines man's role as primarily a cog in the social machine, it needs to be rejected as having an essentially inadequate conception of life and humanity. Unless such charges are made explicit, however, it puts us at a disadvantage, for the socialists also claim to be fighting the emphasis on the economic motive, and to be building an economic structure on which an artistic and healthy life can be raised.

I say all this because of my experience in defending the southern position against the onslaughts of my Socialist friends—some of them very intelligent Socialists with a sound knowledge of economics and a sincere and fine love of the good life. I say it also, not because of any particular love for Socialism, or fear of Socialist displeasure (certainly *not* to placate our own group of professional liberals and pink-tea radicals). As a matter of good tactics, however, I think the position here should be strengthened. (The definition of Socialism as given in the general platform of "I'll Take My Stand," for instance, was very inadequate.) There is no need to lay oneself open to damaging criticism from the outside, especially from England which is rapidly becoming socialist, even if the matter is immaterial with "the brethren" at home, who are already in a psychopathic state of fear of socialism and Bolshevism. To sum up, we need to show a little more intelligent knowledge of socialism, and to give the appearance, at least, of having given it more serious attention before rejecting it.

In the second place, I think that there are just a few hints of underestimating the Puritanism of the South. I say this in spite of such frank and realistic treatments of the matter as in Andrew Lytle's essay, for instance. If one begins to lean too hard on the influence of Virginian sweetness and light, he will certainly be creating a myth out of thin air, or rather out of air considerably befogged. Virginia itself is and has for a long time been predominantly a Methodist state. Incidentally, if someone acquainted with the facts will investigate the history of the break between the Methodist Church, North and South, as well as the break-up of other denominations he will probably find some very interesting and apposite material.

On the other hand, I think that the charge of nostalgia as brought by Hazlitt in *The Nation*[2] and by Mencken in the *Mercury*[3] is quite unfounded and unfair. It is the easiest charge to make—indeed the natural one to make, and I feel that it would have been made regardless of the contents of the book. On the other hand, it is a damaging accusation—and one of the big problems is to convince southerners that they are not making a 'backward' step. They seem (at least the Oxford ones) to [be] more infected with 'progress' than I had thought.

Ransom's essay was a good statement of the general problem.[4] I liked your treatment of the literature question,[5] and I think your criticism of Babbitt is quite fair and true. Have you seen Eliot's *Essays* on Babbitt[6] which have appeared from time to time?[7]

I don't think that we can afford to take a less liberal stand than 'Red' Warren's on the negro question, and I was delighted with Andrew Lytle's essay.[8] I didn't expect so good a one of him. I say the same of Lyle Lanier's.[9] By the way the points he makes about Dewey's position are true, and more than that, they need to be hammered in.

I was frankly disappointed in Owsley's article.[10] I thought it would be the easiest of all the essays to write—I think the style in his treatment is bad, and the tone is not very happy. He is too militant, claims too much, or at least seems to have the attitude of claiming too much. And the case of the South is too strong, I think, to need to have the tone which generally arises from an inferiority complex. This is merely a criticism of the attitude and style. I have no reason to believe that all of his allegations can be proved up to the hilt. (I'm going to start reading up on American history when I go back. I need two years solid reading, at least, before I'll feel competent to say anything about it.)

I was also disappointed at first with Tate's article.[11] On a second reading I was very much impressed, however, but I felt that the conclusions he comes to are apparently a resignation to defeat. As Margaret Moore puts it, 'his essay is one of the best, and one of the most hopeless.'

In the meantime I have read Ransom's *God Without Thunder*.[12] I think that he provides a much sounder statement of the general problem and certainly a much more optimistic one for this particular problem. I was frankly surprized at Ransom's position, and delighted—partially perhaps because his book represents a more mature and sensitive statement of the position I had been working toward; e.g. I had found the same significance in C. C. Ayres' *Science: A False Messiah*. I had made the same interpretation of Kant and Hume—I had found the same hostility and withering scepticism in the attitude of anthropologists, etc., etc. (I am at this time writing Ransom a long letter telling him what I think of his book.)[13]

I don't mind telling you that my personal opinion is that the success of the whole problem depends on just how much the other contributors to the Symposium can accept Ransom's viewpoint. I think that the problem is primarily a religious one. I am quite convinced that Allen Tate is right in saying so, but I am [also] quite convinced that the southerner cannot achieve this sanction and guarantee by 'political means.' I think that his own implied scepticism to the possibility of this is quite well-founded.

The whole problem (to state it much too simply) is that of maintaining or rebuilding a feudal society. Modern society is fundamentally scientific and mechanistic. It is impossible even to return to the Greek ideal—for we have Whitehead's now where the Greeks had Euclid's—and unfortunately men have found out how to apply that science to the work of making sewing-machines and manure-spreaders. The Greek ideal represents a perilous equilibrium once gloriously achieved, and now irrevocably upset. If the southern ideal is feudalistic and medieval, then the problem *is* religious. A medievalism without religion is—*Hamlet* played solely by hopelessly inadequate Rosencrantz's and Guildenstern's.

How are things going on the home front? I have heard one or two of Ransom's debates—had one very favorable account by a friend in New Orleans who heard the debate there. I am very much interested in the whole problem. In fact, I feel completely off-center over here away from things. I hope all goes well. I haven't seen [John Gould] Fletcher lately but I hope to see him in London in a few weeks. Incidentally, I thought his essay on Education very good indeed.[14]

Incidentally, again, I reread your *Tall Men*[15] the other day. I think I bring a more mature taste to this re-reading. There are places which I did not like as well as before, but many other passages sound deeper, and I have a more profound and reasoned appreciation, I think, of the poem as a whole. Please don't get so interested or so busy in other things, no matter how important, that you stop writing poetry. A real poet can hardly have a more important business than writing poetry. (I hardly need tell you that this praise is heart-felt and sincere.)

I expect to come home in July and hope to see you there. [Charles W.] Pipkin wrote me about his interview with you and seemed to have enjoyed it very much. How does he feel about the Symposium attitude now?

Until July I shall be very busy preparing for examinations. I don't expect to do surpassingly well. I really want to get home. I feel like Antaeus after a seven day balloon ride. It doesn't matter much, however. I've written nothing for months. I have sold some sonnets to a magazine in Paris but I've sent off nothing for a long time. I think that I have come to a little more mature attitude, however. That may be something.

Please don't feel that you need to answer this letter at once. I know how busy you are. And as I have said before, I write not so much because I think my advice will be worth anything to you, as rather as an indication of my real interest, and, for myself, a crystallization of my present position.

If more writing is to be done, I think one might have a few words to say on the present European opinion of America.

After allowing duly for exaggeration and misrepresentation, it is rather significant that an Alsatian girl can't believe that I'm an American because I don't rush around with 'Sees, guys' and act like a boor generally, or that an intelligent German student thinks it odd that as an American I don't rush at top speed around the city and bolt my food. And it is significant for the southern position in general that a southern accent can protect one a little from having the onus of these things saddled on him—not, of course, because there is anything intrinsically good about the accent, but because not it but that of New York has been identified with rush, speed, vulgarity, and bragging.

Please believe me to be thoroughly in sympathy with what you are doing, and that I am grateful and feel warmly all the help and encouragement you have given me in the past.

     Sincerely yours,
     Cleanth Brooks

P.S. Apropos of Mencken's review of *I'll Take My Stand*: he names 'Red' Warren as one of the contributors "out of his ken." Someone should suggest to him that it is strange that he should have chosen Red's Life of *John Brown* as one of the ten best books of the year last year and yet not be able to remember it this.[16] It forces one to think what I thought at the time: that no matter how poor (or how good) the book, Mencken would choose any that seemed to be debunking—and that his choice or praise proves nothing more than that one of his chief prejudices has been tickled. But the whole incident reveals his essential shallowness.

In the summer of 1931, having completed his Honours B.A. program, Cleanth came back to America for his four-and-a-half-month vacation. When he returned to Oxford that fall (to pursue a B.Litt. degree himself), he passed through Nashville to see Red and other friends at Vanderbilt. Although he had not achieved much distinction as a poet and had yet to begin his career as a critic, he was already known as a member of the Vanderbilt literary community. John Ransom, who had seemed such a remote and forbidding presence in the classroom had made it a point to call on Cleanth in England the previous spring. Ransom had received a Guggenheim grant for work abroad and was living in Devon, while tutoring at the University of Exeter. He was impressed not only with Cleanth's knowledge of literature but also with his understanding of the issues raised in *I'll Take My Stand*. (Undoubtedly, Ransom had heard much about his former student from Davidson and Warren.) The young man who had once dropped Ransom's class for lack of self-confidence had now been accepted into the fraternity.

II

If Cleanth was spiritually closer to the Fugitive campfire at Oxford than he ever was at Vanderbilt, his formal academic work was still in a very traditional philological vein. During the year that he worked on his B.Litt. degree, he chose as mentor a man quite different from Ransom and company—the Scottish scholar David Nichol Smith. Although Cleanth did not enter Oxford with the intention of concentrating in eighteenth-century literature, he probably would have gone into any period in which Nichol Smith specialized. He followed the time-honored dictum of choosing the man over the field. As a result, he ended up spending much of his third year in England in the British Museum working on an edition of the correspondence of Thomas Percy and Richard Farmer.

Although his name is largely unknown except to specialists in the literary and ecclesiastical history of eighteenth-century England, Thomas Percy was among a select group of scholars who laid the foundation for modern literary study. An Anglican bishop in Dromore in Northern Ireland, Percy was a very minor novelist and a generally undistinguished poet. In *Reliques of Ancient English Poetry*, however, he compiled what was then the most authoritative volume of English ballads, which included the various songs that Shakespeare used in his plays, Elizabethan lyrics, and other related material. When in London, Percy was part of Johnson's circle, and he included among his friends such notables as Oliver Gold-smith, Sir Joshua Reynolds, Thomas Warton, and William Shenstone, as well as Richard Farmer. Percy was a far more dedicated churchman than Jonathan Swift and often worried that his literary labors were diverting him from his clerical vocation. By the time he died in 1811, at the age of eighty-two, Percy had outlived his more famous contemporaries and had helped pave the way for the Romantic movement. He was a friend of the young Walter Scott and an inspiration to Wordsworth and Coleridge. In fact, Percy's biographer Bertram Davis believes that the very title of the *Lyrical Ballads* can be traced to the influence of Percy's *Reliques*.

Cleanth's youthful involvement with Percy's letters was an exercise in pure scholarship. Although there is much that a literary critic could say about the bishop's textual labors and literary influence, such observations were not germane to the editorial task of collecting and annotating the letters between Percy and Farmer. Far from being a dilettante who consid-ered himself above the nitty-gritty of historical and biographical research, Cleanth did such a commendable job with his B.Litt. project that Nichol Smith asked him to help edit the entire body of Percy's letters. Under the general editorship of Smith and Brooks, the first published volume of the series appeared over a decade later in 1944; in 1946 Brooks published his own edition of the Percy-Farmer correpondence.

Successive volumes in this series were published in 1951, 1954, 1957, and 1961. Several factors, including Nichol Smith's death in 1964, created a seventeen-year lull in the project. Since 1977, however, three more of the promised ten volumes have seen the light of day. The tenth and final vol-ume, which was scheduled to to be published in the mid-1990s, has been indefinitely postponed by Cleanth's own death. What had begun as a stu-dent exercise for a young man of twenty-five became a labor of sixty years' duration.

With its emphasis on traditional philological scholarship, the English program at Oxford was not hospitable to literary criticism. (Although Cleanth and Nichol Smith remained good friends for the balance of Smith's life, the Scot had little use for the kind of literary analysis practiced by his students Brooks and Warren.) The University of Cambridge, however, was a different matter. Like Vanderbilt, Cambridge in the twenties produced what George Core calls a "fifth column" of young writers and critics who were challenging the old orthodoxy (Core, "Vanderbilt English," 23). If there was a difference (other than the greater distinction of the department at Cambridge), it is that Cambridge criticism was more fully integrated into the university curriculum, whereas Edwin Mims managed for years to keep Vanderbilt criticism underground, or at least off campus. In 1921 a young Cambridge graduate named Ivor Armstrong Richards joined the faculty of his alma mater as a lecturer in English and Moral Science. By the end of the decade, Richards was making seminal contributions to literary criticism. Moreover, his lectures were so popular that some of them had to be held in the streets—the first time that had happened at Cambridge since the Middle Ages (see Russo, xv).

Although Richards was not particularly well versed in the ideas of either Freud or Jung, he advocated a psychological approach to literary criticism. His principal debt was to Coleridge, who emphasized the balancing and synthesizing powers of the imagination. In his groundbreaking work *Principles of Literary Criticism* (1924), Richards stresses his belief that a poem is finally an experience of the reader. Thus, as Walter Sutton notes, "Richards rules out the possibility of an aesthetic idealism or art-for-art's-sake attitude" (Sutton, 8). He even rules in a note of Arnoldian moralism. Because poetry can establish a creative tension between opposing ideas, it helps to make our thinking more complex and our general approach to life less simplistic.

When Cleanth arrived at Oxford in 1929, the former Fugitives had published very little criticism. Although his interest in close reading and contextual analysis had been inspired by a familiarity with their poetry, his critical insights tended to be random and untheoretical. In Richards he found a man who was at least raising some of the questions that he considered essential to an understanding of poetry. By accepting what he found valid (Richards's approach to individual poems) and formulating objections to what he found specious (Richards's psychological theory), Cleanth was beginning to define his own critical position. After more than half a century, he recalled:

> Later on in that academic year I had an opportunity to test my knowledge of Richards's work. He was invited to lecture in the hall of my Oxford college, Exeter; and for the first time I saw him and heard his voice. I had insisted that several of my friends attend the lecture with me, and to my surprise I found that, while I could follow clearly the argument, to my friends it was almost incomprehensible. They lacked the necessary preparation for what was a pioneering effort that broke with the literary training of the time—with the traditional British training as well as the American. ("I. A. Richards and *Practical Criticism*," 35–36)

Finding the application of Richards's criticism to be more compelling than its theoretical underpinnings, Cleanth was most impressed with *Practical Criticism*, a volume Richards published in 1929. Based on a series of classroom experiments conducted between 1925 and 1928, *Practical Criticism* empirically demonstrates the difficulty that even the best-educated modern students experienced in reading poetry. Richards gave out a total of thirteen unidentified poems to his students and asked for critical responses. When judged by commonly accepted literary standards, five of the thirteen poems should have been considered bad; six good to great; and two borderline. Richards's students—confronting the text without the benefit of history or biography—not only varied widely in their judgments but also fell prey to every conceivable form of misreading. Although it would have been easy enough for Richards to give them the "right" answers, his concern was with nurturing the sort of critical intelligence that would enable his students to come up with those answers on their own.

Like the textbooks that Brooks and Warren would later edit, *Practical Criticism* was at heart an exercise in pedagogy; whatever else it may be, applied criticism is also remedial reading. In letting his students make mistakes, Richards played the role of a diagnostician, who observes a problem in order to discover its causes. Those he found included an inability to discern the plain sense of the poem, a failure to apprehend its rhythm and movement, difficulties in visualizing its imagery; irrelevant associations from the reader's personal life, stock responses to the poem's theme, an excess of sentiment (sentimentality), a deficiency of sentiment (hardness of heart); doctrinal prejudices (usually political or religious), technical preconceptions, and other critical expectations. In identifying these deficiencies, Richards indirectly defined a positive approach to criticism. As Brooks observes, "if one is able to point out a sufficiency of errors made by others, he has at least implied the general lineaments of a sound reading" ("I. A. Richards and *Practical Criticism*," 38).

Although the poems selected by Richards spanned several centuries, his critical approach was particularly well suited to the verse that had been produced in the decade or so prior to the publication of *Practical Criticism*. As John Paul Russo notes, Richards's method

> could cope with the special uses of language and thematics in modernist
> poetry of the Pound-Eliot stamp. . . . High modernist art was oblique, self-
> referential, abstractionist, compressed, ambiguous, allusive, and, in Eliot's

prescriptive term, "difficult." It was linguistically precise and conceptually obscure. The Richardsian method, analyzing the poet's sense, imagery and metaphor, rhythm, tone, form, intention, attitude, and irony was fully prepared to handle compression, ambiguity, self-referentiality, obscurity, and allusiveness. . . . The explication of the modernist poem was not the sole justification of Richards' method, only its immediate historical context. (Russo, 295)

Cleanth soon discovered that he could discard Richards's speculative assertions about what the poem does to the mind of the reader and concentrate on the text itself (the language of a poem is objective and observable, whereas the neural states it produces can only be inferred). In doing so, he found that the most valuable concept Richards had to offer was that of poetic tension. One of the key functions of poetry is to reflect the complexity of actual experience. This can best be done by including in the poem as many diverse elements as possible. It is far too easy to exclude from a poem anything that might seem to run counter to the desired poetic effect. Such exclusion, however, gives us the patent artifice of propaganda and pornography. When the desired effect is achieved too easily, it strikes us as facile and shallow. The greatest poetry (and this includes all genuine tragedy) earns its vision through a dialectical reconciliation of opposites. The metaphor is the vehicle through which this dialectic occurs, and the poetic imagination is the faculty that sets it in motion.

As Brooks would later point out, Richards was not alone in what he chose to emphasize. He had arrived independently at a position quite similar to the one held by the two greatest English language poets of this century—T. S. Eliot and William Butler Yeats. In celebrating the metaphysical poets, Eliot used such phrases as "a degree of heterogeneity of material compelled into unity," "sudden contrasts of associations," "contrast of ideas," "a direct sensuous apprehension of thought," and the "amalgamating [of] disparate experiences." Yeats tended to express himself more epigrammatically, writing in "Ego Dominus Tuus," for example: "The rhetorician would deceive his neighbours / The sentimentalist himself."

It is almost certain that Richards was unaware of the critical writings of Eliot and Yeats at the time he published *Principles of Literary Criticism* in 1924. As Brooks notes: "The times were evidently ripe for a new emphasis on these matters, and the proof that they were ripe lies in the fact that several sensitive literary minds, some of a generation earlier than Richards and others of his own, were also moving in that direction.

The true originality of a thinker does not rest in his ability simply to concoct something novel, but to discover and make fruitful exploration of something that needs to be understood—some concept that the whole culture is in travail to bring forth" ("I. A. Richards and Concept of Tension," 149).

III

When Cleanth was not engaged in intellectual pursuits or playing rugby, he was apt to be enjoying a more leisurely form of recreation. This consisted of renting a flat-bottomed boat called a "punt" and taking it out on the Cherwell, a shallow local river that runs into the Thames. The person who steered the punt (often Cleanth himself) would move the boat along by pushing a long pole against the riverbed, making certain to avoid mud banks and other impediments. Cleanth and a group of his friends from Exeter College would rent a punt at any time during the week when they could afford a break from their studies. They would sometimes pack a picnic lunch or spend the afternoon at a teahouse along the river.

One of Cleanth's punting companions was a young Indian student named Hamayun Kabir. Like so many Oxford-educated colonials, Kabir was a political nationalist and a cultural Westerner. (He experienced indigenous Indian culture firsthand when inhabitants of his home village pelted him with stones for marrying outside his nominal faith.) Kabir was elected head of Oxford's prestigious debating society, the Political Union, and later became Minister of Culture in the Indian government. (He eventually broke with Indira Gandhi because he felt that she was too sympathetic to the Communists.) He and Cleanth were both at Oxford when Mahatma Gandhi made his famous speech at the university in 1931. Cleanth remembers Gandhi as a shriveled little man who wore a loincloth and little else. The Mahatma was accompanied by a devoted female campfollower from the British upperclass.

Since before Cleanth's arrival at Oxford, it had become a tradition for Rhodes Scholars to head for the continent as soon as an academic term was over. For someone who had spent all his life in southern Kentucky, Tennessee, and Louisiana, travel in Europe was more than just a young gentleman's grand tour. It was a means of laying claim to an older cultural heritage. This was particularly true of the second and third vacations Cleanth took during his first year at Oxford. (His first six-week break was devoted to rest and relaxation on the French Riviera.) In the spring

of 1930 he purchased one of the cheap tickets Mussolini was offering to
tourists who would visit Italy. He rode by train from Paris to Naples,
took a steamer to the heel of Sicily (the ticket had to be stamped at the
post office in Syracuse for the return fare to be valid), and then returned
to Paris by train.

That summer, Cleanth packed a trunk full of books and returned to
Europe, beginning with a boat trip up the Rhine. He got off in the Black
Forest and traveled mostly by foot for the next three weeks, observing the
local culture and visiting acquaintances of his Oxford classmates. He
spent three weeks in Munich and three more in Vienna. A boat trip down
the Danube took him to Budapest, where he remained for two or three
days. He than began the long train trip back—passing through Prague,
Leipzig, Dresden, Hannover and finally Holland. Because of the favorable
exchange rate, it was actually cheaper to visit the continent than it would
have been to remain in England.

In 1930 Cleanth spent the Christmas break in Greece and Italy. From
the *S. S. Orama*, "just out of Naples," he wrote to Tinkum on January 7,
1931:

> I wish you had been with me as we toured the temples at Segesta, Sele-
> munte, and Agrigento. They are the first real Greek temples I had ever
> seen. And they are splendid: stone, golden-brown, flawed and honey-
> combed by the rain—mellow-architraves and broken triglyphs—still pre-
> serving the ancient rhythm and grace. That at Segesta stands lonely on a
> little hill, miles from everywhere, with a flock of sheep grazing at the very
> threshold. Those at Selemunte are in utter ruins but, they too, are far from
> the town, and stand on a cliff, with the blue Mediterranean creaming be-
> low them. It is all pastoral and Theocritean, and at the same time very sane
> and fine.

In his second and third years at Oxford, Cleanth confined his vacations
to Great Britain. In the spring of 1931, with his B.A. examination coming
at the end of the next academic term, he boarded at a quiet farmhouse in
the west country, where he read, studied, practiced writing essay exams,
and composed his long letter to Davidson. From the same location, he
wrote to inform Tinkum that while he was staying at a local inn, "a Cor-
nish bar-maid ha[d] been trying to lure me with her blandishments." "The
season is not on yet," he continues, "and so I happened to be the only
guest at the hotel and therefore completely at the mercy of Iris Ianthe
Veronique (that's her name!) and her blooming rosy-cheeked sister. So far

she has carried me off once to see King Arthur's Castle, and once to pick primroses. But now that I've moved out into the country and now that the Easter visitors will soon be here, I suppose that she will lose interest."

During one of his sojourns in the British Isles, Cleanth and a friend from the north of England took a walking tour in the Scottish Highlands. They rode by train from Oxford to Manchester and on to Inverness. There they took a bus to the shores of Moray Firth and saw Cawdor Castle, where Shakespeare set the murder in *Macbeth*. The next day, they began walking west, and from dawn to dusk saw no human faces other than their own. (The Highlands had been largely emptied of human habitation since the English army broke the clans at the Battle of Culloden in the sixteenth century.) They were at a high enough elevation to see the Isle of Skye in the distance. That night they found shelter in a nobleman's hunting lodge, which provided a bed and breakfast to travelers when not being used by its owner. In the early evening, Cleanth and his companion heard a local bagpiper play for a handful of listeners.

Perhaps Cleanth's most important trip from Oxford was the one that brought him to the Café des Deux Magots in Paris on a December afternoon in 1929. This was the occasion of his long-delayed introduction to Allen Tate. At the end of a two-year stint abroad financed by the Guggenheim Foundation (he and Caroline Gordon would sail for New York on January 1, 1930), Tate had already established himself in the international republic of letters. He had met such luminaries as T. S. Eliot, Herbert Read, Morley Callaghan, Sylvia Beach, Gertrude Stein, and Ernest Hemingway; he had even lived rent-free for six months at Ford Madox Ford's apartment in Paris. The dapper and urbane Tate, sporting a toothbrush moustache, was a marked contrast to the bespectacled and scholarly Cleanth. Over forty years later Tate recalled, somewhat flamboyantly, that, through thick glasses, his guest gave one "the fleeting thought that like Eliot's Donne he was looking into one's skull beneath the skin." But Cleanth was also such a mild-mannered gentleman that Tate could not believe he had experienced the "horror and boredom" about which Eliot wrote so movingly (Tate, "What I Owe," 125).

With Cleanth and Allen was Charles Pipkin, chairman of the committee that had awarded Cleanth his Rhodes Scholarship (Hemingway was visible on the sidewalk, holding court with his hands stuffed in a mackinaw). The son of a Methodist minister from Arkansas, Pipkin had earned his M.A. at Vanderbilt and his Ph.D. at Oxford. He had been twenty-six years old and a professor of government at the University of Illinois when President James Monroe Smith wooed him to Louisiana State University in 1926. Five years later, Pipkin was named dean of LSU's newly created graduate school and charged with improving the academic climate of the university. The following year he brought Cleanth Brooks to Baton Rouge.

PART TWO

The Old War Skule
(1932-42)

CHAPTER FIVE

Baton Rouge

On April 10 and 11, 1935, forty writers gathered on the roof of the Heidelberg Hotel in Baton Rouge, Louisiana. John Gould Fletcher, who was rediscovering (or reinventing) his southern roots after years of exile in England, was there. So, too, was John Peale Bishop (Scott Fitzgerald and Edmund Wilson's classmate from Princeton), who was also laying claim to a newfound southern identity. William Faulkner, who considered flying down from Oxford, Mississippi, in his private plane, didn't come; neither did the Agrarians John Crowe Ransom, Donald Davidson, and Stark Young. But five of the contributors to *I'll Take My Stand*—Fletcher, John Donald Wade, Frank Lawrence Owsley, Allen Tate, and Red Warren—did. Among the partisans of the New South, Lambert Davis of the *Virginia Quarterly Review*, William T. Couch of the University of North Carolina Press, and Cleanth's old roommate Hodding Carter, now editor of the Hammond, Louisiana, *Daily Courier*, were there. Literary folk came from as far west as Oklahoma and Texas and, in one notable case, from as far east as England.

If any evidence was needed that the Baton Rouge Conference on Literature and Reading in the South and Southwest was not a provincial affair, it was provided by the presence of Ford Madox Ford. Already in his early sixties, Ford grew to adulthood while Victoria was still on the throne, served as mentor to such diverse writers as Joseph Conrad, James Joyce, and Ernest Hemingway, fought valiantly in the First World War, founded and edited both the *English Review* and the *Transatlantic Review*, and in 1915 wrote one of the most remarkable novels of the twentieth century in *The Good Soldier*. He was a friend of Allen Tate and Caroline Gordon, an admirer of Stonewall Jackson, and a committed British agrarian in the William Morris mold. To attract the attention of Ford Madox Ford, the American South obviously had something to offer that had escaped the notice of H. L. Mencken.

At the time of the Baton Rouge conference, Cleanth Brooks was completing his third year on the English faculty of Louisiana State University. Although he was developing the opinions and forging the alliances that would shape the rest of his career, he was surely among the least significant figures at the conference. The text of the proceedings does not indicate that he said anything, and one can easily imagine his role as that of a young host making the visiting literati feel at home. It was at this conference that LSU announced it was starting a new literary magazine. That magazine, and Cleanth's involvement with it, would be remembered long after the meeting that launched it was forgotten. It was a venture that would cause one observer to say that the center of literary criticism in the Western world had moved "from the left bank of the Seine to the left bank of the Mississippi" (Cutrer, 7).

I

Virtually everybody who has written about the literary scene at LSU during the thirties has found it anomalous if not virtually impossible. The South was the poorest region in a nation sunk in its worst economic depression, and for most of its seventy-five years, Louisiana State University had been a less than mediocre institution, whose primary emphasis had been on the agricultural, mechanical, and military arts (it was fondly referred to as the "Old War Skule"). Under the political leadership of Huey P. Long, however, things would change dramatically. In addition to fighting the Depression with widespread public works projects, Huey was determined to make LSU a showcase for his Louisiana.

If it is difficult to imagine a decent university in the midst of the depression-ridden, pellagra-infested South of the 1930s, it is even more difficult to imagine Huey Long as the patron of such a university. As every good liberal knows, Long was a native American fascist intent only on amassing personal political power. In contrast, universities are supposed to be disinterested bastions of truth, unsullied by political compromise. Unfortunately, such caricatures miss the truth. Even in Hitler's Germany, university education proceeded, with such intellectual giants of the twentieth century as Martin Heidegger paying obeisance to the Führer. The situation in Louisiana was hardly that extreme. Whatever else he might have been, Huey Long was no Führer. At worst, he was an authoritarian demagogue who cared very little about race or creed so long as people voted for him, and because Louisiana was still nominally a democracy, Huey had to provide the people with reasons to do so. These included new roads, free textbooks for school children, unprecedented health care and welfare benefits, and one of the best state universities in the South.

At a time when many universities were facing serious retrenchment, LSU embarked on a $3 million building program. (Long believed that if the people could see what he was doing, they would force their legislators to support it.) "The campus could boast a music building with eighty concert grand pianos, a football stadium enlarged to seat 35,000, a Huey P. Long Field House, and a Huey P. Long swimming pool, at the time the largest in the world. When the Kingfish [so named after a character in the *Amos 'n Andy* radio program] learned that San Francisco had the world's largest indoor swimming pool, he ordered that the one in Baton Rouge be built ten feet longer" (Cutrer, 12).

Even if his personal interests were centered on such high-visibility frills as the football team and the band, Huey was sagacious enough to realize that the lasting reputation of a university lies with its academic program. Recalling those days, Robert B. Heilman writes: "My guess is that what happened at LSU—specifically the remarkable influx of talent—had its ultimate roots in the imaginativeness evident in the very complex makeup of the man who ruled Louisiana for a time. It was an imaginativeness which could grasp ends beyond profit and power" (Heilman, 11–12). On the only occasion when Cleanth Brooks ever saw him, during a program commemorating LSU's seventy-fifth anniversary, Huey Long admitted to an auditorium crowded with local boosters and visiting dignitaries that his enemies had accused him of stealing. Rather than denying the charge, he declared that every university should have someone to steal for it the way he stole for LSU.

Nearly thirty years later, Red Warren, who created an unforgettable fictional portrait of Huey Long in his novel *All the King's Men*, wrote:

> [At LSU] the students [were] like students anywhere in the country in the
> big state universities, except for the extraordinary number of pretty girls
> and the preternatural blankness of the gladiators who were housed be-
> neath the stadium to have their reflexes honed, their diet supervised, and—
> through the efforts of tutors—their heads crammed with just enough of
> whatever mash was required (I never found out) to get them past their
> minimal examinations. Among the students there sometimes appeared,
> too, that awkward boy from the depth of the Cajun country or from some

scrabble-farm in North Louisiana, with burning ambition and frightening energy and a thirst for learning; and his presence there, you reminded yourself, with whatever complications of irony seemed necessary at the moment, was due to Huey, and to Huey alone. For the "better element" had done next to nothing in fifty years to get that boy out of the grim despair of his ignorance. (Warren, "*All King's Men,*" 164–65)

In 1926 the university's president, Thomas Boyd, retired. The man chosen to succeed him was Colonel Campbell B. Hodges, a native of Louisiana and the commandant of West Point. When the Army, however, refused to release Hodges from duty, Thomas Atkinson, dean of the School of Engineering, was named acting president. In 1929 Atkinson suffered a severe heart attack that forced him to resign his position a year later. Hodges, now a general and freed from West Point, was ready to assume the presidency that had been offered him four years earlier. But Governor Long had other ideas. As a state legislator, the general's brother had spearheaded the movement that brought impeachment proceedings against Huey in 1929. Although he had been acquitted, Long was not eager to turn his university over to the brother of a political opponent. Instead, he picked James Monroe Smith, who was then Dean of Education at Southwestern Louisiana Institute at Lafayette.

Smith possessed two essential qualifications for the presidency of LSU—he was unswervingly loyal to Huey Long, and he shared his boss's vision of a world-class university. The first of these qualities assured LSU continued financial patronage from the Kingfish; the second made Smith an effective leader, until some overreaching in the stock market put him afoul of the law. A native of Winn Parish, Smith had earned his Ph.D. in educational administration at Columbia University. The meeting of the LSU Board of Supervisors that ratified his appointment as university president is the stuff of legends. "The story goes that . . . [Huey] glared at Dr. Smith's rumpled attire and handed him a large bill, saying 'God damn you, go out and buy a new suit. At least try to look like a president.' " According to William Ivy Hair, "that something insulting was said is likely, but what makes this version ring false is its depiction of the Kingfish donating money out of his own pocket" (Hair, 211).

Although James Monroe Smith was not himself an intellectual, he valued intellect in others and knew how to put it to work for the good of the university. His principal ally in this effort was Cleanth's old friend Charles W. Pipkin. In many respects Pip was ideally suited to the task. As a native southerner, he could make the case for reform more effectively than even the most tactful Yankee. Like the sociologist Rupert Vance, he hailed from Morrilton, Arkansas, where he was descended from a long line of ministers. Although a secularist himself, Pipkin was closely enough associated with the culture of southern Methodism that Cleanth Brooks, Sr., knew and admired him. (Vann Woodward remembers that when the Pipkin family lived in Arkadelphia, Arkansas, Charles eloquently defended his father, a Methodist minister, against charges of heresy.)[1] Pip's later educational attainments at home and abroad (all at a precociously young age) simply elevated him to the status of local boy made good.

Pipkin came to LSU from Illinois in 1926, the year President Boyd retired. It would be another four years before James Monroe Smith arrived and another two before Pip was named dean of the new graduate school. Although he had spent more than half his life in academia, as either student or teacher, he was still only thirty-two years old at the time of his appointment. Commenting on Pipkin, John Herbert Roper writes, "knowing observers discerned the evangelistic fervor in his demands for reform. To his passion for economic development of the South, his travel in Europe in the 1920s added an equally powerful passion for world peace" (Roper, 19).

Shortly after his untimely death, the obituary notice in the *American Oxonian* described Pipkin's administrative style: "Into a University which . . . for generations had gone its languid way amid a faint smell of magnolia blossoms, he blew like a bracing current of arctic air. . . . He was fresh from Oxford, full of vigor, candor and daring. He deferred to no one, acknowledged no sacred cows, and spoke his mind with a startling lack of regard for what was considered discreet academic policy. He was fluent, witty, affable; but he had a keen eye for frauds and a caustic tongue merciless in their exposure" (Daspit, 5).

It would be a misnomer to call Pip a scholar—his bibliography was too slight. Instead, he was what might be called a public service intellectual, a man who brings a philosophical temper to bear on social issues, usually from a position of power and influence. (FDR appointed so many of these to his administration that they became known as his "brain trust.") Given Pipkin's progressive leanings, one might suspect that he was a more effective version of Edwin Mims. This was not the case; as a child of this century, Pip was infinitely more cosmopolitan than Mims. He also had enough confidence in his own vision and values that he didn't feel threatened by opposing views. Although he did not regard Agrarianism as a practical program for social and economic reform, he respected the intellectual energy of the movement and enjoyed friendly relations with several of its advocates. These included the two fellow Vanderbilt graduates with whom he shared drinks at the Café des Deux Magots on that memorable afternoon in December 1929.

II

Allen Tate is surely overstating the case when he asserts that as far back as 1929, Pip "was planning to bring Cleanth, after his Oxford degree, to Louisiana" (Tate, "What I Owe," 126). There was no graduate school at LSU in 1929, and, as a professor of government, Pip had no influence over appointments in the English department. Nevertheless, he had taken a mentor's interest in Cleanth from the time he chaired the Rhodes Scholarship selection committee that sent Cleanth to Oxford, and he was more than eager to do what he could to advance his young friend's career. Even when he became graduate dean, however, Pip's powers were limited. The graduate school drew its faculty from the existing departments, and its dean had no authority to hire professors on his own. All that he was able to do was to invite Cleanth to give a lecture on campus and make sure that William A. Read, head of the English department, was in attendance. (Because Read had already informed him that there were no vacancies in the department, Cleanth regarded Pip's invitation as little more than a personal and professional courtesy.) The day after his talk, Read approached Cleanth in the library and offered him a position as lecturer in the English department.

When Cleanth joined the LSU English faculty in the fall of 1932, William A. Read was probably the department's only recognized scholar. Already near retirement, Read was a native southerner with a Ph.D. from the University of Heidelberg. When Cleanth arrived in Baton Rouge, he had been department head for twenty years. Read is reputed to have read "the volumes of the *Oxford English Dictionary* as they appeared" and to have known "all that then was known in the field of phonology and most of the field of philology" (Cutrer, 174). (He was particularly interested in place-names and in the language of the Choctaw.) Because he wore a cork prosthesis in place of a leg lost in a hunting accident, he was known as Cork Read.

The other senior professors in the department had achieved their positions largely through longevity. By far the most notorious of these was John Earle Uhler. Although only forty-two when Cleanth arrived at LSU in 1932, Uhler was regarded as the leader of the old boy faction in the department (Read was too busy with his scholarship to concern himself with academic politics). Before completing his doctorate in 1926, Uhler spent most of a decade acting in various stock companies in New York and New England and formed close friendships with such theatrical luminaries as Maurice Evans, John Van Druten, Robert Mantell, and Helen Gahagan (who later married Melvyn Douglas, served in Congress, and lost a historic Senate race to the young Richard Nixon). Although his experience on the stage made him a celebrated performer in the classroom, Uhler was far better known in Baton Rouge as the author of the scandalous best-seller *Cane Juice*.

Many of the younger members of the department regarded Uhler as a prima donna and worse. He considered himself quite a lady's man and acquired the reputation of a womanizer. Because the standards against sexual fraternization were much looser then than now, there is no hard evidence as to how much of Uhler's reputation was deserved (according to Lewis Simpson, he generally stayed away from students and colleagues).[2] With evident glee, Robert Heilman recalls one evening when Uhler's overtures ended in disaster. It was a late afternoon party prior to an early evening football game. The custom at such affairs was for the party goers to get so deep in their cups on a beverage known as "artillery punch" (two parts white wine to one part gin) that they had to make a mad dash to the stadium to avoid missing the kickoff. On the evening in question, Uhler fixed his sights on a young secretary who seemed charmed by his attentions. Later at the game, Heilman recalls seeing that same secretary throwing up into Uhler's hat while his long-suffering wife, Corinne, looked on.[3]

A far more benign member of the old boy faction was Earl Lockridge Bradshear, a native of rural Missouri (always pronounced with a short *a* sound at the end), who wore blue jeans before they were fashionable and wrote Western novels under a pseudonym. (Bradshear was an Americanist who thought that the trouble with Henry James was that he hadn't spent enough time down at the old swimming hole.) Rather late in life, he married a former student, who always referred to him as "Dr. Bradshear."

The only woman professor in the department at that time was Joan Miller, whom Heilman remembers as a bright and energetic member of the old guard, always alluding to the famous people to whom she was related by blood or other connection. Although representing different factions within their own department, Joan Miller and Cleanth Brooks were both named to a nine-member university committee formed in 1935 to investigate charges of misconduct and skulduggery brought against the LSU administration. The committee conducted its investigation by distributing a questionnaire to the university faculty. Although we will never know whether the faculty believed sufficiently in the committee's assurances of anonymity to answer candidly, the answers they did give cleared the administration of all charges. The committee's subsequent report was one of the few instances during his years at LSU that Cleanth was on the side of the established powers.

While he was finishing at Oxford and launching his own career at LSU between 1930 and 1934, Cleanth had had very little direct contact with Red Warren. Although he recalled seeing a picture of a dark-haired California girl on Red's dresser at Oxford, Cleanth did not realize that Red was already secretly married to Emma Brescia, who was called "Cinina" by her friends. The new bride, with whom Red began living on his return to the United States, had been born in Ecuador of Italian parents (her father later became a music professor at Mills College in Oakland, California) and spoke several languages fluently. It was as a young married man that Red had to decide whether to pursue a safe career as a scholar or to take his chances with fiction, poetry, and criticism. Deciding for the latter, he turned down a fellowship to complete his doctorate at Yale and vowed never to contribute an article to a professional journal (see Bohner, 25).

With a new wife to support and his years as a best-selling author still in the future, Red accepted a one-year appointment to teach English at Southwestern College, an exclusive liberal arts school in Memphis. In 1931 he left there to take a temporary position at Vanderbilt. Returning to the scene of his past triumphs, Red might well have thought that he had entered a time warp. Although the Fugitive group had disbanded, Ransom and Davidson were still on the scene, still writing poetry and criticism. At the same time, their activities on behalf of the Agrarian movement were gaining them the sort of publicity that Vanderbilt found embarrassing. Mims, in particular, considered *I'll Take My Stand* an attack on everything he had championed in *The Advancing South* (1926). If Ransom and Davidson were well-established members of the department, Warren was not. Mims regarded him as little better than the upstart Tate, and it is a small wonder that he agreed to even a temporary appointment for Warren. The year Warren graduated from Vanderbilt, Mims resigned from a position teaching night school at the Watkins Institute in Nashville, but when he learned that Red had applied for the job and would be his successor, Mims rescinded his resignation out of pure spite.

Mims seemed to alternate between persecuting the former Fugitives and complaining of their ingratitude toward him. Years later, Cleanth recalled an example of the latter. When visiting Nashville shortly after joining the LSU faculty, he was summoned to Mims's residence on the Vanderbilt campus. There he had to listen to the old man bemoan the fact that "all of your friends are saying such terrible things about me when I've done so much for them." Because he was forced to walk a fine line between agreeing with something he knew to be untrue and denouncing Mims as a liar, Cleanth remembered this as one of the most unpleasant afternoons of his life.

At the end of the 1933–34 school year, Warren's contract at Vanderbilt was not renewed. (Years later, John Ransom wrote to Cleanth: "The letting go of Warren, who asked so little as a reward for staying, is the most nearly criminal thing in the Vanderbilt record"; Ransom, *Letters* 277.) Once again, Pipkin came to the rescue, inviting Red to the LSU campus for a lecture and hoping that W. A. Read would do the rest. Given Red's greater prominence in the literary world, his appointment to the LSU faculty was more nearly a foregone conclusion than it had been for Cleanth. Brooks and Warren were now together for the third time in their careers and ready to embark on a collaboration that would alter the literary history of our time. The only logistical matter to be taken care of was finding something for Red to teach. When he expressed an interest in Shakespeare, Dr. Read told John Earle Uhler to divide his already overly large Shakespeare class. Uhler reported back that that was impossible because he couldn't persuade anyone to leave. Doing a slow burn, Cork Read hobbled down to Uhler's classroom. "Everyone on this side of the room, go with Mr. Warren," he ordered. Turning to Uhler, Read declared, "That is how you divide a class." His administrative chore complete, William A. Read returned to the *Oxford English Dictionary* and the nuances of Choctaw grammar.

III

As Cleanth had confidently predicted to Hodding Carter in 1929, Tinkum was waiting for him when he returned from England. By 1932, however, the Depression made marriage a financially difficult proposition. Tinkum had a job with the social welfare department in New Orleans and could not afford to give up her salary. Until she could find a job that paid as well in Baton Rouge, she and Cleanth would have to delay their marriage.

The situation was further exacerbated when Cleanth, Sr., suffered a
paralytic stroke during his son's first year at LSU. Unable to work and
lacking a pension or disability insurance, he was forced to move himself
and his family in with his son. Faced with the care of two aging and
destitute parents (Social Security did not take effect until 1935) and a
cousin young enough to be his own son, Cleanth found his annual salary
of $2,250 stretched to the limit. (So intent was he on making ends meet
that Cleanth became a diligent reader of mystery novels, believing that if
only he could find the successful formula, he could supplement his professorial income with royalties from best-selling potboilers.) It was only after
Tinkum found a job with the welfare department in Baton Rouge that she
was able to join this household and contribute her paycheck to its upkeep.

The wedding, which finally took place on September 12, 1934, was a
modest affair. The ceremony was held in a Methodist church in Baton
Rouge rather than in Tinkum's Presbyterian church in New Orleans. The
religious mix in the Blanchard household was such that Tinkum felt no
particular loyalty to the church of her upbringing. Ever faithful to southern Methodism, the Reverend Mr. Brooks helped officiate at his son's marriage, and Cleanth and Tinkum continued to attend the Methodist church
for as long as the elder Brooks lived.

Even if they found the luxuries of life inaccessible, the Brookses had
food, shelter, transportation, and inexpensive domestic help. The people
with whom Tinkum dealt in the social welfare system (the mostly black
underclass, some of them former slaves) were in much worse straits. Because the social work staff was overwhelmingly female, the system was
not so much paternalistic as maternal. Tinkum would come home after a
day's work with sad, funny stories to tell. She recalls one old fellow saying,
"Miz Brooks, if I just had two dollars fifty a week, I think I could make
it." Then, there was the woman who said of her mentally deficient daughter, "She ain't much for book larnin', but give her a broom and she knows
just what to do." One can't help comparing Tinkum with those upperclass white women who cared for their slaves in the years before the Civil
War. In the post-civil rights era, such images are unfashionable if not
downright offensive. And yet, as William Faulkner was always quick to
point out, when centuries of injustice cannot be erased overnight, one
simply does what one can under the prevailing circumstances. That may
mean giving an old black man two dollars fifty a week or handing a sim-
pleminded girl a broom.

As a teacher at the state university, Cleanth encountered a wider range of humanity. In the spirit of public education, the poor and the middle class sat next to the children of the rich and powerful. (In a couple of his classes, Cleanth had Huey Long's daughter, a bright but quiet girl who compensated for a lack of original thought by giving back on tests and papers everything her professor had said.) Because of the improvements Huey brought to the Old War Skule, there was less reason for families to pay much higher tuition to send their children to a private university or to a public institution in another state. Cleanth taught four classes a term, while continuing to write in his spare time. The ambition to become a mystery novelist soon disappeared, and the passion to write poetry began to fade. Since discovering the work of I. A. Richards in England, Cleanth had become increasingly interested in the possibilities of literary criticism.

The potential for conflict always exists in a department where energetic young scholars teach next to senior deadwood. For several reasons, this situation was less volatile at LSU than it might have been elsewhere. Although Cleanth represented the first of the new wave, enough subsequent appointments were made that, by the mid-thirties, approximately half the faculty in the professorial ranks were junior to him. Also, being a productive scholar himself, William A. Read felt a greater affinity for his younger faculty than he did for those closer to him in age. Finally, the exhortation to publish or perish was still far enough in the future that writing was considered a means of communication rather than a requirement for professional advancement. (Of course, given the current rage for creative writing and popular culture, Uhler's *Cane Juice* and Bradshear's Western novels would count for more today than they did back then.) It was not until the late thirties that the situation began to change. Robert Heilman recalls: "A friend of mine in another department, adopting a *faux naïf* stance, jested ironically: 'What's this about writing? What do they want me to write? If they tell me what they want me to write, I'll do it'" (Heilman, 10).

For people living in an age of superhighways, modern refrigeration, and nearly universal air-conditioning, it is difficult to imagine the sheer discomfort of life in Baton Rouge in the 1930s. The only relief from the heat and humidity, akin to being locked in a Turkish bath with one's clothes on, was an occasional window fan and nightfall. But the fan and the darkness also seemed to bring in every imaginable insect. Because not even the best of window screens was impenetrable, the prudent individual would retire for the night only after covering his body with insect repellent and his bed with mosquito netting; it also helped to spray every surface of one's lodging with insecticide. One needed to mop up the dead insects as soon as possible; otherwise, a multitude of ants would appear to feast on their remains.

Fifty years later, Robert Heilman recalled driving south in the mid-thirties: "When state and national highways were paved, they had an uneven blacktop surface with a high crown in the middle. Often they were just gravel roads. Detours could wind for many miles over wagon-track back roads; one of these, in north Georgia, made cars ford a stream. . . . If one's reading had suggested a description, it might have been 'Yoknapatawpha without Faulkner.' " Then, there was the approach to Baton Rouge:

> We drove along the coast from Mobile. Nighttime introduced us to the most varied, long-lasting, and vehement outpouring of sounds from nature that we had ever heard, from mosquitoes at one frequency to frogs at the opposite one. The lushness of growth everywhere seemed a little frightening. We drove through our first swarms of what we learned were called lovebugs, were virtually blacked in, and wondered whether all life would mean a stop every fifty miles for a windshield cleanup. Daytime temperatures were a stern probation. We watched heavy rain showers around the gulf, welcomed brief downpours, and found that they only steamed things up. (Heilman, 4)

At first, the demands of a new job did not weigh heavily on Cleanth (it was only after he took on responsibilities that entailed battles with the university administration that the strain began to show). At home the challenges were of a different sort. Cleanth remembers an extended family of three generations doing their best to get along with each other. This included the effort to rear the young cousin, Tookie. Friends recall Cleanth's mother doting on the boy and refusing to admit that his intellectual gifts were less than those of her natural-born sons. For his own part, Cleanth took more pains with the lad than most fathers would with their own children. Eventually, Tookie moved to California and died young.

When Tookie swallowed a class pin in August of 1935, Cleanth sought the assistance of a prominent local physician, Dr. Carl Adam Weiss. Although the old doctor was not available, his son, Carl Austin, was. In a letter written to Red Warren decades later, Cleanth recalled that the junior Dr. Weiss was "a well-spoken young physician . . . , clearly dedicated to his work and quietly competent in his skills"[4] (while interning on a fellowship at the American Hospital in Paris several years earlier, he had patched up a wounded Ernest Hemingway). Three weeks after treating Tookie

Brooks, Dr. Carl Austin Weiss would enter the state capitol in Baton Rouge and change Louisiana forever.

IV

During Cleanth's first year at LSU, the university undertook a short lived project that would lead indirectly to one of the major ventures of his career. The *Southwest Review*, which was published by Southern Methodist University in Dallas, was in danger of going under for financial reasons. LSU, on the other hand, had plenty of money, but no magazine. Pipkin offered to bail out the Dallas quarterly with needed funding in exchange for giving LSU a place on the masthead and a voice in editorial policy. Despite apprehension on the part of the SMU editors, they accepted the life-saving merger and hoped for the best. The fall 1933 issue of the *Southwest Review* announced its new association with LSU.

The liberal New England native John McGinnis had become editor of the *Southwest Review* in 1927, with the liberal Texan Henry Nash Smith as his assistant. Not only did McGinnis and Smith not regard Louisiana as part of the Southwest, they resisted the notion that Texas was part of the South. In particular, they vehemently opposed the anti-industrial vision of the Nashville group. In a long review-essay published in the *Southwest Review* after its merger with LSU, Smith attacked Agrarianism with all of the fashionable progressive arguments at his disposal. He found the rural paradise postulated in *I'll Take My Stand* to be a dangerous pipe dream. For most persons in the real South (as opposed to the region of myth), a return to the land would mean sharecropping or tenant farming. Smith wondered rhetorically how such a fate would be superior to working in a factory. The only way to make the land pay for poor whites would be to reenslave the blacks. In essence, Smith argued, "when the Agrarians are intent upon their myth, they can form no program; when they begin to consider practical measures, they have to turn their backs upon their myth. This is their dilemma" (Smith, 222).

The particular dilemma of the *Southwest Review* in the years 1933 to 1935 was to forge a working relationship between groups of editors who were not only geographically separated but ideologically worlds apart. When Red Warren came to LSU in 1934 and was added to the board of editors from Baton Rouge, the suspicions of the Dallas contingent degenerated into near paranoia. For example, on September 6, 1934, McGinnis wrote to Smith: "We shall have to look to the foundations of the *Review*:

I suspect an invasion of termites—Agrarian termites. We'll wake up some day and find we're just the shell of what we thought we were." [5]

In fact, when Cleanth first wrote Red about the *Southwest Review* (at a time when Red was still teaching at Vanderbilt), his concern was not with advancing the Agrarian cause but with making the magazine more literary. "We are hoping to broaden its scope a little," he wrote, "and to improve the quality of the articles. . . . I am especially interested in pulling up our reviews. What about reviewing some books for us—especially poetry and criticism? (I say 'us,' though I am connected with the magazine in a humble enough capacity; but Pipkin asked me to scout around for some good reviewers.)" In less than two years, Brooks and Warren (in what was their first literary collaboration) completely remade the book review section of the Dallas magazine. Prior to 1935, the reviews were given over to a discussion of undistinguished western and southwestern titles. The single reviewer, J. Frank Dobie, entitled his column "Son-of-a-Gun Stew." (Dobie's idea of criticism was to praise a novel for being "true to cowhorse nature and beautifully written.") When LSU took over the book review function in January 1935, "Son-of-a-Gun Stew" was moved to the back of the magazine, and more current books of genuine literary interest were discussed in a newly created review section toward the front.

Cleanth's own contribution to the revitalized magazine was a review-essay on *Wine from These Grapes*, a volume of poetry published by Edna St. Vincent Millay in 1934. A frequent target of the aesthetic formalists (the term *new criticism*, as it is currently understood, had yet to be invented), Millay would be the subject of John Crowe Ransom's lengthy essay "The Poet as Woman" in 1937. In his more limited treatment, Cleanth recognizes Millay's stature and argues that her work deserves to be treated as major poetry. Unfortunately, her efforts to broaden her emotional range and toughen her vision by including "the ugly, the negative, and the evil" strike Brooks as false, as a willed rather than an earned attempt to achieve maturity. In contrast, the love poems of Millay's earlier volume *Fatal Interview* seem much more natural. Unlike Ransom, Brooks does not blame Millay's limitations on her gender; he simply finds her more convincing when she is trying less hard to sound grown up.

Far from being upset with the new review section, Smith seemed to be delighted with the turn the magazine was taking, although a single review in the spring issue was enough to reawaken his fear of Agrarian termites and to endanger the uneasy collaboration between Dallas and Baton Rouge. The irony of the situation is that the offending review was a highly favorable discussion of *So Red the Rose*, a novel published in 1934 by Stark Young, the founder of the *Southwest Review* (and a book whose chief villain is General Sherman, who had been the first commandant of LSU when the school opened in 1860). Far from feeling institutional loyalty to Young, McGinnis had no doubt written him off as an unreconstructed southerner. Not only had he contributed to *I'll Take My Stand*, but in *So Red the Rose*, he had written an unabashed defense of the antebellum South, anticipating *Gone With the Wind* by only two years.

It is doubtful that Robert Penn Warren had an ideological ax to grind when he asked his young Baton Rouge associate Albert Erskine to review *So Red the Rose*. Had Erskine simply praised the novel as literature, his review probably would have passed muster in Dallas. Instead, he endorsed Young's reactionary social vision and declared the paternalistic slave owners of the Old South morally superior to the capitalist employers of our own time. (This position, which has been articulated by figures as diverse as William Grayson and Eugene Genovese, was also held by Edmund Wilson.) When he read the review, Smith wrote to Warren that its thesis seemed to be "I know this isn't a great novel, but I dare any (liberal) white trash to say so." After Erskine agreed to some minor changes, the Dallas editors grudgingly accepted the review for the spring 1935 issue of their magazine. It would be the last issue published in collaboration with Baton Rouge. LSU had already announced the Southern Literary Conference at which it would launch its own new magazine.

V

The Conference on Literature and Reading in the South and Southwest commenced at 9:30 A.M. on Wednesday, April 10, 1935. After being introduced by Warren, Pipkin welcomed the participants to Baton Rouge. He urged a spirit of "genial tolerance and congeniality," while striking a note of caution: "We do not meet as provincials this morning—how dare we, how could we, meet as provincials, surrounded by the crash of the world, many of whose phases are ended" (see Simpson et al., *Review*, 42–43). In fact, tolerance and congeniality failed to prevail, at least in part because the conferees could not agree on where regionalism ended and provincialism began. If the announced focus of the conference was on the South and Southwest, much of the actual discussion centered on the northeastern metropolis New York City.

It was well and good to speak of southern writers and southern literature, but the fact remained that there was not a large enough reading public in the South to support an indigenous literature. Universities and literary magazines could try to enlarge that public, but the process would be slow. In the meantime, southern writers would either have to appeal to a largely non-southern audience or starve. Consequently, John Peale Bishop argued, we have the spectacle of such southern writers as T. S. Stribling and Erskine Caldwell creating "a criticism of Southern life from standards not Southern but [those of] New York" (see Simpson et al., *Review*, 45).

For a year prior to the Baton Rouge gathering, John Gould Fletcher had experienced growing animosity toward one of his fellow conferees— Lambert Davis of the *Virginia Quarterly Review*. In early 1934 Davis published an essay by Mencken that ridiculed Donald Davidson. When Davis rejected a response by Davidson on the grounds that he had already published too many Agrarian essays, Fletcher began to regard Davis as a scalawag or worse. Consequently, when Davis solicited essays from Ransom, Tate, and Warren for a special southern issue of his magazine, Fletcher insisted that his fellow Agrarians show their loyalty to Davidson by boycotting the project. When the three refused to comply, Fletcher fired off a letter to Davidson in March 1935, stating: "*I do not propose to allow this sort of thing to go on*. The time has come for a showdown. Either Ransom and Tate are CONTRIBUTORS TO THE VIRGINIA QUARTERLY, in which case they are NOT AGRARIANS; or else they are NOT CONTRIBUTORS, in which case *I am still an agrarian*." Not even Davidson himself could pacify the enraged Fletcher. Paul Conkin writes: "Now almost a madman, Fletcher begged a ride down to Baton Rouge with Tate and at the conference made a fool of himself on the platform, with a vicious attack on poor Davis. He rode back to Memphis with Tate, but after the Vanderbilt group left him he collapsed and tried to call his sister in Little Rock to come and bring him home. He was quickly into an asylum" (Conkin, *Agrarians*, 120).

Among the challenges facing those concerned about the future of southern literature was to find a middle ground between the extremes of cultural assimilation and reactionary parochialism. One way out of that impasse was to view southern literature not in regional or even national terms but from an international perspective. If fellow southerners were often too benighted and New Yorkers too biased to appreciate what the Fugitives and Agrarians were doing, perhaps they would receive a more sympathetic hearing overseas. The presence of Ford Madox Ford at the Baton Rouge conference tended to confirm that surmise. According to

Max Webb, "In his decision to attend, Ford felt that his role was one of representing the spirit of literature in contrast with the more regional claims and interests of the other participants" (Webb, 902). That he was not entirely successful in this effort is confirmed by Ford's recollection of "the figure of Mr. John Gould Fletcher from Little Rock, Arkansas, prowling at the back of the audience asking them why they do not lynch me" (see Webb, 901).

If the South was wise to look to the rest of the world, Ford argued, the rest of the world had much to learn from the South. His voice weakened by the gassing he had suffered in the war and his delivery muffled by a thick moustache, Ford pronounced a benediction on the conference:

> Seventy years ago you stood for the fruits of the earth and the treasures of the craftsman, means of wealth that alone can be coterminous with the life of this earth. During those seventy years of the obscuration of your traditions the industrial system rose, dominated humanity, called itself a civilization. It is now crumbling into its final decay. You, on the other hand, continued unmoved to follow out the pursuits and earnings of the husbandman—and measured by human lives, the pursuits and earnings of the husbandman constitute the only wealth that is and must be as durable as humanity itself. . . . Your survival is therefore inevitable: nothing shall put an end to it till this planet falls back into the sun from which it issued. . . .
>
> So the future of the civilization of this hemisphere must lie in your hands as in other continents it will lie in the hands of men similarly minded and of similar traditions. It is for you alone to say what aspect that civilization shall assume. (See Simpson et al., *Review*, 78)

CHAPTER SIX

The Left Bank
of the Mississippi

One Sunday afternoon in late February 1935, James Monroe Smith drove his black Cadillac limousine up to the cottage Robert Penn Warren was renting on Park Drive in south Baton Rouge. He invited Red, Cinina, and their boarder, Albert Erskine, for a drive in the country—an unusual courtesy for a university president to extend to an assistant professor who had yet to complete his first year on the faculty. Smith, however, had concluded that LSU needed a literary quarterly, and he wanted Warren's advice on how to bring this dream to fruition. Red advised Smith that the project could be accomplished for approximately $10,000 a year "if you paid a fair rate for contributions, gave writers decent company between the covers, and concentrated editorial authority sufficiently for the magazine to have its own distinctive character and quality" (Brooks and Warren, *Anthology*, xi). At Smith's urging, Red and Erskine joined forces with Cleanth and Pipkin to draw up a plan for the magazine; the next day, Smith officially authorized the project. The first issue of the *Southern Review* appeared five months later.

I

The beginnings of the *Southern Review* were so hectic that the magazine tended to define itself along the way. Although Pipkin's presence as nominal editor assured that the magazine would give some space to social and political issues, Brooks and Warren were the young workhorses who soon determined the character of the journal. Their experience with the *Southwest Review* had alerted Cleanth and Red to the dangers of provincialism, and their exegetical approach to the difficult texts of early modernism had given them the beginnings of a critical program. Moreover, Red seemed to be either directly or indirectly acquainted with most of the important contemporary writers in the English speaking world. Although many early solicitations fell on barren ground, enough were answered to produce a choice crop of contributors. With strong financial backing, the *Southern Review* was able to pay a cent and a half per word for prose contributions and thirty-five cents a line for poetry. What was even more important to writers who could command higher fees from commercial magazines was the select company they kept in the *Southern Review*.

As with so many other public performances, the art of editing a magazine consists of making the tedious and difficult look exciting and easy. George Core, editor of the *Sewanee Review* since 1973, describes the true state of affairs when he writes:

> Editing a magazine is roughly as romantic as sluicing out a hog pen, and bringing a given issue into existence is less romantic than helping an old sow deliver her farrow. The work is demanding: day after day the staff . . . is taxed by the contingent and the mundane: . . . a contributor (whose wife is a subscriber) moves three times in one year, twice not sending forwarding addresses (later he complains about missing issues; still later his wife sends the wrong forwarding address); various would-be writers send pointless inquiries about editorial advice, style sheets, and free copies; the star boarders at several federal penitentiaries request complimentary subscriptions. (Core, *"Sewanee Review,"* 106)

In addition to putting up with such daily nuisances, Cleanth read ninety manuscripts a week, taught three classes, did his own writing, served on university committees, and maintained a multigenerational household in the depths of the Great Depression. Although he received no additional summer compensation, he was also the person most responsible for keeping the magazine functioning twelve months a year. (Without such vigilance, a quarterly simply cannot exist.) With Red frequently gone from campus (spending a guest semester at another university or the summer in Italy), the day-to-day operation of the magazine fell increasingly to Cleanth and the review's business manager, Albert Erskine. As Red's old friend and boarder, Albert enjoyed an easy collegiality with Brooks and Warren and participated fully in the editorial decisions of the magazine.

Born in Memphis, Tennessee, on April 18, 1911, Erskine was a levelheaded, sweet-tempered young man, described by one contemporary as looking "like a blondish younger brother of Gary Cooper." After studying with Warren at Southwestern College, he had followed Red to Nashville, where he enrolled in the M.A. program at Vanderbilt because of the presence of John Crowe Ransom. After finishing his course work for the master's, Albert returned to Memphis to run the Three Musketeers bookstore and work on his thesis. Then, in the fall of 1934, he became an instructor in the LSU English department (see Cutrer, 63). Shortly thereafter, Erskine wrote his controversial review of Stark Young's *So Red the Rose*. Having been present when James Monroe Smith arrived in his Cadillac and when plans were drafted for the magazine later that night, Erskine could claim to be a founding editor of the *Southern Review*.

The odd man out in this arrangement was the magazine's ostensible editor, Charles W. Pipkin. Not only was Pip too busy as graduate dean to involve himself very closely with the operation of the review, his occasional attempts to steer it more in the direction of social science ran counter to the literary emphasis of Brooks, Warren, and Erskine. In a letter to Allen Tate dated December 1, 1937, Cleanth writes:

> Tinkum and Albert and I have been working up a parody of "The Waste Land" for extremely private circulation. Our *Waste Land* is the Southern Review office, and the dead which have been buried is an MS on social science which we hope will remain interred in the filing cabinet. At present we have only a few scattered fragments, but you can see the relevance of the following: "O keep the Pip far hence that's friend to men / Or with his nails he'll dig it up again"—and Albert has made a really fine contribution by suggesting that the last section deal with the lost MS under the heading "What the Dunder Said."[1]

As he became less a part of the success of the review, Pipkin's position of preeminence on the masthead stirred increasing resentment in the three men who were the magazine's actual editors. Because they were older than Albert and still felt some gratitude to Pip for his role in bringing them to LSU, Cleanth and Red were more diplomatic in handling the situation. Consequently, by the end of 1940, they were elevated from managing editors to coeditors with Pipkin. When Pip refused to allow the upstart Erskine to be promoted at the same time from business manager to managing editor, Albert left Baton Rouge for a position with New Directions publishers in New York.

After his review of Stark Young's novel, Erskine appears to have "retired" from writing to devote himself to editorial labors. Following World War II, he landed a job with Random House and became one of the premier editors of our time. In an interesting reversal of roles, the boy who started as a protégé of Red Warren became Red's editor. Although the extent of Erskine's contribution to Warren's work may never be known, any fair estimate of the Fugitive legacy must take into account the taste and intelligence that Albert Erskine brought to Random House during the postwar years. One can trace a line of influence from Ransom through Warren to Erskine and the many writers Erskine nurtured (a partial list includes Eudora Welty, Ralph Ellison, James Michener, John O'Hara, William Styron, and—during the last fourteen years of his life—William Faulkner). While writing virtually nothing himself, Erskine nevertheless had a significant influence on contemporary American literature. Perhaps for this reason, Cleanth dedicated his last book on Faulkner to "Albert Russel Erskine / A great editor and a true man of letters."

When Erskine left Baton Rouge, he also left an extraordinarily talented replacement in the person of his close friend John Ellis Palmer. A native of Louisiana and a graduate of Louisiana Polytechnic Institute, Palmer was on a fellowship at Columbia University and had actually registered for graduate classes in the summer of 1935 when someone showed him the first copy of the *Southern Review*. John was so much impressed by what he saw that he left Columbia for LSU and a fellowship in journalism, "just so he could be where the *Southern Review* was happening" (see Cutrer, 188).

Before long, Palmer was living with Albert Erskine in an old house in the country and driving to Baton Rouge in a secondhand automobile they bought from one of Pipkin's underlings. (The fact that the car always had something wrong with it did nothing to enhance their respect for Pip and his crowd.) Over half a century later, John Palmer remembered this period to be one of extreme poverty but great excitement. Not only was the *Southern Review* bringing international attention to LSU, but the men who ran the magazine lived as if ideas and words were of central importance to life. Albert and John even planted a small garden on the property they rented to show their solidarity with the Agrarian movement. Palmer earned his second bachelor's degree in 1937 and his master's in 1938. After two years as a Rhodes Scholar, he returned to LSU, where he taught five sections of composition and moonlighted as an editorial assistant and designer for the LSU Press. When Erskine left Baton Rouge, Brooks and Warren were delighted that Palmer was on hand to take his place. For his own part, Palmer was helping to run the magazine that had first brought him to Baton Rouge, and he was also able to drop two of his sections of composition. He remained with the review until entering the Navy in 1942.

It was on the *Southern Review* that the legendary collaboration of Brooks and Warren began taking shape. In editorial conferences held as often as two or three times a week, Red and Cleanth fashioned a literary quarterly that would set the standard for all such magazines in the future. They reminded one not so much of two agreeable colleagues as of two very different parts of the same person.[2] Red Warren was a creative genius, who filled any room he entered with his expansive gestures, staccato brogue, and inimitable Kentucky horse laugh. For him, criticism was not a sullen and lonely art but a social act—the meeting of kindred spirits to talk about books. The circle of friends might be as intimate as himself and one other person, as dynamic as a group of poets calling themselves Fugitives, as recalcitrant as a typical class of university sophomores, or as amorphous as the reading public itself. When Robert Penn Warren was at work, the surrounding area would soon become a god-awful mess. He would jot an idea or an image down on a piece of paper, wad that paper up, and start again with a fresh sheet. Very few of the wads ever made their way to the wastebasket.

In contrast, Cleanth kept a tidier desk and a more orderly mind. If Red's light could be as blinding and diffuse as the sun itself, Cleanth's was more like a laser beam—less primal but more focused. Typically, Red would originate an idea to which Cleanth, with his penetrating logic and encyclopedic knowledge of literature, gave structure and substance. But, as with many generalizations, this antithesis could be reversed. Cleanth (certainly one of the most original critics of the age) was sometimes the source of insight, to which Red (the maker of too many completed works to be a man of inspiration only) supplied shape and closure.

When they collaborated on a textbook, their personalities would blend; when they edited the *Southern Review*, those personalities were submerged. At least since the Renaissance, artists have generally signed their names to their works—both literally and figuratively. The editorial art, however, is almost medieval in nature. It is the destiny of the editor to be anonymous; he lives to make others look good, while rendering himself invisible. (For Cleanth, this meant reworking, and even rewriting, the garbled syntax of many of the articles submitted by Pipkin's friends in the social sciences—John Dewey among them.) Like a Gothic cathedral or a well-made movie, a magazine is a group effort. The editor is not only an architect but one of the bricklayers; he is both director and cameraman. He also has to be something of a public relations expert. The public with whom he deals can include everyone from the local printer to the university bursar, not to mention legions of contributors and would-be contributors. They send manuscripts and queries in every mail and sometimes even call on the telephone or show up in person. John Palmer remembers an afternoon when the secretary of the *Southern Review* came into his office to inform him that Henry Miller was out in the waiting room. The notorious expatriate, whose writings were banned in this country, was trying to sell enough of his work to finance his way west to Taos, New Mexico.

The secretary who announced Miller's presence in the waiting room was Jean Stafford, the future fiction writer who was then best known only as Robert Lowell's wife. In an unpublished memoir of her days in Baton Rouge, she recalls that the review's "quarters included a storeroom with no fan, its windows shut to keep rain from destroying the paper." "I remember the scorched smell there," she writes, "and I remember how, after going in to fetch paper or an early issue, I felt as if I were groping up out of deep anaesthesia; my hair was wet, my eyes were blind[e]d with sweat, I panted like a done-for hound" (see Roberts, 189). Elsewhere in that same memoir, Stafford remembers crawling home at half past four in the afternoon and lying in the bathtub for an hour, "soaking her weary bones and munching frozen cubes of Coca-Cola and mint" (Goodman, 116).

If the general academic progress of LSU under Huey Long seemed an anomaly to the outside world, the existence of the *Southern Review* in Long's Louisiana was even more remarkable. Although Huey had left the governor's chair for the U.S. Senate in 1933 and had his eyes fixed squarely on the White House, he continued to run the state government in Louisiana through a handpicked successor and a powerful political machine. It is certain that James Monroe Smith would never have driven his Cadillac to Warren's cottage that Sunday in February 1935 had he thought that the Kingfish would have disapproved of his mission. In a rather perverse bit of argumentation, Robert Gorham Davis suggested years later in the *New York Times* that Huey needed the *Southern Review* to give him respectability and to provide cover for his political venality. Long partisans argue just as implausibly that Huey was actually a misunderstood patron of art and literature. William Faulkner was probably nearer the truth when, in "Knight's Gambit," he has Gavin Stevens tell his nephew Chick Mallison that "Huey Long in Louisiana had made himself founder owner and supporter of . . . one of the best literary magazines anywhere, without ever once looking inside it probably nor even caring what the people who wrote and edited it thought of him" (Faulkner, *Knight's Gambit*, 229–30).

II

In the mid-1930s the literary review, as we know it today, was in its infancy. The many excellent periodicals that had graced the antebellum South were long gone. In the protracted period of cultural decline that had begun with the Civil War, sophisticated literary journalism was a scarce commodity in the South. One could point to the *Fugitive* and the *Double Dealer*, but neither lasted a full decade. Besides, as Monroe K. Spears reminds us, a little magazine is not the same thing as a critical quarterly. Little magazines "were founded to publish experimental poetry and fiction, and most of them paid little attention to criticism. They were intense and impudent, carefree about deadlines and business arrangements, living very much for the moment" (Spears, *Ambitions*, 111). (Although he is speaking primarily of such avant garde publications as *Broom, Blast, Transition*, and the *Little Review*, Spears's comments could apply with almost as much force to the little magazines of the South.) The literary review, in contrast, is a grown-up enterprise, which intends to be around for the long haul.

According to Spears, "The literary quarterly or critical review is a noncommercial magazine, uncompromisingly highbrow in character, which publishes criticism of literature and to some extent of the other arts in the form of essays, book reviews, and chronicles, together with fiction and poetry selected according to the kind of high standards defined and employed in the criticism" (Spears, *Ambitions*, 110). Such a definition places the literary review somewhere between the little magazine and the scholarly journal. The literary review is descended from such European prototypes as the *Edinburgh Quarterly* and the *Nouvelle Revue Française*. In the early decades of the twentieth century, the relevant models were T. S. Eliot's *Criterion* (1922–39), "which gave most of its space to discussion of fundamental issues in literary and cultural criticism, and the *Dial*, which in its second incarnation (1920–29) was strongly aesthetic in emphasis" (Spears, *Ambitions*, 111). The *Criterion*, however, was published in London and the *Dial* in New York. Despite the existence of such distinguished general interest magazines as the *South Atlantic Quarterly* and the *Virginia Quarterly Review*, the only southern literary quarterly was the *Sewanee Review*, and it was obviously languishing under the eccentric editorship of William S. Knickerbocker.

Thus the *Southern Review* came along at a propitious time. For a sense of what that magazine was trying to accomplish, one need only turn to an essay published in the winter 1936 issue of the review—Allen Tate's "The Function of the Critical Quarterly." Although Tate does not mention the Baton Rouge magazine by name, it is clear that the *Southern Review* aspired to be the sort of publication he was describing. Unlike Spears writing a quarter century later, Tate does not define the quarterly by distinguishing it from the little magazine and the scholarly journal. His points of contrast are the weekly and monthly magazines. "If the quarterly imitates the freshness of the weekly," Tate writes, "its freshness is necessarily three months stale, refrigerated but not new; and if it tries for the liveliness of monthly commentary, its peril is the sacrifice of leisured thought. In either instance the quarterly sacrifices its standards only to attempt a work that it cannot hope to do" (Tate, "Function," 47). The function of the quarterly, according to Tate, is to establish a critical program. This is accomplished not only through critical essays but through creative work as well, because "good creative work is a criticism of the second rate" (47). (What Tate is suggesting is very much akin to Eliot's contention that the function of criticism is to "correct taste.") Deciding on a critical program requires formidable intelligence. Putting it into practice against the impediments faced by nonpopular magazines requires integrity, ingenuity, and an almost superhuman endurance.

Although the quarterly should always keep its transom open to good unknown writers, a critical program cannot be maintained without a stable of regular contributors who share the same standards, if not necessarily the same point of view. Tate argues that the editor should show loyalty to his regular contributors by taking as much as he can of what they offer. The problem is that this principle sometimes runs counter to the even more imperative need to maintain disinterested standards of judgment. This is particularly true when a regular contributor offers an uneven body of work. It is never easy to turn down the inferior submissions of one's talented friends, as Cleanth found out when he rejected a story by Tate's wife, Caroline Gordon.

Gordon describes the experience in a letter she wrote to Mr. and Mrs. Andrew Lytle on May 4, 1941:

> I hurt Cleanth's feelings when he was here. . . . I jumped on him about the way they have been turning my stuff down lately, with letters that might

have been written by the editor of the *Atlantic Monthly*. "This isn't quite it," or "it doesn't quite jell" are the expressions that particularly infuriated me. I am one of their oldest and I thought most valued contributors and then suddenly I begin getting these letters which mean, if I know anything about the editors, "We wish you wouldn't send anything else but we are determined to be polite about it." I won't send anything else, of course, but the whole thing is very puzzling. (See Waldron, *Close Connections*, 199)

An even more difficult case was that of the brilliant but irascible John Gould Fletcher. It is difficult to say when the unbridgeable rift occurred between Fletcher and the editors of the *Southern Review*. Not only had Warren and Fletcher contributed to *I'll Take My Stand*, they had also published favorable estimates of each other's work. Although Fletcher's tirade against Lambert Davis and the *Virginia Quarterly Review* may have created some strains, Fletcher did publish a couple of critical pieces in the first year of the *Southern Review*, and he praised the magazine early and often. By the mid-1930s, however, the quality of his verse had deteriorated. As his poems kept being rejected by Brooks and Warren and the review assignments began to dry up, Fletcher became increasingly resentful of the young editors.

Then, on January 22, 1938, Fletcher fired off an angry letter to Pipkin (which Pipkin acknowledged but did not answer). After summarizing the honors bestowed on his poetry over the years, he then enumerated the various occasions on which Warren or Brooks had rejected his submissions to the *Southern Review*. "That, Pipkin," Fletcher wrote, "is the record."

> In my opinion it proves what I have long suspected: that the "Southern Review," as regards poetry at least, is being run in the interests of a clique—engaged in proving that Donne was a better poet than Shakespeare!—and that T. S. Eliot and his imitators are the only modern poets worth reading! Also it wastes space every issue over people like Dorothy Van Ghent, Lincoln Fitzell, Randall Jarrell, Howard Baker! And it does not contain my work—nor the work of any good American poet! For my part, *I have resolved to have nothing more to do with "The Southern Review."* [3]

Fletcher must have thought that he got the last laugh when his *Selected Poems* (published later that year) won the Pulitzer Prize. But by including in that volume a disproportionate number of poems from his Imagist phase, Fletcher was implicitly conceding the negative judgment Brooks and Warren had pronounced on his more recent work.

Although Fletcher was the most vociferous in expressing his displeasure with the *Southern Review*, others in the Agrarian fraternity were disappointed that the magazine was not more partisan in promoting southern writers. In August 1939 Donald Davidson chided Cleanth for his failure to publish Mildred Haun, a Tennessee mountain girl with a rustic storytelling art. Because more cosmopolitan magazines (including the *Virginia Quarterly Review*) would be likely to dismiss Haun as too primitive, Davidson believed that the *Southern Review* had an obligation to publish her. In a tactful reply, written on October 23, 1939, Cleanth pointed out that he and Red had already published many young writers, "a good 75 per cent [of whom] have been from the South and the Southwest." Although Cleanth conceded that they might have made a mistake in rejecting Mildred Haun, he remained convinced that none of her submissions "were quite competent enough to go as stories." In their effort to correct taste, the editors of the *Southern Review* were not about to issue a free pass to writers from their own region.

III

Probably no submission to the *Southern Review* gave Brooks and Warren more difficulty than one they received from their old mentor, John Crowe Ransom. Shortly after he left his increasingly isolated position at Vanderbilt for a job at Kenyon College in Gambier, Ohio, Ransom completed "Shakespeare at Sonnets," the final essay for a volume he would entitle *The World's Body*. He submitted the essay to Cleanth Brooks on October 18, 1937, asking that it be considered for publication in the winter issue of the *Southern Review*, as Scribner's was planning to publish *The World's Body* in the spring of 1938. As a frequent contributor to the review and a friend of its editors, Ransom probably expected a routine acceptance. Thus, the reaction he got from his former students must have come as quite a shock.

Because their response was not preserved, we do not know precisely what Brooks and Warren had to say about Ransom's treatment of Shakespeare. We do know that Ransom was exercised enough about their letter to enclose it with one he sent to Allen Tate on November 4, 1937. Here, he observes:

> The boys deal pretty pedantically with my poor paper, you will see; I thought when I read it [the letter from Brooks and Warren] I must have mistakenly sent it to the *Yale Review* and got back an epistle from Miss Helen Macafee. I wrote them a pretty warm letter but after thinking over it

withheld it and wrote another. I also revised the thing, adding a bit, taking
account of points of theirs which seemed to me worth anything, generally
improving it; I wanted to do this anyway. The thing is, I believe, that
Cleanth is showing his limitations as a thinker with one thing on his mind
at a time, and he is not providing for Red the suggestions and stimuli that
Red requires. *Those boys are stale.* (I have said this frankly to them.)
Think of an editorial letter in the style of this one, even conceding that it is
written to a friend. I really stepped on their toes a little, come to think
about it. For Red is a Shakespearean, and would not like my irresponsible
knocks for the comfort of the Philistines; and Cleanth is an expert on
metaphysical poetry, and thinks everybody ought to discuss the thing in his
minute terms. They are a bit magisterial, or is it just my oversensitive
imagination? (Ransom, *Letters*, 233–34)

Because his revised essay was published in the *Southern Review* and Ransom remained friends with its editors, one ought not make too much of
the pique expressed in this letter. At the very least, however, it suggests the
widening gulf between Ransom's critical sensibility and that of Brooks
and Warren. Although it is possible to speak of generational conflicts and
to interpret the whole matter in Freudian terms, we are perhaps on safer
ground simply to consider the ideas involved. As one of the seminal forces
in southern modernism, Ransom represents a radical turning away from
the romanticism of nineteenth-century southern letters (the Fugitive flee-
ing from the high-caste Brahmins of the Old South). Part of that romanticism was a kind of Bardolatry.[4] Although Ransom greatly admired Shakespeare as a dramatist, he was more than capable of finding fault with the
construction of Shakespeare's sonnets. To those schooled in the old literary pieties, such an observation was virtual sacrilege. It was a measure of
Ransom's iconoclasm that he stated his position without fear or favor.

Ransom found fault with Shakespeare's minor poetry for its tendency
to accumulate a series of undeveloped associations rather than pursue the
implications of a single controlling metaphor. Ransom is quick to point
out, however, that the antimetaphysical tendency of Shakespeare's verse is
not a flaw when that verse is confined to the context of drama. Analyzed
as a metaphysical poem, for example, Macbeth's "To-morrow, and to-
morrow, and to-morrow" speech is an incoherent hodge-podge of mixed
and imprecise metaphors. Dramatically, however, it possesses undeniable
power. Thus Ransom concludes that "Shakespeare could put a character
into a situation that called for a desperate speech, and give him one. But

he could not seat his character at the table to compose a finished poem, and then let him stand up and deliver it" (Ransom, *Letters*, 302).

Brooks and Warren shared Ransom's general disdain for fuzzy romanticism. They, too, argued for the place of intellect in poetry. Although they probably agreed with Ben Jonson that Shakespeare should have blotted many more lines than he did, they were not willing to give logic the sort of primacy that Ransom insisted upon. For them, what was all important was not the poem's paraphrasable prose content but its psychological coherence. Because they saw all poems as minidramas, they were more willing than Ransom to accept illogic in poetry *as long as it was contextually appropriate*. Brooks and Warren extended to lyric poetry the sort of indulgence Ransom showed toward Macbeth's speech.

If Ransom saw himself as the antithesis of the Romantic tradition (even as it extended backward to include pre-Romantics such as Shakespeare), Brooks and Warren were more interested in forging a synthesis that was less rigid and dogmatic than Ransom's system. Also, as a practical matter, they knew that Ransom's preference for Donne over Shakespeare, qualified as it might be, would only lend ammunition to those who sought to caricature the southern formalists. As it turned out, "Shakespeare at Sonnets" did not enhance the reputation of either Ransom or the *Southern Review*. And when a new edition of *The World's Body* was published in 1968, Ransom added a postscript that all but repudiated the essay his former students had treated so gingerly over thirty years earlier.

IV

If the criticism and poetry in the *Southern Review* were clearly distinguished, the magazine is probably best remembered for the outstanding fiction that appeared in its pages. From 1935 to 1942, the review published seventy-nine stories. Although some of these were by established writers, such as John Peale Bishop, Kay Boyle, Daniel Fuchs, Caroline Gordon, Andrew Lytle, and Katherine Anne Porter, more often the magazine was taking a chance with unknown writers who showed promise. This list included Nelson Algren, Mary McCarthy, and Jesse Stuart, as well as quite a few individuals who have continued to languish in obscurity. When Brooks and Warren published *An Anthology of Stories from the Southern Review* in 1953, they were as impartial in their selection of material as when they were choosing manuscripts for the review a decade or more earlier. The twenty-four authors represented in this volume include a significant number of *Southern Review* discoveries—among them the justly lionized Peter Taylor and Eudora Welty, but also an undergraduate named Louis Moreau, who never published another story after leaving LSU.

From his earliest fiction of the thirties to his Pulitzer Prize–winning novel *A Summons to Memphis* (1986), Peter Taylor claimed the area from Nashville to Memphis as his own postage stamp of soil. Even when he sets a story outside this ambience, Walter Sullivan notes, "Taylor's southerners in exile remain what they are: second- and third-generation Tennessee agrarians who have made an urban progress in the world." If Andrew Lytle was correct in claiming that his was the last generation that intuitively knew the difference between right and wrong, Taylor was the laureate of the next generation. "The attitudes and actions and details [of his fiction]," Sullivan writes, "recreate the uneasy last decade of the hegemony of the southern gentry. His people are the well connected and the well-to-do; the middle-class and poor and black characters who appear in his work are defined by their relationships to the wealthy" (Sullivan, *Blood Sports*, 14). In "The Fancy Woman," a story first published in the summer 1941 issue of the *Southern Review*, the world of the gentry is seen through the eyes of one of these lower-class characters—the mistress of a country "gentleman."

The writer with the most stories in the *Southern Review* was a young woman from Jackson, Mississippi, named Eudora Welty. After publishing her first story, "Death of a Traveling Salesman," in *Manuscript*, a little magazine for young writers, in June 1936, she began to submit her work to the *Southern Review*. Although Brooks and Warren found much to admire in those submissions (first a group of poems and then several stories), they rejected her initial offerings with polite notes of encouragement. When a story called "Petrified Man" was returned in 1937, Welty was so disheartened that she destroyed it. Then, when Red Warren wrote a bit later to say that he had changed his mind, Welty had to reconstruct the story from memory. (Actually, Brooks and Warren had liked the story all along but had deferred to Pipkin, who insisted that it be rejected. Uncomfortable with the decision, Warren simply defied Pipkin with his belated note of acceptance.) "Petrified Man" appeared in the spring 1939 issue of the *Southern Review*; it was later included in the *O. Henry Prize Stories* of 1940.

In an essay entitled "Eudora Welty and the Southern Idiom," which appeared forty years after the original publication of "Petrified Man," Cleanth Brooks comments perceptively on Welty's distinctive gift for colloquial speech. "The beautician named Leota who dominates 'Petrified Man,' " he writes, "is wonderfully vulgar, but she is also wonderful to listen to in the same way as are some of the shabbier characters in Chaucer's *Canterbury Tales*. If the beauty parlor as the town headquarters for female gossip has cheapened and coarsened Leota's mind and spirit, her moving into town has not yet quite sapped the vitality of her country-bred language" ("Eudora Welty," 9).

Any editor would be proud to have had a hand in discovering Peter Taylor or Eudora Welty. "Yet," as Brooks has observed, "an editor worth his salt must take the gamble involved. If the editor insists that every plant to be set out in his chosen garden shall bear much fruit, then he will be safer to get established authors who have already produced a crop. . . . The editor who insists on a sure thing will simply market other people's notions of literature—not encourage experiments or develop new talents" ("Life and Death," 92). One of the best stories by a one-shot author to be published in the *Southern Review* was Louis Moreau's haunting narrative "The Face," which appeared in the second issue of the magazine.[5]

Like so many students at LSU, Moreau came to the university with a limited educational background but plenty of life experience. Cleanth, who was one of his professors, remembers him as a Cajun boy who had a story to tell. Teachers are naturally apprehensive when students ask them to look at their creative work; such efforts are often so inept and self-indulgent that one cannot honestly praise them. But to be too candid is to risk destroying a genuine interest in literature. The discovery of real talent brings a sense of relief, even exhilaration. Wanting to test his own response, Cleanth gave Moreau's story to Warren to read. When Red pronounced it "damn good," they decided to publish it. Having rejected a submission by the Nobel laureate Sigrid Undset (who was a particular favorite of Andrew Lytle), they could boast of the sort of Olympian disinterestedness that would turn down Nobel Prize winners and accept college sophomores, all on the strength of the work itself.

v

Although first-rate poetry, fiction, and new criticism were to be expected in the *Southern Review*, other aspects of the magazine were not nearly so predictable. For example, one is struck by the number of *Partisan Review* intellectuals who appeared in the pages of the Baton Rouge quarterly. (Philip Rahv and Mary McCarthy both published there, while Kenneth Burke, Delmore Schwartz, Sidney Hook, and James T. Farrell were frequent contributors with five or more appearances.) Although *Partisan Review* inhabited an intellectual universe far different from that of the Agrarians, it shared the *Southern Review*'s commitment to literature and ideas. The New York intellectuals may have been technically committed to a future Marxist utopia, but they believed even more passionately in the present existence of the Republic of Letters. That community was not circumscribed by regional boundaries or political loyalties. It included all persons who judged literature of central importance to life. As such, it was a common ground on which Marxists and Agrarians could both stand.

The *Southern Review* began its third year of publication with an exchange of views on Leon Trotsky, which could have easily come from the pages of *Partisan Review*.[6] Frederick L. Schuman began the colloquy with his essay "Leon Trotsky: Martyr or Renegade?" Trotsky had recently taken asylum in Mexico, while many of his alleged accomplices were being subjected to very public trials in the Soviet Union. Even though Trotskyism and Stalinism were both outside the bounds of liberal democracy, liberal democrats were choosing sides for geopolitical reasons. For Schuman the choice was clear: "The democratic West must, for its own security, dry its tears for fallen heroes and accept Moscow's hand" (Schuman, 74).

If ever a magazine could use the disclaimer that the views presented within its pages were those of the authors not the editors, this was it. As a way of broadening the debate, the *Southern Review* sent advance proofs of Schuman's article to several individuals with strong and divergent views on the issues he discusses. These included Malcolm Cowley, John Dewey, Max Eastman, and James T. Farrell. (Trotsky himself failed to respond.) The reactions that had been received by the time the magazine went to press were printed in a special section of correspondence at the end of the issue. The following number (Autumn 1937) featured a long rebuttal of Schuman by Sidney Hook and a correspondence column filled with polemics and ad hominem attacks. It is doubtful that anyone with a definite opinion on Trotsky came away from this debate with a changed mind, but the *Southern Review* established itself as a place where socially engaged intellectuals could talk—even shout—at each other about the issues tearing the world apart.

By 1939, debate over conditions in the Soviet Union had diminished as the world was turning its attention to the more immediate danger posed by Nazism. In its general interest articles, the *Southern Review* stayed abreast of this threat from Germany; however, its most unusual and significant contribution to the understanding of Nazism came from the literary side of the magazine. Like so many people outside Germany, Cleanth Brooks was genuinely perplexed by the ability of such a ridiculous little man as Hitler to stir masses of otherwise civilized men and women into barbaric conduct. If Hitler was in a position to threaten the stability of Europe and perhaps force the United States into a world war, someone ought to look more closely at the way in which he articulated his insanity. Given his interest in rhetoric, Kenneth Burke struck Cleanth as the ideal man for the job. The summer 1939 issue of the *Southern Review* contained Burke's rhetorical analysis of Hitler's *Mein Kampf*.

Burke concludes his essay with the dire warning that America is far from immune to the impulses that led to the rise of Hitler in Germany. Although the Germans had to contend with the resentment of a lost war, there is a sense in which everyone lost the First World War (or at least no one really won it). As the social and economic uncertainties fostered by democratic capitalism intensify, "a certain kind of industrial or financial monopolist may . . . wish for the momentary peace of one voice, amplified by social organization, with all the others not merely quieted, but given the quietus. So he might, under Nazi promptings, be tempted to back a group of gangsters who, on becoming the political rulers of the state, would protect him against the necessary demands of the workers. His gangsters, then, would be his insurance against his workers. But who would be his insurance against his gangsters?" (Burke, 21).

Because the United States would not enter the world war for another two and a half years, Hitler and his philosophy were still remote threats to many Americans. Also, with the widespread popularity of the New Deal, Burke's fears of a homegrown Hitler seemed less plausible than they might have a few years earlier. Nevertheless, a significant number of thoughtful people were convinced that the desire for economic progress, or mere security, was undermining more abstract cultural values. The Agrarians had offered a peculiarly regional version of that argument in *I'll Take My Stand*, a book largely conceived though not yet published when the stock market crashed in 1929. The experience of the Depression only solidified their conviction. As economic conditions worsened, the Agrarians were busy preparing a second symposium—one that spoke even more directly to the national crisis.

CHAPTER SEVEN

The Confederacy of Letters

During his early years at LSU, Cleanth moved through the professional ranks with appropriate speed. After he had served for two years in the rather ill-defined role of lecturer, William A. Read recommended that he be promoted to associate professor.[1] (This was a year before either his first book or the *Southern Review* would see the light of day.) The LSU administration responded by making Cleanth an assistant professor. Because he received no raise in pay, it is not clear whether this was actually a promotion, although it did put him on the promotion track. The following year, his pay was raised from $2,500 to $2,700; then, in 1936, he was finally promoted to associate professor with a raise to $3,600 a year. He would have to wait another six years before getting his next promotion and his next raise. As we shall see, those were six years during which the university was wracked by scandal and related financial hardship.

If the average student at LSU lacked the sophistication of those who attended institutions with more prestige, many of them (such as Louis Moreau) had lived fuller lives and had a greater wealth of experience to bring to the study of literature. Also, as the *Southern Review* became better known, outstanding graduate students began to flock to Baton Rouge.[2] Certainly one of the most unusual of these was a native of Wyoming named Alan Swallow. The son of a banker who had suffered financial reverses during the Depression, Swallow had begun writing poetry while still in high school. As a sophomore at the University of Wyoming, he started a little magazine called *Sage*, which published local writers. Swallow was determined to go into journalism upon graduation, until a letter from Robert Penn Warren changed his mind. Warren had been the judge in a poetry contest sponsored by *College Verse* and had been so impressed

with Swallow's entry that he urged him to attend LSU. In addition to securing a fellowship for Alan, Red "also saw that Mrs. Swallow was hired
as secretary at the *Southern Review*" (Cutrer, 190).

While pursuing his graduate degrees, Alan Swallow purchased a used
handpress with $100 he borrowed from his father and began to publish
inexpensive books of poetry out of his garage. As he had done with *Sage*
at Wyoming, he once again catered to promising local talent. After leaving
Baton Rouge and returning to the West, Alan set up Swallow Press, which
became the publisher of record for, among others, Yvor Winters. Although he was himself a capitalist and the son of a capitalist, Alan Swallow was an avid reader of radical publications and tilted far to the left in
his own politics. Nevertheless, he refused to let his political views affect
his literary judgments. And his personal tastes were hardly proletarian. He
developed a passion for foreign sports cars and fast driving. On one trip
from Denver to the West Coast, he was clocked at 115 miles per hour. The
policeman who stopped him simply suggested that he watch out because
of the presence of a patch of black ice ahead (Heilman, 26).

Another LSU student, who pursued a more conventional academic ca-
reer, was Leonard Unger—the son of a Jewish dry goods merchant from
Nashville. While an undergraduate at Vanderbilt, Unger had studied with
Ransom and Davidson and would have gone on to graduate school in
Nashville had the university not had a curious rule against granting fel-
lowships to town students. After earning his M.A. degree at LSU and his
Ph.D. at the State University of Iowa, Unger enjoyed a distinguished career
at the University of Minnesota, where he edited an influential series of
monographs on American writers. (Ransom considered Unger's study of
Eliot in the series to be "the best thing we have on that poet"; see T. D.
Young, *Gentleman*, 458.) With four poems and two essays (both on Eliot)
in the *Southern Review*, Unger was the student whom Brooks and Warren
published most. Although he parted company with Brooks in his interpretation of the metaphysical poets, Unger never hesitated to acknowledge
the influence of his mentor as both teacher and friend.

During the years that he taught at LSU, Cleanth was also an active
member of the College English Association. In fact, when the managing
editor of the association's journal perused his files in 1970, in search of
what he calls "the organization's quintessential 'self,'" he was struck by
the continuing relevance of an essay Cleanth had published thirty years
earlier in what was then known as the *CEA Newsletter*. That essay, en-

titled "What Are English Teachers Teaching?," was excerpted in the November 1970 edition of the *CEA Critic*, with Brooks's assurance that he still stood by what he had written in 1940.

At the beginning of the excerpt, Brooks agrees with Willa Cather's contention that literature cannot be "taught" in the same way that Latin is "taught." But, he continues, "I think that it might be taught nearly as well as football is taught. I am quite in earnest. The analogy is a fair one. In both cases, native ability will vary greatly from student to student, but good coaching is indispensable; and in both cases, a self-discipline must be acquired in action. No player is developed by merely studying diagrams of plays chalked on the blackboard. But the average student of literature gets little or no practice in trying to evaluate literature for himself. He is condemned to a perpetual skull practice" ("What Are English," 3–4). If his experience in the classrooms of McTyeire convinced Cleanth that students of humble backgrounds could still learn, his experience on the playing fields convinced him how they ought to be taught.

In his daily activities as a teacher, Cleanth displayed an almost idealistic faith in the ability of his students to learn. Like Socrates, he would frame questions in a manner designed to elicit the "correct" response. If the student was within a city block (or even a country mile) of that response, Cleanth would try to draw him closer, exhibiting the patience of an angler reeling in a fish. In an age when students are demanding the right to their own language and the very idea of a correct interpretation of a literary text is scorned, the Brooks method may well seem manipulative, if not benignly autocratic. But it served the genuinely democratic function of bringing learning to the masses. The closest thing to seeing that method in action would be to read Cleanth's critical writings (particularly those in his textbooks). The easy grace of his prose is simply a step up from the pedagogical language of the classroom. All that is missing is the charm and enthusiasm of a young man in seersucker, with open collar, and eyes that would twinkle through the thickest spectacles.

I

Although Cleanth had yet to become a major literary figure, he began to accumulate his share of prestigious speaking assignments, and his association with the *Southern Review* brought him a modest international reputation. His life, however, was not that of a professional drudge; in true Agrarian fashion, he made time for leisure activities (what Ransom had

called the "play forms"). These included the ever-popular charades and a
parlor game in which everyone tried to guess the perpetrator of a "murder" that took place when the lights were out. (Bob Heilman remembers
a game of charades in which a team headed by Cleanth and John Crowe
Ransom was unable to identify the title of Ransom's recently published
book *The World's Body*.) Although tackle football and rugby were young
men's games, touch football could be enjoyed even by otherwise sedentary academics. The interdepartmental competition supplied Cleanth with
his one opportunity to function as quarterback. Heilman recalls that
"Cleanth would devise, and urge upon us, complex reverses and hidden
ball plays, and his characteristically good-natured face would stretch into
sad lines of disappointment in us when in our self-doubt we clung to less
taxing offensive designs. Not for nothing had he come from the Vanderbilt
that invented what was then called razzle-dazzle football" (Heilman, 92).

Tinkum's nephew, Paul Blanchard (born in 1938 and named for his
grandfather), remembers that the Brookses were the only people he knew
in Baton Rouge with a working fireplace. They would soak a porous stone
in a pot of kerosene and place it under the logs to help get the fire started.
When the fire had burned down, they would raise a metal plate under the
logs and scrape the ashes into a container. Paul's other vivid memory is
of Cleanth as a bookbinder. The house would reek with horse-hoof glue
(driving Tinkum to distraction) as Cleanth bound the books in his library. (Fifty years later, he would regret binding the original series of the
Southern Review in cheap lambskin rather than the more durable mo-
rocco.) He even bound a book for Paul—a patriotic volume about the
Army, Navy, and Air Force, published at the height of World War II. When
he couldn't fit the names of all three military services on the spine, Cleanth
suggested that they substitute the catchall title "Defenders."[3]

In addition to the human members of the Brooks household, there was
an extremely neurotic Boston bull terrier named Caesar, whose erratic behavior was blamed on the birth trauma he suffered while being brought
into this world by caesarean section—with Professor Brooks assisting.
Caesar was remarkably even-tempered in that he barked with equal fe-
rocity at friend, foe, and stranger alike. On one occasion, when the visiting
David Nichol Smith encountered him, Caesar "did not so much chew on
Nichol Smith as run all over him, yapping and snarling. . . . When the
Brookses were both busy in the kitchen . . . , Caesar ran up Nichol Smith's
long legs, which, stretched out, formed a sort of ramp from floor to chair,
and began a noisy demonstration on the distinguished guest's middle.

With a very quick but just perceptible turning of the head toward the kitchen to be wholly sure that he was not seen and heard, Nichol Smith made a vehement, sweeping brush-off, hissing fiercely at Caesar, 'Get down, you cur' " (Heilman, 88).

Smith was but one of many visitors to pass through Baton Rouge in those years. Friends of Cleanth and Tinkum remember seeing the Canadian scholar Marshall McLuhan at the Brooks home. Born and reared in the western provinces of Canada, McLuhan could claim a background every bit as rural as that of the Agrarians. Although McLuhan identified himself with the social vision of the Nashville group, his literary views were a bit too moralistic for him to be considered a formalist critic (among the Cambridge literati, he was far closer to F. R. Leavis than to I. A. Richards). Upon returning from Cambridge in 1936, McLuhan taught for the next decade at the Catholic University in St. Louis. Although Missouri is not a southern state, it was close enough to the South that McLuhan could travel in the Old Confederacy and become a kind of honorary Fugitive-Agrarian. Even at that early point in his career, Cleanth recalls, Marshall's thought tended toward grand schematics.

After much coaxing, Cleanth persuaded the university speakers' committee to invite I. A. Richards to lecture at LSU. Thanks to the efforts of Ransom, Brooks, and other formalist critics, Richards was becoming nearly as well known in America as he was in England. Over a period of years, he and his wife Dorothy were frequent guests at the Brooks home. Cleanth remembers them as avid naturalists who enjoyed long walks in the woods. Both Cleanth and Richards were also notorious for their absentmindedness. Once, after a stay with the Brookses, Richards wrote to inquire about a pair of shoes he thought he had left behind. When a search of the house proved fruitless, Tinkum looked at her husband and said, "Cleanth, what do you have on your feet?" Discovering that the shoes he was wearing were indeed too long and narrow to be his, Cleanth's only defense was to say, "But you know my shoes don't fit me" (Heilman, 89).

During those years when he was struggling to develop his own critical position, Cleanth often alluded to this incident, as he saw himself trying unsuccessfully to fill Richards's shoes. Something of his esteem for the Cambridge don can be gleaned from a letter he sent to Allen Tate on April 19, 1934.[4] In remarkably tactful language, Cleanth tries to persuade Tate not to dismiss Richards too hastily. "I am not sure that I understand Richards," he writes. "I certainly do not completely understand him. . . . I have read his *Principles [of Literary Criticism]* at least a dozen times in the last four years—and in so far as I do understand him, I find him to be on your side. . . . I think that his support is worth something and—as regards most of the New York critics—is of some strategic importance."

Because of the light it sheds on Brooks's early debt to Richards, this letter warrants quoting at length. It begins by stating Richards's view of the nature of poetry:

> In the first place, I think that Richards has reduced the subject matter of poetry to "non-science" rather than "non-sense." Poetry, I feel sure Richards would say, is not "a tissue of lies." Poetry uses fictions. And fictions "may be used . . . to deceive. But this is not the characteristic use in poetry. The distinction which needs to be kept clear *does not* set up fictions *in opposition to verifiable truths in the scientific sense.* . . . We may either use words for the sake of the references they promote [scientific use], or we may use them for the sake of the attitudes and emotions which ensue."
>
> . . . Perhaps I do Richards more than justice, but I feel that his mysterious statement about the *Waste Land* and belief can only be interpreted (to put it in your words) as a compliment to Eliot that he has not done what Tennyson did—made poetry a sort of vehicle for inferior scientific generalizations about life. I think the statement is unfortunate because it implies that Eliot is the first poet to have avoided this error, whereas the greatest poets have always avoided it. . . .
>
> Richards, in general, I think is trying to steer a course between the Scylla of the Marxists—poetry is a sort of inferior science—and the Charybdis of the Ivory Tower.

The letter next turns to the question of whether poetry is useful and how the critic is to measure its use without becoming a petty materialist.

> I do not like Richards's utilitarianism, but I must admit that he has made it rather broad. He gives poetry a "use," it is true, but all of us who regard poetry as valuable also give it a use. I believe that his use turns out to be a restatement of the value of poetry—not as a means to ends, as scientific description is a means, but as a value or use which would include contemplation. He attempts to show the importance of contemplation and to relate it up to other activities. I do not think, however, that he reduces poetry to a tool.
>
> What makes me think that Richards is to be interpreted thus is ultimately his own taste—the fact that he has seen the "use" in poets with whom the practical men have nothing to do. His taste seems to me excellent. And his attack on critics who will not respect their terms seems to me thoroughly sound.

Toward the end of his lengthy epistle, Brooks makes the distinction between genuine art and mere propaganda, which, five years later, will be so crucial to his argument in *Modern Poetry and the Tradition.*

> I have had in mind for sometime a contribution to the Communist-poetry controversy which involved a use of Richards. Some of the Communist critics have been using him. Many of them have a holy reverence for science and most of all for psychology. I think that there might be some strategic value in using Richards to dynamite their position: unless my interpretation is badly off. I think that he could be used to show that it is the Marxists who are founding their view of poetry on bad psychology. . . . I think that they are guilty, in his terminology, of "message-hunting." And it is just this message-hunting that is the essence of the Platonic view of poetry. I think that his statement that "It is never what a poem *says* that matters, but what it *is*" comes close to your statement that "The stanza is neither true nor false; it is an object that exists."

As might be expected, the persons who stopped by Baton Rouge most frequently were Cleanth and Red's old Vanderbilt friends, especially the Ransoms and the Tates. And if the Tates were in town, Andrew Lytle was more likely than not to be with them. "We had a good time together," Lytle later recalled, "in the full blood of youth and work." The sensory pleasures were many:

> Pipkin had a wonderful cook, and for lagniappe she and her friends sang the songs we knew and liked to hear. No Christian, only a vegetarian, could forget the savor of her meals. Once the Tates and I with friends swooped through Alabama and descended upon New Orleans. We spent two weeks between Red's house and the hard boards of the Quartier. It was during the depression and the bars were practically empty. We took one over, with its piano, square-danced to "Go In and Out the Window." At three o'clock we ate oysters, Red never less than six dozen and often nine (I remember still my admiration.) Absinthe frappés (actually Pernod) brought us to our feet at nine in the morning. And so it went. (Lytle, 15)

The happiest result of these visits came in June 1938, when one of Cleanth's M.A. students, Edna Barker, became Mrs. Andrew Nelson Lytle.

In addition to the many parlor games played by the Fugitive-Agrarian brethren, there were legendary storytelling contests, often featuring those masters of the oral tradition Red Warren and Andrew Lytle. Although the punch lines in these stories were important, the real art came in the lead-up. Like jazz musicians, individual storytellers could improvise long digressions from the main theme without ever losing the thread of the story.

One favored tale involved the city slicker who had moved into a small country town and won the local belle away from her longtime sweetheart. As was the custom, toasts were proposed to the bride at the wedding dinner. This provided one last opportunity for a contest of wits between the bride's two suitors. When the groom got up to make his toast, he said: "Ladies and gentlemen, I had a wonderful dream last night. I was standing in the middle of a beautiful field. The sun was shining, the grass was green, and flowers were blooming everywhere in multicolored profusion. A gentle wind touched my face like the very breath of God, and I was certain that I had been bodily transported into the realms of celestial delight. And then I beheld an even more wondrous sight. The loveliest white bird upon which my eyes had ever gazed crossed the horizon and began to fly in my direction. If only I could possess that bird, I thought, t'would be bliss divine. The closer it flew, the more splendid did its innocence and purity appear. Against the radiant blue heavens, it was the only patch of white in a cloudless sky. My heart leaped in my bosom as this vision of unspeakable joy drew closer still. As if Joshua had once again made the sun to halt in its orbit, time itself came to a rapturous stop the moment this plumaged goddess alighted upon my unworthy arms. I give you the bride."

It was now the defeated rival's turn to speak. "I don't know no fancy words," he said. "I never went past the third grade, and if I had, I would've passed my pa. I may be a little short on book larnin', but I do know a few things about the lay of the land hereabouts and the critters who live on it. I've seen me a few birds in my time, though none of 'em ever looked like the one in this here feller's dream. It's kind of funny, but I had a dream myself the other night. Me and my old bird dog Buster was out in the field a-huntin'. The cows had pretty well fertilized that field, but me and Buster knew how to step around it. Well, we seen us this sprightly lookin' bird come sashayin' in from the woods. It warn't white but all different colors, and it looked like it had had itself a gay old time lightin' on one tree after another. I could've shot it, but it didn't seem like it would be worth the ammunition. I figgered I'd just try and catch it and keep it fer a pet as long as it would last. Almost had it, too. Reached and grabbed a-holt of it, but the damn thing flew away. And all I got to show fer my trouble are a couple-a pieces of tail."

II

For most people (including millions who will never read a word of south-ern literature), the most distinctive aspect of southern culture is the way the people below the Mason-Dixon Line talk. Although there is a wide variety of regional dialects, what is generically known as the "southern accent" is immediately recognizable. Some (including many native south-erners) regard it as a mark of ignorance that must be purged before one can be considered fully civilized. Others see it as a badge of cultural uniqueness, even superiority, to be flaunted like the Confederate flag at a North-South football game. Not surprisingly, the findings of professional linguists can be used to support either position. As an amateur linguist with near-professional skills, Cleanth Brooks made defense of the south-ern language part of his larger defense of southern culture. The first shot in this battle was fired with the publication of his first book—*The Relation of the Alabama-Georgia Dialect to the Provincial Dialects of Great Britain* (1935).

The origins of this book can be traced back to Cleanth's days at Ox-ford. As a temporary expatriate, he became intensely interested in the roots of his own speech. Then, one day he purchased a copy of Joseph Wright's *English Dialect Grammar* at one of Oxford's many secondhand bookshops. Years later Cleanth recalled that, as he started going through the index, he found that some of the words that Wright "was attribut-ing to remote dialects in counties in England were words I had heard all my life." He also knew that his own "linguistic ancestors must have come from counties where these peculiar pronunciations were used." For example, "I had heard in West Tennessee the word 'navel' pronounced 'nabel'—with a 'b' instead of a 'v'—so I looked in Wright to see in which English counties that pronunciation had persisted into the middle of the 19th century, and I did the same with a good many other words" (Paschall, 3).

This amateur passion for linguistics was deferred when Cleanth re-ceived his degree at Oxford and assumed his new duties at Baton Rouge. But under the influence and patronage of William A. Read, his interest in dialects was eventually rekindled. In a letter to Red Warren dated June 8, 1934, Cleanth writes:

> Just before examinations and for the last few days I have been preoccupied
> with my language study. It goes to the typist tomorrow. I don't think that
> I have told you about it; but I believe that the conclusions, at least, will

be interesting to you. I have taken the dialect of Uncle Remus and of the whites in the section in which Joel Chandler Harris lived and studied it with special reference to its sources. The results are as follows: the negro has made no innovations—he speaks what he learned from the first whites. These whites have made little or no changes—aside from the later influence of the literary language—but speak an English strongly influenced by the provincial dialects of the southwest of England—Devonshire, Somerset, and Dorset, etc.

That's an honorable lineage, isn't it? I honestly believe that I can prove my case. And though the technical aspects are of little interest except to a philologist, I think that the conclusions are of importance to anyone interested in the South—its culture and its civilization.[5]

Published in 1935 as part of the LSU *University Studies* series, Cleanth's book was greeted with generally favorable reviews. Although the validity of the book's general thesis (that American dialects derived from those of England) had already been established by George Phillip Krapp in his landmark study *The English Language in America* (1915), Brooks's particular objective was to apply Krapp's principle to a small section approximately in the center of the quadrilateral formed by the two states of Alabama and Georgia.

This study might well have remained useful only to students of technical linguistics were it not for the fact that in 1939 Hollywood made a film version of Margaret Mitchell's phenomenal best-seller *Gone With the Wind*. Because much of Mitchell's novel was set in the area of the South that Brooks had studied, Susan Myrick—the Georgia newspaperwoman who supervised the speech in the film production—used his book as one of her sources. The March 23, 1940, edition of the Baton Rouge *State-Times* carried a story announcing this fact, along with Cleanth's own reactions to the movie. According to the story, "Mr. Brooks . . . considers the players 'did an excellent job' especially in view of the fact that many are not from the South."[6] What neither Cleanth nor the reporter mentioned was that two of the main players—Vivian Leigh as Scarlett and Leslie Howard as Ashley—were British actors. The ease with which British performers master southern dialects lends a kind of intuitive credence to the notion that southerners speak a purer form of the mother tongue.

When Brooks's first book is mentioned at all today, it is usually in connection with a racial issue that was not even raised until nearly forty years after the book's publication. Brooks's argument that black people, who were brought to America from Africa, learned English from the whites who were already here seemed a commonsense refutation of the quaint myth that southern belles were trying to talk like their black mammies. Certain pronunciations that remain common in Black English can be traced to seventeenth-century England rather than to Africa or to the genetic inability of black people to articulate certain sounds. In his tendentious book *Black English* (1972), J. L. Dillard construes Brooks's argument as a racist attempt to undervalue black contributions to the American language. It is probably more reasonable to conclude, as Monroe K. Spears does, that Brooks saw his linkage of black and white language as "favorable to black self-respect" (Spears, *Ambitions*, 158).

A more vernacular version of Brooks's views on the southern language can be found in his essay "The English Language in the South," published in Stark Young's *A Southern Treasury of Life and Literature* (1937). Here Brooks suggests a reason why the language of the South is more conservative than that of New England. Originally, speech in both regions was greatly influenced by the provincial dialects of Great Britain. The differences, Brooks argues, came over time, "not with laziness and corruption in the South, but with innovation in New England through the influence of spelling, the elocution book, and the diligence of the New England school-ma'am" ("English Language," 355). These influences may be "interpreted as marks of the cultural continuity existing between the New England and the Old. They are susceptible, however, of another account, not quite so favorable perhaps; they may be interpreted as symptoms of a feeling of cultural inferiority—of anxiety, that is, as to status" (356).

In arguing for preservation of the southern dialect, Brooks confidently dismisses questions of status anxiety. "British English is undoubtedly correct for the modern Englishman," he writes. "It is not correct, by virtue of that reason at least, for the Virginian or Tennessean. Moreover, in trying to find a standard for modern America, the best authorities are agreed that there is no virtue in trying to impose an artificial and synthetic criterion. If the Virginian is not to be forced into imitation of the Oxford don, there is logically no reason for him to be forced into imitation of Boston—or, for that matter, of Chicago or Hollywood" (357).

III

Quick as he was to defend the South and its culture from condescending attacks by those outside the region, Brooks also criticized meretricious work within the region. Not only did he and Warren reject the unworthy submissions of southern writers such as John Gould Fletcher and Mildred Haun, but in the first volume of the *Southern Review*, they also carried less than favorable critiques of two of the most prominent southern novelists of the day—Erskine Caldwell and Thomas Wolfe. In both instances, the reviewer was John Donald Wade, who had left Vanderbilt in 1934 to return to his native Georgia.

Wade's discussion of the immensely popular Caldwell is both the longer and the more negative of the two pieces. Caldwell, Wade argues, was intent on turning southern life into a brutal and obscene caricature. Speaking of the inhabitants of *Tobacco Road*, Wade writes, "Liars and thieves, they are filthy, lazy, blasphemous and cruel, and as lecherous as monkeys." He goes on to say, "Shakespeare . . . made his Caliban, but *The Tempest* is not *filled* with Calibans, and the back-drop for the monster's appearances was not London with the double towers of Old Saint Paul's, nor any other place to be pointed out on any map" (Wade, "Sweet," 455). After a somewhat reluctant acknowledgment of Caldwell's powers as a writer, Wade concludes: "It is likely that his entire literary output would be more impressive if—a good southerner still—he were not as plaintively anxious as he is to please the kind and class of people that he has come to be affiliated with—the detached, nervous, thrill-goaded metro-cosmopolitans of his own day" (466).

In his discussion of Wolfe (suggestively entitled "Prodigal"), Wade pays generous homage to his subject's talents. These include "stupendous gusto and energy, and quite remarkable omnivorousness." But Wade adds: "So far, his work has been the record of his own passage through the world. Whether he can transfer his peculiar virtues to books in which he is not himself the protagonist, is something that the performance can only indicate" (Wade, "Prodigal" 194). What Wade finds most disconcerting (and this comes as no surprise to readers of his essay in *I'll Take My Stand*) is Wolfe's lack of identity with his native soil. As Wade puts it: "'*Oh, lost, lost!*' is the refrain, constantly echoed, that this man from Old Catawba, immured now in Brooklyn, N.Y., cries piteously through most that he has written. It would be an interesting thing, and worthy of much wonder, if in his case this should prove inexorable: that to live validly and with satisfying peace he should be driven to a reconciliation with his origins; should be obliged in the vast area of his sympathies, to make room for the people who bred him" (198).

In general, the connection between Wolfe and the Fugitive-Agrarians is a complicated story. If Wolfe failed to show sufficient piety toward the

South to satisfy the likes of John Donald Wade, his approach to literature was an affront to the critical sensibilities of the Nashville group. When Red Warren reviewed Wolfe's sprawling second novel, *Of Time and the River*, in the May 1935 issue of the *American Review*, he decried Wolfe's "attempt to exploit directly and naively the personal experience and self-defined personality in art" (Warren, *Selected Essays*, 183). (This piece, which was called "A Note on the Hamlet of Thomas Wolfe," was reprinted in Warren's *Selected Essays* over two decades later.) Despite this review, and Wade's, Wolfe remained on friendly terms with both Warren and the *Southern Review*. Brooks and Warren lobbied Wolfe for a contribution to the magazine, and they might have gotten one had Wolfe not been in Europe when the request arrived. On October 14, 1935, Wolfe congratulated Warren on the first issue of the *Southern Review* (which, among other things, had included Wade's attack on him), and he sent his protégé Thomas H. Thompson to LSU to study with Warren.

For all his famed hypersensitivity to criticism, Thomas Wolfe felt at least a partial kinship with the Nashville group in general and with Red Warren in particular. He had taught with Warren at a writer's conference in Boulder, Colorado, in the summer of 1935, and the two southerners had become fast friends. (As his former student Robert Lowell would recall in a poem published nearly forty years later, Warren "could make friends with anybody, even showy writer giants that [he] had slaughtered in a review.") In his Pulitzer Prize–winning biography of Wolfe, David Herbert Donald tells of a dinner party that summer in Boulder at which the subject of book reviews had been raised. Wolfe noted that he "had been pleased by favorable reviews but had also learned much from the more critical ones." Turning to Warren, Wolfe said that the one review that had taught him more than any other was written by someone "at this table" (Donald, 335). Later that year, the two southerners ran into each other in San Francisco. "They wandered about the streets at night, and Wolfe was especially delighted by the sights and smells of Chinatown. Both were nonstop talkers, and they 'wrangled back and forth' about the South and about literature, finding themselves, as Warren remembered, in 'not unfriendly disagreement' " (Donald, 340).

Unfortunately, Wolfe's relations with the rest of the Fugitive-Agrarians were not as free and easy. As a native of Appalachia, Wolfe came from a part of the South not represented in *I'll Take My Stand*. His parents were businesspeople rather than farmers, and his friendship with the New South liberals of Chapel Hill made him suspect, if only by association.

Donald Davidson, for example, wrote that "Thomas Wolfe had a divided sensibility which very likely resulted from his education at Mr. Howard Odum's citadel, the progressive University of North Carolina, and from his subsequent unfortunate experience at Harvard." Even more blunt, Allen Tate accused Wolfe of having done "harm to the art of the novel and moral damage to his readers" (see Watkins, 412).

Wolfe's closest contact with the Nashville literati came in December 1936, when he happened to be passing through Richmond during the annual convention of the Modern Language Association. Donald describes the scene as follows: "Striding through the lobby of the Hotel Jefferson, with his overcoat in one hand and a bottle of whiskey in the other, Wolfe spied Warren, went over and clapped him on the back, and said that they should get together for a talk" (Donald, 360). Wolfe recalled that occasion several months later in a letter to Dixon Wecter. "On my trip South after Christmas," he writes, "I stopped off at Richmond and had not been there a day before I ran into Red Warren, Allen Tate, Caroline Gordon, John Crowe Ransom. . . . I spent a very pleasant evening with the Warrens, the Tates, and the Brooks [sic] and Mr. Ransom. In fact, I did almost everything except become a Southern Agrarian. I suppose I don't understand enough about that. But it was good to see Red and to meet all the others" (see Idol, 3). What Wolfe was doing in Richmond at the time is a matter of conjecture. (He may have been on the lam from some legal difficulty in New York.)[7] Whatever the reason, Cleanth recalls that Wolfe "was as surprised to see us as we were to see him, and he seemed amused and even appalled to find that the city was full of literature professors" (see Idol, 4).

In a letter she wrote to her friend Sally Wood the following week, Caroline Gordon recalls the figure Wolfe cut: "He was drunk and dumb and extremely amiable. He kept looking at me and blubbering 'Mrs. Gordon, Max Perkins thinks you're wonderful.' He is so dumb that he can hardly follow a conversation. We were talking about the wonderful whore house scene in Sanctuary. Wolfe assured us solemnly that he had intimate acquaintance with whore houses in many places and that whore house wasn't true to life" (Wood, 204–205). Whether Wolfe was able to discern this condescension or whether he simply got tired of being castigated in print by the Nashville critics, he never again came close to becoming an Agrarian. In fact, his final statement on the matter, in his posthumous novel *The Web and the Rock* (1939), ridicules the "refined young gentlemen of the new Confederacy," who "retired haughtily into the South, to the academic security of a teaching appointment at one of the universities, from which they could issue in quarterly installments very small and very precious magazines which celebrated the advantages of an agrarian society" (Wolfe, 242).

IV

No doubt Cleanth Brooks was one of the refined young Confederates Wolfe had in mind. Although Cleanth had not been a contributor to *I'll Take My Stand*, he soon became involved with the movement that that book helped to spawn. Of the original twelve contributors, Stark Young and Henry Blue Kline soon faded from the scene (Young because he was more involved with his own literary career in New York, and Kline because he was too much of a literary and intellectual lightweight to be taken seriously by the others). With H. C. Nixon and John Gould Fletcher still interested in the cause but physically removed from middle Tennessee (Nixon in New Orleans and Fletcher in Little Rock), a nucleus of eight active Agrarians began meeting frequently to plot everything from the purchase of a county newspaper to the launching of a new political movement. Unfortunately, the need to make a living and the desire to pursue other literary interests kept them from moving beyond the talking stage until three years after the publication of *I'll Take My Stand*.

In March of 1933 Franklin Delano Roosevelt was inaugurated as President of the United States. Although he had been the patrician governor of an urban state, he was the first Democrat to occupy the White House in twelve years, and the programs he advocated offered considerable hope to the farmer. What the Agrarians needed was a national forum from which they could try to influence the policies of the new president. The very month that Roosevelt was sworn in, Allen Tate, who had just arrived back in America from Europe, formed an alliance with the New York journalist and editor Seward Collins. In the late 1920s Collins had been editor of a literary journal called the *Bookman*. Wanting to turn his attention more toward social and political issues, he renamed his magazine the *American Review* and made it an organ for extreme conservative, even reactionary, thought. Although the Agrarians would have the chief voice in this new magazine, it also promoted the views of the Neo-Humanists, the Neo-Scholastics, and a group of British populists known as "Distributists."

Cleanth Brooks was an early contributor to the *American Review*, publishing four essays in that journal between 1934 and 1936. The marriage between the Nashville Agrarians and the *American Review* came to an end, however, when the extreme views of Seward Collins became public. In the course of an interview he gave to Grace Lumpkin in the February 1936 issue of the radical magazine *Fight*, Collins advocated destroying factories and abandoning any attempt to educate the general population; he identified himself as a Fascist and a great admirer of Hitler and Mussolini. "When asked about Hitler's persecution of the Jews, Collins replied, 'It's not persecution. The Jews make trouble. It is necessary to segregate them.' Collins also contended that the Negro must be segregated, although he should be given land to support himself" (Shapiro, 372). The Agrarians did not respond to this lunacy by publicly repudiating Collins (to do so would have been to betray a friend), but they reiterated their utter distaste for Fascism and effectively ended their association with the *American Review*.

Another contributor who distanced himself from Collins after the Lumpkin interview was the journalist and historian Herbert Agar. As London correspondent for the Louisville *Courier-Journal* between 1929 and 1933, Agar had become acquainted with Distributist thought and immediately saw its relevance to the American situation. Upon his return to the United States in 1934, Agar became a friend and ally of Allen Tate, and the two men continued to forge ties after the *American Review* ceased to be an appropriate forum for either Agrarian or Distributist beliefs.

In the meantime, H. C. Nixon had estranged himself from his fellow Agrarians because of his wholesale enthusiasm for the New Deal (including those programs that resulted in greater economic centralization) and his support for black civil rights. John Gould Fletcher, after his disgraceful performance at the Baton Rouge Literary Conference and subsequent hospitalization for depression, was also effectively lost to the Agrarian cause. In a sense, Nixon's and Fletcher's places were taken by Cleanth Brooks and the young poet George Marion O'Donnell. However, Agrarianism by itself, complete with its identifiable sectional bias, no longer stirred interest in the nation at large. No New York publisher could be found for a sequel to *I'll Take My Stand*, and even the University of North Carolina Press turned the project down. The only alternative to being ignored was for the Agrarians to join forces with other economic decentralists under the leadership of Agar.

At the end of a peripatetic summer in 1935, Allen Tate came home to his farm near the Kentucky border (named Benfolly after his brother Ben) and together with Agar, Lytle, and Lanier, planned a volume of essays entitled *Who Owns America?: A New Declaration of Independence*. Tate had deliberately not invited the other Agrarians, knowing that if he did, they would be embroiled in endless disputes. The plan was to present the project as a fait accompli (Tate obtained a contract from Houghton Mifflin) and to flatter such hard-liners as Davidson and Owsley into contributing. Whether they were persuaded by the flattery or by the fact that the train was leaving the station with or without them, the remaining Agrarians swallowed their reservations and climbed aboard. Tate and Agar (who were coeditors) thought it essential to rush the book into print before the 1936 election. Although the New Deal seemed too much in thrall to industrialism, the contributors hoped that their ideas might still become part of the national debate (see Conkin, *Agrarians*, 122–23). When the book was published, Agar sent copies to Roosevelt, Harold Ickes, Cordell Hull, Henry Wallace, and Senator William Borah of Idaho. Roosevelt's speech accepting the Democratic nomination for a second term had come directly out of *Who Owns America?*, Agar claimed with more than a little bravado. "Now let him act on it!" (see Shapiro, 373).

v

Cleanth's contribution to the second Agrarian symposium had appeared earlier that year in the *American Review* as "The Christianity of Modernism." (Agar changed the title to "A Plea to the Protestant Churches" so that *Who Owns America?* would not seem too heavily Catholic.) The argument Brooks makes is familiar to anyone who has read Ransom's "Forms and Citizens" (1933) or *God Without Thunder* (1930)—but with a crucial difference. Ransom's celebration of liturgical ritual in his famous essay, and of fundamentalist dogma in his less widely read book, was finally utilitarian. Ransom longed to recover the sense of beauty and mystery that had vanished from religion, without believing that that beauty and mystery pointed to an objective reality. Brooks shared Ransom's lament but not his skepticism. For that reason he was better able to speak to the wayward churches than was the man who could not publicly affirm the words of the Nicene Creed.

Even at its most eloquent, Ransom's defense of fundamentalism always seemed forced. The Methodist tradition in which he and Cleanth were both reared was more scholarly than evangelical. (It was a tradition in which the phrase "hot gospeller" was a frequent term of derision.) Cleanth recalls with amusement that during his elementary school days, a woman with a quite literal interpretation of Genesis was appalled to catch him drawing pictures of dinosaurs. (She was even more appalled to find that Cleanth, Sr., did not share her concern over his son's soul.) In a sense, Cleanth regards the fundamentalist and the liberal Protestant as opposite sides of the same coin. Both confuse religion and science—the fundamentalist by resisting empirical data; the liberal Protestant by capitulating to it. Perhaps the best way to demonstrate the difference between science and religion, the essay argues, is by considering the difference between science and art.

Brooks is careful to point out that in seeming to equate religion and art, he is not talking primarily about either ritual or architecture. "I am using *art* in the sense of a description of experience which is concrete where that of science is abstract, many-sided where that of science is necessarily one-sided, and which involves the whole personality where science only involves one part, the intellect" ("Plea," 326). Such distinctions are ones that Ransom would certainly endorse; however, Brooks goes one step farther than Ransom. "Religion is obviously more than art," Brooks declares. "A religion is anchored to certain supreme values, values which it affirms are eternal, not merely to be accepted for the moment through a 'willing suspension of disbelief' " (327). The point is that liberal Protestantism has not even reached the level of aestheticism, much less passed beyond it.

In choosing science rather than art as its epistemological model, liberal Protestantism makes several grievous errors. To begin with, it stresses intellect at the expense of emotion. One need not be a "hot gospeller" to realize that mere reason can never lead one to believe anything as mysterious as the Christian faith. The classical proofs for the existence of God may demonstrate that there is an unmoved mover, but not that that primal force became incarnate in the person of Jesus of Nazareth. If religion tries to explain things in scientific terms, it will become increasingly obsolete as science itself is able to explain more of the observable universe. Any religion that does not strike a responsive chord in the *soul* of man is little more than an ethical philosophy. That was the pitfall that Brooks saw for liberal Protestantism.

Unlike science, religion should not try to add to the information explosion. Whereas science is constantly discovering new facts about the universe, religion contends that there are no new truths to be discovered, only old ones to be relearned. " 'The search for God'," Brooks writes, "is all very well for a party of religious explorers; it hardly does for a religion which maintains that it has found Him." Brooks continues: "If there is to be a search at all, it will have to be a search in something of the sense in which the poet explores himself in relation to the truth, pondering over it, relating it to various sets of conditions, but returning to it and working back to it as to a center rather than regarding it as a point on a line along which he continually advances" ("Plea," 327).

Finally, science (or at least technology) is radically humanistic in the sense that it is necessarily man-centered. As the contributors to *I'll Take My Stand* had maintained, industrialism seeks to subjugate nature, whereas an Agrarian sensibility is content to live as much as possible within the limits defined by nature. Liberal Protestantism, particularly in its excessive emphasis on the social gospel, sides with the humanistic, man-centered party. "The fatherhood of God, one feels, is no longer the correlative of the brotherhood of man. The brotherhood of man tends to become an exclusive end in itself. There is little wonder that the most positive affirmation which Liberal Protestantism can make is apt to be some form of socialism" (328).

It is not necessary to know anything about Cleanth's life to evaluate the argument that he makes in "A Plea to the Protestant Churches." Nevertheless, one cannot help noting the bitterly ironic circumstances of his own family situation at the time. As many Protestant churches were bent on remaking the social order, even if it meant ignoring their differences with the officially atheistic creed of Marxism, religious workhorses such as the Reverend Cleanth Brooks, Sr., were put out to pasture ("superannuated" was the accepted euphemism) after they had outlived their professional usefulness. Only sensitivity to his father's continuing denominational loyalty prevented Cleanth from openly criticizing the Methodist Church, much less withdrawing his membership from it.

Because he mentions no churches by name in his essay (citing only the nonsectarian magazine *Christian Century*), one cannot be certain to what extent Cleanth was philosophically disenchanted with the church of his youth. However, during his undergraduate days at Vanderbilt, he had begun attending Episcopal services at the Church of the Advent (where Tennessee Williams's grandfather had once been rector) and had become seriously interested in Anglo-Catholicism while at Oxford. There can be little doubt that by the time he wrote his essay for *Who Owns America?*, Cleanth Brooks was emotionally and intellectually on his way out of the Methodist Church and at least contemplating the road to Canterbury.

CHAPTER EIGHT

An Extended Family

The intellectual ferment created by the *Southern Review* extended from the editorial offices into the classrooms and the teachers' lounges. During the Depression those universities fortunate enough to have money to spend had no trouble attracting promising young faculty. Thanks to the largesse of Huey Long, LSU was one of the prime buyers in the buyer's market. The first half of the thirties saw Brooks and Warren added to the English faculty. Then in 1935, three new Ph.D. graduates arrived—Nathaniel Caffee from Virginia, Thomas Kirby from Johns Hopkins, and Robert Heilman from Harvard. With the later addition of Arlin Turner and Bosley Woolf, the newcomers outnumbered the old guard by the end of the decade.

Although several of the faculty would later gain national prominence, Red Warren was the only one who was already widely known in the Republic of Letters. Despite having rejected a traditional academic career when he decided against continuing his doctoral studies at Yale, Red was making his living as an academic. Because it was virtually unheard of for someone to be hired by a university as a critic and creative writer, his official function at LSU was largely at odds with his true vocation. The disparity may not have been as great as what T. S. Eliot experienced while working at Lloyds of London by day and writing poetry by night, but there was a sense in which Red led a double life. By all accounts, he did so with style and grace.

At least since the Romantic era, the boorish behavior of artists has become legendary—almost a mark of sensitivity, if not genius. Red Warren, however, was always a gentleman. He taught his classes, befriended his students, served his university, and entertained his colleagues. Although he was frequently restless and unhappy, he didn't believe in taking it out on the people around him. When he turned his face toward the world, close friends and casual acquaintances both saw the same man. Forty years after first meeting Robert Penn Warren, Walter Sullivan wrote: "Red is a generous man and a good raconteur even though he talks so fast that his words often run together. . . . In his ordinary conversation, he told stories about almost everything: French immigrants to Kentucky and famous funerals, political campaigns and duels and eating contests, other writers and his own literary experiences, but only rarely did he seem to reveal his own most personal thoughts" (Sullivan, *Allen Tate*, 31–32).

In recalling those Baton Rouge years decades later, Bob Heilman writes: "There was the joyous and laughing Red, whose full face crinkling into merriment meant a fine display of teeth and that long little suck or hiss of breath, an inbound or outbound sibilance, that somehow doubled the sweep of delight" (Heilman, 70). Heilman also remembers the famous parties Red would throw, back when everyone was young and hangovers didn't seem to matter:

> I still have a clear picture of one Warren guest, an instructor in English, standing there with his back against the wall, and a little cross-eyed by now, like a happy late-nighter in a cartoon, and then suddenly starting to slide gently down the wall, his feet moving slowly forward and outward until, never losing contact with the wall, he was seated solidly on the floor, his legs making a big V, and his face coming apart in a slightly puzzled gaze. The Warren party air, though not intent upon such a fall, was comfortable with it; first aid and a comic sense were both there in suitable measure. At such a time all the king's men could reassemble the wall-fall guy. (71)

In looking back on those times, it is easy to minimize the economic difficulties and professional uncertainty, if only because we know how well things came out in the end. The greatest source of continuing unhappiness for Red Warren, however, was a marriage that seemed wrong from the start and only grew worse as time went on. Like so many moody and introspective young people, Red had been disappointed early in love. Worry over his eyesight and his vocation may have brought him to the brink of suicide while he was at Vanderbilt, but what pushed him over the edge was unrequited love for Chink Nichol. (Fannie Cheney believes that another romantic disappointment caused Red to try to drown himself while in California.) It is unclear what attracted him to Cinina Brescia during the year he spent at Berkeley, but their marriage was an accomplished (if secret) fact by the time any of Red's friends back home had met his wife to be. The attitude of those friends was well summed up by Allen Tate when he wrote to Andrew Lytle on July 2, 1928, "We'll lose Red if he marries that girl" (see T. D. Young and Sarcone, 11).

The cultural differences between Cinina Brescia and Red Warren's southern friends were profound. She tried to compensate for her lack of refinement and intellect with behavior that people such as Allen Tate regarded as pretentious. Like Zelda Fitzgerald, she made a fool of herself by trying to compete with a more gifted husband. When her own artistic endeavors failed miserably, she turned to drink, which only intensified her vulgarity and paranoia. In an effort to preserve the marriage and his own sanity, Red tried to deny what he knew people were saying, first behind his back, then eventually to his face. One can only imagine his embarrassment when Cinina, trying to give a clue for the syllable "syn" in "idiosyncracy" during a game of charades, lay on her back simulating sexual intercourse. On another occasion, she got drunk at a party and invited everyone to come to her place the following weekend without consulting Red. A few days later he had to call people to cancel their invitations to the nonexistent party.

In reading letters that Allen Tate sent to Andrew Lytle throughout the early to mid-thirties, one gets the impression that Cinina was bitterly jealous of her husband's friends and tried to drive a wedge between him and them. Correspondence between the Tates and the Brookses tells much the same story. For example, in a postscript to a letter sent to Cleanth on April 5, 1937, Allen writes: "Of course Red will tell you that I have responded enthusiastically to his own enthusiastic plan of getting together this summer. We have exchanged, at this time of year, exactly the same kind of letters for two years,—no, three years, '35, '36, '37. He doesn't know even now that he won't be allowed to come up here. Strange—we know these things better than he does." [1]

Apparently, the Tates and Warrens did get together briefly that summer, but the results were disastrous. In a letter to Cleanth dated June 24, Allen writes:

> Red and Miss Emma came through Middle Tennessee like a bewildered
> Kansas tornado. It is increasingly impossible to talk to Red. He is doing so
> many things he can't put his mind on any of them. Ford wanted to write an
> article, maybe two, for the SR, but Red just started in on him vaguely, and
> at last suggested that he read and review 49 novels for the fall issue. Ford

replied mildly that he reviewed only books that he admires. After all Ford
is one of the great men of letters in the world today, and I do think that
Red oughtn't to have suggested such a routine job to him. I'm really upset
by it. Couldn't something be done? Red didn't mean anything unpleasant;
he just didn't know what he was saying. At that moment he was surveying
mankind from China to Peru, sub specie Californiae, and doubtless had
one eye on the question: Will Miss Emma take me off to the bedroom before or after lunch?

Not surprisingly, Cinina was convinced that her unpopularity was due
to the malice of the Tates, not to any shortcomings of her own. To believe
that theory, however, one must assume that Red Warren's friends were all
so weak-minded that they would turn on his wife simply because Allen
and Caroline Tate persuaded them to do so. In a letter to Cleanth dated
April 30, 1938, Allen wonders "what end the situation will come to. Even
if Red is so infatuated as to believe that the Tates are responsible, . . . I
don't see how that pretext will make his daily life any easier. To blame
somebody else for the trouble doesn't remove it."

On one particularly memorable occasion, Red and Cinina left a party
given by the Brookses to put in an appearance at a wedding reception for
President Smith's daughter. By the time the Warrens returned, Cinina was
deep in her cups and clearly on the defensive. Cleanth was on the other
side of the room when he heard Tinkum make a teasing remark to Cinina
about attending the president's party. The next thing he knew there was
a scuffle of some sort. In a letter to Allen Tate dated March 27, 1938,
Cleanth described the incident as follows: "Tinkum gave C a playful pat
on her seat when she leaned over. C proceeded to kick the hell out of her.
Tinkum still suspected nothing, thinking that C was merely playing and
had not realized how hard she had kicked. Tinkum then moved across the
room, and C followed her, and standing over her, dared her to hit her
again. Perhaps Tinkum should have realized by now that C was really
angry. Anyway, Tinkum tried to pass it off by smiling and tapping her on
the cheek. C then proceeded to box her jaws." As Red ushered his wife
out of the apartment, he was heard to say, "If you ever do anything like
this again, I'm going to leave you."

Cinina's contrite phone call the next day made matters even worse. She
blamed her behavior on too much liquor and too little self-confidence. She
then tried to ingratiate herself with Tinkum by saying that she was a truer
friend to the Brookses than some people who only pretended to like them.

Cinina's neurotic disingenuousness made Cleanth and Tinkum resolve to see as little of her as possible in the future. "At the moment you begin to think that you could pity her," Cleanth wrote to Allen in exasperation, "she does something really revolting." [2]

Red eventually tried to minimize the occasions when his wife and his friends would be together. This motivation, added to his fundamental uneasiness with academic life, may account for his frequent absences from Baton Rouge. He sought academic leave whenever he could get it and began spending summers in Italy, even as the war in Europe made that an increasingly dangerous place for Americans to be. For years thereafter, the American Express office in Rome was the most frequent return address on his letters to Cleanth. In one such communication, dated July 15, 1948, Red casually observes: "Eleanor Clark, whom we knew in Washington and like a lot, was staying in Rome, recovering from a skiing accident . . . and we saw a lot of her."

I

Although LSU had its share of leftists during the thirties and forties, three of Cleanth's friends from that era would turn out to be among the most important influences on post–World War II conservative thought. The oldest of these was Eric Voegelin. Born in Germany in 1901, Voegelin received his doctorate from the University of Vienna in 1922, where he taught until being dismissed for having written books critical of National Socialism. Although Voegelin was a pleasant man and a gifted pianist, his social life was limited by his habit of retiring to bed in the late afternoon and awaking for the day at two or three in the morning. In his *Autobiographical Reflections* (1989), Voegelin speaks warmly of colleagues in LSU's English department. He recalls once seeing Cleanth Brooks "crossing the campus, . . . deep in sorrow and thought." Concerned for his friend, Voegelin asked Cleanth what was bothering him.

> He told me that he had to prepare a chapter on typical mistakes for a textbook on English style that he was re-editing with Robert Penn Warren, and that it was quite a chore to find typical mistakes. I was a bit surprised and told him, "Well, it is very easy to find typical mistakes. Just take any education textbook and you will find half a dozen on every page." He then explained to me that he could not use this method because educationists were far below the level of average literacy, and their mistakes could not be

considered typical for an average English-speaking person. Instead, he was using sociology textbooks and sometimes had to read twenty pages of that stuff before running into a really good example. But even so, he had to worry because social scientists . . . were [also] below the average, though not as far below as educationists. (Voegelin, 60)

Of a very different background from Voegelin was the young southerner Richard M. Weaver. Those who know Richard Weaver only through his writing are likely to picture him as cosmopolitan, even urbane. In fact, for all the subtlety of his mind, he never ceased being a country boy. By all accounts, the figure he cut on the LSU campus was that of a hayseed who didn't quite belong in polite company. He was dirt-poor and showed it in the way he lived and dressed. When he wasn't wearing a beat-up old hat, his hair looked as if he had just gotten up from sleeping in a barn.[3] His clothes were old and shabby, and a vision problem made him look cross-eyed. Nevertheless, Weaver's philosophical mind and unassuming personality caused friends to forget his physical eccentricities.

Weaver began a dissertation in American literature under Arlin Turner, which he continued under Cleanth Brooks when Turner was called away to the war. From 1940 to 1943, while the Second World War was raging abroad, Dick Weaver immersed himself in a study of the American Civil War and its aftermath. His dissertation, directed by Brooks and dedicated to John Crowe Ransom, was entitled "The Confederate South, 1865–1910: A Study in the Survival of a Mind and a Culture." (This project was being completed at a time when another intellectual history of the region—W. J. Cash's *The Mind of the South*—was taking the nation by storm.) Weaver's dissertation eventually became *The Southern Tradition at Bay*, a book published in 1968, twenty-five years after it was written and five years after its author's untimely death. It is difficult to say how much of Cleanth's hand is in this volume or how much he shaped his student's intellectual development. We do know that when Weaver left Texas for LSU, he was a disillusioned former liberal but not yet a conservative. At the very least, working on his dissertation helped to clarify his belief in cultural traditionalism. Through his subsequent influence on intellectuals such as William F. Buckley and Russell Kirk, Richard M. Weaver has made the Agrarian vision a force in contemporary American politics.

The political philosopher who was Cleanth's closest friend was a brilliant but troubled prodigy named Willmoore Kendall. As different from Voegelin and Weaver as those two were from each other, Kendall was born in Konawa, Oklahoma, in 1909, the son of a blind southern Methodist preacher. He learned to read at the age of two by playing with a typewriter. "By five, he was reading to his father; shortly after, driving for him, seeing for him, playing flute to his father's piano" (Wills, 18). While still in his teens, Willmoore published his first book, *Baseball: How to Play It and How to Watch It*, under the pseudonym of Alan Monk. When compiling his bibliography in later years, Kendall would always place this book at the beginning of his list of scholarly publications.

In 1935, with an Oxford M.A. degree in hand, Kendall married his first wife and left for Spain as a correspondent for United Press. His experience there strengthened his hatred for Stalinism and started him down the road to militant anti-Communism. (With typical bravado, he would claim to anyone who would listen that, if the Communists ever took over in America, he would be among the first to be shot.) Returning to the United States, Kendall earned a Ph.D. in political philosophy at the University of Illinois in 1940. His first academic appointment was at LSU.

Those who knew both men have always found it something of a mystery that Willmoore Kendall and Cleanth Brooks became fast friends. It would be difficult to imagine two more different individuals. Cleanth was quiet and unassuming, firm in his convictions but gracious in dealing with opponents. Willmoore was loud and vain, a controversialist who would change his opinions in order to gain advantage in an argument. If Cleanth had a winning manner that drew people to him, Willmoore was just as apt to turn them off with his drunken and boorish behavior. (Once, when he was condemning insurance as a racket, someone asked if he had not made provision for his wife should he die before her. Willmoore's response was that if she couldn't find another meal ticket in six months, that was her tough luck.) The most facile explanation for this unusual friendship is that opposites attract. Beyond that, Willmoore used to claim that he deliberately lost arguments to Cleanth, while Cleanth surmised that he was one of the few people to whom Willmoore had nothing to prove, as he had long since accepted Willmoore's genius as a given.[4]

Because his beliefs were still in a state of flux, Willmoore Kendall was a man of great intellectual curiosity. Although he tried to give the appearance of possessing all human knowledge, he was constantly learning things from people he met. In Cleanth Brooks he found a different kind of thinker from those he had known in Illinois or Europe. While he still considered himself a man of the Left, the fashionable orthodoxies of the Left were making less and less sense to him. What Willmoore lacked was a coherent conservative philosophy to fill the void. As a southern Agrarian, Cleanth clearly had one; he was, for Kendall, at least a novelty if not quite a mentor. As much as poetic justice might demand that Cleanth turn this Oklahoma Trotskyite into a neo-Agrarian, that was not to be. Willmoore scoffed at anything that smacked of cultural elitism and felt no affinity for an antebellum hierarchy that got its vision of life from the novels of Walter Scott. Willmoore was just as faithful to his roots as the Agrarians were to theirs; his were simply different. He was a man of the western prairie, not the Old Confederacy.

The political philosophy that Willmoore Kendall finally adopted was a radical populism based on a belief in absolute majority rule (his dissertation, which later formed the basis for an article in the *Southern Review*, contended that, for all his talk about natural rights, John Locke was essentially a majority-rule democrat). Such a position was more consistent with the rhetoric than with the reality of the Left. From experience, Willmoore discovered that the Left was more interested in speaking for the people than in listening to them. His brand of anti-elitist right-wing populism might lead some to believe that Willmoore's idea of participatory democracy was a lynch mob (except that Willmoore himself was the most likely candidate for lynching in most of the communities in which he lived). If Eric Voegelin and Richard Weaver have had a more profound influence on contemporary political thought, Willmoore Kendall's philosophy has been responsible for winning more elections. Even when he was wrong, he was a man of mythic proportions. According to Saul Bellow, who used him as the model for his character Willis Mosby, Willmoore Kendall "made some of the most interesting mistakes a man could make in the twentieth century" (see Wills, 17).

II

Of the literary folk living in Baton Rouge at this time, none owed a greater debt to the *Southern Review* than Peter Taylor. Peter was born in the west Tennessee town of Trenton in 1917. His family moved to Nashville in 1924 (the year that Cleanth entered Vanderbilt) and to St. Louis in 1926; in 1932 (when Peter was fifteen), the family moved back to Tennessee and settled in Memphis. A generation younger than Cleanth, Peter Taylor was farther removed chronologically from the frontier past of his native region. In a sense, though, that past was personally closer, as Peter's family had helped shape the history of the land from which they came. His maternal grandfather, Robert Taylor (who coincidentally shared the same name as Peter's paternal grandfather), served a term in Congress, three terms as governor, and one as U.S. senator. When he was the Democratic candidate for governor in 1886, his Republican opponent was his brother, Alf Taylor (and running against both of them on the Prohibitionist ticket was their father, Nathaniel Green Taylor). "To this day, wry stories are still told about the two brothers stumping the state together, telling tales, fiddling, and pulling tricks on each other, in what came to be called Tennessee's 'War of the Roses' " (Griffith, 3).

Shortly after he graduated from high school in 1935, Taylor boarded a freighter in New Orleans and worked his way to England. Before leaving port, he climbed a fire escape to get a better look at Huey Long, who was delivering a radio address from a hotel in the French Quarter; that evening, Peter tasted New Orleans nightlife for the first time (see Cutrer, 201). When he returned to Louisiana to live five years later, he had already discovered his vocation as a writer. That discovery began when he enrolled as a freshman at Southwestern College in Memphis during the spring of 1936. His freshman English teacher was Allen Tate, who immediately recognized that Taylor "had a perfection of style at the age of eighteen that I envied" (Tate, "Peter Taylor," 9). Believing that his student could learn more elsewhere, Tate recommended that Peter transfer to Vanderbilt in the fall and study under John Crowe Ransom. During that year at Vanderbilt, Peter formed a close friendship with his fellow student Randall Jarrell and became, in effect, a second-generation Fugitive-Agrarian. In the fall of 1937, however, when Ransom left Vanderbilt for Kenyon, Peter Taylor returned to Memphis to sell real estate.

In the fall of 1938 Taylor rejoined Ransom by enrolling at Kenyon, where he was reunited with Randall Jarrell (now a young professor and rising poet) and first met an eccentric young man who would be his college roommate and lifelong friend. That man was Robert Traill Spense Lowell IV. Descended from one of the most distinguished families in Boston, Lowell was rebelling against his Brahmin heritage in general and his unhappily married parents in particular. His general sensibility can perhaps be inferred from his favorite nickname, "Cal," after the Roman emperor Caligula and the Shakespearean monster Caliban.

While Lowell was marking time as an undergraduate at Harvard, his psychiatrist—Merrill Moore, the former Fugitive who had married Cleanth's old girlfriend Ann Leslie Nichol—suggested that both his liter-

ary ambitions and his mental health would be better served if he transferred to Vanderbilt to study under Ransom. Because Ransom was already
on his way to Kenyon at that point, Lowell never matriculated at Vanderbilt, although he did audit some classes in the spring of 1937. It was during that year that Cal appointed himself protégé to Ford Madox Ford and
began following Ford around the country. In April, with the fall term at
Kenyon still several months off, Cal appeared at Benfolly, the Allen Tate
home in Clarksville, Tennessee, where Ford, his mistress, and his secretary
were all staying. Knocking over Tate's mailbox when he drove up, and
stopping just long enough to urinate on a tree in the front yard, Cal invited
himself to join the already crowded household. When Tate facetiously told
him that they would have to put him up in a tent, Cal went to the local
Sears, Roebuck store and bought a pup tent, which he pitched on the
lawn, and stayed for the next three months.

Lowell began his three years at Kenyon sharing a room in Ransom's
house with Randall Jarrell. Before too long, however, he ended up room-
ing with Peter Taylor in a literary enclave called Douglass House. Taylor
remembers Lowell as being "not unappealing as a person, but . . . awful
looking. He never cut his hair, he never took a bath. His shoes often had
the soles divided, and were just flapping. He looked terrible. Though he
had what he called his good suit, which hung in our closet at Kenyon
always, as a sort of sacred object" (see McAlexander, *Conversations*, 35–
36). Lowell played tackle on a spectacularly unsuccessful football team,
majored in classics, and continued to write poetry (often on the back of
papers diagramming football plays). As Jim Prewitt in Taylor's autobiographical story "1939," Lowell comes across as arrogant and insecure but
generally likable. Despite his bohemian ways and indifferent grooming,
the real-life Lowell was capable of charming virtually anyone.

Upon receiving his B.A. degree at Kenyon (Phi Beta Kappa, summa cum
laude, and class valedictorian), Lowell thought seriously enough about
graduate work at Harvard to write a letter of inquiry to the university's
president, his cousin Lawrence. Unfortunately, the situation in his immediate family was such that Merrill Moore advised Cal against returning to
Boston; the logical alternative was to continue his southern odyssey and
enroll at LSU. In his letter of recommendation to Brooks and Warren,
Ransom wrote: "Lowell is more than a student, he's more like a son to
me" (see Hamilton, 72). That "son" arrived in Baton Rouge in the summer of 1940. In describing the scene to his maternal grandmother, Cal

wrote: "In place of Mrs. Curtiss, the Casino, the wharf, the ocean etc. are immense twentieth-century-Mexican dormitories, iron pipes blazing with crude oil, palm-beachy trees and Huey Long's two million dollar sky-scraper capitol" (see Hamilton, 75). Upon making his first appearance at the Brooks house, Cal was greeted by a typically manic Caesar. "I think," said Peter Taylor, "it is best to keep these two highly bred Bostonians apart."

The one thing Baton Rouge offered that Cal Lowell had not found at Kenyon was a religious heritage radically different from that of his up-bringing (like the Lowells themselves, Kenyon College espoused a rather bland and respectable version of the Episcopal faith). According to Peter Taylor, "In Louisiana, very French, Catholicism was in the air" (see Hamilton, 78). Lowell began to inhale this Catholicism through his reading of Hopkins, Newman, Pascal, and Gilson. Then, one day, Red Warren asked the university's Catholic chaplain, the Reverend Maurice Shexnayder, to speak to his sixteenth-century literature class on the subject of the Refor-mation. Cal Lowell, who was one of the students in the class, followed Father Shexnayder into the hall and asked him for instruction in the Catholic religion.

The simplistic puritanical faith of the Louisiana Cajuns was a far cry from the intellectual tradition represented by the Catholic writers Cal had been reading. (Father Shexnayder himself had probably forbidden more books than he had read.) Nevertheless, the Roman Church offered Cal the sense of order and discipline that he sorely needed at this point in his life. And, like so many other artists before and since, he found in the ritual of the mass an aesthetic gratification not to be had in his dour Protestant upbringing. The virtually monastic regimen that Cal observed after his baptism was almost a caricature of the convert's zeal: "Mass in the morn-ing, benediction in the evening, two rosaries a day. Reading matter was vetted for its 'seriousness'—'no newspapers, no novels except Dostoyev-sky, Proust, James and Tolstoy.' " Once, when he was served soup on Fri-day, "he tasted meat stock, or thought he tasted meat stock, so he took the soup and dumped it in the sink" (Hamilton, 79).

The religion practiced in Baton Rouge, and adopted so enthusiastically by the prodigal Lowell, was close to that of the Irish scrubwomen of Bos-ton. By becoming a Catholic, Cal could continue the rebellion against his family that brought him south in the first place. That rebellion may have been exacerbated when he was advised not to return to Harvard after completing his studies at Kenyon. If southern poets such as Ransom and Tate came to replace the weak father Lowell had known in his childhood home, the Catholic Church may well have been a substitute for his domineering mother. Bob Lowell was a rather feckless naval officer who brought no additional luster to his distinguished family name—for which the bitterly disappointed Charlotte Winslow Lowell never forgave him.

One of the most awkward evenings of Cleanth's life was spent when he was invited to a "dinner party" at the Lowell home in Boston. When he arrived, he found that he was the sole guest. The dinner table conversation included Mrs. Lowell asking him rather pointedly whether he thought that "their ugly duckling" would eventually make something of himself. A bit later, Mr. Lowell turned to his wife and said, as if they were the only ones in the room, "You know, my dear, I rather like this fellow." Breaking bread with the Lowell parents was enough to explain to Cleanth why Cal turned out the way that he did.

III

As happy as they were to acquire a student of Lowell's promise, Brooks and Warren were even more pleased to secure the secretarial services of Lowell's new wife, Jean Stafford. When Ransom wrote to his friends at LSU to recommend the young couple in the summer of 1940, the *Southern Review* had just lost its secretary, Mae Swallow; Cleanth wired back: "PLEASE ADVISE BY WESTERN UNION IF MRS. LOWELL KNOWS SHORTHAND. LETTER FOLLOWS."[5] Although her shorthand was only passable, Jean was a first-rate typist and bookkeeper, who almost immediately began to bring order to the chaotic operations of the review.

The South was just as strange a place for Jean Stafford as it was for her husband. A native westerner, she had grown up in Colorado, the daughter of a strange and shabby family (her father was a half-mad aspiring writer who lost a small fortune in the stock market). Cal had met her at a writers' conference in Boulder, where she was attending the University of Colorado, in the summer of 1937. (As the featured speaker, Cal's idol, Ford Madox Ford, distinguished himself by delivering an inaudible ninety-minute speech on his relationship with Jozef Korzeniowski, whom he failed to identify as Joseph Conrad.) Despite, or perhaps because of, the disapproval of the Lowells, the romance flourished, even surviving an accident in which Cal crashed his car into a brick wall and broke Jean's nose. The wedding took place on April 2, 1940, at the historic Episcopal church St. Mark's in the Bowery, in Greenwich Village, New York. The honeymoon consisted of a train ride back to Ohio, where Cal finished his final two months at Kenyon. Shortly thereafter, the couple moved to Baton Rouge, where they sublet an apartment from Red and Cinina Warren.

According to one of her biographers, Jean

> complained later that in those days before people routinely installed air-conditioners, the mildew and damp macerated book bindings and made the *Encyclopaedia Britannica* she had sent to Baton Rouge so "edematous" that all the volumes would no longer fit into the wooden case in which they were stored; that the humidity warped phonograph records and gave salt "the consistency of gritty sherbert"; and that "every surface was covered with a mysterious fungoid slime." She also loathed the numerous cockroaches "the size of hummingbirds" that abounded in their apartment and "ravenously devoured the glue in the spines of books, particularly the collected works of Cardinal Newman." (Goodman, 116)

In a letter written in June 1940, Jean sounded similar complaints in describing her first few weeks in the South to Peter Taylor, who would soon join the Lowells at LSU. "It is hot and steamy," she writes, "but there are no snakes. There are, however, cockroaches. Cal killed one as big as a calf last night. . . . The job isn't bad and Erskine and Brooks are nice to work for. The office looks like a hogsty with an accumulation of manuscripts (there are some here, really, that were sent in 1938) and magazines and review books and third class matter for Mr. Warren" (Stafford, 27).

On June 26, 1940, Jean wrote to her college friend and sometime lover James Robert Hightower about the intellectual ambience of her new home: "Talk in academic gatherings is of . . . (1) language requirements for the degree PhD (2) the deficiencies of the Freshman English curriculum and (3) the necessity of subordinating historical scholarship to criticism or vice versa. . . . Sat. night we ate at the Brooks's . . . and had food in our laps in a brightly lighted and much too small room and we were there for six hours hearing those three things. . . . Now mind, they were all delightful, charming, amusing people *but* it is a university. It is academic. It is that and nothing more" (see Hulbert, 112).[6]

Peter Taylor came to visit the Lowells in August and was persuaded to enroll in the LSU graduate program the following month. He and a casual girlfriend moved in with Cal and Jean, and for the next year, Peter and Jean grew closer, as Cal's devotion to Catholicism and his difficult personality made him an increasingly remote figure. It was also during this time that Jean developed a drinking problem, which would plague her for the rest of her life. Peter remembers one evening in particular, when Cleanth Brooks drove the Lowells and him to a big party at the Warrens' country house.

"We were scared to death of him," Taylor recalls, "because he was maybe ten years older than we were, and we thought it was great stuff being out with Cleanth Brooks." The evening turned into a social disaster, as Cal, Jean, and Peter all had too much to drink. They sat in the backseat going home and did their best to carry on an intelligent conversation about the metaphysical poets. (Although Cleanth was far from a teetotaler, he invariably knew his limit.) At one point, as she was opening her purse, Jean said, "Well, I think John Donne—," and promptly threw up into the purse. If that wasn't bad enough, the movement of getting out of Cleanth's car caused Peter to vomit on the back of the vehicle. He was so embarrassed that he tore off the jacket of his new gray flannel suit and began wiping off the car as Cleanth pulled away, trying not to notice what was happening. When Peter and Cal entered the apartment later that night, they "could see Jean back in the bathroom, washing dollar bills" (see Roberts, 191).

At the end of the academic year, the Lowells left Baton Rouge for New York, where Cal went to work for the Catholic publisher Sheed and Ward. Cal's marriage had survived some rough times, including an evening in New Orleans when, enraged, he had hit his wife, breaking her nose for the second time. The increasing ardor of his religious practice also widened the breach between husband and wife, a theme that Stafford would treat in her autobiographical short story "An Influx of Poets."

Throughout her frequent illnesses, bouts of alcoholism, and marital strife, Jean Stafford always maintained her witty and sardonic view of life. This is evident not only in her published fiction but also in her letters to friends, including Cleanth and Tinkum Brooks. Several letters to the Brookses in the years immediately after her departure from Baton Rouge reveal the essential Jean Stafford and also suggest her continuing affection for her former employer and his wife.[7]

In an undated letter from the early forties, Jean describes her husband's continuing obsession with religion:

The janitor spent an evening with Cal quoting St. Thomas to him in Latin. He is a Catholic refugee from the Rhineland. This, if nothing else, recommends our building to Cal. There was a period when he regarded the place as needlessly luxurious and seriously wanted, after I had described the environs of the Catholic Worker, to go down and live on Mott Street.[8] I argued the general insanity of such a move, the bedbugs, the proximity to the Bowery, the high rate of tuberculosis, scurvy, etc., the stink, the general affectation of it, but nothing would convince him and I truly believe we would be living there now if it hadn't been that a priest whom he much admires stopped in at Sheed and Ward and laughed at the idea, saying that Cal's metier was obviously intellectual not sociological. Mrs. Sheed has little use for the Catholic Worker, I'm happy to say (she's English, and the worker people are all strong isolationists and this doesn't go down very well with her) and I'm pretty well shut of that now. Blessedly, I have the flu lately which has kept me in bed for a week and so I have been able to postpone any more "good" work but it is blackly written on the books that soon I am to go help in a friendship house in Harlem, run by a Russian Baroness. It sounds much more attractive than Mott Street anyhow.

Later in that same letter, Jean tells of a recent visit to the Tate residence. Because of a mix-up, the Lowells arrived around noon, while the Tates were not due back until five. Consequently, "we spent the afternoon with Caroline's Aunt Louli who belongs in a booby hatch. She used to be a Christian Scientist but now is interested only in vitamins. We sat in the garden and she often said, 'I'm soaking up B through the back of my head by the galore.' At lunch she sprinkled all our food with grated carrot and passing something would say, 'Have some D.'" The letter concludes, as it began, with an account of eccentricity closer to the hearth: "Cal is about to quit typewriting school and is going to practice at home. I don't look forward to that because he has not yet developed any rhythm and is slow as a tortoise. He is very patient with himself and over and over again writes: Aga, baba, gaga, mugwump, the last being, I think, his own interpolation."

Another of Jean's undated letters from the early forties brings news of a sculptor and his wife who had previously lived in Baton Rouge:

I had lunch not long ago with De Mila Ferguson and it may interest you to know (I expect that Red has told you this, though) that she and Duncan are now Trotskyites, bonafide members of the party and all, and that De Mila in all seriousness several times used the expression "come the revolution." When it comes, she assured me, she has taken precautions that her mother and father will not be shot. She has this promise in writing from the party leaders. Every third farmer in the south is to be killed. I could scarcely believe my ears. She said Duncan at last had something to work for, that the head of Trotsky he just finished was his best work because it was his only really inspired work.

By the end of the decade, Robert Lowell and Jean Stafford had gone their separate ways. Each would marry twice more before dying within two years of each other in the late seventies. Both remained on friendly terms with Cleanth and Tinkum Brooks. (When her third husband, A. J. Liebling, was writing a book on Earl Long, Jean put him in touch with the Brookses as experts on Louisiana.) The man who was initially concerned about whether his future secretary knew shorthand would one day boast that among the secretaries of the *Southern Review* "was no less a literary figure than Jean Stafford" (Brooks, "Life and Death," 97). But there was also a gap in age and sensibility between the distinguished new critic and the young writer who threw up in his car that night in Baton Rouge. Tinkum's younger sister, who became a close friend of Stafford, once told Cleanth and Tinkum that *her* Jean was a woman they never knew.

IV

In the summer of 1937 Cleanth and Tinkum made an automobile trip from Baton Rouge to Benfolly. Because Memphis was on their route, Albert Erskine asked if he could have a ride to his old hometown. (As Cleanth recalls, Albert didn't think that the Brookses should make such a long car trip by themselves.) When they got to Memphis, however, Albert decided to remain for the rest of the trip, hoping to renew his acquaintance with the Tates and to see the legendary Tate home for the first time. Much to their surprise the trio from Baton Rouge discovered that Allen and Caroline's houseguest was the acclaimed short story writer Katherine Anne Porter. Although she had published three stories in the *Southern Review*, this was the first time that the Brookses or Erskine had ever met Miss Porter. What they found was a woman of extraordinary beauty and charm who, in her late forties, had already lived a full and varied life. Cleanth and Tinkum retired at their accustomed hour that evening, but Albert and Katherine Anne "remained on the gallery talking in the moonlight (it was a full moon) until four in the morning. Only Allen Tate in his room off the gallery lay awake listening through the open window to everything they said and thinking that they ought to go off to New Orleans together and have an affair" (Givner, 305).

The truth about Katherine Anne Porter has always been elusive. In many ways, she was a self-created character who, like Jay Gatsby, sprang from her Platonic conception of herself. She was born on May 15, 1890, in the rural community of Indian Rock, Texas, although for years she lied about her age—often placing her birth after the death of her mother in 1892. Her given name was Callie Russell Porter, and her family was of yeoman stock, not the aristocratic pedigree of which she often boasted. She was first married at the age of sixteen and would have three more husbands and numerous lovers, although her biographer speculates that she "was unable to find any pleasure in sex" (Givner, 92). She did not take the name "Katherine Anne" until she divorced her first husband at the age of twenty-five. As a young woman, she suffered near-fatal bouts with tuberculosis and influenza and lived in Mexico during a time of revolution. And yet, she died in a rest home at the age of ninety. Politically, Katherine Anne Porter was always a woman of the Left. She protested the convictions of Sacco and Vanzetti, demonstrated outside the prison on the night they were executed, and published a book on their case half a century later. She even admits to having been a member of the Communist Party in Mexico in the 1920s until she was expelled for violating party discipline. But she was also a lifelong anti-Semite, who claimed to have danced with Hitler, Goebbels, and Göring at a dinner party in Berlin during the 1930s.

Despite the contradictions in her life (perhaps because of them), Katherine Anne Porter was a brilliant writer of short fiction. By the time her work began appearing in the *Southern Review*, she was well enough established that she could command higher fees from better-known magazines. But she was willing to let Red and Cleanth have the pick of her work because she knew that they would not insist that she compromise her standards. (Her story "The Leaning Tower" had been originally accepted by a more commercial New York magazine, but Katherine Anne withdrew it in favor of the *Southern Review* when the editor of the first magazine wanted her to change the ending.)

When she began publishing in the *Southern Review* in the mid-1930s (she had a story in the first issue of the magazine), Katherine Anne was living in Europe with her third husband, a foreign service officer named Eugene Pressly. Although this marriage had been less traumatic than her first two, Pressly chafed at his wife's independence and resented her literary career; in turn, his drinking became increasingly hard for her to tolerate. Perhaps most important, Katherine Anne was ready to return to the

United States and make yet another in her lifelong series of new beginnings. In the spring of 1937 Caroline Gordon wrote to Red Warren that "Katherine Anne has cast Gene off, with a twist of the wrist as it were. She kept writing about how she was enjoying life and how it was necessary to embrace her particular demon in poverty, chastity and obedience and so on, whereupon Allen said he feared for Gene. I'm surprised he lasted as long as he did." When she met Albert Erskine that summer, Porter was still married to Pressly; she divorced him in the spring of 1938 and married Albert ten days later.

On April 30, 1938, Allen Tate wrote a letter to Cleanth in which he offered the following "brief meditation on K. A. and Albert":

> Of course Albert, being young and merely sophisticated without experience of the world, doesn't know that La Belle Dame sans merci has him in thrall. It's a nice state to be in—what man wouldn't want to be in it for a few months? But married to her? No! I predict that in less than two years K. A. will get the wild mustang look in her eye, and charge off, perhaps gathering in another Albert, and in less than a wink Albert I will be as if he never existed. We've known K. A. for going on fifteen years, and she has gone through this same pattern five times. She always comes out of it with a kind of moral virginity, ready to try it again because she forgets that she has tried it; but the men lie gasping on the sand. What has become of them all? Somehow they are never heard from again. As soon as the relation becomes solid, and of predictable permanence, she runs off. Like [the] heroine, that is to say like herself, at the end of one of her long stories, she flies off to seek Truth, which is another way of saying romantic irresponsibility.

The marriage of Albert Erskine and Katherine Anne Porter came as a shock to Cleanth Brooks, who was surprised at how quickly their romance had bloomed. What made the match even more improbable was the fact that Katherine Anne was twenty-one years older than Albert (she had been married for five years to her first husband before Erskine was even born!). But Katherine Anne Porter was no ordinary older woman. Rather than fading, her beauty seemed to increase with age. She was no slave to cosmetics, no freak of nature cursed with perpetual youth. Through her forties and fifties and even into her early sixties, she remained a stunning woman, with "soft unblemished skin and . . . beautiful violet eyes, which were becoming a smoky blue-gray" (Lopez, 227). She also maintained a youthful zest that may have been a function of immaturity. (In some ways, Albert was the more serious of the two.) As an artist, she had a passion for life that a young man of Albert Erskine's disposition found irresistible. The sense of ethos is sometimes so strong that one feels an instinctive bond with certain writers. In Andrew Lytle's opinion, Albert fell in love with Katherine Anne's story "Old Mortality."[9]

The protagonist of "Old Mortality" is Miranda, a modern girl who has grown up with the romantic image of her Aunt Amy, a charming, capricious southern belle who died of tuberculosis shortly after her marriage. In the first section of the story, Miranda's attitude toward the legend of Amy is one of childish credulity; in the second section, she has progressed to an adolescent skepticism; by the story's third and final section, she is eager to reject the mythology surrounding her aunt as the fantasy of an earlier generation. At the end of the story, Miranda's resolve to live her own life is gently undercut by the superior wisdom of Porter's narrative voice. "Let them tell their stories to each other," Miranda thinks. "Let them go on explaining how things happened. I don't care. At least I can know the truth about what happens to me, she assured herself silently, making a promise to herself, in her hopefulness, her ignorance" (Porter, "Old Mortality," 192).

In a sense, Katherine Anne Porter was both Miranda and Amy. Like her modern protagonist, Porter was determined to live her own life on her own terms, but part of that life consisted in transforming the images of the Old South into the art of fiction. Like the other great writers of the Southern Renascence, she captured the ambivalence of the current generation about the passing of the old order. By constantly creating an unreal personal past in her manic rush to an equally unreal future, Katherine Anne became the creature of her own legend.[10] Like a male Miranda, Albert Erskine passed from early credulity through skepticism to a kind of tough-minded resignation.

Shortly after meeting Albert, Katherine Anne separated permanently from Eugene Pressly and by September had moved from New York to New Orleans; in October, Albert took the bus from Baton Rouge to spend his first weekend alone with the woman of his illusions. "When he left, Porter was rapturously in love and wrote him in a dazzle of joy. She said she missed him fearfully, as if she had known him all her life, seen him every day, and suddenly found him gone" (Givner, 307). Still, she was fearful of being nearer to him on a permanent basis and steadfastly resisted the idea of marriage. Unfortunately, their separation only caused them to idealize each other the more. After they were apart over Christmas, Katherine Anne finally weakened and agreed to a marriage that her experience and common sense told her could never work.

In describing the union of Albert Erskine and Katherine Anne Porter, Joan Givner writes:

> No marriage can have been based on slighter knowledge. The partners had known each other for eight months, but during that time they had spent only a few weekends together. The letters had served not to deepen their knowledge of each other but to obscure it. Porter refused to take stock of the age difference between them and Erskine did not even know how old she was. He had thought she was approaching forty, and when he found out, during the marriage ceremony, that she was nearly fifty, he was horrified. . . . [From the beginning,] the marriage was a total and unmitigated disaster. (Givner, 311)

Katherine Anne remembers their first summer together as "a long season of rain, terrible heat, and terrible suffocating unhappiness. There were violent rows in which Erskine would vent his rage by driving at terrifyingly high speeds. . . . And all the while they were wishing each other dead or separate, the wedding gifts and hearty good wishes kept creeping in—bitter ironic comments on a former state of mind and feeling" (Givner, 311).[11]

At first, even their closest friends were not aware how badly the marriage was going. Katherine Anne and Albert moved into an apartment across the hall from Cleanth and Tinkum (the elder Brookses now occupied a house of their own) and saw quite a bit of their new neighbors. In particular, Katherine Anne was drawn to Tinkum, with whom she exchanged recipes and confidences (their ensuing correspondence reveals a little-seen domestic side to Katherine Anne's personality). When Stark Young came to visit not long after the marriage, he had great fun referring to Katherine Anne as "Mrs. Erskine" and pretending not to know of her more public identity.[12] But the difference in years produced continual public embarrassment, as strangers would innocently mistake the Erskines for mother and son. Although Albert had none of the character flaws of her previous husbands, he inevitably had to take second place to Katherine Anne's writing and her desire for new beginnings. Just as she had longed to leave Europe for America, Katherine Anne was now just as intent to leave Louisiana for the Yaddo writer's colony near Saratoga, New York. When she did so in 1940, it was without Albert Erskine, whom she always called her "New Orleans husband," even though their life together had been spent in Baton Rouge.

The letters that Tinkum Brooks received from Katherine Anne after her departure from Louisiana reveal a woman of keen intelligence and profound loneliness. On May 5, 1941, Porter comments on the moral deficiencies of two acquaintances who were trying, rather late in life, to become "pure artists":

> A pure artist is pure from the beginning, at least in intention and in practise [sic] so far as he is able, and he always knows when he fails. It is like living a virtuous life on any other plane: you may not be up to it, but if you stop trying, you are damned. They seem a little late to me. My Catholic training reminds me that it is never too late to mend and God will accept your sincere repentance on your death bed; but Art is not so forgiving. The worst of it is their befuddlement about morals. I remember stories of my old Wobbly and radical friends in Mexico, who stole bottles of milk off backsteps of little poor houses in the towns they were bumming through, and stole fruit and bread from little street stands where poor men were trying to make a living: and they roared with laughter saying they called it sabotaging the Capitalist system. (See Brooks, "Woman and Artist," 18)

On October 11 of that same year, Katherine Anne speaks of the energy she was putting into a house that she hoped would give her some semblance of stability.

> My beautiful house is hungry as any growing child, and keeps the cupboard bare. I had planned as well as I could to keep a tiny margin between me and downright want, but it just closed up suddenly with me caught fast in the vise. . . . However, money came suddenly and went again as suddenly, but made a difference, a great and happy one. . . . In my weaker moments I sometimes wonder why such natural and simple things as I want and need are so very hard to come by, but I am very willing to work for what I want and do pay cheerfully for it so long as I can possibly manage. . . . It seems most wonderfully worth doing, what else would I want to do? I can think of nothing, quite literally. For the first time in my life I can't see—don't want to see, wouldn't accept for a moment—any second choice, any alternative. (See Brooks, "Woman and Artist," 19)

Although she would live for another forty years, Katherine Anne Porter's best work was behind her by the time she left Baton Rouge. Her *Collected Stories* won the Pulitzer Prize for fiction in 1965, but only one of those stories had been written after 1944. She moved many more times after she had "settled" in Yaddo—eventually dying in the Carnegie Hill Nursing Center in Silver Spring, Maryland, in 1980. Her stay in Baton Rouge had been brief, but it had produced two faithful friends in Cleanth and Tinkum Brooks. Also, some of her most memorable fiction had been published in the pages of the *Southern Review*. After the first issue of that magazine appeared, with her story "The Circus" in it, Katherine Anne sounded a note of enthusiasm tinged with apprehension. "Do send me a subscription to *The Southern Review*," she wrote to Red Warren from Paris. "It is the best magazine I know, judging from the first number. I can't do without it. I hope that nothing has occurred that will change or destroy your plan" (see Cutrer, 69).

1. Cleanth Brook's maternal grandfather William Witherspoon (*left*) plays chess with his friend M. B. Hurt.

2. Cleanth Brooks's maternal grandmother, Elizabeth Weir Witherspoon.

3. The Reverend Cleanth
Brooks, Sr.

4. Cleanth Brooks's mother, Bessie
Lee Witherspoon Brooks.

5. Cleanth Brooks (*left*) and his brother Billy, ca. 1912.

6. Tinkum as a child.

7. Emily Price Blanchard
(Tinkum's mother).

8. Cleanth Brooks, ca. 1928.

9. *Left to right:* Cleanth Brooks,
H. S. A. Potter, Hamayun Kabir,
and an unidentified fellow student,
Oxford University, 1931.

10. Cleanth Brooks at the Kenyon School of Letters, Gambier, Ohio, 1948.

11. Cleanth Brooks, Lady Astor, Burgess Meredith, and an unidentified fourth individual at the Library of Congress in the 1950s.

12. Honorary Consultants in American Letters, Washington, D.C., April 1958. *Left to right:* Cleanth Brooks, Librarian of Congress L. Quincey Mumford, Eudora Welty, Librarian Roy P. Basler, John Crowe Ransom, and Richard P. Blackmur. Unable to attend were Elizabeth Bishop and Maxwell Anderson. (Photograph courtesy Library of Congress)

PART THREE

A New Criticism
(1936-47)

CHAPTER NINE

What Is Poetry?

Back in the mid-thirties, while they were doing the writing and editing that would make them world famous in the profession of letters, Cleanth Brooks and Robert Penn Warren were earning their keep primarily as classroom teachers at a land grant university in the South. As Brooks recalled the situation forty years later: "Our students, many of them bright enough and certainly amiable and charming enough, had no notion of how to read a literary text. Many of them approached a Shakespeare sonnet or Keats's 'Ode to a Nightingale' or Pope's *Rape of the Lock* much as they would approach an ad in a Sears-Roebuck catalogue or an editorial in their local newspaper." A student to whom Red was teaching *King Lear* mournfully shook his head and muttered: "I just don't like to read about bad people" (see Brooks, "Forty Years," 5). The practical question Cleanth and Red faced was how to teach literature (particularly works of some difficulty and sophistication) to such students.

The available textbooks were of little help. James Dow McCallum's *The College Omnibus*, published by Harcourt Brace in 1933, was the standard anthology both at LSU and elsewhere. The volume contained complete texts of Lytton Strachey's biography of Queen Victoria, Thomas Hardy's *The Mayor of Casterbridge*, J. M. Synge's *Riders to the Sea*, and Eugene O'Neill's *Emperor Jones*; sections were also devoted to essays, short stories, and poems. The poets represented were John Keats, Alfred Tennyson, and Robert Browning from the nineteenth century; and Thomas Hardy, A. E. Housman, William Butler Yeats, John Masefield, Siegfried Sassoon, Amy Lowell, Robert Frost, Carl Sandburg, Elinor Wylie, and Edna St. Vincent Millay from the twentieth.

One could obviously criticize this text on historical grounds. With none of its selections written before 1800, it gave its readers no sense of the development of English literature prior to the Romantic era. From the standpoint of criticism, it was even more deficient. Anyone teaching Keats's "Ode to a Nightingale" would have to be content with a short biographical introduction to Keats and a dollop of impressionistic response. ("The song of the nightingale brings sadness and exhilaration to the poet and makes him long to be lifted up and away from the limitations of life. The seventh stanza is particularly beautiful"; McCallum, 670.) A reasonably competent college English teacher might be expected to know when Keats lived and to have a vague emotional reaction to the poem already. What he might not have was an effective means of explaining to a classful of college sophomores (most of whom probably have never been "half in love with easeful death") what this poem has to say that would be of any interest to them. Reading the poem with dramatic emphasis (in the manner of Edwin Mims) might heighten appreciation but not understanding. For a conscientious teacher, it was simply not enough to say what Louis Armstrong said of jazz: "If you have to ask what it is, you wouldn't understand if I told you."

Fortunately, many students, then as now, had dirty minds, so the poems with double entendres, such as *The Rape of the Lock*, were easier to teach. In fact, the sort of analytical skills necessary to discern Pope's hidden meanings were precisely what students needed to read poetry in general. If McCallum's *Omnibus* and the other existing textbooks were not teaching such skills, Warren argued that he and Brooks would simply need to provide their own text. Consequently, at the suggestion of W. A. Read, Warren prepared a thirty-page mimeographed booklet on metrics and imagery. This class handout was first used by Brooks, Warren, and a graduate student named John T. Purser in the spring semester of 1935; by the fall of 1936, the three had published a critical anthology of poetry, fiction, drama, and expository prose under the title *An Approach to Literature*.

As Thomas W. Cutrer has pointed out, the depth of the Depression was not a propitious time to bring out a new textbook, especially with the McCallum anthology being so recent and so widely accepted. Nevertheless, Marcus Wilkerson, director of the new LSU Press, approved of the idea, and President Smith promised financial backing. (The enthusiastic young Purser had to be dissuaded from seeking the political influence of his friend O. K. Allen, who had succeeded Huey Long as governor; see Cutrer, 181.) Perhaps because the book represented such a radical departure from the McCallum approach, it was not greeted with universal approval, even in Baton Rouge. (When threatened traditionalists started referring to it as "The *Reproach* to Literature," Brooks and Warren picked up on the joke and began calling it that in their private conversations.)

Not only was the *Approach* short on biographical and historical information but—horror of horrors—it included a generous selection of southern writers, where McCallum had none. Many of these were either Agrarian allies of Brooks and Warren or contributors to the *Southern Review*. Even if this could be seen as cronyism, the cronies of Brooks and Warren included some of the finest writers of the day. Thomas W. Cutrer believes that "Brooks and Warren were making an attempt to remove their native region from the educational imperialism which had been its lot since *McGuffy's Reader, Webster's Dictionary*, and the Yankee schoolmarm invaded the South in the nineteenth century" (Cutrer, 182). It is therefore ironic that among the first schools to adopt the new book were the universities of Maine and New Hampshire.

Like the McCallum text, *An Approach to Literature* contains an abundance of primary material, but it also includes critical introductions that examine the various genres as analytically as an auto mechanic would examine the engine of a car. Browning's dramatic monologue "Porphyria's Lover" becomes a kind of touchstone throughout the text. The "General Introduction" contrasts Browning's poetic treatment of his material with the way the same situation might be presented in a coroner's report, a legal indictment, and a newspaper story. Later, in introducing the section on poetry, the editors use Browning's text as an example of the special character and effects of figurative language. Finally, the "Introduction to Drama" asks us to imagine how "Porphyria's Lover" would look if turned into a play.

It could be argued that in treating literature as a series of technical problems, this text takes some of the magic out of the reading experience. Brooks and Warren were, in fact, accused of being "cold-blooded analysts who found no pleasure—certainly no joy—in literature." Even if this were true, which it is not, their pedagogical approach made literature an accessible mode of discourse rather than a forbidding mystery that could be admired but never known; moreover, they were intent on making it accessible *as literature*, not as an adjunct to sociology. As Brooks recalled over forty years later, "We were trying to apply the grease to the wheel that squeaked the loudest. Besides, the typical instructor, product as he was of the graduate schools of that day, had been thoroughly trained in literary history, or so we assumed" (*Community*, 82).

The success of *An Approach to Literature* was such that by 1939 most major textbook companies were trying to buy the copyright from the LSU Press (Brooks and Warren had not even offered the book to a commercial house in 1935). F. S. Crofts (later Appleton-Century-Crofts) won out and acquired both the plates and the rights for two percent of future royalties. In 1975 (forty years after its original publication) the book went into its fifth edition. Had Brooks and Warren never published another textbook, the longevity of *An Approach to Literature* would have earned them a niche in the history of modern English pedagogy. Encouraged by what they had done, Cleanth and Red were soon at work on a book that would revolutionize the teaching of literature for more than a generation.

I

The first edition of *Understanding Poetry* appeared in 1938 with no grandiose ambitions, even if the title itself claimed more than Brooks and Warren had originally intended. They had wanted simply to call the book *Reading Poems*; however, the marketing division of their publisher Henry Holt convinced them that that title was too modest. (It is interesting to note that when Wright Thomas and Stuart Gerry Brown called their new critical textbook *Reading Poems*, Leslie Fiedler accused them of a nominalistic rejection of the very concept of poetry.) In fact, the phrase "understanding poetry" is a perfect statement of the book's purpose—its end is critical *understanding* rather than vague appreciation, and the object of that understanding is *poetry*, not literary history or biography.

After a ten-page "Letter to the Teacher" and a twenty-five-page "Introduction," Brooks and Warren divide their text into seven sections of poems, each preceded by an editorial foreword. (There is also an "Afterword" following the second section, as well as three "notes" of several pages each in section 4.) The distinctive feature of this approach is that the divisions are made according to literary rather than historical or geographical considerations; the categories are narrative, implied narrative, objective description, metrics, tone and attitude, imagery, and theme. The main body of the book contains critical discussions of thirty-seven poems and the texts of over two hundred others (many of which are accompanied by exercises). This is followed by a twenty-three-page glossary, heavily emphasizing matters of technique.

Nearly fifty years later, Warren observed that his labors with Brooks were "quite literally . . . collaborative":

We sat down and argued out general notions and general plans for the book—only to find as work developed that we were constantly being thrown back to revise original ideas. But very early Cleanth had made a fundamental suggestion. After an introductory section of general discussion, we would get down to individual poems and start with narrative, including folk ballads. Folk poetry has one great pedagogical advantage. It springs from a nonliterary world and some event that has had some special appeal to the imagination of that world. . . . Our whole effort was to show how the non-bookish poetry could lead straight to the bookish: that is to a narrative poem, say, by Frost. (Warren, "Brooks and Warren," 2)

(Among the folk poems included was the old favorite of their Oxford days—"Frankie and Johnny.")

In their introduction, Brooks and Warren compare poetry with other kinds of discourse that students (and, indeed, all human beings) habitually use. Unlike technical language, poetry does not give an objective description of facts but expresses an attitude toward experience. Thus in its function it resembles ordinary human speech far more than technical discourse does. As Brooks and Warren point out, "it is highly important to see that both the impulse and methods of poetry are rooted very deep in human experience, and that formal poetry itself represents, not a distinction from but a specialization of, thoroughly universal habits of human thinking and feeling" (Brooks and Warren, *Understanding Poetry*, 9).

To be useful, any definition must identify differences as well as similarities; for that reason, the introduction to *Understanding Poetry* falls short of giving a completely satisfying definition of poetry. (It is only incrementally in the text of the book itself that the differentia begin to appear.) Nevertheless, the introduction does strive to clear away misconceptions that are probably based on faulty definitions acquired in high school and elsewhere. The most prevalent of these is that poetry exists for moral instruction. To believe this is to identify the value of a poem with the "truth" of its message. According to this principle, it would be impossible for one to admire both Longfellow's "Psalm of Life" and Wordsworth's "Expostulation and Reply" because these two poems express contradictory attitudes toward life. (Neither could one admire both the Catholic Dante and the Protestant Milton.) Moreover, even the most sententious message hunter might balk at a tin-eared alteration in the rhythm and language of a favorite poem. Even if the "meaning" seemed unaffected, a clumsy revision would clearly lessen the pleasure to be derived from the poem.

The opposite extreme from reducing poetry to message hunting is to equate it with beautiful language. If poetry exists simply to paint a pretty picture in words, it should never be used to depict anything disagreeable. Unfortunately, that would necessitate purging Sophocles and Shakespeare (and certainly Chaucer) from the poetic canon. Hamlet's "To be or not to be" soliloquy paints a whole series of disagreeable pictures. The effectiveness of a passage of poetry has much less to do with fine sentiment or flowery speech than with contextual appropriateness. *"The poetic effect depends not on the things themselves but on the kind of use the poet makes of them"* (18; emphasis in the original).

One might easily come away from this introduction thinking of poetry as *language skillfully used to express an attitude about experience.* That, of course, is more nearly a definition of rhetoric than of poetry. In a sense, Brooks and Warren see poetry as a kind of rhetoric—one based on dramatic tension rather than on didactic assertion or appeals to pathos (although both of these latter elements appear in many good poems). As Brooks would later do in *Modern Poetry and the Tradition,* he and Warren make the analogy between a poem and a drama. "Every poem," they write, "implies a speaker of the poem, either the poet writing in his own person or someone into whose mouth the poem is put, and . . . the poem represents the reaction of such a person to a situation, a scene, or an idea" (23).

Part of the excitement generated by *Understanding Poetry* lay in its being a genuinely *critical* text, which did not hesitate to attack canonical writers, including that favorite whipping boy of literary modernists, Percy Bysshe Shelley. Although the book includes nine of Shelley's poems, the only one analyzed is "The Indian Serenade." Brooks and Warren correctly note that one's response to this poem is predicated on one's reaction to its speaker (the question of ethos). What makes both the speaker and his message suspect is Shelley's failure to demonstrate or dramatize the emotions the speaker expresses. The famously egregious line "I die! I faint! I fail!" (which seems like a reversal of the normal sequence of actions) might be a statement of emotion genuinely earned; it might also be the hysterical utterance of a self-indulgent adolescent. There is nothing in the poem to convince us which it is.

Brooks and Warren offer Shelley's poem as an example of sentimentality. This is defined as "the display of more emotion than the situation warrants" (*Understanding Poetry,* 322). Although we cannot be certain whether Shelley was prompted to write his poem by a genuine and sufficient emotion he experienced, that is quite beside the point. He does not demonstrate the basis for this emotion in the poem. (In literature the burden of emotional proof must always rest with the writer himself.) The editors find it "symptomatic of this sentimental attitude that there is nowhere in this poem a sharp and definite image. The poet apparently does not perceive anything sharply and compellingly and he does not cause the reader to perceive anything very compellingly. This obsession with the sweet thrill is so strong here that the mistress herself is not described—even by implication. But the poet does describe himself and his own feelings—in detail" (322).

In addition to Shelley's "The Indian Serenade," Brooks and Warren find fault with Francis Mahoney's "The Bells of Shandon," Adelaide Anne Proctor's "The Pilgrims," and Sidney Lanier's "My Springs." But their severest comments are reserved for Joyce Kilmer's popular lyric "Trees." In their discussion of this fireside favorite, Brooks and Warren demonstrate that it is sometimes possible to learn as much about poetry from bad poems as from good ones. As far as consistency of metaphor is concerned, Kilmer is what Tolstoy once accused Chekhov of being—worse even than Shakespeare.

Kilmer's controlling metaphor compares a tree with a person. When we try to visualize this comparison, however, we see that Kilmer must have had several different people in mind. In the second stanza, the tree is a sucking babe drawing nourishment from Mother Earth; in the third, it is a supplicant reaching its leafy arms to the sky in prayer. (If this is a single human being, Brooks and Warren point out, it is an anatomically deformed one.) In the fourth stanza, the tree is a girl with jewels (a nest of robins) in her hair; and in the fifth, it is a chaste woman living alone with nature and with God. There is no warrant in the poem to say that it is different trees that remind the poet of these different types of people. What Kilmer has given us is a series of fanciful analogies that could be presented in any order without damaging the overall structure of his poem. The undeniable popularity of "Trees" lies in the fact that "it appeals . . . to a stock response that has nothing to do, as such, with poetry. It praises God and appeals to a religious sentiment. Therefore people who do not stop to look at the poem itself or to study the images in the poem and think about what the poem really says, are inclined to accept the poem because of the pious sentiment, the prettified little pictures (which in themselves appeal to stock responses), and the mechanical rhythm" (*Understanding Poetry*, 391).

Even before *Understanding Poetry* began making its impact in the classroom, it was hailed by the critics as the first wave of a pedagogical revolution. In the inaugural issue of the *Kenyon Review*, John Ransom wrote: "Mr. Brooks has established his place among the subtler critics, while he keeps to himself his own versifying, and Mr. Warren is one of the really superlative poets of our time" (Ransom, "Teaching," 82). Ransom goes on to note that "The analyses [of *Understanding Poetry*] are as much of the old poems as of the new poems, and those of the old are as fresh and illuminating as those of the new; or at least, nearly. What can this mean but that criticism as it is now practiced is a new thing? . . . Probably we need the new critics for the sake of understanding our classics even more, and much more, than we need them for securing our possession of the strange moderns" (83).

Although *Understanding Poetry* was not itself a historical text (and was ignorantly accused of being antihistorical), its treatment of works from various periods implied a radically revised history of English poetry. By celebrating irony as a sign of emotional maturity and labeling more straightforward expressions of emotion as sentimentality, Brooks and Warren were shaping a canon that valued the metaphysicals and high modernists more than the Romantics. (Although a few poems were included from the Restoration and eighteenth century, none was analyzed.) All that was required now was for someone to make this revised history and new canon explicit. Cleanth did precisely that in 1939 when he reworked his literary essays of the previous decade into his first full-length book of criticism, *Modern Poetry and the Tradition*.

II

In dedicating *Modern Poetry and the Tradition* to Allen Tate, Brooks acknowledged the practical and theoretical debt he owed to his friend. Next to Richards and Eliot, Tate was the critic who had most influenced Brooks's thinking about the nature of poetry. (After noting the "deep disagreements" between Brooks and Ransom, René Wellek writes, "Cleanth Brooks is clearly much more in sympathy with Allen Tate"; Wellek, 206, 207.) In particular, Tate's concept of tension enabled Brooks to view poetry dynamically, while avoiding an undue emphasis on either its denotative or connotative functions. Tate steered a middle course between the hot-blooded emotionalism of the Romantics and the cold-blooded rationality of Yvor Winters, while eschewing the static dualism that Brooks found so troubling in Ransom's poetic theory.

From a practical standpoint, it was Tate more than anyone else who enabled Brooks to find a publisher for his book. In a letter dated August 8, 1938, Tate begins by praising the manuscript of *Modern Poetry and the Tradition*, while offering a few friendly suggestions for change. He then writes:

> I believe the first person to try is Couch at Chapel Hill.[1] He is awfully stu-
> pid, and he should be warned that the stenographer or the professor of
> sociology would not be a competent reader of the ms—least of all the Pro-
> fessor of English, a fellow named Coffman and a perfect blockhead. If I
> were you, I would suggest readers myself: Ted Spencer at Harvard, Mark
> Van Doren, etc. It would seem to me proper to point out to him that the
> ordinary professor of English has as stock in trade the views that you are
> opposing, and would automatically say no, even if he understood what
> you are talking about.—I will make this point in my letter to him. Please
> wire me the day you send him the ms.[2]

A little over a year later, in the fall of 1939, *Modern Poetry and the Tradition* was published by the University of North Carolina Press.

Essentially, Brooks accepts Eliot's notion that English poetry took a wrong turn at the end of the seventeenth century, but he argues that the modernists—under the influence of the French Symbolists—have begun to reverse the dissociation of sensibility. Brooks contends that the eighteenth and nineteenth centuries developed certain aesthetic assumptions that the metaphysical poets did not hold and that the modern poets have rejected. Perhaps the most important of these assumptions is that there is an inherently poetic subject matter. Brooks traces this belief back to Hobbes's view that the poet is a mere copyist, not a maker. If it is the poet's function simply to hold the mirror up to nature, he can please his audience most by holding that mirror up to pleasant objects.

Another shared assumption of the eighteenth and nineteenth centuries was that intellect was somehow antagonistic to the poetic faculty. Despite superficial differences between the neoclassic and Romantic critics, both saw metaphysical wit as a trivialization of the deep emotion and high seriousness of poetry. Better to whisper sweet nothings into the ear of one's beloved than tax her mind with ingenious metaphors and conceits. Better to worship God in utter simplicity than to write religious poems with puns in them. In opposition to this prejudice, the best critical minds of the seventeenth and twentieth centuries were of one accord. Like I. A. Richards, Brooks believes in a poetry that can accommodate a wide range of human experience—a poetry of inclusion, not of exclusion.

To Brooks's mind, the exclusion of intellect and wit not only limits the potentialities of poetry, it also leads inevitably to sentimentality. "The sentimentalist," Brooks writes, "takes a short cut to intensity by removing all the elements of the experience which might conceivably militate against the intensity. . . . To put the matter in terms of the poet's accuracy and fidelity to experience, the sentimental poet makes us feel that he is sacrificing the totality of his vision in favor of a particular interpretation. Hence the feeling on reading a sentimental poem that the intensity is the result of a trick" (*Modern Poetry*, 37). Rather than writing poetry of high seriousness, the sentimentalist is the one who actually trivializes his experience by simplifying it beyond credibility. The poet who uses wit and irony is fundamentally more serious; he *earns* his vision by testing it against the complexity of genuine experience.

Like most of the other new critics, Brooks takes metaphysical poetry as his paradigm because it is the most extreme example of a poetry of inclusion—not just an equal opportunity but an affirmative action poetry. The failures of metaphysical poetry "are failures to reconcile discordant materials—not failures based on a too precious exclusion of discordant materials" (42). In fact, the more dissimilar the terms of a metaphysical conceit appear to be, the more one is impressed by their reconciliation. Even Dr. Johnson (who was no great admirer of metaphysical poetry) likened "a successful comparison to the intersection of two lines, pointing out that the *comparison is better in proportion as the lines converge from greater distances*" (see *Modern Poetry*, 43). The synthesizing faculty that enables a poet to make these lines converge is, as Coleridge reminds us, the imagination. When critics dismiss certain metaphysical conceits as mere flights of fancy, they are saying the imagination was not equal to the task, that the synthesis was incomplete. Sentimental metaphors are produced by comparing terms that are too obviously similar. They are the fruit of a banal or timid imagination.

Although Brooks more fully discusses his conception of poetry in *The Well Wrought Urn* (1947), it should be clear already that he regards metaphor as being the very essence of a poem. (Here he differs with Housman and others who see it as simply a figure of speech used to dress up a prose statement—prose in drag, if you will.) Above all others, Brooks contends, "the metaphysical poets reveal the essentially functional character of all metaphor. We cannot remove the comparisons from their poems, as we might remove ornaments or illustrations attached to a statement, without demolishing the poems. The comparison *is* the poem in a structural sense" (*Modern Poetry*, 15). What makes the metaphysical conceit different from the sentimental metaphor (other than its superior inclusiveness) is its effect on the reader. Although the sentimental metaphor may seem apt on first reading, closer acquaintance will reveal the disparities that the poet has been unwilling to acknowledge; hence, it doesn't wear well. Because the metaphysical poet has acknowledged the disparities from the outset, has actually built his poem around them, his metaphor usually seems more apt with successive rereadings. Or as Brooks puts the matter, "if it does not explode with a first reading, it is extremely durable" (45).

In addition to sentimental verse, another form of the poetry of exclusion is propaganda art. Very few propagandists are confident enough of what they believe in to subject it to ironic contemplation; in fact, the focus of propaganda art is not contemplation but action. Using different terminology to make a similar point, Allen Tate distinguishes between what he calls imaginative and Platonic poetry. The latter variety may express "a cheerful confidence in the limitless power of man to impose practical abstractions upon his experience" or it may despair of that power (see *Modern Poetry*, 46). In contrast, the truly imaginative poet is not out to change the world and is not going to be disillusioned at failing to do so. (To quote W. H. Auden: "Poetry makes nothing happen.") Even when the Romantic poet scorns science, he is trying to do what science does—explain and control the world. The truly imaginative poet is simply content to experience the world and to translate that experience as fully as possible through the medium of language.

The common view of literary history at the time that Brooks wrote *Modern Poetry and the Tradition* was that the Romantics had effected a literary revolution by breaking with the neoclassic concept of decorum prevalent in the eighteenth century and that the modernist poets of the early twentieth century had taken that revolution several steps farther. Following Eliot's lead, Brooks disputes this view, for one thing, seeing the Romantic revolt as being a bogus revolution: "The Romantic poets, in attacking the neoclassic conception of the poetic, tended to offer new poetic objects rather than to discard altogether the conception of a special poetic material" (52). In their failure to be sufficiently revolutionary, the Romantics simply perpetuated the dissociation of sensibility introduced into English poetry at the end of the seventeenth century by the influence

of Hobbes. At its worst, this led to the twin sins of didacticism and sentimentality, both of which were carried to ridiculous extremes during the
Victorian era. The modern poets approved of by Brooks and Eliot are not
extending the Romantic revolution so much as reversing the dissociation
of sensibility to which the Romantics were just as prone as their neoclassic
predecessors and Victorian heirs. These "moderns" are actually counter-
revolutionaries or neometaphysicals.

As he moves farther into his discussion of the twentieth century, Brooks
makes clear that not all contemporary verse belongs in his canon of "modern poetry." When the revulsion against Victorianism did not lead to a
rediscovery of the metaphysical approach, it usually tended in one of two
other directions—either toward the Imagist insistence on an objective description of things or toward the kind of primitivism that defines local
color as the essence of poetry. (In his rejection of these two extremes,
Brooks shows most clearly the influence of Fugitive poetics on his thinking.) The problem with Imagism (what Ransom calls "physical poetry")
is that it was too concerned with the materials of poetry while being
largely indifferent to questions of structure. If Imagism allowed us to write
poems about steam engines, it did not say nearly enough about what to
do with the steam engines once they had made their way into the poem.
To argue for no ideas but in things is not quite the same as arguing for no
ideas at all.

III

After establishing his theoretical framework in the first four chapters of
Modern Poetry and the Tradition and devoting most of chapter 5 to holding up the three major Fugitives as role models, Brooks spends his next
three chapters discussing the strengths and weaknesses of other prominent
modern poets. In chapter 6, for example, he argues that Auden (still in his
leftist phase) might well be a rare example of a propagandist of inclusion;
that MacLeish is a more talented Sandburg, who might yet develop a semblance of structural complexity; and that Frost, for all his sobriety and
sensitivity, cannot seem to move beyond a kind of "licensed whimsy."

Over half a century later, these judgments cry out for modification.
Brooks was prescient enough in his praise of Auden, who became more
inclusive and less propagandistic as he grew older. MacLeish, however,
seems a less formidable presence today than he did in the thirties—certainly of much less importance than Ezra Pound, Hart Crane, and Wallace

Stevens, three figures whom Brooks mentions but does not discuss. Even more regrettable is Brooks's too easy dismissal of Frost. Neither in *Modern Poetry and the Tradition* nor in *Understanding Poetry* does he recognize the dark undertones in "After Apple-Picking." Moreover, one would be hard pressed to find a more perfect metaphysical poem of any era than Frost's "The Silken Tent" (which was not published until two years after *Modern Poetry and the Tradition*). Although Brooks is not naive enough to fall for Frost's country bumpkin persona, it would be many years before he would give the New England bard sufficient credit for the complexity lurking beneath his apparent simplicity.

What has clearly stood the test of time is Brooks's remarkably perceptive reading of *The Waste Land*. So much has been written about that poem since 1939 that it is easy to forget how incompletely it had been understood before Brooks came along. The explication he gives of the poem is as lucid as any beginning student could possibly want. To accomplish this, Brooks devotes eighty percent of his chapter on *The Waste Land*. The final pages of that chapter, however, are of immeasurably greater importance. Here, Brooks argues for a startlingly revisionist interpretation of the poem. To read *The Waste Land* as a statement of despair or unbelief, he contends, is to stay far too close to the surface of this supremely ironic text. Instead *The Waste Land* is at least an inchoate affirmation of Christian faith. Making this point, Brooks writes:

> Eliot's theme is not the statement of a faith held and agreed upon (Dante's *Divine Comedy*) nor is it the projection of a "new" system of beliefs (Spenser's *Faerie Queene*). Eliot's theme is the rehabilitation of a system of beliefs, known but now discredited. . . . To put the matter in still other terms: the Christian terminology is for the poet a mass of clichés. However "true" he may feel the terms to be, he is still sensitive to the fact that they operate superficially as clichés, and his method of necessity must be a process of bringing them to life again. The method adopted in *The Waste Land* is thus violent and radical, but thoroughly necessary. (*Modern Poetry*, 170–71)

When Brooks originally wrote this account of *The Waste Land*, he sent a copy to Eliot. On March 15, 1937, Eliot wrote back to say of the essay, "It seems to me on the whole excellent." He goes on to say: "I think that this kind of analysis is perfectly justified so long as it does not profess to be a reconstruction of the author's method of writing. Reading your essay made me feel, for instance, that I had been much more ingenious than I had been aware of, because the conscious problems with which one is concerned in the actual writing are more those of a quasi musical nature, in the arrangement of metric and pattern, than of a conscious exposition of ideas" (*Community*, 99–100).

In looking back on what he had to say about *The Waste Land* from the perspective of half a century, Brooks concluded in 1989 that Eliot had written a prophetic poem; by this he meant primarily "an utterance of a deep and important truth, often thought of as divinely inspired" (*Community*, 112). But he also intended the colloquial meaning of the term as well. Citing authorities as diverse as Eric Voegelin, Christopher Lasch, E. D. Hirsch, and Walker Percy, Brooks shows how contemporary man (at least in America) is cut off from history, tradition, and faith. If anything, Eliot may have expressed that truth too brilliantly in *The Waste Land*. According to Brooks:

> The artist who insists on speaking of how or when the world will end faces a dilemma. It is that of the famed playwright-actor who rushed onto the stage before a packed first-night house, shouting "The theater is on fire! Rush for the exits!" and was wildly applauded. What an opening! the audience thought. What a play! What an actor! He almost makes you think that the theater is really burning! Indeed, the more frantically he pleaded with the audience to leave, the more lustily they clapped their hands. Art had triumphed over fact, appearance over reality. Something similar happens when we read *The Waste Land*: the nightmarish vision of a civilization breaking up is done so well that we almost believe the breakup is real. But, of course, we know that it isn't. (*Community*, 110)

Perhaps it is the function of the critic to convince the audience that there is truth as well as artifice in the poet's message, that the theater really is on fire.

In *Modern Poetry and the Tradition*, Brooks's discussion of Eliot is followed by a chapter on Yeats as mythmaker. Here again, Brooks makes the work of a difficult modern poet understandable without compromising its complexity. Because of his aversion to the modern industrial world, Yeats is a kindred spirit of the Agrarians. And like the southern formalists, he believes that the poetic imagination can divine truths that are inaccessible to science. "'I am,' Yeats tells us, 'very religious, and deprived by Huxley and Tyndall . . . of the simple-minded religion of my childhood, I had made a new religion, almost an infallible church of poetic tradition, of a fardel of stories, and of personages, and of emotions, inseparable from their first expression, passed on from generation to generation by poets

and painters with some help from philosophers and theologians' " (see
Modern Poetry, 174).

Although there is a good deal of truth to this statement, Yeats was not
content simply to replace orthodox religion with poetic tradition and folk
culture. In his book *A Vision*, he devised an elaborate personal mythology,
complete with a philosophy of history based on the phases of the moon.
Whether Yeats believed in this system more literally than he did in the
religion from which he had been weaned by Tyndall and Huxley is finally
a question for the biographer rather than the literary critic. What Brooks
as critic demonstrates is that the myth informs Yeats's poetry and that *A
Vision* can serve as a very useful gloss on that poetry. Because the myth
itself consists of the clash and resolution of antitheses, one can see where
it would appeal to a critic who admires the metaphysical poets.

Reading the chapters on Eliot and Yeats back-to-back, one cannot help
noticing the marked difference between their respective mythologies. For
all the difficulty of Eliot's style and the novelty of his approach, he uses
symbols and beliefs that are in the public domain. If Eliot's mode of communication presents problems for the ordinary reader, the content of what
he is saying is really quite traditional and orthodox. While it is often easier
to grasp the prose sense of Yeats's verse, its deeper meanings are more
obscure. That obscurity can be penetrated by someone who, like Brooks,
takes the time to master Yeats's private mythology. Or the lazy among us
can simply let an explicator such as Brooks do our work for us. But does
this not raise a question of evaluation? It is reasonable, if irksome, for a
poet to expect his readers to master vast amounts of public information
in order to understand and appreciate his work. But to ask those same
readers to master a private system of thought may be too much. If the
formalist critics are correct in saying that we should not need to know the
details of a poet's life to evaluate his verse, then we should not need to
know the details of his *personal* metaphysics either. This is a point that
one might have expected Brooks to make.

Modern Poetry and the Tradition concludes by returning to the dissociation of sensibility as the key issue in English literary history. Brooks
argues, for example, that Hobbes is responsible not only for the wrong
turn that poetry took at the end of the seventeenth century but also for the
death of tragedy on the English stage. By emphasizing paradigmatic simplicity, the scientific worldview of Hobbes robbed poetry of the dialectical
tension that made metaphysical verse so rich. That same tension, Brooks

argues, is essential to tragedy. In order to appreciate tragedy, we must be able simultaneously to admire and judge the tragic hero. The Elizabethans could do this (just as they could admire and judge dashing rogues). The heroic drama of the Restoration, however, more nearly resembles melodrama. When character is purged of ambiguity, pathos is still possible, but tragedy is not.

By linking the poetry and drama of the seventeenth century so closely, Brooks lays the groundwork for one of his own dominant critical metaphors—the poem as drama. Although he would develop the implications of this concept much further in *The Well Wrought Urn*, he is content here with emphasizing the fact that seventeenth-century poetry is even at the most literal level quite dramatic. This is true not only of metaphysical poetry, but also of the verse of Carew, Marvell, Herrick, and other "sons of Ben." "Even the meditations of George Herbert are not ruminations; they are attempts made by the poet to explore his own religious experience" (*Modern Poetry*, 213). The characteristic that these poets, the Cavaliers and the metaphysicals, all shared was the use of wit as a structural device. For this reason, Brooks sees the schools of Donne and Jonson as differing more in subject matter than in technique.

If there is a countertradition in the English Renaissance, it is represented by the Spenserians. These poets stood apart, Brooks argues, because they "tended to approach the poem as an allegorical construct, that is as an abstract framework of statement which was to be illustrated and ornamented by overlaying the framework with concrete detail" (220). In two significant respects, the Spenserians can be said to anticipate the dissociation of sensibility that infected English poetry at about the time of the Restoration—they wrote in a deliberately archaic diction that suggested a poetry of exclusion, and they used wit for decorative rather than structural purposes.

If tragedy fared so badly after the Elizabethan era, one might ask why comedy remained so healthy well into the eighteenth century. More to the point, could wit really have been purged from literature when the appeal of the great Restoration comedies lay in little else? Brooks responds to this objection by distinguishing between the ironic wit that is characteristic of tragedy and the satiric wit that sustains comedy. Tragedy "represents something of a tension between unsympathetic laughter and sympathetic pity—between the impulse to condemn the protagonist and the impulse to feel pity for him" (214). Perhaps the last significant character in seventeenth-century literature to exhibit tragic tension was Milton's Satan. The Puritan in Milton condemned the Prince of Darkness, while the rebel secretly admired him. Although such an attitude raises logical and theological problems, it is the very essence of the tragic imagination. The epistemological simplification introduced by Hobbes could accommodate a criticism of others, but not the criticism of self authored by a truly introspective wit. Yeats said that we make rhetoric out of our arguments with others and poetry out of our arguments with ourselves. By this definition, the writing of true poetry became much more difficult after the dissociation of sensibility.

If *dissociation of sensibility* seems too grandiose a term, Brooks talks of the "segregation of impulses." He argues that this accounts for neoclassic tragedy being "too noble and too easily didactic" and for the love poetry of the era being too baldly sentimental. We find only superficial breaks with this tradition as we move into the nineteenth century. The pre-Romantics may have thought of themselves as severing the bonds of neoclassicism; however, they too thought of poetry as essentially descriptive and didactic. They were simply descriptive and didactic about more rustic and exotic topics. This was also true of most of the major Romantics most of the time. Shelley is of course the bête noire of the new critics, with other poets being judged acceptable according to the degree to which they avoided his narcissistic lyricism. According to Brooks, "Wordsworth has as little of the dramatic as does Shelley, and where we find an attempt at the dramatic, it is the personal self-dramatization of Byron—the self-conscious actor, not the objectifying dramatist" (217). Although Coleridge achieves a kind of tragic grandeur in *The Rime of the Ancient Mariner* and Keats gives us concrete and sensuous imagery, the Romantic poet who comes closest to approximating metaphysical wit is William Blake. His use of metaphor in poems such as "London," "The Mental Traveller," and "The Scoffers" would have been appreciated in the Age of Donne, but in his own time Blake "remains an isolated and exceptional figure" (235).

When writing *Modern Poetry and the Tradition*, Brooks could find no equivalent to Blake, nor any other happy exception to the dissociated sensibility, in the Victorian era. He mentions Gerard Hopkins and Emily Dickinson as "poets who transcended Victorianism," but omits a discussion of them. He says that Matthew Arnold achieved success "within certain rather narrow limits" (241), but fails to specify either the success or the limits. The one neometaphysical poet of the Victorian era to whom

Brooks gives more than passing attention is Thomas Hardy, and Hardy is perhaps best characterized as a premodern or—to use Daniel Joseph Singal's terminology—a modernist by the skin of his teeth.

Of the two most eminent Victorians, Brooks writes Tennyson off as being too didactic and dismisses the ostensibly dramatic qualities of Browning's poetry as superficial. He approvingly cites F. R. Leavis's observation that Browning's poetry "belongs to the world he lives in." According to Leavis, "there are kinds of strengths a poet is best without. And it is too plain that Browning would have been less robust if he had been more sensitive and intelligent" (see *Modern Poetry*, 241). Although Brooks and Leavis have a point about much of Browning's huge corpus, one cannot help thinking that their opinions were somewhat colored by the anti-Victorianism that pervaded literary circles until well after World War II. Certainly in *The Poetry of Experience* (1957), Robert Langbaum makes a strong case for Browning's best poetry being as ironic and paradoxical as any produced by the metaphysicals and moderns.

One of the charges leveled against the new critics is that their yoking of the poetry of the seventeenth and twentieth centuries is itself an arbitrary act of metaphysical violence. In reconstructing literary history, one can account for the dissociation of sensibility by placing the blame on Hobbes. But how did poetry get back on track at the beginning of the twentieth century after floundering for more than two hundred years? The intriguing answer Brooks offers is that "the course of science has come full circle from the age of Hobbes to the age of Einstein. . . . By removing the curse of *fiction* from poetry, [modern science] allows the poet to develop *his* kind of *fiction* in accord with its own principles, unconfused by those of another" (*Modern Poetry*, 217). With scientists (particularly in the realm of theoretical physics) transformed from imposing dogmatists into genial relativists, poetry need no longer suffer from an epistemological inferiority complex.

IV

Despite a few strongly stated opinions to the contrary, the critical reception of *Modern Poetry and the Tradition* was generally favorable. One point on which the admirers and detractors of the book agreed, however, was that nothing less than the history of English verse (what we now call the canon) was at issue. One objection frequently raised was that Brooks's critical standards were too narrow to accommodate the multiplicity of poems that had pleased many and pleased long. Writing in the *Sewanee Review*, Stuart Gerry Brown complained that "it is surely not a very penetrating criticism which would by implication exclude 'Lycidas,' 'The Triumph of Dulness,' *The Dunciad*, some of Johnson's satire, the theft of the boat in *The Prelude*, some of the lyrics of *In Memoriam* or the radio plays of MacLeish from the sphere of the dramatic and perhaps even the serious and complex" (Brown, 550–51).

It was in their dismissal of the Romantic poets that Brooks and the other new critics inspired their most spirited opposition. Probably the most effective brief for the Romantics was filed by Richard H. Fogle in his essay "Romantic Bards and Metaphysical Reviewers," first published in *English Literary History* in 1945. In essence, Fogle argued that the new critics were themselves guilty of a dissociated sensibility. "By the doctrine of Irony," he wrote, "the New Critics claim to have reunited emotion and intellect, which the eighteenth century and the Romantics had divided. Actually they have drawn them farther apart than ever. They have banished emotion completely, although giving her lip-service, so that only intellect remains, mutilated by this forcible separation" (Fogle, "Romantic Bards," 248).

In *Modern Poetry and the Tradition*, Brooks had made some damning generalizations about the poetic theory of the Romantics, while providing little supporting evidence. By quoting directly from the critical writings of Wordsworth and Shelley, Fogle suggested that Brooks was attacking straw men. The only plausible case that the new critics could make against the Romantics was that they failed to practice what they preached, and Fogle believed that that argument withers under scrutiny. The new critics, for example, faulted the consistency of Shelley's imagery by reducing imagery to the level of simplistic visual representation and then treated that technique as if it were the sum total of poetic art. Moreover, in their zeal to purge direct statement from poetry, the new critics ended up banning rather than championing intellect. Fogle pointed out that direct statement "may itself contribute to the sum-total of poetic effect" and that shunning it may encourage "the poet to make a fetish of unintelligibility" (242).

When Fogle revised and expanded this essay for his book *The Imagery of Keats and Shelley* (1949), Brooks had already published *The Well Wrought Urn*, with its extensive analyses of Wordsworth's "Intimations" ode and Keats's "Ode on a Grecian Urn." But Fogle ignored the degree to which Brooks had altered his canon to make room for certain approved Romantics, arguing instead that all of the Romantics would be approved if the new critics would simply apply their own standards correctly. He contended, for example, that Brooks's notion of irony was "a mere attitude without a situation, or a rigid, predetermined formula, or sometimes a new invention to enable you to go wading without getting your feet wet." Fogle went on to say that he found "irony, within the present meaning of the term, in the studious understatement of the conclusion of *Michael*, in the self-realization which underlies the apparent breaking-off of *Kubla Khan*, in the breadth of understanding beneath the excitement of *Ode to the West Wind*" (Fogle, *Imagery*, 276). But he thought Brooks unlikely to agree.[3] Fogle concluded by observing: "Mr. Brooks has somewhere expressed the fear that critical relativism may lead us to confuse Edgar A. Guest and Shakespeare; critical absolutism, one may feel, has already confused Edgar A. Guest and Shelley, in an almost equal failure of values" (278).

Another point of controversy was whether early modernists had actually recovered the metaphysical tradition of seventeenth-century verse. Rosemund Tuve suspected that Brooks and the other new critics were simply creating a usable past by interpreting the intentions of the metaphysical poets according to the standards of our day rather than theirs. Writing in the *Modern Language Quarterly*, she criticized our unwillingness to accept a concept that the seventeenth-century poets "would never have questioned—the *use* of poetry to make *statements* which they believed *true* (however small the truth), *to a reader* whom they tried to convince of this truth by such means as they thought effective *to that end*." Tuve concluded, rather coyly, that "if the reader thinks this an untenable theory of poetry, he will enjoy in Mr. Brooks's book one of the most brilliant of recent confutations of it" (Tuve, 150).

In an otherwise laudatory review published in the *New Republic*, W. H. Auden also questioned Brooks's apparent dismissal of the relationship between poetry and belief. One need not subscribe to what Auden called the "social-significance heresy" to realize that a poet's worldview is an important consideration in assessing his work. Auden, for example, believed that Dante was superior to Yeats because of his ability to "coordinate his experience and the general experience of his time." Yeats, unfortunately, was locked in a private myth that simply abused industrial civilization without providing sufficient enlightenment about it. "In consequence much of his work fails, in spite of his amazing verbal gift, to stand up under that 'ironic contemplation' which Mr. Brooks [and Auden himself regard] . . . as an acid test of poetry" (Auden, 187).

John Ransom's official response to *Modern Poetry and the Tradition* (published in the *Kenyon Review*) was what one might have expected—effusive general praise for Brooks, followed by reservations about several of his specific points.[4] Brooks was, according to Ransom, "very likely, the most expert living 'reader' or interpreter of difficult verse" (Ransom, "Apologia," 248). It was the inferences Brooks drew from his readings that Ransom found suspect. For example, after declaring Brooks's discussion of *The Waste Land* to be "superlative," Ransom let the other shoe drop.

> Mr. Brooks seems to regard symbolist poetry as a twin to metaphysical poetry, and therefore perfectly traditional, but I cannot follow that reasoning. Among many learned and resolutely well-disposed commentators of Eliot none has made so magnificent an attempt as Mr. Brooks to piece out a logical frame implicit in the poem, but this frame is too thin for me, and not continuous. The symbols used in the religious poetry of the 17th century were both public, or conventional, and, in any single poem, systematic. Mr. Eliot's symbols are esoteric, which means, according to my experience, that they belong to a fraternity of mystics and are a good deal less than definitive; and they are to an incredible degree eclectic, or miscellaneous, which means that they are not systematic. (250)[5]

Even as he quarreled with Brooks over particular points of theory and interpretation, Ransom must have been heartened by the fact that their arguments were conducted entirely within the realm of criticism. As we look back from the perspective of over half a century, it is clear that the despair Ransom initially felt over the prospects for criticism in the academy was spectacularly premature. Two years prior to the original publication of his seminal essay "Criticism, Inc.," Brooks and Warren had founded the *Southern Review*, and two years later Ransom himself would found the *Kenyon Review*. Moreover, "Criticism, Inc." appeared only a year before the first edition of *Understanding Poetry* and two years before *Modern Poetry and the Tradition*. By the time that Ransom published his essay "Wanted: An Ontological Critic" in 1941, such critics were already beginning to reshape literary study in America.

It was not unusual for an English major in the forties or fifties to encounter the new criticism by reading *Understanding Poetry* as a sophomore, progress to the more sophisticated articles in the *Kenyon* and *Sewanee* reviews as a junior and senior, attend one of Ransom's summer programs at Kenyon before entering graduate school, work his way through an advanced degree program by teaching Brooks and Warren to a new generation of sophomores, do a new critical reading of some venerable masterpiece of English literature as an M.A. thesis or Ph.D. dissertation, land a tenure-track job at a state university by reworking his best graduate seminar papers into essays for the critical quarterlies, and spend his prime years teaching three sections of freshman composition and one of Brooks and Warren while trying to publish his way into the Ivy League. Even if the path to professional advancement is quite different now, it is difficult to imagine what the university study of literature would have been like if the new criticism hadn't come along.

CHAPTER TEN

The Man Who Knew MacArthur

In September 1935 Robert B. Heilman, a new Ph.D. from Harvard, arrived in Baton Rouge to assume his first job as an assistant professor of English at LSU. A week after hitting town, Heilman decided to walk the block or two from his apartment to Louisiana's skyscraper state capitol. He wanted to see the legislature in action, especially because it was rumored that Senator Huey Long would be in attendance. It was a Sunday, the day before Labor Day, when Bob Heilman found his seat in the visitors' gallery. He could see the Kingfish, surrounded by bodyguards, working the floor. A driven little man who relished the power he wielded, Long suggested "a degree of aloof amusement at the show he was stage managing" (Heilman, 6). When Huey and his lackeys left the chamber after half an hour or so, the legislature was still officially in session, but the show was over.

"A few seconds later," Heilman recalls, "there was a strange outburst of sounds in a rapid but irregular sequence. Firecrackers, I thought, puzzled. Then men came running back into the chamber below us and ducking behind desks" (6). What Heilman had heard was a string of gunfire that had left the Kingfish mortally wounded and his assailant, Dr. Carl Austin Weiss, a bullet-riddled corpse. The young Dr. Weiss (who had attended Tookie Brooks only a few weeks before) was but one of many Louisianans angry enough to want Long dead. As the Kingfish consolidated his power in the 1930s, his enemies increasingly believed that he could be brought down only through violence. Fifty years later, Betty Carter said that when she heard a man in a white suit had just shot Huey Long, her first thought was "Where's Hodding?" [1]

Although Huey rallied briefly, he died in a Baton Rouge hospital a day and a half later. The news of his death brought multitudes of the dispossessed from around the state to view the body of their slain hero and to camp out on the capitol grounds in the days before his funeral. The one thing about which Long's partisans and antagonists could agree was that the state would be vastly different with him gone. His machine was still in place, but none of his surviving henchmen was bright enough to run it as ruthlessly as the Kingfish had. In death as in life, he cast a giant shadow over the state. In fact, a few days after Long's death, Cork Read hobbled over to Bob Heilman's apartment to tell his new employee that school might not open on schedule the following week. At first, Heilman thought that Read meant the official period of mourning would be extended. But he soon realized that Read and others were afraid that the whole damn state was about ready to fall apart.

                              I

Shortly before his assassination, Huey Long observed: "If anything happens to me, the people who try to wield the powers that I have created will all land in jail" (see Johnston, 16). One such individual turned out to be James Monroe Smith. Whether one sees Smith as primarily a villain or a victim, he was clearly a man out of his depth. As a toady to Huey Long, he could be relied on to follow orders; but on matters not involving Huey, Smith was remarkably willing to defer to the faculty. When Cleanth and other reformers suggested the formation of a faculty council, Smith endorsed the idea. He was also the man who appointed Pipkin graduate dean and approved the *Southern Review*. Unfortunately, Smith became convinced that he could make himself and the university rich by playing the stock market. He had begun his speculation while still in Lafayette by purchasing shares of Morrison's Cafeteria stock. That was with his own money, however. At LSU, Smith had access to public funds, so his activities there were limited only by his own imagination.

Believing that war was imminent in Europe, Smith purchased 2 million bushels of wheat, using $300,000 in university bonds as collateral. The scheme might have worked had British Prime Minister Neville Chamberlain not capitulated to Hitler's territorial demands at Munich, thus making war seem less likely. When the bottom started falling out of the wheat market and Smith's brokers demanded more collateral, he simply walked into a Baton Rouge print shop with a stolen $1,000 bond and said, "Print me three hundred of these." And when the brokers would not accept the phony bonds without a legal opinion concerning their validity, Smith covered his purchases by using the university's name to borrow $300,000 from a New Orleans bank. After a Baton Rouge banker objected to so much business going out of town, Smith obligingly borrowed $100,000 from the local bank. Needless to say, neither of these loans had been authorized by the LSU Board of Supervisors. A short time later, the subterfuge was discovered, and on June 25, 1939, Smith and his wife fled for Canada (see Johnston, 100, 102).

No doubt James Monroe Smith was a criminal who deserved to be punished for abusing the public trust, but in the political atmosphere of Louisiana he was also something of a pathetic figure. Smith was only one of many officials who convinced himself that the public good could be purchased through private graft. And if Hitler had not pulled the wool over Chamberlain's eyes at Munich, Smith might well have made a tidy profit for the university and gotten a dormitory named after him. Instead, he was brought back from Canada under indictment, and his name was chiseled off the dormitory then under construction. Huey Long, whose dishonesty was much greater and much more successful than Smith's, died at the height of his power, a hero to millions. Smith lived long enough to see his world fall apart. The May 11, 1940, issue of the *Saturday Evening Post* carried a picture of him standing in a field at the Angola State Prison, wearing the striped uniform of an inmate. After his release, he held a series of insignificant jobs under assumed names. But his past always caught up with him. Unable to earn a living or to make a new start in the world, he went to the penal authorities at Angola and asked for the job in the prison library he had held while serving his time. A few years later James Monroe Smith died in obscurity, a broken and forgotten man.

After Smith's resignation as president, the LSU Board of Supervisors appointed the Law School dean, Paul M. Hebert, to serve as acting president. The choice was applauded by Cleanth and other faculty reformers. Hebert was a man of integrity and genuine collegiality. Not only was it unthinkable for him to flash thousand-dollar bills (an essential part of a public official's wardrobe during the Long years) or to play the stock market with stolen money, Hebert was also unlikely to sacrifice important academic principles for political favor. Unfortunately, the virtues that made him a nearly ideal leader to the reformers caused Hebert to be suspect in the eyes of the power brokers who still wanted to run the university. Also, as a Roman Catholic of French origin, Hebert represented a minority constituency within the state.

In contrast to the violence in state government and the scandal at the upper reaches of the university administration, power changed hands peacefully in the English department. On January 17, 1941, William A. Read announced his retirement as department head, and Cleanth was asked to chair a committee to select his successor. Because Read had run the department for nearly thirty years, various interest groups were more than ready to fill the vacuum he was leaving. John Earle Uhler had been tapped as heir apparent by James Monroe Smith, but his propects had vanished with Smith's downfall. The only chance that Uhler and his cohort Earl Bradshear had to influence the department was to see that someone sympathetic to their side was appointed to replace Read. For reasons that were never fully apparent, they backed Tommy Kirby, the Hopkins Ph.D. who had come to the department in 1935. (Perhaps old school ties influenced Uhler's choice.) The blessing of the old guard was enough to cause Cleanth and his principal ally Bob Heilman to look for an alternative. The man they settled on was Aldophus Jerome Bryan, a Harvard Ph.D. who had been instrumental in bringing Heilman to LSU. (Might old school ties have been decisive here as well?) Bryan was neither a new critic nor an academic reformer, but at least he had no affiliation with the Bradshear-Uhler faction.

When Hebert appointed Tommy Kirby as department head, it appeared as if the old guard had dealt the reformers a stunning setback. In point of fact, Kirby proceeded to run the department with the independence of a federal judge enjoying lifetime tenure. He remained chairman for thirty-two years and soon formed a closer alliance with Brooks and Heilman than he had had with Bradshear and Uhler. At a personal level, Kirby and his charming southern wife, Josie, were warm friends of the Brookses and the Heilmans, even as the old boys in the department saw their ranks and power dwindle. (Over a quarter century later, Cleanth wrote to Kirby: "In my balmier moments I may picture myself sitting on the veranda of the Prince Murat house, watching with one eye Leroy, our old yard boy, trim the camellias and with the other eye watching Josie and Tinkum shoot bluejays out of the oaks, while you and I converse on the state of letters.")[2] Alas, the English department was atypical of the larger institution; on the campus as a whole, those who jealously guarded the status quo greatly outnumbered the small band of activists intent on making LSU into a real university.

II

One of the most energetic reformers on campus, and one of Cleanth's closest allies outside the English department, was Charles Hyneman, who chaired the LSU Department of Government from 1937 to 1942. Charlie Hyneman was comfortable dealing with the theoreticians in his own department (Eric Voegelin and Willmoore Kendall among them), but he could also speak to practicing politicians in their own language. One of Hyneman's most promising graduate students at this time was a young Minnesotan named Hubert Humphrey. The doctoral dissertation (on the "Political Philosophy of the New Deal") that Humphrey wrote under Hyneman's direction was an able combination of the theoretical and the practical, and he and Hyneman planned to collaborate on several books before Humphrey's political career took him out of academia.

A man of plainspoken amiability, Hyneman was that rarest of creatures—a commonsense idealist. He knew the world for what it was but tried to make his own corner of it a little better. During his time at LSU, Hyneman was the driving force behind the local chapter of the American Association of University Professors. He knew Roberts Rules of Order backwards and forwards, and he was an effective public speaker. Others in the reform movement were content to plan strategy, while allowing Hyneman to be their most visible spokesman. One of the most active strategists was Cleanth Brooks, whom Robert Heilman remembers as "an instinctive quarterback, . . . [who] loved the metaphor of the quarterback sending the fullback crashing through the enemy line" (Heilman, 92).

On one notable occasion, however, Cleanth was left standing in the middle of the field without protection. One of the marks of distinction coveted by almost every university is its own chapter of Phi Beta Kappa. Historically, land grant institutions, which are focused on the agricultural and mechanical rather than the liberal arts, have had a difficult time making their case for membership in the fraternity. When LSU decided to apply, Charles Hyneman pointed out that the only people officially qualified to file the application were those members of the LSU faculty who were themselves Phi Beta Kappas. No doubt, the university administration expected these individuals to sing the praises of the Old War Skule in the sweetest and most unbroken harmony. Instead, the committee candidly surveyed the situation and concluded that Louisiana State University did not yet deserve a chapter of Phi Beta Kappa. Charles Hyneman had chaired the committee, and Robert Heilman had written its report; but, as committee secretary, Cleanth was the only one who had signed the document. He recalls that shortly thereafter, his brother (who was not even connected with the university) told him that even he had heard that the powers that be were very displeased and were holding Cleanth personally responsible.

The Phi Beta Kappa report paints LSU as a provincial institution largely indifferent to academic standards. Part of the problem lay in the pervasive military heritage of the university. "We appear to have all of the disadvantages of the [military] camp and none of the advantages," the report asserts. "We have noise, show, intellectual conformity, pride of position, all disguised by flag-waving symbolism, the true import of which few people seem to realize. But still we seem to exert over the students none of the essential authority which they need" (Brooks, *Report*, 53). This lack of authority was evidenced in the power that students could wield against faculty simply by launching complaints with the administration. Professors were thus in the paradoxical situation of feeling pressure from both above and below. As the report puts it: "If the faculty feel, on the one hand, that they are somewhat at the mercy of superiors, [to] whom they must cater to an extent beyond that normally implied by the office, they also feel, on the other hand, unusually subject to the force of student opinion" (56).

The Phi Beta Kappa report contains flashes of wit not usually found in committee prose. In characterizing the Arts College, the report surmises that "it is perhaps the absence of a clear conception of what it is doing and where it is going that is responsible for an apparent welcome to all comers, so that, throughout the University, it enjoys a reputation as an asylum for misfits, lame ducks, and cast-offs" (27). In commenting on the lack of minimum standards for students in liberal arts, the report concludes that it need not attempt to define "minimum knowledge" to "point out how far away from it we are when upperclassmen constantly use the phrase 'in olden times' to refer indiscriminately to everything from 1000 B.C. to 1890 A.D." (29).

Faculty reformers saw the public discredit brought to LSU by the James Monroe Smith scandals as a blessing in disguise; they hoped that this would be the occasion for a thorough reexamination of the academic climate at the university. The reformers first made their proposals for change shortly after President Smith was extradited from Canada. On the very day of Smith's return, the university's alumni president, Tom W. Dutton, made a statewide radio broadcast calling on Earl Long (Huey's brother, who was now governor) to "depoliticize" the university. As a gesture of encouragement, a group of nineteen faculty members sent Dutton an open letter praising his speech and urging a wholesale reform of the university.

In response to this manifesto, 176 faculty members issued a counterstatement indicating that things were essentially fine as they were. Across the campus, the opposition branded "the Nineteen" (as the reformers came to be known) as radical agitators and, most damning of all, Yankee troublemakers. Although charges of radicalism and carpetbaggery were fighting words in the South at this time, the accusations would never have stood up to scrutiny. The Nineteen included persons of divergent political views and regional provenance. By the same token, a goodly number of northerners (if no known radicals) were among the 176. In terms of sheer numbers, there were more than nine defenders of the status quo for every reformer (one person did sign both documents), but, given the political climate at LSU, it took far more courage to be a dissident than a cheerleader. Also, the apathetic majority (those who signed neither document) far outnumbered the activists of both camps combined.

For as long as Paul Hebert remained at the helm of the university, the Nineteen could count on a sympathetic ear, if not official endorsement. Unlike the dissidents, Hebert believed that LSU was a sound institution academically (he cited the *Southern Review* as evidence) and needed only to get its financial affairs in order to become a first-rate university. Nevertheless, he did not endorse the counterstatement of the loyal 176 or take any punitive action against the Nineteen. Of more importance, he agreed to the formation of a faculty senate to deal with matters of curriculum.

As various unsatisfactory candidates were rumored to be in line for the permanent presidency of LSU, the reformers continued to back Hebert. In fact, one Sunday afternoon, Cleanth and a few other concerned faculty members drove several hundred miles to lobby James Smitherman, head of the board of supervisors, at his home in Shreveport. After expressing gratitude for the interest his guests had shown in the university, Smitherman deftly turned the conversation away from academic politics. Upon discovering that two of his visitors (Brooks and Heilman) were professors of literature, he kindly showed them his wife's poetry and introduced them "to the maker herself." "He was like a plantation owner letting an oil prospector in on a hidden gusher in the back forty," Heilman recalls. "I am not sure whether we were to assay the crude on the spot or send in a laboratory report by mail. On the scene I limped in clichés while Cleanth managed benign words, in which the chilly critical spirit was somewhat muffled in the folds of courtesy" (Heilman, 86).

In March 1941 the board of supervisors announced that Campbell Blackshear Hodges, the man who had been offered the job fourteen years earlier, was to be the new president of LSU. In a letter to Donald Davidson, written on March 19, Cleanth tried to take the most optimistic view possible of this development.

> We're not certain what the election of a major general means. The first re-action on the part of the faculty was one of bitter disappointment. We felt that the acting-president was doing a good job, and that, confirmed as permanent president, he would aid in—at least allow—the reformation of the University. Since the election, I have heard from trustworthy sources a number of things which put the Board's action in a better light: that they had tried to get some real educators and had been refused—that General Hodges is rigidly honest—that the Board knows that the University Administration (deans, etc.) needs cleaning out—that the Board intends to clean it out and will be receptive to faculty suggestion. I am hoping for the best. The situation may actually be far better than I think, but then it may be worse.[3]

In terms of sheer honesty, Hodges could hardly be faulted. If James Monroe Smith was a visionary corrupted by overreaching, General Hodges was a man of cautious rectitude. (After the reforms he instituted had been in place for a few years, Cleanth wrote to Red Warren: "It seems that poor LSU either errs on the side of corruption, or in reaction to that, goes into the other extreme of being so careful to save the university money that it demands five forms typewritten in order to buy a lead pencil.")[4] Hodges had attended West Point with General MacArthur and was referred to contemptuously as "the man who knew MacArthur." Like his more famous classmate, LSU's new president saw himself as a benevolent despot. Unfortunately, he knew next to nothing about running a university. Hence he relied on the lower administration for advice and then imposed their will on the faculty. In a hierarchical organization such as the Army, this method of governance may be effective, but university faculty members are not enlisted men. If the Army had lost an educator, dissidents complained, LSU had gained a general.

In his March 19 letter to Davidson, Cleanth's greatest hope was expressed in his final paragraph: "We have in the last few months set up a university senate and have organized the college faculties according to a plan in which I had a hand. The Board has vested in this organization legislative powers with regard to educational policy. In the elections to the various central committees we have had very good luck. The organization is beginning to get good committees appointed and they are beginning to bore in. If this system is not killed, we may come out all right after all."

The hope of the reformers was dashed, however, when the senate took on the dean of the Teachers College. In what was essentially a question of turf, the Teachers College had traditionally required prospective teachers to major in education. (The Phi Beta Kappa report describes the situation as follows: "If the Arts College has sinned in welcoming an unwieldy mass of mediocre students with a heterogeneous collection of course offerings unrelated to its own objectives, it has been sinned against by a Teachers College aggrandizing itself in defiance of tradition, reason, and decorum"; Brooks, *Report*, 39.) The senate wished to change this policy by allowing the future teachers to major in any discipline, so long as they met the requirements for certification. When the dean of the Teachers College complained to General Hodges, it was like a senior officer informing his commander of a mutiny in the ranks. Showing bold and decisive leadership, Hodges simply dissolved the senate. Political interference in the university had been replaced by military occupation.

III

If Cleanth's forays into academic politics bore little fruit locally, his scholarship and criticism were making their mark far from the parochial confines of Baton Rouge. Because of his views on both the nature of poetry and the shape of English literary history, he was in demand as a speaker at major northeastern universities. One of his most important lectures during this period was delivered before the English Institute at Columbia University in 1940. Because his first critical book, *Modern Poetry and the Tradition*, had been published the previous year, Brooks's general position on the nature of poetry was already well known. What he was concerned with on this occasion was the harm that varieties of misreading had done, not to modern verse, but to older works in our literary tradition. The needed corrective is suggested by the title of his talk—"The Poem as Organism: Modern Critical Procedure."

Brooks begins by rejecting the notion that poetry is statement (this rejection would become one of the leitmotifs of his criticism). Unfortunately, poets in the eighteenth century conceived of it as being precisely that. In composing his *Essay on Man*, Pope revised a poetically rich line in order to make a more ostensibly logical statement of fact. Originally, Pope had the poet and his friend: "Expatiate freely o'er this scene of man, / A mighty maze of walks without a plan." The final version reads: "A mighty maze, but not without a plan." In his discussion of this change, which was strongly defended by Dr. Johnson, William Empson argues that Pope has been overly punctilious. Empson believed that Pope's original antithesis "was jaunty and secure because it implied that it was worth looking about, whether the maze had a plan or not; and because in either case, it was possible to understand a great deal about *the scene of man*, merely not by falling into absurdities" (see Brooks, "Poem as Organism," 22).

If eighteenth-century poets often fell prey to a kind of naive literalism, this is a pitfall that has bedeviled critics in virtually all eras. For example, when Shakespeare's Cleopatra implores the asp to untie "this knot intrinsicate / Of life . . . ," far too many scholars gloss "intrisicate" as meaning merely "intricate." I. A. Richards, however, points out that "Shakespeare is bringing together half a dozen meanings from *intrinsic* and *intrinse*," in addition to the various connotations of "intricate" and "involved" (see "Poem as Organism," 23). The difference between an old-line scholar and critic, even one as perceptive as Dr. Johnson, and the new breed of exegetes lies in their different conceptions of language. For Johnson, "words tend to be fixities, hard definite cores of meaning, linked one to another in accordance with fairly exact laws. By contrast, for Empson, words are plastic, their meanings much less definite, and as a consequence the relations among them are almost limitless in their complexity" ("Poem as Organism," 23).

If the new critics differ from the old in their conception of language, both share the conviction that it is possible to speak intelligibly about the craft of poetry. In the Romantic era many readers (one hesitates to call them "critics") came close to rejecting this notion out of reverence for the spontaneity and mystery of poetic composition. Because they are unable or unwilling to speak of poetry as such, these readers turn their attention to the personality of the poet—after all, they reason, the purpose of poetry is to enable the poet to express his emotions. Such a conception, however, is both too narrow and too broad to suit Brooks. It is too narrow because it would exclude the work of poets who were trying to do something other than give vent to private feelings (in *Paradise Lost* Milton was trying to justify the ways of God to Man). It is too broad because people can express their emotions in a variety of ways other than by writing poetry. If sincerity of feeling were the only criterion for judging poetry, a good bit of doggerel would have to be hailed as great verse. Formalist critics, like their neoclassical forebears, believed themselves to be on firmer ground trusting the work and not the maker.

Beyond his growing eminence at professional meetings, the most pervasive mark of Brooks's influence continued to be the way that literature was taught in the college classroom. Not only were *An Approach to Literature* and *Understanding Poetry* successful textbooks in their own right, but they also foreshadowed the direction in which competing textbooks would be heading. Even those that continued to shun a new critical bias, such as James Dow McCallum's *Revised College Omnibus* (1939), began adding more analysis than they had previously deemed necessary.

The success of *Understanding Poetry* was such that in 1943 Brooks and Warren published a companion volume entitled *Understanding Fiction*. In their "Letter to the Teacher" at the beginning of this book, the authors indicate that the teaching of fiction presents different pedagogical problems from the teaching of poetry. For one thing, "most students read some kind of fiction of their own free will and for pleasure," whereas they often have to be forced to read poetry. The difficulty is that their choices in fiction are frequently made for superficial reasons. Even when they abandon formulaic potboilers for high literature, it is likely to be for incidental qualities of theme or subject matter. It is the teacher's duty to enable the student to appreciate the right works for the right reasons.

For the new critics, organic resolution is achieved in fiction much the same way that it is achieved in poetry—through the clash and reconciliation of opposite forces. The dogmatist (or melodramatist) paints a world of black and white with clearly defined heroes and villains. In contrast, the true literary artist (be he poet or fictionist) will depict his world with enough ambiguity that his vision will be earned rather than merely asserted. "The artist is sporting enough to put the best case possible for the opposition. But this is not mere sportsmanship. The artist realizes that, if the opponent—'villain' or 'idea'—is a straw man, the conflict will lack interest" (Brooks and Warren, *Understanding Fiction*, xvii). Although an ironic attitude can lead to "a smug and futile skepticism," this is not what Brooks and Warren endorse. Their ideal reader wants to see the conflicts of the story resolved, "but he does not want it to be too easy or too soon. He wants to see the knockout, but he does not want to see it until the fifteenth round. And, if he feels that the fight has been fixed, he will want to stop at the box office on the way out and demand his money back" (xviii).

It is frequently argued that the new criticism is ideally suited to the analysis of poetry (particularly short poems of the metaphysical or modernist variety) but is less effective when applied to other genres. Because a line-by-line explication of any but the shortest work of fiction would be prohibitively cumbersome, Brooks and Warren are necessarily more general in *Understanding Fiction* than in *Understanding Poetry*. Still, their emphasis is on the disciplines of craft, so much so that their appendix ("Technical Problems and Principles in the Composition of Fiction") can be used in either the literature or the creative writing classroom. Because the *Southern Review* was most noted for its fiction, Brooks and Warren had formed critical principles concerning this genre before they ever undertook a textbook on it (six of the thirty-four stories in *Understanding Fiction* originally appeared in the review).

Their discussion of Hemingway's "The Killers" illustrates the method Brooks and Warren employ in *Understanding Fiction*. They demonstrate that one can divine the meaning of Hemingway's story through nothing more than a careful analysis of the text. After offering four pages of such analysis, however, they ask a much broader question: "What is Hemingway's attitude toward his material?" (*Understanding Fiction*, 320). Answering that question requires a five-page discussion of some of the characteristic themes, situations, and personalities in Hemingway's other works. (Brooks and Warren even compare his philosophy of life to one found in an essay by Robert Louis Stevenson.) Strictly speaking, this may not be an example of biographical criticism, in that Brooks and Warren say nothing about Hemingway's personal life. Nevertheless, to make comparisons between different works by the same author is to go beyond the bounds of a given text. To speak of something as broad as the Hemingway hero or the Hemingway code is to focus on the personality of the author, at least insofar as it is evident in an entire body of work. Such an approach is not inconsistent with the new criticism as long as generalizations are inferred *from* the works rather than imposed *upon* them. There are, of course, such things as a Hemingway hero and a Hemingway code, but they exist for the literary critic only to the extent that they are embodied in individual novels and stories.

IV

In the summer of 1940 the *Southern Review* commemorated the centennial of Thomas Hardy's birth with a special issue devoted exclusively to the British poet and novelist. Although ordinarily such ventures are celebrations of the figure in question, the contributors to the *Southern Review*, were more interested in correcting taste than in singing praise. In a letter to one potential contributor, Cleanth himself put the matter as follows: "Although the mere fact of devoting an issue to Hardy implies a belief in Hardy's importance, it does not imply that only eulogy is appropriate to the occasion; it is hoped, in fact, that the essays collected in this issue will do something toward making a precise definition of his status as an artist, his limitations as well as his achievements." This task was assumed with utmost seriousness by John Crowe Ransom, R. P. Blackmur, Howard Baker, Allen Tate, Morton Dauwen Zabel, W. H. Auden, F. R. Leavis, Bonamy Dobrée, Delmore Schwartz, Katherine Anne Porter, Donald Davidson, Jacques Barzun, Arthur Mizener, and Herbert Muller.

Although Davidson, Mizener, and Muller wrote on Hardy's fiction and Porter on his criticism, the rest of the essays discussed his poetry. Despite genuine admiration for a few of his poems, Hardy was roundly criticized for prolixity, didacticism, and technical lapses. When getting down to specific texts, however, the critics could not agree about which poems represented Hardy at his best. (Leavis picked six poems and Zabel seven, but no single poem appeared on both lists.) If the effect of this special issue was to debunk the reputation of a venerable writer, that was probably not its intention. As Tate notes: "After Thomas Hardy had become a great figure on the British model—that is to say, a personage to whom one makes pilgrimages—criticism of his work languished; . . . critics had very little to say, except that one admired him" (Tate, "Hardy's Philosophical Metaphors," 329). When literary tastes change, it is often our most immediate predecessors whose stock plunges the most. Having been in his grave only twelve years, Thomas Hardy seemed less contemporary than a figure as historically remote as John Donne.

In its issue of June 10, 1940, *Time* magazine noted that "Neither in the little old town of Dorchester, where he lived, worked and died, nor in London, where his ashes rest in Westminster Abbey, was the anniversary [of Hardy's birth] marked so impressively as it was in Baton Rouge, Louisiana" (*Time*, "Wessex," 92). "More exacting than the *Yale Review*," *Time* continues, "less staid than the *Virginia Quarterly*, richer than Ohio's new *Kenyon Review, The Southern Review* has applied no standards save excellence, has been subject to no political pressure whatever." Calling the essays in the Hardy memorial issue "the most discerning criticism of Hardy's verse and fiction that has ever appeared," the article goes on to say that the contributors to this issue "testify to the breadth and integrity of U.S. literary talent. And they prove, if any proof was necessary, that there exists in the U.S. a national community of scholars and artists alive to their own time and country, and capable of preserving the traditions of the West" (94).

As the *Southern Review* continued to grow in international esteem, its nominal editor, Charles W. Pipkin, became increasingly disengaged from the operation of the magazine. One might attribute this to his responsibilities as graduate dean, except that Pipkin's performance there was slipping as well. Those who observed him on a daily basis knew that Pip was a sick man who had lost his intellectual dynamism and his self-confidence. He was hitting the bottle pretty hard, and as a result became ever more quarrelsome and paranoid. On one occasion, he accused Cleanth and Red of taking the magazine away from him. In an attempt to mollify his mentor, Cleanth offered to let Pip have complete control of the next issue. That wouldn't do, Pip replied, the deadline was too soon for him to line up contributors. Cleanth then offered to let him have any future issue he wanted. Neither of them mentioned the matter again.

If Pipkin's drinking was evident to quite a few people on campus, the reasons for it were not. Despite his professional brilliance, Pip's personal life was deeply unhappy. Although he was rumored to be having an affair with a female law professor, he was never able to remain exclusively heterosexual for very long. Although did his best to stay in the closet while in Baton Rouge, the out-of-town debaucheries of this "friend to men" became more frequent and harder to disguise. While serving as a visiting lecturer at Columbia University in 1931–32, Pip roomed with Vann Woodward, a fellow Arkansan who was pursuing graduate study. According to Woodward's biographer, John Herbert Roper, "Pipkin was drinking heavily and was both promiscuous and ambivalent in his sexual life. The source of so much excitement about scholarship and reform back in Arkansas and Louisiana was in New York essentially a playboy" (Roper, 52). In fact, Pipkin was so intent on concealing the side of his personality that Woodward had seen that he paid his young friend's passage to Europe, hoping that Vann would remain silent about what he had seen and heard in New York.

At his best, Pipkin was frequently unconventional—consider his unorthodox strategy for bringing Brooks and Warren to Baton Rouge—and at times he could be downright weird. When Warren was still teaching at Vanderbilt, Pip wrote to ask if he could stop by when he was in Nashville. After dinner, he mentioned the possibility of LSU's involvement with the *Southwest Review.* "But along the way in the conversation Pipkin asked if Warren had any new poems handy. This seemed a trifle odd, or polite, for Pipkin had not shown any previous interest in Warren's poetry or other contemporary poetry. . . . After a little time with the new poem, Pipkin said that he would like to print it in the *Southwest Review.* . . . He would like to pay for the poem now and collect from the *Southwest Review* later. He produced fifteen dollars" (Brooks and Warren, "Original," 36). Warren cannot remember whether the poem ever appeared in the *Southwest Review,* much less if Pipkin was compensated by its editors.

Cleanth recalls that Pipkin's drinking and his homosexuality became more pronounced after a Louisiana girl he was courting rejected his proposal of marriage. Although his friends were tempted to believe that things might have turned out better for Pipkin had he married this girl, it is debatable that he could have been saved by a good woman's love. In any event, his health worsened during the summer of 1941, and on August 4 of that year, he died of a heart attack in the Hotel Dieu Hospital in New Orleans. The following day, Red Warren sent a letter to Cleanth Brooks and John Palmer from Chapala, Italy, which began as follows:

> You can well imagine my shock this afternoon when I went to the hotel for my mail and found a telegram telling of Pipkin's death. It came from his secretary, and gave no information beyond the statement that he was to be cremated in Memphis this morning. . . . The whole thing has been a sad, bitter, nasty business, and I suppose that this is the predictable end—at least, it is the one which has been predicted for some time. Heart attack or stroke or suicide or the case of pneumonia. My one-time feelings for him have long since been converted into the feelings which we have shared; and now I only have the thought that he is probably a lot better off than he was.

When Jean Stafford heard the news of Pipkin's passing, her pronouncement was even more severe than Warren's. "A more terrible spectacle than [Pipkin's] life I cannot imagine," she wrote to her confidante Robert Hightower. "I had actually seen him not above a week ago and had known, minutely, what his life had been for the last 10 years—impotent intellectually, homosexual, perpetually drunk and [I] considered how this person

I had seen, being eased into a car like an old man, the color of leather from jaundice, was perhaps at this moment being judged" (see Roberts, 202). Whatever the divine verdict may have been, those who knew Pipkin in this world mourned the youthful promise that had been cut short long before his death at age forty-one. He had been instrumental in sending Cleanth to Oxford and in bringing both Cleanth and Red to Baton Rouge. For those reasons alone, the *Southern Review* would not have been possible without him, even if its excellence owed little to his direct efforts. It was a legacy that would outlive him by less than a year.

V

It is an irony of literary history that the fortunes of the *Southern Review* rose and fell with those of the Long machine. The money that launched the review and sustained it through its early years had come from James Monroe Smith. Although Smith's departure did not discredit the enterprise, it deprived the magazine of its most powerful institutional patron. (Paul Hebert realized the inherent value of the review and the good that it was doing for the reputation of the university, but his tenure as acting president was relatively brief.) When Campbell Hodges took over, his primary mission was to restore the fiscal integrity of the university in both fact and appearance. The question was not whether the *Southern Review* was a good magazine but whether LSU considered it worth supporting in the manner to which it had become accustomed.

Outside the English department, quite a few professors and administrators had long seen the review as an expensive luxury. President Smith had tried to build support for the magazine by distributing it free to the faculty, but the effect was to make it seem to many like another piece of university junk mail. Even the good notices the review received cut both ways. For all it did to enhance the image of the university, the magazine also inspired envy on the part of colleagues who were not being lionized in the press. Professors who published without pay in academic journals could not understand why the *Southern Review* compensated its contributors from university funds. (Conversely, those who wrote for the review often could not understand why it took so long for them to get their checks.) When they began seeing the names of LSU students and faculty (including occasionally those of the magazine's editors) among the contributors to the review, some in the university suspected cronyism and demanded an investigation.

In one of his last decisions as acting president, Paul Hebert convened a committee to consider some questions about the financial dealings of the *Southern Review*. Perhaps in reaction to the excesses of the Long era, the bean counters were now in ascendancy. In its report, issued on February 8, 1941, the committee urged much stricter control over the distribution of complimentary and sample copies of the magazine and questioned the propriety of the editors accepting compensation for their own contributions to the review. This second point drew a spirited response from Brooks and Warren, who quite understandably felt that their integrity was under attack. If the editors could be trusted to judge the manuscripts of others, they reasoned that they could also judge the value of their own work; because they were capable of publishing in much better paying periodicals, they were hardly profiteering off the university. Having established what they considered to be an important principle, Brooks and Warren agreed voluntarily to refrain from publishing any more of their own writing in the *Southern Review*.

With the appointment of General Hodges on July 1, 1941, it was not just the policies but the very existence of the review that was being questioned. Early in the fall semester the editors were informed that their magazine might well be suspended indefinitely; within months that prospect became even more likely because of events far from Baton Rouge. On the first Sunday in December, when Cleanth was visiting his parents, his sister-in-law called to inform him that the Japanese had bombed Pearl Harbor. Although the attack itself shocked the world, it had seemed likely for some time that America would go to war. When Cleanth had visited Germany a decade earlier, while on holiday from Oxford, Nazism was still so much of a national joke that he had declined his landlady's offer to show him Hitler's headquarters. Now that the future of civilization itself was being threatened by this demented Austrian paperhanger, life would be changed both abroad and at home. Male students and faculty of a certain age (Cleanth included) quickly became subject to the military draft; the economy began gearing up for war, and many peacetime activities were reexamined. (There was even talk of suspending major league baseball!) In such an atmosphere, with a major general at the helm of the university, a mere literary magazine seemed more of a frill than ever.

It remains an open question whether the review could have continued had it been willing to make greater concessions to wartime austerity. (What Cleanth and Red did not realize at the time was that LSU profited from the war by teaching military personnel in a program financed by the federal government.) Although Brooks and Warren offered to reduce costs by eliminating one sixteen-page signature per issue, they were adamant that further reductions would radically change the character and quality of the magazine. Reducing the rate of payment would limit their potential contributors, and increasing the price of each issue probably would lose as much money as it would gain by decreasing the number of subscribers.

While this debate raged, intercollegiate sports continued as it had in the heyday of Huey Long, and the team's tiger mascot continued to live in a heated cage and enjoy choice cuts of meat. In fact, the cost of supporting the tiger was nearly as great as the cost of supporting the review. But then, Mike the Tiger had never signed a letter criticizing the university administration or issued a report questioning the fitness of LSU to sponsor a Phi Beta Kappa chapter. Hodges was too new on the job to hold any grudges against the dissident Nineteen, but many who were advising him did. (The only deans to vote against killing the *Southern Review* were Paul Hebert, now back in the law school, and Colonel Troy H. Middleton, dean of administration and future president of the university.) As Hodges told Cleanth, "I either have to do what my deans advise me to do or get new deans."

As a kind of swan song, the winter 1941–42 *Southern Review* was among the best issues of any literary magazine ever published. Devoted entirely to discussions of William Butler Yeats, it included essays by R. P. Blackmur, L. C. Knights, T. S. Eliot (in his only appearance in the magazine), F. O. Matthiessen, Delmore Schwartz, Horace Gregory, Donald Davidson, John Crowe Ransom, Kenneth Burke, Morton Dauwen Zabel, Allen Tate, Arthur Mizener, Austin Warren, Howard Baker, and Randall Jarrell.[5] The enthusiastic response to this issue was tempered by Brooks and Warren's announcement in their editorial that the magazine would probably suspend publication with the spring 1942 issue. They expressed gratitude to the administration of LSU for its financial support and its "understanding of the ends to which the *Review* has attempted to dedicate itself." "The editors are confident," they concluded, "that the magazine's contributors and readers will share with them this feeling of gratitude, but they are also confident that the contributors and readers will agree with the administration and with the editors that the pursuit of these ends, in times such as these, must be curtailed" (Brooks and Warren, "Editorial" [Winter 1941–42]).

Unfortunately, what was meant as irony was so understated that many readers assumed that Cleanth and Red had gone down without a fight.

Allen Tate expressed his consternation in a letter to Andrew Lytle, dated January 26, 1942:

> Part of my time, a large part, since I got back from [the convention of the Modern Language Association in] Indianapolis has been spent working up publicity about the *Southern Review*. So far we've got editorials and articles in *The Nation*, the *New Republic*, and *Time*. And in Indianapolis I got a petition up with 231 names to the President of LSU. (By the way, I saw it passed to Knickerbocker, and he refused to sign it.) We were seriously hampered at first by the preposterous statement of the editors announcing the suspension. We've had to tell everybody that the editors didn't really mean that they agreed with the university policy. The announcement is a perfect example of Cleanth's humorless political intrigues. (See T. D. Young and Sarcone, 178)

In its meeting of March 10, 1942, the LSU Board of Supervisors officially suspended support for the *Southern Review* and the two other magazines sponsored by the university (the *Journal of Southern History* and the *National Mathematics Magazine*). The widespread publicity generated by Tate and other friends of the review had gone for naught. Because the magazine had been supported almost entirely by LSU, its only hope of survival lay in finding alternative sources of funding. The John Simon Guggenheim Foundation, the Rockefeller Foundation, the Carnegie Corporation, and the Rosenwald Fund all expressed sympathy but offered no money. Agnes Scott College in Decatur, Georgia, thought about acquiring the magazine but could not come up with the funding. The only hope that was left was some kind of merger with the *Kenyon Review*.

The possibility of such a merger was broached by John Crowe Ransom when he first heard rumors of the demise of the *Southern Review*. The arrangement would have had LSU paying Kenyon to fill the unexpired subscriptions to the Baton Rouge journal (the money otherwise would have to be refunded to subscribers). A joint magazine, with a neutral title, would be published at Gambier with the editorial assistance of at least one of the old *Southern Review* editors. LSU would provide no operating subsidy, only a course off from teaching for the Baton Rouge editor and modest secretarial help. Although such a solution would have been quite favorable to LSU, Hodges apparently wanted the university out of the magazine business entirely and uncharacteristically vetoed the recommendation of his advisers, who thought the merger a good idea.

The original series of the *Southern Review* ended in the spring of 1942 with a 258-page issue in which the editors published their accumulation of accepted manuscripts. At the same time, they were forced to return many excellent submissions on which they had yet to pass judgment. This was all done even as "the painters and floor sanders began to take possession of the *Southern Review* offices, stacking files and furniture in the corridors" (Cutrer, 251). Cleanth remembers quite vividly the day that a couple of burly janitors came in and emptied the records of seven years in giant waste drums. The man who knew MacArthur showed as much sensitivity in dealing with these documents as he had in reducing to scrap metal the two ten-pound Parrott rifles General Sherman had captured at Charleston in 1865 and bequeathed to the university in 1868. Discovering where the files were dumped, Cleanth grabbed a flashlight one sweltering summer night, crawled up into the attic of Allen Hall, and salvaged for posterity what was left of the *Southern Review*.

CHAPTER ELEVEN

The Mating Dance

Just as the *Southern Review* was valued more highly in the literary world at large than it was in Baton Rouge, so too were Brooks and Warren more greatly honored the farther away they were from LSU. That was probably one of the reasons why Red managed to be away as much as he could. Not only was he gone during the summers, teaching in Colorado or writing in Italy, he also had a sabbatical for the academic year 1939–40 and unpaid leave for the spring of 1941. If LSU basked in the reflected glory of his growing literary reputation, it benefited only intermittently from his presence on campus. Still, Red liked much about Baton Rouge and wanted to stay there, provided he could get the recognition he deserved. That seemed to be happening up through 1936, when he and Cleanth were promoted to associate professor. But for the next six years, both men appeared to be on an academic treadmill. The textbooks that bore the names of Brooks and Warren were being adopted across the nation; their critical writings were changing the way that people looked at literature, and the *Southern Review* was winning international praise. But still, Cleanth and Red were unable to win elevation to the same rank as senior deadwood such as Bradshear and Uhler.

The available information suggests that Cleanth and Red had the support of Read and Kirby and the majority of their colleagues, but that their promotions to full professor were continually blocked by the upper administration. No doubt the worsening Depression and the political chaos in both the state and university made the late thirties and early forties an unpropitious time for professional advancement. Nevertheless, the record of those years was one of broken promises. In a letter to Paul Hebert sent from Rome on March 7, 1940, Warren wrote:

The situation is this. Mr. Cleanth Brooks and I, with the permission of
Dr. Read, had an informal talk last winter with Dr. Smith on the subject of
our promotion. At that time Dr. Smith said that he would look into the
matter and would give us some word on it during the spring. Later, in the
spring, I saw Dr. Smith in connection with another matter, but the subject
of the promotion was again raised. . . . He replied, "The promotions are
on the books for next year"—that is, for 1940. I then asked him if I could,
with confidence, proceed on that assumption. He said, "Yes, definitely."[1]

On April 2, William A. Read officially recommended to Dean Fred Frey
that both Cleanth and Red be promoted to full professor with a raise from
$3,600 to $3,800. Once again, the answer was "not this year."

By 1942, Red had had enough. With the *Southern Review* on its way
out and his status on campus still in neutral, he accepted a $200 raise and
an appointment as director of creative writing at the University of Minnesota. The offer, which LSU refused to match, carried with it the rank of
full professor. That same year, Cleanth finally received his long overdue
promotion and a salary of $3,895 (he didn't make it to $4,000 until
1944). His joy was considerably lessened, however, by the loss of the
Southern Review and the departure of his friend and collaborator. Even
as he was himself getting feelers from other schools, Cleanth was keenly
aware of his continuing responsibility to two parents who had now lived
in Baton Rouge longer than anywhere else in their adult lives.

One measure of Cleanth's growing reputation was the increasing demand for his services on other campuses. In addition to tentative inquiries
about permanent relocation, there was a steady stream of invitations to
lecture, as well as opportunities for guest appointments. In 1941 he taught
summer school at the University of Texas; in 1942, with the *Southern Review* a thing of the past, he headed north to Ann Arbor for the summer
session at the University of Michigan. The contrast couldn't have been
more striking. If the LSU administration considered him a troublesome
dissident and his literary activities of only marginal importance, the students and officials at Michigan treated Cleanth as if he were an academic
celebrity. It was during this summer session that he tested several of the
readings that found their way into *The Well Wrought Urn* in 1947. As a
consequence, he dedicated that book to the students in his summer course.

By freeing him to publish more widely, the suspension of the *Southern
Review* probably enhanced Cleanth's marketability within the academic
world. The void that had been created at LSU also presented an opportunity for some other publication to take the place of the Baton Rouge quar-

terly. Unfortunately, that prospect was not immediately apparent. Upon hearing rumors of the review's impending demise, Allen Tate described the situation in nearly apocalyptic terms. In a letter dated December 26, 1941, he wrote to Cleanth: "John has gone off after positivism and aesthetics: the Kenyon is only a branch of philosophy or rapidly becoming that. The Partisan was never very good; it too will probably fold up or be suppressed. With the passing of the SR the kind of literary criticism that we have all been interested in is liquidated. . . . It is a calamity of the first order." In less than a year, Alexander Guerry, Vice Chancellor of the University of the South, would set out to reverse that calamity.

Although the University of the South had supported the *Sewanee Review* for fifty years, the magazine had always been of erratic quality. Under William S. Knickerbocker it had declined, even as Knickerbocker's personal behavior made him an increasingly objectionable presence on campus. With Knickerbocker on the verge of forced retirement or resignation, Guerry dreamed of making the *Sewanee Review* into the sort of magazine that might rival the *Kenyon Review* and take the place of the *Southern Review*. All that was needed to bring this about was the right editor. On the recommendation of Andrew Lytle, who was then teaching at the Sewanee Military Academy, Guerry offered the job to Allen Tate. When Tate initially declined the position, Guerry set his sights on Cleanth Brooks.

Convinced that Cleanth was the man for the job, Guerry sent him a telegram on July 28, 1942, urging him to assume the editorship of the review. This was followed by a meeting in Chicago on July 31. Although Cleanth did not want the position, Guerry was reluctant to take "no" for an answer. He wrote letters to Cleanth on August 5 and 12, sent him a second telegram on August 14, spoke with him on the phone on August 16, and followed up with a third letter on August 18. All that he got for his trouble was Cleanth's agreement to have his name appear in the magazine as "associate editor." With Knickerbocker gone, the acting editor of the review was T. S. Long, a professor in Sewanee's English department, but the real force behind the refurbished magazine was Andrew Lytle, who had been cajoled into assuming the post of managing editor.

Cleanth's reasons for rejecting the editorship of the *Sewanee Review* are not difficult to fathom. Despite Guerry's enthusiasm for the review, literary magazines were an endangered commodity at this time. Although President Gordon Chalmers had brought Ransom to Gambier to edit the *Kenyon Review* only a few years earlier, that magazine was now facing financial setbacks. In January 1942, when the possible merger of the *Ken-*

yon and *Southern* reviews was being discussed, Ransom informed Red Warren that the Ohio magazine was on a reduced budget and might actually be discontinued (it was already paying half its former rates and trying to get by with a student secretary). Tate had turned down the editorship of the *Sewanee Review* largely because it did not pay its contributors, and that issue had yet to be resolved. Cleanth was understandably reluctant to step into a situation that Tate had found unacceptable and one that might conceivably pose some of the same problems he had recently faced in Baton Rouge.

These objections might very well have been outweighed had Cleanth been eager to get back into editing or to make a long-term commitment to Sewanee. Neither was the case. Had the *Southern Review* been continued, Cleanth probably would have remained with it indefinitely; now that it was gone, a burden had been lifted from him. Even as he had fought for the merger of the *Kenyon* and *Southern* reviews, he had told Hodges that from a personal standpoint he almost preferred that the merger not happen. Given the demands that his editorial labors had made on his time and energy, he was not at all certain that he had gained more than he had lost. Once the *Southern Review* was gone, Cleanth began doing other work that would have to be put aside were he to take over another magazine. He had also reached a point in his career when he could reasonably expect to receive other offers of employment. Even if the Sewanee position had been an improvement over his situation in Baton Rouge, it was not the best he could hope for. Rather than using Sewanee as a stepping stone to something else, Cleanth was content to bide his time at LSU until he was ready to make a permanent career move.

I

Although he never published a full-length survey of contemporaneous criticism, Brooks's various essays and reviews establish both his affinities with and differences from the other major critics writing in English. (René Wellek believes that one of Brooks's most enduring legacies is as a "critic of critics.") Typically generous to those with whom he disagrees, he readily concedes the strengths of an opponent's argument and strives whenever possible to find common ground. At the same time, he does not shrink from defending his own position or pointing out the erroneous assumptions of others. Although many readers are familiar with Brooks's spirited polemics in *The Well Wrought Urn*, some of his most discerning and judicious criticism of other critics is contained in two unanthologized essays from the early forties—one dealing entirely with William Empson, the other primarily with Yvor Winters.

Brooks's piece on Empson, which appeared in the summer 1944 issue of *Accent*, is filled with genuine admiration for the British critic. He notes the attack on Empson's (and, by implication, his own) critical method comes from two radically different sources—the impressionists, who believe that we murder to dissect, and the pedants, who believe that the meaning of a poem can never be known until all possible scholarship has been exhausted. Empson inadvertently made himself vulnerable to the former camp when he said of poetic analysis that "it has made something which seemed to me magical into something that seems to me sensible" (see "Empson's Criticism," 213). Is Empson then denying that the appeal of poetry is to the feelings or doubting that its glory lies in its magic? Not necessarily. "What the conventional critic tends to take refuge in," Brooks writes, "is a kind of *black* magic: it is secret, dark, and not to be peered into. But poetry, fortunately, is a white magic, and the more closely that we look into it the better. Its 'magic' has nothing to fear from the closest inspection" ("Empson's Criticism," 214).

Those who would delay criticism until the work of the scholar is done are also fundamentally mistaken. Scholarship will always go on as new facts are discovered, and those facts will inevitably alter literary judgments. But if we wait until all facts are known, no critical judgment would ever be made. As any reader of Eliot's "Tradition and the Individual Talent" knows, literary history is as much a product of the critic as of the scholar. When critical theories and literary tastes change, the tradition itself is altered. Scholarship may give us a better understanding of Milton, but scholars wouldn't be studying Milton in the first place if there had not been a *critical* judgment that his poetry was worthy of attention. That critics sometimes get their facts wrong means that they are human, not that they are engaging in a worthless endeavor.

In his discussion of Yvor Winters (published in the Spring 1944 issue of the *Kenyon Review*), Brooks finds much less to admire than he did in his essay on William Empson. Certainly, Winters is to be praised for his attempt to talk sense about poetry and to correct deficient taste (the book under consideration is *The Anatomy of Nonsense*, published in 1943). The problem is that Winters's specific judgments are far different from those that other critics might reach by applying the same principles. "It does very little good to agree on a theory of the relations of color," Brooks writes, "if one person is continually turning up with green where others see red, or blue, where they see yellow" ("Cantankerous," 284).

Almost as substantial as his differences with Winters are Brooks's disagreements with John Crowe Ransom. (Brooks will challenge the positions of both Winters and Ransom in *The Well Wrought Urn*.) To see how fundamentally Brooks and Ransom diverged in their conceptions of poetry, one need only compare the implicit premises of "Shakespeare at Sonnets" with those of "The Reading of Modern Poetry," a paper that Brooks and Warren delivered before the Modern Language Association in Richmond, Virginia, in December 1936. (That the *Southern Review* published Ransom's essay, while Ransom chaired the panel at which Brooks and Warren read their paper, suggests the collegiality that persisted in the midst of these theoretical arguments.)

"The Reading of Modern Poetry" is at least as much about varieties of misreading. At the outset, Brooks and Warren list fourteen specious objections often raised against modern poetry. Rather than examining each of these individually, the authors subsume them under two large categories— stock responses to poetry in general and associations derived from one's personal history (the influence of Richards's *Practical Criticism* is evident here). "These two general types of misreading," they write, "grow out of the same fundamental misconception of the nature of a poem. This misconception neglects the fact that a poem, in so far as it is successful, is a unified construct, a psychological whole; and since a poem is an organism it is not only greater than, but different from, the sum of its parts" (Brooks and Warren, "Reading," 438–39).

Although Ransom would not have denied that a poem should possess organic unity, his theory tended toward a dualism of form and content (his preferred terms were *structure* and *texture*). Whereas Ransom, in "Shakespeare at Sonnets," praises only the dramatic effectiveness of Macbeth's "Tomorrow" soliloquy, Brooks and Warren laud it as poetry. Those who think that poetry should present only beautiful and pleasing pictures would hardly approve of the image of an idiot slobbering and mouthing. "But anyone alive to the meaning of the image [i.e., anyone who understands poetry] realizes that the poetic force lies in the horror of this brute parody of the human and rational" (440).

One of the stock responses that encourages the misreading of poetry (particularly modern poetry) is the expectation of a logical progression of imagery. Brooks and Warren note that one critic (obviously Ransom, although they do not mention him by name) "considers it a deadly attack on some modern poems to say that the parts of a poem 'form a psycho-logical, not a logical unity.' " The answer to this is that "every successful poem creates a *psychological* unity, and not even the simplest metaphor fails to violate a *logical* unity. The distinction between the two kinds of unity is extremely important: psychological unity is the aim of every poem; logical unity is a device to achieve this aim, and may or may not be used" (442). It is this theoretical position, not a blind adoration of Shake-speare, that must have accounted for the reservations Brooks and Warren expressed toward Ransom's argument in "Shakespeare at Sonnets."

II

Cleanth Brooks was thirty-five years old when the Japanese bombed Pearl Harbor. In addition to his age and his weak eyesight, his family respon-sibilities ought to have been sufficient to exempt him from military ser-vice. But as the war became more desperate, the selective service became less selective. By early 1943, Cleanth had been classified 1-A, and the prospects of his entering the Army seemed likelier with each passing day. On March 2, 1943, Tommy Kirby sent a notarized letter to Presi-dent Roosevelt appealing the 1-A classification and pointing out the spe-cial circumstances of Cleanth's family situation. He concluded by saying, "Mr. Brooks's case impresses me as one in which the usual provisions for dependency will prove highly inadequate unless we assume that our gov-ernment intends that not only a wife incapable of support but also aged parents should feel the full impact of the war in a way not expected of most citizens." [2]

As cogent as Kirby's reasoning may have seemed, the draft board was not prepared to excuse Cleanth for reasons of family responsibility. It was only after seriously elevated blood pressure was discovered during his draft physical that he was declared temporarily unfit for military ser-vice. Although he treated the blood pressure with medication and was technically subject to recall, the government made do with younger and healthier warriors. If being free of military obligation removed one worry, the health condition that earned him that freedom created additional problems for Cleanth. His stoic imperturbability was such that even close friends were prone to underestimate the stress of his situation at LSU. The political battles within the department and the university and the struggle to maintain the *Southern Review* had all taken their toll. Moreover, as he saw his father deteriorate physically during the last decade of his life, Cleanth was painfully aware that high blood pressure ran in the family.

In describing the elder Brooks's condition to President Roosevelt, Kirby wrote: "I believe very sincerely that, if Mr. Brooks leaves his father for any lengthy period, it will materially hasten his death." In fact, the situation was graver than Kirby or anyone else realized. Less than four weeks after the draft appeal was written, Cleanth Brooks, Sr., was dead. In the obituary that appeared in the annual report of the Louisiana Conference for 1943, W. E. Trice writes: "Through suffering the depth and strength of a man's spirit is tested. No man could have met this test more nobly and triumphantly than Dr. [sic] Cleanth Brooks. Always this was a gentle spirit, but he became even more kindly, courteous, patient, and understanding as the last years and days of his life slipped away. . . . His memory will continue to guide and bless those who were privileged to know him during the days of his active ministry; and the courage of his unconquerable spirit will inspire all those who knew him during those tragic days of his suffering" (Trice, 81).

Cleanth, Jr.'s, love and respect for his father were due to more than a mere filial devotion. Cleanth, Sr., had been responsible for his son's early love of learning and had guided his childhood education. One could hardly have asked for a better moral or intellectual model. And yet, there was something tragically incomplete about the elder Brooks's life. A sense of his vocational frustration can be gleaned from an undated letter he typed on the stationery of the Noel Memorial Church in Shreveport, which was the next to the last pastorate in which he would serve. "My life at Noel has been a cruel disappointment," he writes. "There has been a diffidence that could be felt, like the Egyptian darkness. I never quite so well knew what was the significance of the name of the wife of Giant Despair. . . . When a man is speaking out of his heart the things that the Spirit moves in his heart, and when he expects the Spirit to move in other hearts, and then the Spirit seems to be dumb in others, there is a feeling that the diffidence is not only an antagonism to you but to the Spirit himself."

The controversy in question has long since been forgotten. All that is left is the tension between human bitterness and unquestioning faith that is evident in virtually every sentence of this tortured epistle.

> As I write here in a very crucial hour, I do not know what the result of this meeting will be. It may humanly speaking be the determining point in all my ministry, and in all my living. It does anew and seriously raise the ques-

tion of dependence on Almighty God. My prayer is to Him as the God of
my life. Yet the thing that I would choose, that seems so clear to me, that
seems so just that it looks as if any other course would be rank injustice
sufficient to sink any institution—that course may not be best. I am pray-
ing that I may be in His gracious keeping, that His leadership may be
for me and mine and that I may be able to pray in faith the old prayer
"Choose our changes for us."[3]

It has often been remarked that one should never take the vow of poverty without also taking the vow of celibacy, as the burden of a religious
calling ought not to be imposed on a man's family. Because the Reverend
Mr. Brooks was a Protestant clergyman, his family did bear the burden of
his vocation. They lived from hand to mouth during the years of his ministry and assumed responsibility for his care when the church cut him
loose. (His accomplishments had been rewarded with neither adequate
recognition nor a living wage.) Shortly before his own death, Cleanth, Jr.,
dreamed about his father. The senior Brooks came to him, his pockets
sagging from a heavy weight. When Cleanth asked him for money, the
Reverend Mr. Brooks began pulling large silver coins from those pockets,
emptying them handful after handful at his son's feet.[4]

None of his three sons followed Brother Brooks into the ministry,
and only Cleanth, Jr., chose a white collar career. John Kirkby ("Jack")
Brooks, who was the product of his father's marriage to May Browder,
left Tennessee for Arizona, where he became a cowboy and later a rancher.
He was a rugged man who fought wildcats, but he also designed an intricate cattle brand and classified the plants on his ranch according to a system of his own devising. Jack told cowboy stories that entertained not only
his own children but his nieces and nephews as well (late in life, Cleanth
tried unsuccessfully to have them published). Cleanth's full brother, Bill
Brooks, traveled even farther west, pursuing the American Dream all the
way to California, where he enjoyed a long and rewarding career as an
automobile mechanic.

III

During the academic year 1945–46 Cleanth was on leave from LSU to
accept a visiting appointment at the University of Chicago. For more
than a decade, the dominant personality at that institution had been its
brilliant and controversial president Robert Maynard Hutchins. A man
more different from Campbell Hodges could hardly be imagined. Called

"the boy wonder," sometimes with admiration and sometimes with contempt, Hutchins had moved from the deanship of the Yale Law School to the Chicago presidency at age thirty. Although Chicago at that time was a prestigious research university, which emphasized empiricism and modern thought, Hutchins distrusted both.

With the assistance of his acerbic protégé Mortimer Adler, Hutchins began to fashion an undergraduate curriculum based on the Great Books model. When the sociologist Edward Shils arrived on campus in the early 1930s, he "began to hear rumors that Hutchins was seeking to impose scholastic philosophy on the University of Chicago, that he wished to suppress the social sciences, that he wished to put down science and reduce scientific study to the study of the classical scientific writings of antiquity and early modern times" (Shils, 212). Given the fondness of Hutchins and Adler for Thomistic philosophy, observers quipped that at the University of Chicago, "Jewish professors teach Roman Catholicism to Protestant students!" (see Shils, 220).

Hutchins's influence in the English department was felt largely through the presence of Richard McKeon, who was brought to Chicago at Adler's urging to head the Humanities Division. McKeon, Elder Olson, Norman Maclean, and R. S. Crane formed the nucleus of a group known as the "Chicago critics." In their reverence for Aristotle (or their own eccentric interpretation of the *Poetics*), the Chicago critics staked out a position similar to that of the Vanderbilt critics in intention, but radically different in approach. The disagreements between Cleanth Brooks and Ronald Crane, which—on Crane's part—were vigorously stated in print, did not damage their personal friendship (Crane had been instrumental in bringing Brooks to Chicago). But the more Cleanth tried to operate within the prescribed Chicago curriculum, the more dissatisfied he became. The emphasis on logic and metaphysics was all well and good for a philosophy course, but Cleanth was convinced that there was a point at which literary criticism needed to move beyond theory and to deal with individual literary texts. That wasn't happening at Chicago.

Marshall McLuhan, who corresponded frequently with Cleanth at this time, was deeply disappointed with the program at Chicago. Viewing the history of Western education from medieval times to the present as a battle between the dialecticians and the rhetoricians, McLuhan saw himself and the southern critics he most admired as defenders of the rhetorical tradition. Unfortunately, with the ascendancy of empirical science, American universities were largely controlled by dialecticians. (What was even more alarming than the preeminence of science was the extent to which scientific epistemology was corrupting the traditional humanistic disciplines.) Although Hutchins seemed to be making a stand for rhetoric at Chicago, McLuhan believed that too many of the administrators charged with carrying out his policies were dialecticians at heart.

In a letter dated February 17, 1946, Marshall wrote to Cleanth: "Today arrived offprints of a paper I'd forgotten about. Perhaps a few extra copies may be of use to you, so I'm sending 9 under separate cover. The subject is Hutchins." The paper in question was "An Ancient Quarrel in Modern America," published in the January 1946 issue of the *Classical Journal*. Although it dealt only with the theoretical arguments for and against the Chicago program, Marshall's letters to Cleanth are quite candid about the program's practical shortcomings. On May 10, 1945, he characterizes "the adolescent *Philosophes* of Chicago" as "a parcel of non-contemporary minds." Evidently referring to a recently completed critique of the Chicago program, McLuhan writes on March 29, 1946: "I came increasingly to feel that Hutchins was beyond any hope from our point of view, and my tone, therefore, became uncompromising. I'm sure that he'll put this in the hands of Adler, McKeon, and Crane, but nothing is to be gained by playing ball with those lads. Intimidation might work, provided there was enough scope to it."

No doubt Cleanth's unhappiness in Chicago was personal as well as philosophical. After more than a decade of marriage, he was once again living the lonely life of a bachelor. His relationship with Tinkum was as affectionate as ever, but for some time she had been needed in Baton Rouge, where she was helping to run her father's lumber business as it faced the special demands of war. (In a letter to Red the previous spring, Cleanth wrote: "Tinkum has been working very hard at her father's plant. She's up at six and usually doesn't get home until about six in the afternoon. We have had no social life to speak of for months. By the weekend we are too tired and sleepy to do much more than catch up on sleep.") As Cleanth recalls, Tinkum would look after her father's business for a few weeks, then come up to Chicago to look after him.

The loneliness of this long-distance relationship is apparent in the letters that Tinkum sent to Cleanth. In one of these, she writes: "Cleanth, my precious darling, . . . I've spent the last few days keeping a stiff upper lip missing you terribly and wanting to go to you, but trying to keep my private griefs out of the general trouble pool." On another occasion, Cleanth's absentmindedness threatened possible financial trouble.

Tinkum writes: "I got your letter today, with the insurance stuff & will take care of it. You mention including a signed check·on the Chicago bank. There was no check in the letter. I can handle it through the B. R. [Baton Rouge] bank, but I hope the signed blank check hasn't gone astray." By the end of winter quarter, the cold weather, the marital isolation, and the uncongenial curriculum had taken their toll on Cleanth. After informing the officials at Chicago that he would not finish out the year, he headed south to Tinkum and the Louisiana spring.[5]

IV

The intellectual hostility between the Chicago neo-Aristotelians and the Nashville critics might at first seem puzzling. The Chicagoans shared almost all of the negative prejudices of the new critics, along with the fervent belief that only an intrinsic or ontological approach to literature would do. In fact, the apparent affinities between the two groups were such that in "Criticism, Inc.," John Crowe Ranson said of his Chicago counterpart that if criticism were to gain acceptance in the universities, "the credit would probably go to Professor Ronald S. Crane . . . more than to any other man" (Ransom, *Essays*, 95). Despite this olive branch, the Nashville and Chicago schools never really joined forces to overthrow the reigning establishment. They were too busy attacking each other like Bolsheviks and Mensheviks.

One of the earliest and most measured attempts to differentiate the neo-Aristotelian approach from that of the new critics was Hoyt Trowbridge's "Aristotle and the 'New Criticism,' " published in the autumn 1944 issue of the *Sewanee Review*. According to Trowbridge, the true Aristotelian "considers the poem, in its internal character, as an autonomous thing. It is conceived as a whole made up of parts; the analysis distinguishes the parts, the material constituents out of which the work is made, and establishes the principle of their unification—the 'form' or governing principle which determines the order and connection of the parts and unites them in a single coherent whole" (Trowbridge, 547). One might conclude from their emphasis on textual analysis that Brooks and the other new critics were attempting the sort of autonomous criticism that Trowbridge attributes to Aristotle. The neo-Aristotelian objection is that Brooks and company did not limit themselves severely enough to matters of form (i.e., generic rules of composition) and thus violated the integrity of the text as a verbal artifact. (This contention would seem novel, even perverse, to the many detractors who have accused Brooks of ignoring values in favor of "mere" textual analysis.)

The problem with the neo-Aristotelians' circumscribed view of criticism is that it takes far too literally what is at best a useful metaphor—that of the poem as artifact. As W. K. Wimsatt notes, "if anything about poetry is clear at all it is that a poem is not really a thing, like a horse or a house, but only *analogically* so" (Wimsatt, *Icon*, 50). To treat the analogy as literally as the neo-Aristotelians would like is to pretend that the poem is something other than the act of a poet speaking. "What can the predicate of a definition of poetry be," Wimsatt asks, "if it does not contain terms drawn from the rest of human experience? A way of criticism which does not balk at so radical an analogy as that between poetic discourse and 'thing' ought not to balk at other ways of trying to connect poetic discourse with the materials of life to which it refers" (50).

Eight years after the publication of Trowbridge's essay, the neo-Aristotelian elders published their summa—a collection of twenty-one essays, running to 647 pages and some 300,000 words. Entitled *Critics and Criticism: Ancient and Modern*, this volume included R. S. Crane's provocative essay "The Critical Monism of Cleanth Brooks." If a truly *literary* criticism is inductive and pluralistic, Crane argues, one that is deductive and monistic must be suspect. Like Trowbridge, Crane accuses Brooks of basing his critical theory on a misreading of Coleridge. What follows from this "misreading" is a view of poetry at once so broad that it can encompass various kinds of prose discourse and so narrow that it can exclude much of the most admired verse of the ages.

The charge that Brooks has misread Coleridge is a particularly disingenuous one for a neo-Aristotelian to make. Because the Chicagoans believe that Coleridge was responsible for much of what was wrong in modern literary criticism, they would probably have found a correct reading of his work to be even more reprehensible. In any event, what is at issue is the distinction that Coleridge makes in the *Biographia Literaria* between "poetry" and "poems." In chapter 14 of his masterwork, Coleridge defines poetry as an activity of the imagination, "that synthetic and magical power" that "reveals itself in the balance or reconciliation of opposite or discordant qualities: of sameness, with difference; of the general, with the concrete; the idea, with the image; the individual, with the representative; the sense of novelty and freshness, with old and familiar objects" (see Crane, 85–86).

Crane proceeds to argue that "poetry" thus conceived "is a much wider

term than 'poem,' since, on the one hand, what is essential to poetry may
be found in writings, like those of Plato, Jeremy Taylor, and Thomas Burnet, which lack not only meter but also 'the contra-distinguishing objects
of a poem,' and since, on the other hand, no poem of any length either can
be or ought to be 'all poetry.' " Crane then proceeds to make a crucial
distinction: "The definition of poetry, therefore, is the same as the definition of what 'the poetic genius' does with whatever materials it operates
upon: whenever 'opposite or discordant qualities' of any sort are balanced
or reconciled, poetry results, though we may call it, judging by other criteria, poetry (in the narrower sense) or philosophy or pictorial art. Poetry
is thus architectonic thought, but a 'poem,' or 'poetry' in its limited meaning, is a composition in words of a special kind" (87).

Crane accuses Brooks of ignoring the Coleridgean distinction between
poetry as a quality of the imagination and poems as special kinds of composition. If the poetic imagination, as it manifests itself in irony, wit, and
paradox, is the defining characteristic of that mode of composition we call
"'poetry' in its limited meaning," there is no reason for not saying that
the prose writings of Plato, Taylor, and Burnet are actually poems. For
that matter, we do not even need to confine ourselves to those texts that
might be found in an anthology of literature. "The syntheses of science,
too, can be described, omitting questions of their truth, in much the same
terms as Brooks uses to distinguish the 'poetry of synthesis.' " Crane then
moves in for the kill by stating that $E = mc^2$—"the formula in which
Einstein brought together in a unified equation the hitherto 'discordant'
qualities of mass and energy, [is] . . . judging it solely by Brooks's criterion
for poetic 'structure,' . . . the greatest 'ironical' poem written so far in the
twentieth century" (104–105).

Forced by his theory to admit Einstein to the poetic canon, Brooks must
also undervalue verse lacking in irony, wit, and paradox—regardless of
what other virtues it might possess. This charge was hardly original with
the neo-Aristotelians. Certainly, after *Modern Poetry and the Tradition*,
Brooks seemed particularly vulnerable to such an accusation. Had he not
canonized metaphysical and modern poetry, while regarding everything
in between as some sort of Hobbesian error? As we shall see, *The Well
Wrought Urn* was an attempt to answer this charge by broadening the
new critical canon without any sacrifice of principle, but by doing so,
Brooks left himself open to the charge of excessive ingenuity. If he was not
entirely wrong in finding irony, wit, and paradox in the most indispensable poetry of the eighteenth and nineteenth centuries, he was placing too

much emphasis on these qualities—in effect, liking the right poems for the wrong reasons.

Crane's essay is so prolix and dogmatic that one might assume his case to be more substantial than it actually is. To begin with, the charge that Brooks is advancing an inadequate definition of poetry really begs an important question. Nowhere in *The Well Wrought Urn* (or, for that matter, *Modern Poetry and the Tradition*) does Brooks pretend to define "poetry" or "poems," much less confuse the two. By any reasonable definition, including a neo-Aristotelian one, the texts he considers in that book are examples of the type of composition we call "poems." Moreover, most readers, regardless of their critical persuasion, would probably agree that these texts are among the better poems the modern English language has to offer. Brooks is not concerned with definition but with evaluation. Edwin Mims could tell his students that the poems Brooks discusses are good, even great, but he could not tell them why. In trying to answer that question, Brooks is indeed guilty of critical monism.

If monism may lead to an occasional overemphasis on a particular quality, critical pluralism presents at least as many difficulties. As Brooks demonstrates in "Criticism, History, and Critical Relativism" (one of the appendices to *The Well Wrought Urn*), allowing different criteria of judgment for poems from different eras leads us down a slippery slope. At what point do we stop subdividing the eras? A similar proliferation of genres, each with its singular set of standards, would be admirably empirical and pluralistic (two favored qualities of the neo-Aristotelians). We could thus *describe* poems with endless specificity, but we would be at a loss to say that one poem was better than another.

The critical pluralism of the neo-Aristotelians also fails to rise to a level of generality beyond that of the individual poetic genre. It can, for example, describe the properties of a narrative, a lyric, or a satire, but it seems unable to tell us why all of these specific genres can be classified as "poetry." To do that, of course, would be to fall prey to critical monism. Perhaps without realizing it, Crane does precisely that when he cites approvingly Coleridge's definition of a poem as "that species of composition, which is opposed to works of science, by proposing for its *immediate* object pleasure, not truth" (see Crane, 88).

Is Crane's monism really more satisfactory than Brooks's? All that it has to recommend it is a more slavish adherence to Coleridge. It certainly does not define poetry by any principle as objective as its generic structure (formal cause) or its language (material cause). Instead, we have only the effect that the poet intends to produce in the audience. This is not a quality that inheres in the poem. Rather, it is a combination of efficient cause (the poet's intention) and final cause (the poem's effect). As Wimsatt points out, Aristotle himself would have objected to the exclusion of truth as one of the ends of poetry. If the definition seems too exclusive at one end, it is surely too inclusive at the other. If a poem is any composition whose immediate object is pleasure, we have excluded Einstein from the poetic canon. But in place of $E = mc^2$, we must admit erotic pornography as among the most immediately pleasurable "poetry" in our literature.

Even if Brooks's particular monism is subject to fewer pitfalls than is the position of the neo-Aristotelians, one might still question his choice of paradox as the supreme (though not defining) quality of good poems. When he says at the outset of *The Well Wrought Urn* that "the language of poetry is the language of paradox" (*Urn*, 3), Brooks realizes that few people will readily agree with him (which is one reason why he had to write the book). Crane is precisely the sort of doubter he had in mind. "Why all the to-do about 'irony' in poetry?" Crane writes. "Why not look for 'irony' everywhere? For, if we look, it will assuredly be found" (Crane, 102). An effective response to this objection is made by Anthony J. Tassin. "Most assuredly irony is everywhere," Tassin admits, "but the *manner* of its presence in poetry is different. It is there by indirection, by metaphor. This is what makes the poem a poem and not exalted rhetoric. . . . [Brooks's conception of irony is] no mere verbal piddling. It is more than linguistic; were it only verbal, irony would be synonymous with the pun, which is only one minor type of irony" (Tassin, 135).

If we said that Brooks believes the language of poetry is the language of metaphor, we would not be contradicting but clarifying the emphasis he places on paradox. (Remember, in *Modern Poetry and the Tradition*, Brooks says of the metaphysical conceit that "the comparison *is* the poem in a structural sense"; *Modern Poetry*, 15.) Moreover, by speaking of metaphor, we limit the discussion of irony and paradox to a literary context, thus avoiding the necessity of considering Einstein's theory of relativity to be a great ironical poem.[6] Brooks's emphasis on metaphor as the vehicle through which poems exhibit the poetic imagination is monistic only in regard to structure. (Although poetic structure is surely Brooks's primary critical interest, one can find discussions of tone, meter, rhythm, sound patterns, balance, and the other aural traits of verse in *Understanding Poetry* and his other writings; see Tassin, 137.) To accuse an architect of being insufficiently interested in interior decoration is hardly fair. But even that analogy won't do. In the structure of *poetry*, Brooks would argue, form and function are one.

                    V

By the mid-forties, the *Sewanee Review* was taking great strides toward filling the void left by the *Southern Review*. Alexander Guerry finally managed in late 1943 to persuade Allen Tate to take over editorship of the magazine. (This was after making three more attempts to sign Cleanth in the spring of that year—in letters of April 9 and May 11 and, in an incredible display of bad taste, in a note of condolence on the death of Cleanth, Sr., sent on May 18.) When Tate officially became editor of the *Sewanee Review* in 1944, the changes he effected were immediate and dramatic. Lytle had begun the transformation from the Knickerbocker era by publishing fiction for the first time in 1943 and increasing the amount of space given to poetry. Tate redesigned the format of the magazine, began paying contributors, introduced prize competitions, and quadrupled the circulation of the review.

It was during this period that Cleanth Brooks became a frequent presence in the magazine (a status that continued under successive editors for half a century). Two of the essays that later appeared in *The Well Wrought Urn* (the ones dealing with Pope's *The Rape of the Lock* and Keats's "Ode on a Grecian Urn") originally appeared in the *Sewanee Review*. Also, in the winter of 1946, Cleanth made one of his rare appearances as a published poet. Writing more complexly textured verse than in any of his previous efforts, he based this poem—"The Maelstrom"—on Poe's classic horror story "A Descent into the Maelstrom."

If Brooks's poetic output was too meager to assure his prominence in the world of letters, his criticism and editorial labors were another matter. In the decade between 1935 and 1945, he had produced seven books. The dialect study and *Modern Poetry and the Tradition* were entirely his own work. Before Warren's departure from LSU, he and Brooks edited the three textbooks we have already discussed. Then, in 1944, Brooks and David Nichol Smith brought out the first volume of the Percy letters. Finally, in 1945, Cleanth published his fourth textbook, a collaboration with Robert Heilman entitled *Understanding Drama*.

If fiction seemed less suited than poetry to close reading, drama presented an additional set of difficulties. Not only is drama a full-length narrative mode, but it is primarily a performance art, meant to be experienced in the theater rather than the study. The essence of the new criticism is to discuss the individual work as a literary artifact—to identify its principles of construction, to define those characteristics of form and technique that make it uniquely what it is. Often the most effective way of saying what something is is to say what it is not. In *Understanding Poetry* Brooks and Warren went to great lengths to differentiate poetry from more purely denotative types of discourse; in *Understanding Fiction* their initial task was to show how well-constructed fiction differs from other types of narrative. By the same token, Brooks and Heilman devote their introductory essay of thirty-four pages to enumerating "The Problems of Drama." By this they mean the special limitations that make drama different from other genres of literature—particularly fiction and lyric poetry. The term *limitations* is meant in a purely descriptive rather than a pejorative sense. If anything, these limitations make drama a more concentrated form of storytelling; to paraphrase Frost's famous analogy, it is definitely a case of playing tennis *with* a net.

Brooks and Heilman acknowledge the truism that drama is primarily dialogue. It does not follow, however, that most forms of written dialogue are necessarily dramatic. As negative examples, they cite dialogue from a courtroom transcript and the imaginary "conversation" Walter Savage Landor composed between a famous French bishop and the mistress of Louis XIV. As one might expect, the courtroom transcript does little to advance action or character; Landor's dialogue reveals character but it does not develop any discernible plotline. Even the shooting script of a movie (here represented by an excerpt from the script for *The Great McGinty*) differs significantly from the text of a play. Because movies are largely a visual medium, the good screenwriter specializes in suggestive action, leaving the director to fill in shading and nuance.[7]

After discussing some of the burdens uniquely placed on dialogue in drama (the comments on poetic language as a "natural" form of speech are particularly good), Brooks and Heilman proceed to specific examples. The introductory section concludes with Oscar Wilde's *Lady Windermere's Fan* as an illustration of the general points the editors have been making. Part 2 ("Simpler Types") consists of *Everyman*, Plautus's *The Twin Menaechmi*, and Lillo's *The London Merchant*. In part 3 ("The More Mature Types"), we find Sheridan's *The School for Scandal*, Ibsen's *Rosmersholm*, Shakespeare's *Henry IV, Part I*, and Congreve's *The Way of the World*. Appendix A provides analyses and questions about fifteen plays not reprinted in the book, while Appendix B gives us "An Historical

Sketch of the Drama." The book concludes with two glossaries—one defining dramatic principles, the other common literary terms. Although it never attained the near-canonical status of the textbooks edited by Brooks and Warren, *Understanding Drama* did go into a second edition in 1948. It provided, according to the *American Oxonian*, "a sound and scholarly approach in place of the superficial and hit-or-miss attack that tends to result from the use of a bare [chronological] anthology" (see Walsh, 332).

VI

One might have expected Cleanth's record of professional accomplishment and his growing stature in the academic world to have improved his status at LSU. And in some respects, it did. He had the support and respect of both his department head and his dean. (Dean Hatcher, of Arts and Sciences, announced that the three faculty members he would most like to honor were Eric Voegelin in Political Science, T. Harry Williams in History, and Cleanth Brooks in English.) Unfortunately, enough of his former nemeses were still around to make LSU a trying place to live and work. For example, while Cleanth was on leave in Chicago, the Bradshear-Uhler faction plotted a coup in the English department.

Although the precise issue has long since been forgotten, correspondence between Tommy Kirby and Cleanth suggests that a good deal of malicious talk was taking place. In a letter sent from Chicago some time in the fall of 1945, Cleanth suggests that Kirby have the complainers put their charges in writing and then threaten to sue them for libel. He also indicates that he will soon send a "persuader" in the form of a photostat. In a letter dated November 21, 1945, he indicates exactly what the "persuader" was. Back in 1934, Cleanth recalls, Uhler wrote in a widely circulated magazine article that "about ten per cent of the white population of the South has colored ancestry, though, of course, they are blocked out enough to 'pass.' " "On this computation," Cleanth concludes, "at least two of the board of Supervisors can boast of such ancestry—unless, of course, they are not 'typical' of the South, or are—perish the thought!—damnyankees."[8] Apparently, Kirby managed to handle the local unpleasantness without use of the "persuader."

What proved more difficult was keeping Cleanth at LSU when more prestigious northern schools began seeking his services. On November 20, 1945, Harold W. Thompson of Cornell wrote to Kirby informing him that Cleanth might be considered for a professorship at that university or possibly for chairmanship of the English department. F. S. Crofts, the publisher of *An Approach to Literature* and *Understanding Fiction*, was a Cornell alumnus who had tried for years to interest Cleanth in a position at his alma mater. (In a letter to Cleanth dated June 8, 1940, Red Warren mentions that Crofts had told him of "the flirtation which Cornell had begun with you.") In 1945 Cornell had a badly divided English department in search of a chairman with both a scholarly reputation and a healing touch. Although Cleanth was acceptable to all factions and could have had the job for the asking, he was reluctant to take on administrative responsibilities, especially because Yale was offering him a full professorship at $7,000 a year, a rather substantial increase over the $4,000 a year he was making at LSU.

Having lost Warren to Minnesota, Kirby was determined to do whatever it took to keep Cleanth in Baton Rouge; as a kind of stopgap measure, he came up with a special professorship named in honor of W. A. Read. Although the salary of $5,500 was considerably less than what Yale was offering, Cleanth was committed to staying at LSU for another year, and Kirby used that time to urge the administration to come up with a better deal. (In communications with Kirby, Cleanth even suggested a nominal administrative title and wondered aloud whether Yale might be receptive to a split appointment.) Delighted to have a position named in his honor, Cork Read wrote to Dean Hatcher: "The offer of the chair to my brilliant young friend, Professor Cleanth Brooks, will meet with the approbation of distinguished men throughout the world. What a happy choice! I am extremely fond of him, and I have long admired the extraordinary range and versatility of his scholarship."

By the fall of 1946, it had become apparent that the officials at Baton Rouge lacked either the will or the means to compete with the challenge from New Haven. Because of financial corruption and provincial shortsightedness, LSU had squandered the chance for excellence that had seemed to be within its grasp in the 1930s. Its highest aspiration now was to a kind of comfortable mediocrity. Yale, in contrast, was one of the world's great universities. "On a very beautiful moonlit spring night in 1947," Robert Heilman recalls, "the Brookses and we were driving back to Baton Rouge from what had been an especially pleasant party at a country home in Mississippi. Trying as one does at such times to strengthen the irrational barriers against departure—the apparently rational ones are always the most fragile—and knowing that anything rhetorical would not do, I came up with something no more eloquent than 'You would miss all this very much'" (Heilman, 94). But, as Heilman must have known, the mating dance from Yale was too seductive to be resisted. Not having entered the clergy, Cleanth refused to see poverty and obscurity as necessary virtues, and he could pursue his secular calling to greater effect in the not-so-alien North.

CHAPTER TWELVE

The Interior Life
of the Poem

In March 1947, while Cleanth Brooks was preparing to make the transition from LSU to Yale, Reynal and Hitchcock published his second major collection of critical essays. If Brooks's reputation as a critic can be said to rest on a single book, that book is *The Well Wrought Urn: Studies in the Structure of Poetry*. Almost immediately, it became the object of both admiration and controversy in English departments across America and, to a lesser extent, in England as well. Properly speaking, the book did not take the academic world by surprise. Most of its contents had been previously published, and the position it articulated was generally consistent with that of Brooks's earlier books, particularly *Understanding Poetry* and *Modern Poetry and the Tradition*. The unique contribution of *The Well Wrought Urn* was to combine the virtues of those two earlier volumes, while answering some of the charges leveled against Brooks's approach to criticism.

The main argument of *Modern Poetry and the Tradition* was engaging and internally coherent. It also represented a departure from the limited historicism that dominated literary study in the academy. But at the same time, it appeared to require concessions that many devotees of literature were not willing to make. Although he did avoid Ransom's folly of undervaluing Shakespeare, Brooks seemed to be asking his readers to regard most of the English poetry of the eighteenth and nineteenth centuries as an inferior aberration of taste. This was a tall order, which most readers were not willing to accept. Although a critical theory that is indiscriminate is useless, one that excludes too much will have only a few eccentric followers.

Whether or not Brooks was consciously trying to keep from being thought of as an elitist curmudgeon in the tradition of Yvor Winters, he did begin to reconsider his sweeping dismissal of eighteenth- and nineteenth-century verse. Consequently, in *The Well Wrought Urn*, Brooks readmits some universally admired poems to the canon by rereading them according to the standards of the new criticism. As Robert B. Heilman notes: "In arguing for the applicability of his method to poems of different times and traditionally incompatible modes, [Brooks] denies that his method is only a front for a sort of mafia effort to set up a new underground power and leave the old order with nothing but uninfluential respectability" (Heilman, 137).

Heilman places Brooks's intentions in the proper perspective when he says that "to declare the literary work self-contained or autonomous was less to deny its connections with the nonliterary human world, past and present, than to assert metaphorically the presence in the poem of suprahistorical uniqueness along with the generic or the hereditary or the culturally influenced" (138). Brooks has had the effrontery to take the usual platitudes about the timelessness of literature quite seriously.

On the surface, the charge of dogmatism seems to be the most damning one leveled against Brooks. In an age that often seems to worship tolerance and open-mindedness, would it not be wiser to allow a plurality of critical approaches than to try to define, much less evaluate, something as various as poetry? This plea would carry more weight if the new critics were able to enforce their position with brute force. Because there *is* a plurality of critical approaches from which to choose, the new critics can prevail only if readers find their arguments to be persuasive. The truly illiberal position is the sort of dogmatic relativism that holds that there are no objective values. In the world of the deconstructionists, "the work is no longer an entity, a benevolent despot whose power is to be critically understood; rather the text is a by-blow of the hypostatizing imagination, an insufferable tyrant against which everyman acts as his own successful Robespierre by recognizing that nothing is really there but a stimulus to any libertine excitability" (Heilman, 136).

I

One of the qualities that has enabled *The Well Wrought Urn* to endure when other seasonal classics have fallen by the wayside is the ease with which the book moves between general theory and specific practice. Brooks's critical principles inform his readings, and his readings illuminate his principles. This symbiosis is evident as early as the first chapter, where Brooks illustrates his concept of poetic language by referring to important poems by Wordsworth, Pope, and Gray before reaching back in time to Donne. Brooks's basic assumption (boldly announced in the title of his first chapter) is that poetic language is "The Language of Paradox." He tells us that "it is a language in which the connotations play as great a part as the denotations. And I do not mean that the connotations are important as supplying some sort of frill or trimming, something external to the real matter in hand. I mean that the poet does not use a notation at all—as the scientist may properly be said to do so. The poet, within limits, has to make up his language as he goes" (*Urn*, 8). Whereas the scientist (really the technologist) is constantly purging his language of ambiguity, the poet thrives on ambiguity, because it allows him to approximate more closely the rich texture of actual experience.

The title *The Well Wrought Urn* is itself remarkably suggestive and ambiguous. Brooks's reference is to the penultimate stanza of Donne's "The Canonization," where the speaker argues that the love he shares with his woman, although it be of no great moment in worldly terms, can serve as an example and inspiration to future lovers (just as the humble lives of saints can be a source of religious inspiration): "We'll build in sonnets pretty roomes; / As well a well wrought urn becomes / The greatest ashes, as half-acre tombes. . . ." "The poem," Brooks writes, "is an instance of the doctrine which it asserts; it is both the assertion and the realization of the assertion. The poet has actually built within the song the 'pretty room' with which he says the lovers can be content. The poem itself is the well-wrought urn which can hold the lovers' ashes and which will not suffer in comparison with the prince's 'half-acre tomb' " (16).

As lucid as it is, Brooks's discussion of Donne's technique does not take us beyond the argument he made in *Modern Poetry and the Tradition*. What it does do is set the terms for his analysis of other poets. The conventional wisdom holds that Donne's use of metaphor is an eccentric anticipation of modernists such as Yeats and Eliot, not an extreme instance of qualities to be found in all poetry worthy of the name. Brooks challenges this conventional wisdom by comparing the imagery of Donne's verse with that of Shakespeare's *Macbeth*.

Brooks's intentions are obvious from the original title of his essay, when it was first published in the *Yale Review*: "Shakespeare as a Symbolist Poet." In a virtuoso display of critical acumen, Brooks traces two patterns of imagery (ill-fitting clothes and the newborn babe) throughout *Macbeth*. The fact that these are recurring images, which help develop the major themes of the tragedy, suggests that Shakespeare was anything but an inspired madman devoid of conscious artistry. These images, Brooks admits, "are not the only symbols, to be sure; they are not the most obvious symbols: darkness and blood appear more often. But with a flexibility which must amaze the reader, the image of the garment and the image of the babe are so used as to encompass an astonishingly large area of the total situation" (*Urn*, 45–46).

Although readers generally have found Brooks's exegesis to be persuasive,[1] a common criticism of his approach is that he is explicating, however brilliantly, passages that are not self-sufficient artifacts. Brooks is not so much comparing apples and oranges as trees and orchards. In *Macbeth*, Shakespeare is writing in poetry, but he is not writing a poem, at least not in the same sense that the other nine writers Brooks deals with are. One need not be a neo-Aristotelian nitpicker to point out that a play that is meant to be performed on a stage is experienced differently from a short poem by Donne or Wordsworth. This is not to say that there are not instructive similarities. In *Modern Poetry and the Tradition* Brooks had shown how great poetry and great tragedy take a similar view of life and had also argued that there is a sense in which a poem can be considered a drama. These useful analogies, however, establish similarities, not identity. If we take the analogies too literally, we run the risk of ignoring crucial differences. As Arthur Mizener notes in an otherwise enthusiastic review of *The Well Wrought Urn*: "Brooks has, I believe, a tendency to undervalue the symbolism of the visible action of the performed play. . . . I am not sure it is not because the storm symbolism, like the sleep symbolism, of *Macbeth* is largely part of what happens, and only in a comparatively minor way the spoken poetry of the play, that Brooks leaves it untouched" (Mizener, "Equality," 321, 322).

When we are clearly dealing with works of a similar order (perhaps different varieties of apples), *The Well Wrought Urn* is much more convincing in establishing common qualities. Put simply, the excitement generated by the book was due in large part to Brooks's ability to tell us why good poetry is good. It is one thing to be moved by John Milton; it is quite another to understand how this particular *maker* has constructed verbal artifacts that have pleased many and pleased long.

In his discussion of the twin poems "L'Allegro" and "Il Penseroso," Brooks uses his characteristic method to provide such an understanding.

He finds that like the metaphysicals and the moderns, Milton was fascinated by the balance of similarities and differences that makes metaphor work. If the metaphysicals were primarily interested in showing occult resemblances between seemingly dissimilar objects, Milton comes at the issue from the other direction in his twin poems. He is trying to reveal contrasts, although he cannot do so effectively without also establishing similarities. "Milton could not afford to exploit mere contrast," Brooks writes. "If he had, the two halves would have been driven poles apart. . . . We are almost justified in putting the matter in this way: by choosing the obvious contrast between mirth and melancholy, Milton obligated himself to bring them as close together as possible in their effect on the mind. For the tension between the two choices depends upon their presentation as choices which can appeal to the same mind" (*Urn*, 50).

Typically, Brooks will raise a critical crux early in his discussion of a poem, proceed to a detailed analysis of the poem, and then return to the crux in the light of that analysis. (In his discussion of *Macbeth*, he shows how the clothes metaphor explains the otherwise confusing reference to daggers "Unmannerly breech'd with gore.") The crux in Milton's companion poems is the dissimilarity between the speaker's bombastic banishment of melancholy at the beginning of "L'Allegro" and the style of the rest of the poem. Although this shift in tone has bothered critics for centuries, the best explanation thus far offered has been that of E. M. W. Tillyard, who used purely biographical evidence to surmise that the youthful Milton was engaging in a kind of academic burlesque. Accurate though this surmise may be, it does not tell us why Milton opted for burlesque or what effect that decision had on the two poems in question.

After guiding us through a close reading of the companion poems, Brooks concludes that the "reprehension of Melancholy as loathsome [at the beginning on "L'Allegro"], and the identification of her with the blackness of midnight are associated with a consciously stilted rhetoric which forms an ironical contrast with the freer and more casual rhythms in which the pensive man's actual experience of melancholy is expressed [in "Il Penseroso"]. It is the most delicate kind of qualification that a poet can give. For those who feel with Tillyard that the opening *is* bombastic, the presence of the bombast thus becomes meaningful" (*Urn*, 59). Not only does this explanation help us make sense of Milton's verse, it also demonstrates the superiority of a criticism rooted in the text to one dependent on biographical inference.

In order to demonstrate that paradox is the universal language of poetry, Brooks must discuss a representative selection of poems that are widely admired but generally thought to be free of paradox. The first of his texts to fall clearly into this category is Herrick's "Corinna's going a-Maying." By examining the complex attitude that the speaker of this poem takes toward the carpe diem theme (whether or not this was the biographically known attitude of Parson Herrick), Brooks questions whether any true poem can ever be reduced to its paraphrasable prose content.

Brooks entitles his chapter on "Corinna" "What Does Poetry Communicate?" and answers that question by asserting: "The poem communicates so much and communicates it so richly and with such delicate qualifications that the thing communicated is mauled and distorted if we attempt to convey it by any vehicle less subtle than that of the poem itself" (*Urn*, 67). Taken too literally, that statement could mean that criticism is virtually impossible. If any critical analysis less subtle than the poem itself is inadequate, only the most discriminating minds are capable of criticism, and that criticism necessarily will be expressed in a prose that is very different from the language of poetry. Faced with such a challenge, the prospective critic might well throw up his hands, read the poem verbatim, and say *that* is what it communicates. Brooks does not go that far, although he realizes that any critical theory that would reduce a poem to its prose paraphrase is incapable of answering the exasperated sophomore who asks: "Then, why didn't the poet just come out and *say* what he meant?"

II

Brooks's method of reading may make the ostensibly difficult simpler, but it also makes the ostensibly simple more difficult. Readers who thought that they understood Pope's *The Rape of the Lock* to be a straightforward satire (if that is not a contradiction in terms) about the vanity of the aristocracy (particularly aristocratic women) find Brooks urging them not to understand Pope too quickly. Belinda is every bit the shallow tease that Pope makes her out to be, and we are right to condemn her as such. But her beauty also commands a certain admiration. The mock-epic structure that Pope uses to tell this story is perfectly suited to the world of artifice and hypocrisy he is describing. What keeps the telling from becoming too heavy-handed is Pope's appreciation of the uses of artifice and hypocrisy, especially when dealing with something as ephemeral as beauty and as elemental as sex. Pope would have agreed with La Rochefoucauld that hypocrisy is the tribute vice pays to virtue.

One of the brilliant effects of Pope's mock epic is its deft modulation of tone. The poet captures the superficial world of Belinda without becoming so myopic as to think that it is the only world that exists. Not only does he pronounce an understated judgment on Belinda's values through his subtle use of the zeugma, but he further censures those values by showing at one point how unjustly more serious crimes are punished in the world outside Belinda's boudoir: "The hungry Judges soon the Sentence sign, / And Wretches hang that Jury-men may Dine." As Brooks notes, "A lesser poet would either have feared to introduce an echo of the 'real' world lest the effect prove to be too discordant, or would have insisted on the discord and moralized, too heavily and bitterly, the contrast between the gay and the serious. Pope's tact is perfect. The passage is an instance of the complexity of tone which the poem possesses" (*Urn*, 95).

When moving from the naturalistic to the supernatural, Pope maintains his sense of balance and decorum. Because the rape of the lock is a violation that must be resisted even as it is secretly desired, the sylphs that he conjures up to "protect" Belinda's virtue are appropriately ineffectual. In Brooks's opinion, Pope's sylphs make more poetic sense than do the powerless angels Milton dispatches to watch over Adam and Eve in *Paradise Lost*. The sylphs are meant to be ridiculous creatures fighting a truly dubious battle over ultimately insignificant issues. We laugh with Pope rather than at him; he is deliberately ironic, where Brooks believes Milton to be unintentionally ludicrous.

It is easy to admire Brooks's critical method when he makes the difficult simple. Any reader who has gotten bogged down in *The Waste Land* (and who hasn't?) cannot fail to be impressed with the lucidity of Brooks's reading. Although he goes well beyond mere explication, the explication itself is a wonder to behold. This is generally true whenever Brooks is writing about poems of obvious and conventional difficulty—specifically those of the metaphysicals and moderns. But one might question whether it is worth the effort to explain a poem as seemingly transparent as Gray's "Elegy Written in a Country Churchyard." Brooks's detractors would even argue that finding hidden complexities in such a poem is a gratuitous display of ingenuity. The problem, however, is that without some display of ingenuity, it is difficult for the critic to account for the greatness of a poem that appears to do little more than convey a straightforward prose message.

If the greatness of Gray's "Elegy" lay in its message, then all poems that "say" what the "Elegy" seems to say would be of equal value. And yet literary history tells us that of the many "graveyard" poems of the late eighteenth century, only Gray's has stood the test of time. Brooks argues that we can account for the greatness of the "Elegy" only by studying the how rather than the what of the poem's meaning. In fact, the whole point of Brooks's structural (not structuralist) analysis is to demonstrate that the how not only expresses but helps to determine the what. By creating a dramatic context, the entire poem conditions our reading of any particular line. For that reason, something as ostensibly trite and prosaic as the epitaph at the end of Gray's "Elegy" can take on unsuspected nuances of meaning. Unlike, say, Matthew Arnold, Brooks is less interested in the philosophical truth or rhetorical originality of a passage of poetry than in its *dramatic* appropriateness to the larger structure of which it is a part.

That there is a dramatic situation in Gray's "Elegy" is incontestable. A speaker observes and comments on the country churchyard in which generations of the humble villagers have been laid to rest. He seems to regret that so many of these people died before realizing their true potential in life but questions whether any earthly glory can mean much to the dead. (In what may be an overly brilliant exegesis, William Empson charges Gray with being a subtle apologist for social inequities;[2] Brooks, while finding this charge specious, also recognizes the ambiguity of Gray's attitude toward worldly fame.) The real drama comes, however, when the speaker imagines a particular individual committed to the earth. When a "kindred spirit" inquires about the deceased, the unlettered swain who tends the graveyard remembers only that he was a loner when he was alive and then points to the epitaph on the tombstone. That epitaph becomes part of the drama because we must imagine it as written not by the poet, but by an unidentified character in the town. What is more, we read it over the shoulder of the kindred spirit. (As Brooks argues, our reading of the poem up to this point has made us, too, kindred spirits with the man in the grave.)

Not content with the situation as Gray has depicted it, Brooks suggests that the dead man is none other than the speaker himself—as he imagines he will be after taking his appointed place in the graveyard. Although there is no explicit warrant in the text for concluding that this is so, the dead man's epitaph expresses directly the attitude toward life that the speaker has only hinted at earlier in the poem. Unlike the hapless peasants buried in the churchyard, this youth has *deliberately* turned his back on fame and fortune, concluding that they are not worth the effort to attain. Even if Brooks has gone too far in literally identifying the dead man as the speaker's projection of his future self, there is clearly a kinship between the two figures. Although we are all united in death, we remain divided over the proper attitude to take toward this fact. Through the "kindred spirits" Gray has created, the experience of one possible attitude is fully dramatized.

Brooks's best-known and most admired application of the doctrine of dramatic propriety is probably his discussion of Keats's "Ode on a Grecian Urn." Unlike Gray, Keats is not the sort of poet whom a critic of Brooks's persuasion need strain to defend. Keats may not be as witty as Donne or as densely allusive as Eliot, but his originality of metaphor and sensuousness of imagery set him apart from all other Romantics, and the Grecian Urn "Ode" is generally regarded as one of his best poems. But this wonderfully concrete artifact ends with an apparently sententious bit of philosophizing that even Keats's greatest admirers have found hard to defend. If the concluding equation of beauty and truth is inconsistent with the rest of Keats's poem, then it is an affront to logic; if it is not inconsistent, one suspects that it is probably superfluous. Brooks manages to resolve this dilemma by taking seriously Keats's metaphor of the urn as a dramatic speaker. He asks if we might not read the "Ode" in such a way that the statement "Beauty is truth, truth beauty" rises as naturally from the dramatic context of the poem as Lear's statement "Ripeness is all" does from the conflicts of Shakespeare's play.

Perhaps a more fundamental problem with the last two lines of the poem is determining what they might mean at a prose level. If the idea itself is merely gibberish, then its appropriateness to the poem becomes irrelevant—unless, of course, one wants to argue that Keats was deliberately writing nonsense verse (inviting a comparison not to *King Lear* but to Edward Lear). Brooks indicates the dilemma as follows: "One can emphasize *beauty* is truth and throw Keats into the pure-art camp, the usual procedure. But it is only fair to point out that one could stress *truth* is beauty, and argue with the Marxist critics of the 'thirties for a propaganda art. The very ambiguity of the statement, 'Beauty is truth, truth beauty' ought to warn us against insisting very much on the statement in isolation, and to drive us back to a consideration of the context in which the statement is set" (*Urn*, 140–41). Not surprisingly, Brooks discovers that rather than forcing us to accept either "conflicting" reading of the poem, this procedure allows us to synthesize both readings at a higher level of ambiguity.

The "message" that one gleans from examining the urn is riddled with paradox. Keats calls the urn a "sylvan historian," although Brooks reminds us in the title of his essay that the history in question is "without footnotes." The specificity of conventional historical accounts is absent from the scenes depicted on the urn. What we have is no facsimile representation of actual events but an unchanging paradigm of the richness of life—what Keats calls a "cold pastoral." "The sylvan historian," Brooks notes, " . . . takes a few details and so orders them that we have not only beauty but insight into essential truth. Its history . . . has the validity of myth—not myth as a pretty but irrelevant make-belief, an idle fancy, but myth as a valid perception into reality" (151).

The urn does not answer the specific historical queries raised by the speaker in the first stanza of the poem because it has a far more universal truth to communicate. This truth includes not only what the urn depicts, but what it implies as well. By showing a group of people in a forest environment where they obviously do not live, the urn implies the existence of a deserted town. According to Brooks:

> If the earlier stanzas have been concerned with such paradoxes as the ability of static carving to convey dynamic action, of the soundless pipes to play music sweeter than the heard melody, of the figured lover to have a love more warm and panting than that of breathing flesh and blood, so in the same way the town implied by the urn comes to have a richer and more important history than that of actual cities. . . . The poet, by pretending to take the town as real . . . has suggested in the most powerful way possible its essential reality for him—and for us. (149).

Truth, for Keats, is something far more general and far more beautiful than mere facts. Or, to put the matter differently, myth is all the history that we know or need to know. If we are sensitive to what the entire poem has been saying (largely in terms of paradox), "we shall be prepared for the enigmatic, final paradox which the silent form utters" (151). Thus our response to those closing lines is a way of testing whether we have been reading the poem correctly. Had Keats simply meant that beauty is truth and written his "Ode" as a declaration of pure aestheticism, the poem would have been much less complex and its concluding statement of theme clearly beside the point. (That that theme is so often simplistically misread indicates how a reader's preconceptions can distort his understanding.) However, by stating the theme as a paradox that cannot be adequately understood except in terms of the entire poem, Keats refuses to allow the *careful reader* a too facile understanding of that theme.

The inevitable corollary to Brooks's position is that poems that *can* be understood too facilely are not really very good. As we have seen, the high value he places on complexity prompts him to emphasize the element of paradox in poems previously thought to be simple and straightforward. If this approach works well enough for poems such as "Corinna's going a-Maying" and Gray's "Elegy," it is less successful when applied to Wordsworth's "Intimations of Immortality" (or perhaps it would be more accurate to say that the approach is all too successful in revealing the structural inconsistencies of this poem). Brooks does a commendable job of discussing the function and development of Wordsworth's imagery. Whereas most critics would insist on reading the Intimations "Ode" in the light of Wordsworth's autobiography and judging it according to Romantic standards, Brooks tries to read it as he would a poem of the seventeenth or twentieth century. In so doing, he concludes that Wordsworth frequently wrote better (i.e., more paradoxically) than he knew and that his craft would have been even more fully realized had he maintained the courage of his metaphors. In effect, Brooks inverts the conventional wisdom that sees poetic form as a matter of conscious manipulation and message as a product of divine inspiration. In Wordsworth the play of language sounds natural and spontaneous; it is his ideas that occasionally seem willed and artificial.

Like many poets before and since, Wordsworth depicts birth as a glorious dawn. In the Intimations "Ode," however, that dawn is more an ending than a beginning. The child enters the world "trailing clouds of glory" because his celestial preexistence has been far more wonderful than anything he will experience on earth. In a very original use of light imagery, Wordsworth has the child moving not toward darkness but toward prosaic daylight, what he calls the "light of common day." Because he does not posit a Never-Never Land where one can remain perpetually a child, the logic of Wordsworth's poem is quite bleak. It is only when he tries to find a way out of this dilemma that that logic succumbs to wishful thinking.

While acknowledging the devastating effects of aging on one's spiritual well-being, Wordsworth tries to suggest that all is not lost. "The childhood vision," Brooks explains, "is only one aspect of the 'primal sympathy'; this vision has been lost—is, as the earlier stanzas show, inevitably lost—but the primal sympathy remains. It is the faculty by which we live. The continuity between child and man is actually unbroken." Unfortunately, the symbolism of the poem asserts this point without really dramatizing it. "If we make a desperate effort to extend the implied metaphor—if we say that celestial light is the flame which is beautiful but which must inevitably burn itself out—the primal sympathy is the still-glowing coal—we are forced to realize that such extension is overingenious. The metaphor was not meant to bear so much weight" (*Urn*, 137).

It is hardly an exaggeration to say that Brooks regards paradox, irony, and wit as inherent qualities of a good poem, whether or not the poet intends to be paradoxical, ironic, and witty. Thus, through some anomaly of the imagination, even the most earnest and bombastic of poets can occasionally achieve uncharacteristic levels of subtlety in their verse. A prime example is the poet laureate of the Victorian era, Alfred Lord Tennyson, who Brooks tells us "was not always successful in avoiding the ambiguous and the paradoxical" (153). Brooks sees this failure as a "saving grace"—especially in the highly nuanced lyric "Tears, Idle Tears."

Although Brooks does not make this point explicitly, the mastery of language Tennyson displays in "Tears, Idle Tears" demonstrates the fatal limitation of a biographical approach to criticism. An examination of Tennyson's personal history and of the rest of his verse (which is surely a part of that personal history) proves that "Tears, Idle Tears" is a poem most untypical of its author, but we are left with no clue as to why Tennyson wrote so well on this particular occasion. The theme of "Tears, Idle Tears," Brooks notes, does not differ significantly from that of a much more conventional Tennyson poem—"Break, Break, Break." Thus the demonstrable superiority of "Tears, Idle Tears" is a function of neither subject matter nor vision. According to Brooks, "the lyric quality, if it be genuine, is not the result of some transparent and 'simple' redaction of a theme or a situation which is somewhat poetic in itself; it is, rather, the result of an imaginative grasp of diverse materials—but an imaginative grasp so sure that it may show itself to the reader as unstudied and unpredictable without for a moment relaxing its hold on the intricate and complex stuff which it carries" (*Urn*, 162).

Brooks's discussion of individual works ends with his analysis of Yeats's "Among School Children." Although Yeats's poem is thematically quite similar to Wordsworth's Intimations "Ode," Brooks argues that the "inner logic" and "economy of symbol" of "Among School Children" make it a much denser and more suggestive poem (165); it is at once more concrete and more difficult than Wordsworth's "Ode." At the outset, we observe a situation that seems transparently autobiographical. An old man is inspecting a school when he suddenly recalls the tale of a childhood experience that made a lasting impression on a lady friend. Whether the old man is Yeats and the lady friend Maude Gonne is finally irrelevant; the situation becomes the occasion for a meditation on the curse of aging. Mutability is depicted in all its ugliness and decay ("Old clothes upon old sticks to scare a bird"). Although Yeats alludes to the doctrine of preexistence, it is but one of several philosophies mentioned—none of which can forestall the ravages of time.

Nothing that Brooks says in this essay would come as much of a surprise to readers of *Modern Poetry and the Tradition*. By tracing the development of English poetry from Donne to Yeats, Brooks closes the circle at the point where the metaphysicals and the moderns come together. His perceptive and sensitive reading reminds us of the excellence of Yeats's poem and goes a long way toward identifying the reasons for that excellence. More tough-minded than Wordsworth's Intimations "Ode," "Among School Children" is also more than just a lament for the loss of youth. A statement about the nature of art itself, the poem dramatizes in its magnificent final stanza the loss of morbid subjectivity experienced by the artist when he becomes one with his art. It is not a flight from the physical ("Body is not bruised to pleasure soul") but an experience of total incarnation. Using the concluding images of the poem, Brooks notes that "our staple study of literature consists in investigations of the root system (the study of literary sources) or in sniffing the blossoms (impressionism), or—not to neglect Yeats's alternative symbol—in questioning the quondam dancer, no longer a dancer, about her life history (the study of the poet's biography)" (*Urn*, 175). The interest of the true literary critic, however, must always be with the dance itself.

III

By calling his summary chapter "The Heresy of Paraphrase," Brooks stakes out a position that separates him not only from didactic critics but also from such formalist allies as John Crowe Ransom and Yvor Winters. Strictly speaking, all but the most ardent propagandists would agree that paraphrase is to poetry what heresy is to theology—a partial truth that becomes an untruth when abstracted from its qualifying context. But the connotations of the word *heresy* suggest a good deal more; those who were branded as heretics by the Church were not simply in error but perversely antagonistic to truth. Although Brooks is too much of a gentleman to say that of those who disagree with him, he gives no quarter to those who argue for a paraphrasable prose content in poetry.

The folly of paraphrase, he argues, becomes evident whenever the reader tries to "formulate a proposition that will say what the poem 'says.'" As such a proposition approaches adequacy, it will increase in length, be filled with reservations and qualifications, and begin to express itself in terms of alternative metaphors (see *Urn*, 181). A heresy that emphasizes one part of the faith can be useful as long as we strive to see it within the context of the entire faith, that is, when it ceases any longer to be a heresy. Those who would reduce poetry to some paraphrasable prose content are the equivalent of the Puritan reformers who regarded dogma as all and ritual as a vain adornment.

As Brooks has suggested in his discussion of "Corinna's going a-Maying," the temptation to think of poetry as prose in drag is probably due to nothing more sinister than their superficial similarity—poetry and prose are both constructed with words. To keep that similarity from leading us astray, Brooks asks us to compare poetry with certain nonverbal art forms. "The structure of a poem," he writes, "resembles that of a ballet or musical composition. It is a pattern of resolutions and balances and harmonizations, developed through a temporal scheme" (*Urn*, 186). Perhaps sensing that these analogies are not quite adequate, Brooks reintroduces a point made in *Modern Poetry and the Tradition*, that "the structure of a poem resembles that of a play." Conceding that plays too are constructed with words, he is nevertheless confident that "most of us are less inclined to force the concept of 'statement' on drama than on a lyric poem; for the very nature of drama is that of something 'acted out'—something which arrives at its conclusion through conflict—something which builds conflict into its very being. The dynamic nature of drama, in short, allows us to regard it as *an action* rather than as a formula for action or as a statement about action" (186–87).

Brooks's quarrel with Winters and Ransom is that both men are essentially dualists. Winters reacts against the vague impressionism of the Romantics by overemphasizing the rational content of poetry. In *The Anatomy of Nonsense*, he makes the quite sensible point that the denotation of a word will set limits to the range of connotations it may evoke. (The word "*fire*," for example, "will seldom be used to signify *plum-blossom*"; see *Urn*, 217.) From this observation, Winters posits a dualism of denotation and connotation, of intellect and emotion. Thus the rational statement or paraphrasable content of a poem is primary. If this is the case, then the difference between poetry and other verbal constructs consists of such accidental features as meter and rhythm, which are nothing more than the sugarcoating or the decorative adornment for what is really important—the moral message of the poem.

If Winters sought to reduce criticism to a kind of neoclassic moralism with Dr. Johnson as its patron saint, Ransom was more interested in the logical development of metaphor we associate with the poetry of Donne. That position, and Brooks's difficulties with it, go back at least as far as the controversy over "Shakespeare at Sonnets." Although Brooks takes a back seat to no man in his admiration for Donne, he believes that Ransom admires Donne for the wrong reasons. He notes "Ransom's tendency to praise . . . Donne's logical rigor, not for its function in the development of the [poem's] tone, but as an end in itself" (*Urn*, 220). What we have is a dualism in which the purpose of the poem is to convey a logical argument through the vehicle of an extended metaphor.

This truly is a narrow conception of poetry. If Brooks can be accused of trying to subsume too much of the canon under his notion of paradox, Ransom is frankly excluding most of the verse that has been admired over the centuries. As Brooks demonstrates, this would leave us with neither good poetry nor good logic. At best, Donne's brilliant figures constitute a kind of sophistical argument. "The logic of 'The Canonization,' for example, will hardly satisfy the friend to whom it is addressed. . . . The real structure of 'The Canonization' transcends the logical framework of its images. . . . It involves mixed metaphor and rapidly shifted figures" (220). (For that matter, consider Ransom's own poem "The Dead Boy," which in the course of twenty lines compares a recently deceased child to a green bough, a black cloud, a sword beneath his mother's heart, a pig with a pasty face, and the first fruits of his family.) This is not to say that Donne is not a great poet, only that his greatness has nothing to do with logical unity; his poems achieve a unity of dramatic tone. A kind of pseudologic may help to characterize the speaker's voice, but the paraphrasable argument of the poem is incapable of standing on its own.

One can hardly take issue with Brooks's contention that a paraphrase, no matter how skillfully constructed, is at best a poor substitute for the poem itself. Still, the interpretative literary critic really has no tool other than paraphrase. An impressionistic reader can emote, a literary judge can rank, and a cultural historian can measure; but once one starts to *interpret* a poem, the only recourse is to talk about it in a prose that is not the language of the poem itself. The error of Winters and Ransom is not that they use paraphrase but that they mistake a particular aspect of the poem for the whole poem. Even some of Brooks's staunchest admirers believe that his emphasis on poetic structure leads to a similar pitfall.

Writing in the *Sewanee Review*, Arthur Mizener makes the following point:

> Mr. Brooks is giving us something like a paraphrase of the poem's structure. When such a paraphrase is used badly—there are examples in the magazines all the time—it turns the poem into a game, as chess, once a religious ritual of some seriousness, has become a game. When it is used well, as Mr. Brooks uses it, it teaches us how to see the variety in unity of a poem's attitudes. Mr. Brooks ought not to ask us to compare his brilliant paraphrases of a poem's structure with a poor paraphrase of a poem's attitudes and, on this evidence, decide that the former is a legitimate method of dealing with poetry and the latter not. (Mizener, "Desires," 469)

If Brooks insists on judging poems as good or bad without reference to their moral content, one might ask how he makes distinctions among explicitly didactic poems. Herbert J. Muller suspects that Brooks would simply purge didactic poetry from the canon on the grounds that it is not susceptible to "ironical contemplation." That, of course, is nonsense; Brooks is not in the business of legislating morality out of poetry. To do so would be to practice a poetics of exclusion (something that Ransom accused the Imagists of doing). However, if we are to allow ideas and values a place in poetry, we must have some way of discerning when those ideas and values are handled well and when ill. How can two poems with essentially the same moral outlook be of vastly different aesthetic worth? Brooks's answer is that it is precisely when a didactic poem does submit itself to "ironical contemplation" that it earns its vision. He notes, for example, that "Dante, in dramatizing his faith, was willing to portray more than one pope in hell. Surely there is more than mere propagandizing for a dogma and an institution in a view that can envisage Christ's vicar among the damned. . . . Dante was quite willing to expose his preachment to something very like 'ironical contemplation' " (*Urn*, 204).

IV

Brooks's reluctance to reduce poetry to moral posturing does not make him a relativist; in fact, the tendency of his position is toward a kind of

aesthetic absolutism. (If the moralist wishes to consult poetry in formulating a philosophy of life, he has Brooks's blessing, so long as he does not
call what he is doing "literary criticism.") Brooks's attack on critical relativism is rooted in the belief that "in giving up our criteria of good and
bad, we have . . . begun to give up our concept of poetry itself. Obviously,
if we can make no judgments about a poem *as a poem*, the concept of
poetry as distinct from other kinds of discourse which employ words becomes meaningless" (*Urn*, 198). Even at the time Brooks was writing,
which was long before the advent of deconstruction, some literary scholars were already willing to define literature as "'anything written in
words,' it being obvious that any narrower criterion would be hopelessly
subjective" (198).

The most respectable alternative to the critical absolutism that Brooks
endorses is the relativism of the historical scholar. Because literary tastes
change so much over time, does it not seem reasonable to evaluate each
writer according to the standards of his own age and leave the absolute
judgments to God? The problem with that position is that once you have
given in to historical relativism, where do you draw the line? There are
not only literary periods but subperiods as well. Do we judge a poet according to the standards of a century, a generation, a decade? Even if we
can define the boundaries of a literary era, who defines the standards of
that era? "And what of that not too rare rebel against his period, a Gerard
Manley Hopkins among the Victorians, or a John Milton among the poets
of the Restoration? Do they not have the right to demand judgment in
terms of a special modification of sensibility? In short, does not the logic
of the principle push us on to acceptance of the proposition that each poet
is to be judged in terms of his own individual sensibility?" (210).

As everyone who has ever taken an introductory course in philosophy
knows, relativism is a self-contradictory position. If any set of standards
is as valid as any other, it becomes impossible to make normative judgments. In fact, there is no reason to say that the multiplication of critical
norms should stop with the individual poet. Why not with the individual
reader? Certainly the most democratic form of criticism would be to celebrate what is most popular; the spirit of the age would be found in the
best-seller list. The minute we begin to cite some authority other than
sheer numbers, we fall back on standards that are making at least an implicit claim to objective validity.

If dogmatic relativism raises philosophical problems, aesthetic absolutism raises practical ones. Because Brooks does not claim that his critical

principles are the product of divine revelation, we must conclude that they are themselves historically conditioned. Cleanth Brooks happened to reach intellectual maturity at a time when the literary climate was reacting against Romanticism and rediscovering the virtues of Donne and company. It is one thing to express a preference for the metaphysicals and moderns, as Brooks does in *Modern Poetry and the Tradition*; it is something else to define poetry (or at least good poetry) in terms of that preference, as he seems to do in *The Well Wrought Urn*.

Even if Brooks can find some poems of the eighteenth and nineteenth centuries that meet (or can be made to meet) his criteria, much of the admired verse of those eras would prove more recalcitrant. As Monroe K. Spears points out, "had he chosen *The Dunciad* instead of *The Rape of the Lock*, or *Locksley Hall* instead of *Tears, Idle Tears*, probably verdicts would have resulted that would have outraged many readers" (Spears, "Mysterious Urn," 57). For that matter, Spears argues, it is doubtful that a poem such as "Tears, Idle Tears" would be published today. "Not because the excellent qualities Mr. Brooks finds in it are not there, but because its form and diction and modes of feeling express and appeal to sensibilities different from our own. Our view of a poem of the past is never absolute: consciously or not, we make adjustments, change our expectations, modify our standards; a poem is too deeply immersed in its own time for true absolutism to be possible" (56).

A similar attack on Brooks's notion of aesthetic absolutism was launched by Herbert J. Muller in the summer 1949 issue of the *Sewanee Review*. Although Muller believed that Brooks's discussion of irony and paradox helps us to understand and appreciate much of the great poetry of the Western world, he was not willing to accept the implication that complex poetry is necessarily superior to simpler kinds. What, he wonders, would Brooks's theory make of the Twenty-Third Psalm, the opening lines of the prologue to *The Canterbury Tales, The Song of Roland*, Celtic romance, and the poetry of Pushkin? Moreover (and here Muller sounds very much like R. S. Crane), irony and paradox can be found in modes of discourse that we would not think to call poetry (Muller, 360–61).

Muller raises two other major objections to Brooks's position. The first is that in so strenuously avoiding the pitfalls of critical didacticism, Brooks fails to consider the aesthetic effects of the propositions that poems make. A modern audience can esteem Dante's *Divine Comedy* or Milton's *Paradise Lost*, but its reaction is going to be different from that of a society that shared the religious beliefs of Dante or Milton. That Dante put popes in Hell is not so much an example of ironic contemplation in the modern sense as it is an indication of the intensity of Dante's belief. A critical approach that fails to judge the truth claims of poetry ultimately trivializes both poetry and criticism.

Finally, Muller questions whether Brooks's argument against the slippery slope of relativism has much relevance to the real world in which people are called upon to render judgments. To admit that opinions are relative to circumstances and subject to change is not the same as saying that all opinions are equally valid. "I know of no fixed principle," Muller writes, "by which one can demonstrate conclusively that Donne is a greater poet than Chaucer, Milton, Kalidasa, or Li Po, and I see no necessity for a fixed hierarchy; yet I can say flatly that all these poets are superior to Eddie Guest" (369).

In his response (published immediately following Muller's essay), Brooks pursues a strategy that is typical of his argumentative style—he contends that he and Muller are in essential agreement and that apparent differences are a result of misunderstanding. By admitting that we can sensibly rank some poets higher than others, Muller concedes the necessity for critical standards. When the critic applies such standards, he is not claiming a special and personal knowledge of absolute truth; he is simply making judgments that others are free to accept or reject as they will. The critic's responsibility is not to claim infallibility of taste but to make clear the reasons for his judgments of individual texts. Brooks has done this in *The Well Wrought Urn*. His detractors may well challenge his readings of particular poems, but in so doing, they are also making judgments they are obliged to defend.

Brooks believes that the contention he is indifferent to the truth claims of poetry is also based on a misconception. Here, Muller succumbs to the biographical or intentional fallacy. Knowing what Dante or Milton believed as individuals, and even what they intended to say as poets, does not tell us authoritatively what their poems actually say. For that we must go to the texts themselves. Although an audience's response to a poem is conditioned by the truth claims the poem makes, Brooks prefers to focus his attention on the ways in which those claims are expressed. As he and Warren pointed out in *Understanding Poetry*, a competent and sensitive reader should be able to respond to both Longfellow's "Psalm of Life" and Wordsworth's "Expostulation and Reply," even though these poems articulate opposite views of the world. In *Practical Criticism*, Richards demonstrates how many adventitious factors can affect literary response. The duty of the critic and the teacher of literature is to differentiate legitimate from extraneous standards of judgment.

Finally, Brooks questions the method of argument that attributes positions to him that he has never taken. Those who attacked *Modern Poetry and the Tradition* were certain that Brooks was simply dismissing the bulk of admired poetry written in the eighteenth and nineteenth centuries. He wrote *The Well Wrought Urn* at least in part to demonstrate that they were wrong. To refute Muller, must he now write a book of essays on the Twenty-Third Psalm, Chaucer's Prologue, *The Song of Roland*, and so on? If he did, one suspects that he would find in those poems subtleties that most other critics have ignored. The question remains, however, whether those subtleties account for the greatness of the indicated poems—whether irony and paradox are indeed the *essence* of poetry or simply secondary characteristics. Whatever the answer may be, not even Muller denies that Brooks's approach helps us to see in a poem qualities that we scarcely suspected were there.

In *The Well Wrought Urn* itself, Brooks makes a pragmatic argument for holding to absolute critical values. Such a stance, he contends, would not make literary study narrower but would actually help to redeem it and the humanities in general from the charge of irrelevance. His argument is that teachers of the humanities sacrifice the uniqueness of their discipline when they avoid raising normative questions. If literary study is nothing more than a branch of cultural history, professors of literature "must not be surprised if they are quietly relegated to a comparatively obscure corner of the history division. If one man's taste is really as good as another's, and they can pretend to offer nothing more than a neutral and objective commentary on tastes, [literary scholars] must expect to be treated as sociologists, though perhaps not as a very important kind of sociologist" (*Urn*, 213).

Among those who would not think of reducing literature to a minor branch of cultural history are some who see nothing wrong in making it a handmaiden of philosophy or religion. If poetry can be said to reveal truth and to deal with absolute values, it seems reasonable to locate those truths and values in the realm of metaphysics. The problem with this position is that it introduces at a higher level the dichotomy that would make poetry a fancy way of communicating paraphrasable ideas. Brooks rejects this notion by contending that "a poem does not *state* ideas but rather *tests* ideas. . . . A poem . . . is to be judged, not by the truth or falsity as such,

of the idea which it incorporates, but rather by its character as drama—
by its coherence, sensitivity, depth, richness, and tough-mindedness"
(229). To judge poetry in these terms, however, is to be far more inclusive
than analyzing it for the presence of wit, irony, and paradox.[3] Indeed,
Brooks is tempted to agree with I. A. Richards that poetry can provide us
with a "discipline in coming to terms with the world in relation to ourselves" (*Urn*, 231). If poetry can do that much, it doesn't need to try to
compete with philosophy and religion.

Even as his view of the function of poetry seemed to become broader as
he came to the end of *The Well Wrought Urn*, Brooks remained leery of
claiming too much for poetry. Certainly, no one would want to argue
that the best poets are necessarily the best people. There is too much empirical evidence to the contrary. (Shortly after Brooks published *The Well
Wrought Urn*, the case of Ezra Pound raised again the question of whether
we can honor the poetry while reviling the poet.) But then, no form of
intellectual or moral training can guarantee virtue. Otherwise, Dante
would have put no popes in Hell. All other factors being equal, one who
is able to regard the world with the ironic contemplation required by great
poetry is less likely to succumb to facile dogmatism—either of the true
believer or the moral relativist. At its best, poetry can help us confront the
world in a spirit of sympathetic understanding. Although it is possible to
reject or compartmentalize that understanding, just as it is possible to be
a religious apostate or hypocrite, poetry has something unique and un-
translatable to say to those who will listen. That is all the critic knows or
needs to know. For Brooks, it is enough.

PART FOUR

South of Boston
(1947-64)

CHAPTER THIRTEEN

A Connecticut Yankee

When John Crowe Ransom left Nashville for Gambier, Ohio, in 1937, he was making his home outside the South for the first time since his service in World War I twenty years before. But he was also moving from a more urban to a more bucolic environment. Nashville had become one of the principal cities of the New South, and, as the years went by, one had to get farther and farther out of town to find a landscape unblemished by commerce. Gambier, in contrast, was a small midwestern village, located fifty miles from Columbus, the nearest city to rival Nashville in size. The Ohio countryside immediately reminded Ransom of rural Tennessee, except that the seasons were far more pronounced. To experience autumn in north central Ohio was to learn to love nature all over again. Moreover, Kenyon College itself soon became one of the literary capitals of the Western world. Since its founding by the Episcopal Diocese of Ohio in 1824, the school had languished in comfortable Broad Church respectability. But when Ransom arrived on campus, serious students of literature followed him. By 1948, the *Kenyon Review* had established itself as the foremost literary quarterly in the English-speaking world. The time was right to bring some of the magazine's most distinguished contributors together to train the nation's next generation of literary critics.

With support from both Kenyon College and the Rockefeller Foundation, the Kenyon School of English held its first session in the summer of 1948. Although the new criticism was gaining status in the academy, it still did not dominate many English departments. Because few students enjoyed the mobility and resources of Robert Lowell and Peter Taylor, those who attended universities without a first-rate critic had to educate themselves or give up literary criticism altogether. Now they could spend half a summer studying and living with some of the top critics in England

and America. Even if the atmosphere was more formal and hierarchical, the sense of excitement was not unlike what the Fugitives must have experienced a generation earlier. As George Lanning recalls, the faculty were regarded as pioneers, while he and his fellow students felt like the first settlers:

> We had come to help make order out of the wilderness of literary criticism. Perhaps we were like the early Beats—as improbable as that yoking may at first appear. But I mean that we possessed the kind of exhilaration that they had to start with. And we knew, too, that on every side, even in our midst, was the Enemy, the wooly headed Beast of primitive criticism in whose territory we proposed to settle. He was fighting back hard—very hard, just then. Vigorously, we "explicated" in and out of class; we got so that we could spot a Precious Object at a thousand yards; and where we couldn't find an ambiguity we made one. (See T. D. Young, *Gentleman*, 388)

Mornings were devoted to classes (which met between 8:30 and 12:30, Monday through Saturday), while the afternoons were reserved for library work, informal conferences, and recreation (the softball games, with Allen Tate exhibiting his prowess at shortstop, became legendary). Countless glasses of beer were consumed at Dorothy's, a local hamburger joint, and movies were shown on campus certain nights. Each Wednesday evening a public forum featured one or more of the faculty discussing a literary topic. Although Ransom had been unable to land T. S. Eliot, the teaching staff that first summer included Eric Bentley, Richard Chase, F. O. Matthiessen, William Empson, Ransom himself, Austin Warren, Allen Tate, and a forty-one-year-old full professor from Yale named Cleanth Brooks.

Although this was an eclectic group, all of its members were committed to criticism as opposed to mere historical or philological scholarship. The range of interests represented can be gleaned from the program for the forums that summer. From June 30 through August 4, one could hear Matthiessen on "The Social Responsibilities of the Critic," Ransom and Austin Warren on "Some Critical Strategies," Bentley on Charlie Chaplin's *Monsieur Verdoux*, Empson on "The Relevance of Verbal Analysis in Criticism," Brooks on Milton's metaphors, and Tate and Chase on whether it is the artist's fate to be isolated from his culture. At a personal level, Cleanth relished the opportunity to spend some time with his friends John and Allen and to form new ties with the rest of the faculty. One of the most distinguished of these new acquaintances was Francis Otto Matthiessen.

F. O. Matthiessen could easily have been mistaken for a banker or an insurance executive. (When his classmate Henry Luce was starting his publishing empire, he wanted to make Matthiessen his treasurer, but the idealistic "Matty" was already devoted to scholarship and socialism.) His former student Kenneth S. Lynn describes Matthiessen in even more pedestrian terms: "A short, stocky man, largely baldheaded, and wearing rimless glasses, he looked to me like a grocer" (Lynn, 107). Through his teaching and his scholarship, particularly his masterwork *American Renaissance* (1941), Matthiessen probably did as much as any individual to establish the respectability of American literature in the academy. ("When Matthiessen entered Yale in the fall of 1919, *Moby Dick* was shelved under 'Cetology' in the university library"; Lynn, 103.) In addition to being a noted scholar, Matthiessen was a dedicated teacher whose tutorials at Harvard became legendary.

Although he was never an ideologically tendentious critic, Matthiessen was an earnest political activist who spent countless hours canvassing voters and speaking out on behalf of his socialist views. Shortly after finishing his duties at Kenyon in 1948, he went to Philadelphia, where he seconded the nomination of Henry Wallace as Progressive Party candidate for president. (Cleanth told Matthiessen to say hello to his mother-in-law Emily Price Blanchard, who was a delegate from Louisiana.) With the defeat of Wallace and the increasing hostility of the Cold War, Matthiessen saw his dreams of world peace disappear. He also despaired that the age-old gap between the patrician and frontier strains in American culture would ever be bridged (his personal attempts to make contact with the working class were painfully awkward). In his lecture "The Responsibilities of the Critic" (delivered at Kenyon and elsewhere), Matthiessen made his most explicit attempt to distance himself from what he considered the aestheticism of the new critics.

Like so much of Matthiessen's work, this lecture is characterized by a tone of sweet reasonableness. It pays sincere tribute to the Kenyon critics and to the older generation of Eliot and Richards. But Matthiessen also believes that criticism has spent too much time cultivating its own garden. "My views," he writes, "are based on the conviction that the land beyond the garden's walls is more fertile, and that the responsibilities of the critic lie in making renewed contact with that soil" (Matthiessen, 6). The specific responsibilities Matthiessen cites include an awareness of the art of one's own time, an interest in popular culture, and a commitment to academic freedom.

To oppose any of these was to run the risk of seeming irresponsible, a charge against which the new critics could have easily defended themselves. Certainly, the quarterlies that came into existence as a result of the new criticism had done much to promote contemporary literature by publishing recent fiction and poetry. One need only consider Eliot's enthusiasm for the British music hall and his correspondence with Groucho Marx to realize that the supposed boundaries between elite and popular culture were quite often traversed. And anyone who ever taught or studied in a department headed by Edwin Mims could be expected to value academic freedom from having experienced its absence. One might nevertheless wonder to what extent these worthy pursuits are specifically responsibilities of the *critic*. Criticism, after all, is performed by a human being who has many other roles; in addition to being a critic, he may be a spouse, a parent, a teacher, a religious communicant, and a citizen. All of these roles entail certain responsibilities, but those responsibilities are not all the same. No doubt, Matthiessen was aware of this objection and believed that some cross-fertilization was necessary to keep the soil of criticism from going barren.

Matthiessen's most problematical assertion, however, is that the critic must also be concerned with politics. And by this, he means the correct kind of politics. "It is at this point," Matthiessen writes, "that my divergence becomes most complete from the formalists who have followed in the wake of Eliot as well as Eliot himself, whose reverence for the institutions of monarchy and aristocracy seems virtually meaningless for life in America" (10). Matthiessen goes on to agree with Vernon Parrington's insistence on the primacy of economics in society, but, unlike Parrington, he meant the primacy of Marxist economic analysis. Although acknowledging that the Marxists of the thirties made exaggerated claims, Matthiessen still believed "that the principles of Marxism—so much under fire now—can have an immense value in helping us to see and understand our literature" (11).

While working on *American Renaissance*, Matthiessen suffered a nervous breakdown, and his periodic bouts of depression worsened after the death of his beloved companion Russell Cheney in 1945. On March 31, 1950, Matthiessen checked into a "nice airy" room at the Manger Hotel near Boston's North Station. He had recently finished reading the galleys for one book and completed the draft of another; in the preceding year, he had drawn up a detailed will. Before leaving his apartment, he had tidied his desk and written letters to his closest friends. Alone at the Manger Hotel, Francis Otto Matthiessen composed a brief suicide note and jumped twelve floors to his death. The next morning, "his mangled body, still faintly breathing, was found on Nashua Street [and] taken to the morgue" (Rackliffe, 91). On a table in his hotel room, he had left his Skull and Bones key, symbol of Yale's oldest secret society.

I

The summer at Kenyon followed Cleanth's first year at Yale. When he left Baton Rouge in September of 1947, the world had been at peace for two years. Returning veterans were filling college classrooms that had been virtually empty the year before (they were also producing children who would flood the nation's campuses in the 1960s). Harry Truman, a much vilified political hack from Missouri, had become president upon the death of his Olympian predecessor two years earlier. Although Truman was given virtually no chance of winning the White House on his own in 1948, he had already made history by dropping the atom bomb on Japan and proposing the most sweeping civil rights measures in the history of the country. Several states in the solidly Democratic South considered leaving the party of their fathers if Truman were nominated for another term in office. The shopping center and the subdivision would soon transform the American landscape to a degree unimagined even in the worst Agrarian nightmares. That year the Pulitzer Prize in Poetry was awarded to Robert Lowell for *Lord Weary's Castle*, while the prize in fiction went to Robert Penn Warren for *All the King's Men*, a tale of political corruption in an unnamed southern state.

On August 25, 1947, Cleanth wrote to Red Warren from Baton Rouge to say that he had "lost a week in sorting and burning papers and in packing and mailing to New Haven some 2000 pounds of books. But the worst is over. Since we move by van, the other preparations will not take so long—there'll be next to no crating, etc., to do." He hoped to leave Louisiana by car on September 8th and to be on the road five to six days. In a letter from New Haven dated September 14th, he informed Red that he and Tinkum had made it to town the previous day but were still waiting for the van with their furniture to arrive.[1]

In comparison to the tropical summers in Baton Rouge, the weather in

New Haven was quite mild (the average summer temperature there is seventy degrees). The town itself had been founded in 1638 by a charismatic Puritan minister named John Davenport and a wealthy Puritan layman named Theophilus Eaton. Along with five hundred of their followers, they had come from London to Boston, where Indian fighters returning from the Pequot Wars told them of the good harbor to the south. "In the words of one historian, they 'had decided to found a colony with the minimum of pioneering discomfort, by virtue of the maximum of financial preparation.' They laid out a town in a grid pattern of nine squares, with the Green at the center. At first they lived in dugouts in the ground, but soon they built 'fair and stately houses' " (Wiencek, 325–28). In the early 1660s, Edward Whalley, William Goffe, and John Dixwell—three of the judges who had signed the death warrant against Charles I—fled to New Haven to escape the wrath of Charles II, newly restored to the throne. Not only are these men buried in New Haven, but three prominent streets in the city are named for them.

New Haven was the site of a famous colonial victory, when Benedict Arnold (who had not yet defected to the British) demanded the keys to the town powder house on behalf of the Revolution. Nathan Hale lived in New Haven while pursuing a degree from Yale. Around the corner from where Hale roomed as a student, Eli Whitney later developed the cotton gin (which hastened the Civil War) and the principle of interchangeable parts, which made the assembly line possible; nearby, Noah Webster compiled his first dictionary. Well before the dawning of the nineteenth century, New Haven had made the transition from a Puritan to a Yankee culture. During the last decades of the nineteenth century, the city produced Winchester repeating rifles, carriages, hardware, pianos, corsets, bicycles, and cigars. Over the years, the rising economic forces so shaped the character of the town that all that is now left of the original colony of New Haven is the grid around which it was built. The Green is surrounded on two sides by commercial buildings; on another side by a church, a library, and courthouse; and on the fourth by Yale University.

Yale itself is not quite as old as New Haven and was not even located there originally; founded as the Collegiate School in Branford, Connecticut, in 1701, it ranks behind Harvard University and the College of William and Mary as the third oldest institution of higher learning in the United States. Initially, classes were held in nearby Killingworth, Milford, and Saybrook; in 1716 the school moved to New Haven and was renamed Yale College after its first benefactor, Elihu Yale. In 1947 the university, four years shy of its 250th anniversary, had a reputation for both academic excellence and cultural homogeneity. For the children of the WASP aristocracy, a Yale education was the rite of passage between prep school and a career on Wall Street or in the upper levels of government service. (Yale also produced its share of teachers and scholars and, in the nineteenth century, had been known as the "mother" of new colleges throughout the Midwest.) Although Yale did not have a chapel for Catholic students until 1938 nor hire its first Jewish faculty members until 1946, it did admit blacks and women to its graduate school in the late nineteenth century—long before Harvard or Columbia.

Like so much of American society, Yale was profoundly changed by the Second World War. Because the university had agreed to admit all who had successfully applied in earlier years but had gone off to war, the freshman class of 1946 was twice the normal size. "Students were jammed into Quonset huts; but many had come there from barracks in any case. They were older than the normal freshmen, and more serious; competitive, with time to make up for—some of them used to command, young lieutenants demoted to 'heeling' school activities" (Wills, 14). This class, which was beginning its sophomore year when Cleanth arrived in 1947, was also more religiously and ethnically diverse than any in the school's past. In 1949 the *Yale Daily News* made history by electing its first Catholic chairman in William F. Buckley, Jr., and its first Jewish managing editor in Thomas H. Guinzburg.

In 1930 Yale instituted a housing system based roughly on the Oxford-Cambridge model. After living their freshman year in dormitories, the undergraduates move to one of twelve residential colleges—Berkeley, Branford, Calhoun, Davenport, Timothy Dwight, Jonathan Edwards, Morse, Pierson, Saybrook, Silliman, Ezra Stiles, and Trumbull.[2] Each of these units, which can accommodate approximately 250 students, has its own library, dining hall, kitchen, common rooms, and squash courts. A master and his family live in each college, with twenty or more faculty members appointed as fellows of the college. The fellows perform tutorial services and associate informally with the students of their college. Despite some traditions and rivalries, these units were never allowed to develop the independent character of their British counterparts, and today their composition is largely decided by computer. Cleanth, who became a fellow of Davenport College in the spring of 1948, always regretted that Yale did not take the next step and emulate the curriculum of Oxford and Cambridge—if only on an experimental basis in a single college.

Sometimes individuals with no official ties to Yale would develop an attachment to certain colleges. For example, whenever Robert Frost was in town, he would stay at Pierson College. During his first few years in New Haven, Cleanth would occasionally get a call about 11 P.M. from the obviously weary mistress of Pierson. Mr. Frost was in town and wondered if the Brookses would like to come over for some conversation. As if summoned to a papal audience, Cleanth and Tinkum would get dressed and walk the block or so from their residence to Pierson. A notorious insomniac, Frost would hold court until his visitors pleaded fatigue or mentioned the obligations of the next morning (he might go through several sets of guests during a given night). Cleanth remembers Frost as a bitter old man who had something nasty to say about virtually everyone he knew.

Another prominent American poet who passed through New Haven during those years was Wallace Stevens. In a letter to Allen Tate dated March 31, 1949, Stevens ruefully recalls one such occasion: "About a year ago, I met Cleanth Brooks and his wife in New Haven under circumstances which made a wreck of the thing. After reading a paper at Yale [which was inaudible to all but the first two rows of a packed house] I went to dinner and the Brookses were there. Either the cocktails were too good or too many, with the result that I got to talking to Brooks about the fact that Louisiana was not a part of the United States at the time of the Revolution, etc. The worst of it is I was probably not very respectful to his wife, who of course took his part" (Stevens, 634).

Whatever indiscretions Stevens committed probably paled to insignificance when compared to the antics of the bacchanalian Welshman Dylan Thomas. Although his work was known in America, Thomas did not come to this country until the winter of 1950. On the afternoon of February 28, he gave a reading at Yale and afterward attended a dinner party in one of the upstairs rooms at Mory's. This was Thomas's first encounter with American academics, and the ambience itself was relentlessly collegiate. Mory's had originated as a public eating house in the middle of the nineteenth century. According to legend, it was discovered by members of the class of 1863 when returning from boat races in the New Haven harbor. The owners, Frank and Jane Moriarty, twice moved their establishment to bring it closer to the Yale campus. After the Moriartys died, the business passed through several hands, the last being those of Louis Linder, who retired in 1912. By this time Mory's and Linder himself had been immortalized in song by the Whiffenpoofs, a men's chorus that would sing for their supper at "the place where Louie dwells." Rather than allow the traditions of half a century to be lost with Linder's retirement, a group of Yale men bought the restaurant and moved it to its present location at 306 York Street. To this day, it remains a nominally private dining club. The walls are adorned with oars from crews past and photographs of several generations of Yale athletes (including a youthful George Bush in his baseball uniform). The tables are carved with the initials of countless Yale men, and various choral groups (now of both genders) serenade diners during the school year.

Recollections of Dylan's night at Mory's differ. According to John Malcolm Brinnin, the Welshman's guide during his tour of America, the academics were generally cold and aloof toward their guest. "With the exception of Cleanth Brooks, who conveyed by his presence more than by anything he said a sympathetic recognition of Dylan's dilemma, and of Norman Pearson, who was the talkative host of the party, all the professors sat around in a brooding druidic circle apparently awaiting an oracle" (Brinnin, 38). Cleanth, however, remembers things differently. He is convinced that Brinnin expected something terrible to happen and was simply imagining the fulfillment of his own worst nightmares. Dylan was apparently uneasy among so many university professors. To compensate for his sense of social and intellectual inferiority, he began telling bawdy stories about Queen Victoria on the chamber pot as soon as he had a couple of drinks under his belt. "He became very truculent," Pearson recalls. "I can believe that it became as unhappy for him as for the group" (see Ferris, 235). Compared to Dylan's later legendary misbehavior, that evening was a mild if awkward occasion.

Cleanth saw Dylan only one more time before his tragic death from alcoholism in 1953. The director of one of the art galleries in Washington, D.C., organized a program on the poetry of Thomas Hardy. Dylan and W. H. Auden were to read from Hardy's verse, and John Ransom was to make some brief critical remarks. Not too long before the day of the program, Ransom contracted laryngitis and asked Cleanth to fill in for him. It was an imposing enough task to be the interlude between readings by two celebrity poets, but the situation became even more frantic when a phone call on the day of the program informed the museum director that Dylan had missed his train from New York. Much to everyone's surprise, he did catch a later train and arrived both sober and on time. The audience was composed largely of society women in their sixties; however, when Dylan Thomas began to read Hardy's poem "The Going" in his resonant

Welsh voice, they melted like bobby-soxers raving over the current teen idol Johnnie Ray.[3]

If Dylan was only a casual acquaintance, Cleanth's friendship with the other panelist, Wystan Auden, went back over a decade. In 1939, when Auden was in the United States and traveling from the East Coast to Taos, New Mexico, Cleanth wrote him, care of his titular father-in-law, Thomas Mann, to suggest that the poet take the southern route and stop in Baton Rouge. When Auden arrived, he was accompanied by his young lover, Chester Kallman. In an effort to entertain their British visitors, Tinkum Brooks and Katherine Anne Porter drove Auden and Kallman to see a nearby antebellum mansion. When Cleanth later saw the two women laughing hysterically, he was told that a bee had flown into the car and that Chester had reacted like a girl frightened by a mouse. Cleanth saw a good deal more of Auden over the years, and the two eventually joined forces in an unsuccessful attempt to preserve the traditional Anglican liturgy. A true propagandist of inclusion, the young firebrand Marxist became something of a High Church Tory in his later years.

Although there were no antebellum plantations in Connecticut, one could find within a thirty-mile radius of New Haven hundreds of occupied dwellings older than any in Louisiana. If a southerner felt out of place in such an environment, it was not because he had been transported from a traditional to a synthetic culture but because he was in a strange land that was in some ways even older than his own. Like a Yale undergraduate named John C. Calhoun at the dawn of the nineteenth century, Cleanth had made a home among the Connecticut Yankees.

II

When Cleanth Brooks came to Yale, he joined what was generally regarded as the best English department in the world; however, it had not attained its distinction through literary criticism. The senior men in the department were historical scholars of the old school. Although each of the major periods was covered, Yale's greatest strength lay in the eighteenth century; by the 1940s, the department could claim a trio of world-class eighteenth-century scholars in Chauncey Brewster Tinker, Frederick A. Pottle, and Frederick W. Hilles.

Tinker had received all three of his degrees from Yale (in 1899, 1901, and 1902, respectively) and had stayed on to become a powerful force in the English department for half a century. Tinker will be best remembered as the scholar who did the most to bring James Boswell out from under the formidable shadow of Samuel Johnson, establishing Boswell's reputation as a man and artist, not just a biographer and sycophant. Tinker's book *Young Boswell* (1922) began the modern reevaluation of Boswell; it was followed two years later by Tinker's impressive edition of the *Letters of James Boswell*. Not only a considerable scholarly endeavor, this project required Tinker to track down more than a hundred unpublished letters "scattered from Switzerland to California" (Buchanan, 35). Later that same decade, Tinker discovered a wealth of Boswell papers in Malahide Castle in Scotland. His protégé and former student Fred Pottle began the massive task of editing the papers in late 1929; in 1949 these documents and other Boswell artifacts were sold to Yale. That same year, Yale appointed twenty-four leading British and American scholars to an advisory committee for the publication of the Boswell papers. The recently hired Cleanth Brooks was among them.

Cleanth's appointment to the Boswell advisory committee was a tribute to the reputation he was beginning to earn as one of the general editors of the Percy letters. Although that project and his book on the southern dialect (which had been reviewed favorably in *American Speech* by Yale's senior linguist, Bob Menner) helped to establish Cleanth's credibility among Yale's old guard of historical scholars, the real impetus for his appointment to the faculty had come from young associate professors who saw the limitations of the old historical approach to literature. At the time *Understanding Poetry* was published in 1938, the standard freshman English course at Yale, which had been instituted shortly after the turn of the century, consisted of three months of Shakespeare, followed by "five modern greats"—Carlyle, Ruskin, Tennyson, Browning, and Arnold. Reflecting back on those times over half a century later, Louis Martz (another protégé of Tinker who had been kept on the faculty) asked in exasperation: "Can you imagine teaching Carlyle's 'Heroes and Hero Worship' in 1939?"[4] As valuable as this approach might have been at one time, it was no longer working in the undergraduate classroom; *Understanding Poetry* offered a way out of this dilemma.

The man who was largely responsible for introducing *Understanding Poetry* at Yale was Maynard Mack. A young specialist in both Shakespeare and the eighteenth century (he would later write the definitive life of Alexander Pope), Mack was another Yale graduate (B.A., 1932; Ph.D., 1936) who had been kept on the faculty. In 1938 he taught "Brooks and Warren" in a special freshman seminar in modern poetry and encouraged his colleague John Pope to make *Understanding Poetry* the basis of an entirely revamped freshman program in 1940. Maynard had met Cleanth when they were both spending the summer of 1940 at the University of Texas. Now that Yale was going to introduce the new criticism into its curriculum, it seemed only logical to entice one of the leading new critics into joining the department. While the younger men (particularly Maynard Mack) were leading the effort, the senior faculty seemed remarkably acquiescent.

On December 8, 1944, Cleanth delivered one of the annual Bergen Memorial lectures at Yale. By all accounts, this presentation was well received. Titled "Shakespeare as a Symbolist Poet," it was published the following summer in the *Yale Review* and later became the second chapter of *The Well Wrought Urn*. Whatever else it might have accomplished, it disabused anyone who heard it of the notion that the new critics were a band of eccentrics who knocked Shakespeare for the greater glory of Donne. No doubt, Cleanth's own southern charm and courtliness won over some doubters. (Tinker did not suggest that anyone throw a stool at the speaker, as he had when he heard Tate deliver a controversial lecture several years earlier.) He was even invited back to New Haven to teach in the following summer session. Unfortunately, Cleanth had to decline that assignment because it would overlap by a couple of weeks the beginning of fall quarter at the University of Chicago, where he had agreed to teach in 1945–46.

Before the end of the fall quarter at Chicago, Cleanth had firm offers of permanent employment from both Cornell and Yale; he also had reason to believe that his guest stint at Chicago might lead to a job there. However, his ultimate choice was never in doubt. Although Chicago and Cornell both would have been preferable to LSU, each school had its drawbacks—Chicago its rigid neo-Aristotelian curriculum and Cornell the administrative duties that would have come with being department chairman. Even if all other factors had been equal, Yale's academic preeminence would have tipped the scales for Cleanth. (As he put it in a conversation shortly before his death: "If you've been playing in the bush leagues and the best team in the majors calls you up, you go.") Although Yale wanted him to join the faculty in the fall of 1946, Cleanth was sensitive about the manner of his leaving LSU. He thought it would look bad if he departed immediately after taking a year off to teach at Chicago; also, he needed a year to help his mother plan for her future and to make his own clean and dignified break from the Old War Skule.

The addition of Cleanth Brooks to the Yale faculty in 1947 culminated a radical change in direction for the English department (even if that change had been developing incrementally for the better part of a decade). Only the year before, a version of the new criticism had established a significant beachhead elsewhere in the university when Dean William C. DeVane brought the European scholar René Wellek to New Haven from the University of Iowa to form a program in comparative literature.[5] A theorist and historian of criticism whose own position was quite compatible with that of Brooks and Warren, Wellek helped give a kind of continental respectability to a movement that had been regarded up to that point as a largely Anglo-American phenomenon.

The sense of academic hierarchy at Yale was such that the senior members of the English department could have stood firm against the new criticism had they been so inclined. Although they did not adopt it themselves, they allowed younger men to make it the basis for undergraduate teaching in English. Fred Pottle, who wrote an attack on the new criticism in his book *The Idiom of Poetry* (1946), taught a much more inclusive course in criticism, which began with Aristotle and ended with I. A. Richards. Among the old guard, only Chauncey Brewster Tinker expressed visceral opposition to the new way of doing things ("Tink" had been deeply offended when the Yale poet Andrews Wanning published an essay depicting him as a literary dinosaur and I. A. Richards as the wave of the future). The depth of his feeling was revealed when Louis Martz (one of Tink's former students) asked his old mentor to help him snare a course in literary criticism called "Approaches to Poetry" when the incumbent teacher of the course, Ray Short, left Yale. "The trouble with you young fellows," Tink exploded, "is that you are all off a-whoring after I. A. Richards."[6] By the time Cleanth arrived on the faculty, Tinker had been retired for two years. He had also mellowed to the point of writing Cleanth a friendly letter welcoming him to Yale. Even after his retirement, Tinker remained as a fellow of Davenport College, where he and Cleanth developed a genuine sense of collegiality, at least in part because of their similar views on religion.

As a full professor, Cleanth was a rank above his friends Mack and Martz and was privy to the deliberations of the old guard. He remembers being greatly impressed when the full professors had to choose between two junior colleagues who were up for promotion and tenure. In casting his vote, Fred Pottle said that he was going against the man he liked better personally because he believed that the other candidate could bring greater distinction to the department. Pottle's vote, and the appointment, went to a young critical theorist named William K. Wimsatt. Over the years, Wimsatt did bring great distinction to the department and became a close personal and professional friend of Cleanth Brooks. Over forty years later, a Yale graduate student from the early fifties recalled that "one of the local sights was William K. Wimsatt, a hulking and rumpled six foot five inches [actually 7'0"] looming over the dapper five-foot-six-inch Brooks, as they ambled across campus, talking away about (we knew) momentous matters" (Rollin, 374).

In addition to being a brilliant new critic (and a formidable eighteenth-century scholar), Bill Wimsatt was also an ardent defender of the Old South. One of his collateral ancestors, Wilmer McLean, "had owned a farm near Manassas Junction, stretching along the banks of Bull Run at the time of the first of the two battles fought there. In fact, a shell had come crashing through one of his windows during the opening skirmish, and after that grim experience he had resolved to find a new home for his family, preferably back in the rural southside hill country, 'where the sound of battle would never reach them.' He found what he wanted at Appomattox Courthouse—a remote hamlet, better than two miles from the railroad and clearly of no military value to either side" (Foote, 945–46). It was in Wilmer McLean's house, on Palm Sunday 1865, that Lee surrendered to Grant. (For the rest of his days, McLean would boast that the Civil War began in his front yard and ended in his parlor.) The Federal troops later trashed the house and seized much of the family furniture. When Mrs. McLean saw a reconstruction of the surrender at the Smithsonian museum years later, she recognized her dining room table, which the museum refused to return. Although his home state of Maryland had been physically restrained from seceding, William Kurtz Wimsatt was as much a neo-Confederate as any of the Nashville Twelve.

III

In 1949 Brooks published "Irony as a Principle of Structure," one of the most widely cited essays never to appear in one of his books. Theoretically, this essay breaks no new ground. It makes the familiar argument that the essence of poetry lies in juxtaposition and context, not in any qualities intrinsic to the words and subject matter of the poem. In *The Well Wrought Urn*, Brooks had argued that paradox is the language of poetry. In this later essay, he substitutes the term *irony*; however, his position is essentially unchanged. What he is referring to is "the *obvious* warping of a statement by the context" ("Irony," 730). Not only does poetry render the abstract concrete through the vehicle of metaphor, it can purge an otherwise general statement of abstraction through the pressure of context. Making the same point he had made in his analysis of Keats's "Ode on a Grecian Urn," Brooks writes, "the statements made—including those which appear to be philosophical generalizations—are to be read as if they were speeches in a drama. Their relevance, their propriety, their rhetorical force, even their meaning, cannot be divorced from the context in which they are embedded" (731).

"Irony as a Principle of Structure" shows Brooks's style at its best; that style is conversational in the truest sense of the term. One has the feeling that the critic is *conversing* with the reader rather than lecturing to him (those who are familiar with Brooks's speaking voice cannot help hearing it in his writing). Robert Heilman has characterized the Brooks style as "unfailingly considerate of the reader—easy, exact, diaphanous, unpretentious, never gesticulating or calling attention to itself." Heilman goes on to note that "in its discipline it is in contrast with the accident-prone clumsiness or the swishing in-house jargon of the downright scholar, and with a worse evil—the egotistic-opaque that beclouds current exercises in theory (the concepts with which I deal, says the theorist in effect, are too difficult and profound to be reduced to public language). But a central sweet reasonableness is no bar against the firm, the crisp, the epigrammatic" (Heilman, 141).

One of the virtues of "Irony as a Principle"—and of Brooks's style, in general—is its insistence on illustrating critical ideas by applying them to the reading of specific poems. (As we shall see in a later chapter, the reading Brooks gives here to Wordsworth's "A slumber did my spirit seal" has become a touchstone by which a wide range of scholars have defined their positions vis-à-vis that of the new criticism.) Also, like Donne's "well wrought urn," Brooks's prose can become an instance of the doctrine it expounds. In talking about the importance of metaphor in poetry, he employs some striking metaphors of his own.

At one point, Brooks writes that "the elements of a poem are related to each other, not as blossoms juxtaposed in a bouquet, but as the blossoms are related to each other in a growing plant. The beauty of the poem is the flowering of the whole plant, and needs the stalk, the leaf, and the hidden roots" ("Irony," 729). Elsewhere, he writes: "Invulnerability to irony is the stability of a context in which the internal pressures balance and mutually support each other. The stability is like that of the arch: the very forces which are calculated to drag the stones to the ground actually provide the principle of support—a principle in which thrust and counterthrust become the means of stability" (732–33). Perhaps most memorably, he compares the metaphors in poetry to the tail of a kite "—the tail that makes the kite fly—the tail that renders the kite more than a frame of paper blown crazily down the wind" (729).

Another notable effort that Brooks undertook during his early years at Yale was a concerted attempt to rescue John Milton from his more traditional admirers by reinterpreting his achievement on solid new critical grounds. The modernist backlash against Milton was probably to be expected, considering the high esteem in which his work had been held during the preceding two centuries. In his famous review of H. J. C. Grierson's anthology of metaphysical poems, T. S. Eliot maintains that the dissociation of sensibility that set in at the end of the seventeenth century "was aggravated by the influence of the two most powerful poets of the century, Milton and Dryden" (Eliot, *Essays*, 247). Eliot makes his case for the metaphysical poets in part by depicting Milton as the precursor of Romantic verse with its overheated emotion and impassioned rhetoric, divorced from wit.

Brooks's most substantial effort to make Milton palatable to the new critics came in 1951 with his edition of *The Poems of Mr. John Milton*. Along with providing a scholarly edition of Milton's early verse, Brooks and his coeditor, John Edward Hardy, wrote a series of critical essays over five times as long as the primary text. In their extended summary essay, "The Progress and Form of the Early Career," the editors argue that Milton's superficial similarities to Spenser have been wrongly stressed to the exclusion of his more fundamental affinities with the metaphysical poets. Although Donne and Milton approach their materials in a markedly different manner, both are fully committed to metaphor. Brooks and Hardy offer the following comparison and contrast:

> One has to get into a poem of Donne's through a consciousness of the complexities of metaphor. There is no other way. The articulation of the conceits *is* the poem—its "meaning" and its form; the mechanical effects are habitually designed to sharpen rather than to soften the impression of ingenious precision in the images. One usually becomes conscious of what is conventional in a Donne poem only *after* he has discerned the unique pattern of its imagery, its self-contained form. But with Milton the reading process is likely to be reversed. The reader feels that he is on ground of

> familiar and easy contours. And he may go on for some time, through
> many readings of a poem, before he is even vaguely aware of an underlying
> complexity of metaphorical structure. (Brooks and Hardy, *Poems of
> Milton*, 261)

In "Milton and the New Criticism," an essay published in the *Sewanee
Review* the same year that *The Poems of Mr. John Milton* appeared,
Brooks again argues that Milton's use of metaphor is not fundamentally
different from Donne's. The point is not to turn Milton into Donne but to
suggest that there are common traits possessed by all true poets; Donne is
a useful touchstone simply because his approach to metaphor demonstrates characteristics we might miss in the work of a less flamboyant
craftsman. By examining selected passages in *Comus, Paradise Lost*, and
Paradise Regained, Brooks demonstrates that the connection between individual metaphors and total context is as functional in Milton's poetry
as in Donne's. In contrast, scholars such as Douglas Bush would have us
believe that Milton's distinctiveness lay in his engagement with sublime
themes and in the grandeur of his moral vision.

In "Eve's Awakening" (1954) Brooks notes that Milton's ideas can actually be an impediment to the appreciation of his poetry. One of the problems that modern readers experience in *Paradise Lost* is the gender psychology that informs Milton's depiction of the Fall. If we are to accept
Milton's poem on its own terms, it appears that we would have to accept the notion that man is superior to woman and that a wife should be
subservient to her husband. Brooks correctly notes that such ideas "set the
modern reader's teeth on edge" (*Shaping Joy*, 349). (And this was long
before feminism had become such a significant force in literary studies!)
The problem is compounded by the fact that in his personal life, particularly in his treatment of his first wife Mary Powell, Milton had proved
himself to be something less than a poster boy for twentieth-century feminism. Brooks tries to rescue *Paradise Lost*, if not Milton himself, by looking more closely at what actually happens in the poem.

Beginning with her first moments of consciousness, Eve reveals a nar-
cissism that will ultimately prove her undoing. She is much taken with the
image of herself and, at least at first, finds the watery image of Adam more
pleasing than his reality. It is only as she comes to know Adam better that
she realizes: "How beauty is excelled by manly grace / And wisdom, which
alone is truly fair." By putting these words into Eve's mouth, Milton emphasizes the superiority of the manly virtues to female vanity. If that were
all there was to it, then Milton would stand convicted of simplistic male

chauvinism. The truth, however, is that Adam himself is bewitched by images and falls short of the supreme rationality that would have preserved him in a state of Grace. In sacrificing himself to remain with his wife, Adam demonstrates a more chivalric version of the character flaw that drove Eve to disobedience. What is finally most important to Milton, Brooks argues, is not the superficial differences between men and women but their common tendency to be less than what they ought to be. "The Cavalier poet Lovelace has dealt with the essence of the situation in his little poem 'To Lucasta, on Going to the Wars': 'I could not love thee dear so much, / Loved I not honour more.' Adam cannot love Eve as much as he ought unless he loves God more: unless he loves God more, ultimately he cannot love Eve at all" (*Shaping Joy*, 363).

In "Poetry and Poeticality" (a lecture delivered at the University of Manchester in 1966), Brooks uses a paradox at the heart of Milton's greatest epic to illustrate a central truth about the nature of poetry. Since at least the time of Blake, readers have noticed that Milton's Hell is a far more interesting place than his Heaven and that his Satan is a far more engaging personality than his God. In terms of morality, the doctrine of the "Fortunate Fall" has always left orthodox believers a bit uneasy. In terms of aesthetics, however, it is a necessary truth. Literature cannot exist in Heaven or in an earthly paradise; it requires conflict and a vision of evil. Not only does this give us a truer picture of life, it also helps us see why, in the words of the *Exultet*, we deserve so great a redeemer.

IV

While Cleanth's reputation was flourishing at Yale, Red Warren was also finding greater professional acceptance in the North than he had known in the region of his birth. Joseph Warren Beach had put together a first-rate program at the University of Minnesota, and the students Red taught were generally much better prepared than those he had encountered at LSU. Still, Baton Rouge had been an exciting place to live, and the memory of his years there continued to haunt Red even as he tried to accustom himself to the Minneapolis winters. In 1946 Red Warren laid permanent imaginative claim to the Louisiana of Huey Long with his great novel *All the King's Men*. Although he called his protagonist Willie Stark and never named the state in which the novel was set, no one doubted that Red was writing about Huey. In fact, he raised Huey Long to such mythic proportions that it was years before critics began turning their attention to less topical aspects of the novel. With *All the King's Men*, Warren crossed the border between high and popular literature; not only did he win the Pulitzer Prize for fiction, he also created a mass audience for future best-selling novels. Having earned fame, fortune, and critical favor, he was at the top of his profession.

At the same time, Red Warren was a profoundly lonely man. Although Minnesota had treated him well, it would never be home. The excitement of the *Southern Review* was now only a fond memory, and his always fragile marriage was coming apart at the seams. The more Red accomplished professionally, the more bitter and envious Cinina became. He had gallantly defended her (and, when that was impossible, remained silent) for nearly two decades. As her drinking got worse, he became more protective. Finally, Cinina agreed to see a psychiatrist. In the course of her treatment, her doctor convinced her that she was trapped in a bad marriage and that she would never recover until she broke herself free of Red. Rather than feeling any sense of loyalty to the man who had stood by her for twenty years, Cinina grandly announced that the marriage was over. When the news got out, Red's friends had to restrain themselves from sending him heartfelt congratulations.

Although separated from Cleanth by the length of the Mississippi River, Red kept in close touch with his old friend through the mail. By the time Cleanth had moved to New Haven, the two were once again collaborators; in 1949 their fourth textbook, *Modern Rhetoric*, was published by Harcourt Brace. (This is probably the only time that a writer has followed up a best-selling, Pulitzer Prize-winning novel with a freshman English text.) Although *Modern Rhetoric* has gone into three editions, it has not had nearly the historic impact of *Understanding Poetry*. The reason is obvious to anyone who examines both books. Whereas *Understanding Poetry* launched a pedagogical revolution, *Modern Rhetoric* was counter-revolutionary, if not reactionary.

In terms of its organization and content, *Modern Rhetoric* seems clearly designed for a course in freshman composition, but even admirers of the book believed that it was too advanced for such an audience. The book is probably most effective when Brooks and Warren are playing to their strengths as literary critics, as in the chapter they devote to the importance of metaphor. Not only is metaphor the essence of poetry but also one of the most natural devices for anyone using language. Metaphor that is based on clear perception and clear thought can serve as an antidote to much current misuse of the language. There is, for example, "an important negative relation" between jargon and metaphor. "It is the very lack of concrete words and of metaphorical vividness and particularity that makes jargon cloudy and ineffective" (Brooks and Warren, *Modern Rhetoric*, 408).

The problem is that academia itself spawns jargon, leading far too many people to believe that the use of abstract words makes one sound learned. Brooks and Warren counter this notion by citing Orwell's translation of a familiar passage from Ecclesiastes into the language of bureaucracy. In the Scriptures, we read: "I returned, and saw under the sun, that the race is not to the swift, nor the battle to the strong, neither yet bread to the wise, nor yet riches to men of understanding, nor yet favor to men of skill; but time and chance happeneth to them all." According to Orwell, that passage might well be written today as follows: "Objective consideration of contemporary phenomena compels the conclusion that success or failure in competitive activities exhibits no tendency to be commensurate with innate capacity, but that a considerable element of the unpredictable must invariably be taken into account" (see *Modern Rhetoric*, 409).

With yet another book to his credit and the ordeal of his marriage over, Red was poised to make a new start in life, both professionally and personally. The film version of *All the King's Men*, which was made in 1949, extended the audience for his work even beyond the tens of thousands of readers who had put the novel on the best-seller list. Moreover, Red himself had won the Robert Meltzer Award from the Screen Writers Guild for his work on the movie script; this fact alone suggested that his ambition to be a successful dramatist was not out of the question. In the fall of 1950 Thornton Wilder, who was a longtime fellow of one of Yale's colleges and a good friend of Cleanth, suggested that the university might revitalize its School of Drama by hiring more creative writers to teach playwriting. At that point, Warren was living in New York and teaching part-time in the Yale English department. Because Marc Connelly was leaving the School of Drama, there was a permanent opening in that program. A. Whitney Griswold, the new president of Yale, called Red to his office one Saturday afternoon and invited Cleanth to come along. Although he would be officially listed as Professor of Playwrighting, Warren was promised another course in the English department. Thus, for the fourth time in their careers, the same campus was home to Brooks and Warren.

When the Yale registrar called Cleanth in late April 1951, hoping to locate Red, who had not turned in his grades, Cleanth discovered that his friend was in Reno getting a divorce. The following year, Red Warren and

Eleanor Clark were married at her mother's home in the Connecticut countryside. It was a small private ceremony with Albert Erskine as best man and Albert's former wife, Katherine Anne Porter, as matron of honor. Tinkum's nephew Carver Blanchard, who was then ten, remembers wrestling in the front yard with Eleanor's nephew, Nate Jessup, shortly before the marriage vows were exchanged in the parlor. On the way over, Cleanth had had to stop the car to allow his dog Pompey (who was half Great Dane, half German shepherd, and a worthy successor to Caesar) to relieve himself. Pompey, with a mind of his own and energy to match, tried to run away, pulling Cleanth against a barbed wire fence. By the time the Brooks contingent arrived at the wedding, Cleanth's shirt was soaked with blood, and he had to borrow a clean one from Red. Despite this slapstick beginning, the marriage turned out to be a spectacular success. Red was happy, perhaps for the first time in his life.

Later, on August 1, 1953, Red wrote the following letter to Tinkum Brooks:

> This is to say that Rosanna Phelps Warren arrived, in a most melodramatic fashion, in the middle of the living room floor, last Monday at about ten p.m. No doctor present, but a neighbor, M. Carleton called doctors and ambulances, etc. So we sat on the floor for some twenty-five minutes until they arrived. To compound the matter, the ambulance had a collision on the way to Bridgeport (we had planned to have a decorous affair for the arrival in New Haven, but there wasn't time to waste), but managed to go ahead on its power. Eleanor had a pretty rough time that night, for they had to take about a hundred stitches after the explosive advent. While this was going on Rosanna nearly died, but a doctor saw her in time—this in the hospital—and got her through. She spent several days in an incubator, but is now out and is fine. . . . Eleanor is abed, and will be so for some time, but feels all right. And we have a good nurse to take care of both the ailing ladies. Rosanna ails only from hunger. She is mighty little but seems determined to catch up. And she is very pretty.

In addition to personal contentment, family life brought the end of a long dry spell during which Red was unable to write poetry. Two years after his marriage to Eleanor, he published *Brother to Dragons: A Tale in Verse and Voices*, which was his first poem in a decade. This closet drama, written in blank verse, tells the story of the brutal murder of a slave on the Kentucky frontier. Because the murderer was a nephew of Thomas Jefferson, Warren turns a grisly slice of history into a parable of American innocence. The poem, which Randall Jarrell considered "Warren's best book," was dedicated to Cleanth and Tinkum Brooks. In a letter to Red, dated August 4, 1954, Cleanth expresses his opinion of the work:

> The curious thing about that fine poem, and the only thing about it that has ever shocked me, was its ability to short-circuit so many otherwise fine critical intelligences. I could not have predicted it, but I think that I am now beginning slowly to discern why. I am tempted to say that it is the first really 'new' poem since *The Waste Land*. (I am not trying to praise it in calling it 'new': I am simply calling attention to what I am convinced is a historical fact.) Allen's reaction is a nice case in point: he has been utterly frank with you and me in indicating his dislike for it. But I am convinced now that what is involved is more than a particular blind spot in Allen. It is something that Allen shares with others—it is a blind spot in the age. (Not *all* of the age, thank God!)

                                     V

Just as some of Vanderbilt's more creative minds found their way to Baton Rouge in the thirties and forties, a group of *Southern Review* alumni began to form around New Haven in the fifties. When Cleanth arrived in 1947, Albert Erskine had just begun his association with Random House; for many years, he and his wife Marisa lived in the Connecticut countryside, where they continued to be close friends of Cleanth and Tinkum. Red Warren arrived in 1950. Then, in 1954, John Palmer became the fourth *Southern Review* editor to join this community of LSU expatriates.

Twice during the previous twelve years, John's career as an editor had been interrupted by military service. He had left the *Southern Review* for a naval commission in World War II. After the war, he was without a job when Allen Tate resigned as editor of the *Sewanee Review*. Because Cleanth was already being wooed by Yale, he declined the opportunity to succeed Tate but backed Palmer for the job. John began editing the *Sewanee Review* in 1946. Although he was called back to active duty during the Korean War, he continued to run the magazine from his post in Washington from 1950 to 1952. It was only after he was reassigned to the U.S. Embassy in London that he was forced to turn over the editorship to Monroe Spears. By 1954, John Palmer was once again an unemployed civilian. That same year, the editorship of the *Yale Review* became vacant. Although President Griswold was urging Cleanth to take the magazine, he was pursuing too many other projects to want to slip back into the editorial harness. Cleanth told Griswold that Palmer was not only available but had done an outstanding job as editor of the *Sewanee Review*. John edited the *Yale Review* for the next twenty-five years, taught a light load in the English department, and served as dean of Silliman College.

Another of Cleanth's friends from LSU was on the political science faculty. The same year that Cleanth arrived in New Haven, Willmoore Kendall came to Yale. Willmoore (or "Ken" as he was known to his Baton Rouge friends) was a walking embodiment of the adage that the more things change, the more they remain the same. The Trotskyite of the late thirties and early forties was now an abrasive right-wing nativist. (Years later, Cleanth remarked: "I may have helped push him to the right, but I certainly didn't mean to push him quite so far.")[7] If his politics had turned nearly 180 degrees, Kendall's personality was still much the same. Recently divorced, he occupied a bachelor's suite in Pierson College, where he had been appointed a fellow shortly after being hired. When the master of the college gave a lecture upon his return from Europe, Ken could not resist the impulse to contradict his every assertion. As he later reported to Cleanth, "I guess I've done it again." Before long, Kendall became so unpopular with his colleagues that he was granted virtually unlimited academic leave so that they could be rid of him.

If Kendall failed to endear himself to the Yale faculty, he nevertheless made some ardent disciples among the student body. By far the most famous and influential was William F. Buckley, Jr. Bill Buckley was a sophomore when he took Willmoore Kendall's political science seminar; perhaps for the first time in his somewhat insular upbringing, he encountered intellectual challenge rather than indoctrination. ("When his freshman composition teacher, Richard Sewall, suggested that he take a challenging metaphysics course, Buckley replied, 'I have God and my father. That's all I need' "; Judis, 59.) Kendall's staunch anti-Communism, his eccentric genius, and his sheer outspokenness made him an unusual figure at Yale. The university's reputation for cautious conservatism was so extreme that it often tried to stress its liberality. In doing so, however, it made itself a target of more committed and ideological conservatives such as Buckley and Kendall.

Although Cleanth never had Bill Buckley as a student, he followed Bill's career closely and admired his debating skills. At the invitation of Bill's younger brother Reid, who did take a couple of his classes, Cleanth and Tinkum were invited to dinner at the Buckley home in Sharon, Connecticut, one evening in the mid-fifties. The Brookses were to follow Reid by car across Connecticut but got lost on the last leg of the trip. They asked for directions, only to arrive at a house with so many cars parked around it that they were sure it was a hotel. Actually, they were simply part of a large gathering, which included Mr. and Mrs. William F. Buckley, Sr., their ten children, and assorted guests. Tinkum and Mrs. Buckley, a gracious and sweet-tempered woman who had matriculated for a time at Sophie Newcomb College, immediately took to each other. Although Will Buckley was a Texan who had lived in many different places during his years as an oil speculator, his wife was very much the southern belle. In addition to maintaining a home in Connecticut, the family also had a house in Camden, South Carolina, and seemed by temperament and conviction more southern than yankee. Moreover, like true aristocrats, they took their wealth for granted. The night that Cleanth visited, the family was very excited about a new painting they had acquired. In showing it off, however, they did not mention the identity of the artist, much less the price they had paid. Although no expert, Cleanth knew enough about painting to recognize that the Buckleys owned an original Botticelli.

During the Korean War, Willmoore Kendall took a leave of absence from Yale to work for an Army think tank. Having served with the CIA for a time between his departure from Baton Rouge and his arrival at New Haven, he was committed to defeating Communism by any means necessary. (He would be one of the few prominent academics to defend Senator Joseph McCarthy a few years later.) One of the strategies being developed for use in Korea was psychological warfare. With the atom bomb, America's technological superiority was assured, but Truman was understandably reluctant to use the bomb again. (MacArthur's eagerness to do so helped cause his celebrated rift with the Commander in Chief.) If America could win the hearts and minds of the enemy population, victory would be assured at a much smaller cost in blood and treasure. Kendall was convinced that, if anyone knew anything about the connotations of language, it was his old friend Cleanth Brooks. He invited Cleanth down to Washington to meet some generals. The idea was to construct such cunningly worded leaflets that when they were dropped behind enemy lines, mass defections would ensue. Cleanth was skeptical about this scheme, and it never moved beyond vague theoretical discussions. It is significant to note, however, that there was a time in the early fifties when respected government officials actually thought that the new criticism might be a tool for helping win the Cold War.

CHAPTER FOURTEEN

The Backlash

If the new criticism had simply been the latest rage to sweep literary studies, it could have been tolerated with no more than the standard amount of academic envy and backbiting. What was intolerable to many, however, were the sweeping claims made on behalf of this new movement. Not only were ontological critics answering John Crowe Ransom's want ad; they saw themselves as being the *only* true critics on the contemporary scene, if not in the entire history of literature. These upstarts were not just claiming a piece of the turf; they seemed to want it all. Given the popularity of *Understanding Poetry* in the undergraduate classroom and the tremendous influence of the *Kenyon, Sewanee,* and *Southern* reviews among the rising generation of graduate students and younger academics, talk of a southern or new critical mafia was not all lighthearted banter.

I ··

Although the resistance of old-line scholars to this brash insurgency was to be expected, the vehemence with which it was often expressed spoke as much of desperation as of conviction. The cry of the old guard reached a particularly shrill pitch on December 29, 1948, when Douglas Bush, the outgoing president of the Modern Language Association, addressed the members of his organization on the manifold sins of the new criticism. As a historical scholar, Bush accused the new critics of being ignorant of and indifferent to the circumstantial evidence that makes literary works cultural as well as verbal artifacts. In their cavalier disregard for literary history, the new kids on the block were constantly heading down blind alleys and going off on tangents that careful scholarship would have warned them against.

Bush supports his argument by citing some inaccuracies in the work of Ransom and Tate, apparently believing that such anecdotal evidence would cause his listeners to laugh the new critics out of court. Of course, using the same logic, one might argue that, because Homer occasionally nodded, the greater body of his work—indeed the entire corpus of Greek poetry—was of no value. But Bush seems to have been less interested in observing the rules of evidence than in giving a pep talk to the home team. In his demonology, the new critics stand condemned as dilettantes who are not quite up to the serious work of scholarship. (What scholars were to do with historical facts once they are assembled is not entirely clear.) To be sure, Bush says that critics and scholars have much to learn from each other, but he offers no examples of that ever having happened. In fact, when he reads the new critics, he gets the impression "that they would gladly teach but have little more to learn" (Bush, "New Criticism," 14).

Bush levels two other, seemingly contradictory, charges against the new criticism—that it is simplistic and esoteric. The first of these charges is made in an oft-quoted one-liner: "For a select though large number of literary students the new criticism has been an advanced course in remedial reading" (13). The honest answer is that Bush is quite right. As we have seen, the origins of *An Approach to Literature* were in a class handout that Brooks and Warren used at LSU. Bush's students at Harvard may have been able to navigate the linguistic intricacies of Eliot and other high moderns, not to mention the archaic diction of the metaphysicals, with no pedagogical help beyond the citing of historical allusions, but the less privileged undergraduates at LSU—and, judging from the popularity of *Understanding Poetry*, at other institutions, such as Yale—did need an advanced course in remedial reading.

Having begun his speech on a note of authentic snobbery, Bush concludes on one of fake populism. He argues that "the new criticism, with all its virtues, assumes that literature exists for the diversion of a few sophisticates; that this criticism, with all its portentous seriousness, has really a good deal of the frivolous; that it looks, in short, too much like an intellectualized version of art for art's sake" (19–20). Ever the moralist, Bush sounds a somber warning: "Such academic criticism obviously appeals to an inner circle of initiates, but it is not likely to make converts from the world at large, and literature and the humanistic tradition surely need converts now more than ever before" (21). Thus, even if its practitioners did manage to get all their facts straight, the new criticism would still be dismissed as remedial hermeneutics or elitist word games.

Although Brooks is mentioned only in passing in Bush's presidential address, the historical scholar would take dead aim at the new critic four years later in the pages of the *Sewanee Review*. (That Bush would be given space in a journal so associated with the new criticism is itself a refutation of the supposed hostility of the new critics to the old scholars.) The source of Bush's specific complaints was an essay on Marvell's "Horatian Ode" that Brooks had published in the winter 1947 issue of the *Sewanee Review*.[1] Although Brooks's reading of Marvell's poem would seem to represent the blending of historical evidence and critical insight that Bush called for in his presidential address, he finds Brooks's conclusions overly ingenious and politically tendentious.

The poem in question was written by Marvell as a celebration of Oliver Cromwell's rise to power and triumphal return from Ireland. In his essay Brooks attempts to determine what the poem actually says about Cromwell, as opposed to what political historians tell us the poet personally thought about the British Lord Protector. "For to ascertain what Marvell the man thought of Cromwell," Brooks writes, "and even to ascertain what Marvell as poet consciously intended to say in his poem, will not prove that the poem actually says this, or merely this. . . . There is surely a sense in which anyone must agree that a poem has a life of its own, and a sense in which it provides in itself the only criterion by which what it says can be judged" (see Keast, 322).

Here, as in *The Well Wrought Urn*, Brooks explores the ambiguity and complexity of poetic language to determine the *speaker's* attitude toward his subject. In doing so, Brooks emphasizes the dramatic character of the "Horatian Ode." "It is not a statement—an essay on 'Why I cannot support Cromwell' or on 'Why I am now ready to support Cromwell.' It is a poem essentially dramatic in its presentation, which means that it is diagnostic rather than remedial, and eventuates, not in a course of action, but in contemplation" (see Keast, 336). For purposes of illustration, Brooks cites Shakespeare's *Macbeth* as an example of a similarly sophisticated contemplation of an ambiguous personality. "What, for example, is our attitude toward Macbeth?" Brooks asks. "We assume his guilt, but there are qualities which emerge from his guilt which properly excite admiration." Far from palliating or compensating for Macbeth's guilt, these qualities "actually come into being through his guilt, but they force us to exalt him even as we condemn him. . . . The kind of honesty and insight and whole-mindedness which we associate with tragedy is to be found to some degree in all great poetry and is to be found in [Marvell's] poem" (336).

Not surprisingly, Douglas Bush found Brooks's analysis to be Procrustean and antihistorical. What is curious about his attack, though, is that he and Brooks seem almost to switch roles. There is far more historical commentary in Brooks's essay than one would expect from a new critic (or at least from the caricature of the new critic drawn by Bush and company) and far more textual explication in Bush's rejoinder than one would expect from a historical scholar. Readers are certainly free to determine whether Brooks or Bush is closer to a correct—or at least persuasive—interpretation of Marvell's poem. But if this exchange demonstrates anything about the methodological debate these men were waging, it is that Brooks's version of new criticism is innocent of the charges leveled against it.

To begin with, Brooks is careful to adduce historical evidence about Marvell's attitude toward Cromwell before examining a single line of the ode. Based on Marvell's public behavior and on his other writings, one might think it probable that the ode would be "the utterance of a constitutional monarchist, whose sympathies have been with the King, but who yet believes more in men than in parties or principles, and whose hopes are fixed now on Cromwell, seeing in him both the civic ideal of a ruler without personal ambition, and the man of destiny moved by and yet himself driving a power which is above justice" (see Keast, 324–25). This supposition is made not by Brooks but by Marvell's editor H. M. Margoliouth. Far from challenging Margoliouth's historical characterization, Brooks finds it plausible and just; he simply believes that a careful reading of the ode will amplify Margoliouth's generalizations and show us more specifically how Marvell balanced his Royalist principles with his personal admiration for Cromwell.

Bush begins his attack by egregiously misstating Brooks's thesis. He argues that Brooks "is forcing the evidence to fit an unspoken assumption—namely, that a sensitive, penetrating, and well-balanced mind like Marvell could not really have admired a crude, single-minded, and ruthless man of action like Cromwell" (see Keast, 342). Bush would have us believe that Brooks reads the ode as an attack on Cromwell "as a sort of Puritan Stalin" (342), when, in fact, Brooks demonstrates how the language of Marvell's text reflects the ambivalence we know the *historical*

Marvell to have felt.[2] In contrast, Bush denies Marvell any ambivalence (except, as we shall see, in his treatment of Charles I's martyrdom). He accuses Brooks of always making "a pejorative choice among 'ambiguous' possibilities" (343). But the quotation marks around "ambiguous" actually give the game away. Bush's real objection is that Brooks sees ambiguities that would make pejorative judgments (or qualifications of positive judgments) of Cromwell possible. If Bush finds such a reading far too clever, what does he give us instead?

The image of Marvell that Bush endorses is an antihistorical caricature; Bush's Marvell was no more than a party hack currying Cromwell's favor. That Marvell's treatment of the execution of Charles I reveals the Royalist sympathies we know the poet to have had might appear to present a problem to Bush. Not so. He simply discovers in that section of the ode an irony that he denies it possesses anywhere else. Besides, "for too many readers," the account of Charles's execution "disturbs the center of gravity of the poem" (see Keast, 348). This would seem particularly true of readers bent on giving the ode the most simplistic reading possible.

Bush actually sides with such readers when he observes triumphantly that the "Horatian Ode" was excluded from the 1681 edition of Marvell's verse. The poem would not have been acceptable during the Restoration, Bush seems to be saying, precisely because it was unambiguous in its praise of Cromwell. But, of course, the point is that Marvell's ambivalence would not have been entirely pleasing to rabid partisans of either side. That Marvell couched his reservations about Cromwell in language too subtle to excite a Royalist mob does not mean he had no reservations. Bush even neglects to mention Brooks's discovery that the ode was circulated among Royalists during the 1650s. One need only recall that a goodly number of readers in every generation have failed to note the irony in Swift's "A Modest Proposal" to realize that audience response is not always a reliable guide to the meaning of a work of literature. For that matter, a competent historical scholar should realize that a printer or editor often selects the contents of a given edition of poetry on grounds that have nothing to do with literature or politics.

Brooks responded to Bush in the *Sewanee Review* the following year. His brief essay stresses the historical basis of his reading of Marvell and tries to counter several of the specific points Bush had raised against him. Nevertheless, Brooks concedes that "nothing is more boring to the reader than such a point-by-point refutation." He realizes that "Mr. Bush is stalking bigger game. He has not written his reply merely to argue over a few niceties of interpretation of a poem—important as that poem is. Mr. Bush means to vindicate the biographer and the historian against the mere critic and to show that 'historical conditioning has a corrective as well as a positive value' " (see Keast, 353). (Accepting Bush's implicit challenge, Brooks has entitled his piece "A Note on the Limits of 'History' and the Limits of 'Criticism.' ") For several reasons, Brooks does not believe that historical information can solve critical problems. "In the first place it is often inadequate and problematical. In the second place, the objective facts that can be pegged down and verified do not in themselves yield a judgment: the 'historian' finds himself working with probabilities and subjective evaluations almost as much as the 'critic.' If the critic does well to remind himself how heavily he leans upon history, the historian does well to remind himself how often he is making a critical evaluation" (355).

II

Those who are familiar with Brooks's work, and not just the cartoon images promulgated by his detractors, know him to be a conscientious and genuinely learned scholar. Although he did not possess the creative gifts of Ransom, Tate, or Warren, he probably knew more than any of them about the history of English poetry. He may have shared Tate's disdain for unimaginative pedantry, but he always maintained a tone of civility and sweet reasonableness. Whenever he engaged historical scholars in debate, it was for the purpose of showing them how much they needed each other and how much literature needed them both. A case in point is his essay "The New Criticism and Scholarship," originally published in 1946 in *Twentieth-Century English*, a volume edited by none other than William S. Knickerbocker.

Brooks begins his discussion by pointing out that historical scholarship as we know it is itself a relatively recent development. In the English tradition, it can be traced to Bishop Percy's old correspondent Richard Farmer, who argued in the eighteenth century that those who would understand Shakespeare must acquaint themselves with "all such reading, as was never read." In the ensuing century and a half, this revolutionary insight has become orthodox wisdom. Linguistic and historical scholarship have made modern literary study possible by establishing accurate texts and by ascertaining both the denotative and connotative meaning of those texts for the audiences that originally read them. Without the foundation of scholarship, criticism could never be more than subjective speculation.

If the new critics have occasionally pointed out the limitations of relying too exclusively on historical scholarship, they are merely saying that man cannot live on bread alone, not that he can live without bread. "Indeed," Brooks notes, "in proportion as nuance and connotation are allowed to have importance, in proportion as ironic inflection, word play, or rhythmical variation take on significant meaning, in proportion as symbol and metaphor bulk large in determining 'what the poem says'—in short, in proportion as the critic makes use of the characteristic methods of William Empson or R. P. Warren, he needs to know precisely and exactly what the poet wrote. . . . The new criticism, therefore, properly understood, is the criticism that is *on principle* least hostile to orthodox scholarship" ("New Criticism and Scholarship," 372).

As an example of how the scholar and the critic can, indeed must, work hand in hand, Brooks offers a reading of Bishop Corbet's poem "The Faeryes Farewell." This whimsical meditation on the character of English life (or at least the English sensibility) when Protestantism replaced Catholicism as the national religion can be read in a variety of contradictory ways. Is the equation of Catholicism with the fairies meant to denigrate the seriousness of the Catholic faith? Is it meant to condemn the severity of Puritan moralism? Is the poem perhaps a defense of the Anglican via media? Any of these readings is possible, and the complexity of the poet's attitude toward his subject matter suggests that they may not be mutually exclusive. But the critic interested in determining what Corbet actually wrote would do well to consult the *Oxford English Dictionary*, a history of the age in which the poem was written, and such biographical information as can be found about Bishop Corbet.

It is the province of the literary scholar to uncover the sort of linguistic, historical, and biographical evidence Brooks says we need. Where the scholar differs from the critic is in the use to which he puts this evidence. The scholar will educe from the evidence what Bishop Corbet intended to say in his poem and then conclude that that is what the poem says. In contrast, the critic will examine the evidence and then provide a close textual reading of the poem. Such a reading would not be possible, however, if we did not know the meaning of the word *housewife* in Corbet's time, if we failed to recognize topical allusions to sectarian propaganda, or if we could not identify the family servant fondly mentioned in the poem's final stanza. One suspects that the universal appeal of a poem may well decrease as the need to understand such specialized historical references increases, but then, most modern readers would experience difficulty navigating their way through Shakespeare without footnotes. We should thank the scholars for providing us with textual aids, so long as we realize that such aids only suggest rather than exhaust the meaning of a work of art. As essential as it may be, scholarship is a preparation rather than a substitute for critical reading.

A decade and a half later (after he had become unquestionably the foremost apologist for the new criticism), Brooks attempted once again to defend both the validity and the essential conservatism of his approach to literature. His essay "Literary Criticism: Poet, Poem, and Reader," published in Stanley Burnshaw's *Varieties of Literary Experience* (1962), begins with a clever rhetorical maneuver. Brooks repeats some of the hoary charges laid against the new critics in Douglas Bush's presidential address to the Modern Language Association. Then he notes that "it may be amusing to reconsider, in the light of these strictures, the first great critical document of our Western tradition. Aristotle was certainly no timid aesthete. As a many-sided and healthy Greek of the great period, he took all knowledge to be his province. He was very much concerned with politics and morality as his *Nicomachean Ethics* and his treatise on politics testify. And what does he say about Greek tragedy? Does he praise Aeschylus for his profound insight into the human soul? Does he call attention to Sophocles' deep concern for moral problems?" ("Literary Criticism," 96).

As anyone who has read the *Poetics* knows, Aristotle's concern was almost entirely with matters of formal structure—whether the play had a beginning, a middle, and an end; whether the recognition and reversal were plausibly motivated. Even the moral pronouncements of the play were to be judged not by their doctrinal correctness but by their dramatic propriety. Is Brooks claiming that Aristotle was really a new critic or that the new critics are the true Aristotelians? Not quite. "My point is a more modest one," he writes: "I invoke Aristotle's example simply to suggest that a man who has a proper interest in politics, history, and morals may still find it useful to concern himself with the structure of literary works and with defining the nature and limits of aesthetic judgment" (97). (Douglas Bush, who was in the audience when this essay was first delivered as a paper, good-naturedly conceded that Brooks had scored a point.)

Not content simply to claim an impressive literary pedigree, Brooks goes on to demonstrate empirically the critical advantages of concentrating on the literary text rather than on all of the extrinsic issues that so captivate historical and biographical scholars. (Although a poem as topical as Marvell's "Horatian Ode" cannot even be understood without some

knowledge of British political history, information about the circumstances of a poem's composition will not tell us whether the poem is any
good as a work of art.) Readers of Richard Lovelace's "To a Grasse-
hopper," dedicated to his friend Charles Cotton, might well be curious to
know more about Cotton and his relationship with Lovelace. But once we
assume that the critic ought to know these things, we are virtually imply-
ing that such knowledge can "turn an obscure poem into a clear poem—
and a poor poem into a good poem." Unfortunately, such a principle can
be applied just as easily to doggerel as to canonical literature. "Even the
verse from the newspaper agony column beginning 'It is now a year and a
day / Since little Willie went away' might move us deeply if we actually
knew little Willie and his sorrowing mother. But only the unwary would
take the triggering of such an emotional response as proof of the goodness
of the poem" (105).

A philological scholar examining Lovelace's poem might comment
learnedly on the poet's indebtedness to his Greek source. A historian of
ideas might identify the themes of the poem in order to place them within
an intellectual or philosophical tradition; the moralist would want to
know if the poem is advocating truth and virtue. But one can think of all
sorts of poems that are scholarly, philosophical, or moral—no doubt
some that are all three—which are also wretched works of art. "If one
tries to save the case by stipulating that the doctrine must not only be true,
but must be rendered clearly, acceptably, and persuasively, he will have
come perilously close to reducing the poet's art to that of the mere rhetorician" (107). The only way out of this impasse is for the critic to concentrate on Lovelace's handling of those features that are distinctively poetic.
As we have seen in his previous works, Brooks ranks metaphor as being
foremost on this list.

Brooks's reading of "To a Grasse-hopper" is the sort of lucid exegesis
we have come to expect from the author of *The Well Wrought Urn*, but
the point he is making here is a broader one. Critics can choose to concentrate—as the subtitle of the essay makes clear—on the poet, the poem, or
the reader. Only the second of these approaches is concerned with the
nature and quality of the literary artifact. To focus on the poet or the
reader to the exclusion of the poem will provide us with biographical and
psychological information but no peculiarly literary understanding; to
pursue all three approaches is to risk being distracted from the task at
hand. "Even where we know a great deal about the author's personality
and ideas," Brooks concludes, *"we rarely know as much as the poem*

itself can tell us about itself; for the poem is no mere effusion of a personality. It is a construct—an articulation of ideas and emotions—a dramatization. It is not a slice of raw experience but a product of the poet's imagination—not merely something suffered by him but the result of his creative activity. As a work of art, it calls for a reciprocal imaginative activity on our part; and that involves seeing it for what it *is*" ("Literary Criticism," 114).

III

Few attacks on the new criticism were more virulent than those launched by democratic nativists, who detested any philosophy that seemed to espouse art for art's sake. In 1940, for example, Archibald MacLeish warned apolitical scholars and writers that their indifference to the war in Europe threatened the very freedom that made their scholarship and writing possible. In an impassioned tract called *The Irresponsibles*, MacLeish contrasted the quietism of present-day literary intellectuals with the political activism of John Milton. Himself a New Deal bureaucrat, MacLeish set an example of social engagement that few of his fellow writers could match.

In 1941 Van Wyck Brooks leveled a more comprehensive indictment of literary modernism in a curious book called *The Opinions of Oliver Allston*.[3] Having long since dropped out of the literary vanguard, V. W. Brooks was deep into his curmudgeon phase. Under the guise of presenting the views of his late friend Oliver Allston (actually a fictional persona for himself), the author waxed nostalgic for the nineteenth century and before. In the golden ages of the past, a great writer was "a great man writing, not a mere artificer or master of words. . . . A great man writing is one who bespeaks the collective life of the people, of his group, of his nation, of all mankind" (V. W. Brooks, 216). Not surprisingly, "Oliver Allston" finds modernism to be a departure from this venerable tradition. Rather than producing primary literature (the red-blooded humanistic kind), modernism spawned a kind of enervated, self-regarding coterie literature, divorced from the concerns of real people. "Allston" saw the new criticism as a predictable outgrowth of this coterie literature and condemned it accordingly.

Having hit upon a rhetoric of attack, however, "Allston" has little interest in trying to understand what his target really is saying. For example, he takes out of context John Crowe Ransom's statement that Cleanth

Brooks "prefers poetry to science because he judges poetry is capable of the nicer structures." To this Van Wyck Brooks responds:

> Do not these critics deceive themselves? Very few great poems have as nice a structure as the greatest bridge, and moreover there is this difference between them,—if the structure of a bridge is not nice, the bridge is worth a great deal less than nothing, for not only will the bridge collapse but people will be drowned, while a "poem" like *Hamlet* can be, as Eliot says, a "failure" because it is not like a bridge, and yet remain one of the world's great poems. A critic who prefers poetry to science for this reason only, or chiefly, is therefore one who really prefers science; and this is undoubtedly the truth about all these critics. (243)

It is not a scientific or technological bias but the very existence of a system and methodology that Van Wyck Brooks finds so objectionable about the new critics. What he endorsed was an impressionistic criticism that judged literature by its content rather than its form. Those works he considered life-affirming were good, whereas those that reflected the death drive must be "rebuked." His critical statements are thus subjective assessments of his own likes and dislikes; argument and analysis give way to flat assertion. Even when what is being asserted seems true or prophetic (as when one applies the comments of "Allston" on the early modernists and new critics to the postmodernists and deconstructionists), the resulting body of criticism can never do more than preach to the converted. In the case of the later Van Wyck Brooks, the preacher was attacking a literary revolution he himself had helped to launch.

If the attacks of Van Wyck Brooks–Oliver Allston could be dismissed as the subjective babblings of a glorified journalist trying desperately to rewrite the literary history of this century and his own role in it, the same could not be said of Alfred Kazin. *On Native Grounds*, Kazin's "interpretation of modern American prose literature," appeared in 1942, when its author was still in his twenties and America had just entered the war against Hitler. As a New York intellectual devoted to cultural criticism, Kazin tried to maintain a balance between aesthetic and social concerns. In so doing, he believed that he was continuing the mainstream of American criticism.

Kazin believed that historically (from Emerson and Thoreau to Mencken and Van Wyck Brooks), "criticism had been the great American lay philosophy, the intellectual conscience and intellectual carryall" (Kazin, 400). Critics such as Poe and James, who were more interested in craftsmanship than in citizenship, were exceptions to the rule. By the

1930s, however, the two most dominant schools of American criticism had broken away from the liberal democratic center to create a dangerous polarization in our literary culture. According to this interpretation, the Marxists and the southern formalists were opposite manifestations of the same phenomenon. Kazin even goes so far as to brand these two groups as totalitarian, a characterization that would have reminded readers at this point in history of the recent Hitler-Stalin pact.

In likening the southern formalists to the Marxist critics, Kazin puts himself in the anomalous position of seeming to compare conservatives to Communists. The reductiveness of Marxism as a mode of *literary* criticism had become so apparent by the early forties that even independent leftists such as Kazin were using it as a negative paradigm. Kazin's point is that both the Marxists and the southern formalists had arrived at their positions because of a profound alienation from liberal democratic culture. That point is made most emphatically in the following passage:

> Allen Tate's South was remarkably like Michael Gold's Russia—an ideal embodied in a culture, a community to be used as a standard of order and fellowship against the Enemy. Each was a great literary myth, to be appreciated in its own terms only by the literary intelligence. But with one difference, the vital difference between a culture believed by its adherents to be alive and militant, the very center of moral energy in a changing world, and a culture whose grandchildren mourn it in the country of their enemies—"a buried city," as Tate once wrote—yet one they must defend and whose example they are ready to apply in the face of all those forces that once destroyed it. (Kazin, 428–29)

In Kazin's mind, the irony of southern formalism is that it celebrates a traditionalism without a tradition; he doubts that most actual residents of the modern-day South would recognize the Agrarian myth as possible or even desirable. Thus, when he examines the position of the southern formalists, Kazin finds an orthodoxy that "was so palpably a convenience, a foothold, a margin of security, that it made a joke of the historic legends it ran after, and belied them. This was the perfect manufactured traditionalism, the apex of desire: it called for faith, but it had no faith; it called for order, which it could find only in poetry; it summoned men to the tasks of philosophy as if philosophy were a dignity of mind rather than the relation of ideas to the human situation" (443).

Because of their inability to speak effectively to the general public on matters of substance, the new critics must speak increasingly to each other on matters of form. Kazin believes that one of the consequences of this phenomenon is that the southern formalists assigned an exaggerated importance to the office of the critic. "It was a neoclassicism of attitudes," he writes, "a neoclassicism resting on an incommunicable distaste for the world and a desperate satisfaction with itself. The new critics, as Van Wyck Brooks said, doubted the progress of everything save criticism—their own criticism" (432). If Nero fiddled while Rome burned, the new critics were playing word games while all of Europe was ablaze.

Although Kazin speaks mostly of Ransom and Tate, he also finds fault with their contemporaries Eliot, Blackmur, and Winters (whom he apparently regards as honorary southerners). When he mentions the next generation of critics, it is primarily to take issue with Cleanth Brooks's assertion that textual analysis had "done much to enlarge our view of the imagination" (see Kazin, 435). Not surprisingly, Kazin believes just the opposite to be true. Although he probably would disdain the politics of Edmund Burke, he seems to agree with Burke's concept of the moral imagination—this is what fires Kazin's own cultural criticism and what he finds so lacking in the work of the southern formalists. According to Kazin, the new critics' "conception of the imagination was such that they could understand it only in terms of technical analysis: the level on which the imagination gets into a particular poem and is to be studied there. To them the imagination was not the summation and projection of a writer's resources, the very distinction of them; it was rather a kind of machine which did its work in poetry, and only in poetry of acceptable tension and difficulty" (437).

Despite the power and grace of his rhetoric, Kazin's position was vulnerable at several points. In reviewing *On Native Grounds* for the spring 1943 issue of the *Sewanee Review*, Cleanth Brooks notes some of the major problems with Kazin's book. For one thing, while attacking the southern formalists for an excessively narrow view of literature, Kazin goes too far in the other direction, characterizing modern American literature as "at bottom only the expression of our modern life in America."

It is the qualifying "only" that troubles Brooks: "If modern literature is 'at bottom only the expression of our modern life in America,' then how distinguish between literature and other expressions of our modern life, such as neon signs, the advertising sections of the popular magazines, and telephone books?" Brooks believes that Kazin, no less than the new critics, operates with an aesthetic definition of literature. The difference between them is that the new critics are willing to talk about their definition, while Kazin allows his to remain implicit. "Mr. Kazin's manoeuver," Brooks

argues, "is to assume that anybody knows what literature is, and that consequently anyone who talks about problems of form is simply a cold
rhetorician who is, *ex hypothesi*, interested in nothing but 'literature.' The
'new formalists,' as he terms them, thus become anti-democratic obscurantists" ("Mr. Kazin's America," 56).

Kazin's procedure is to praise the new formalists for being brilliant and
then to caricature their position so grossly that anyone believing him
would have to think them fools. When speaking of the southern critics,
Kazin assumes that they are concerned with literary form completely divorced from human content. In contrast, Kazin prefers those critics who
see in a work of literature "not the specific formal properties but only the
amount and range of human life brought to the reader." One might conclude from this that Kazin and the critics he admires are concerned only
with content and not form. The problem with this position is twofold.
First, in positing a form-content dualism, Kazin falsifies the organic unity
of a work of literature. Second, his own discerning comments about style
reveal that, no less than the formalists he condemns, Kazin, too, is concerned with *how* "the amount and range of human life [is] brought to the
reader." As Brooks points out, even the extreme naturalist "uses words,
which imply some kind of selection, and which, as words, are finally symbols, not the objects themselves" (57).

In comparing the southern formalists with the Marxist critics, Kazin
charges that both groups are blinded by myth. Turning that charge back
at him, Brooks asks whether Kazin might not have his own myth of
American experience. The evidence would suggest that "Mr. Kazin's
America" is large enough to encompass the pieties of New England
(Van Wyck Brooks on Emerson) and the Midwest (Carl Sandburg on Lincoln), but not those of the South. In Kazin's America, the vision of Sinclair
Lewis and H. L. Mencken is accepted at face value; while Allen Tate is
dismissed as a regional chauvinist, John Crowe Ransom as a Eurocentric
elitist, and William Faulkner as an inveterate romantic. But accuse Kazin
himself of being victim to literary myth, and Brooks suspects that his critical principles would forbid him even to discuss the question, "for the nature of myth and the senses in which it is true and its relation to 'reality'
are, like questions about literature, technical questions that imply an Al-
exandrian coldness, an academic thinness of blood, a detachment and ex-
clusiveness that suggests a contempt for democracy" (60).

To show a proper respect for democracy during a time of world war presumably requires forsaking the "luxury" of criticism, or at least what Kazin would regard as a narrowly aesthetic criticism. It is, of course, but a short step from such a position to the one that Campbell Hodges took when he suspended the *Southern Review*. Brooks charges that Kazin is discounting the importance not just of criticism but of literature itself. True, Kazin has not gone as far as "Herr Hitler" or even "Mr. Van Wyck Brooks, . . . when he urged us to imitate the Nazis by burning those books which irritated him. Mr. Kazin . . . implies only a discreet program of voluntary birth control" (61). By thus wrapping himself in the flag, Alfred Kazin proved that cultural criticism can sometimes be the last refuge of a scoundrel.

IV

Throughout the 1940s the main organ through which the democratic nativists attacked the new critics was the *Saturday Review of Literature*. In the September 6, 1941, issue of that magazine, Howard Mumford Jones had published an essay titled "The Limits of Contemporary Criticism." Jones found two trends he saw dominating critical discourse, political and aesthetic; what he failed to find was an approach that treated literature as "an end in itself, not a means toward something else" (Jones, 4). Although this was precisely what the new criticism claimed to do, Jones considered it part of the problem rather than the solution (R. P. Blackmur and T. S. Eliot came in for particular scolding). "It is doubtless useful," Jones writes, "for a certain kind of literary technician to be made aware of unsuspected ambiguities lurking beneath the fair surface of the English language, but inasmuch as books are made for men, not men for books, the weakness of the introspective and analytical schools of criticism has been the disproportionate emphasis they have laid upon literary and linguistic technology" (3). Seeing Jones's article as a direct attack on what they were trying to accomplish, Brooks and Warren took the unprecedented step of responding to that article in an editorial in the autumn 1941 issue of the *Southern Review*.

They begin by challenging Jones's assumption that reading is easy. "That assumption," they argue, "rests in turn upon the further assumption that the 'meaning,' the real content, of a piece of literature, as contrasted with the 'meaning' of scientific or other rigidly expository prose can be abstracted in a paraphrase" (Brooks and Warren, "Editorial" [Autumn 1941], viii). Moreover, in "setting up the opposition between a concern with the 'mechanisms of literature' and a concern with its ethical and political relationships, Mr. Jones has, as it were, used the forensic trick of the false option: in the left hand he clutches 'form' and in the right he clutches 'content,' and he has heeded the Biblical injunction not to let his right hand know what his left hand doeth" (xii). Brooks and Warren were planning to follow this editorial with one in the next issue "on the subject of Van Wyck Brooks, MacLeish and company."[4] Only the imminent suspension of the magazine forced them to curtail this along with so many other plans. Brooks got his second chance for a response, however, when he reviewed Jones's *Ideas in America* in the spring 1946 issue of the *Sewanee Review*.

Like Van Wyck Brooks, Jones believed that contemporary American literature was sick and dispiriting because it had listened too long to what Emerson called "the courtly muses of Europe." (Presumably, by recovering its indigenous roots, our songs and stories would become more red-blooded and uplifting.) Commenting on this notion, Cleanth Brooks writes, "Mr. Jones's conception of literature seems to be more than a little reminiscent of that of another great American whose belief in nobility, I believe, has never been questioned. During the late depression Mr. Herbert Hoover was reported to have remarked that what we needed to end the depression was the creation of a great poem" ("Mrs. Colum," 338). Although Jones may not have been quite this naive, he did argue that America was suffering from a crisis of the spirit, which could be cured by recovering the nineteenth-century optimism of Henry Wadsworth Longfellow and Louisa May Alcott.

Brooks believed that in seeing literature as therapeutic, Jones misconstrued its true nature and function. In any event, the age was long since past when even a poet as popular as Longfellow or Whittier could dominate the national consciousness. "Though I put the virtues of Maud Muller second to none," Brooks writes, "I do not believe that Mr. Jones can so dress her up as to compete with her real rival, the latest Hollywood queen" (342). When positive values are put forth by an Eliot or a Faulkner, Jones will have nothing to do with them because they seem too foreign to his provincial conception of true Americanism. (Eliot, after all, was a Royalist and an Anglo-Catholic, while Faulkner was a southern gothicist and probably a neo-Confederate.) Ironically, in denouncing the negativism of modern American literature, democratic nativists such as Jones themselves became the most crotchety of naysayers.

The defenders of democratic culture were not always content to confine their attacks to the *literary* judgments of their opponents. For example, when the Fellows of the Library of Congress, a group heavily stacked with aesthetic formalists, bestowed the 1948 Bollingen Prize for Poetry on Ezra Pound, a disgruntled Robert Hillyer all but denounced the new critics as Fascists. At the end of the war, Pound had been confined to a mental hospital under indictment for treason. It was bad enough that he had made radio broadcasts for Mussolini during the war, but the poem for which he was being honored—*The Pisan Cantos*—compared the Italian dictator to Thomas Jefferson, ridiculed the American war dead, and made scurrilous references to Jews. In articles published in the June 11 and June 18, 1949, issues of the *Saturday Review*, Hillyer questioned whether the Library of Congress should be honoring a poet such as Pound and a poem such as *The Pisan Cantos*.

For several months the literary world in America was divided by this controversy. Allen Tate and John Berryman drafted a letter of protest to the *Saturday Review*, which was signed by eighty men of letters (Cleanth Brooks not only signed the letter but helped to distribute it). When Norman Cousins, the editor of the *Saturday Review*, refused to run the letter unless he was given the names of everyone who refused to sign it, Tate and Berryman sent it to the *Nation*, where it was published on December 17, 1949.

Among the several letters that Cousins did run was one written by Cleanth Brooks himself. Published on October 29, 1949, the letter begins by summarizing Hillyer's argument; then, in his final paragraph, Brooks moves in for the kill:

> Mr. Hillyer ought to list the names of these vicious persons [the traitor-critics]. His responsibility to the public demands it: in order to protect itself, the public needs to know definitely who these men are. An effective Paul Revere cannot afford to be mealy-mouthed. Moreover, in this case vagueness serves not only to screen the wicked esthetes but to compromise those possibly innocent writers who have blundered into the "subsidized quarterlies" through misapprehension. If the list is produced and published, such innocent persons will be freed from suspicion. Surely the process of proving "guilt by association" must be quite as repugnant to Mr. Hillyer as it is to most right thinking Americans. By all means, let us have the names. ("List," 24)

Not surprisingly, Hillyer declined to accept this obvious invitation to a libel suit.

Brooks offered a more thoughtful rebuttal to Hillyer in a lecture delivered at the Jewish Theological Seminary in the winter of 1949. Hillyer's position, Brooks argued, was similar to one urged by Matthew Arnold when the Victorian intelligentsia was experiencing a crisis of faith because of Darwin's theories of biology. Because science had undercut the epistemological bases of religion, Arnold reasoned, it was impossible for any intelligent person to hold to the superstitions of the past. The ebbing of the sea of faith left a spiritual and emotional void that could be filled only by literature. It must be a literature of high seriousness, however, because it now had to do the work of religion. Viewed in this light, literature carried a great responsibility for nurturing the human spirit. Those who denied that responsibility were, at best, irresponsible and, at worst, traitors to mankind.

To divide the literary world between the moralistic and the amoral, however, is to beg an important question. Many of the new critics (Brooks and Eliot among them) still subscribed to an orthodox religious faith. Having weathered the assaults on religion made by Darwin, Marx, and Freud, they saw no need to make literature into a secular faith; they could allow it to be itself. "On the one hand," Brooks writes, "I see a group of muddled and confused writers and critics who wish painfully, though vaguely, to affirm what they find around them, who are uneasy with anything but conventional literary forms and nervously apprehensive when presented with anything more than transparent salestalk for democracy. In the group to which Hillyer gives the back of his hand, I find, however, the true conservatives and traditionalists, though they are to be described as radical, not conventional conservatives" ("Metaphor," 132).

Shortly after the controversy died down, Hillyer resigned from his position at Kenyon College and faded into obscurity. Although he published two more books of poetry before his death in 1961, he is remembered today chiefly for his attacks on Pound and the Bollingen Prize. Future political controversies were minimized when the Bollingen Foundation decided to disassociate itself from the Library of Congress and bestow its subsequent awards under the auspices of Yale University. (In 1950 the prize went to John Crowe Ransom, in 1957 to Allen Tate, and in 1966 to Robert Penn Warren.)[5] Although Robert Gorham Davis tried to keep the controversy going, by the time his essay "The New Criticism and the Democratic Tradition" appeared in the *American Scholar* in the winter of 1949–50, Ezra Pound and the Bollingen Prize were no longer news.[6]

V

Among the critics who came to prominence after World War II, few posed a more formidable challenge to the new criticism than Leslie Fiedler. As a Jewish intellectual who earned his B.A. at NYU and wrote for *Partisan Review*, he was of the same cultural ambience as Alfred Kazin. However, Fiedler also had received his Ph.D. from the University of Wisconsin and had taught at the Kenyon School of English. When he chose to issue his own critical manifesto, it was published not in a left-wing New York magazine but in the *Sewanee Review*. "Archetype and Signature," which appeared in the spring of 1952, made an eloquent case for Fiedler's own brand of mythic or archetypal criticism, but it also found serious fault with the critical orthodoxy of the day.

One way of differentiating the various attacks on the new criticism is to note the different terminology used by its attackers. Douglas Bush called it "remedial reading"; Van Wyck Brooks saw it as a form of "coterie literature"; Alfred Kazin found the label "southern formalist" damning enough; F. O. Matthiessen hinted that the whole movement was "socially irresponsible"; and R. S. Crane regarded it as "monistic." For Fiedler, the devil term was "anti-biographical"; he believed that the formalists had gone too far in trying to separate the artifact from the artificer. As his prime exhibit, he cites the Thomas and Brown anthology *Reading Poems*, which prints poems without the names of their authors (listing them instead in the back of the book).

Although he readily admits that a poem cannot be regarded as the sum total of its author's intentions, Fiedler believes that the "anti-biographers" have distorted that valid insight into the rather extravagant contention "that nothing the poet can tell us about his own work is of any *decisive* importance" (Fiedler 1:533). As if to dispel doubt as to which antibiographers he had in mind, Fiedler declares that "the notion of 'intention' implies the belief that there is a somehow existent something against which the achieved work of art can be measured; and although this has been for all recorded time the point of view of the practicing writer, every graduate student who has read Wimsatt and Beardsley's ponderous tract on the Intentional Fallacy knows that we are all now to believe that there is no poem except the poem of 'words' " (1:533).

Fiedler concedes that biography has been misused by everyone from romantic subjectivists to dusty pedants. But a doctrinaire antibiographical stance would prevent critics from comparing several works by the same author or even discussing the tendency of William Shakespeare and John Donne to pun on their own names. If Fiedler were saying no more than this, there would be no real quarrel between him and the new critics. His objections, however, are more deep-seated, even metaphysical. He argues, for example, that the title of Thomas and Brown's *Reading Poems* "reveals the dogma . . . [that] in a world of discrete, individual 'experiences,' of 'close reading' (a cant phrase of the antibiographist) as an ideal, one cannot even talk of so large an abstraction as poetry" (1:534). That Brooks and Warren's infinitely more popular anthology was entitled *Understanding Poetry*, not *Understanding Poems*, would seem to refute Fiedler's argument, but his charge that the new criticism is excessively nominalist warrants further scrutiny.

What is most curious about Fiedler's attack is that his objections to the new critics are almost the exact opposite of those raised by the neo-Aristotelians. The Chicagoans did not believe that their Nashville counterparts were sufficiently discrete and pluralistic in their reading of poems. Fiedler, being much more the neo-Platonist, does not believe that the formalists are monistic or mystical enough in their conception of poetry. Thus, even though "Archetype and Signature" does not target the neo-Aristotelians, it is a much more powerful indictment of them than of Brooks, Warren, and company.

In the second part of his essay, Fiedler speaks of myth (whether residing in the Jungian unconscious or in a Platonic realm of pure essences) as the universal material of song and story. This material becomes literature when the signature of an individual writer is imposed upon the universal myth or archetype. (The theory is actually more complex, as there are communal and personal elements in both the archetype and the signature.) Thus Fiedler believes that depth psychology and cultural anthropology are of greater value than semantics or prosody in analyzing a work of literature, although how such analysis can provide a basis for critical *evaluation* is a point that he ignores. In *Literary Criticism: A Short History* (1957), Brooks argues convincingly that, regardless of their other contributions, myth critics offer no criteria for literary judgment; that, for Fiedler, the archetype constitutes "a privileged poetic subject matter in disguise," while the signature makes the poem not "an object to be known . . . [but] a clue to an event in the poet's psyche" (Brooks and Wimsatt, *Literary Criticism*, 713).[7]

Although *Literary Criticism: A Short History* did not appear until five years after Fiedler's essay, Brooks's initial response to "Archetype and Signature" came almost immediately in the *Sewanee Review*. In the winter 1953 issue of that magazine, Brooks added a few words about Fiedler in the brief piece in which he was defending himself against Douglas Bush (both the Bush and Fiedler essays had appeared in the *Sewanee Review* the previous year). Although he admits that Bush and Fiedler would find each other to be strange bedfellows, Brooks notes that both are trying to restore biographical and historical considerations to the criticism of literature. Summarizing Fiedler's "neat, almost jaunty survey of recent literary history," Brooks writes: "If I may fill in some names, Mr. Fiedler might see Mr. Bush as the thesis (the old fashioned historical scholarship), me as the antithesis (the doctrinaire antibiographer), and himself as the triumphant synthesis" (see Keast, 357). There are, however, other ways of looking at the situation. Eschewing dialectics for dichotomy, Brooks sees formalism as the only pure criticism and all other approaches as hybrids of nonliterary disciplines.

"In their concern for the break-up of the modern world," Brooks writes, "Mr. Bush, Mr. Fiedler, and a host of other scholars and critics are anxious to see literature put to work to save the situation" (see Keast, 357). Although Brooks professes to share the desire of his adversaries to restore our disintegrating, deracinated culture, he thinks it dangerous to confuse religion and poetry (as in his response to Hillyer, Brooks again blames Matthew Arnold for this heresy). Such confusion ultimately serves neither God nor art: "though poetry has a very important role in any culture, to ask that poetry save us is to impose on poetry a burden that it cannot sustain. The danger is that we shall merely get an ersatz religion and an ersatz poetry" (358).

Paradoxical as it may seem, an orderly separation of the various realms of culture may be the surest guard against cultural fragmentation. The person who does criticism may also do many other things without feeling that he has to call these other things criticism. For Brooks and his fellow new critics, literature does not need to be less than politics or more than religion. As experience redeemed in form, it is already of central importance to life.

CHAPTER FIFTEEN

The Squire of Northford

When Edwin Mims was forced to retire as head of the Vanderbilt English department in the spring of 1942, one might have expected his successor, Walter Clyde Curry, to welcome the department's prodigal sons home with open arms. After all, Curry himself had been a minor Fugitive and was closer to the new critics than to Mims in his pedagogical style. By 1942, however, Curry was far better known as a medievalist than as a poet, and his administrative manner was largely indistinguishable from his predecessor's. It was not until after Curry's own retirement in 1955 that Vanderbilt officially tried to make amends to the poets who had once studied and taught there.

By then, the department chairman was Randall Stewart, a specialist in nineteenth-century American literature who had been an undergraduate at Vanderbilt before World War I, when the Fugitive group was still in its formative stages. (With a doctorate from Yale and nearly twenty years as a professor at Brown, Stewart could hardly be suspected of southern provincialism.) Not long after he took office, Stewart began to plan a reunion of the surviving Fugitives for some time in 1956; his primary ally in this venture was a young South Carolinian named Louis D. Rubin, Jr., who was executive secretary of the newly formed American Studies Association. Rubin secured a grant of $4,000 for the project from the Rockefeller Foundation. Following several months of preparation, ten of the original Fugitives, along with ten other invited guests,[1] gathered on the Vanderbilt campus on May 3–5. After thirty years, the young bohemians who had been such an embarrassment to Eddie Mims were coming home.

Beyond the receptions and public readings, the real business of the meeting was to allow the Fugitives to comment on the literary movement they had spawned; this was done in four closed tape-recorded sessions. As one of the invited guests, Cleanth Brooks was responsible for moderating the first and fourth of these sessions. Because the men involved included some world-class talkers, his role as moderator was largely perfunctory. Still, the fact that he was included in this reunion indicated Cleanth's growing significance within the Vanderbilt literary tradition. It was the first time that he had been officially invited back to campus since his graduation twenty-eight years before.

The literary situation had changed considerably in the forty years since the original Fugitives had gathered at the feet of Sidney Hirsch to discuss philosophy and poetry. ("When the Reunion opened," Louis Rubin recalls, Hirsch "was not present but remained at home sulking in his tent until Merrill Moore went over and fetched him"; Rubin, "Gathering," 670.) In addition to other literary genres, poetry now had to compete with radio, television, and motion pictures. As Cleanth observed in his remarks at the reunion, "I have a friend who says that the age of the printed book is over. He says he's already given it a name—he says the Gutenberg period is finished" (see Rubin, "Gathering," 658). The audience in Nashville laughed at this dire prediction. Because *Understanding Media*[2] would not be published for another eight years, it is doubtful that many people in that gathering had ever heard of Marshall McLuhan.

After nine years at Yale, Cleanth was convinced more than ever of the advantages of his present institution over any that existed in the South, but even at Yale he had not seen "this very precious thing which Vanderbilt once had." Whether any useful lessons could be drawn from the experience of the Fugitives was another matter. "There is probably nothing that any of us can do," he observed, "to insure the emergence of another group like the Fugitives. Inspection of last year's bird's nest will not tell us how to make Vanderbilt once again a nest of singing birds. The fortunate circumstance of the concurrence of so many talented men is unpredictable and rarely repeated" (see Purdy, 222).

As the final session ended, Red Warren offered an analogy to explain why he and his cohorts wrote and criticized literature:

> There was a sociological survey made several years ago . . . of juvenile delinquency among young girls, girls in New York City. And they had many thousand interviewed, and asked them why they did it. And there were about seven or eight hundred said, "My mother doesn't like me," and about two thousand of them said, "My father doesn't like me" . . .—and another seventeen hundred said, "Well, they quarrel at night, and I have to go outdoors to keep from hearing their quarrels," and "I don't like my

baby brother," and one thing and another. This got down to four thousand, nine-hundred and ninety-nine of them. And then they had one more little girl to talk to—and they asked her why she did it, and she said, "I likes it. . . ." Well, I think that's what the Rockefeller Foundation's going to find out—. . . We haven't got any alibis. (See Purdy, 223)

I

Like the Warrens of Fairfield County, the Brookses had decided early in their stay at Yale that the convenience of being near the university did not outweigh the disadvantages of urban life. They resolved that when the opportunity presented itself, they would move out into the country, preferably into a house with some history and character. Finding the right house in the right location was not easy. The right house, they concluded, was a structure built in 1720 on the outskirts of Wallingford, northwest of New Haven. This was one of three houses that had belonged to the Street family. The patriarch of the clan was a seventeenth-century Puritan divine who served as chaplain of Wallingford. In appreciation of his ministry, the town gave him some property, which went vacant until it was inherited by his grandson. Of the three houses eventually built on the site, one had been moved, and a second significantly altered. Although Cleanth and Tinkum fell in love with the third house, they were far from enamored of the location. Railroad tracks ran practically through the front yard, and the adjoining lots belonged to other people, who might well build on them.

Over a year's time, the Brookses had a contractor move the Street house, board by board, from Wallingford to some isolated property in the country village of Northford, about ten miles north of New Haven. When they moved out to Northford, they persuaded Willmoore Kendall to come with them. The ninety acres that were for sale were more than the Brookses needed or could afford, but they were leery of what might happen if a developer purchased the property surrounding them. The solution was for Ken to buy that property and to build his own country house. He responded with enthusiasm, hiring a professor from the Yale School of Architecture to plan his new home.

Cleanth and Tinkum substantially redesigned their old house; they added a bedroom and a kitchen to the downstairs and had bathrooms installed both upstairs and down. Of the three bedrooms, two were equipped with their own fireplaces. The house was heated by a total of five

fireplaces, two of which were big enough to contain bake ovens. The
Brookses enlarged the basement and later constructed another building
separate from the house. This addition contained a study, a garage, and a
sizable attic. Cleanth figured that it took the entire decade of the fifties to
do everything that he and Tinkum wanted done to the house. But the effort and expense were worth it. The place was on forty acres back from
the road. With a river running through it and plenty of grass to mow, the
owner of this property could live pretty much like a British country gentleman of two centuries ago. For nearly thirty years, this was one of the unofficial country homes of the Yale English department.

In a letter to Glenway Wescott, sent from Northford on September 19,
1951, Katherine Anne Porter writes: "I came here to visit my dear Tinkum
and Cleanth Brooks rather suddenly after long planning and talk about it,
and they have a beautiful old house with fireplaces like yours, in a landscape that makes me feel as if I were sitting in the midst of an illustration
from a history of New England—even a little old cemetery with winged
skulls on the red granite (or sandstone?) tombs" (Porter, *Letters*, 404).

By 1955, Katherine Anne was herself living in nearby Southbury, Connecticut, and seeing her fellow Baton Rouge exiles often. In a letter written to Gertrude Bechtel on September 20, 1955, she describes one such
gathering:

> On Sunday my dear old friends Cleanth and Tinkum (Edith) Brooks and
> John Palmer came over from near New Haven, and I did a big old fash-
> ioned mid-day Sunday dinner for them: pork roast—half a fresh ham—
> with sweet potato purée, hot home rolls and currant jelly and plenty of
> gravy and little golden squash very delicately cooked with sweet butter,
> and baskets of fruit with five different cheeses. . . . Alas we did not have the
> stout burgundy, the only wine that can stand up to such a combination of
> food, but cocktails before, beer with, and whiskey afterwards, before the
> big fire in the large, many-windowed room that lets the whole lively
> landscape in. (Porter, *Letters*, 489)

Not long after the move to Northford, Cleanth and Tinkum joined the
local Episcopal parish. For many people brought up in a generically Protestant environment, this would not have been a particularly momentous
move. For a person on his way up in society, switching from the Methodist
to the Episcopal Church might be like moving up from a Chevrolet to a
Buick. For Cleanth, it was a good deal more than that; because he had
been reared in a Methodist parsonage, his confirmation as an Episcopalian constituted a significant break with his personal past. Although he

did not see it as a repudiation of his father, Cleanth waited until the elder
Brooks had been in his grave for nearly a decade before making the move.
Looking back on his father's beliefs and temperament, Cleanth became
convinced that the Reverend Mr. Brooks was closer to the Episcopal
Church than to southern Methodism. At a time when much of the Protestant world was falling prey to secular humanism, the Anglican tradition—with its sacramental worship and its magnificent Tudor liturgy—
seemed like a safe harbor. Although he was not ready to join Allen Tate
on the road to Rome, being an Anglo-Catholic put Cleanth in the company of T. S. Eliot and, in a sense, John Wesley himself.

Tinkum also became a faithful communicant of her new church. As
founding member of the altar guild in their small parish in Northford, she
helped care for the communion chalice and clerical vestments, and she
spent many a Saturday afternoon arranging flowers for the following morning's worship—often with the assistance of her young neighbor Rosanna
Warren. Although Red and Eleanor belonged to no church and subscribed
to no orthodox religious creed, they were traditional enough in their beliefs to think that a child should have godparents. Rosanna's two god-
mothers were Katherine Anne Porter and Tinkum Brooks. Because Katherine Anne was constantly traveling, Tinkum became the most important
surrogate parent for the girl her friends and family called "Roposie." (In
a letter to Tinkum dated November 2, 1955, Red writes: "Yes, it is certainly our wish that you and Cleanth adopt Rosanna and [her younger
brother] Gabriel if we should die while they are children.") Apparently,
the affection was reciprocated. In an undated letter to Cleanth written
some time in the late fifties, Red notes that "Roposie tells me she is planning to move in with you and Tinkie. When I remark to her that we shall
miss her, she ponders that question, then magnanimously suggests that we
live across the field from Tinkie's and drop in occasionally."[3]

During the 1952–53 school year, Tinkum's nephew Carver Blanchard
lived at Northford. He remembers life there as being like something out of
a nineteenth-century boy's adventure book. The region was still wild with
plenty of woods to explore. Carver attended an old country school, where
the fifth and sixth grades were taught in the same room. Every afternoon,
when Carver got home from school, the Brookses' dog, Pompey (who was
as big as ten-year-old Carver), would almost knock him over anticipating
the mischief the two might find. One day Pompey came running up with
a completely plucked chicken in his mouth. Because the dog could not
have done such a neat job himself, Carver surmised that he must have

grabbed the chicken out of a farmer's hand. At another time, Pompey cornered a woodchuck, which Carver then shot with his bow and arrow. Because he was reading books about trapping at the time, he implored Cleanth to skin and gut the animal for him and stretch the fur out on a board (when the stench became unbearable, Tinkum discreetly got rid of the pelt). Carver remembers Cleanth performing the task so obligingly that it was not until years later that he realized how disagreeable a chore it must have been. A few summers later, when Carver came back to Connecticut to visit, he found that Pompey was gone. The dog had become such a town nuisance during mating season that Tinkum had had him put to sleep. When Tinkum informed Carver that Pompey had died, the fourteen-year-old boy left the room in tears.

That year in Northford, Carver helped haul cement blocks for Willmoore Kendall's new house. He remembers sitting around the Thanksgiving dinner table while Ken read passages from *The Book of Common Prayer* in his rolling baritone voice. Carver also served as an altar boy in the local Episcopal parish. (As the priest was responsible for three country churches each Sunday, he would celebrate the Eucharist at two of them, while Cleanth—now a licensed lay reader—read morning prayer at the third.) When Carver turned eleven, the Elizabethan scholar Leslie Hotson solemnly asked him how it felt to enter his second decade. All the while, Carver was coming to know some of the leading literary figures of the age as family friends. One day, after hearing a particularly loud yawn in the house, he asked his aunt in all his boyish innocence "if that was Pompey or Mr. Warren?"[4]

By the time that Carver was away in college and no longer coming regularly to Northford, Rosanna Warren was spending more and more time with Cleanth and Tinkum. Some of her earliest memories were of the old boards in their house. She recalls feeling the grain of the wood against her fingers. At night when she was staying over, she would get up in her room and peek through where the floor panels didn't quite fit together and watch the adults conversing downstairs. She stared in wonder at the huge pots in the fireplace and at the piles of manuscript in Cleanth's study. The giant oak tree in the backyard was a special place where Rosanna and her brother Gabriel would pretend to be squirrels. A swing was hung from that tree on a chain three stories high. For a young girl, swinging out over the pond by the oak was like taking a magic ride over the ocean.

In a letter to Tinkum, dated September 19, 1958, Red conveys Rosanna's concern to her godmother over a recent injury. "I thought you were unbreakable," Red writes, "and sort of wish you were. Roposie is very sympathetic and proposes to send you her best two pictures to cheer you up. . . . She mourns for your condition—but human nature being what it is she is a little bit excited at knowing somebody important enough to have a wheel chair all for themselves. She says she hopes you will make Cleanth push you a lot."

According to Rosanna, the discipline in the Brooks household was always more implied than overt. No one ever doubted for a moment that Tinkum ruled the hearth. By making all of the important domestic decisions, she freed Cleanth to concentrate on his writing. (Rumor has it that she would even get her shotgun and dispatch animals who were making too much noise when her husband was in his study.) Outside the house, Cleanth was the master of the grounds. He would take Rosanna on long walks in the woods and patiently identify the various kinds of wildflowers they would see.[5] From the spring until the fall, he would come home from the university and spend countless daylight hours mowing acres and acres of grass. One can only imagine how many critical books and essays must have taken shape in his mind as he was perched atop his tractor mower. So fully did he live Ransom's ideal of the Agrarian as country gentleman that he would summon Pompey with a post horn (John Edward Hardy used to say that whenever he heard that horn, he expected Allen Tate to come bounding out of the woods).[6] It wasn't long before friends began referring to Cleanth as the "Squire of Northford."

II

Unfortunately, at this point in American history, many people were identifying the southern way of life with a racial caste system that seemed both anachronistic and morally repugnant. When the United States Supreme Court ruled in 1954 that segregated schools were unconstitutional, a historic southern dilemma became a national obsession. A year later, the bus boycott in Montgomery, Alabama, launched the career of a young black minister named Martin Luther King, Jr. By October of 1957, federal troops had been called to Little Rock, Arkansas, to integrate that city's school system. Red Warren, who had written a defense of black equality under the law in I'll Take My Stand, was but one of many southern intellectuals who were forced to reconsider whether such equality was possible within a segregated society. The product of Warren's meditation was a book-length essay published in 1956 under the title *Segregation: The Inner Conflict in the South*.

In researching his book, Warren had traveled to Kentucky, Tennessee, Arkansas, Mississippi, and Louisiana, where he had talked to white and black people who represented every shade of opinion on the issue of race. Although he came away with no illusions about the ability of law to alter the attitudes and customs of centuries, he was convinced that the South must change. For white southerners, the essential problem was not to learn to live with the Negro—it was "to learn to live with ourselves" (Warren, *Segregation*, 63). Even as he wrote those words, Red must have realized that many of his oldest friends would feel that he had gone over to the side of the carpetbaggers. The battle against industrialism had been lost; everywhere one looked in the national press, southern tradition was vilified and ridiculed. If there was one last stand left to be taken, it was against federal intervention in the life of the southern community. In 1956 the integration decision was still new enough that some advocates of states' rights believed that it could be successfully resisted. Across the South, white citizens banded together to support local control of local institutions. One of the resistance organizations was the Tennessee Foundation for Constitutional Government. Its most impassioned and articulate spokesman was Red Warren's old and dear friend Donald Davidson.

Perhaps the best assessment of Davidson's position on the civil rights struggle is offered by Walter Sullivan, who was his colleague at Vanderbilt during the turbulence of the fifties and sixties. According to Sullivan:

> It seemed to be Mr. Davidson's misfortune that his political adversaries were able to define their conflict with him almost totally in terms of race; but in fact he collaborated in the definition. He told me that when he first came to Vanderbilt, he was friendly with the black professors at Fisk University, met with them socially as well as professionally, but ceased his intercourse with them when the push for racial equality began. In his judgment, the civil rights movement was a vehicle for political upheaval. Even had he not believed this, he would have opposed the movement on its merits, and his stubborn devotion to a platform built on the hypothesis of white supremacy caused both him and his friends a good deal of pain. (Sullivan, *Allen Tate*, 26)

Perhaps in the hope of establishing dialogue between racial liberals and conservatives, Warren had sent Davidson a copy of *Segregation*. In a letter to Cleanth dated February 17, 1957, Davidson reveals how deep the cleavage had become between himself and Red. Among other things, he accused Warren of being ill informed, cold-blooded, careless about the company he kept, a traitor to the South, and a sellout to Henry Luce (most of *Segregation* had been originally published in *Life* magazine). His intemperate rhetoric reveals Davidson's habit of personalizing philosophical disagreements. If his friendship with Red was not ruptured by politics, it was clearly strained. Caught in the middle, Cleanth tried valiantly to make peace.

In a letter to Davidson dated March 28, 1957, Cleanth writes:

> I take it that on the tortured integration issue I am somewhere in between you and Red. (I am certainly mixed up and torn several ways. I wish that I could be surer of a clear position.) Theologically, I have to say that all men are equal—that is, all have souls precious in God's sight. Incidentally, though I have full confidence in the theological case, I have very little in the anthropological or sociological, and it seems to me that an important confusion has been the attempt on the part of the integrationists to ground on a *scientific* basis what can be asserted only metaphysically and theologically.
>
> But what are the consequences of the acceptance of the theological principle? Not surely all that the integrationists would argue for, though perhaps some. This for me is the area of great difficulty—the more so, since I believe in local government and an organic society and since I distrust abstraction and the change of morals by legislation. I have to admit too, that my feelings have probably been exacerbated by living in the East and viewing at first hand the frequently unconscious moral complacency of this section. . . . Perhaps living in the South, I would take a different tack and make a different emphasis. I don't know.[7]

Not all southerners had such difficulty coming to terms with social change. In 1961 Yale hired a southern historian whose liberalism was already legendary. During a distinguished career at Johns Hopkins, C. Vann Woodward had established himself as the profession's foremost authority on the modern South. His books included *The Strange Case of Jim Crow* (1953), which Martin Luther King proclaimed "the Bible of the civil rights movement" (see Roper, 198) and *The Burden of Southern History* (1960), which Woodward dedicated to his good friend Robert Penn Warren. In fact, when Yale decided to recruit Woodward, George Pierson, the chairman of the history department and a fellow of Davenport College, asked Cleanth to have Red call his friend to disabuse him of the notion that Yale was a preppy undergraduate school uninterested in scholarly research.

When Cleanth pleaded that he was on his way to New York, Pierson asked if there were not telephones in New York. (Apparently, the message got through, because Woodward accepted the Sterling Professorship of History.) Vann freely admits that his appreciation of irony in human affairs has been deepened by his reading of Brooks and Warren. Rather than accusing the new critics of being divorced from history, Comer Vann Woodward was convinced that the literary imagination is an essential means of apprehending historical truth.[8]

III

If the students Cleanth taught at Yale were generally of a higher quality than those at LSU, there were no stars of the magnitude of Robert Lowell or Richard Weaver. Nevertheless, of the thousands of students who passed through New Haven, several have attained prominence in the Republic of Letters. (One of them, A. Bartlett Giamatti, later became President of Yale and Commissioner of Baseball.) Cleanth was a remarkably popular teacher among both graduate and undergraduate students. Perhaps more important, many of these students remembered him fondly years later. As time goes by, one's opinion of spellbinding lecturers and classroom entertainers quickly diminishes if there was no substance behind the performance. The impact of a class with Cleanth Brooks seems to have grown more powerful over time. Over thirty years later, one of his earliest students at Yale—Reid Buckley—remembered what it was like:

> It was an eight o'clock class, the excruciating hour designed to separate true acolytes from dilettantes. Mr. Cleanth Brooks, co-author of *Understanding Poetry*, on which my generation cut its critical teeth, was almost always there in the classroom before the first of us, a short roundfaced man whose eyes blinked from behind thick lenses and who stooped forward as he walked so that his astonishingly tiny feet seemed always to be trying to catch up to his center of gravity. He was dapper. The leather of his Oxfords shone, his charcoal gray flannels held a knife's edge crease, and his brown herringbone Harris tweed jacket was cut with the insouciant perfection of the great Ivy League haberdashers. Only his ties were on occasion rebellious, a reminder of the West Tennessean blood that coursed beneath his exquisite manners.
>
> They distinguished him as they do today. In that musical Mississippi accent, he revealed to us the disciplines of rhythm, language, and imagery that, when perfectly harnessed, can produce the magic of a poem. In sug-

gesting his reading of, say, a sonnet by Yeats, he shunned any semblance of imposing it. He would begin, "On . . . the one hand," presenting his views, followed inevitably, by, "On . . . the o-ther hand, presenting an opposing, or different, view. (As he grew older, we, his ex-students, grinned to hear him begin, "On . . . the o-ther hand," so scrupulous had he become about the opinions of others.) (Buckley, 22)

Like so many of Cleanth's students, Reid Buckley remembers being a frequent guest at Northford. And like many of those guests, he has vivid memories of Cleanth and Tinkum as a couple. He recalls their communicating without even having to look at each other.[9] (As age began to take its toll, Tinkum increasingly became Cleanth's eyes, while he became her ears.) Several generations of students felt thoroughly at home with the Brookses. There always seemed to be the smell of freshly baked bread coming from Tinkum's oven. And knowing how wretchedly most students ate, she insisted that they take a loaf home with them. During the years that Cleanth and Tinkum might have started a family of their own, their financial and emotional resources were taxed by caring for Cleanth's parents and the wayward Tookie. They later spent their parental love on Tinkum's niece and nephews and on her goddaughter, Rosanna, while playing the role of aunt and uncle to Cleanth's students.

These roles were temporarily mixed when Tinkum's nephew Paul Blanchard enrolled as an undergraduate at Yale in 1956. It had been a decade since Paul had had regular contact with Cleanth and Tinkum; throughout the late forties and early fifties, he had seen them primarily at Christmas dinners presided over by the imperious Emily Price Blanchard. (Years later, Paul realized how sorely his grandmother's pretensions must have taxed the patience of Cleanth, who was dutifully repaying Tinkum for having helped care for his family for so many years.) It was an eye-opening experience for Paul to see his aunt and uncle living like New England gentry. The intellectual ambience and general sophistication of Northford were quite different from anything he had known while growing up in Baton Rouge. Because Paul was on a limited income, Cleanth gave him clothes from his own wardrobe and unlimited use of a 1952 Plymouth.[10]

Perhaps Cleanth's most brilliant student at Yale was a native of Peterborough, Canada, named Hugh Kenner. After leaving Yale, Kenner produced studies of Wyndham Lewis, T. S. Eliot, Samuel Beckett, James Joyce, and Buckminster Fuller, among others. His monumental book *The Pound Era*, published in 1972, is still considered by many to be the definitive work on high modernism. After earning his B.A. and M.A. degrees at the University of Toronto, Kenner arrived in New Haven in 1948, already an accomplished scholar at the age of twenty-five. As Hugh recalled over forty years later, his friend and mentor Marshall McLuhan had told him quite emphatically that he must continue his education with Cleanth Brooks. So Hugh and Marshall climbed into Hugh's car—McLuhan, who owned neither an automobile nor a television, did not drive—and headed from Toronto to New Haven in the late spring of 1948. Marshall seemed not to know or care that the application deadline for graduate school was well past. Nor did he know whether his old friend was even in town. Fortunately, they did find Cleanth, who was able to get Hugh into Yale despite the lateness in the year.

Although Cleanth was nominally Hugh's dissertation adviser, he claims to have done no more than give his student a free rein to pursue his research on Joyce. (Kenner himself recalls Cleanth giving him shrewd practical advice on how to construct a document that would meet with the least possible resistance from Yale's graduate faculty.) Before his degree could be conferred, however, the entire English department was invited to examine Kenner on any facet of British or American literature. Hugh recalls being besieged by an army of old men in wheel chairs, most of whom he had never seen before.[11] Not too long into the examination, it became apparent that some of the faculty were less interested in original thought than in stock responses. "Mr. Kenner," William C. De Vane solemnly intoned, "I am going to ask you a series of questions and I expect you to answer each of them in one sentence. Now *What was the principal contribution of Coleridge to English poetry?* Remember, One sentence!" Kenner began, " 'Well, technically,' only to be interrupted: 'Mr. Kenner: technique is a part of poetry; but *a very small part!*' " Hugh "next ventured on a Jamesian sentence, which was not what he wanted either" (Kenner, 251). "*Coleridge—liberated—the imagination*," De Vane thundered. "Now remember that, Mr. Kenner!"

"And here Cleanth moved in deftly," Hugh recalls, "perceiving—and sharing—my dismay: a doctoral oral at a major university reduced to that kindergarten order of cliché!"

> He guessed, too, that many examiners would agree; what they'd value was familiarity with the remote, even the second-rate: the style of the period. So, What, he asked, did I remember about William Congreve? (His dates are 1690–1728. What does *anybody* remember about him?) Well, I responded, chiefly the passage Dr. Johnson admired. Ah, went on Cleanth suavely, What was it he admired about it? I replied, "He said there was

nothing to equal it in Shakespeare. It is a description of a temple; and, said Johnson, you can show me no such description of material objects, without an intermixture of moral notions, which produces such an effect. . . ."

And on the examiners that did produce the effect Cleanth had been aiming for; I was not the fumbler I had earlier seemed to be. Only he and I knew that he'd known that his question wouldn't stall me; that the Congreve passage had come up in a conversation between us, not many weeks before. (Kenner, 252)

IV

Although the dating of historical trends is often arbitrary, many observers regard the year 1957 as a turning point in the fortunes of the new criticism. As we shall see later in this chapter, that was the year that Northrop Frye's *Anatomy of Criticism* unmistakably established myth criticism as the main challenger to aesthetic formalism. That same year, W. K. Wimsatt and Cleanth Brooks published their own version of the evolution of criticism from antiquity to the present. Although *Literary Criticism: A Short History* was far from a programmatic defense of the philosophy of its authors, the book's very existence suggested that the new critics were now in a position to establish their own canon rather than simply attack an earlier consensus.

On October 12, 1956, I. A. Richards, who was now teaching at Harvard, wrote to his wife, Dorothy, to inform her that "an incredibly heavy pile of proofs arrived at the Office yesterday. Proof of Cleanth Brooks' + a certain Wimsatt's big book entitled *A Short History of Criticism* [sic]." Richards goes on to say: "I've flipped a few of the unmanageable sheets over and see that I got more space than Aristotle. . . . Dear Cleanth—very loyal: he sides with ME (as against Ransom) in plenty of places. So there is a lot we'll be talking of tomorrow" (Richards, *Letters*, 133, 134).

The allusion to an upcoming conversation refers to a program in which the two critics were to participate the next day. On October 14, Richards reported back to Dorothy about the proceedings, suggesting something of the pressure under which Cleanth operated:

Back O.K. from Philadelphia. Rather successful, though I say it. Big gathering, over 500. Three addresses in the morning. Ransom, Cleanth, and then me. Lucky they put me last, for I did save the situation. Neither Ransom nor Cleanth have any audience appeal. Ransom getting a bit old, 68, and without much gift of phrase or freshness of thought. Cleanth confided

to me (on the way back towards Yale) that Ransom really ought to prepare
his utterances better: I thought so too. Cleanth not very lively either. The
dear little man is hopelessly *overworking*, revising his many textbooks
(4 of 'em all due to be brought up to date together—if he doesn't the Publishers threaten to drop them!). Also finishing his vast *Short History of
Criticism* [sic] which (I think I told you) sort of culminates in ME. (Richards, *Letters*, 134)

W. K. Wimsatt was in charge of writing the first three-quarters of the
critical history, while Brooks handled section 4, a sequence of seven chapters dealing almost exclusively with Anglo-American criticism in the twentieth century. In the first chapter for which he was responsible, Brooks
examined various modern theories of tragedy and comedy. He begins by
noting that "each age tends to find in some one of the literary genres the
norm of all literary art. The 17th century . . . found the highest poetry to
be embodied in the epic. The later 18th century saw in the lyric the 'most
poetic kind of poetry,' for man's interests had shifted, with the burgeoning
Romantic movement, from an externally known world to the knowing
and expressive self." "When men's minds are dominated by a lyric norm,"
Brooks continues, "their conceptions of the other genres are affected. Like
metamorphosed rocks, the other genres under the heat and pressure of
lyricism, change their structure and appearance" (*Literary Criticism*,
556). The consequence for tragedy is that the critical emphasis shifted
from Aristotle's concern with plot to assessments of the protagonist's
character.

Because the effects of comedy are more readily observable than those
of tragedy, the smiling mask has been more frequently analyzed than the
frowning one. Although these analyses have included sociological and
philosophical observations, the tendency in the twentieth century has been
toward a psychological focus. Consequently, Brooks concentrates much
of his discussion on Henri Bergson and Sigmund Freud, along with objections that Max Eastman and Arthur Koestler have raised to Freud. Although he handles this material with lucidity and grace, Brooks is clearly
uneasy with any critical position that is based on an analysis of audience
response. He is particularly troubled by the implications of Koestler's contention that *Oedipus Rex* could be transformed into a French farce without any change in its cognitive layout. "There is obviously some loose and
easy sense in which an author can do this," Brooks writes; "otherwise it
would not be possible to produce parodies and ironic paraphrases" (580).
But Koestler seems to be saying more than this; he comes close to asserting

one of I. A. Richards's more questionable doctrines—that art is concerned exclusively with the emotive rather than the referential use of language.

In his next chapter, Brooks focuses on the relationship of the imagination to reality, an issue which has been one of the central concerns of the literary theory of the past two centuries. Nineteenth-century Romanticism popularized the notion that the poet is not so much a maker or craftsman as he is a visionary or seer. According to this theory, language can create an alternative reality that is far preferable to the mundane world in which most people are condemned to live; thus literature is not so much an apprehension of reality as an escape from it. The poetic imagination becomes a substitute for religion, except that the object of piety is not the created universe but man's own powers of self-transcendence.

The effort to create an alternative reality through the incantatory use of language was never entirely successful. It led to surrealistic effects that could be technically impressive but finally unintelligible. Often the "reality" that lay behind these poetic utterances was an exotic or even private system of myth. The emphasis was on occult wisdom rather than on anything that might be derived from the empiricism of social science. ("Suffice it to say," Brooks writes, "that the French symbolists were interested in the magic of the Rosicrucians rather than that of the Trobriand Islanders, and in the ritual practices of the heretical sects of the Middle Ages rather than in those of the present-day tribes of the Congo and Amazon"; *Literary Criticism*, 597.) In far too many instances, the poets who pursued this path also led lives of personal excess (Poe, Baudelaire, Hart Crane, Dylan Thomas, and the British decadents, to cite only the most notorious examples) or abandoned poetry altogether, as did Arthur Rimbaud when he burned his manuscripts and left Europe to become an ivory trader and gunrunner in Abyssinia.

v

In his next three chapters, Brooks identifies some of the issues that were at the heart of the new critical revolution. The first of these chapters—"I. A. Richards and a Poetics of Tension"—begins with a consideration of various theories of aesthetics. Like Richards, Brooks finds any attempt to define aesthetic gratification in purely hedonistic terms to be far too crude. He is drawn to Richards's equation of the aesthetic response with synaesthesis because this consists of an inclusive harmonization of discordant impulses. He parts company with Richards, however, by insisting that synaesthesis is not subjective fancy but an appreciation stimulated by qualities actually existing within the art object. Brooks notes that Richards himself backs down from his extreme subjectivist position when he suggests that we submit poetry to the test of ironic contemplation: "For, though the reader supplies the ironical squint, the subsequent collapse in the defective poem is a structural collapse" (*Literary Criticism*, 621). Regardless of the source of the harmonic tension he identifies, Richards's position bears clear affinities with Eliot's emphasis on the importance of a unified (or reassociated) sensibility.

Another valuable contribution that Richards has made to critical understanding is in his distinction between the emotive and referential uses of language. Unfortunately, he undercuts the value of that distinction by trying to make it absolute; he sees poetry as completely self-referential in the sense that it can be judged only in terms of the context that it establishes for itself. Brooks is willing to go along with the severance of poetry from all reference if Richards means no more than that "the reader of Shakespeare did not need to worry about the inaccurate Scottish history in *Macbeth*, or that the reader of Coleridge had no cause to be disturbed by such scientifically impossible descriptions as that which places a star within the nether tip of the moon. On this level, the severance between poetry and history and poetry and science had been made by the ancients. But Richards, going further, seemed to be arguing that poetry was literally nonsense, though, for reasons bound up with his psychologistic theory, a peculiarly valuable nonsense" (626).[12]

If Richards errs in attempting to maintain a rigid dualism, Brooks sees a different instance of this same fallacy in the practice of one of Richards's severest critics—John Crowe Ransom. By distinguishing between the structure and the texture of poetry, Ransom in effect identifies texture as the distinguishing characteristic of poetry. (After all, scientific—or purely referential—discourse also possesses logical structure.) Ransom's point is that our pleasure in reading a poem derives from the resistance that its irrelevant local texture poses to the resolution of its logical argument. The problem with this theory is that it gives us no reason for preferring one irrelevant detail of local texture to another. Ransom might argue plausibly enough that Marvell's "To His Coy Mistress" is "the fine poem that it is because the lover's argument runs such an obstacle race before it can come to its conclusion." But, as Yvor Winters points out, this same principle would hold that Crashaw's "The Weeper" is "a finer poem still, its argument being even more besettingly impeded by the irrelevance of its texture" (*Literary Criticism*, 628). If some "irrelevant" details are more suitable to a poem than others, then those details are anything but irrelevant.

The question of meaning in poetry forms the crux of Brooks's next chapter—"The Semantic Principle." If we dismiss the notion that poetry is pure emotive sound, we must identify its cognitive function. Although it can often tell us valuable things about the world in which we live, that is at best an extrinsic or ancillary benefit. What the poem articulates is itself. If it helps us see the world in a different way, it is because poetic language is more concrete and more ambiguous than the language of pure reference. By incorporating multiple perspectives, poetic language can actually say more than scientific language can. As William Empson and others have demonstrated, the ambiguity in poetry is not the result of imprecise words but of juxtapositions that allow words and phrases to mean several different things at once. Paradoxically, ambiguity makes poetic language more precise because it allows us to see the world in its complexity and plenitude rather than reducing it to abstraction.

Contrary to popular belief, emotional complexity does not necessarily make a poem more difficult or remote. By the same token, poems that appear eloquently simple on the surface may well convey an understated complexity. The seemingly simple statement "Ripeness is all" carries great force within the context of Shakespeare's *King Lear*. Speak the same phrase at a fruit and vegetable stand to someone who has never heard of *King Lear*, and the response will be quite different. The "simple eloquence" of Shakespeare's language is owing to the context of the entire drama. Even a play as ostensibly pure in its intention as *Romeo and Juliet* complicates itself by placing Mercutio in the bushes. As Robert Penn Warren points out in his essay "Pure and Impure Poetry," Shakespeare's play would have been simpler in a superficial sense without Mercutio and his bawdy jests or Juliet's nurse and her earthy common sense. But Warren doubts that the play would have been as great. Its vision is earned because it is able to incorporate elements that violate the simplicity of its dominant mood. Mercutio is an implied presence in all poems, and the sooner the poet makes peace with him the better.

In his chapter "Eliot and Pound: An Impersonal Art," Brooks considers the extreme reaction against Romanticism that developed in the early part of this century. If the Romantics equated poetry with the spontaneous overflow of powerful emotion, Eliot saw it as an objective and impersonal medium through which one might communicate virtually anything. To be effective, however, that communication must operate through indirection and suggestion in the manner of the metaphysical poets or the French symbolists. The complexity of poetry should not be a function of fuzzy thinking or bardic excess but of conscious craftsmanship. Poetry has emotions and ideas to convey, but they are drained of their power and meaning if stated too directly. They must take us unawares in the guise of metaphor, but the poet must not cloak his meaning too completely. One ought not write about dullness by being dull or about insanity by being irrational—this would constitute what Yvor Winters called the "fallacy of imitative form." (In one of his most controversial judgments, Winters charged Eliot with such an error when he employed fragmented language to write about the fragmentation of modern culture in *The Waste Land*.)

In his penultimate chapter, Brooks notes that the genre of literature that has come most clearly into its own in the twentieth century is prose fiction. Although its origins go back at least to medieval times, the novel rose in popularity with the rise of the middle class during the eighteenth century. It was not until the time of Flaubert and James, however, that critics began speaking of the novel as a high art form, nearly on the same level as poetry and drama. Not surprisingly, much of the theorizing about poetry that we have seen in the twentieth century has also been applied to fiction. Like Pound and Eliot, the novelists of high modernism reacted against romantic lyricism. In striving for an objective and impersonal narrative structure, they experimented with fragmented chronology, multiple points of view, and the various techniques for showing rather than merely telling a story. The objection that is often raised against this approach is that it reduces fiction, which should be directly related to life, to the level of self-conscious aesthetic experiment. Literature, we are assured by critics who possess more conviction than logic, is more than mere words on a page. Such critics "frequently write as if the author could lay upon the page warm, quivering chunks of life, if he were only gifted enough, and if he only chose to" (*Literary Criticism*, 695).

Rather than ending his section of the book with a smug celebration of the triumph of the new criticism, Brooks devotes a final chapter to discussing myth and archetype. Although there is much to be said about the role of myth in literature, Brooks raises objections to the various critics who have pursued this approach. To say that literature emerges from primordial patterns that exist in the racial subconscious is to make a controversial psychoanalytic assertion. Even if the theory of archetypes could be proven true, its usefulness for literary criticism would be limited. Archetypal analysis is, finally, a somewhat more esoteric form of historical scholarship. Instead of concentrating on the poet's biography or the social conditions in which he lived, the myth critic focuses on those elements of literature that exist prior to biography and sociology as such. At most, the mythic approach provides a new and fascinating means for cataloging different types of songs and stories. But cataloging is a prelude to criticism rather than a form of criticism itself.

VI

As we have seen, the new criticism was subject to constant attack from the moment it became a presence in the literary world, but it was not until the publication of Northrop Frye's *Anatomy of Criticism* in 1957 that a newer criticism shattered the hegemony of aesthetic formalism. Frye's objective was nothing less than to reinvent the entire concept of literary study. In a sense, his book was the mirror opposite of the new criticism. For the new critics the two principal enemies were science and romanticism, whereas Frye's system claimed a kind of scientific objectivity, while expounding a view of literature that was romantic almost to the point of gnosticism. Surely, it is no accident that Frye's first significant book of criticism was a study of the cosmic poet William Blake. If Frye himself resembles any nineteenth-century figure, however, it is Casaubon, the earnest pedant in George Eliot's *Middlemarch*, who devoted his life to searching for the "key to all mythologies."

Because *Anatomy of Criticism* was published too late to be considered in *Literary Criticism: A Short History*, Brooks's first official response to Frye's masterwork was in a review in *Christian Scholar*. He gives a succinct and lucid overview of the book's argument and pays generous tribute to its many strengths. On the matter of fundamental principles, however, he takes sharp issue with Frye. His first objection is with the *Anatomy*'s apparent attempt to turn criticism into a value-neutral social science. Brooks does not believe that Frye is successful in doing so or that he should be.

Brooks then argues that far from being value-neutral, the criticism Frye endorses implies a dubious standard of judgment:

> The ultimate difficulty of archetypal criticism is that it cannot tell us the difference between a good work and a bad, since an inferior novel, for example, may on occasion make use of the richest archetypal material and yet remain an inferior piece of art. This is the point that Jung has already

made: *Moby Dick* is a great novel and Rider Haggard's *She* is not, but they both incorporate archetypal material. Indeed what literary work does not? In so far as Frye has really classified all the possibilities of narrative structure, all the varieties of the hero, all the symbolic progressions, it will be impossible for any fictional product of the human mind not to find its proper pigeonhole. (Review of *Anatomy*, 173)

By 1965, Frye's influence was such that the English Institute organized a formal assessment of his work. While most of the essays solicited for this project were predictably laudatory, W. K. Wimsatt weighed in as devil's advocate. While justly praising Frye for his liveliness and wit, Wimsatt found the substance of his thought to be problematical. To cite one telling example of his cavalier approach to reality, Frye bases much of his theory of genres on an analogy to the four seasons. And yet, as Wimsatt notes, "man's consciousness of seasonal change has varied much in various ages and climates" (Wimsatt, "Northrop Frye," 103). Despite Frye's grand schematics, much of the literature of the Western world presupposes three or even two seasons. In Wimsatt's opinion, "The four seasons, as they function in Frye's system, are just about as primitive as the four strokes of a piston in a Rolls Royce engine. Except that Frye's Rolls Royce will not actually roll" (104).

Unfortunately, deductive generalities are the stock in trade of mythographers such as Frye. Wimsatt identifies the central fallacy of their approach as follows:

> The Ur-Myth, the Quest Myth, with all its complications, its cycles, acts, scenes, characters, and special symbols, is not a historical fact. And this is not only in the obvious sense that the stories are not true, but in another sense, which I think we tend to forget and which mythopoeic writing does much to obscure: that such a coherent, cyclic, and encyclopedic system, such a monomyth, cannot be shown ever to have evolved actually, either from or with ritual, anywhere in the world, or ever anywhere to have been entertained in whole or even in any considerable part. We are talking about the myth of myth. (97)

VII

A series of lectures Brooks gave in June 1955 (which were published as *The Hidden God* in 1963) suggests that his sensitivity to the moral and religious dimensions of literature was greater than his detractors would have us believe. The lectures examine the religious dimension in the work of Hemingway, Faulkner, Yeats, Eliot, and Warren. It is significant that of the five only Eliot could be regarded as an orthodox Christian. Brooks's intention was to show Christian readers (his audience was the Faculty Conference on Theology at Trinity College, Hartford, Connecticut) that they could learn much about the world from writers who did not share their dogmatic faith.

Although he mentions the great Protestant theologian Paul Tillich only in passing, Brooks's position is congenial with Tillich's. Religion, according to Tillich, is quite simply an expression of man's ultimate concern; by this definition, we are all religious in different ways. Indeed, a poet or philosopher who has confronted the deep existential questions of life can be more religious, even if he is an atheist, than the complacent churchgoer who has never experienced the dark night of the soul. Tillich believed that existentialist philosophy raised all of the significant religious questions in a language uniquely relevant to the concerns of our age. He also believed that Christianity provided the answers to those questions. Tillich's life work was devoted to making this connection clear by translating Christian dogma into the language of existentialism. In *The Hidden God* Brooks is translating the existential concerns of modern literature into the language of Christianity.

The eclecticism of Cleanth's work and his continuing professional stature so impressed his colleagues that his name immediately came to mind when an old Yale alumnus named Neil Gray left the university a bequest to promote the proper use of language. Because Yale did not have a department in the specified field of rhetoric, it was up to the English department, now chaired by Louis Martz, to determine what to do with the money. Cleanth probably had been more concerned in more different ways with the uses of language than had anyone else in the department. Because he clearly deserved an endowed chair, he was named in 1961 to be Yale's first Gray Professor of Rhetoric.

Back at home, a snake appeared in the Garden of Northford in the person of Willmoore Kendall. When the Brookses took him in as a neighbor, it was on the assumption that Ken loved the bucolic life as much as they did. Unfortunately, that love of nature lasted only until Ken discovered that he could make money by selling gravel off his place. Before long, trucks were violating the serenity of Cleanth and Tinkum's right-of-way. Pleas to Kendall's better nature led only to arguments and friction. On one memorable occasion, he called Tinkum after he had been drinking hard and tried to dispute the location of the property line. Upon meeting him at the creek, Tinkum could tell that Ken was in no position to discuss anything. With her characteristic plainspokenness, she told him to go home and sober up. His companion, the town drunk, observed: "You know, Miz Brooks, that's what I've been trying to get him to do all night."

During his absences from Yale, Kendall would rent his house to a variety of tenants, some of whom would do their best to antagonize the neighbors. Because he was such a disruptive force on campus, those absences occurred with increasing frequency as Yale granted him academic leave whenever he asked for it. When a disgruntled colleague told Dean Bill DeVane that he should insist upon Ken's returning from one extended leave, DeVane replied that he was afraid he might. Finally in 1961, Willmoore Kendall made academic history when Yale agreed to buy up his tenure rights. Ken was soon off to the University of Dallas, a conservative Roman Catholic institution, where he spent the final years of his troubled life in relative happiness and local sainthood. Although he eventually became reconciled with many of the friends he had alienated over the years, the Brookses were not among them. When Carver Blanchard allowed that there was something Snopesean about Willmoore Kendall, Cleanth assured him that he was being too hard on the Snopeses.

On February 12, 1962, nearly nineteen years after the death of his father, Cleanth's mother suffered a fatal heart attack. She had lived in Baton Rouge until 1949 and in Memphis from 1949 to 1956. (An attempt to live with Cleanth and Tinkum shortly after they moved to New Haven turned out badly because of profound differences in culture and values.) In 1956 Mrs. Brooks moved to Inglewood, California, to be near her two younger sons, William and Tookie. All three of her sons were at her bedside when she died. In the obituary he wrote for her in the annual *Journal of the Louisiana Conference* of the Methodist Church, Cleanth observed: "My mother was by temperament more akin to Martha than to Mary. She was energetic and ardent, not afraid to use her hands, too humble about her capabilities otherwise, but in any case anxious to be of positive help—to do something. Many a parsonage she left in spick-and-span shape only to find the task to do over again at the parsonage to which she had just come. . . . Hers was not an easy life. She suffered hardships and some disappointments, but she persevered in faith and hope and ended her days in sunshine and serenity" ("Mrs. Cleanth Brooks," 273).

At the suggestion of Donald Davidson, Cleanth spent the summer of 1963 at the Bread Loaf School of English in Middlebury, Vermont. Although detractors depicted him as the most provincial of southern chauvinists, Davidson had himself taught at Bread Loaf since the 1930s. He gloried in the regional diversity of American life and believed that the Vermont farmer had just as much right as his southern cousin to maintain cherished customs and folkways. In fact, Davidson was probably happier in Vermont than in an increasingly cosmopolitan Nashville (1964 would be his last year at Vanderbilt.) In his essay "Still Rebels, Still Yankees," Davidson writes with genuine affection of the prototypical New England agrarian, whom he calls Brother Jonathan. In his contribution to *I'll Take My Stand*, Davidson had argued that art, at least of the traditional kind, requires the nurture of a life lived close to the soil. Having found such a life at Bread Loaf, he naturally wanted to share it with old friends. If literary fashion and even history itself had passed him by, friendship and a sense of the old verities were all he had left to fall back on.

Cleanth returned to Vanderbilt to speak at a literary symposium on April 28–30, 1964. Conditions on campus had changed since the Fugitive Reunion in 1956. Not only was Davidson on his way out, the English department was again without a head. Randall Stewart had announced his retirement (he would die suddenly from a heart attack later that year), and the effort to replace him was already underway. (Although a few old friends and local admirers wanted to see Cleanth in the position, he was too deeply entrenched at Yale to consider the possibility.) [13] The surviving correspondence shows Cleanth eager to advise the university officials who would select the next department head, although it is clear from their response that they were listening to him out of little more than perfunctory courtesy. [14] The Vanderbilt administration was content to have him lecture on literary topics and even to entertain him royally when he was in town, but the new regime was no more willing than the old to value his opinion on anything they considered important. [15] With his estrangement from the New South deeper than ever, Cleanth would soon claim the traditional South with a seminal study of the greatest writer that region had ever produced.

CHAPTER SIXTEEN

A Postage Stamp of Soil

In November of 1948 Cleanth wrote to Red Warren: "I had a very pleasant meeting with Faulkner in New York last week. He strikes me as a thoroughly fine person *as a person*, some of the legends to the contrary notwithstanding."[1] The meeting in question was set up by Albert Erskine, who had informed Cleanth that Faulkner was in New York. With his literary stock on the rise, Faulkner was traveling more, but his presence so close to New Haven was a rare occurrence. As Faulkner's editor at Random House, Albert promised Cleanth an introduction if he would take the train down to Manhattan and meet them at a bar. Because this was one of Faulkner's many drying-out periods, he nursed a single bottle of beer all afternoon.

The conversation began on a tentative note, with Cleanth avoiding any direct mention of literature. He spoke of his place in the country and of the local hunting club's asking permission to run dogs through his land. The talk moved from coon hounds to Dixiecrats (Faulkner loved the one and despised the other), before eventually drifting on to Faulkner's work. Cleanth allowed as how he never understood why Uncle Buck, who seemed to have won the poker game in "Was," ended up losing a slave he wanted to keep and winning a wife he wanted to avoid. "It wasn't in that poker game that it happened," Faulkner replied, "but in one I haven't written yet. I have so many stories in my head." The critic and the novelist never met again, and no one will ever know how many of the stories in Faulkner's head went unwritten.

I

In the fall of 1992 Lance Lyday reported that "William Faulkner and his writings have now been the subject of more than 6,000 essays and reviews, more than 300 books, and about 500 dissertations—more than the total amount of critical attention devoted to any other writer in English except Shakespeare" (Lyday, 183). For most of Faulkner's career, such notice would have been unimaginable. During the time that he was producing the novels on which his future reputation would rest, Faulkner's praises were sung by a few fellow writers and literary intellectuals, but both the general public and the critical establishment regarded him as a gothic curiosity—when they were not ignoring him altogether.

Although the reversal in Faulkner's critical reputation was the better part of a decade in coming, the process began in 1939. In January of that year, Robert Cantwell wrote a cover article on the Mississippi novelist for *Time* magazine. In the summer issue of the *Kenyon Review*, George Marion O'Donnell published an influential essay that saw the world of Yoknapatawpha as being divided between the Sartorises and the Snopeses. (Although this simplistic dichotomy would later become a cliché of Faulkner criticism, O'Donnell was the first serious literary scholar to argue that Faulkner had a coherent vision of the world.) Finally, in November, the *Atlantic Monthly* carried Conrad Aiken's brilliant defense of Faulkner's much-maligned prose style.

This initial burst of critical appreciation gathered momentum in the early forties with an essay by Delmore Schwartz in the *Southern Review* (Summer 1941) and influential articles by Warren Beck—in the *Antioch Review* (Spring 1941), *College English* (May 1941), and the *Rocky Mountain Review* (Spring-Summer 1942). Unfortunately, Faulkner published no books between *Go Down, Moses* in 1942 and *Intruder in the Dust* in 1948. At the same time, his earlier books were going out of print and, in some cases, the very plates on which they were printed were melted down for war material. Students excited by the new wave of critical interest in Faulkner were forced to seek their primary texts in the remainder bins of secondhand bookstores.

It was not until after World War II that Faulkner's work once again became widely available to a public that had previously ignored or reviled it. In 1946 readers were persuaded to take a second look at Faulkner's fictional county by the publication of Malcolm Cowley's *The Portable*

Faulkner—a selection of stories and novel excerpts set in Yoknapataw-pha. In editing the *Portable Faulkner*, Cowley paid scant attention to the formal distinctions between novels and stories. He believed that Faulkner was less the careful craftsman than the grand mythmaker. Thus Cowley arranged the contents of his volume chronologically, giving us a history of Yoknapatawpha County over a period of two centuries. To a large extent, Cowley's argument was an extension of the one that O'Donnell had made in the *Kenyon Review* seven years before. The main difference was that Cowley was reaching a much larger audience and had the accompanying texts to back him up.

The next phase of Faulkner's career began in 1950, when he became the fourth American to win the Nobel Prize for Literature. In his famous speech accepting the prize, Faulkner spoke of certain eternal verities that it is the duty of the writer to preserve. The affirmative, even moralistic, tone of the speech was such that a novelist who had been long denounced for his pessimism and depravity was now being hailed as some sort of Christian humanist.

The year after Faulkner won the Nobel Prize, Harry M. Campbell and Ruel E. Foster published the first of the 300 books to be devoted to Faulkner's work.[2] By the end of the decade a dozen other books had been produced, including highly useful studies by Irving Howe, William Van O'Connor, Olga W. Vickery, and Hyatt H. Waggoner. By 1960, Faulkner had joined Hemingway as one of the two surviving novelists from the prewar era against whom the achievement of the postwar generation was measured. Like Hemingway, Faulkner was now removed by more than two decades from his best work, even as he was being honored for his past achievement. The influence of both men on our literary tradition was due not only to their own work but to the intelligent interpretation of it by literary critics.

Although Brooks read Faulkner's first novel, *Soldier's Pay*, shortly after its publication in 1929 and taught courses in Faulkner at a time when his classroom texts had to be obtained from secondhand bookshops, his career as a Faulkner critic began rather late. His first essay on Faulkner, a discussion of *Absalom, Absalom!* in the *Sewanee Review*, was not published until 1951, a year after Faulkner received the Nobel Prize. As Brooks told the story to me years later, Monroe Spears, who had just taken over the editorship of the *Sewanee Review* from John Palmer, wrote in the contributors' notes to the magazine that Cleanth Brooks was writing a book on Faulkner. Because that was an inaccurate surmise on Spears's part, Cleanth's first inclination was to ask that a correction be run in the next issue. On second thought, he decided that it might not be such a bad idea for him to write a book on Faulkner. That was the rather accidental genesis of *William Faulkner: The Yoknapatawpha Country*, a volume that has set the standard for the hundreds of books and thousands of essays on Faulkner that have appeared since.

II

From the fifties on (actually from Cowley's *The Portable Faulkner* on), one of the major tendencies in Faulkner criticism has been to see the Yoknapatawpha saga whole. Published in 1963, the year after Faulkner's death, Cleanth Brooks's *William Faulkner: The Yoknapatawpha Country* was the first important book to attempt this task after the canon was complete. At the outset, Brooks declares that his intention is to describe William Faulkner's "characteristic world." Like Cowley, he examines Faulkner's little postage stamp of soil as if it had a real history and a real geography. At the same time, he is careful to show how the world of Yoknapatawpha is realized in individual novels and stories, which have an integrity of their own independent of their contribution to the larger saga.

Although the bulk of his book is devoted to discussions of these individual works, Brooks uses his first three chapters to establish a general context for his study. In his first chapter, for example, he identifies Faulkner as a provincial writer. By this Brooks does not mean that Faulkner was a country bumpkin who was limited in his knowledge of the sophisticated world away from home. Rather, like William Butler Yeats and Robert Frost, Faulkner was so rooted in a particular region that he was able to expose the shortcomings of the larger urban and commercial culture. (It is this observation that has caused Brooks's detractors to accuse him of making Faulkner into an honorary Agrarian.)

Two of the most prevalent ways of misreading Faulkner are to see him as either a sociologist or an allegorist. Readers looking for a report on conditions in the South will find Erskine Caldwell more reliable or more persuasive or, perhaps, only more accessible. Studies exposing Faulkner's lack of verisimilitude are as plentiful as they are facile. What they fail to realize is that, for Faulkner, setting is a point of departure rather than the final purpose of his art. Nevertheless, to understand the function of place in his fiction, it is helpful to know something about the place itself. In a sense, Faulkner is an historian, but his history—like that of Keats's Grecian urn—is written without footnotes. At the same time, it is too deeply grounded in observed reality to be reduced to one-dimensional symbols. After citing a particularly labored interpretation of the killing of a pig in *The Sound and the Fury*, Brooks asks in exasperation, "Shall there be no more innocent consumption of pork chops and spareribs in Yoknapatawpha County because someone has read *The Golden Bough*?" (*Yoknapatawpha Country*, 8).

If the general influence of Agrarianism is evident in Brooks's description of Faulkner as a provincial, one detects the more specific presence of Andrew Lytle—or perhaps Frank Owsley—in the second chapter of *The Yoknapatawpha Country*. Persons unfamiliar with the South often imagine it as populated by only three groups of people: aristocratic whites, poor whites, and blacks, a tripartite division that leaves out the rather large category of yeomen farmers. Readers who identify all nonaristocratic whites in Faulkner's fiction as white trash miss much of the social nuance in the world of Yoknapatawpha. Brooks tries to illuminate the rich particularity of that world by discussing the role of the "plain people" in such diverse works as "Shingles for the Lord," *The Mansion, Light in August*, "An Odor of Verbena," "Shall Not Perish," *As I Lay Dying*, "The Fire and the Hearth," *Sanctuary*, and *Intruder in the Dust*.

The last of Brooks's preliminary chapters discusses "Faulkner as Nature Poet." Making many suggestive comparisons between Faulkner's fiction and Wordsworth's poetry, Brooks argues that the cultural backwardness of the American South was actually an aesthetic advantage. Like Wordsworth a century earlier, Faulkner did not yet inhabit a "post-Christian" world. Although he might not have practiced the ritual or preached the dogma of orthodox Christianity, he believed instinctively in Original Sin and the depravity of the will. These beliefs in no way restrained his love of the natural world, but they did limit the philosophical inferences he was apt to draw from his experience of nature.

Brooks begins his consideration of specific novels with a discussion of *Light in August* (1932). Not only is this novel universally regarded as one of Faulkner's finest efforts; it is also a book that illustrates the function of the community in Faulkner's fiction. Readers who ignore the importance of the community in *Light in August* are apt to find the book a pastiche of brilliant writing, which lacks the unity and coherence we usually demand of novels. (Brooks notes that even such perceptive and sympathetic critics as Conrad Aiken and George Marion O'Donnell fell into this category.) Elaborating on this point, Brooks writes:

> One way in which to gauge the importance of the community in this novel is by imagining the action to have taken place in Chicago or Manhattan Island, where the community—at least in Faulkner's sense—does not exist. . . . The plight of the isolated individual cut off from any community of values is of course a dominant theme of contemporary literature. But by developing this theme in a rural setting in which a powerful sense of community still exists, Faulkner has given us a kind of pastoral—that is, he has let us see our modern and complex problems mirrored in a simpler and more primitive world. *Light in August* is, in some respects, a bloody and violent pastoral. The plight of the lost sheep and of the black sheep can be given special point and meaning because there is still visible in the background a recognizable flock with its shepherds, its watchdogs, sometimes fierce and cruel, and its bellwethers. (*Yoknapatawpha Country*, 54)

In addition to tracing broad themes in the novel, Brooks also corrects what he regards as misconceptions about narrower matters. For example, he points out that the evidence we have for the presence of Negro blood in Joe Christmas is meager and inconclusive (what matters is that Joe does not know who or what he is). Also, the contention that Joe is the victim of a lynching misstates the actual circumstances of the novel. Joe is killed not by a mob but by an isolated individual. Percy Grimm's brutality is an expression not of the will of the community but of his own profound alienation from it. The proper interpretation of such details finally marks the difference between tragedy and comedy. "Tragedy," Brooks writes, "always concerns itself with the individual, his values, his tragic encounter with the reality about him, and the waste which is suffered in his defeat. Comedy involves, on the other hand, the author's basic alignment with society and with the community" (72). Despite its pathos and horror, Brooks sees *Light in August* as ultimately a comic work.

If *Light in August* is one of the works on which Faulkner's reputation will rest, the same could not be said of *The Unvanquished*, which for years after its publication in 1938 was dismissed as a collection of slick *Saturday Evening Post* stories posing as a novel. Andrew Lytle had challenged that characterization in an influential essay published in the *Sewanee Review* in 1955, and Brooks continued the effort at rehabilitation. If *Light in August* shows the plight of marginal characters in a traditional society, the situation in *The Unvanquished* is almost exactly the opposite. Colonel John Sartoris, his son Bayard, Drusilla Hawk, and Miss Rosa Millard are individuals who belong in a traditional society, but the upheavals of war and Reconstruction have destroyed that society. Colonel Sartoris, the antebellum aristocrat, has no clearly defined place in the postwar world. Bayard finds the duties of a son toward his father and the passage from childhood to adulthood to be more difficult in a world where the old rules no longer prevail. But the characters most uprooted are Drusilla and Rosa, who are effectively desexed by the war. Drusilla, in particular, is caught in a double bind. Even as the war denies her the traditional life of a young woman, the older members of the community judge her harshly for her unconventional ways. Because Faulkner sees Drusilla as a victim, he can share the basic values of the community without joining in its judgment on her.

One of the problems with seeing the Yoknapatawpha saga as a continuous story is that certain novels depicting a character in old age were actually written earlier than others depicting that same character in his youth. (We probably do not know enough about Faulkner's habits of composition to assert that he had the entire history of his mythical county in mind from the outset, although Brooks suspects that this may be close to the truth.) In the 1929 novel *Sartoris*, for example, Bayard, who will be a vital youth in *The Unvanquished* (published nine years later), is depicted as a tired and ineffectual old man. If we assume that Faulkner planned this degeneration of Bayard's character from the outset, we have even more powerful evidence of the deracinating effects of modern life. Brooks calls his chapter on *Sartoris* "The Waste Land: Southern Exposure," and he argues that it is Faulkner's lost generation novel. The characters who figure most prominently in its pages are Bayard's manic grandson Young Bayard and the Prufrockian Horace Benbow. According to Brooks, "the special problems of the twenties and a good deal of the mood of the waste land are here placed in a small Southern town that is still suffused with the atmosphere of the post–Civil War period" (*Yoknapatawpha Country*, 114).

Faulkner's reputation for depravity is an ironic by-product of his traditional moral sensibility. Because of his pragmatic belief in Original Sin, he is able to recognize evil in the world. This is particularly true in his two novels about Temple Drake—*Sanctuary* (1932) and *Requiem for a Nun* (1951). Although Brooks finds much to admire in both novels, he does not believe that the "dramatic presentation" in *Requiem* is "quite full enough, articulate enough, convincing enough to bring the whole work to success" (140). *Sanctuary*, however, is a different matter. Because of its popularity, even notoriety, some highbrow critics tend to write this novel off as a mere potboiler. In reality, it is one of those rare modern books to bridge the gap between popular and elite culture. (Faulkner accomplished that feat only in this one novel, although his indirect influence on popular culture was immense.) After discussing *Sanctuary* as both gangster novel and mystery novel, Brooks identifies its contribution to the Yoknapatawpha canon: "In nearly every one of Faulkner's novels, the male's discovery of evil and reality is bound up with his discovery of the true nature of woman. Men idealize and romanticize women, but the cream of the jest is that women have a secret rapport with evil which men do not have, that they are able to adjust to evil without being shattered by it, being by nature flexible and pliable. Women are the objects of idealism, but are not in the least idealistic" (127–28).

One of Faulkner's greatest achievements as a writer was his ability to depict different social classes with full imaginative sympathy. Although his heritage and his values were aristocratic, some of his most fully realized fiction displays an understanding of poor whites that is tinged with neither condescension nor sentimentality. This is particularly true in *As I Lay Dying* (1930), his tale of the quixotic odyssey of the Bundren family. Brooks regards this novel as "a triumph in the management of tone." "Faulkner," he writes, "has daringly mingled the grotesque and the heroic, the comic and the pathetic, pity and terror, creating a complexity of tone that has proved difficult for some readers to cope with" (141). What keeps the black comedy of this novel from wearing thin is Faulkner's incisive probing of the motivations of the Bundren clan. Being of a low social class does not make the Bundrens simple people. "As a commentary upon man's power to act and to endure, upon his apparently incorrigible idealism," Brooks concludes, "the story of the Bundrens is clearly appalling—appalling but not scathing and not debunking. Heroism is heroism even though it sometimes appears to be merely the hither side of folly" (166).

III

As George Marion O'Donnell noted in 1939, the central cultural conflict in Yoknapatawpha County involves the fall of the aristocratic Sartoris

family and the rise of the white trash Snopeses. We are first introduced to
the Snopeses in Faulkner's pastoral novel *The Hamlet* (1940). According
to Brooks, the pastoral mode is used in this novel, as it had been elsewhere
in Faulkner's work, "to underscore [the] double effect of irony and wonder" (*Yoknapatawpha Country*, 173). He describes its aesthetic function
as follows:

> Because the world of *The Hamlet* is—at least at an initial glance—so dif-
> ferent from the reader's normal experience, Faulkner's first problem is to
> make it credible to his reader. It cannot be presented as normal and every-
> day, but must be made to seem, in its very strangeness, solid and lifelike.
> Thus we find that Faulkner has stylized and formalized his world of
> Frenchman's Bend almost as much as Jonathan Swift stylized and formal-
> ized the country of Lilliput, but again like Swift, he has rendered it in al-
> most microscopic detail. One might say that the narrator of *The Hamlet*
> has a touch of Gulliver in him, but scarcely a hint of the modern anthro-
> pologist investigating the customs of the Trobriand Islanders. (174)

Although its primary story is of the rise of Flem Snopes within the mundane and vernacular world of commerce, *The Hamlet* finally inhabits the
realm of myth. This mythic world includes not only the tall tale tradition
of the frequently anthologized "Spotted Horses" episode but also Faulkner's treatment of the recurring themes of love and honor. Within this
world, the impotent and acquisitive Flem is contrasted with his arche-
typally feminine wife, Eula. But perhaps the most radical embodiment of
pure and uninhibited love is the idiot Ike's devotion to his cow. Faulkner's
lyrical treatment of this absurd situation is itself a tour de force of irony
and wonder.

Seventeen years later, in 1957, Faulkner published *The Town*, which is
the second installment in the Snopes trilogy. Because the mythic world of
the earlier novel has been reduced to more human proportions, the passion and delusion that we see in *The Town* are more domestic, even prosaic. The focus of this novel is the Harvard-educated lawyer Gavin Stevens. Because of Gavin's obvious decency and intellect, some readers
mistake him for Faulkner's spokesman. In *The Town*, however, he is
blinded to reality by his doomed and chaste love for Eula Varner. Brooks
makes sense of Gavin's erratic behavior by seeing it as a manifestation of
courtly love. Although Brooks does not know whether Faulkner ever read
Denis de Rougemont's *Love in the Western World*, his fiction is filled with
characters who devote themselves to a romantic quest that is noble to the

degree that it is hopeless. Such individuals include characters as different as Bayard Sartoris in *The Unvanquished* and Emily Grierson in "A Rose for Emily." Because of his Platonic devotion to Eula Varner Snopes (and later to her daughter Linda), Gavin Stevens is one of the most extreme and fully developed examples of this pathology.

By the time we get to *The Mansion* (1959), the emphasis has shifted again. Calling his chapter on *The Mansion* "Faulkner's Revenger's Tragedy," Brooks shows how Linda Snopes (daughter of Eula and her lover Manfred de Spain, and the foster daughter of Flem Snopes) displays her ostensibly liberal compassion by arranging the release of Mink Snopes from prison. Knowing of Mink's long-standing grudge against Flem, Linda figures that she can do away with her hated foster father without having to raise a finger against him. Although she is no longer a member of the Communist Party, Linda maintains a sentimental attachment to the cause of the downtrodden. This enables her to rationalize a series of actions that amounts to premeditated murder. Considering Faulkner's view of men and women, it is not surprising that Gavin Stevens is far more shaken by this experience than Linda is.

With *Go Down, Moses*, published in 1942, Faulkner is still in the realm of myth. Like *The Unvanquished*, *Go Down, Moses* is a novel composed largely of previously published short stories (the original title of the book was *Go Down, Moses and Other Stories*). By far the most famous of these is the novel's fifth chapter, "The Bear," which has often been published by itself, sometimes with its difficult fourth section removed. The aim of Brooks's discussion is to demonstrate the unity of *Go Down, Moses* and to correct errors that result from reading "The Bear" in isolation. *Go Down, Moses* might have been more prosaically entitled *The McCaslins* because the book deals to varying degrees with the white and black descendants of an old slave owner named Carothers McCaslin.[3] The destruction of the wilderness and the legacy of slavery are the novel's dominant themes. The dilemma the McCaslins face is how to live in a world afflicted by these curses.

Readers familiar only with "The Bear" are apt to overemphasize the undeniably important role of Isaac (Ike) McCaslin in *Go Down, Moses*. The first chapter, "Was," begins with Ike as an old man but quickly flashes back to a story involving his father, mother, and uncle eight years before his own birth. This is followed by "The Fire and the Hearth" and "A Pantaloon in Black," two episodes featuring black protagonists. Although Ike is mentioned in passing in "The Fire and the Hearth" (in a manner that crucially affects our interpretation of a key scene in section 4 of "The Bear"), he does not appear in his own right until the fourth chapter, an elegiac tale of the wilderness entitled "The Old People." Taken together with sections 1–3 and 5 of "The Bear," "The Old People" depicts Ike's initiation into manhood in the context of a disappearing wilderness. Many readers of these episodes see Ike as a primitivist saint heroically defending an older and better way of life against the encroachments of technology. Section 4 of "The Bear" even suggests that Ike is a principled foe of racism atoning for the sins of his grandfather (although the racial theme does not seem at first glance to have much to do with Ike's hunting idyll).

In "Delta Autumn," the episode that follows "The Bear," we see Ike as an ineffectual old man (he has been described earlier as "uncle to half the county and father to no one.") His lonely stand against civilization has not prevented the desecration of the forest by sawmills and logging camps (the men must now drive a couple of hundred miles to find land on which to hunt). Also, Roth Edmonds's mixed-blood mistress (who, by virtue of being the great-great-granddaughter of Carothers McCaslin, is also Roth's distant cousin) accuses Ike of having destroyed her lover's character by bequeathing to his family land that did not belong to them. Far from atoning for the sins of his grandfather (which are not miscegenation and incest so much as a coldhearted and prideful denial of love and its obligations), Ike has made possible a repetition of these crimes generations later. Whether or not we accept this woman's interpretation of things (with its hint of Sophoclean irony), the fact that it even has a place in *Go Down, Moses* "effectively undercuts any notion that Faulkner is asking the reader to accept Isaac's action as the ideal solution of the race problem or even to regard his motivation as obviously saintlike" (*Yoknapatawpha Country*, 274).

In the title episode of *Go Down, Moses*, which immediately follows "Delta Autumn" and concludes the volume, Faulkner presents a less abstract and more human bond between the races. Here, Miss Belle Worsham shares the grief of her Negro friend Mollie Beauchamp,[4] whose grandson Butch has been executed for murder in Chicago. Although Gavin Stevens has helped raise money for the return and burial of Butch's body, he is made uncomfortable by the blatant emotionalism of Mollie and Miss Belle. "It may seem odd," Brooks concludes, "to have this book close on an episode in which Mollie and her white counterpart, Miss Worsham, dominate the action, especially when one remembers how much of the book has to do with [Mollie's husband] Lucas' striving with his fate and with Isaac McCaslin's initiation, self-discipline, and attempted expiation. But the actions of Lucas and Ike are unthinkable except against the background of such a community [as Faulkner depicts], and it is the women who most typically embody and express its claims" (278).

Intruder in the Dust (1948) was the first of Faulkner's novels to appear after *The Portable Faulkner* had created a new and larger audience for the Yoknapatawpha saga. Because it concerns a black man (Lucas Beauchamp) who is unjustly accused of murder and almost lynched, many critics (particularly in the North) read it as a racial tract. Viewed in those terms, the novel expresses a politically incorrect ambivalence toward both Lucas and the community of which he is a part. This is particularly true if one makes the mistake of again seeing Gavin Stevens as Faulkner's spokesman. Although Brooks acknowledges that *Intruder in the Dust* is not one of Faulkner's better efforts, he argues that the fault lies not with its political message but with the implausible contrivances of the novel's plot. If we move beyond plot and theme, however, and concentrate on character, *Intruder in the Dust* can be appreciated as a tale of initiation similar to *The Unvanquished* or "The Bear." According to such an interpretation, Charles Mallison, not Lucas Beauchamp or Gavin Stevens, is the most important character in the novel.

The first of Faulkner's great novels (many would say his greatest) was published with much less fanfare two decades earlier. On the surface, *The Sound and the Fury* (1929) would appear to be a case study of a single southern family. Because the Compsons are so emphatically southern, some readers have erroneously interpreted their plight as symbolizing the condition of the region as a whole. Not surprisingly, Brooks takes issue with that reading. He argues that "the real significance of the Southern setting in *The Sound and the Fury* resides, as so often elsewhere in Faulkner, in the fact that the breakdown of a family can be exhibited more poignantly and significantly in a society which is old-fashioned and in which the family is still at the center. . . . What happens to the Compsons might make less noise and cause less comment, and even bring less pain to the individuals concerned, if the Compsons lived in a more progressive and liberal environment" (*Yoknapatawpha Country*, 341).

Brooks contends that each of the four sections of the novel presents a different conception of time and exhibits a different mode of poetry. For Benjy, the idiot, past and present are hopelessly jumbled, while the future scarcely seems to exist. Quentin, the romantic, is in bondage to a highly neurotic vision of the past. Jason, the businessman, runs a constant and losing race with the clock. Only Dilsey, the black cook, living in the eternal security of her Christian faith, is totally comfortable with time. In terms of language, the poetry of Benjy's section is that of immediate sensory experience. Quentin is more of a decadent, who speaks in a private, even symbolist, tongue. The prosaic Jason achieves the poetry of perfect self-expression. (In Brooks's view, "Faulkner does more in these eighty pages [of Jason's section] to indict the shabby small-town businessman's view of life than Sinclair Lewis was able to achieve in several novels on the subject"; 339.) And finally, Dilsey gives us the simple eloquence of an unlettered faith.

In addition to misreading *The Sound and the Fury* as a parable of the South, some observers also make the mistake of regarding it as a primitivist tract, with Dilsey playing the role of the noble savage. Brooks will go so far as to admit that "Dilsey's poverty and her status as a member of a deprived race . . . may have something to do with her remaining close to a concrete world of values so that she is less perverted by abstraction and more honest than are most white people in recognizing what is essential and basic" (344). Dilsey's moral authority, however, cannot finally be explained by the theories of Rousseau. She "is no noble savage and no *schöne Seele*. Her view of the world and mankind is thoroughly Christian, simple and limited as her theological expression of her faith would have to be. . . . Dilsey's goodness is no mere goodness by, and of, nature, if one means by this a goodness that justifies a faith in man as man. Dilsey does not believe in man; she believes in God" (343). The Compson family believes in neither. This, not their residence in the South, is the source of their tragedy.

Because *The Yoknapatawpha Country* is not organized chronologically, there is no compelling reason for Brooks to complete his book with a discussion of Faulkner's last novel, *The Reivers* (1962). Coming immediately after a masterful discussion of *The Sound and the Fury*, this essay might strike many readers as anticlimactic. Nevertheless, there is much in *The Reivers* that links it with the rest of the Yoknapatawpha saga. If it is a less singular achievement than Faulkner's greatest novels, it is in some ways more typical of the fictional world he has created. Brooks compares it to other initiation stories, such as *The Unvanquished*, "The Bear," and *Intruder in the Dust*. (Because of its concern with what it means to be a gentleman, Brooks argues that "*The Reivers* is a sort of latter-day 'courtesy book'"; 351.) Moreover, "there is the heroic journey, as in *As I Lay Dying*. . . . There is also the complicated wager, such as that found in the story 'Was,' and the elaborate bargaining, as is carried out by Ratliff in *The Hamlet*" (350).

The bonding of the sensitive boy and the adult bum, the reformation of the good-hearted whore, and the romance of the automobile—all recollected from the elegiac perspective of old age—are hardly original themes, and in the hands of a writer less skillfull than Faulkner, they might easily have degenerated into bathos and sentimentality. If *The Reivers* does not reveal the depths of Faulkner's world—"the violence, isolation, and agony to be found in *Light in August, The Sound and the Fury,* or *Absalom, Absalom!*" (367)—Brooks believes that it does represent that world in its full social breadth. "The fact that the spirit of *The Reivers* is comic and that most of its characters are good and kindly people is scarcely evidence of a late mellowing. . . . The truth of the matter is that Faulkner's world has always had room in it for a wide range of experience and that Faulkner has never offered his world as proof of any special thesis about human nature other than the marvelous capacity human beings have for goodness and evil" (366).

IV

In between his chapters on *Intruder in the Dust* and *The Sound and the Fury*, Brooks has placed a discussion of the novel he regards as Faulkner's masterpiece, *Absalom, Absalom!* (1936). The reworking of two earlier essays (published in the *Sewanee Review* and the *Yale Review*, respectively), this chapter would not be Brooks's final word on the novel. In the notes to *The Yoknapatawpha Country*, he devotes nearly twenty pages (what amounts to a series of mini-essays) to elaborating various points made about *Absalom, Absalom!* in the body of the text. Then, in *Toward Yoknapatawpha and Beyond* (1978), he comes back to the novel in two of the three essays printed as appendices and a couple of shorter notes. Even though Brooks was supposed to have left Yoknapatawpha behind in this sequel, he returns to *Absalom, Absalom!* as compulsively as Shreve and

Quentin return to the story of Thomas Sutpen. For Brooks, *Absalom, Absalom!* is not only Faulkner's supreme achievement as an artist but also his most American work, for in it he confronts the American dream of innocence.

If Faulkner's conservative social vision is most often comic, he was capable in his greatest novels of creating truly modern tragedies. Such is the case with *Absalom, Absalom!* But to read this book as a tragedy of the South is to misconstrue Faulkner's meaning. Thomas Sutpen is a completely self-made man, whose character has neither been formed nor constrained by any organic community. To be sure, he is not a rebel against the community in the sense that Joe Christmas is. He simply tries to establish his identity (which includes his role in society) according to his private obsessions. In so doing, Thomas Sutpen becomes a victim of his own innocence.

Brooks's description of the fall of Thomas Sutpen (which makes up the first half of his chapter on *Absalom, Absalom!*) is an incisive and persuasive indictment of the nontraditional sensibility. Far from being Procrustean and thesis-driven, such an interpretation almost seems to be demanded by the manner in which Sutpen's story is told. All that Quentin and Shreve know about this legendary figure is what Quentin has learned from various people in the community. As far as it goes, the conventional wisdom about Sutpen is correct. The pathos of the story comes from nothing we learn about Sutpen but from what we discover about the suffering of his children. They, even more than Sutpen himself, are victims of their father's mania.

As sound as it may be, Brooks's discussion of Sutpen's downfall is only part of his analysis of *Absalom, Absalom!* The rest of his chapter on this novel concerns the structure of the narrative itself. In addition to its other virtues, Brooks believes that *Absalom, Absalom!* is Faulkner's most successful detective story. Not only do Shreve and Quentin become "authors" of Sutpen's tragedy, but as readers we too are drawn into the game, as we are required to sort through contradictory information and alternative conjectures. Through his own bit of textual sleuthing, Brooks concludes that Quentin has learned the essential facts about Charles Bon's life and death in an encounter with the aged and dying Henry at Sutpen's Hundred.

In his concluding comments, Brooks sounds like nothing so much as the new critic demonstrating how meaning is realized through form:

Absalom, Absalom! is in many respects the most brilliantly written of all Faulkner's novels, whether one considers its writing line by line and paragraph by paragraph, or its structure, in which we are moved up from one suspended note to a higher suspended note and on up further still to an intolerable climax. The intensity of the book is a function of the structure. The deferred and suspended resolutions are necessary if the great scenes are to have their full vigor and significance. Admittedly, the novel is a difficult one, but the difficulty is not forced and factitious. It is the price that has to be paid by the reader for the novel's power and significance. There are actually few instances in modern fiction of a more perfect adaptation of form to matter and of an intricacy that justifies itself at every point through the significance and intensity which it makes possible. (*Yoknapatawpha Country*, 323–24)

After such a statement, one wonders what is left for Brooks to say about *Absalom, Absalom!* The answer is, nothing that changes his basic view of the novel. Much of his later commentary has been devoted to the purely expository task of untangling the mystery of how we know what actually happens in the plot. Brooks pursues that task painstakingly in extensive notes at the end of *The Yoknapatawpha Country* and in an even more extensive appendix at the end of *Toward Yoknapatawpha*. The intricate detail of his analysis defies paraphrase or summary and, in any event, would have little meaning to someone who knew the novel less well than Brooks himself. This attention to plot has led some detractors to accuse Brooks of taking Faulkner's world too literally. But the point Brooks is making is that the imagination must be literal before it can become symbolic. Keats's "Ode on a Grecian Urn" is a great poem at least in part because the empty town, which is only implied, seems as real as the forest that is fully described.

In addition to unraveling the plot of *Absalom, Absalom!*, Brooks has been intent on refuting the notion that Thomas Sutpen is a typical southerner of the planter class. The evidence he provides comes both from Faulkner's novels and from historians who have studied the southern aristocracy. According to Brooks, the crucial distinction between Sutpen and the class he seeks to join finally comes down to fundamentally different approaches to life. At his worst, the southern aristocrat could be a more despicable human being than Thomas Sutpen. Although there are some striking surface similarities between Sutpen and Carothers McCaslin, Brooks admits that the McCaslin patriarch is more wicked. But even in his sinning, McCaslin is not the bourgeois parvenu that Sutpen proves to be. Carothers "sustains no special downfall: he dies in bed. He has no 'design' and no interest in founding a dynasty." Brooks believes that "he would have been amused to learn that his two white sons had turned out to be Southern abolitionists, and that his grandson, the hero of 'The Bear,' had repudiated the whole McCaslin inheritance, preferring to live as a poor carpenter" (*Yoknapatawpha Country*, 427, 428).

Next to the importance he places on community, Brooks's assertion that Sutpen does not typify the southern aristocrat is probably the most controversial point in his criticism of Faulkner. His position was challenged by both Olga W. Vickery and Ilse Devoir Lind shortly after Brooks had articulated it in the *Sewanee Review* in 1951. Over a quarter century later, in an appendix to *Toward Yoknapatawpha and Beyond*, Brooks was still holding his ground, this time citing historical authorities from Eugene Genovese to C. Vann Woodward. It is only in a few incidental traits, Brooks argues, rather than in his essential personality, that Thomas Sutpen resembles the slave-owning aristocrat. Whatever their failings, the planters were generally paternalistic, not only toward their slaves, but also toward their poor white neighbors, many of whom were distant kin. The Sutpen children, particularly Judith, possess these aristocratic virtues. Their father can manage only the external trappings.

Even if the presence of Charles Bon creates a difficult situation for Sutpen, it is one that a more pragmatic man might have handled. "With his hundred square miles of plantation and his respectable marriage to Ellen Coldfield, Sutpen could probably have outfaced any charge of bigamy, and by letting the community know that Bon was part-Negro, could have disposed of any notion that Henry was not his legitimate heir" (*Toward Yoknapatawpha*, 298). On the basis of these conjectures, Brooks concludes that "the conditions of antebellum society in the South, as reflected in Faulkner's novel or as presented in history, did not, then, of themselves determine Thomas Sutpen's fate. His case was more special and, as in every authentic tragedy, was finally attributable to his own character. In sum, it was Sutpen's fanatical insistence that events conform to his private dream that brought about his downfall" (298–99).

V

From the outset, the critical response to Brooks's study of Faulkner involved more than a disinterested assessment of the strengths and weaknesses of a particular book. Almost from the moment that *The Yoknapa-*

tawpha Country was published, scholars and critics began choosing up
sides in a battle to claim Faulkner for their own. Orwell once said that
"Dickens is one of those writers who are well worth stealing." The same
is true of Faulkner. In the years since World War II, Faulkner's stature in
world literature (insofar as it can be measured by the amount of scholarly
attention paid to his work) has been so large that any group that can claim
him as a kindred spirit can also claim to be on the side of the titans, if not
necessarily the angels.

By far the most vitriolic and mean-spirited attack on Brooks's Faulkner
appeared in the newly formed *New York Review of Books.* Writing in the
January 9, 1964, issue of that magazine, Marvin Mudrick signaled his
intentions from the outset by calling his review "The Over-Wrought Urn."
"After decades of the bowler-hat and furled-umbrella litcrit that made his
academic reputation," Mudrick begins, "Cleanth Brooks has reverted
with a rebel whoop to the Confederacy. His Faulkner book is a Southern blend of vitriol, tart courtliness, regional piety, genealogies back to
Adam, the stupefying trivia of life in a small town, and uninhibited hero-
worship." Summing up the thesis of his essay, Mudrick writes, "The book
is, like its subject, both formidable and provincially eccentric" (Mudrick,
8). Although other critics have had a similar reaction to *The Yoknapatawpha Country,* few have put the matter as bluntly. "To be a provincial in
America," Mudrick sneers, "is to be a fraction of a fraction" (8). In a
sense, this piece announced what would become the semiofficial position
of the *New York Review,* to be elaborated nearly three decades later in a
more extended but equally wrongheaded polemic by Frederick C. Crews.

As might be expected, reviewers more sympathetic to Brooks's position argued that his emphasis on community in Faulkner was both accurate and illuminating. Admitting the countertendency of the zeitgeist,
James H. Justus writes in *Modern Language Quarterly* that "the virtues
of a traditional society (or their viability in a nontraditional one) have
been questioned since early Eliot, and they no doubt will be questioned
this time. The fact is that Brooks's thesis is well-documented and sensi-
tively elucidated. To be sure, it does not work equally well for all of the
novels. It is more obviously relevant to *Light in August, The Unvanquished, The Town, Intruder in the Dust,* and *The Reivers.* But Brooks
rides his thesis gracefully" (Justus, 232).

In one of the most balanced (if not necessarily most accurate or fairest)
estimates of Brooks's achievement, David Littlejohn argues that Faulk-

ner is large enough to encompass multitudes. In his book *Interruptions* (1970), Littlejohn writes:

> Not all of Faulkner is open to [Brooks]: as hugely human as the novelist is, each of us may take to himself his own share, his own Faulkner. Brooks finds, and offers us, primarily the wise, Man-affirming tragi-comedian, the creator of Uncle Ike and the Reivers, the voice behind the voice of V. K. Ratliff (surely the most humanely ingratiating narrative presence in literature). What he most admires are the ancient, smiling eyes behind the triumphs of Lena Grove, the Bundrens, the Mink Snopes of *The Mansion*. This Faulkner, conscious, loving, community-rooted Faulkner, the Faulkner who "leaves us not knowing whether to laugh or cry," he understands like a brother. (Littlejohn, 133)

There is, however, another Faulkner—one who is neither a brother to Brooks nor a cousin to the Agrarians. Littlejohn describes this other Faulkner with obvious affection and kinship: "The ocean-floor pressure at which Faulkner's packed, desperate imaginative life was led, the ocean-slow inexorable pace, the drunken roll of words, the more-than-sexual sex; all the mad driven fury *against* which Brooks's humane and affirming Faulkner was so obviously fighting—none of this is here. In making 'The Yoknapatawpha Country' too solidly a human 'Community,' [Brooks] neglects to remind us that it was also a Region of the Mind" (134).

Another way of putting the matter would be to say that, throughout his career, Brooks's criticism was generally corrective in nature; he tried to suggest possibilities ignored by those more attune to the conventional wisdom. This is not to say that the conventional wisdom is wrong, only that it is incomplete. If Brooks did not stress the Dionysian side of Faulkner's genius, it may have been because he didn't think it necessary to do so. For too many years, Faulkner had been dismissed as nothing more than a gothic sensationalist. Brooks has simply had the effrontery to argue that there was also an Apollonian side to his personality. To say, as Littlejohn does, that the Yoknapatawpha Country is "also a Region of the Mind," is to imply that it is more than a mere region of the glands.

13. Fugitives' reunion, Nashville, May 1966. *Left to right, back row:* Allen Tate, Cleanth Brooks, William Cobb, Rob Roy Purdy, Richard Croom Beatty, Frank Lawrence Owsley, Randall Stewart, Brainerd Cheney, R. D. Jacobs, Alec Stevenson. *Middle row:* Willard Thorp, Andrew Lytle, Jesse Wills, Alfred Starr, Louis D. Rubin, Jr. *Front row:* Robert Penn Warren, Dorothy Beethrum, Merrill Moore, Jonh Crowe Ransom, Sidney Hirsch, Donald Davidson, Louise Cowan, William Yandell Elliott. (Photograph courtesy Louis D. Rubin, Jr.)

14. Cleanth Brooks (*center*) as cultural attaché, London, mid-1960s.

15. Cleanth Brooks (*right*) as cultural attaché, London, 1965.

16. *Left to right:* Cleanth Brooks, Evangeline Bruce, and George Balanchine, London, 1965.

17. Cleanth Brooks and Allen Tate at Tate's seventy-fifth birthday party, Monteagle, Tenn., November 1974.

18. Cleanth Brooks at the U.S. Air Force Academy, April 1978.

19. Cleanth Brooks in his study at Northford, 1979. (Center for Southern Folklore copyright © 1979; photo by Bill Ferris)

20. Cleanth and Tinkum Brooks.

21. *Left to right:* Cecil Taylor, Tinkum Brooks, Cleanth Brooks, and George Core at the fiftieth anniversary celebration of the *Southern Review*, Baton Rouge, October 1985.

22. Robert Penn Warren and Cleanth Brooks at the fiftieth anniversary celebration of the *Southern Review*, Baton Rouge, October 1985.

23. Brooks and Warren, Baton Rouge, 1985.

PART FIVE

A Moveable Feast
(1964-85)

CHAPTER SEVENTEEN

Albion Revisited

The scene was Westminster Abbey, February 4, 1965. Thomas Stearns Eliot, poet and churchman, had died the previous month and had been quietly laid to rest in the family graveyard at East Coker. Now it was time for the dignitaries of the English-speaking world to pay their respects to the dominant poet and critic of the century. There was no more fitting place for this ceremony to be held than the mother church of Anglicanism. Protestants point proudly to the fact that the Collegiate Church of Saint Peter had been established at Westminster by Elizabeth I in 1560. But Anglo-Catholics are quick to note that a community of monks had lived there in 785, two centuries before the split between Eastern and Western Christendom and nearly three hundred years before the Norman Conquest. (Edward the Confessor, the last Anglo-Saxon king, had built a church on this site and saw it consecrated in 1065.) Since William the Conqueror, every British sovereign has been crowned at Westminster.

Queen Elizabeth II and Prime Minister Harold Wilson both sent representatives to the memorial service for Eliot. President Lyndon Johnson dispatched a delegation headed by Lionel Trilling and Cleanth Brooks. Men in black robes with chains and medals on their necks led the invited guests to their seats, each of which was marked with a name. After Mrs. Eliot was escorted to her place, the service began with a prelude of organ music. Then a choir of twenty boys and a few men marched in, followed by eight clergymen in black funeral copes with silver and gold embroidery. While seated between the altar and the pulpit, Tinkum Brooks realized that the man behind her was quite familiar. It was only when the vested beadle came with his wand to escort him to the pulpit that Tinkum recognized this man as Sir Alec Guinness. He was bald and twenty years older than she had remembered him, and when he got to the pulpit he had to put on his glasses to read from Eliot's verse. But the poetry, as spiritual as a psalm, and Sir Alec's magnificent voice made the next fifteen minutes timeless.[1] The choir then sang an anthem by Stravinsky with words from "Little Gidding"—"The dove descending breaks the air." The stone in Poet's Corner read: "Thomas / Stearns / Eliot / OM / Born 26 September 1888 / Died 4 January 1965 / 'the communication / Of the dead is tongued with fire beyond / the language of the living.' "

Outside the church, Cleanth noticed an old man with a white goatee and piercing eyes standing as rigid as a cigar store Indian. People who tried to engage him in conversation were simply ignored, more out of distraction than rudeness. One can only imagine that the old man was lost in memories of half a century earlier, when he and Tom Eliot and modernism itself were still in the first flower of youth. At the age of seventy-nine, Ezra Pound had flown from Venice to London to say good-bye to the friend who considered him the superior craftsman. "He looked like someone from another world," Tinkum recalled, "—emaciated, wispy, but that striking head still handsome. Dressed strangely, just sort of bundled up and with a dark gray astrakhan hat on. Someone was obviously taking care of him and took him off." Later Pound said of Eliot: "His was the true Dantescan voice—not honored enough, and deserving more than I ever gave him. . . . Who is there now for me to share a joke with? . . . Let him rest in peace. I can only repeat, but with the urgency of fifty years ago: READ HIM" (see Matthews, 178).

I

The chain of events that led Cleanth Brooks to the choir loft in Westminster Abbey began one day about dusk in November 1963. He had just arrived at his office in Davenport College when he heard the phone ringing. Fumbling with his keys, he managed to get the door open and answer the phone before his caller hung up. It was someone in Washington calling about a job at the American embassy in London. At first, Cleanth thought that one of his colleagues or former students had applied for a federal job and had given him as a reference. Gradually, however, he began to realize that the United States government wanted him to assume the post of cultural attaché in London. He wasn't certain what the position entailed, but he did know that it would involve a leave of two years from Yale. He had already been accepted for a Fulbright appointment at the University of Bordeaux and was looking forward to brushing up on his French while living in the wine country. But the prospect of living in England for the first time in thirty years seemed attractive. And if his government thought enough of him to offer the job, he was loath to turn it down.

The opportunity to know T. S. Eliot better may not have figured in Cleanth's calculations, but he did call on Eliot shortly after arriving in London. The great man's office at Faber and Faber was much as it had been described to Cleanth, complete with Eliot's personally inscribed photograph of Groucho Marx. Not wanting to seem like the eager academic trying to gather material for a scholarly article, Cleanth steered the conversation away from literary topics. He mentioned that he was on the committee to hire a new rector for his parish and was having difficulty finding the right man for the job. Eliot, who had been in a similar situation, jokingly remarked: "Whatever you do, you mustn't hire a spike." [2] Cleanth would have stayed longer except for the fact that Eliot was experiencing obvious difficulty breathing. Not wanting to cause his host any more discomfort, Cleanth fabricated some pretext for leaving. They parted on a cordial note, with Eliot promising to have the Brookses over for dinner soon. Shortly thereafter, Cleanth heard that Eliot was in a nursing home. Not long after that, he was dead.

Although Brooks published more on Faulkner than on Eliot, his engagement with the poet goes back over a much longer period of time (to his review of Eliot's *The Use of Poetry* in the January 1934 issue of the *Southwest Review*). One of his most useful and perceptive discussions of Eliot can be found in *The Hidden God* (1963). The task that he set for himself in that essay was almost the exact opposite of the one he faced with the other four writers considered in that volume. In discussing Hemingway, Faulkner, Yeats, and Warren, Brooks had to demonstrate the relevance of non-Christian writers for a Christian audience. Because Eliot was himself a devout and orthodox Christian, the audience of believers would automatically assume that he was talking their language. But if they were looking for conventional sermons or inspirational parables, they were likely to go away disappointed. In his essay "Discourse to the Gentiles," Brooks argues that Eliot's witness to the modern world was so powerful precisely because he was so much a part of that world.

By 1955, when Brooks gave the lectures that became *The Hidden God*, the reading public was so accustomed to thinking of Eliot as a Christian poet that they had to be reminded that his most famous poem was written prior to his conversion. Brooks had endeavored to show that a genuine religious sensibility permeated the poem in his groundbreaking discussion of *The Waste Land* twenty years earlier. In fact, the Eliot who wrote *The Waste Land* might well be viewed as a secular prophet similar to the other writers considered in *The Hidden God*. That he completed the pilgrimage from despair to Christian affirmation would seem to confirm Tillich's view that Christianity provides the answers to the malaise of our time and that those who have fully experienced that malaise are paradoxically closer to God for having done so. If the medieval Christian of Aquinas's time could conceive of Heaven as simply a more wonderful version of Earth, the modern Christian is more likely to come to God as a refuge from the horrors of earthly existence.

In terms of technique, the most obvious link between Eliot's preconversion and postconversion poetry is his reliance on suggestion and indirection. If Dante could assume that he was writing for a world that shared a reverence for Christian symbolism, Eliot could not. He had to find new ways of expressing old truths. Regardless of whether one uses the old symbolism or devises a new one, the need to speak of spiritual things symbolically remains the same. As Tate pointed out in his discussion of Poe, the angelic imagination is a liability to a poet. Because we are earthbound creatures, we can ascend to Heaven only on the ladder of analogy. Both the believer and the nonbeliever are similarly prisoners of their own finitude. Thus the technique of indirection that Eliot learned from the French Symbolist and English metaphysical poets was not merely a sleight of hand designed to lure the secular world toward the Kingdom of God. "With regard to the apprehension of the eternal," Brooks writes, "all of us, even the professing Christians, are gentiles. We cannot see directly and face to face. We must use symbols and analogies" (*Hidden God*, 96–97).

While serving as cultural attaché a decade later, Brooks delivered a lecture entitled "T. S. Eliot: Thinker and Artist" at the University of Kent in Canterbury. In this talk, he tried to illustrate Eliot's approach to poetry by considering his treatment of the urban scene. By writing so insistently about the modern city, Eliot rejects the Romantic notion that poetry should depict the beauties of the world and remain close to nature. In response to Arnold's assertion that "it is of advantage to a poet to deal with a beautiful world," Eliot remarks that the true advantage for a poet is "to be able to see beneath both beauty and ugliness; to see the boredom, and the horror, and the glory" (see *Shaping Joy*, 40). Eliot possessed this ability to an extraordinary degree.

To see how far Eliot's poetics were removed from Romanticism, one need only consider his assertion that "prose has to do with ideals; poetry with reality." Although this "statement has proved puzzling to many a reader who has been brought up on just the opposite set of notions," Brooks writes, "Eliot's observation seems to be profoundly true. Discursive prose is the medium for carrying on arguments, drawing conclusions, offering solutions. Poetry is the medium *par excellence* for rendering a total situation—for letting us know what it feels like to take a particular action or hold a particular belief or simply to look at something with imaginative sympathy" (*Shaping Joy*, 42).

Moving forward another decade to a festschrift for W. K. Wimsatt published in the mid-seventies, we find Brooks reexamining some of his opinions on Eliot and radically qualifying the view of English literary history he set forth in *Modern Poetry and the Tradition*. In his earlier book, Brooks had pretty much accepted at face value Eliot's notion of the dissociation of sensibility. By the time he wrote the essays in *The Well Wrought Urn*, he had revised that position sufficiently to discern evidences of wit and irony in the verse of Wordsworth and Keats and to adopt Coleridge's view of the poetic imagination. Eliot's debt to the French Symbolist poets is obvious, but it is no longer quite so obvious that either the French Symbolists or Eliot owe more to the British metaphysical poets than they do to their more immediate predecessors in the Romantic era.

Eliot is an anti-Romantic largely in his insistence on writing urban poetry and in his rejection of the notion of inherently poetic subject matter. But neither he nor the French Symbolists employ two defining characteristics of the metaphysical poets—logical or pseudological poetic structure and the extended metaphor or simile. In its use of elliptical or implied connections, Eliot's verse more nearly resembles a poem such as Wordsworth's "She Dwelt among the Untrodden Ways" than anything written by John Donne or Andrew Marvell. According to Brooks, "We may sum up the relations between metaphysical poetry, Romantic poetry, and the French poets that Eliot praises in this way: in general structure, the French poets are much closer to the Romantics than they are to the metaphysicals. What they do share with the metaphysicals—or at least what Eliot believed they shared—are striking instances of heterogeneity, a powerful sense of disparity, and obscure and sometimes farfetched analogies" ("T. S. Eliot as Modernist," 362). In claiming the metaphysicals as his poetic forebears, Eliot was in part creating a usable past. He was thus freed from having to acknowledge the extent of his kinship with a Romantic tradition that he had rejected on philosophical grounds.

A dozen years after this revisionist essay was published, Brooks tried to

assess Eliot's connection with something far more local and concrete than
the English poetic tradition—the culture of the American South. Because
few modern poets were more deracinated than T. S. Eliot, it might initially
seem ludicrous to think of him as in any sense a southern poet. Still, he
spent his childhood in St. Louis, an environment that was southern
enough for him to grow up speaking "with a nigger drawl," even though
his family considered themselves "northerners in a border state and
looked down on all southerners and Virginians." Eliot regarded himself
as someone who was "never anything anywhere and who therefore felt
himself to be more a Frenchman than an American and more an Englishman than a Frenchman and yet felt that the U.S.A. up to a hundred years
ago [he wrote this in 1928] was a family extension" (see Brooks, *Community*, 214). Despite these protestations, Brooks asserts that Eliot might
be claimed as at least an honorary southerner.

Eliot's longest documented trip to the Old Confederacy was in 1933,
when he gave the Page-Barbour lectures at the University of Virginia. The
first of these lectures contains expressions of sympathy for the South in its
attempt to maintain a traditional way of life, along with specific words of
praise for *I'll Take My Stand*, which had been published three years before. (Aware that his hosts included New South enemies of Agrarianism,
Eliot was certainly not engaging in ritualistic flattery.) In fact, when one
reads the printed version of the lectures—*After Strange Gods: A Primer
of Modern Heresy* (1933)—they sound like cosmopolitan addenda to the
Agrarian manifesto. Unfortunately, Eliot never consented to having this
volume reprinted. Fifteen years later, he developed some of the same
themes in this book in the more diplomatically worded *Notes toward a
Definition of Culture* (1948). Although Brooks finds much to admire in
the second book, he regrets that the first one is no longer widely available.
With its suggestion that modern man is whoring "after strange gods" and
its forthright acknowledgment that there is such a thing as heresy in the
modern world, Eliot's book goes against the grain of much contemporary
thought.

II

Cleanth and Tinkum Brooks departed for London on Tuesday, June 16,
1964. They left New York on a Pan Am flight at 10:00 A.M., and were on
the ground in London six and a half hours later. Cleanth's deputy met
them at the airport, and they sailed through customs flashing diplomatic

passports. They were then driven to Westminster and put up in what would be the first in a series of temporary lodgings. Common sense had told them to leave their furniture at home, but they had foolishly listened to a government official who convinced them that they would feel more at home if they had it shipped with them. While they could have rented any number of suitable furnished apartments in London, they had a terrible time finding an unfurnished place large enough for everything they had brought with them.

Even as their domestic situation remained unsettled, Cleanth was at his desk in the embassy the day after his arrival. When he was taken to lunch at the Saville Club that day, the first person he saw was Herbert Agar, the coeditor of *Who Owns America?*, by now a longtime resident of London. Throughout his two years on the job, Cleanth would serve as a liaison between Americans in England and the various cultural institutions of Great Britain, although sometimes the process worked the other way around. For example, one day he was contacted by a British nobleman of modest means who lived in a house that was said to have been built with wood from the *Mayflower*. The man was constantly besieged by tourists who wanted to see the house. He didn't mind showing it to them for free, but he needed some money for upkeep of the place. Of even more importance, he wanted to know if someone could confirm the historic origins of the house. Although Cleanth had no expertise in this area, he was expected to find the answer. When he located the relevant authority, it turned out that the pilgrim fathers must have sailed to the New World in somebody else's house.

In a letter to her family dated July 6, 1964, Tinkum describes some of the social gatherings that were part of embassy life. On Friday, July 3, the ambassador, David Bruce, gave a reception at his home at 11:30 in the morning. According to Tinkum, "the Embassy wives were asked to come early, park their hats, gloves & bags, and help as hostesses. I chatted with the ambassadors (and wives) of about 10 countries and had a long talk with Mrs. Shima, the Jap amb's wife—adorable. I saw, but didn't talk to, Prince and Princess Radizwill, Jackie K's sister. I thought the bee-hive hairdo was on the way out, but Lee R and Mrs. Bruce were well brushed out, so I suppose it's still in." At three that afternoon, they went to a garden party for the Queen Mother at Lancaster House. "It was to honor exchange teachers from America & the Commonwealth and only they met her. But we got a very good look and a nice tea. She wore powder blue chiffon, head to foot, and looked—well, just plain pretty—not handsome or stylish but lovely and soft. The poor lady was still shaking hands and having a gracious word with what looked like 200 slobs when we sneaked off."

On November 29, 1964, Cleanth wrote a letter to Red Warren about his first five months on the job: "The job is not so bad, or rather it won't be so bad if I can find ways to get through the paper work more speedily and cut down on seeing so many people including the time-wasters, the narcissi, and occasionally the clinically insane. (I talked an hour with an Indian gentleman of this sort last week.)" Later in that same letter, he notes that "part of the problem has been the predicament of the man who is being killed with kindness—genuine kindness but also genuine killing—too many luncheons that knock out the middle of the day—too many dinners and cocktail parties. But the worst of that appears to be over."

Although their housing problems had not been solved, Cleanth and Tinkum had resigned themselves to the situation. After spending several months occupying the house of an absent government official, they had had to move again in September, finally settling in a flat in Mayfair. The building apparently had been purchased as a tax dodge, and the owners didn't care whether they rented any of the space or not. The only other tenant was a sheikh from Bahrain. Given those circumstances, Cleanth was understandably concerned about leaving Tinkum by herself on the few occasions when his job took him out of town overnight. (She could have been murdered, and no one would have been around to hear her screams.) Fortunately, Bob Heilman, who had left LSU to head the English department at the University of Washington not long after Cleanth left for Yale, was in London on a sabbatical, and he and his wife, Ruth, stayed with Tinkum when Cleanth was out of town. Although the Brookses suffered no physical harm, their apartment was burglarized once, with the thief netting items of primarily sentimental value—Cleanth's gold watch, Phi Beta Kappa key, and the like.

The Brookses' flat faced the back door of the Dorchester Hotel, which meant they got to hear the night shift at the hotel revving up their motorcycles as they prepared to leave at 1:30 in the morning. In a letter to her mother dated November 9, 1964, Tinkum lamented that they would "never have a window open on the street side at night." Because of construction faults in the building, it took them several days to get a telephone installed, at which point they were warned (correctly, as it turned out) that it probably would stop working the first time it rained. "The plumbers, the electricians, the disposal man, the door-fixers have all been here to correct faults," Tinkum continues. "Some minor nuisances, like a tub draining too slowly, can't be corrected. The disposal had to be removed and two men worked on it with chisels and hammers, chipping out the concrete which had completely stopped it up—the builders' men had used it to wash out concrete and plaster pans." Also, the closet in one of the bedrooms was too shallow to take coat hangers. "The builder explained that the new mode was to have them hang on the slant." And so it went.

On those evenings when Cleanth was not committed to some embassy function, he and Tinkum would often attend the theater or the ballet. In a letter to her mother dated November 29, Tinkum praises a production of the ballet *Giselle*, featuring Rudolph Nureyev and Margot Fonteyn. She also has good words for an amateur production of *Electra* and *The Trojan Women*. In a letter of December 18, however, she is scathing in her criticism of Laurence Olivier's controversial portrayal of *Othello*. In addition to making Othello a simian creature ("a real head-waggling grinning Sambo") rather than the noble Moor, Olivier shamelessly overemphasized the play's sexuality. "I found particularly unsettling the clothes he wore," Tinkum writes, "—not Venetian garments at all but something rather jungly—a loose very short shift and he postured so as to make you think you were about to see all. I suppose he had on underwear but the effect was to make you think he hadn't and didn't care."

Because Cleanth and Tinkum were planning to spend their thirty-first Christmas together in Spain, they opened their presents in London on Sunday, December 20. Writing to her mother that evening, Tinkum noted that "everyone had been not only generous but very ingenious in sending us things that are lovely, useful and take up no room." Cleanth was delighted with his present of opera glasses. "They work just fine," Tinkum writes, "and are very masculine looking in their little black case. Now he will get an even better look at Margot Fonteyn's legs."

III

After Eliot, the British poet who most engaged Brooks's imagination was William Butler Yeats. Brooks's treatment of Yeats in *The Hidden God* was understandably quite different from his discussion of the other writers of the post-Christian world. Hemingway, Faulkner, and Warren all wrote with a religious sensibility that might have put them very close to God in Tillich's terms. None of them, however, arrived at this sensibility by going to church or by affirming the historic creeds of Christianity. Eliot differed

from them by coming to Christian orthodoxy through the dark night of
the soul. Yeats was neither a skeptic nor a crypto-Christian but a believer
in magic and the occult. He was living proof of Chesterton's observation
that the man who does not believe in the Christian God does not believe
in nothing but in everything. In his *Autobiographies* Yeats had declared
himself "very religious"; he had also claimed that having been "deprived
by Huxley and Tyndall . . . of the simple-minded religion of [his] childhood," he had had to create a new and eclectic religion from poetic tradition and the folk literature of the Irish people (see *Hidden God*, 46). Of
course, as Brooks demonstrated in *Modern Poetry and the Tradition*,
Yeats is being a little disingenuous here. Regardless of how much his verse
owed to folklore, it was even more deeply rooted in the very private mythology of *A Vision*.

If many of the modernist theologians of Christianity attempted to de-
mythologize the ancient doctrines to make them more palatable to a scientific age, Yeats went in the opposite direction. Whenever his poetry dealt
with Christian themes, which was quite often, he tried to remythologize
Christianity to make it more acceptable to the poetic imagination. As a
result, Yeats wrote with the verve and passion of the inspired heretic (his
best-known transformation of Christian myth is his vision of the anti-
Christ in the apocalyptic poem "The Second Coming"). Much of the lecture on Yeats from *The Hidden God* consists of sympathetic citations from
Yeats's Christian verse. My only regret is that Brooks makes no mention
of "The Magi," which is not only a beautiful poem but one with which
the orthodox believer would have no quarrel. Here, Yeats makes the pilgrimage of the ancient wise men a metaphor for the religious quest of all
men. The speaker imagines the Magi ("In their stiff, painted clothes, the
pale unsatisfied ones") continuing their search, not only beyond the na-
tivity in Bethlehem but beyond the crucifixion in Jerusalem, as well. As
they proceed on their mission, the speaker sees "all their eyes still fixed,
hoping to find once more, / Being by Calvary's turbulence unsatisfied, /
The uncontrollable mystery on the bestial floor."

In a discussion of Yeats as literary critic, written over a decade later,
Brooks notes what so many other readers have discovered—that the great
poet also wrote a masterful prose, frequently summing up the character of
another writer's work in a memorable phrase or sentence. Although Yeats
could be crotchety and eccentric in his tastes, he was almost always persuasive in his judgments. Beyond random observations, he was also a systematic thinker, who operated from settled principles and a coherent view

of poetry. Fortunately, one need not master the esoterica of *A Vision* to grasp Yeats's approach to criticism.

Summarizing Yeats's position, Brooks writes: "What prompted the poem, what set the poet dreaming, may have been any of a hundred things—his enemy or his love or his political cause—but these incitations do not ultimately matter. The verses that he writes 'may make his mistress famous as Helen or give a victory to his cause,' but men will not honor him because he has been a devoted servant to his mistress or served well his cause. They will do so only because they 'delight to honour and to remember all that have served contemplation' " (*Shaping Joy*, 134). If a tragedian projects an emotion such as sorrow through the characters he creates, it is not a sentimental or self-regarding sorrow. "The artist's 'shaping joy has kept the sorrow pure, as it had kept it were the emotion love or hate, for the nobleness of the arts is in the mingling of contraries, the extremity of sorrow, the extremity of joy, perfection of personality, the perfection of its surrender, overflowing turbulent energy, and marmorean stillness' " (124–25).

If Yeats is careful to distinguish between poetry as a mode of contemplation and propaganda as an incitement to action, the later Auden was even more insistent on this distinction. Even during his early Marxist phase, Auden possessed a sufficient gift for irony that Brooks called him a "propagandist of inclusion" in *Modern Poetry and the Tradition*. By the time that Auden had embraced Anglican Christianity and a more conservative politics, his sensibility had become in some ways even more classical than Eliot's. In discussing Auden's criticism, Brooks mentions his scholarly essays on everything from the relationship of masters and servants to the theological implications of the murder mystery. What he finds most significant, however, are Auden's polemics against those who would make art into religion, ideology, or even therapy. Not even Aristotle escapes Auden's censure. To the extent that he understands Aristotle's notion of catharsis, he finds it wrong. Paraphrasing Auden, Brooks writes: "You do get a purgation of the emotions from witnessing a bullfight or a professional football match, but not from a work of art." Nor is poetry prophecy. "Shelley's claim for the poets that they are 'the unacknowledged legislators of the world' is, says Auden, 'the silliest remark ever made about poets' " (*Shaping Joy*, 136–37).

Auden's view of what poetry ought to be is consistent with the general position of Nietzsche, Yeats, Richards, Ransom, and Brooks. He believes in achieving unity through the inclusion and reconciliation of discordant elements. Whatever that accomplishes, however, is neither an escape from life nor "the blueprint for a better life." As he writes in his unforgettable elegy for Yeats, "poetry makes nothing happen." Far from making him a cloistered aesthete, Auden's position actually frees him to confront the problems of civilization without the delusion that a knack for reading and writing verse gives him a special wisdom denied to lesser mortals. Brooks sees Auden's position as "a positive source of strength, [which] has enabled him to avoid most of the traps laid for the historical critic, the moralistic critic, and the archetypal critic" (142).

If Auden's approach to poetry aggressively attacks Romanticism while Yeats's sublimely transcends it, the verse and criticism of Alfred Edward Housman would seem to embody both the charm and limitations of the romantic sensibility. Without gainsaying any of Housman's faults, Brooks argues that in certain respects the elegiast of Shropshire was more a man of our age than we or he had realized.[3] Although he was of the same generation as Yeats (born six years earlier and died three years earlier), Housman strikes most readers as being closer to Tennyson or even Wordsworth. Brooks suggests that a far more apt comparison would be to Hemingway. Both writers are adept at showing sensitive young men facing disillusionment with a kind of bravado that passes for stoicism. The hard-drinking, tough-minded losers who inhabit the world of both writers evoke a kind of pathos that is never far from sentimentality, and that actually becomes sentimentality when either writer loses control of his art. The enduring appeal of Hemingway and Housman may lie in their ability to touch the adolescent who lives in all of us.

IV

On April 20, 1965, Cleanth wrote Red Warren to tell him that Tinkum had been in the hospital for nearly three weeks. She had passed all of the physical exams required by the U.S. government before leaving for England, but during her first ten months in London she had begun to feel progressively worse. Finally a British surgeon discovered and removed a tumor on her liver. It had been growing there for over thirty years and was now large enough to cause real discomfort. Fortunately, however, it was benign. Cleanth reported that she was recovering nicely, despite being sore and restricted to light exercise. "I am sure," he writes, "that from now on she is going to feel like a new woman."

Cleanth himself experienced a vexing health problem during his service in London. While on a speaking tour in Scotland, he noticed a soreness in his big toe as he was retiring to bed for the night. The pain increased to the point where he was unable to sleep. By morning, he was scarcely able to move. Upon examining him, the hotel doctor informed Cleanth that his kidneys were not properly excreting the uric acid in his body. As a consequence, the acid was spreading and settling in his joints. Although this condition could be controlled by medication, Cleanth had to cancel his remaining lectures and stay off his feet for several days. Donald Davidson, who was visiting London shortly thereafter, wrote to Allen Tate on February 1, 1966, to report on their friend's condition: "Cleanth has been suffering from an unexpected attack of the gout, but was in good spirits—though both he and Tinkham [sic] can think of little now but getting through with their pesky duties and returning to the U.S." (see Fain and Young, 400).

On a brighter note, Tinkum's letters home are filled with news about parties, lectures, encounters with famous people, and occasional travels around Europe. The trip to Spain over Christmas 1965 had turned out to be cold and only intermittently enjoyable. In fact, one suspects that reading Tinkum's letter of January 5, 1965, would have been more pleasurable than actually being there. Consider her description of the capital city:

> Madrid, where we landed, is the highest capital in Europe—2000 feet. It's not really a very attractive city, nor a very old looking one. It was nothing much until 200 years ago and like Washington is a "made" official city. Most of the buildings look anywhere from 75 years to 2 minutes old. The exception is the Royal Palace (now a museum) which is the size of Versailles, maybe larger and has one gold-leafed, tapestried room after another, not very beautiful but reeking of wealth. Tapestries, both Spanish and Flemish, are one of the great things in Spain and we saw them everywhere. They are beautiful, their colors seem brighter than others I've seen and the workmanship is so fine that sometimes you have to get close to be sure it's not an oil painting.

The Brookses took two other major excursions away from the British Isles during Cleanth's service in London. The first was a trip to Greece in May of 1965. On this trip, they met the Nobel Prize–winning poet George Seferis and his wife. (The Seferises entertained in the traditional Homeric manner, providing their guests with food and drink while not joining in themselves.) Although Tinkum was still recuperating from her operation, she wrote to her family in a letter dated June 2, 1965, that her "health improved marvelously on the trip—it was just the right mixture of exercise and rest—a stiff morning's walk and then an afternoon on the bed—and the sun and the complete change of scene—all very healing." The first day in Athens, she had struggled to get to the top of the Acropolis, but the last night she made it without any difficulty. The only sour note was sounded after they returned to London and discovered that the people to whom they had rented their house in Northford had had a $600 septic tank installed in the kitchen because the plumber had assured them that "the Brookses would want it done—they always wanted the job done right and only the best."

By April of 1966, Cleanth had accumulated enough earned leave that he and Tinkum were able to take an extended Easter vacation in the Middle East. In Lebanon they found a desert where six million sheep were being moved to better grazing land (the better grazing consisted of a few tufts of grass amid vast expanses of sand). In Damascus, where the streets were clogged with pilgrims returning from Mecca, the Brookses came upon the tracks of Saint Paul, including the house of the man who had taken him in after he was struck blind and the prison wall down which he had escaped in a basket. "Jerusalem," Tinkum told her family in a letter dated April 20, 1966, "is a fine place to visit in many ways, being just about the cleanest place we were ever in, at home or abroad. The city fathers see that it is kept clean, and the cleaners go through the bazaars and old narrow streets three times a day. Not a fly, not a crumb, but life goes on vigorously, the streets swarming with children."

The two years the Brookses spent in England were turbulent ones back home in America. The worst of the urban race riots took place in the summers of 1964 and 1965. Also, Americans who thought that they were voting for peace in Vietnam when they returned Lyndon Johnson to the White House saw a continuing escalation of the war effort with no end, nor even a clearly stated goal, in sight. One Sunday in February 1965, when Cleanth and Tinkum were on their way to evening prayer at St. Mark's Church, they saw a group of young Communists gathered outside of Grosvenor Square across from the American Embassy. They were carrying placards urging the United States to get out of Vietnam and shouting that hoary cliché "Yankee Go Home." A hundred British bobbies patrolled the sidewalks and guarded the embassy steps. On their way back from evening prayer, the Brookses noticed that the protest was beginning to break up. A couple of policemen were telling the few remaining stragglers: "All right now. The demonstration is over. Please leave now." The weather was cold enough that the bobbies met no resistance.

The mid-sixties was also a time of revolutionary change in what had previously been some of the most conservative churches in Christendom. Because of its size and age, the changes in the Roman Catholic Church were considered most newsworthy. But a kind of mini-Vatican II was also taking place within the Anglican Communion. When John Hines became Presiding Bishop of the Episcopal Church in 1965, he spearheaded an effort to turn that church to the left politically and socially and to overhaul the majestic language of the *Book of Common Prayer*. (It used to be said that Episcopalians were Catholics who flunked Latin, but with tin-eared vernacular liturgies being introduced in both churches, even literate English seemed to be an endangered tongue.) On the doctrinal front, theologians of various denominations were beginning to question the historic dogmas of Christianity. (Some even called themselves "Christian Atheists" and proclaimed the death of God.) The most notorious dissident in the American Episcopal Church was the Bishop of California, James A. Pike. In March 1965 Cleanth and Tinkum met his British counterpart, the Bishop of Woolwich, John A. T. Robinson.

If the Episcopal Church in the United States seemed a bit somnolent at times, the Church of England was downright moribund. Tinkum noted that on a typical Sunday morning at St. Mark's, there might be forty people at church, "all aged, most of them crippled and using canes." In his book *Honest to God* (1963) Bishop Robinson suggested that the solution to this problem was a "religionless Christianity." Robinson's secularist rejection of supernaturalism was really nothing more than a candid endorsement of the trend that Cleanth had identified in liberal Protestantism when he wrote his essay for *Who Owns America?* thirty years before. In a letter to her family, dated March 7, 1965, Tinkum observes in her characteristically blunt manner: "I'm sure you can have lots of good things and lots of good people without religion, as most of my dear relatives can testify, but I don't see how you can have Christianity without it." She goes on to say of Robinson: "He's a very handsome young man in an almost too pretty way, covers his bald spot by combing his hair sidewise over it and didn't say the blessing at dinner."

Later that month, the Brookses entertained C. P. Snow and his wife at a dinner party they held in their flat. Although a left-wing admirer of the

Soviets, Snow was also something of a puritanical moralist. In a spirit of friendly counsel, he told Cleanth and another embassy official that the Russians were a virile and family-minded people. Thus the American State Department would do itself a favor if it would stop sending so many homosexuals as cultural ambassadors to Moscow. "He didn't name our fairies," Tinkum writes in a letter home, "but Cleanth was ready with a list of them—Tennessee Williams, James Baldwin, Gore Vidal and a dozen others. I believe the message will get home."

Among other things, the assignment in England gave Cleanth the opportunity to renew his acquaintance with friends from his years at Oxford. The first time that his old tutor Nevill Coghill came to dinner was a revelation. During his student days, Cleanth had found Coghill to be something of a cold fish. What he realized now was that the character trait he had taken as aloofness was more shyness or insecurity. Not only did Cleanth begin to enjoy a more cordial relationship with Coghill, he was also enlisted in a project involving Nevill's former student Richard Burton and Burton's new wife, Elizabeth Taylor. The Burtons had agreed to come to Oxford to do a production of Marlowe's *Dr. Faustus*, with Burton playing the title role and Taylor appearing as Helen of Troy. As part of the occasion, Cleanth would give a lecture on Marlowe's play.

The reading that Brooks planned to give of *Dr. Faustus* (in an essay that eventually made its way into *A Shaping Joy*) was based on Aristotle's dictum that a play should have a beginning, middle, and end. Among the more honored dramas in the English language, Marlowe's *Faustus*—like Milton's *Samson Agonistes* and Eliot's *Murder in the Cathedral*—seems to begin and end strongly but to lack a proper middle. Brooks questions that popular assumption; he observes that the judgment we pronounce on *Dr. Faustus* depends on our interpretation of the protagonist's action in signing away his soul early in the play. If this is a final and irrevocable action, then everything else that Faustus does is anticlimactic and inconsequential. The playwright is simply filling time until the grand finale, when his tragic hero is dispatched to Hell. This, however, is not the case with Marlowe's drama. There are several occasions in the course of the play when Faustus is given an opportunity to repent. (Even Mephistopheles concedes that the damnation of Faustus is far from a done deal.) It is the doctor's *continuing* unwillingness to be saved rather than his signature on a legal document that seals his fate. In Faustus's pride, "he can believe in and understand a God of justice, but not a God of mercy" (*Shaping Joy*,

378). The hardening of Faustus's heart constitutes his damnation. The evidence of this hardening also constitutes the middle of Marlowe's play.

Unfortunately, Coghill's project was delayed a year when the Burtons were summoned to Hollywood to do the film version of Edward Albee's *Who's Afraid of Virginia Woolf?* By the time they were free from that obligation, Cleanth was already back at Yale. Although working with the most glamorous couple in show business would have been a fascinating experience, Cleanth was relieved that his lecture did not have to compete with Burton's dynamic stage presence and with Taylor's still voluptuous body for the attention of the Oxford theatergoers.

Besides seeing old British friends, Cleanth also kept running into various American colleagues who were in England to pursue scholarly projects. These included not only the Heilmans but Arthur Mizener of Columbia, Chester Kerr (director of the Yale Press), and Bill and Margaret Wimsatt, who arrived in October of 1965 to spend Bill's sabbatical year in London. It was a delight to see the Wimsatts, who were Cleanth and Tinkum's best friends in the Yale English department. The previous spring, the Wimsatts' nineteen-year-old son, Alexander, had had an operation for cancer, but the surgery had been judged successful, and the disease appeared to be in remission. No sooner had Bill and Margaret arrived in London, however, than they were phoned by Alexander's doctor, who informed them that there had been a recurrence and that their son would soon die. In addition to the tremendous burden of grief and anxiety, the Wimsatts had to resolve many practical difficulties. They had rented their house in New Haven to a family with three children, whom they did not want to evict without arranging alternative lodging. Also, they had a younger son in school in London. Finally, there was the question of resolving Bill's professional obligations during a year when he could neither do research nor fit back into Yale's teaching schedule, which had been rearranged for his sabbatical. Writing to her family on October 12, 1965, Tinkum reported that "[the Wimsatts have] spent every evening with us, staying late, hating to go back and face each other in that hotel room I suppose. They've been extraordinarily composed, both very strong people and committed Roman Catholics."

At the end of two years, Cleanth's appointment as attaché came to an end. The embassy would have been happy to have kept him on longer, but he was reluctant to ask Yale to extend his leave. Also, he was eager to get back to several scholarly projects that had been placed on hold while he was doing his diplomatic duties. Besides, a cramped flat behind the Dorchester Hotel was a poor substitute for the comforts of Northford. Even the chores of home seemed inviting after spending so much of the preceding two years living out of a suitcase. On May 11, 1966, Tinkum wrote her family to say that she and Cleanth would be back in the United States by the end of the month. "Some day when I'm mowing the lawn or felling a tree or cleaning the river," she writes, "I may look back on these London days with longing, but right now my feeling is 'Let me at that mower.'"

CHAPTER EIGHTEEN

The Attack on
Tory Formalism

Cleanth had kept his distance from LSU since leaving for Yale in 1947. But with the passage of time and the demise of the administration that had undervalued him, the wounds of an earlier day had begun to heal. On January 12, 1968, he wrote to Tommy Kirby to express his feelings about a recent trip to his old hometown: "I was glad to get another glimpse of LSU, even in the rain, the morning that we drove up some two weeks ago. I was also very happy to hear Josie's voice over the telephone and to feel that at least something of personal contact had been made. We put in our few hours there stopping for a few minutes at the Press, paying a call on an uncle of Tinkum's who is retired and not well, a visit to our old yard boy, Leroy McCelos, and his family, and a visit to my parents' graves at Roselawn."[1] When Kirby offered Cleanth a visiting professorship for the spring semester of 1969, he was delighted to accept.

In a letter to Bob Heilman dated August 23, 1969, Cleanth reflects on his experiences that spring:

> The amazing thing for me was that LSU had changed so little. Physically, of course, it was almost unrecognizable, and Baton Rouge's urban sprawl and traffic volume have become almost unbelievable. We lived in an immense and comfortable apartment within a walled grotto on the edge of a colored district in north Baton Rouge—a few blocks from our old retainers, Leroy and Emma McCelos (who became our temporary retainers again). As Leroy would say, "I used to go hunting in the fields where this apartment house is now." One of the pleasantest things was to look out of our screenless (because airconditioned) windows, beyond the wall and see

the fishermen going up and down that little colored street calling "Buffalo, garper-goo, sacolait."[2]

Not all was sweet nostalgia, however. Some of the same pettiness and corruption that the Nineteen had decried thirty years earlier was still there. Members of the last Sugar Bowl team and associated administrators had been given watches. A board member had blocked the raise of a young professor whose politics he disliked. And both state and local government appeared to have the same proportion of scoundrels as in the heyday of Huey Long.

Cleanth told Heilman he was impressed with the students he taught that semester. (He was assured that they were not handpicked but represented the average undergraduate.) They were better trained than the ones he remembered from the thirties and forties, and all were friendly, courteous, and eager to learn. Moreover, they lacked the intellectual façade and pretension sometimes evident at Yale. He also found the faculty to be generally more intelligent and better educated than in his day. "But," he concludes, "the brilliance and energy which you and I remember about the place is, I'm inclined to say, pretty well gone. Or am I simply now in love with the past?"

I

Almost immediately after his return from England, the Episcopal Church began abandoning those things that Cleanth had found most attractive about its tradition. The left-wing political agenda of the church hierarchy drove a steady stream of previously faithful conservatives into other denominations while failing to replace them with the liberals and radicals being wooed. Still, most ordinary parishioners were content to let the activists have their own way outside the parish walls as long as they didn't try to change what was happening inside. By the late sixties, however, two of the Episcopal Church's most cherished traditions—an all-male priesthood and *The Book of Common Prayer*—were also under assault. Theological traditionalists were more alarmed by the first of these developments; the second proved more vexing to ordinary worshipers.[3] The reason for this is simple. To a large extent, the Anglican Church was defined by its prayer book. Roman Catholics could look to the pope and the church hierarchy for guidance in faith and morals. Fundamentalists had a literal belief in Scripture. Anglicans and Episcopalians prayed what they believed in church every Sunday.

In its 1964 convention the American church authorized the Standing Liturgical Commission to begin the next major round of revision. In 1967 *The Liturgy of the Lord's Supper* was approved for trial use; this was followed in 1970 by *Services for Trial Use*, a paperback volume with a green banana cover that struck many as a thoroughly vulgarized version of *The Book of Common Prayer*. Reaction to this liturgy was so strong that it appeared for a while as if the revisionists were on the defensive. In the spring of 1971 a group of traditionalists met at Andrew Lytle's house in Sewanee to form the Society for the Preservation of the Book of Common Prayer (SPBCP); by 1973, the society had grown to 30,000 members. Three years later, that number had swelled to 100,000. The leadership of the society was centered in the English department at Vanderbilt, where Walter Sullivan, John M. Aden, and Harold Weatherby directed the fight.[4]

Not surprisingly, Cleanth joined the board of directors of the SPBCP. As a devout churchman and a lover of the English language, he was appalled by the tepid theology and the vernacular language of the "green book." Although some of the options offered in 1973 and 1976 were meant to placate the traditionalists, the SPBCP thought that the revisionists had not backed down nearly enough. Some traditional language had been put back into the book in alternative liturgies, but most of the text was written in a flat approximation of modern English. Moreover, a liturgy that had once been a unifying force in a diverse church now accentuated and even exacerbated historic divisions. The variety of liturgical options made the notion of *common* prayer an anachronism, even as a useful fiction. The modernists had won so complete a victory that they were willing to make a few meaningless concessions to the traditionalists until they all died off or left the church in dismay. The draft book of 1976 was approved as the official prayer book in 1979.

Although there was no realistic chance of reversing the ordination of women or throwing out the new liturgy, the Prayer Book Society (what had once been the SPBCP) fought to have the 1928 prayer book retained as an alternative form of worship. The General Convention allowed this in principle but left the implementation up to the discretion of individual bishops and rectors. In "God, Gallup, and the Episcopalians," an essay published in the summer 1981 issue of the *American Scholar*, Cleanth Brooks gave his assessment of the situation. He began by challenging the canard that defenders of the old book were idolators who were more interested in ritual than in what the ritual represented. The fallacy of that argument was that the reformers were not trying to replace verbal prayer with an immediate (angelic?) perception of God Almighty. They were simply substituting one set of words for another. "The issue, then, is not whether we can discard language in our worship, but whether the language of the 1979 revision is superior to that of the traditional book" ("God, Gallup," 316).

If some modernization was desired, Brooks wonders, why did the Episcopal Church not turn to the great modern writers among its own membership? In the new version, the Psalter, which is intended entirely as poetry, repeatedly sacrifices beautiful figurative language for a sophomoric literal-mindedness. "In the old Prayer Book, verse 1 of Psalm 69 reads: 'Save me, O God, for the waters are come in, even unto my soul.' The 1979 Prayer Book renders it thus: 'Save me, O God, for the water has risen up to my neck. . . .' The cry sounds like that of a careless bather who has let himself be caught offshore by the incoming tide. The reader will exclaim, 'Save me, O God, from such a translation' " (318). Similar howlers can be found throughout the 1979 Psalter.[5]

Although the traditionalists repeatedly asked the Church to conduct a referendum on the prayer book, the request was routinely denied. Finally the Prayer Book Society hired George Gallup to conduct a poll in the spring of 1979, just months before the new liturgy was to be considered for final approval. As Brooks explains:

> The results showed that the laity overwhelmingly favored the traditional book. Preference for the traditional Prayer Book was approximately three to one (63 percent to 23 percent), with those in favor of the traditional book feeling more strongly about their choice than those who favored the revised book. By contrast, 80 percent of the clergy preferred the revised book (14 percent the traditional book). The results would indicate that the opposition to the 1979 Prayer Book was not merely that of a group of disgruntled English professors. The laity lined up solidly with them against the bishops and the rest of the clergy. ("God, Gallup," 323)

Four decades after his attack on liberal Protestantism in *Who Owns America?*, Cleanth Brooks saw his direst prophecies come true in a church to which he had devoted much of his adult life. In his final years, he and the young New Haven poet Jonathan Leff joined Maynard Mack and other like-minded traditionalists at St. John's Episcopal Church at eight o'clock Sunday morning to worship with dog-eared copies of the 1928 prayer book. When Cleanth asked his priest—Father Peter Rodgers—if the Bishop of Connecticut knew what they were doing, Father Rodgers replied: "I wrote and told him, but he never wrote back."

II

One of the projects delayed by Cleanth's service in London was an anthology of American literature that he and Red Warren had contracted to do for St. Martin's Press. Because the book required more historical commentary than either Cleanth or Red felt comfortable with, they asked their colleague R. W. B. Lewis to join them as a third collaborator. They divided responsibility for various periods and various figures and pursued their own individual research until Cleanth returned to the United States and they were able to make their editorial labors a truly social experience. Lewis recalls convening for two or three days at a time at the Warren homes in Fairfield, Connecticut, and Brattleboro, Vermont, at the Brooks estate in Northford, and at his own master's living quarters in Calhoun College. On those occasions, they would discuss and criticize each other's individual contributions and work on parts of the book that were genuinely collaborative. Lewis describes how the "Letter to the Reader"[6] was composed:

> We were at the Warrens' Vermont place during a summer week, and in
> between swimming in the mountain pool and striding along the country
> roads, between chatty meals on the screened porch and leisurely drink-
> times on the terrace, we met in a small cabin across the lawn from the
> main house and worked away. Warren sat at a rustic table with a type-
> writer in front of him; Brooks and I shifted and prowled about. Warren, an
> erratic typist at best, would listen to different tentative formulations of this
> sentence or that, and when the right one struck him he would tap it out
> haphazardly onto the page. The resulting script, full of x-ed out lines and
> proximate spellings, was turned over to Brooks, who took it back home
> and rewrote it in his own style. That version was then emended, separately,
> by Warren and me, and Brooks thereafter gave it a final run-through.
> (Lewis, 569)

This experience convinced Lewis of "an irreducible subsurface regionality in American literary folk." In fact, as the three colleagues began discussing the mid-nineteenth century, Lewis got "the eerie but enlivening sensation that we were, between us, reenacting the Civil War." Brooks and Warren seemed to him to become increasingly southern. "To my ear their very accents thickened," Lewis recalls; "and though I am in fact Chicago-born, I felt myself becoming more and more northern and even, like Emily Dickinson, beginning to 'see New Englandly.' When Warren presented us with his selection of Melville's war poems, I remarked that to judge from this lot—all of them springing from northern defeats and disasters—one would be in doubt as to which side had actually 'won' the war" (570).

The book that was finally produced from this collaboration—*American Literature: The Makers and the Making*—ran to two million words, a fourth of which consisted of commentary by the editors. Lewis figured that he, Warren, and Brooks wrote about 500 typescript pages each. The result was not just a standard classroom anthology but also a critical history of American literature from the seventeenth century to the present. Although the editors decided early on to take collective responsibility for the book and not claim individual authorship for various parts, we know that Cleanth Brooks wrote introductions for the periods 1743–1826 ("An Emergent National Literature") and 1914–1945 ("The Moderns: Founders and Beyond"). He was also responsible for a section on early American travel writing and for individual essays on Thoreau and Poe. In addition, he wrote about the development of poetry in America and the rise of southern literature.

Because Warren and Lewis divided most of the nineteenth-century poets between themselves, Brooks's first sustained discussion of poetry after Poe comes in the second volume of the anthology, with a look at the nativist strain in early twentieth-century American verse. Although this poetry had been summarily dismissed in *Modern Poetry and the Tradition*, Brooks is now more inclined to judge individual poets and individual poems on their own merits. A writer who followed the "wrong" tradition might still produce good, even great, work, just as someone with the "right" literary opinions could turn out inferior verse. Although the early Brooks was never rigidly Procrustean, the necessity of defending a thesis prompted him to think in terms of categories and movements. Putting together a comprehensive anthology of American literature occasioned a reassessment and reevaluation of figures major and minor. The most dramatic example of this in *American Literature: The Makers and the Making* was Red Warren's discovery of unsuspected richness in the verse of Whittier, which he had previously written off as little more than fireside doggerel. If Brooks experienced no conversion nearly so radical, he manifests a newfound appreciation for Edwin Arlington Robinson and Robert Frost.

In contrast to the nativist branch in twentieth-century American verse is the high modernist tradition, which sprang from the Imagist movement in post-Victorian London. That the movement originated overseas as a collaboration of Englishmen and American expatriates suggests the decreasing importance of national boundaries in the literature of the new century; American writers had matured to the point where they were beginning to influence British literature rather than simply be influenced by it. In a chapter entitled "From Imagism to Symbolism: The Crisis in Culture," Brooks shows how Imagism arose as a reaction to the "rhetorical" and "poetic" excesses of Victorian verse. With empirical science claiming a kind of epistemological supremacy, poets were no longer regarded as visionaries, much less "the unacknowledged legislators of the world." If they were not to be dismissed as anachronisms, they would have to reinvent their language and discover a function that would not put them in competition with scientists.

It could be argued that the major Fugitives combine aspects of both the nativist and the high modernist traditions. Like Frost (and, for that matter, Yeats and Faulkner), they arrived at the universal through the regional. From a technical standpoint, however, Ransom, Tate, and Warren were clearly part of the revolt against Victorian excess. In *American Literature: The Makers and the Making*, they are treated apart from the two major groupings of twentieth-century poets. Because his later verse (from the mid-fifties on) is generally considered his best, Warren is included among fourteen post–World War II poets. Ransom and Tate appear earlier in a section devoted to southern literature. In his discussion of these two figures, Brooks shows how their most southern poems enable Ransom and Tate to comment on the more general malaise of the modern world.

Ransom's "Antique Harvesters," written in 1927, has the distinction of being an Agrarian poem that existed before the Agrarian movement itself. At one level, the poem is a realistic description of poverty in the rural South. The speaker in the poem, however, remains faithful to the Southern myth. We might say that his fidelity is an earned vision because it does not require any self-deception regarding actual conditions in the region. "The myth is put forward very frankly as a myth," Brooks writes. "The Old South is invoked as a lady, now not young, though the speaker claims that she still has a heart of fire. She is still to be praised even though the company of those who render the praise has dwindled" (*American Literature*, 2646).

Ransom avoids sentimentality by distancing himself from his subject through the ironic use of archaic diction. Biographically, we can trace Ransom's fondness for such diction to his study of the classics at Oxford.

More important, Ransom's "'classical' quality is the response of a particular mind reacting to a special cultural situation, where a balance between loving engagement and cool detachment is appropriate and where the very motive of his poetic expression is to effect a mediation between intellect and emotion and between the local scene in its temporal particularity and a universal and timeless condition" (2647). The dualism that Ransom sees in the experience of the modern southerner is only a more pronounced form of the dualism that he sees at the very heart of human nature.

The original version of Allen Tate's "Ode to the Confederate Dead" was published in 1927, the same year as "Antique Harvesters" (a revised version appeared in 1930). Tate's "Ode" also deals with a regional myth, although the contrast is more clearly one of an heroic past and an ineffectual present. In his own gloss on the poem, Tate contends that he is writing about the modern condition of solipsism. This situation is captured brilliantly in the image of the jaguar leaping for his own reflection in the jungle pool. If the classical Narcissus was a victim of excessive self love, Tate depicts a beast unwittingly bent on his own destruction.

The modern man, who stands at the gate of the cemetery, is aware of the great gulf that separates him not only from the heroic war dead but from the natural world itself. This man possesses sufficient self-awareness to recognize his plight. Also, he can imaginatively recover the passion and commitment of the dead soldiers ("knowledge carried to the heart") when he is standing in their midst. Unfortunately, his is a vision that cannot last. If Ransom's speaker maintains a sense of his own absurdity in defending "archetypes of chivalry" that are little more than dreams in the modern world, Tate's protagonist cannot even sustain a ritualistic tie to the old myths; he possesses the will to believe but not the necessary faith. The reader of "Antique Harvesters" might conclude that the myth of the South has never been more than an aesthetic construct. If that myth seems particularly fragile in the twentieth century, it is because of the superior skepticism of the modern mind. In Tate's poem, the Old South is more a palpable reality that has been lost. (Although both are symbols, Tate's serpent in the mulberry bush seems far more literal than Ransom's ghostly fox.) Only a paradise that is real can be lost. Only an object of contemplation—like the picture on the Grecian urn—can last forever.

III

If the new criticism seemed passé by the mid-sixties, it was not because it had been replaced by a monolithic newer criticism. It had simply been challenged for a quarter century by approaches that had nothing in common except their differences with the new formalism. The myth criticism practiced by Northrop Frye and others tried to elevate literature to the realm of magic. On the other extreme, the New York intellectuals most closely associated with *Partisan Review* continued to place literature within a social and political context. Despite their disagreements with the southern formalists—as revealed most tellingly in Alfred Kazin's *On Native Grounds*—the New Yorkers were secure enough not to make a target of the new criticism, even as they themselves published in new critical journals.

Probably the most sustained theoretical assault on the new criticism in the late sixties and early seventies came from two different Yale graduates—Stanley Fish and E. D. (Donald) Hirsch.[7] A native of Providence, Rhode Island, Fish received his A.B. at the University of Pennsylvania in 1959 and his M.A. at Yale in 1960. He completed his Ph.D. at Yale in 1962 (serving for a time as a reader for Cleanth Brooks). Fish rose from instructor to full professor at the University of California at Berkeley during the sixties and early seventies, a time when that campus was synonymous with political turmoil and cultural experimentation. For his own part, Fish helped launch a revolution in English studies by applying newly fashionable critical theories to some classic works of seventeenth-century literature, including the poetry of John Skelton and Milton's *Paradise Lost*. Fish moved into the Kenan chair at Johns Hopkins in 1974. In 1985, he became chairman of English at Duke and has since gained nationwide fame (or infamy) for the changes he brought to that staid old department. He was the inspiration for Professor Morris Zapp (author of "Textuality as Striptease") in David Lodge's satirical novel *Small World* (1985) and one of the prime villains of Dinesh D'Souza's best-selling jeremiad *Illiberal Education* (1991).

Although reader response theory of one sort or another is as old as criticism itself, Fish breathed new life into it with two revolutionary books—*Surprised by Sin: The Reader in Paradise Lost* (1967) and *Self-Consuming Artifacts: The Experience of Seventeenth-Century Literature* (1972). In the preface to the 1971 paperback edition of *Surprised by Sin*,

Fish writes: "Meaning is an *event*, something that happens, not on the page, where we are accustomed to look for it, but in the interaction between the flow of print (or sound) and the actively mediating consciousness of a reader-hearer" (Fish, *Surprised*, x). If nothing else, this theory suggested a way of dealing with literature as a temporal art form rather than as a body of decorated discursive statements. Form matters precisely because it helps determine our response to a work of literature. In fact, we cannot even speak of form except in terms of response. "If the meaning of the poem is to be located in the reader's experience of it," Fish writes in *Surprised by Sin*, "the form of the poem is the form of that experience; and the outer or physical form, so obtrusive, and, in one sense, so undeniably there, is, in another sense, incidental and even irrelevant" (341).

The theoretical problems with this position should be obvious. While it is often difficult to agree on an author's intention or on the clear meaning of a text, those tasks are infinitely easier than cataloging the varieties of response elicited by a work of literature. I. A. Richards demonstrated that point amply in *Practical Criticism*. Of course, Fish is no more interested than Richards in empirical cataloging as such; he is concerned instead with how a text operates in the experience of *a sensitive and well-informed reader*. Fish defines such a reader in the course of analyzing "Why is Iago evil?," the opening sentence of Joan Didion's *Play It as It Lays*. "There are at least four potential readers of this sentence," Fish writes, "and these range from 'the reader for whom the name Iago means nothing' to the reader 'who is aware that the question has its own history, that everyone has had a whack at answering it, and that it has become a paradigm question for the philosophical-moral problem of motivation' " (see Cain, *Crisis*, 53). Clearly, Fish believes that it is this last reader whose experience determines the meaning of the sentence. As David H. Hirsch has noted, the practical consequence is that Fish is continuing to practice the new criticism with "a slightly different rhetorical posture." "What Fish actually did in his criticism," Hirsch writes, "was to seek out image patterns, ironies, and paradoxes, just as the New Critics had instructed him, but instead of attributing 'meanings' to an author or a text, he attributed meanings to the mind in the act of reading" (D. H. Hirsch, 4).

Charged with the twin sins of subjectivism and elitism, Fish modified his theory in the mid-seventies. Now it was no longer the isolated ideal reader but an "interpretative community" that defined meaning. Because such a community shared common values and common strategies, the possible interpretations of a given work, while various, were not unlimited. As William E. Cain notes, Fish does not say how these communities came into being or what holds the members together other than a common approach to literary interpretation.[8] Also, because a reader's response to language is not confined to literature as it has been traditionally defined, Fish's method could be applied to all sorts of nonliterary texts. Fish has elaborated an approach to literature that cannot even tell us what literature is.

While Stanley Fish was virtually obliterating textual autonomy by locating meaning in the mind of the reader, Donald Hirsch was denying the autotelic text by championing the author. Hirsch spent a decade on the Yale faculty before moving to the University of Virginia in 1966. The following year, he staked out his critical position with *Validity in Interpretation* (1967), a controversial treatise that he dedicated to William K. Wimsatt (his mentor at Yale) and Ronald S. Crane. Hirsch's purpose was to identify meaning firmly with the author. Only by doing this, he believed, could we avoid the relativism and "cognitive atheism" currently afflicting humanistic study. So insistent was Hirsch on the referentiality of all language that he denied any special status to literary language. In his second major book, *Aims of Interpretation* (1976), he writes: "No literary theorist from Coleridge to the present has succeeded in formulating a viable distinction between the nature of ordinary written speech and the nature of literary written speech" (E. D. Hirsch, *Aims*, 90). In his attempt to avoid the pitfalls of relativism, Donald Hirsch surely became the most literal-minded literary theorist since Yvor Winters.

In *Validity in Interpretation* Hirsch argues that a text can be complex and richly ambiguous but it cannot convey a meaning other than what its author intended—it either conveys authorial meaning or it fails to communicate at all. For Hirsch, meaning consists of more than mere intention, but intention is always an essential component of meaning. To demonstrate his theories, Hirsch cites two plausible readings of Wordsworth's poem "A Slumber Did My Spirit Seal"—one by F. W. Bateson and the other by Cleanth Brooks. Bateson's reading sees the poem as a great pantheistic affirmation, as it describes Lucy being reabsorbed into the earth of rocks and stones and trees. Brooks reads the poem as a bitterly ironic meditation on death. Hirsch asks how we are to confront two such contradictory readings of the same text.

One way to do this would be to assume that Brooks's reading includes Bateson's: there is a gesture of affirmation, but it is superseded by the forces of negation. On the contrary, we could argue that Bateson's reading includes Brooks's, that the speaker's bitterness and sorrow are swept away by spiritual exultation. A third alternative might say that Brooks and Bateson are partially right but that their positions must be fused to produce a satisfactory reading of the poem. The problem with all three "inclusivist" readings is that they all regard the submeanings of the text as "blocks which can be brought together additively" (E. D. Hirsch, *Validity*, 229–30). Because Brooks and Bateson find radically different emphases in Wordsworth's poem, there is no way that either could subsume the other's reading or that both could be partially correct. To Hirsch's mind, the only logical solution is that one of the two is right or that both are wrong.

In judging between Brooks's reading and Bateson's (or, for that matter, between any alternative readings of a given text), one must apply certain criteria. The criterion of legitimacy determines whether a reading conforms to the general norms of the language in which the text is written; the criterion of correspondence asks whether all of the linguistic components in the text have been accounted for; and the criterion of generic appropriateness ascertains whether the conventions of a particular type of discourse have been followed. According to all three criteria, the readings of Brooks and Bateson seem equally plausible. The fourth, and tie-breaking, criterion is that of coherence.

If the other three criteria determine plausibility, coherence ascertains probability. When we know nothing of the author and his characteristic beliefs, we must appeal to the general sentiments of mankind or the prevailing opinion of the society in which the text was written. (That is why Hirsch believes it so important to date anonymous texts.) By those standards, Brooks would seem to be more nearly on target. Most people do not see the return of their beloved to the earth as a cause for rejoicing. Wordsworth, however, was no ordinary man. We know enough of his beliefs, particularly as they were expressed in other poems, to judge Bateson's reading more probable. An author's intention, no matter how noble, does not give him the right to violate the norms of legitimacy, correspondence, and generic appropriateness. But once those norms have been observed, authorial intention can tell us far more than either critical ingenuity or impressionistic reading about the meaning of a given text.

If we wish to identify certain benchmark years in recent American criticism, we could say that the position of the new critics was solidified with the publication of *The Well Wrought Urn* in 1947. It faced its severest challenge from Northrop Frye's *Anatomy of Criticism* exactly ten years later. Then, after another decade had passed, Hirsch and Fish mounted a second major assault with their first books in 1967. As we shall see in a later chapter, all of these attacks would soon be eclipsed by a radical new movement from Europe, which took root at Yale when a German scholar named Paul de Man joined the comparative literature faculty in 1970.

IV

Political challenges to the new criticism, which had come primarily from democratic nativists in the forties, were launched with increasing virulence from the radical Left beginning in the late sixties. The Marxists of the thirties had tempered their rhetoric as part of the Popular Front initiative of the forties; in the fifties they went underground in response to the anti-Communist sentiment of the era.[9] By the mid-sixties, however, a younger and more antinomian New Left had formed in the United States in the wake of the civil rights and antiwar efforts. College campuses became the center of New Left activity, and many professors and students in the humanities began to reexamine their professional conduct in light of their political commitments. One product of that reexamination was a volume entitled *The Politics of Literature: Dissenting Essays on the Teaching of English*. Edited by Louis Kampf and Paul Lauter in 1972, this self-styled antitextbook resembled nothing so much as an Oedipal assault on everything that its contributors had been taught about the study of literature. Even though new criticism was no longer dominant in 1972, the New Left scholars were bent on extirpating its lingering influence from the profession.

   In one of the most strident essays in the volume, the Maoist agitator Bruce Franklin writes his own spiritual autobiography under the title "The Teaching of Literature in the Highest Academies of the Empire." Employing a characteristically inflammatory rhetoric, Franklin says that aesthetic formalism "is the expression of the mentality of Mussolini's son, who was thrilled by the beauty of the bursting bombs he dropped on the Ethiopian villages." Without even bothering to examine the premises of the new criticism, Franklin brands it a "crude and frankly reactionary formalism" (Franklin, 113). He notes that it arose in the thirties as a counterforce to proletarian culture and enjoyed its complete ascendancy during the anti-Communist fifties. Presumably, the apolitical stance of the new critics was a mere subterfuge to protect the social and political status quo while pretending to an Olympian disinterestedness. One suspects that Franklin would not have been surprised to have learned of Willmoore

Kendall's scheme to employ Brooks and Warren in psychological warfare against North Korea.

A far less tendentious assessment of the new criticism is offered by Richard Ohmann, an English professor at Wesleyan University, editor of *College English*, and "well-known proletarian metacritic" (Kampf and Lauter, 416). Ohmann pays generous tribute to the humanistic contributions of the new critics and discounts attempts to brand them as proto-Fascists. Lacking the conspiratorial mentality of Bruce Franklin, he does not pretend to discern an explicit political agenda in the new criticism. To cite the Agrarian sympathies of a few of the southern new critics would prove only that they were romantic pastoralists. (By the early seventies, anti-industrialism had become a cause of the Left, in any event.) Ohmann concedes that "there are indeed many remarks by Eliot, Tate, Ransom, and others praising monarchy, aristocracy, the ante-bellum South, etc. But the criticism and literary theory, in sharp contrast to these political manifestos and asides, are square in the middle of the bourgeois liberal tradition" (Ohmann, 149). "To conduct the assault on [the level of partisan politics]," Ohmann observes, "quite properly invites the kind of response Tate offered . . . : that Eliot voted Labor, that an American New Critic voted for Norman Thomas, that Tate himself voted for FDR" (158). The political consequences of the new criticism are largely indirect and unintended.

The new critics enjoyed their greatest success during the postwar expansion in academia, when college professors were becoming a part of the comfortable bourgeoisie. The humanistic fervor with which the new critics promoted a disinterested formalism caused them to believe that the interpretation of poems and, indeed, the general life of the mind were powerful forces for social good. By the late sixties, things had changed. With society divided by social conflict at home and war abroad, activists such as Richard Ohmann believed that the literary critic's contribution to society must include more than merely analyzing the nuances of an autotelic text.

In his influential book *Literary Theory: An Introduction* (published in 1983), the Marxist critic Terry Eagleton argues that the new criticism had converted the poem "into a fetish": "If I. A. Richards had 'dematerialized' the text, reducing it to a transparent window on to the poet's psyche, the American new critics rematerialized it with a vengeance, making it seem less like a process of meaning than something with four corners and a pebbledash front" (Eagleton, 49). Eagleton deplores the political consequences of such aestheticism. "Reading poetry in the New Critical way," he contends, "meant committing yourself to nothing: all that poetry taught you was 'disinterestedness,' a serene, speculative, impeccably even-handed rejection of anything in particular. It drove you less to oppose McCarthyism or further civil rights than to experience such pressures as merely partial, no doubt harmoniously balanced somewhere else in the world by their complementary opposites. It was, in other words, a rec-ipe for political inertia, and thus for submission to the political status quo" (50).

In one sense, the new criticism actually represented an egalitarian force in English studies. At one time, only the classics were deemed worthy of serious academic attention. Because everyone in the university was ca-pable of reading works in his native tongue, there seemed little reason to waste time teaching courses in English literature. Once such courses did make their way into the curriculum, they were confined to dead authors whose place in the canon seemed relatively secure. It was the new critics and the New York intellectuals (both of whom shared a "high" concep-tion of literature) who secured a hearing for works written not only in living languages but by living authors. Although standards of taste devel-oped in the critical quarterlies still maintained a distinction between texts worthy of study and mere junk, those standards were technical rather than chronological, and they did much to take literature off the museum shelf.

Those who fault the new critics for a lack of social engagement seem to assume that society can be improved if only the proper (i.e., politically correct) attitudes are expressed in literature and literary criticism. In fact, this is rarely the case. With the exception of a few notable works of pro-paganda, such as *Uncle Tom's Cabin*, Auden was closer to the truth when he said "poetry makes nothing happen." Even when literature does change fundamental beliefs, the reaction is often delayed. Thoreau's writ-ings had an immense impact on the politics of the twentieth century, but they did not succeed in ending the Mexican War or freeing the slaves in their own time. Similarly, we may have to wait a while longer to assess the social legacy of the southern new critics.

Thoughtful scholars on the Left have come to realize that the Agrarians offered a more trenchant critique of bourgeois American society than any produced by the literary followers of Marx.[10] William E. Cain (F. O. Mat-thiessen's foremost contemporary interpreter and a man who is hardly a political conservative, much less a reactionary) believes that the southern men of letters would have better fulfilled the social responsibilities of the critic had they remained truer to their original Agrarian vision.[11] What he finds most attractive in their position is their critique of industrialism (which, along with John Fekete, he wishes they would call "capitalism") and their commitment to a broad-based cultural criticism. For example, he enthusiastically approves of the following statement made by Ransom in *I'll Take My Stand*: "We cannot recover our native humanism by adopting some standard of taste that is critical enough to question the contemporary arts but not critical enough to question the social and economic life which is their ground" (see Twelve Southerners, xxxvi). Unfortunately, Ransom seems to have reversed his position by the time he published *The World's Body* in 1938.

In contrast to Ransom, Donald Davidson, the least reconstructed of the major Agrarians, appears never to have lost sight of the difficulties faced by the arts in an industrialized society. In his contribution to *I'll Take My Stand*, "A Mirror for Artists," Davidson writes: "Education can do comparatively little to aid the cause of the arts as long as it must turn out graduates into an industrialized society which demands specialists in vocational, technical, and scientific subjects" (Davidson, "Mirror," 37). On the next page, Davidson notes "the almost overwhelming difficulty of communicating the humanities at all under systems of education, gigantic in their scope, that have become committed to industrial methods of administration—the entire repulsive fabric of standards, credits, units, scientific pedagogy, over-organization" (38).

For William E. Cain, "the unsettling truth seems to be not merely that the New Critics gave up something when they left Agrarianism behind. They appear in addition to have taken strides toward an embrace of the enemy, filtering their notion of criticism, the English department, and the academic discipline through commercial and professional/managerial values that they once strove to delegitimize and displace" (Cain, *Matthiessen* 41).

What Cain fails to consider is the possibility that the new criticism represented an extension rather than a repudiation of the Agrarian movement. (For that matter, it is a trifle disingenuous for leftist critics who function within the academy to condemn the new critics for functioning within the academy.) The sad truth is that the economic prescriptions of *I'll Take My Stand* and *Who Owns America?* were rejected by the American public. (Some would say that they never got a fair hearing.) Nevertheless, some of the values underlying those political manifestos were translated into the spectacularly successful pedagogical movement called the "new criticism." Grant Webster was exaggerating only slightly in saying that when the Agrarians failed to take over the country they decided to take over the academy instead.

Despite what their detractors might say, the new critics were not disengaged aesthetes trying to mold obedient citizens for the corporate state. If anything, their position was more deeply subversive than that of those who wore their social consciences on their sleeves. If the Agrarians believed that the humanizing activities of art, manners, and religion were more essential to civilization than unbridled economic growth, this attitude was reflected in the high value that the new critics placed on the literary text. Literature was worthy of study in its own right and did not have to be justified on utilitarian grounds. In addition, by stressing paradox, irony, and ambiguity in literary study, the new critics were cautioning us against accepting facile and simplistic explanations of any aspect of reality. Finally, by making us more careful students of language, they made it more difficult for authoritarian and venal interests to manipulate society with clichés, euphemisms, and jargon. Since the demise of the new criticism, we have seen a devaluation of art, a decline in the moral imagination, and an accelerated corruption of the language. Whatever their shortcomings, the new critics realized that the enemies of literature were the enemies of humanity itself.

V

During the time that Cleanth Brooks taught at Yale University, that institution probably changed more than it had during its previous two and a half centuries of existence. The university increasingly diversified its enrollment in the years after World War II, although Yale's historical ethos was still strong.

Over thirty-five years after his own graduation, Calvin Trillin, the son of an immigrant working-class Jew from Missouri, recalled the university he attended in the 1950s. "There had long been a tradition at Yale," Trillin writes, "of the bright, hardworking outsider who emerged as a class leader and may even have saved the Harvard game in the final seconds." By the time Trillin himself arrived at Yale, "the appearance of the bright outsider was no longer accidental. There was a broad and conscious movement into the white middle class and toward the West, a sort of *apertura* to the yahoos" (Trillin, 33). Trillin's father, who read Owen Johnson's worshipful potboiler *Stover at Yale* within a decade of its publication in 1911, began early to save money from his grocery store in Kansas City to send his son to Yale. "What my father saw as the most important reason for Yale's existence," Trillin writes, was "to turn the likes of us into the likes of them" (36).

By the mid-sixties, the concept of a homogeneous Yale experience was pretty much a thing of the past. With the appointment in July 1965 of R. Inslee ("Inky") Clark as director of undergraduate admissions, the administration of Yale accelerated efforts to reduce the number of private school students accepted and to recruit minority and scholarship students. Even Yale's traditional status as an all-male undergraduate institution was being seriously questioned. The pressure from students and faculty for coeducation, which had begun when Whitney Griswold was president of the university, continued under Griswold's successor, Kingman Brewster, who persuaded the institution's governing body (the Yale Corporation) to authorize the admission of women undergraduates in the fall of 1969.

As popular as this reform was, it met with something less than universal approbation. Cleanth Brooks had come into contact with too many bright women in his time to believe them incapable of competing intellectually with their male counterparts. If anything, he feared that they were too good. During two decades at Yale, Cleanth had struggled to convince male students, many of them future tax lawyers and stock brokers, of the value of literature. He now envisioned a situation in which women would dominate the class discussion and claim the subject for their own. Although his more progressive colleagues regarded this as a patronizing attitude, Cleanth remained adamant in his position. He recalls that a few years after the admission of women, he was teaching a class on Faulkner in which the men scarcely said a word. One day midway through the semester, he asked the women to remain silent for a day and give the "poor boys" a chance to catch up.

As skeptical as he may have been about the admission of undergraduate women to Yale, Cleanth had experienced no difficulty dealing with the few women he encountered in the coeducational graduate program. In the late fifties, a young poet named Judith Banzer had been told by her mentor, Leonie Adams, that she must go to Yale to study with Cleanth. (The poet Marianne Moore told Judith that "Cleanth Brooks certainly understood poetry.") Nearly forty years later, Judith recalled the experience:

> I well remember the first day of class with Cleanth. I had never seen a picture of him and because he was so powerful a critical force then, I somehow expected that he would be ten feet tall with Dionysian locks,

breathing fire. Instead, I found myself walking along the corridor in search
of the proper classroom with a rather short and slender, clearly very gentle
gentleman with kindly eyes, silver hair, a smart bow tie, and a very big
briefcase. "Good morning," he said with a mellifluous southern accent,
"are you lost?" "It's my first day of class at Yale," I said. "I've come here to
study with Cleanth Brooks and I'm looking for his classroom." "Well,
now, you just come along with me," he said, and though it is a deadly
cliché, I must report that he said this "with twinkling eyes." (Farr, 250)

Before long, Cleanth became a father figure for Judith, taking a keen
interest in her both personally and professionally. When this girl from
New York fell in love with a young Virginian named George Farr (who
had taken a Brooks class as an undergraduate), she went to Cleanth for a
seal of approval. George Farr passed on both personal and regional
grounds. Even as Cleanth was busy persuading the LSU Press to publish
Judith Farr's dissertation on Elinor Wylie, he urged her not to neglect her
poetry. If his solicitude was framed in the courtly manner that feminists
find condescending, Judith never thought to be offended. As one pores
over her lengthy correspondence with her former professor (watching it
gingerly move to a first name basis), one sees her calling on him for rec-
ommendations and advice as readily as any male student might. (Once
when she was denied a promotion she deserved, Cleanth told her that she
would eventually make her detractors regret their decision. "Darling," he
admonished her, "remember what President Kennedy always said—'don't
get mad, get even.'") Although she learned a good deal about literature
from Cleanth, Judith Farr's own criticism struck out in a different direction, relying far more heavily on psychoanalysis (her book *The Passion of
Emily Dickinson*, published in 1992, is considered a landmark study). She
now teaches at Georgetown University, where she became the first female
full professor in the 200-year history of the school.

Judith Farr completed her education and began her career at a time
when the conventions in both literature and society were leaving Cleanth
Brooks behind. Many in the rising generation of literary scholars were
contemptuous of the new criticism and its reverence for the work of art.
Cleanth, however, refused to elevate the critic above the artist, as tempt-
ing as that might have been for a renowned critic to do. Behind his
back, graduate students who were convinced that they had discovered a
greater wisdom would say: "We've got to get a shovel and bury Cleanth
Brooks." [12]

For his own part, Cleanth was appalled by the decline in decorum among students and faculty alike. While he continued to wear a suit and tie to class, he noticed that his students often didn't bother to put on a clean pair of jeans. And some of the professors looked as if they had just stepped out of a hobo jungle. What was even worse was the decline in basic civility. When General Westmoreland was invited to speak to the Yale Political Union in the spring of 1972, protestors prevented him from being heard. It fell to Vann Woodward, a liberal opponent of the Vietnam War, to argue that free speech belongs to all sides in a debate, not just to the side one happens to agree with. Once, on a trip south to Sewanee, a few of his friends had asked Cleanth if he looked forward to retirement. He raised himself halfway out of his chair and banged the chair down on the floor for emphasis. "I can't wait to get out of that place," he said. "I can't wait to get out."[13]

VI

Like everyone else around Yale, the *Southern Review* expatriates had had to come to terms with the radically changing culture of the university. Denounced as dangerous agitators during their years at LSU, they now found themselves to be part of an embattled establishment. Perhaps because of his intimate association with students during his years as dean of Silliman College, John Palmer tended to be sympathetic with the undergraduate dissidents. Red Warren thought that Kingman Brewster had done a masterful job of averting the sort of damage that had been done to Harvard and Columbia. (New Haven's most serious brush with student rebellion came during a trial of seven Black Panthers in 1970.) Only Albert Erskine (who grew more strident in his convictions with the passing years) remained outspokenly conservative in his political views. As might be expected, Cleanth was somewhere in the middle—appalled by the nihilism of the campus radicals and apprehensive about the integrity of the university but unwilling to stand with such right-wing demagogues as George Wallace and Spiro Agnew.

These different shades of opinion were not nearly as strong as the bonds that united the southerners in exile. The adolescent Rosanna Warren discovered this one afternoon when her mother forced her to practice the piano much against her will. In something of a petulant mood, Rosanna began banging out the first song she turned to in her practice book. Eleanor rushed back in the room, waving her arms for her daughter to stop. Rosanna had inadvertently turned to "The Battle Hymn of the Republic" at a time when her parents were entertaining the Brookses, the Erskines, the Wimsatts, and Eudora Welty.[14]

Walter Sullivan describes another revealing encounter, which occurred in 1971 at the annual meeting of the Modern Language Association in Chicago. Cleanth had organized a panel to discuss Allen Tate's essay "A Southern Mode of the Imagination." The morning before the panel, Sullivan and Tate joined Cleanth, Bill Wimsatt, and Louis Rubin for breakfast at the Palmer House. As Sullivan recalls:

> Perhaps because we were all southerners, we began to talk of the Civil War. . . . Allen, remembering work he had done fifty years before, spoke of Stonewall Jackson and Jefferson Davis, praising one and damning the other. He and Bill lamented the loss of Jackson which, they thought, had caused the loss at Gettysburg, which in turn had led to the loss of the war. They had not yet said that they wished the South had won, but they were tending strongly in that direction, when R. W. B. Lewis, who along with Louis and Allen and Cleanth and me was to be on the Tate panel, sat down at our table. Lewis reprimanded Allen and Bill for their Confederate fervor; he said the southern cause had been corrupt and the war had ended as it should have.
>   Bill and Allen were sitting across from each other and both of them stood up. Bill was big, easily six and a half feet tall, and heavy. He made Allen appear even smaller than he was, but he did not surpass Allen in indignation.
>   "You don't know anything about it," Allen said to Dick Lewis.
>   "Absolutely nothing," Wimsatt added. "Don't try to discuss it."
>   Dick was surprised into silence. Allen and Bill sat down and, as if there had been no interruption, they continued to lament the demise of the Confederate South. (Sullivan, *Allen Tate*, 65–66)

Within four years, Bill Wimsatt was dead. Allen Tate hung on for a little more than seven years, most of it spent in a bedridden purgatory with an oxygen mask on his nightstand and a picture of T. S. Eliot on his wall. The Modern Language Association itself increasingly became captive to some of the same truculent ideologies that had invaded Yale. The new criticism seemed as dead as the Confederate South, and the very concept of humane learning was under attack. Cleanth had fought many battles over the preceding four decades, but, at sixty-five, he had neither the optimism nor the innocence that had sustained him at twenty-five. There were still books to be written and arguments to be joined, but his days on the Yale faculty were coming to an end.

CHAPTER NINETEEN

A Place to Come To

After forty-three years of college teaching, Cleanth Brooks officially retired in the spring of 1975. Writing to her mother on June 13, Tinkum contemplated some of the changes that she and her husband would have to look forward to:

> We face the fact that when Cleanth stops teaching altogether and we become part of the completely "retired" world, our life will be quite different. We will seldom see socially people other than those who retired from Yale at about the same time that we did. Younger people will think occasionally that they should have the dear old Brookses over, but that will play out in a year or two. Nobody will ask Cleanth's advice about literary matters, about a major appointment in a university, beg him to serve on a committee, ask him to give a notable lecture, etc. I don't mean that life would stop—he'd still have his own writing—but writing can be a more demanding, energy-consuming thing than teaching, and writing in a vacuum, without the stimulus of other minds, can be very hard indeed.[1]

One way that Cleanth maintained ties to the Yale community was by dining often with the friends of three decades. Even before his retirement, he began having lunch each Monday at Mory's with a group of colleagues from the English department. The weekly ritual was initiated in the 1970s by James Osborne, one of Yale's outstanding eighteenth-century scholars (like Cleanth, he had studied at Oxford under David Nichol Smith). The group has never had a constitution or bylaws, and its composition has changed with the death and illness of some members and the addition of others to take their place. At the time of Cleanth's death, he was one of seven retired professors in the group. The others were Maynard Mack, Louis Martz, the Old English specialist John Pope, the Jacobean scholar

Eugene Waith, the Shakespearean George Hunter, and the medievalist Fred Robinson. (Until his confinement to a nursing home, René Wellek was a regular participant, even when he had to be helped into the dining area in a wheelchair.) The newest member is the critic Claude Rawson, who came to Yale in 1986.

Because these men first began their Monday gatherings when most of them were still teaching, they were viewed by department radicals as a sort of conservative caucus formed to bolster their waning influence in the English department. The men's wives were probably closer to the mark when they claimed that the purpose of the group was to stay current on campus gossip.[2] Often members would bring visiting guests. As Claude Rawson discovered on one occasion, it was always best to introduce those guests, regardless of how well known they might be. When Rawson brought the British critic Frank Kermode to lunch, Kermode greeted Cleanth warmly by name. Cleanth reciprocated the warmth and engaged Kermode in a lively discussion for over an hour. It was only after Kermode left to catch the Yale shuttle to his temporary residence that Cleanth turned to Rawson and asked, "What was your friend's name?"[3] If the memories of some of the group members had been dulled by age, their intellectual curiosity remained keen. All could fit easily around a single table, and the good fellowship might remind one of the early Fugitive meetings or even of the circle that gathered around Samuel Johnson in the taverns of eighteenth-century London. Because the Episcopal Church once sponsored a group called the "Girls Friendly," Jim Osborne suggested that this band of senior citizens be called the "Boys Friendly."

During all the years that Cleanth and Tinkum had been gone from Baton Rouge, they maintained close contact with their old yardman Leroy McCelos and his wife Emma. Leroy was a simple, hardworking man, who did his best to support a wife and five children. Distrusting banks, he kept his life savings in a mattress in his house. After he reached a premature old age, armed thieves forced Leroy to turn that money over to them. Throughout a life of hardships, he attended the True Light Baptist Church, where he served as deacon. In a letter to "Mr. and Mrs. Brooks," dated 11-18-80, Leroy reported: "I have retired in June I had a stroke in April Its called a sugar stroke. I Lost the use of Left hand an Leg. But It is Doing Fine Now."[4] The letter was enclosed with a package of Louisiana pecans. Less than a year later, on October 12, 1981, Leroy was dead.

In addition to keeping in touch with the Brookses through the mail,

Leroy had been a guest at Northford on several occasions. When he was staying there in Cleanth's absence, Tinkum would always make sure that someone else was in residence as well. This was out of respect, not fear. Richard Wright remembers feeling humiliated and, in a sense, unmanned when white prostitutes undressed in his presence while he was working as a hotel bellboy. Tinkum was not about to treat Leroy as if he were invisible. Nevertheless, the racial caste system established barriers that were not easily breached. Even though members of the McCelos family ate countless meals with the Brookses, Cleanth and Tinkum never allowed them to reciprocate that hospitality. Carver Blanchard remembers stopping by the McCelos house with his aunt and uncle one afternoon. When they were invited to stay for dinner, Tinkum said, "No, Emma, we couldn't do that." Out of the corner of his eye, Carver noticed platters of fried chicken in the dining room and a table set for eight.[5]

It will probably never be known how much money Cleanth and Tinkum sent to Leroy and Emma over the years, but their largesse continued at least through the end of 1981. At that point, Cleanth had been diagnosed with skin cancer and was undergoing radiation treatment. In a letter dated January 8, 1982, Emma and her daughter, Linda, wrote to Tinkum Brooks to suggest the time had come to end a patronage that may have grown awkward for all concerned.

> For many, many years you and Mr. Brooks have extended your kindness and expressed your love for us in various ways, for which we have been extremely grateful. Had it not been for many of your gifts I (Linda) would not have been successful in many of my endeavors.
>
> We are aware of the great expense involved in medical care, etc. Inflation has really taken its toll. So please have no regrets about discontinuing the check.

The radiation treatments were successful, and the Brookses continued to prosper financially. Cleanth knew that his textbooks had sold well, but he always turned his royalty checks over to Tinkum, who managed the family income. She was a shrewd businesswoman, who invested money wisely with the aid and counsel of Albert Erskine. When the local water company wanted the rights to some land she owned, she held out until she was paid several times what the land would have brought for any commercial purpose. Cleanth later recalled with amazement the evening Tinkum showed him a financial statement telling him he was worth over a million dollars.[6]

I

In 1978 Cleanth Brooks published his second book on William Faulkner.[7] If the focus of *The Yoknapatawpha Country* might be described as "The Faulkner Everyone Knows," *Toward Yoknapatawpha and Beyond* deals with the unknown Faulkner. This book examines what Faulkner was doing when he was not laying claim to his "little postage stamp of soil." Where Brooks's earlier book made a strong positive case for the importance of the Yoknapatawpha fiction, this later volume makes a strong negative case for the same judgment. Even if Brooks is correct in saying "nothing that the mature Faulkner ever wrote is without interest" (*Toward Yoknapatawpha*, xii), the non-Yoknapatawpha material commands our interest largely because of the light it sheds on Faulkner's major work. (Can one imagine Cleanth Brooks writing or the Yale University Press publishing, in the last quarter of the twentieth century, a 430-page study of James Branch Cabell, the southern romantic whom the early Faulkner most resembles?) *Toward Yoknapatawpha and Beyond* is the intrinsic critic's tribute to the biographical approach to literary study.

Although Faulkner did not create Yoknapatawpha County until his third novel, *Sartoris*, it exists in embryonic form in Charlestown, Georgia, the imaginary setting of his first novel, *Soldier's Pay* (1926). If *Soldier's Pay* looks forward to the great novels of Faulkner's major period, it is also clearly an outgrowth of his earlier poetry and experimental prose. The interest in pagan mythology that he derived from the British decadents informs the characterization of several major figures in this novel. In the severely wounded war veteran Donald Mahon, the novel's ostensible protagonist, we have a faun, who is contrasted with the satyr-like Januarius Jones; two of the most important female characters, Emily and Cecily, are both nymphs. Although Faulkner would agree with his early model, Swinburne, that paganism has no place in the modern world, it is not the "pale Galilean" but religious skepticism that has triumphed. (Believing this to be the case, Brooks focuses much of his attention on Donald's father, an Episcopal priest who has lost his faith.) Set in the aftermath of World War I, *Soldier's Pay* is Faulkner's Waste Land or Lost Generation novel.

The difference between the early and the maturing Faulkner can be easily seen if we compare and contrast *Soldier's Pay* with Faulkner's first genuine Yoknapatawpha novel, *Sartoris* (1929). Both novels take place in 1919 and treat the malaise of the returning soldier. In *Sartoris*, however, this theme is played out within a richly developed social and historical context. As Brooks explains, reference is made "to Jefferson's history, to the Sartoris family tradition, to the continuities of the countryside, and to the relatively unchanged cultural state of the yeoman whites and Negroes. In *Soldier's Pay* there are no more than mere hints of these matters. . . . Except for the Negroes, Charlestown, Georgia, might just as well have been Charlestown, New Hampshire, or Charlestown, Indiana" (*Toward Yoknapatawpha*, 99).

Faulkner's second novel, *Mosquitoes* (1927), brings together a group of sophisticates who converse for several days about art and sex. (The clever dialogue has prompted Brooks to wonder if Aldous Huxley's *Chrome Yellow* [1921] was one of Faulkner's models.) Although the ideas expressed are of some topical interest, the enveloping action is so mannered and lifeless that *Mosquitoes* is generally considered to be Faulkner's worst novel. Nevertheless, literary historians and biographers (particularly Joseph Blotner) value the book for its fictional portraits of real-life characters. Probably the most significant of these is Dawson Fairchild, who is evidently modeled on Faulkner's New Orleans associate and mentor, Sherwood Anderson. While never renouncing his friendship for Anderson or denying his literary achievement, Faulkner believed that the Ohioan was finally too provincial. Anderson had taught Faulkner to find inspiration in his own regional roots. But Faulkner never forgot that the truest regionalism manifests the universal through the local and subjects itself to international standards of judgment. This is a truth that Dawson Fairchild (i.e., Sherwood Anderson) failed fully to grasp; as a result, he never completely broke free from the limitations of local color.

Faulkner made his first foray into Yoknapatawpha County when he wrote *Flags in the Dust*, which was published in a shortened form as *Sartoris*. (The original version did not see the light of day until a decade after Faulkner's death.) At about the same time, he used his home turf as the setting for two short stories, "Miss Zilphia Gant" and "A Rose for Emily." Both stories are about strong-minded spinsters who have been victimized by an overbearing parent. Miss Zilphia's mother, who has hated and distrusted men ever since her husband left her, is horrified when she discovers her adolescent daughter lying innocently beside a boy under a blanket. (Variations on this theme can be found in *Soldier's Pay* and *Elmer*.) Although Zilphia finally does secure a husband, her mother drives him off before the marriage can be consummated. Through a Memphis detective agency, Zilphia keeps track of her former husband, who has remarried and fathered a child. Not knowing that his new wife has died in childbirth, the husband himself is fatally struck by a car on the way to see her in the hospital. Miss Zilphia suddenly appears, claims the child, and returns triumphantly to Jefferson. She has become a widow without ever really being a wife and a mother without ever losing her maidenhead. The victory is a Pyrrhic one, however, as Miss Zilphia comes increasingly to resemble her mother (now dead) in both dress and manner.

"A Rose for Emily" is a far better known and more accomplished story. It is also, in Brooks's opinion, one of the most misunderstood works in the Faulkner canon. Much of that misunderstanding comes from attempts to make Miss Emily into a metaphor for the Old South. Even if typical southerners are not literally guilty of murder and necrophilia, some commentators see the region as symbolically guilty of these crimes. They, and others of their mind-set, view the Compson family and Thomas Sutpen as symbols of a decaying southern aristocracy. In each case, however, we see a deviation from the southern ideal rather than a symbolic incarnation of it. But figures such as Miss Emily and Thomas Sutpen are more than mere deviants; by their very isolation from the community, they help the community to define itself. *Absalom, Absalom!* is not so much the story of Thomas Sutpen, fascinating though that might be, as it is the story of a society that has made a myth of Thomas Sutpen. For that same society, Miss Emily "had been a tradition, a duty, and a care; a sort of hereditary obligation upon the town" (Faulkner, *Collected Stories* 119). Through his use of a choric narrator, who serves as spokesman for the townspeople, Faulkner shows us a community that is capable of cherishing, if not fully understanding, even its most eccentric members. It is the presence of the community through this choric narration that makes "A Rose for Emily" a more subtle and complex story than "Miss Zilphia Gant."

After discovering the literary possibilities of writing about the people and places he knew best, Faulkner set most of his remaining fiction in Yoknapatawpha County. The first notable exception to that practice was *Pylon*, a novel that he wrote in a burst of energy between October and December of 1934. If the role of the community is the great theme in Faulkner's Yoknapatawpha fiction, the absence of community is a crucial factor in *Pylon*. Unlike the central characters in *Light in August* and "A Rose for Emily," the aviators in *Pylon* have no identifiable society from which they are alienated or by whose standards they can be judged. Faulkner might have gained something had he set this novel in Jefferson rather than in the more cosmopolitan ambience of New Orleans. (Brooks notes that the flyers have much in common with the young Bayard Sartoris, while the Reporter vaguely resembles Horace Benbow.) But Faulkner obviously wanted to write a different kind of book in *Pylon*. Although the flyers have a personal past, they feel no compulsion to accept or repudiate a communal history. For this reason, Brooks finds their story to be in some ways more nihilistic than that of *Sanctuary*, the most brutal and hopeless of the Yoknapatawpha novels.

In 1939, four years after the publication of *Pylon*, Faulkner took another hegira from Yoknapatawpha (*Absalom, Absalom!* and *The Unvanquished* had appeared in the interim) with one of the strangest books he would ever write. *The Wild Palms* appears on the surface to be two totally unrelated novellas arbitrarily printed between the same covers. The title narrative is the tragedy of two adulterous lovers who are destroyed by their passion for each other. Harry Wilbourne is a young internist who gives up his career and all other interests in life to run away with Charlotte Rittenmeyer, the wife of another man. When Charlotte dies from an abortion she had insisted Harry perform on her, he rejects the opportunity to commit suicide, so that he can survive in prison focused on her memory. Harry is the true courtly lover, who is absurdly out of place in the modern world.

In alternating chapters, Faulkner tells the story of a very different kind of modern naïf (Brooks calls his chapter on *The Wild Palms* "A Tale of Two Innocents"). The "Tall Convict" is a poorly educated man who uses the *Detective's Gazette* as his manual for planning a train robbery. He is like a grown-up Tom Sawyer, except that he attempts a real rather than an imaginary crime. His motivation, we are led to believe, is a desire not for money but for heroism and romance. He unwittingly experiences plenty of both when the prison authorities send him out during a flood to rescue a pregnant woman who has taken refuge in a tree. After delivering the baby and experiencing all sorts of adventures while battling nature, the unnamed convict brings the woman to safety and returns the boat he has been issued to the state prison. Although a very simple man, the Tall Convict possesses an instinctive sense of chivalry and honor.

From the very beginning, one of the paradigmatic figures in American literature has been that of the unfallen Adam. From Hawthorne on, our greatest writers have warned of the dangers of such innocence. Harry Wilbourne and the Tall Convict are perhaps different versions of the American Adam—one suffering from excessive contemplation and self-absorption, the other from a complete lack of intellect and self-awareness.

"We read [*The Wild Palms*] badly, however, if we assume that Faulkner asks us to choose between the young convict and the young doctor. Both men are in part victims of the societies which produced them, and of the age in which they grew up. In both cases there was a wastage. Our culture seems to offer little scope for the heroism latent in the naive young hillman, or the almost ascetic dedication to passionate love latent in the young sobersides intern. These are propositions which the Convict probably did not learn and the young physician may have learned only partially. Nevertheless, they constitute Faulkner's judgment on our time" (*Toward Yoknapatawpha*, 229).

A *Fable* (1954) is the last of Faulkner's non-Yoknapatawpha novels and the only one to be published after he won the Nobel Prize. Unlike *Mosquitoes*, it cannot be dismissed as juvenilia; it was the work of a mature artist who continued to write good (if no longer great) books until the year before his death. If *A Fable* is the failure that so many critics regard it to be, it is because Faulkner attempted something that was not suited to his particular talent. Leaving Yoknapatawpha County for a foreign setting was only part of the problem; Faulkner also abandoned realistic narrative for the unfamiliar realm of fantasy and parable. Moreover, as Brooks demonstrates, *A Fable* lacks the philosophical consistency and mythic vision that makes a story such as Dostoyevsky's "The Grand Inquisitor" more than an illustrated sermon. Although it contains some fine dramatic scenes, *A Fable* suffers from wooden allegory, an unsuccessful mixture of the fabulous and the mundane, and thematic confusion. Like so many mortals, Faulkner was never able to decide whether Christ was God as well as Man. Such ambivalence can be the source of great drama (the heart in conflict with itself) when one is writing about doubting humanity. But when one presumes to depict Christ himself (however disguised), that ambivalence must be resolved. Instead, Faulkner gives us a mawkish secular humanism clothed in magic.

The final chapter of *Toward Yoknapatawpha and Beyond* is a general discussion of Faulkner's concepts of time and history. In the first half of this discussion, Brooks attempts to correct what he regards as an excessive emphasis on Faulkner's debt to Henri Bergson. From both internal evidence in the fiction and his own statements in interviews, it is clear that Faulkner knew and agreed with Bergson's concept of time as a kind of eternal flux. But that notion was hardly original with Bergson. In the Western tradition one can trace it back at least as far as Augustine's *Confessions*. Moreover, if one takes Bergson too literally, the only arts that do not falsify time are music, dance, and motion pictures. No art whose medium is words will do. "Since nouns are names and clot the dynamic flow of reality into little static pseudo-entities ('things'), a poem or a story necessarily denies the true nature of reality" (*Toward Yoknapatawpha*, 261). From the very beginning of literature, writers have had to use the static instrument of language to convey the dynamic flow of action. Centuries before Faulkner (or Bergson), this difficulty was confronted by Homer, Sophocles, Dante, and Shakespeare. "It has been solved, more or less satisfactorily, over and over again. One of Faulkner's favorite poets, by writing what was to become perhaps Faulkner's favorite poem, the 'Ode on a Grecian Urn,' solved it very much to Faulkner's own special satisfaction" (260).

For Faulkner, history was not a record of names and dates but a system of myth—what Robert Penn Warren called "the myth we live." As a Mississippian, Faulkner was drawn to the myth of the Old South; he viewed it with the ironic contemplation we reserve for those things we take seriously. (To accept the myth unblinkingly or to dismiss it contemptuously would have been opposite ways of treating it too lightly.) If the southern myth was focused on the past, the American myth (or dream) pointed to the future. At times, Faulkner was as disappointed by the meretriciousness of the American future as he was by the squalor of the southern past. A distrust of millenialism was deeply ingrained in the southern character and reinforced by the experience of military defeat. (It was not until the Vietnam War that the rest of America began to share the sense of tragedy that the South had known since 1865.) The Fall from Grace came not in a garden in Mesopotamia but on a battlefield called Gettysburg.

II

As we have already seen, critics have been sharply divided in their willingness to agree with Brooks on the importance of the community in the Yoknapatawpha saga. In *The Unwritten War* (1973) the leftist scholar Daniel Aaron evolves an interesting conspiracy theory to explain why Brooks is so far off the mark:

> Only after the flurry of Agrarianism petered out did the Neo-Confederates
> come to a proper appreciation of William Faulkner. Some of them knew
> him, of course, in the 1930s as one of the talented representatives of the
> Southern literary "renascence," but a decade passed before they canonized

him belatedly as "the most powerful and original novelist in the United States and one of the best in the modern world," and inadvertently made his achievement ancillary to their own social and aesthetic dicta. The exegeses of Warren and especially of Cleanth Brooks influenced Faulkner scholarship so profoundly, in fact, that the differences between him and the Nashville group have become obscured. (Aaron, 311)

A similar but more reasoned challenge to Brooks's position was issued by Thomas L. McHaney in a long and thoughtful review of *Toward Yoknapatawpha and Beyond*. McHaney begins by pointing out that Brooks's attention to Faulkner came almost exclusively after the Mississippian had won the Nobel Prize, rather than during those years of obscurity when the critic's "intelligent and sympathetic readings" could have done the most good (McHaney, 30). More surprising is the fact that the original series of the *Southern Review* paid scant attention to Faulkner. Although Delmore Schwartz did write an essay on Faulkner's fiction for the final volume of the magazine, four of the six novels that Faulkner published between 1935 and 1942—*Pylon* (1935), *The Unvanquished* (1938), *The Wild Palms* (1939), and *Go Down, Moses* (1942)—went unreviewed. Only *Absalom, Absalom!* and *The Hamlet* were mentioned briefly in omnibus reviews.

McHaney attributes what he regards as Brooks's inadequate treatment of Faulkner to two factors. First, Brooks began writing about Faulkner so late because he was a traditional academic, more apt to comment on writers safely in the canon than on problematic contemporaries. Second, when Brooks did take up Faulkner's cause, he did so as a displaced southerner needing to convey a nostalgic and idealized view of his home region to cosmopolitan students and colleagues at Yale. Beginning in 1951 with essays on *Absalom, Absalom!* (in the *Sewanee Review*) and *Light in August* (in the *Harvard Advocate*), Brooks began developing the theory about Faulkner and the community that would become the cornerstone of *The Yoknapatawpha Country*. Whether writing out of group loyalty or more personal compulsions, he discovered (or contrived) a Faulkner that many readers find too conventional and too benign, a Faulkner without thunder.

At the 1981 Faulkner conference in Oxford, Mississippi, Brooks attempted to set the record straight about the affinities between Faulkner and the Nashville group. In a talk entitled "Faulkner and the Fugitive-Agrarians," he responded explicitly to Daniel Aaron and implicitly to all the critics who had attacked the thesis of *The Yoknapatawpha Country*.

He notes that, far from being latecomers to the Faulkner bandwagon, several of the most prominent Fugitives had recognized the Mississippian's genius even before the Agrarian movement had gotten under way.

In 1926, four years before the publication of *I'll Take My Stand*, Donald Davidson had favorably reviewed *Soldier's Pay* on his book page in the Nashville *Tennessean*; this was followed by a mixed review of *Mosquitoes* in 1927 and an enthusiastic endorsement of *Sartoris* in 1929. Like Brooks, Warren read *Soldier's Pay* at Oxford in 1929 and favorably reviewed Faulkner's first collection of short stories, *These Thirteen*, in 1931. Ransom published George Marion O'Donnell's historic essay on Faulkner in the *Kenyon Review* in 1939 and planned a special Faulkner issue of the review in 1945. (The project was dropped only because there was not enough good Faulkner criticism to fill an entire issue of the magazine!) Although Tate did not write about Faulkner until relatively late, his correspondence with Davidson refers to the novelist as early as 1932. Even McHaney notes that Brooks and Warren included a discussion of "A Rose for Emily" in *Understanding Fiction*. All of this attention came prior to Malcolm Cowley's rediscovery of Faulkner in 1946.

Whether the Fugitive-Agrarians discovered Faulkner early or late is finally less important than whether they read him properly. Clearly, Faulkner followed no party line. But then, neither did the Nashville critics. Anyone who knows about the arguments surrounding the production of *I'll Take My Stand*, or has read the book itself, knows that the Nashville Twelve could agree on little among themselves. Upon examining the careers of individual Agrarians, "one can find plenty of detachment, soul-searching, and critical examination in the writings of Ransom, Warren, and Tate" (*Prejudices*, 7). As a case in point, Brooks cites Tate's novel *The Fathers*, which exposes the deficiencies as well as the virtues of the Old South. (Although Aaron concedes as much in his own discussion of *The Fathers*, he persists in his cartoon image of the Agrarians as a whole.) By the same token, Faulkner was balanced (or schizophrenic) enough to present an equally mixed view of southern culture. Along with his criticism of the region was a genuine love for its history, manners, traditions, and values. Faulkner's critique of the southern myth, Brooks argues, was nothing in comparison to his indictment of the more general American Dream.

Obviously, Brooks could not expect to persuade all of his detractors with this moderate and cogent defense of his position. One might have expected, however, that they would at least have taken notice of what he had to say. In an essay published in the *New York Review of Books* nearly thirty years after Marvin Mudrick's snide hatchet job, Frederick C. Crews repeated all of the hoary clichés about Brooks and his fellow Agrarians. Although Brooks's essay on Faulkner and the Fugitive-Agrarians was contained in one of the books he was purportedly reviewing, Crews made no mention of that essay. He compounded his error by listing *The Yoknapatawpha Country*, which had just been reissued by the Louisiana State University Press, as "out of print."[8]

However we may interpret the historical causes for an Agrarian—or even Brooksean—reading of Faulkner, the durability of that reading is demonstrated by the repeated attempts to refute it. As Lance Lyday points out, "the most direct and systematic challenge to Brooks's interpretation" (Lyday, 187) came as recently as 1990 in *Faulkner's Marginal Couple: Invisible, Outlaw, and Unspeakable Communities* by John N. Duvall. The thesis of this book is that the really important communities in Faulkner's fiction are not the officially sanctioned ones but those formed by two or three marginal individuals seeking solace in their mutual rebellion.

Although we can certainly debate the extent of Faulkner's esteem for traditional community values, Brooks's interpretation of the world of Yoknapatawpha is at least grounded in observed reality. Duvall, on the other hand, insists on judging the limited good in this world by a standard of utopian perfection. "What is wrong with *Faulkner's Marginal Couple*," writes Lyday, ". . . is best illustrated in Duvall's reference to the 'hollowness' of Martha Armstid's charity in the opening chapter of *Light in August*, when she makes clear her disapproval of Lena Grove's lifestyle. Duvall evidently envisions a good society as one in which no such judgments would be made, but it doesn't seem to occur to him that a far more likely alternative [in the last decade of the twentieth century] would be a society in which a Martha Armstid wouldn't open her door to a stranger at all, much less provide her a room for the night, food, and her hard-earned eggmoney" (188).

It is because that "far more likely alternative" is the world in which we live now (and have lived for some time) that critics as diverse as Brooks and Duvall (born fifty years apart) yearn for some sustaining sense of community. That they can both find what they are looking for in the work of Faulkner may be one reason for the continuing appeal of that work. Although he was never an unblinking defender of the old order, Faulkner was capable of telling an interviewer from England that "if it came to fighting I'd fight for Mississippi against the United States even if it meant going out into the street and shooting Negroes" (see *Time*, "Curse and

Hope," 47). (One finds no chauvinism that intense, or indiscreet, in the writings of the Agrarians.) The fact that Faulkner could make such a statement and yet write with sensitivity about race should make us cautious about applying facile labels to his social vision.

There is no question that, like all of his fellow modernists, Faulkner wrote about a broken and disordered world. Nevertheless, he had a concrete and experienced standard against which to measure the brokenness and disorder. Brooks believes that that standard was the southern community at its best. That it was often not at its best, Faulkner knew only too well, but he was neither a nihilist nor an unbridled individualist. "Even lack of purpose and value take on special meaning when brought into Faulkner's world, for its very disorders are eloquent of the possibilities of order" (*Yoknapatawpha Country*, 368). Art creates those possibilities through a kind of magic; criticism discerns them through a kind of science. Together they provide what Allen Tate called "knowledge carried to the heart."

III

The ravenous grave finally claimed Allen Tate on February 9, 1979. A heavy smoker for decades, he was finally confined to his bed by emphysema in 1975. Over the next four and a half years, his body grew emaciated from inactivity and the ravages of illness. Already having lived several years longer than his doctors had predicted, he might have continued wasting away indefinitely had other afflictions not complicated his treatment. When he suffered a urinary tract infection in early 1979, Tate's third wife, Helen (a former nun he had married in 1966), checked him into the Vanderbilt University hospital. His doctors had to perform a medical balancing act, giving him enough antibiotics to kill the infection but not more than his weakened condition could sustain. The official cause of death was listed as "systemic failure," which is to say that his body was all used up. His funeral in Nashville was conducted according to the rites of the Roman Catholic Church (which he had officially joined in 1950). After a ninety-mile drive into the mountains of east central Tennessee, his mortal remains were laid to rest in a cemetery not far from where he had edited the *Sewanee Review* thirty-five years before. His passing was pushed off the front pages in Nashville by the death of Elvis Presley's father.

With Tate gone, only three of the original twelve Agrarians remained. John Gould Fletcher had taken his own life in 1950.[9] A year later,

Henry Blue Kline succumbed to uremic poisoning. Frank Owsley suffered a fatal heart attack not long after the Fugitives Reunion in 1956. Stark Young was gone by January of 1963; he was followed by John Donald Wade later that year, H. C. Nixon in 1967, Donald Davidson in 1968, and John Crowe Ransom in 1974. As the semicentennial of *I'll Take My Stand* approached, Lyle Lanier, Andrew Lytle, and Red Warren (all now in their seventies) were the only contributors still alive. Walter Sullivan and William C. Havard (a former graduate student at LSU who was now head of Vanderbilt's political science department) decided that the university should officially commemorate this fifty-year anniversary. The question was whether Vanderbilt's current leaders would be any more receptive to the idea than their predecessors had been to the original movement half a century earlier.

After Randall Stewart's retirement, the Vanderbilt English department would never again have a strong head in the tradition of Mims and Curry. For the students and faculty who had suffered under those two autocrats, that was all to the good. The only drawback was that the department became increasingly factionalized as various faculty members put in brief stints as department chairman. Stewart's successor, Russell Fraser, lasted for only two years. An outsider who was unacceptable to the department's conservative wing, he left Vanderbilt for a professorship at the University of Michigan in 1967. At that point, the university's director of admissions, Thomas Daniel Young, was named chairman. Dan Young had earned his doctorate from Vanderbilt in 1950 and had distinguished himself as an expert on the Fugitives and Agrarians (even as he chaired the English department, he was writing John Crowe Ransom's biography). When Young became Gertrude Conaway Vanderbilt Professor of English in 1973, he was succeeded as chairman by the linguist Rupert Palmer, who served two three-year terms. In 1979 Palmer passed the reins to James Kilroy, a universally well-liked specialist in Victorian and modern Irish literature. For fifteen years, the new guard and the old guard had fought over curriculum, tenure and promotion decisions, and virtually every other aspect of departmental policy. The old guard had the power of seniority, but the new guard—growing in numbers every year—could afford to bide its time.

A sizable faction within the English department and the university administration regarded the Fugitive-Agrarian–New Critical heritage as a provincial embarrassment. When Walter Sullivan tried to bring Cleanth Brooks to campus as a guest professor shortly after his retirement from Yale, new guard faculty blocked the effort. And when Walter first approached Chancellor Alex Heard with plans for the fifty-year Agrarian reunion, Heard accused him of thinking that nothing had ever happened at Vanderbilt except the Fugitives and Agrarians. (Years earlier, the Vanderbilt library had refused the gift of Tate's papers, only to see them sold to Princeton for $70,000.) Heard eventually backed the project, and an Agrarian symposium was held on the Vanderbilt campus in the late fall of 1980. Scholarly papers were presented on October 30 and 31 by Charles P. Roland, John Shelton Reed, Lewis P. Simpson, Robert B. Heilman, and Louis D. Rubin, Jr. The conference concluded on the morning of November 1 with a panel of Lanier, Lytle, and Warren, moderated by Cleanth Brooks. It was Cleanth's third official invitation to Vanderbilt in the fifty-two years since his graduation.

If Agrarianism had seemed quixotic in 1930, it remained so in 1980. In 1976 Jimmy Carter had become the first southerner elected president since James K. Polk in 1845, but Carter, a nuclear engineer and agribusinessman, was clearly a product of the New South. (Eugene McCarthy had characterized him as a "third-generation Snopes.") Besides, the Tuesday after the Agrarian conference, Carter would lose a landslide election to Ronald Reagan, whose faith in industrialism and economic growth was seemingly unlimited. During the panel discussion, Lyle Lanier made several favorable references to Barry Commoner, candidate of the ultra-left-wing Citizen's Party. Where the Agrarians of the 1930s had thought that they could influence the New Deal, Lanier was now reduced to praising a fringe candidate who would get no more than a handful of votes. Nevertheless, the Agrarian symposium was more than a mere exercise in nostalgia. Even though the ideas in *I'll Take My Stand* were farther from adoption in 1980 than they had been fifty years earlier, some of the warnings issued in that book now seemed prophetic.

Ironically, the Agrarians had been denounced originally as ultraconservative if not downright reactionary. If progress and industrialism were synonymous, then anyone who questioned industrialism opposed progress. But as the ravages of pollution and urbanization became apparent, those who preached concern for the natural and human environment were increasingly seen not as reactionaries but as radicals. Welfare state liberals were the ones most intent on cleaning up the environment, while the banner of "conservatism" was being claimed by champions of laissez-faire industrialism (e.g., the Reagan wing of the Republican Party). Was the political spectrum actually circular, with the Agrarians being so far "right" that they were now "left?" Not quite. The new ecological aware-

ness may have seemed like a vindication of the Agrarians, but it was far
from a triumph for their cause. The left wing of the Democratic Party was
not about to urge a return to the family farm (which had largely disappeared by 1980, anyway) and would later be among the forces seeking to
ban the Confederate flag.

Although Agrarianism failed politically, it was never primarily a political movement. The major contributors to *I'll Take My Stand* were men of
letters, and it is by their literary achievement that they should be judged.
As Louis Rubin and others have pointed out, the Agrarian metaphor was
a part of that achievement. As poets and critics, the Vanderbilt brethren
also helped make the academy a more hospitable place for literary artists.
By 1980, however, the principal beneficiaries of that hospitality were
writers and theoreticians who held the Fugitives and new critics in contempt. A cynic might say that the men from Nashville were back where
they began, once again on the outside. But even if their success had been
fleeting, the mark they made was permanent, and the need they filled
would never go away. In one of the symposium papers, George Core
observed:

> There is a constant need for men of letters who can mediate between the
> academy, the reading public, and the literary estate; men who can practice
> criticism with enough ease and authority that one can suspend his disbelief
> in the artifice and artificiality of art and in the subordinate critical enter-
> prise that art—especially literature—necessitates. The job is perpetual, and
> the augean stable needs to be cleaned out at least once every generation.
> That is our present plight. In such circumstances we might well wish that
> the Agrarians were starting over." (Core, "Agrarianism," 139).

IV

On March 29, 1977, Red Warren wrote the following urgent message to
Cleanth: "LISTEN! We've just heard an awful rumor that you are selling
your place here. Is that true? You simply can't upset us that way. It is not
Christian. It is not even Episcopalian. It's not human."[10] Although the
rumor Red had heard was premature, Cleanth and Tinkum had indeed
decided that the time was fast approaching for them to sell the property
at Northford that had been their home for over twenty-five years. Until
the move to Northford, Cleanth had never lived under one roof for more
than a few years at a time. His early childhood was spent in one Methodist
parsonage after another; that was followed by his student days at Mc-

Tyeire, Vanderbilt, Tulane, and Oxford. Even in Baton Rouge, he had lived in several different residences. Northford finally became the home he had never had, a place to put down roots and grow old. Unfortunately, growing old carries with it some liabilities.

At first, hiring and training the local teenagers to perform occasional chores around the place had been no great task. But as Cleanth and Tinkum became less capable of looking after the property themselves, they became more dependent on young people who had other interests and more lucrative ways of making spending money. The remoteness of the location, which had once been part of its charm, started to become a drawback. Cleanth's eyesight had deteriorated to the point where he could no longer drive. Tinkum wondered what would happen if she suddenly took ill. In New Haven, they could call an ambulance and give an easily recognized address; at Northford, they would have to tell the medical dispatcher how to navigate country roads ten miles out of town. A sense of the isolation of the rural winters can be gleaned from a letter that Cleanth sent to Hodding Carter less than a year after his return from London. "Tonight Tinkum and I are snowbound indeed," he wrote on February 8, 1967. "A real blizzard has whipped around the house all day, piling up the drifts, and thoroughly blocking our long lane of some quarter of a mile that leads to the highway. Fortunately, I did not have a class today and I am trusting that the man who has promised to plow us out will get here sometime between now and morning so that I can take my nine o'clock class."

After leaving Northford, the Brookses made the mistake of thinking that they would be happy living in a condominium. Even though they got rid of a lot of personal property (Cleanth gave the bulk of his library to the University of Southern Mississippi), they felt crowded and confined in an apartment. So, in September 1981, they moved into a two-and-a-half-story house at 70 Ogden Street, a couple of miles west of the Yale campus. On the first floor, the house had a kitchen, dining room, parlor, study, half-bath, and screened-in porch. The second floor had four bedrooms (one of which was turned into a second study) and two bathrooms; the half-floor attic room also had its own bath and could accommodate a houseguest. In addition to a utility room, the basement had a large area that could easily be turned into a recreation room. Although the house had a small backyard and only a stoop in front, a second-floor patio opened off the master bedroom. There was considerably more living space than at Northford, and a large family could have occupied the house with relative ease. In a letter dated August 25, 1982, Cleanth wrote to Red: "Our house on Ogden Street has proved to be a good summer house. . . . The big screened porch has been delightful and the attic, with windows open along the attic door swung wide, have kept the warm air pushed out of the house. Accordingly, we haven't had any of the window air conditioners that we inherited with the house reinstalled. I'm happy not to be bothered with them."

Some southern acquaintances who were surprised that the Brookses remained in Connecticut after Cleanth's retirement found it even harder to understand why Cleanth and Tinkum did not move South after they sold Northford. The reason was simple. Over a period of more than thirty years, the Brookses had acquired more close friends around New Haven than in any single city in the South. No doubt, some southern chauvinists looked upon Cleanth's service at Yale in much the same way as the southern aristocrats in *All the King's Men* looked upon Jack Burden's employment with Willie Stark—he might be gaining wealth and fame working for the enemy but his heart was really with them. It is true that Cleanth and Tinkum never lost their southern accents and many of their southern loyalties. In this regard, their "southernness" may have been more pronounced than that of people who stayed in the Sunbelt and became homogenized along with it. The solution to their biregionalism seemed to be to maintain residency in New Haven while traveling in the South (and elsewhere) as much as possible. Cleanth's being in constant demand as a guest professor and lecturer didn't hurt matters any.

In a manner of speaking, Cleanth began his career as a gypsy scholar when he taught summer school at the University of Texas in 1940. Even after he got to Yale, he did guest stints at the University of Southern California, the Kenyon and Indiana schools of English, and elsewhere. He had sabbatical leaves, a Guggenheim grant for his Faulkner book, and two years of unpaid leave to serve as cultural attaché in London. When he decided several years in advance that he would retire in 1975, he took advantage of a university policy that allowed him to teach half-years during his final three years of service. During the semesters he was not on campus, he was able to teach at other universities. This peripatetic existence continued for nearly a decade after his retirement. During this time, he taught twice at the University of Tennessee, twice at the University of North Carolina, once at Tulane, and once at Millsaps College in Jackson, Mississippi. He also held research fellowships at the University of South Carolina and at the Humanities Center in Research Triangle Park, North

Carolina. To paraphrase the title of Red Warren's final novel, Cleanth was increasingly finding the South a place to come to.

v

A little over a month before the Agrarian symposium in 1980, Cleanth and Tinkum's old friend Katherine Anne Porter died at the age of ninety. Although they had not been neighbors for many years, the Brookses remained fond of Katherine Anne, forgiving her her various foibles as one would forgive a child. Cleanth was happy to see her attain both fame and fortune (if not critical acclaim) with the belated publication of her novel *Ship of Fools* in 1962. When a stern moralist reminded her that the best things in life cannot be purchased with money, Katherine Anne replied that she had already had those things, but now she wanted the things that money *could* buy.

In the years before she was confined to a nursing home, she maintained two adjoining apartments in College Park, Maryland. Although Cleanth and Tinkum never spent a night in the guest apartment, they tried to stop in and see Katherine Anne whenever they were in town. If it were lunchtime, she insisted on cooking for them despite her advancing age and failing eyesight (Cleanth and Tinkum would hold their breath as Katherine Anne carried hot pans off the stove). One time when they arrived for a scheduled visit, the maid announced on the intercom that Miss Porter was unavailable. When they were unable to convince the maid that they were old friends who were expected, Cleanth and Tinkum finally drove on. Weeks later, they received a letter from Katherine Anne. "Darlings," she explained, "I forgot that I had promised to give a talk that afternoon. I simply panicked. Please forgive me." To the end, Katherine Anne was one of the most charming and irresponsible women the Brookses had ever known.

If Cleanth could make excuses for Katherine Anne and other eccentric friends, he was far harder on himself. Although he realized that he was accepting more speaking commitments than he needed to, he felt honorbound to show up wherever and whenever he said he would. Once during a guest semester at LSU, he appeared for a public lecture looking as if he belonged in a hospital bed. Although he tried gamely to give his talk, he realized halfway through that he could not continue. Fortunately, Don Moore, an LSU professor, agreed to read the remainder of the text. Rather than immediately retire to his sickbed, Cleanth stayed in the auditorium until the talk was over. As a result, he was laid up with the flu for the next couple of weeks.

As the Modern Language Association became increasingly radicalized from the late sixties on, Cleanth began to feel more at home at the annual meetings of the South Atlantic Modern Language Association (SAMLA). For as long as anyone can remember, SAMLA has been the largest and most active of the regional modern language groups. Not only are its conventions well attended by professors teaching at universities within the region, but faculty from across the country who earned degrees from one of the SAMLA schools regard these gatherings in early November as a kind of homecoming. This is especially true when the meeting is in Atlanta (in alternate years, when the convention is held in some other regional city, it is generally not as well attended). With his old school ties to Vanderbilt and LSU and his more recent guest appointments in various southeastern schools, Cleanth became a kind of renaturalized southerner. After the first two days of scholarly sessions—on Thursday and Friday—many departments host parties or cash bars during the cocktail hour. Then the conferees (sometimes in groups of six or eight or even larger) proceed to dinner. During the time that Cleanth regularly attended SAMLA, his most frequent Friday evening dinner companions were Louis Rubin of Chapel Hill, Lewis Simpson of LSU, George Core of the *Sewanee Review*, and Walter Sullivan of Vanderbilt.

Louis Rubin believes that Cleanth became more consciously southern the longer he lived in the North. The alternatives were either to renounce his heritage or to embrace it more ardently. As an exile, he did not have the luxury of simply taking his home region for granted. Because his students and colleagues were predominantly from the North, their impressions of the South were largely derived from Erskine Caldwell, Margaret Mitchell, W. J. Cash, and the evening news. New Haven may not have been the most hospitable ground on which to take one's stand for southern culture, but that made it all the more imperative to do so. The annual trips to SAMLA helped Cleanth revalidate his identity as a southerner. They also kept him in touch with southern reality rather than with the myths that all too often sustain the patriot in his exile.

One of his most notable appearances in the South came in April 1984 when Cleanth became the twenty-eighth distinguished scholar to deliver the annual Dorothy Blount Lamar lecture at Mercer University in Macon, Georgia. This series had been established nearly three decades earlier "to provide lectures of the very highest type of scholarship which will aid in

the permanent preservation of southern culture, history, and literature."
The first lecturer, in 1957, had been Donald Davidson, whose discussion
of southern writers in the modern world helped call attention to the regional artist in his own land. (The emergence of southern literature as an
academic discipline was a product of the fifties and sixties.) In 1975 Walter Sullivan had used this forum to declare a requiem for the Southern
Renascence, while in 1981 T. D. Young had celebrated the continuing
relevance of the Agrarian vision. Given this tradition, one might have expected Cleanth to speak on southern poetry or criticism. Instead, he returned to the topic of his first book and an enthusiasm he had never really
abandoned—the language of the American South.

That an identifiable Southern idiom had survived the homogenizing effects of the mass media gave Cleanth cause for optimism. When even the
Europeanized intellectual Walker Percy maintained an ear for the inflec-
tions of southern speech (particularly for the locutions of an aristocrat
such as Binx Bolling's aunt in *The Moviegoer*), the language of the South
clearly had staying power. In his final lecture, Cleanth identified the greatest threat to the continuing idiom: "It is not education properly understood but miseducation: foolishly incorrect theories of what constitutes
good English, an insistence on spelling pronunciations, and the propaga-
tion of bureaucratese, sociologese, and psychologese, which American
business, politics, and academies seem to exude as a matter of course. The
grave faults are not the occasional use of *ain't* but the bastard concoctions
from a Latinized vocabulary produced by people who never studied
Latin" (*Language*, 53). As he had observed over two decades before,
"the dying flesh of language may produce a spiritual gangrene" (*Shaping
Joy*, 16).

Even if he was not giving a lecture or serving on a panel, Cleanth was
constantly being sought out by graduate students and young scholars,
who wanted to quote him on whatever project was engaging their attention at the moment. Louis Rubin remembers socializing with Cleanth one
afternoon when they were accosted by a graduate student who wanted to
discuss the current place of Erskine Caldwell in southern literature. Rubin
felt it was too late in the afternoon to take up such a dreary topic; Cleanth,
however, offered his point of view with great patience and generosity. On
many other occasions, Cleanth would return to his hotel after a late dinner, notice that it was already past midnight, and decide to turn in so that
he would be alert for a 7:30 breakfast appointment with a total stranger.[11]

In addition to being an extraordinarily gracious man, Cleanth simply loved to talk; because he was also a good listener, no one ever accused him of being garrulous or self-indulgent. Lewis Simpson remembers flying back to Boston with Cleanth from a southern literature conference in Portland, Maine, in 1978. Cleanth was delighted that the two would have a layover of several hours before catching their connecting flights. In fact, Cleanth even tried to get Simpson to change his flight so that he could spend the weekend at Northford. "Think of all the talk we could get in over the weekend," he said, beaming at the prospect. Not being up for such a marathon, Lewis declined.

Four years before, in 1974, Simpson, Cleanth, and Louis Rubin had attended a Faulkner symposium at the University of Alabama. After a full day of papers and discussion, the three had joined other conferees for a reception at a local country club. If Rubin and Simpson counted on grabbing a couple of drinks and then heading back to the hotel, they would soon be disappointed. As the young Faulknerians gathered around Cleanth, he proceeded to hold court; with someone always willing to replenish his drink, he was able to field questions nonstop for well over an hour. "How does he do it?" Simpson asked. "That's what they teach you at Vanderbilt," Rubin replied.[12]

In a letter to Red Warren, dated December 3, 1980, Cleanth reports that after the Agrarian symposium in Nashville, he and Tinkum had spent four days at SAMLA "mostly dining, lunching, drinking, and chatting with old friends." He spent most of the following week getting in and out of a hospital, where he was treated for an incipient hernia; from there, he returned to his research at the National Humanities Center in North Carolina. Describing his day to Red, he writes: "It's just as well that Tinkie had me outfitted in blue shirts, for I am working a blue collar's hours these days. I rise at 6:20 a.m., catch the van at 8:15; and take the returning van at 5:00 p.m. When I get home at 5:30, I am ready for a drink, the newspaper, the 7:00 TV news, and nothing much else."

One of Cleanth's fellow passengers on the van from his apartment complex to the center was the director of the enterprise, a young philosopher named William Bennett. Although both he and Cleanth were nominal Democrats, Bill Bennett was far more favorably inclined toward the newly elected Republican president, Ronald Reagan. Through friendly political banter and serious discussion of issues on which they both agreed, Bennett and Cleanth developed a respect for each other (Bill would occasionally ask Cleanth to read and comment on speeches he was scheduled to deliver before various audiences). Not long thereafter, when Reagan had to ap-

point a new director of the National Endowment for the Humanities, a
bitter battle ensued between supporters of Bill Bennett and those backing
another of Cleanth's friends, Mel Bradford of the University of Dallas.[13]
Bennett got the nod and went on to become a significant political figure,
serving as secretary of education under Reagan and drug czar under
George Bush.

Cleanth's cordial relations with various Republicans failed to mitigate
his general dislike for the breed. One of Paul Blanchard's most vivid
memories of his uncle came in 1974 when Gerald Ford had just assumed
the presidency after the resignation of Richard Nixon. Outside of the political community in Washington, little was known about Ford other than
that he had been in Congress almost his entire adult life and had played
football at the University of Michigan. When a group of people began
speculating on the sort of president Ford would make, Cleanth said, "I'll
show you what Gerald Ford is good for." He then jumped up, crouched
in a four-point stance, and began shouting "hut, hut, hut," as if he were
centering a football. This display was memorable not because it was particularly clever or particularly original, but because it was so out of character for the ordinarily proper and reserved Professor Brooks.[14]

As much as Cleanth abhorred the damage that radical politics had done
to the academy, he never became a conservative ideologue. (After partici-
pating in a symposium sponsored by the Partisan Review, he observed,
only half in jest, that PR was now to his right.) True to his Agrarian roots,
he remained an environmentalist. Also, as a small town boy who had
spent his adult life in academia, he never lost his native distrust of big
business. He saw a modified welfare state as the only humane way of dealing with America's underclass. To his mind, Reagan and Bush were fiscal
profligates who ran up the national debt while ignoring the nation's long-
term social and economic problems. Never much of a Cold Warrior,
Cleanth did not even give the Republicans credit for the fall of Communism, which he saw as largely the consequence of the Soviet system's own
excesses. With the exception of voting for Norman Thomas for president
in 1948, he quietly pulled the Democratic lever over the years, while partisans of both the far Left and the far Right erroneously pigeonholed him
as a southern reactionary. If his support for the Democratic nominee had
often been lukewarm, Cleanth enthusiastically backed his fellow southern
"moderate" Bill Clinton in 1992.

Cleanth's disdain for the national Republican Party had become particularly intense because of the experience of his good friend Ben C. Tole-

dano two decades earlier. Toledano was, for many years, a lawyer and politician in New Orleans; he was also a book collector and an ardent devotee of southern literature. (He named his daughter Cleanth Brooks Toledano.) Cleanth first met Walker Percy in Toledano's home in the early 1960s, and he always made it a point to spend time with Ben C. and his wife, Roulhac, whenever he was in town. After making a surprisingly strong run against the Democratic machine in a race for mayor of New Orleans, Toledano was encouraged to run for the U.S. Senate in 1972. In an abrupt change of strategy that came out only as the Watergate case began to unravel, the Nixon administration decided not to help any Republican candidate running against a southern Democrat who had supported the war in Vietnam. As a result, Ben C. Toledano and several other Republican candidates went down to humiliating defeat.

As he was traveling through the South, Cleanth occasionally crossed paths with even older friends. While serving as the Andrew W. Mellon Professor of the Humanities at Tulane in 1976, he picked up his phone one evening to hear a familiar voice on the other end. Without even bothering to say "hello," his caller blurted out: "Cleanth, did you ever notice how all of the stories in Joyce's *Dubliners* come from the *Metamorphoses*?" It was Marshall McLuhan. Despite having become an international celebrity in the sixties, Marshall was still something of the wide-eyed country boy from Canada trying to impress the southern critics he admired so.

A few years later, during one of his stints at the University of Tennessee, Cleanth entertained the visiting Margaret Wimsatt. Thinking that this proper New England lady might enjoy meeting such an unreconstructed southerner as Andrew Lytle, he took her to Monteagle to call on Andrew in the log cabin that has been in his family since before the turn of the century. At one point in the evening, Margaret asked about an oil painting on the wall. "That was my great-aunt," Andrew replied. "She died a maiden lady. Told the undertaker to inscribe on her tombstone—'Returned to the great post office, unopened.' "

VI

Although she never published an essay, delivered a lecture, or expressed herself publicly on the great issues of the day, Tinkum Brooks was a forceful presence in the literary world. For over fifty years she helped to make her husband what he was. No doubt Cleanth would have been an important critic had he never met her, but he would have been a different man. (One need only compare Red Warren's two marriages to see what a difference a writer's domestic circumstances can have on his life and work.) Two years after her death, Robert B. Heilman wrote of Tinkum:

> Her sharpness of observation came across in candor and tartness. She could be plain and direct, or wry, or ironic. Though she could be sardonic, she was never bitter. Obviously she and Cleanth shared fundamental feelings and ideas, shared the ideas that people live on. But she had, at least now and then, a somewhat different perspective. Hence they could disagree overtly, and occasionally did. But the big thing here was the openness and ease, the essential urbanity and civilizedness, of expressed differences and challenges. It was rather a lesson to those of us who tended to withhold disagreement lest it lead to disagreeableness. Cleanth could say, "Tinkum, you're not being fair," or "Tinkum you're missing the point," and Tinkum could say, "Cleanth, don't be stuffy"—sharply, on both sides, yet without discomfiting cantankerousness, or awkward confrontation. It was simply a fundamental amiable candor, a direct counter-criticalness, allowed by a basic compatibility of thought and feeling. (Heilman, 101)

Whenever people referred to Tinkum's plainspokenness, they were apt to be thinking of a clever put-down or witty observation. At times, however, her candor allowed her to bestow praise that more circumspect people might withhold. Once, in the midst of an evening's conversation involving herself and Cleanth, Monroe and Betty Spears, and an Episcopal priest from Tennessee, Tinkum suddenly said, "Monroe, say some poetry." Although Monroe knew reams of poetry from Matthew Prior to W. H. Auden, he was caught so off-guard that he drew a temporary blank. Then, reverting to his South Carolina roots, he began reciting one of the anonymous battle songs of the Confederacy, concluding with these rousing lines: "And when our rights were threatened, the cry rose near and far: / Hurrah for the bonnie blue flag that bears a single star!" "What did I tell you?" Tinkum proclaimed. "Doesn't he have the most beautiful speaking voice you ever heard?"[15]

Like all couples who have stayed married for most of their lives, Cleanth and Tinkum maintained certain tacit understandings. One of these was that she could continue smoking so long as she did it out of his presence. Cleanth himself had been a heavy cigarette smoker up through the mid-1950s. Then one night, when he was working late on the history of literary criticism he was writing with Bill Wimsatt, he noticed that he was out of cigarettes. He started for his car, intending to drive to an all-night convenience store and buy a new pack, when he realized that his addiction was a bit absurd. At that point, he quit cold and never smoked again.

Tinkum, however, lacked either the desire or the will to quit. Cleanth's former student and literary executor, John Michael Walsh, remembers a party in the Ogden Street house, when Tinkum came out to the screened-in porch to sneak a cigarette. Walsh, who had previously seen her only in Cleanth's presence, was surprised to see Tinkum light up. He was even more surprised to see her stub the cigarette out the minute Cleanth called her from his post in the living room. Another time, when Tinkum drove Walsh to the train station in New Haven, she borrowed a cigarette from him. "All this time I've known you, and I never knew you smoked," Walsh said. "Cleanth doesn't like it in a woman," Tinkum replied.[16]

When Tinkum became the family chauffeur after Cleanth's vision deteriorated beyond the limits of safe driving, tales of her own exploits behind the wheel began to proliferate. Passengers in her car would be amused by Tinkum's anger whenever she saw the highway patrol stop a motorist for speeding, even as Cleanth admonished her that the policeman was only doing his job. Tinkum herself had a heavy foot on the accelerator but could usually talk her way out of a ticket. On one occasion, she slowed down when she saw a patrol car but speeded back up when it left the interstate. At the next entrance ramp, the same cop came back on the road and pulled her over. After a minute or so of Tinkum's distressed southern belle routine, he let her go with a warning.

Back when Cleanth had his license, he was a slower and more cautious driver than his wife, but riding on the same road with him could still be an adventure. Louis Rubin remembers the time when he and William Styron and Red Warren tried to follow Cleanth to a radio station to make some tapes for the Voice of America. Cleanth, with his thick spectacles and faulty peripheral vision, was driving a Volkswagen bug, whose license plate said "TINKUM." To the consternation of other motorists, he kept making left turns from the extreme right lane. The best of drivers would have had a difficult time following him. And Red Warren was far from the best of drivers. In addition to having only one eye, Red insisted on turning his head to look directly at whomever he was talking to. After they made it to the radio station without harm, Rubin, Styron, and Warren were soon doing a taped interview for worldwide consumption. Although Cleanth's turn would come, it was all he could do to restrain himself from joining in the interview at hand. He kept leaning closer and closer to pick up the conversation. Had he leaned any farther, his chair would have toppled over.[17]

When they went to SAMLA, Cleanth and Tinkum wisely parked their car in the hotel garage and left the driving to the cabbies of Atlanta (even those cabbies sometimes had difficulty finding the obscure restaurants where George Core would make dinner reservations). After the conviviality of eating, drinking, and talking with old friends had run its course, Cleanth and Tinkum would shut the world out and ride back to the hotel as if they were alone. On one such evening, Lewis Simpson, who was riding in the front seat of the cab, heard something that sounded like poetry coming from the back. Glancing in the rearview mirror, he noticed that Cleanth had his arm around Tinkum and was speaking love poems in her ear. She tried to seem annoyed but was actually relishing the attention from her old beau.[18] For the rest of the cab ride, it was 1929. They were back in New Orleans, and the young poet from Tulane was again wooing the girl with the comic strip name.

CHAPTER TWENTY

Claiming Criticism

The arrival of Cleanth Brooks at Yale in 1947 solidified a radical change in direction for the English department. The historical scholarship that had dominated the program for as long as anyone could remember remained strong, but it no longer defined the shape of literary study at Yale. Throughout the fifties and much of the sixties, the new criticism enjoyed a preeminence in New Haven that it was starting to lose elsewhere in academia. If Cleanth was the brightest star in this firmament, additional light was shed by Maynard Mack, Louis Martz, and Bill Wimsatt, along with René Wellek in Comparative Literature. (Red Warren also taught in the School of Drama from 1950 to 1957 and in the English department from 1961 to 1973.) But just as the aesthetic formalists had supplanted the old historicists after World War II, newer and more radical theoreticians began to challenge the hegemony of the new critics in New Haven by the end of the 1960s. Not only were the Yale graduates Donald Hirsch and Stanley Fish spreading apostasy from their posts at Virginia and Berkeley, but the very term *Yale critic* was starting to mean something very different from what it had when Wimsatt, Brooks, and company exemplified the species.

By 1972, Harold Bloom, Geoffrey Hartman, J. Hillis Miller, and Paul de Man were all teaching literature at Yale. Although each pursued a somewhat different approach to criticism, all were identified with a revolutionary European movement called "deconstruction." If there was a specific moment when deconstruction arrived in America, it was probably during a literary symposium at Johns Hopkins in October 1966, when the French critic Jacques Derrida gave his first American lectures. Although the precise nature of deconstruction has been the subject of considerable debate in the three decades since the Johns Hopkins symposium, what seems inarguable is that deconstruction, like the new criticism before it, became for a time the touchstone against which other critical approaches defined themselves. According to Frank Lentricchia: "The traditional historicists, the Chicago neo-Aristotelians, the specialists in American literature, the Stanford moralists, the myth critics of the Frye type, old-line Freudians, critics of consciousness (such as were left), the budding structuralists, and the grandchildren of the New Critics now gathered under the umbrella of Murray Krieger's contextualism—all have found themselves united against a common enemy in a Traditionalism which, though imposed upon them by Derridean polemic, has seemed to suit these strange bedfellows just fine" (Lentricchia, 159–160).

Bloom, Hartman, Miller, and de Man seemed to encourage the literary world to identify them as a new school of Yale critics by publishing a volume entitled *Deconstruction and Criticism* in 1979. This book featured essays by the so-called gang of four and by Derrida himself. This was clearly the high point of group activity, however. While the personal ties among the four remained strong, they increasingly staked out positions different from each other. Only de Man (who died in 1983) and Miller (who left Yale for the University of California at Irvine in 1986) continued to think of themselves as deconstructionists. Hartman (who is a man of considerable wit) has referred to his colleagues as "boa-deconstructors," while Bloom has tried to distance himself from the movement (he even quipped that the title *Deconstruction and Criticism* was his own "personal joke, which no one can ever understand: I meant that those four were deconstruction, and I was criticism"; see Lehman, 148).

Although Geoffrey Hartman aligned himself politically with the newer generation of Yale critics, he actually wanted to reverse the emphasis on interpretation that had characterized new critical and deconstructive discourse. In the title essay of his book *Beyond Formalism* (1970), Hartman chides the new critics for being too concerned with the interpretation of language and not enough with the human reality behind the text. He begins by citing F. W. Bateson's attack on the "Yale formalism" of Wimsatt, Wellek, and Brooks: "Bateson defined *formalism* as a tendency to isolate the aesthetic fact from its human content, but I will here define it simply as a method: that of revealing the human content of art by a study of its formal properties" (Hartman, 42). As valuable as that enterprise might be, Hartman wanted to move beyond it. "Taking his lead from ancient scriptural interpreters," writes Vincent B. Leitch, "Hartman wanted to move criticism from text and theme to life-world and vision—from philology to philosophy and hermeneutics, from formalist exegesis to phenomenological and anagogical criticism" (Leitch, 164). Just so that there would be no mistake about what he was endorsing, Hartman concludes "Beyond Formalism" with the following rhetorical flourish:

> The dominion of Exegesis is great: she is our Whore of Babylon, sitting robed in Academic black on the great dragon of Criticism, and dispensing a repetitive and soporific balm from her pedantic cup. If our neo-scriptural activity of explication were as daring and conscious as it used to be when Bible texts had to be harmonized with strange or contrary experience, i.e., with history, no one could level this charge of puerility. . . . To redeem the word from the superstition of the word is to humanize it, to make it participate once more in a living concert of voices, and to raise exegesis to its former state by confronting art with experience as searchingly as if art were scripture. (Hartman, 56, 57)

Just as René Wellek, from his position in Comparative Lit, offered support to an earlier generation of new critics at Yale, Paul de Man soon became the acknowledged leader of the deconstructionists, godfather of what William Pritchard called Yale's "hermeneutical Mafia." With his urbanity and sophistication, de Man struck all who knew him as the very flower of European civilization. Were one to make "a movie of de Man's life as conceived at the time of his death," writes David Lehman, "it would have been an American success story, another chapter in the twentieth-century saga of European intellectuals who fled their bloodied native ground and flourished on American soil" (Lehman, 151–52).

If de Man was the major theoretician of deconstruction at Yale, J. Hillis Miller was the movement's most vocal advocate. The son of a Baptist minister from Newport News, Virginia, Miller had been a thoroughly conventional scholar and critic prior to his arrival at Yale in 1972. Under the influence of de Man, however, he soon began repudiating (or perhaps deconstructing) his earlier allegiance to the criticism of consciousness, an approach to literature that placed great stress on authorial intention. When Cleanth Brooks retired in 1975, the direction of literary study at Yale had shifted to the point where Joseph Hillis Miller was named the new Gray Professor of Rhetoric.

I

For all of the controversy generated by deconstruction, the concept remains elusive. Because deconstruction depends on a structuralist notion of linguistics, it has sometimes been called "poststructuralism" (although, properly speaking, poststructuralism includes any and all approaches developed after structuralism.) Like the structural linguists, Derrida and his fellow deconstructionists reject the mimetic notion of language. Subscribing to the position of Ferdinand de Saussure, they see language as an arbitrary and conventional system of signs that bears no necessary relationship to an external reality. If I. A. Richards denied the referentiality of literary language, the deconstructionists have taken the next step and denied the referentiality of all language. When we analyze a text, it is to discover how language works rather than to discern some objective truth about the world.

Because of its extreme relativism, deconstruction presents itself not as a philosophy but as a strategy for reading. Where the new critics thought that a text often transcended authorial intention, the deconstructionists believe that that is always the case. The author may attempt to communicate a message, but language always speaks with a tongue of its own. It is the function of the critic to decipher that tongue, and the only limit he faces is that of his own ingenuity. When the new critics argued that context determined meaning, they were thinking of the context of a clearly delineated text. For the deconstructionists, all of language—not just the words of a particular poem or novel—constitutes the relevant context. For that reason, the pun and other sorts of wordplay are familiar features of deconstructive writing. Because potential meanings exist within the text irrespective of the author's intention, the reader who is clever enough to discover a variety of meanings is every bit as creative as the original author. If the new critics think of the poem as a verbal icon, the deconstructionists are iconoclasts. When Marc Wortman published an article on the conflict between the deconstructionists and the new critics in the December 1990 issue of the *Yale Alumni Magazine*, he entitled it, quite appropriately, "Shattering the Urn."

According to J. Hillis Miller, the opposition is essentially between a metaphysical and an antimetaphysical approach to criticism. By metaphysical, he means

> the system of assumptions coming down from Plato and Aristotle which
> has unified our culture. This system includes the notions of beginning, con-
> tinuity, and end, of causality, of dialectical process, of organic unity, and
> of ground, in short of logos in all its many senses. A metaphysical method
> of literary study assumes that literature is in one way or another referen-
> tial, in one way or another grounded in something outside language. This
> something may be physical objects, or "society," or the economic realities

of labor, valuation, and exchange. It may be consciousness, the Cogito, or the unconscious, or absolute spirit, or God. (Miller, 100–101)

In contrast, "an anti-metaphysical or 'deconstructive' form of literary study attempts to show that in a given work of literature, in a different way in each case, metaphysical assumptions are both present and at the same time undermined by the text itself. They are undermined by some figurative play within the text which forbids it to be read as an 'organic unity' organized around some version of the logos. The play of tropes leaves an inassimilable residue or remnant of meaning, an unearned increment, so to speak, making a movement of sense beyond any unifying boundaries" (101).

In terms of reading literature rather than merely theorizing about it, the central issue involves the autonomy and closure of a given text. The deconstructionist critic Jonathan Culler tackles this issue in a direct assault on Brooks's reading of Donne's "The Canonization" and the concept of poetry it implies. "For New Criticism," Culler writes, "an important feature of a good poem's organic unity was its embodiment or dramatization of the positions it asserts. By enacting or performing what it asserts or describes, the poem becomes complete in itself, accounts for itself, and stands free as a self-contained fusion of being and doing" (Culler, 200–201). Culler readily admits to the existence of paradox and self-referentiality in poetry, but, unlike Brooks, he sees these elements as impediments to closure and unity. (In this regard, he seems to be echoing Ransom's objection to the note of irresolution that paradox introduces into a poem.) To put the matter succinctly, a poem can never completely refer to itself because that reference then becomes a part of the poem. Total self-consciousness and self-possession are no more possible in art than in life.

In his discussion of "The Canonization," Brooks had asserted that "the poem itself is the well-wrought urn which can hold the lovers' ashes." Culler argues that

> if this is so, if the poem is the urn, then one of the principal features of this urn is that it portrays people responding to the urn. If the urn or hymn is the poem itself, then the predicted response to the hymn is a response to the representation of a response to the hymn. This is confirmed by the fact that by far the most hymnlike element of the poem is the invocation of the lovers by those who have heard the hymn or verse legend of their love. The earlier stanzas of the poem, in which the lover argues, as Brooks says, that "their love, however absurd it may appear to the world, does no harm to

> the world," can scarcely qualify as a hymn; so if the poem refers to itself as
> a hymn it is including within itself its depiction of the hymnlike response—
> the response to the hymn it claims to be. (Culler, 203–4)

By resisting closure, the poem reaches beyond itself to include the critical responses it elicits within its total frame of reference. As Culler puts it: "In celebrating itself as urn the poem incorporates a celebration of the urn and thus becomes something other than the urn; and if the urn is taken to include the response to the urn, then the response it anticipates, such as Brooks's, becomes a part of it and prevent it from closing. Self-reference does not close in upon itself but leads to a proliferation of representations, a series of invocations and urns, including Brooks's *The Well Wrought Urn*" (204).

One can scarcely quarrel with Culler's logic, although the point he is making is less profound than it might seem. I doubt that Brooks or any other new critic would argue that complete autonomy or closure is possible in any literary text (such qualities are probably not to be found outside of theoretical mathematics). The connotations of poetic language—what Ransom called the "irrelevant local texture"—are always resisting the logical and denotative structure of the text. To achieve even an approximate balance and unity is a minor miracle. When Brooks says of "The Canonization" that it "is an instance of the doctrine that it asserts," he is speaking metaphorically rather than establishing a logical equivalence. As with all metaphors or analogies, there are elements that resist comparison. Donne's poem is not completely an instance of the doctrine it asserts any more than the two lovers in the poem are *in all respects* identical with two canonized saints. Had Brooks simply said that "The Canonization" *helps to illustrate* the doctrine it asserts, he would have made essentially the same point without leaving himself open to Culler's deconstructive hairsplitting.

At first glance, the differences between the new critics and the deconstructionists may seem to be only ones of degree. But that is like saying that the difference between conjugal love and promiscuity is only one of degree. The major new critics courted philosophical untidiness at least in part because they could sense what was at the end of the slippery slope. Even as they argued for the relativity of textual meaning, they never doubted that meaning was an objective quality of the real world. They believed that connotations enriched language without obliterating denotations. They could argue against a moralistic reading of literature precisely because their own sense of moral certitude was so strong. They could step out of the confines of historical and cultural determinism because they believed that history and culture would be waiting for them when they got back. For the new critics, the values of Western civilization were so palpable that they could afford to take those values for granted. It is the pride of the deconstructionists that they take nothing for granted. The new critics warned us against confronting complex works of literature in a spirit of naive realism. The deconstructionists hold that any belief in reality is necessarily naive.

At its best, deconstruction can open up possibilities of textual meaning that timid or conventional readers might be reluctant to entertain (the first reader to intuit that Satan was the real hero of *Paradise Lost* was functioning as a deconstructionist). At its worst, the movement is an affront to both literature and criticism. For all their caution about the intentionalist fallacy, the new critics never doubted that literature was largely a product of the creative intelligence. Many were themselves poets, and all revered the creative calling. The deconstructionists deny the qualitative distinctions between great literature and other written texts. Whatever dizzying feats of interpretation they can manage, they are prevented on principle from rendering an aesthetic judgment. Moreover, the very usefulness of their interpretations is constantly undercut by an impenetrable jargon that is finally as contemptuous of the reader as it is of the creator of the text they are explicating.

II

Like the prodigies of earlier generations, Harold Bloom stayed on at Yale after receiving his doctorate and worked his way from instructor to full professor over the course of two decades. During the sixties and seventies, he helped rehabilitate the Romantics, including his beloved Shelley, who had taken such a beating from the new critics. Bloom championed the neo-Romantic Wallace Stevens and lauded the later, more open, poetry of Red Warren. His psychobiographical meditation *The Anxiety of Influence* became a controversial classic almost overnight in 1973. "As a teacher," Colin Campbell writes, Bloom is "known as sage, genius and comic rolled into one—Zarathustra cum Zero Mostel" (Campbell, 26). Possessing almost total recall, he can dazzle party goers by reciting *Paradise Regained* verbatim. As his fame grew, Bloom broke with the English department and became a "free-floating 'professor of the Humanities'" (Campbell, 25). Always flamboyant and opinionated, Harold used to stop his former teacher and colleague on the street and say: "You are indomitable, Cleanth, you are just indomitable."

The deconstructive movement in criticism tells us very little that is useful about the critical stance of Harold Bloom. As we have already noted, his connection with that movement was more attenuated than that of Hartman, Miller, or de Man, and his reaction against the new criticism was more visceral than that of any of the other latter-day Yale critics. Frank Lentricchia puts the matter most aptly when he writes: "Ever since the publication in 1959 of his first book, Harold Bloom has been preoccupied with the task of defining a revisionist poetics against the New-Critical position associated with some of the most illustrious of his former graduate teachers at Yale. In the neo-Freudian language of his recent tetralogy on the theory of literary history, W. K. Wimsatt, Cleanth Brooks, and Robert Penn Warren are Bloom's dangerous precursors, the impossibly demanding father-figures who must be symbolically slain in an act of 'misprision,' or willful misreading" (Lentricchia, 319).

For the most part, Bloom's assault on the new criticism has been designed to rehabilitate the reputation of those Romantics whom the new critics had practically read out of the canon. What is involved here is more than a question of literary taste, as important as that may be, but finally one of metaphysics and even religion. (In 1986 Hillis Miller told Colin Campbell that he "retains the low-Protestant eye that dislikes stained glass windows and ritual. . . . It is curious, Miller says, how he and his low-Protestant tradition have run smack into the old New Criticism, whose spirit is decidedly high-Protestant and Anglo-Catholic"; see Campbell, 48.) Steeped in the literature and culture of his own Jewish heritage, Harold Bloom has championed a radically Protestant poetics in opposition to what he regards as the Anglican and Roman Catholic sensibility of the new critics.

In the introduction to the 1971 revised edition of *The Visionary Company* (his monumental study of the British Romantics), Harold Bloom unequivocally states that the conflicting traditions in English verse derive from radically different religious sensibilities. Romantic poetry, he argues, can be traced to the nonconformist vision that informed the left wing of British Puritanism. "It is no accident," he writes, "that the poets deprecated by the New Criticism were Puritans, or Protestant individualists, or men of that sort breaking away from Christianity and attempting to formulate personal religions in their poetry." Bloom sees this tradition as beginning with aspects of Spenser and Milton, reaching its apogee in the

Romantic and Victorian eras, and continuing into the twentieth century in the work of such poets as Hardy and Lawrence. In contrast, "the poets brought into favor by the New Criticism were Catholics or High Church Anglicans—Donne, Herbert, Dryden, Pope, Dr. Johnson, Hopkins in the Victorian period, Eliot and Auden in our own time. . . . What distinguishes [the two main traditions of English poetry] are not only aesthetic considerations but conscious differences in religion and politics. One line, and it is the central one, is Protestant, radical, and Miltonic-Romantic; the other is Catholic, conservative, and by its claims, classical" (Bloom, *Visionary*, xvii).

The theological differences that Bloom has identified account for differences in epistemology. Because they were heirs of the inner-light tradition of British Protestantism (however much they may have rejected church dogma), the Romantics were poets of spiritual inspiration. If Allen Tate could accuse Poe of the fallacy of angelism, the same was even more true of Shelley. The sacramental vision of the High Church party was more comfortable with concrete images that served as outward and visible signs of the inward and invisible essences the poet wished to convey. The metaphysicals and the high modernists were content to climb the ladder of analogy rather than ascend to Heaven in a mystical ecstasy. As we have seen, Eliot's notion of the dissociation of sensibility initially seemed to marginalize the most admired English verse of some 250 years. What was infinitely worse in Bloom's mind was the subsequent effort to legitimize that verse by making it compatible with a new critical, High Church sensibility. In 1959, Bloom had written: "When we have reached the stage at which Brooks can find Milton of the Minor Poems more metaphysical than Spenserian, and this for the sake of critically redeeming those poems, then it is surely time for a judicious counterattack" (Bloom, *Shelley's Mythmaking*, 149). Sounding a similar note a dozen years later, he asserts in *The Visionary Company*: "Academic criticism of literature in our time became almost an affair of church wardens; too many students for instance learned to read Milton by the dubious light of C. S. Lewis's *Preface to Paradise Lost*, in which the major Protestant poem in the language becomes an Anglo-Catholic document" (Bloom, *Visionary*, xviii).

Bloom is willing to let the "church wardens" claim the metaphysical poets of the seventeenth century, but he vehemently denies that the metaphysical school has made a comeback by way of French Symbolism. Bloom believes that American poetry in particular has been predominantly Romantic in a line that extends from Emerson through Whitman to Wallace Stevens and Hart Crane. In making this assertion, he cleverly (or shamelessly) claims the authority of one of the leading anti-Romantic critics of our time—Yvor Winters. "In an age during which a formidable array of minor poets-turned-critics convinced the academies that twentieth-century verse had somehow repudiated its immediate heritage, and mysteriously found its true parentage in the seventeenth century," Bloom writes; "in so odd and unnatural a time the voice of Winters was heard proclaiming, with perfect truth, that almost all poetry written in English since the age of sensibility, of the mid-eighteenth century, was inescapably Romantic, whatever its contrary desires." In a parting shot at his scholarly nemeses, Bloom adds: "A man who can tell us, accurately and powerfully, what he dislikes, does us a greater service than our host of church-wardenly purveyors of historical myths of decline" (Bloom, "Central Man," 25).

Other scholars, far different from Bloom, have expressed dismay at what they take to be the religious stance of some new critics. In a joint review of Ransom's *Beating the Bushes* and Brooks's *A Shaping Joy*, the self-described "secular critic" and Palestinian revolutionary Edward W. Said infers the following from the texts in question: "Poetry shares some characteristics with logical discourse, but we read poetry because if offers a more than literal organization of a more than determinate content—not because it is more true or more immediate. In other words, the New Criticism alleged that literature had almost the freedom from time and space enjoyed by prophetic utterance" (Said, 5). A bit later Said suggests that one who reads Ransom and Brooks comes away with the impression that "literature for them is primarily made by Anglo-Americans, that Yeats and T. S. Eliot exhaust what one needs to know about modern culture, and that a pastoral community of Protestant scholars is the most satisfying. Indeed, one has the impression that nothing short of religious awe will do for the study of literature. Hence, analyzing a poem is fairly similar to reliving a miracle" (5, 12).

III

In the midst of all the radical assaults on the new criticism, we are apt to forget that aesthetic formalism was itself initially a revolutionary movement in literary studies, only to be reminded of that fact whenever the new criticism is attacked on conservative grounds. This was the case not only with Donald Hirsch but also with a student of Yvor Winters named Gerald Graff.[1] Almost from the time that he earned his Ph.D. at Stanford in 1964, Graff was aggressively challenging the antirationalism of the new critics. Like his mentor, Graff believed that poetry was a mode of discourse that made statements and communicated ideas. Although it should accomplish certain ends that scientific discourse never attempted, poetry must first be intelligible and referential. Analogies to nonverbal art forms may be useful in stressing what poetry does in addition to denotation, so long as they are not taken too literally. To say that a poem should not mean but be, that it communicates only itself, or that it is an experience rather than a statement is (to use one of Winters's favorite terms) sheer "nonsense." Not only does such a position defy logic, it also proscribes some of the most admired poetry ever written.

Graff introduced his position to the literary public in 1966 in the second volume of the resurrected *Southern Review*. His essay, "Statement and Poetry," begins with a facile summary of the "anti-propositional" stance of Eliot, Richards, Tate, and Brooks. All four of these major new critics (and numerous textbook authors who have followed their lead) betray a pervasive skepticism toward logical and rational thought in poetry (except, of course, as a feature of dramatic propriety). To Graff's mind, this skepticism reveals an amusing contradiction. As conservative thinkers, many of the new critics are hostile on principle to logical positivism; however, in their approach to literature, they have implicitly "accepted and embraced the characteristically positivistic assumption that reason and logic have no part in determining values, that rational and logical norms of truth are applicable only in the realm of quantitatively measurable phenomena" (Graff, "Statement," 502). In contrast, Graff argues that "rational and discursive modes of thought are not alien to poetry":

> On the contrary, many great poems depend upon them both for content and structure. Furthermore, poems often *do* assert philosophical generalizations and mean them, and the truth or falsity of these generalizations is not irrelevant to the aesthetic value of the poems. Intellectual and moral values are essential constituents of aesthetic values, and it is only by an arbitrary gesture that one can erect rigid boundary lines between them. It is likewise arbitrary to say that poems are not propositional but dramatic. Good poems tend to be both—they state (or imply) propositions and dramatize attitudes toward those propositions at the same time. Both the stated and the dramatized elements are aesthetically important. (503)

To illustrate his point, Graff quotes and discusses Edwin Arlington Robinson's poem "Hillcrest." According to new critical doctrine, this is a bad poem, or perhaps no poem at all. Lacking a dramatic situation, it is essentially an instance of versified doctrine. Nevertheless, as Graff analyzes what the poem says and the manner in which structure and prosody reinforce statement, we are forced to concede that Robinson has achieved the sort of maturity, complexity, and coherence that the new critics demand of poetry. If these ends can be accomplished through means that the new critics deplore, it may be that the new critical conception of poetry is fundamentally wrong, or at least excessively narrow. It is one thing to censure the didacticism of Longfellow's "Psalm of Life" or the collected works of Edgar Guest; it is something else to legislate ideas out of poetry.

Graff's essay serves as a needed corrective to some of the excesses of the new criticism. On occasion, Brooks and others have made absolute statements that can be disproved by obvious exceptions. One of the best things that can be said on their behalf is that in practice they are constantly violating whatever seems most absurd or extreme in their theoretical pronouncements. Clearly, Graff has demonstrated that undramatized statement does have a place in poetry. How large a place remains open to question. One cannot help noting that "Hillcrest" is a special case, not only for poetry in general, but for its author's canon in particular. Far more typical of Robinson's most memorable work are "Richard Cory," "Miniver Cheevy," and "Mr. Flood's Party"—short dramatic poems that express a complexity of attitude not idea. To be sure, one can extract propositions from each of these poems. "Richard Cory" tells us that money can't buy happiness; "Miniver Cheevy" that decadent romanticism is an evasion of life; and "Mr. Flood's Party" that growing old is hard to do. Stated in such a way, these propositions seem trite; they also oversimplify the experience of the poem in question. It may be that the more complex the proposition, the more amenable it is to a poetry of statement. Apparent clichés, however, can be redeemed only by a dramatic context that allows us to experience them as truth rather than as truism.

In 1970 Graff published a revised version of his dissertation under the title *Poetic Statement and Critical Dogma*. The fourth chapter of that book uses the work of Cleanth Brooks to illustrate what Graff considers to be the internal inconsistencies of "new critical organicism." To say that a poem does not state but tests ideas, Graff argues, is to introduce a false contradiction that Brooks himself is unwilling to maintain in practice. An idea cannot be tested in poetry (or anywhere else) unless it is first stated, or at least implied. "Ideas, unlike physical substances, are not inert," Graff writes; "to 'test' an idea is to become committed to some intellectual point

of view which emerges from the test" (Graff, *Poetic Statement*, 91–92).
The test may make the idea more subtle and complex, but it does not
make it any less an idea. To say that a poem is less concerned with asserting the truth of an idea than with dramatizing what it feels like to hold the
idea is to invite serious difficulties. It can lead to subjectivism or to an
excessively high regard for sincerity, which is to say variations of the affective and intentionalist fallacies.

The principle of dramatic propriety is invoked by Brooks and other
new critics as a means of judging a poem solely by intrinsic standards.
Graff argues that, here again, Brooks frequently avoids in practice what
he asserts in theory. When Brooks demands that the attitude expressed by
a poem be mature, complex, inclusive, and faithful to the facts of experience, he is not excluding his personal beliefs from the act of judgment.
Graff points out that "admiration for inclusive awareness is itself an expression of a view of reality." He then quotes Morris Weitz, who had argued that "Brooks prefers the inclusive, the nonsimplification of attitudes,
because he *believes* it to be a *truer* conception of human experience than
the exclusive or sentimental simplification of attitudes" (see Graff, *Poetic
Statement*, 97). Far from quarreling with this position, Graff notes that a
slavish fidelity to dramatic propriety would allow any incoherence, sentimentality, or bathos into a poem—so long as it was "in character." (This
is what Graff's mentor Winters referred to as the "fallacy of imitative
form.") It is not Brooks's reverence for inclusiveness and maturity to
which Graff objects; it is the attempt to ground those values in a specious
notion of dramatic propriety.

The final point of new critical dogma that Graff attacks is the belief
that poetic statement transcends logic because it is expressed in the language of paradox. This position asserts too narrow a view of poetry and
too wide a view of paradox. Like most opponents of the new criticism,
Graff is unwilling to concede that paradox is the language of all poetry, or
even all good poetry, but he leaves that argument for others to make. His
major objection is to the notion that paradox in poetry somehow represents a violation of logic. Graff argues that time and again Brooks sees
examples of what Robert Graves and Laura Riding call "supra-logical
harmony," when in fact the poet is simply presenting the same entity in
different relations or different contexts.

In examining the second stanza of Wordsworth's "She Dwelt among
the Untrodden Ways," Brooks concludes: "Though Lucy, to the great
world, is as obscure as the violet, to her lover she is as fair as Venus, the

first star of evening." Graff maintains that in making this contrast Wordsworth has not violated or transcended logic: "once the implicit logical
connections between images are discovered, their unity turns out not to
be supralogical at all" (Graff, *Poetic Statement*, 106). Echoing John Crowe
Ransom, Graff argues that there can be no resolution in a poem or any
other mode of discourse "which is apprehended outside the context of
logical relationships" (108). As Ransom had argued in a critique of Brooks:
"Opposites can never be said to be resolved or reconciled merely because
they have been got into the same poem, or got into some complex of affective experience to create there a kind of 'tension.' . . . If there is a resolution
at all it must be a logical resolution. . . . When there is no resolution we
have a poem without a structural unity" (Ransom, *New Criticism*, 95).

Graff continued to expose what he regarded as the fallacies of new criticism in a short essay in the spring 1979 issue of *Critical Inquiry*. Although
this piece, entitled "New Criticism Once More," is ostensibly a response
to René Wellek's earlier essay "The New Criticism: Pro and Contra,"
Graff's argument can easily be understood on its own. His first bone of
contention has to do with the way new critics use history. For Graff, the
problem is not that the new criticism is ahistorical,[2] but that the new critics have a fully developed philosophy of history that is both anachronistic
and tendentious. Graff believes that the dissociation of sensibility is a
modern concept that Eliot and his followers have projected back into history. "The New Critics were so deeply concerned with the post-industrial
crisis of dissociation," Graff writes, "that they read this issue into every
work they encountered, including those which happened to have been
written before intellectuals had become preoccupied with it. . . . If being
historically conscious means trying to understand the past on its own
terms, then the New Critical revision of the history of English poetry . . .
was not very historically conscious, for it reinterpreted the past in terms
of modernist interests and biases" (Graff, "New Criticism," 570–71).

The second objection Graff voices is his oft-stated concern over the new
critical aversion to ideas in poetry. He believes that the new critics, like the
Romantics, have been so intimidated by the truth claims of science that
they have retreated too hastily from the notion that poetry provides any
verifiable truth about the world. They find it much safer to stay within the
text of the poem than to do battle with science over the nature of reality.
Cultural revolutionaries, phenomenologists, deconstructionists, and others share this reluctance to fighting empiricism on its own terms. The con-

sequence of this position, however, is to widen the gap that C. P. Snow discovered between the two cultures of science and the humanities and to exacerbate the dissociation of sensibility "that we all say we want to have done with" (Graff, "New Criticism," 574).

Graff's final point is one that R. S. Crane had made thirty years earlier and reiterated several times since. In asserting as a given that paradox was the language of poetry, the new critics were taking the "high priori road." As Graff puts it: "By starting out with the assumption that *all* poetry must be the 'language of paradox,' or some comparable thing, the New Critics, in effect, knew the meanings of poems before they read them" (574). This presumptive approach to literary analysis may account for some of the strained interpretations that one occasionally finds in the writing of the new critics.

In 1979, the same year as his piece in *Critical Inquiry*, Graff published *Literature Against Itself*, a collection of essays on the current state of literary study. One of his chapters, entitled "What Was New Criticism?," repeats charges made as far back as his Ph.D. dissertation. Among the fresh perspectives that it offers, however, is the notion that new criticism was doomed to inconsistency because it arose in opposition to two antithetical forces in literary culture—hedonistic impressionism and genteel moralism. In fighting the impressionists, the new critics argued that literature provided a unique kind of knowledge that was more concrete and, hence, more objective than scientific knowledge. In fighting the moralists, the new critics railed against the heresy of paraphrase and acted as if literature consisted of nonreferential objects of aesthetic contemplation. Even if they were not guilty of logical contradiction, the new critics pursued opposed emphases that seemed to pull them in different directions at once. While their belief that literature constituted a special form of knowledge smacked of an Arnoldian gnosticism that made the poet priest of a new religion, their denial of fixed meaning in texts left the door open for the cognitive anarchy of deconstruction. It was only the tact of critics such as Brooks that kept them from the extremes to which their position sometimes seemed to be tending.

Employing the totalistic rhetoric of his mentor Winters, Graff not only condemns the new critics for their own lapses but holds them accountable for the excesses of those who did not know when to stop. He casts them in the role of liberal parents who have begotten radical progeny. In a commentary on Yale criticism, past and present, Graff writes:

When the New Critics assigned literature a different "ontology" from that
of conceptual discourse, they privileged literature (while leaving its relation
to reality obscure) and deprived criticism of authority. Recent critics have
gone a step further and denied the privileged authority of *all* discourse, literary *and* conceptual, so that the New Critical opposition between literature and discursive language disappears—but only because both are cut off
from reality. Contemporary criticism has closed the gap between the literary and the nonliterary, not by returning literature to the real world but by
transforming the "real" world into a literary fiction. Literature ceases to be
alienated from the world because alienation has been made total. In all
this, the critic remains where he was—a tragic seeker for what is by definition out of reach. (Graff, "Fear and Trembling," 475)

IV

If Brooks was slow in responding to the specific attacks of the newer critical theories, he never wavered in his conviction that aesthetic formalism
provided the most nearly adequate means of interpreting and evaluating a
work of literature. Rather than simply reiterate that belief, he preferred to
demonstrate its utility with close readings of an ever wider range of texts.
This was evident in 1971 when he gathered twenty-two of his more recent
essays (most had been written in the previous decade and about half
within the preceding five years) in *A Shaping Joy*. That some of these essays take us into realms of theory and sociology is meant as a rebuke to
the caricature of the new criticism, not as an abandonment of its basic
principles. In his introduction to this volume, Brooks writes: "Though experience is ultimately a seamless garment and everything is related to everything else, the form of the achieved work is properly distinguished from
the process that went into its making and from the effects that it produces
on a particular reader or company of readers. Studies of the creative process and socio-psychological reports on reader response do have their own
interest and they are valid literary studies. But it is the examination of the
work itself that seems to me to have the best claim to be called a specifically 'literary' criticism" (*Shaping Joy*, xv).

Having stated this principle, Brooks vacates the critical office long
enough to devote his first essay to a consideration of the uses of literature.
Countering the affective approach to criticism, he argues that it is not primarily the function of literature to give pleasure. Properly understood,
pleasure should be a by-product of any experience of literature, but it is a
gift that comes most freely when unsought. In fact, the truest lovers of

literature are likely to be those most intensely interested in how literature works. Brooks makes his point through the following analogy: "The young men who really love automobiles literally can't leave them alone. They are continually tinkering with their jalopies and hotrods, equipping them with cut-outs, experimenting with special kinds of carburetors, end-lessly taking them to pieces and putting them back together again. These are the true amateurs of automobiles— . . . not the business man who never looks under the hood of his car and does not care to look as long as the car continues to get him to the office on time" (3).

One of the strong temptations of critical theory (especially since the Romantic era) has been to see literature as a form of self-expression. When considered as such, it can be therapeutic for the author and cathartic for the audience. (Edmund Wilson made the former case in *The Wound and the Bow*, while Aristotle made the latter one in the *Poetics*.) Although he does not deny that literature can serve an expressive function, Brooks be-lieves that its primary use is to convey a particular kind of knowledge. Specifically, literature lets us know what it feels like to live a certain kind of life or to hold certain kinds of beliefs. In doing so, it broadens our un-derstanding and sympathies. To the extent that it merely propagandizes for a certain style of life or a given system of beliefs, it is abandoning what it does best for what can be done more effectively with didactic rhetoric.

Although he has always shunned the label, there is a sense in which Brooks is a moral critic. He properly suspects the *moralistic* notion that literature exists to promote a specific religious or political party line. However, to the extent that it broadens our sensibilities, literature re-moves certain impediments to virtue. Conversely, when literature and lan-guage are coarsened or deadened, they can easily become instruments of manipulation and mendacity. Brooks is making essentially the same ar-gument Orwell did in his brilliant essay "Politics and the English Lan-guage." "The death of language is serious," Brooks writes. "One of the uses of literature is to keep our language alive—to keep the blood circu-lating through the tissues of the body politic. There can scarcely be a more vital function" (16).

When Brooks eventually did strike back at his attackers, it was in the fall 1979 issue of the *Sewanee Review*. There he pointed out that those intent on attacking a straw man image of the new critic usually saw him as the straw man. Opponents of the new criticism were quick to notice all of the issues that Brooks and company failed to deal with, without ac-knowledging that no critical approach can be comprehensive within the confines of a single essay or a single textbook. Using a favorite homely metaphor, Brooks declared himself concerned with applying grease to the wheel that squeaked the loudest; he did not so much ignore the rest of the machine as take it for granted. Unfortunately, his attackers conveniently forgot all of the qualifications and disclaimers he issued. One opponent who should have known better was his former student Hugh Kenner.

In an act of questionable taste, Kenner had taken the occasion of a series of memorial lectures for John Crowe Ransom to characterize the new criticism as a mere classroom strategy masquerading as a full-blown approach to literature. However, the very terms of that attack rested on certain premises that Kenner left unexamined. In a left-handed tribute to the new criticism, Kenner argued that students in the forties and fifties needed the type of remedial reading it offered. Now it was time for the new critics to get out of the way and let the cultural historians do their job. The problem, of course, is that a teacher's job is never done. Just because the students of the forties and fifties had been taught to read a text more carefully didn't mean that students of the sixties and seventies had acquired the skill. If anything, plummeting literacy rates would suggest the opposite. Also, it is interesting to note the extent to which those who would supplant the new critics begin by practicing what looks suspiciously like new critical explication.

Kenner's complaint finally comes down to a lament that the new critics are so ruthless in identifying the central meaning of a text that they pay insufficient attention to "peripheral information." Without saying how one is to distinguish central from peripheral information, he illustrates his own critical approach by analyzing a passage from Shakespeare's *Cymbeline* in light of some information regarding the idiom of Warwickshire. Unfortunately, the learned Kenner falls prey to anachronism. By consulting the *Oxford English Dictionary*, Brooks demonstrates that the idiom to which Kenner refers could not have predated the nineteenth century. In a curious reversal of roles, Kenner is guilty of the sort of historical carelessness often attributed to the new critics, while Brooks grounds his interpretation in solid philological scholarship.

If Kenner, like Homer, occasionally nods, the differences that separate him from his old teacher are finally ones of emphasis and nuance. Both critics are worlds apart from the deconstructive ingenuity of J. Hillis Miller. Brooks uses Miller's virtuoso analysis of Wordsworth's poem "A Slumber Did My Spirit Seal" (published in the January 1979 issue of the *Bulletin of the American Academy of Arts and Sciences*) as an example of where "close reading" stops and a kind of fanciful free association begins. Although Brooks alludes to his own account of this poem written thirty years earlier, he fails to mention that that account, along with the response to it, has become a kind of touchstone for contemporary critical theory.

In "Irony as a Principle of Structure" (1948), Brooks had argued for a bitterly ironic interpretation of Wordsworth's poem. F. W. Bateson responded with an affirmative pantheistic reading of this same text in the second edition of *Wordsworth: A Reinterpretation* (1952). As we have seen, Donald Hirsch used these two conflicting readings to make a theoretical point about the primacy of authorial intention in *Validity in Interpretation* (1967). Paul de Man discussed the same poem in "The Rhetoric of Temporality" (1969). Like Bateson and Hirsch, he discounted the presence of irony in the text, but not because of any reference to Wordsworth's characteristic beliefs; De Man was interested instead in making a philosophical point about the difference between the temporal structures of irony and allegory. In "Beyond Formalism" (1967) Geoffrey Hartman attempted a formalistic analysis of "A Slumber," based on a history of style. (In order to understand why Wordsworth wrote as he did, Hartman argues, we must understand that he was reacting against the "pointed" style of the eighteenth century.) Thus, by the time Miller took his turn at this brief lyric, there seemed little more of a conventional nature that could be said about it. As Brooks observes, "Miller's first several paragraphs serve only as a runway for the takeoff into what amounts to an intercontinental—possibly interplanetary—flight" (*Community*, 90).

Brooks does not necessarily object to Miller's conclusions about "A Slumber," but he accuses the deconstructive critic of engaging in a pretentious display of learning to make a rather obvious point. Brooks and Miller both agree that the meaning of the poem hinges to a large extent on the connotations of the word "thing" as it is applied to Wordsworth's Lucy. According to Miller, Heidegger sheds some light on this issue. But Brooks notes that an even more relevant source is an old folk song "that Wordsworth may well have known, as he could not have known the writings of the yet unborn Heidegger" (*Community*, 91). The first stanza of that song goes:

"Can she bake a cherry pie, Billy Boy, Billy Boy?
Can she bake a cherry pie, charming Billy?"
"She can bake a cherry pie quick as a cat can blink its eye,
But she's a young thing, and cannot leave her mother."

Turning to the *OED*, Brooks surmises that "thing" usually refers to a person in a positive or neutral sense when it is preceded by an adjective; otherwise, it has a pejorative connotation. In the song addressed to Billy Boy, the prospective bride is called a "young thing"; in Wordsworth's poem, the line "She seemed a thing that could not feel" contains no qualifying adjective.

If we give up the notion of an adequate or persuasive reading and allow critics to find whatever they wish in a text, then criticism begins to resemble Robert Frost's definition of free verse—playing tennis with the net down. "Granted an agile mind and a rich stock of examples from the world's literature," Brooks writes, "granted modern theories about the doubleness of the human mind and the ways in which secret meanings can underlie surface meanings (and sometimes one can 'mean' one thing by uttering its opposite), it is possible to construct readings that make a kind of glittering sense. The real trouble is that the game is almost too easy to play. With so lax a set of rules to govern the play, one might be able to do something with even 'Humpty Dumpty sat on a wall' or 'Hey diddle diddle the cat and the fiddle' " (*Community*, 93).[3]

Looking to the opposite end of the critical spectrum, Brooks defends himself and his fellow new critics from the attacks of Gerald Graff. Referring to Graff's *Literature Against Itself*, Brooks writes: "Almost everything that has happened in literary criticism since the heyday of Henry Seidel Canby and George Lyman Kittredge gets roundly swinged—the Structuralists, the Deconstructionists, the proponents of an affective criticism, the Northrop Fryes and the Hillis Millers, the Jacques Derridas and the Frank Kermodes, and many another. They make up a strange assortment of bedfellows. A more apposite figure might be a motley group of wrongdoers hustled before the bar" (94). Just as Brooks feels inclined to applaud Graff for his choice of enemies, he finds himself on the list "cast in the role of Pandora who, though not meaning any harm, nevertheless foolishly opened the fateful box and loosed all the present evils upon the literary world" (94). The problem with Graff's scenario is not only that it uses the logically dubious argument of the slippery slope, but that it fails to consider the forces in European philosophy that were actually responsible for the ills that both he and Brooks deplore.

Rather than explore the philosophical origins of the newer critical theories, Brooks devotes the balance of his essay to attacking Graff. Should Graff be correct in arguing for the referential character of literary language, no useful critical theory can be based on that argument alone. Experience tells us that our response to literature is based on far more than our assessment of its truth claims. Even if it is the case that "all literature is didactic," Brooks asks, "how would Graff distinguish between a poem and a sermon or a poem and an essay?" (95). Brooks and his fellow new critics focused on those characteristics that made literature different from other modes of discourse; Graff, like Yvor Winters, was more concerned with those qualities that literature shared with other types of language. If both positions necessarily concentrate on only part of the truth, Brooks is convinced that the new criticism tells us more about the distinctive character of literary art and provides a more illuminating approach to individual texts.

V

Brooks issued his most comprehensive challenge to the newer critical theoreticians in the Paul Anthony Brick lectures, delivered at the University of Missouri in April 1982. The titles of his three lectures—"The Primacy of the Author," "The Primacy of the Reader," and "The Primacy of the Linguistic Medium"—clearly suggest the nature of his targets. Although no sane person would question the importance of the author, the reader, and the linguistic medium in the total experience of literature, Brooks is disturbed by the effort to give any of these elements *primacy* over the text itself. As we have seen, he has made this argument in various forms almost from the beginning of his career. What made the Brick lectures different from earlier statements of his position was the specific character of the challenges he was facing. In arguing against Harold Bloom and Stanley Fish, one stresses different points than in doing battle with Douglas Bush.

Brooks begins his challenge to the primacy of the author by emphasizing the unique ways in which literature differs from other forms of discourse. In some ways, this position is counterintuitive. Literature has always been used as scripture and as therapy. It can serve as entertainment and propaganda. (Plato would have banned the poet from his ideal republic because of the ability of literature to stir dangerous emotions.) It so often does the work of other types of discourse that we are sometimes apt to think that literature has no independent existence at all. What makes it special, in Brooks's opinion, is that it works upon us indirectly. No doubt, Milton was sincere in saying that the purpose of *Paradise Lost* was to "justify the ways of God to man." In reality, his poem accomplished both more and less than that. Among other things, it was "a wonderful interconnected story of events in heaven and hell and upon earth, with grand and awesome scenes brilliantly painted and with heroic actions dramatically rendered" (*Community*, 171). Nevertheless, a sermon probably would have done a more effective job of explaining the divine purpose. Countless readers, from William Blake on, have declared Lucifer the true hero of the poem and found Milton to be "of the Devil's party without knowing it." If we judge *Paradise Lost* solely in terms of authorial intention, then it has failed dismally for a good many readers over the centuries.

Quite inadvertently, Descartes radically reduced the importance of literature by establishing a rigid distinction between the truth of experience and the truth of contemplation. As science came to explain so many of the phenomena that people had once understood only through religion, truth increasingly was defined as that which is empirically verifiable. As we have seen, Matthew Arnold's response to this situation was to grant science supremacy in the physical world, abandon religion altogether, and establish literature as the source of ethical values. At the same time, the French critic Hippolyte Taine was forging a sociological interpretation of literature and other cultural artifacts. For him the task of criticism consisted of defining an idea, an institution, or a work of literature in terms of its race, milieu, and moment. When Brooks began his own academic study of literature, the influence of Arnold and Taine was pervasive. What was left out of the equation was any means of judging a poem as a work of art.

The problem with a moralistic or a sociological view of literature is that both approaches assign to poems, plays, and stories a function that can be more reliably served by baldly expository prose. If we wish to accumulate facts about Periclean Athens, we can find better sources than *Oedipus Rex*. By the same token, history and sociology will not tell us how to value a literary text as a work of art. "A detailed knowledge of the eighteenth century and of the life of Colley Cibber," writes Brooks, "surely will not reveal why his *Love's Last Shift* is inferior to *The Rape of the Lock*, from the pen of his contemporary and enemy, Alexander Pope" (*Community*, 175). Only by applying objective aesthetic standards can we distinguish between the work of Pope and of Cibber. We may then want to go back and learn as much as we can about both men and the times in which they lived, but the point is that we study these men because of their achievement as artists. Had John Keats not written the poems that he did, his life would have been that of any other poor medical student of the time. Biographers and readers alike are fascinated by Keats's life primarily because they are enthralled by his poems. Such glory in the work, they reasonably assume, must come from a glory in the man.

Brooks begins the second of the Brick lectures with some unfinished business from the first. For several years, his old student and longtime colleague Harold Bloom had asserted the primacy of the author in a manner that few historical scholars would recognize. Bloom's theory of literary influence had little to do with the pedantic task of cataloging verbal echoes or surveying an author's personal library. Rather, he saw poetic creation as a kind of Oedipal struggle in which later writers achieve originality by throwing off the influence of their strong forebears. Among other things, this theory is a direct challenge to Eliot's notion that a poet gains his true voice and personality by finding his place within the ongoing literary tradition. As Brooks is quick to point out, Bloom's assumption that poets strive for originality is a critical prejudice no more verifiable than Eliot's opposite assumption. "Such knowledge as I have of the history of English and American literature shows no such general pattern," Brooks writes, "nor have I found this impulse notable among the contemporary poets whom I have known personally. . . . I expect that the competitiveness among men of letters is mostly with their living contemporaries rather than with their dead ancestors" (*Community*, 245).

According to Denis Donoghue, the differences between Bloom's approach and that of his new critical fathers can be characterized as follows: "Bloom's practical criticism is indifferent to the structure, internal relations, of the poem, or to its diction, syntax, meters, rhythm, or tone: it is chiefly concerned to isolate the primal gesture which the critical paradigm has predicted" (see *Community*, 246). The reason for this is that Bloom is finally not interested in literary criticism as such. He has identified himself as a "Jewish Gnostic, trying to explore and develop a personal Gnosis and a possible Gnosticism, perhaps one available to others." Such a stance helps to explain the eccentric nature of Bloom's interest in literature. "Far from accepting reality," Brooks writes, "Gnosticism is ultimately disappointed with it and means to circumvent it, escape from it, or remake it to suit its own vision. We move to the more aggressive, political mode when the love of poetry is seen as 'a love of power' [Bloom had defined it as such]—not as contemplation, but as an assertion of the ego" (*Community*, 247).

Having dispensed with Bloom (or at least stated his position on Bloom's literary theories), Brooks turns his attention to the work of another influential former student—Stanley Fish. At one level, Fish's interest in the reader represents a legitimate and venerable tradition in criticism. When well-respected critics can produce a variety of interpretations of a well-known work (Brooks cites a recent book featuring different readings of Keats's "Ode on a Grecian Urn"), there is some truth to the notion that meaning is in the mind of the reader. In fact, if one of Fish's pedagogical experiments tells us anything significant, the situation may be even more dire. Coming into his class at Johns Hopkins one morning, Fish failed to erase the names of several prominent linguists that had been written on the blackboard in a previous class in linguistic theory. Instead, he drew a framing line around this list of six proper names and wrote at the top of the frame "p. 43." He convinced his class in seventeenth-century religious poetry that this list of six proper names constituted a poem of the type that they had been studying. Paraphrasing Fish's account in *Is There a Text in This Class?*, Brooks writes:

> Nothing daunted, the members of the class began to interpret the assemblage of names in terms of Christian symbolism. The name "Jacobs" brought to their minds the story of Jacob's ladder, regarded by Christians as a type of the ascent to heaven. "Rosenbaum" ("rose tree"), they assumed, must surely refer to the Virgin Mary, the rose of Sharon, mother of the Man-God through Whom the ascent could be made. "Ohman," the last name in the list, they variously interpreted as meaning "omen," "oh man," or even "amen." With a little straining, therefore, these three words could be fitted into a Christian poem about man's need for salvation through the acceptance of Jesus Christ as his Lord and Savior. . . . This example proved—to Fish, at least—that readers do not *decode* poems. They *create* poems. Given their notion of what a poem is, along with their expectations about what they ought to be able to find, they proceeded to find those expectations realized in whatever is singled out to be read as a poem. (*Community*, 249–50)

Not surprisingly, Brooks believes that this experiment proves only the gullibility of Stanley Fish's students. The problem is that they came to the "text" on Fish's blackboard with inadequate notions of what to expect from a seventeenth-century poem. How could a well-informed student confuse the jumble of words on the board with a poem by Donne, Marvell, or Herbert? Where is the logical structure or figurative language typical of seventeenth-century religious poets? Although Brooks does not make this point, one could more easily imagine the students believing that they were reading a poem by William Carlos Williams or e. e. cummings.

With only Fish's testimony to rely on, the cynical reader might wonder whether Fish was really tricking his students or whether they were simply letting him think that that was the case.

Two other aspects of Fish's critical philosophy come under scrutiny— his concept of reading as a series of perceptual units and his notion of interpretive communities. The first theory holds that our reading proceeds by jerks rather than in an unbroken flow; hence we are constantly forming provisional judgments that are later modified, sometimes even contradicted, by larger syntactical units. Because these earlier provisional interpretations are part of the reader's experience of the work, they remain part of its total meaning. (Of course, an intentionalist might point out that syntax is deliberately crafted by an author; while an autotelic critic would note that it is a characteristic of the text itself.) Fish believes that this conception of the reading process "supports his conviction that language is truly indeterminate and that it proves that the reader normally generates all kinds of out-of-the-way interpretations and meanings." Brooks concludes that "for someone like Fish, whose specialty is coming up with the new and unexpected meaning even in familiar texts, such a method of reading becomes a very serviceable tool" (*Community*, 252).

As previously noted, Fish avoids the charge of complete relativism by locating authority in "interpretive communities." It is not clear, however, how such communities come into existence (does someone issue a charter?), how many there are, and whether a given reader can belong to more than one. If the term *interpretive community* simply refers to readers of a given critical persuasion, it is not clear what the concept has added to our total store of knowledge. Brooks agrees with the British reviewer who wrote the following:

> What is significant in [Fish's] theory is how he identifies the class which he aggrandizes [that is, the new interpretive community]. It does not consist of aesthetes, independent thinkers, *amateurs des livres*, poets' poets, but it is the unified class of the faculties of university English departments, with special privileges [going] to the more ambitious and the more assertive. Fish's arbiter of critical truth is characteristically someone with students to teach, colleagues to convince, a hearing to gain for himself, and who, if he does well in all this, will be, in Fish's words, "a candidate for the profession's highest honors." (See *Community*, 253)

Perhaps remembering his ambitious young grader, Brooks notes that "Fish's reference to 'a candidate for the profession's highest honors' does give off a faint whiff of the world of business success. It might almost have been spoken by a bright young advertising executive, confident that he can market any attractive new product" (254).

VI

In his climactic lecture at the University of Missouri, Brooks directly confronts the challenge that recent critical theories pose to traditional concepts of literature and the humanities. On the surface, he argues, structuralism and deconstruction would seem to be in radical opposition to each other; "whereas structuralism attempts to reveal the deep structure that underlies the surface meanings of any literary construct, deconstruction, using a more radical analysis, deconstructs *that* very structure, revealing its lack of any relation to anything beyond itself" (*Community*, 17). Not only is this a profoundly antihumanistic notion, it also contradicts the experience of literature that readers have known throughout the ages.

To reduce literature to a linguistic medium—mere words on a page—raises more questions than it answers. Brooks cites René Wellek's observation that much of what we discuss in literary criticism—motifs, themes, images, symbols, plots, genre patterns, character and hero types, not to mention the comic, the tragic, the sublime, and the grotesque—has at most a tangential relationship to the linguistic medium in which it is expressed. To see that this is the case, we need only consider the power exerted over the imagination by many great writers—Homer, Dante, Shakespeare, Goethe, Tolstoy, and Dostoyevsky, to name only a few—even in loose or poor translations. (Leslie Fiedler makes a similar point in extolling popular works that seem to lose none of their mythic appeal when translated from one genre to another.) In fact, the attitude of deconstruction toward language itself is a mass of contradictions. Several years after the Brick lectures, David Hirsch wrote of the deconstructionists: "Language, they insist, speaks itself, but they sign their essays and books 'Jacques Derrida,' 'Roland Barthes,' etc., not 'Monsieur Language' " (D. H. Hirsch, 19).

In Brooks's opinion, the current crop of critical theorists are more interested in metaphysics (or perhaps in denying metaphysics) than in examining individual works of literature. It would be easy and comforting to dismiss them as etherealists whose impact on the real world was marginal. In fact, however, they have captured the spirit of the age with a kind of bone-chilling accuracy. Alvin Kernan, whom Brooks quotes, puts the matter as follows:

The world may learn something about its own future from the effects of structuralism on literature. For structuralism is not merely one of many critical squabbles which enliven a small institution, but the working out, in the area most suitable to the issue, of a view of man which is already having profound effects. What once was character is becoming a role or a lifestyle: advertising has replaced goods with media messages; television "theatricalizes" the news; and politics has become the art of image making. Structuralism did not cause these changes—but it is the philosophy which justifies and explains a world in which the center can be and is thought of as a deficiency. (see *Community*, 20)

It is simplistic to argue, as some ultratraditionalists have done, that the new criticism paved the way for deconstruction by stressing the multiplicity of meanings that can coexist in a literary text. Brooks and his fellow new critics may have been relativists in regard to meaning, but they have always been absolutists on the question of value. Brooks made the case for aesthetic absolutism in *The Well Wrought Urn* and reiterated it in his subsequent debate with Herbert Muller; it is on this point that he and the deconstructionists would disagree most radically. By denying the objective reality of all values (logical, ethical, and aesthetic), the deconstructionists take the position that literature (or textuality in general) is a game that exists for its own sake. By speaking so insistently about such things as maturity, complexity, and fidelity to experience, Brooks judges literature by standards that are derived from human life. His point is that these values are embodied *in a particular way* in art. The didactic critic or the propagandist is so concerned with the thematic bottom line that he ignores the unique manner in which values live in art. "Literature tells the *truth*," Brooks writes, "but, as Emily Dickinson says in one of her poems, it tells it at a 'slant.' It tells the truth through a *fiction*, but it is a truth nonetheless. Literature has something to say about *reality*, and is in fact one of the clearest available windows for looking out on to reality" (*Community*, 25).

Because literature tells the truth at a slant, its relationship to reality is not always mimetic. Sometimes the very quality of distortion (as in a political cartoon) can enable us to recognize that which has grown too familiar. As prime examples, Brooks cites Lewis Carroll's Alice books. At one level, the humanoid animals in these fantasy tales satirize specific aspects of Victorian life and customs, but Carroll is also trying to "provide us with universal truths about human nature." His satire "often reveals things about ourselves that we usually fail to perceive. To mention only a few instances: the hypocritical Walrus and Carpenter, who weep over the fate of oysters as they devour them; the White Knight, who bubbles over with quixotic schemes which he will never put into operation; . . . the rhetorician Humpty Dumpty, who uses language in a way of his own and boasts, 'When I use a word, it means just what I choose it to mean— neither more nor less' " (27). Even the fatuous civilities of our communal life come in for ridicule. "The characters in the book," Brooks writes, "constantly 'deconstruct' courteous expressions if not other aspects of the language" (27).

Lewis Carroll's sense of the absurd can tell us much about reality be- cause it is firmly rooted in a sense of the normal and the normative. (Suc- cessful satire is our most moral but least moralistic form of writing.) In contrast, deconstruction extols the absurd without being able to recognize it as absurd. If Brooks and his fellow new critics can sometimes be mis- taken for church wardens, the deconstructionists live in a world without Logos. In an unpublished and undated letter to the critical theorist Mur- ray Kreiger, Brooks argues that the deconstructionist view of language stems from an atheistic view of the world. "I have for some time," he writes, "been interested in the connection that the post-structuralists make between the emptiness of words and the death of God. . . . Indeed, I and some of my friends here in the Yale department are inclined to believe that their literary theory is in good part an outcome of their philosophy of nihilism and despair." He continues in this vein for two more paragraphs:

> I, at least, think that they have accepted the reports of the demise of God too glibly. The most truly learned man that I have ever met, Eric Voegelin, is well equipped to dispute their claims. Voegelin seems to take for granted what they dismiss, and though he has not addressed himself—so far as I know—directly to the matter, he has in glancing asides, derided some of their own gods, e.g., Heidegger and Freud. Though he seems more sympa- thetic with Nietzsche, his view of Nietzsche's statement "We have mur- dered God" is sharply different from, say, Miller's.
>
> In any case, the post-structuralist literary criticism that I have read seems amazingly extravagant. As you have indicated, so often the poem (or story) is used simply as a take-off pad from which they bolt off into outer space. Their triumphs, at least thus far, have been in theory not in any practical help to the reader.[4]

PART SIX

Toward Sunset
(1985-94)

Ogden Street

On July 23, 1985, Red Warren wrote to Cleanth: "Last night Eleanor and I were settling down for her music and my reading when the radio announced for 10 P.M. a recording of your Jefferson Lecture. So we caught it at 10. I had read it before, but I had no idea how it would sound to an audience. But Eleanor simply jumped up, literally, with delight. So deep, so available, so astute. I simply had not caught—certainly not fully—the effectiveness. . . . Later E[leanor] remarked that a few generations back 'Cleanth would have been a great theologian and preacher.' Well, I am glad he was saved for our time. When he is more sorely needed." [1] Red was referring to a talk on "Literature in an Age of Technology," which Cleanth had delivered in Washington, D.C., on May 8, 1985, and again in New Orleans on May 14 as that year's Jefferson lecture, sponsored by the National Endowment for the Humanities. (The thirteen previous lecturers had included Sidney Hook, Barbara Tuchman, Edward Shils, Vann Woodward, Saul Bellow, John Hope Franklin, Erik Erikson, Lionel Trilling, and Red Warren himself.) Coming fifty years after the publication of his first book, Cleanth Brooks's appointment as lecturer was a fitting, if belated, tribute to a longtime champion of the humanities.

The issue that Brooks posed in his lecture is one that has plagued Western civilization at least since the time of Descartes—how do we find a place for art (in this case, literature) in a world where science reigns supreme? One way of approaching that dilemma, Brooks argues, is to remind ourselves of those questions for which science still does not provide an answer. Fortunately, the frontiers of science no longer seem as limitless as they did only a century ago (when Matthew Arnold suggested that the only way of combatting the dehumanizing force of empiricism was for poetry to masquerade as religion). The matter was put quite well by Victor F. Weisskopf, a distinguished physicist at the Massachusetts Institute of Technology, who wrote that "important parts of human experience cannot be reasonably evaluated within the scientific system. There cannot be an all-encompassing scientific definition of good and evil, of compassion, of rapture, or tragedy or humor, or hate, love, or faith, of dignity, and humiliation, or of concepts like the quality of life or happiness" (see Brooks, *Community*, 265).

The truth that is told by art is usually both more and less than what we can derive from scientific discourse. Like Keats's Grecian urn, art gives us history without footnotes. In his poem "The Convergence of the Twain," for example, Thomas Hardy describes the sinking of the *Titanic* without ever telling us that this disaster occurred on April 15, 1912, "that it happened on the *Titanic*'s maiden voyage; that she was, at forty-six thousand tons, the largest ship afloat; that over fifteen hundred lives were lost; that the ship, though warned of ice ahead, was traveling at high speed; or that she was regarded as unsinkable, with double bottoms and sixteen watertight compartments" (*Community*, 91). What strikes Hardy as being of greater interest than any of these factual details is the sheer coincidence and contingency of nature. Coming from vastly disparate origins, a Belfast shipyard and the ocean off the coast of Greenland, the ship and the iceberg followed a split-second timetable that brought them together in a disastrous collision on the high seas. Had Hardy given us more specific detail, we might have lost sight of the general shape of the action.

If poetry conveys a special kind of truth, it is in large part because of its mode of presentation. Like Keats, Brooks "hate[s] poetry that has a palpable design upon us." Or, in the somewhat more folksy way that he puts it, we should beware of those who would sell us "salvation in a jug." As his prime example, he cites Longfellow's "Psalm of Life." Because Longfellow's message is presented too directly, it strikes Brooks as versified platitudes. The only way that such moralism can be justified in poetry is if it is not meant to be taken seriously. A poet can get away with virtually anything if it is meant ironically and his true meaning is sufficiently hid. Poetry does indeed have a design on us. It is only when that design becomes palpable that it is offensive. Poetry should allow us to *discover* the truth rather than hitting us over the head with it.

This method of indirection is brilliantly exemplified in Robert Frost's "Provide, Provide," which redeems itself from didacticism by presenting all sorts of sage advice tongue in cheek. The cynical voice of the poem tells us that "Some have relied on what they knew; / Others on being simply true. / What worked for them might work for you." The validity of a course of action is defined in purely pragmatic terms, the implication being that anything as mundane as knowledge or loyalty is not likely to bring success in the sophisticated modern world. It is a world in which Abishag, who was once the pride of Hollywood, is reduced to scrubbing the front steps with a rag and pail. "Better to go down dignified / With boughten friendship at your side. / Than none at all. Provide, provide." The Boy Scout's motto is turned on its head.

The last poem that Brooks discusses is Yeats's "Prayer for My Daughter." If we remember that this poem was first published in 1919, the year after the end of World War I, it seems downright prophetic. Indeed, Brooks suggests that we might want to read it in tandem with John Maynard Keynes's *The Economic Consequences of the Peace*. Keynes's book is clearly prophecy *with* footnotes. It "foretold the disastrous consequence of the Treaty of Versailles, predicting what would happen under the peace terms to the economy of defeated Germany and the consequent ruin of the rest of Europe" (*Community*, 269). While not dealing directly with the imminent catastrophes of the public world, Yeats conveys a sense of foreboding as the speaker broods over the bed of his infant daughter. In the midst of all the chaos in the outside world, he wishes his daughter an ordered, ceremonious, and innocent life. The key word in his invocation is "innocence," although Yeats means by it "neither the babe's lack of experience nor the blind indifference of nature, but the soul's clear-eyed mastery of experience and of itself." The poem that Yeats gives us is "not the bare skeleton of an abstract argument, but that argument fleshed out into an entity that possesses a life of its own" (*Community*, 272).

In a sense, the Jefferson lecture was the high point of Cleanth Brooks's career. Viewed in a different light, it was simply another day on the job. Even though he had been retired from Yale for over a decade and had not been a visiting professor anywhere for a year, his speaking schedule remained as hectic as ever. When he gave the Jefferson lecture, he had just returned from Japan, where he had spoken at an international Faulkner conference (the Japanese and French Faulknerians seemed to him much more impressive than the Americans). The year before, he had lectured on American literature at the University of Amman in Jordan. The State Department official who helped arrange the trip suggested that while he was in the Middle East, Cleanth might also want to speak in Damascus. But when his Jordanian hosts took him to the Syrian border, no one was there to greet him. Because terrorism against Americans in the Middle East had been on the rise throughout the late seventies and early eighties, Cleanth was not about to let the car that had brought him from Amman leave him stranded at the border. After an hour of increasing tension and apprehension, he was ecstatic to see his Syrian escorts arrive. Apparently the bureaucrat on the American desk in Damascus had forgotten that there was an hour's difference in time between Syria and Jordan.

On October 16, 1985, Cleanth turned seventy-nine. The year had begun with Ronald Reagan taking the oath for a second term as president in a ceremony kept private so as not to distract attention from the Super Bowl being played later that afternoon. On a single day in January, Eric Voegelin and Charles Hyneman died; in February the literary world marked the centennial of the first American publication of *Huckleberry Finn*.[2] Later that year, Edmund Lee Browning, primate of Hawaii and an ecclesiastical liberal, was elected presiding bishop of the Episcopal Church. In the fall, Louisiana State University Press published *The History of Southern Literature*, while the university itself was preparing to celebrate the fiftieth anniversary of the founding of the *Southern Review*. After all these years, Red Warren and Cleanth Brooks were coming home.

I

Who among us has not dreamed of returning in triumph to the place where he was scorned? Only the very modest or the very lucky have not at some time felt unappreciated. When General Hodges sent university janitors to clear out the offices of the *Southern Review*, Cleanth Brooks and Red Warren both knew that life in Louisiana would never be the same for them again. Both eventually left for better jobs in the North, but the memory of Baton Rouge went with them. Years later, Red observed that "After Louisiana nothing has been real" (see Simpson, "Continuity," 8). What even the author of *All the King's Men* might have found surprising was the degree to which the Louisiana he once knew had remained the same for fifty years. Although Huey had been dead for many years, his son had been in the Senate for half his life. Waves of reform had periodically swept through the state, but the reformers committed the cardinal sin of being uninteresting. In 1985 the state was ruled by a populist demagogue who might have taught the Kingfish a thing or two. Edwin Edwards was a flamboyant womanizer who went on gambling sprees to Las Vegas several times a year; his administration was riddled with graft, and he considered a federal indictment a rite of passage.

What *had* changed in Louisiana was the attitude of LSU toward the *Southern Review*. The revived magazine had now been in existence almost three times as long as the original series. When the University prepared to celebrate the 125th anniversary of its founding, the emphasis was on events that had taken place during its seventy-fifth year—the Conference on Literature and Reading in the South and Southwest and the establishment of the literary magazine that James Monroe Smith hoped would put LSU on the map. On October 9–11, 1985, the Baton Rouge campus commemorated twenty years of the new *Southern Review* and honored those who had started the original magazine half a century before. If the Agrarian symposium at Vanderbilt in 1980 could be seen as the belated vindication of an idea, LSU's conference on Southern Letters and Modern Literature was more of a personal homage to two men who had played the tired old role of prophets without honor. As so many of the literary giants of 1935 had faded into obscurity, Brooks and Warren had grown in stature. They had also grown old.

Earlier that year, Red had marked his sixty-second year as a professional writer by publishing *New and Selected Poems: 1923–1985*. Because his reputation will almost surely rest on the poems published since 1954, they constitute the bulk of the volume (287 of 322 pages); and because the poems are printed in reverse chronological order, the more recent work enjoys pride of place. Still, the sheer length of his career is a wonder in and of itself. As Louis Rubin has pointed out, when Warren published his first poems in 1923, Thomas Hardy, Joseph Conrad, Anatole France, Henri Bergson, and George W. Cable were still alive. "Nobody much had ever heard of William Faulkner, Thomas Wolfe, or Hart Crane. *The Great Gatsby* would not be published for another two years, [and] Eudora Welty was a thirteen-year-old in Jackson, Mississippi" (Rubin, "RPW," 137). By October 1985, about the only literary honor Warren had not won was the Nobel Prize. The standing ovation he received from the people of Baton Rouge was a particularly bittersweet tribute. The obscurantists who had let him go so many years earlier were themselves gone. At least one high-ranking member of the current university administration was at every session in 1985. By living long and well, Red Warren had achieved the best revenge.

If Red was the star of the occasion, second billing would almost certainly have gone to Eudora Welty. The southern literary community was pretty much agreed that, with Faulkner gone, Warren and Welty were the two most prominent writers of the South. The general populace, which usually did not read poetry or criticism, knew Warren and Welty as popular fiction writers—even if that knowledge did not extend beyond *All the King's Men* and "Why I Live at the P. O." Although no celebrity, Cleanth was far from unknown. Many prominent Louisianans now in their fifties and sixties still remembered having their eyes opened to the complexities of poetry in Brooks's sophomore literature class;[3] the Brooks and Warren textbooks and *The Well Wrought Urn* had long since become standard references for the specialist and nonspecialist alike. If literary fashion had passed the new critics by, no one would have suspected it that weekend at LSU.

One significant difference between the literary conference in 1935 and the one fifty years later was the presence of several prominent black writers at the second gathering. James Olney, who had taken Don Stanford's place on the *Southern Review* when Stanford retired in 1983, knew a good deal about African-American literature and made significant efforts to feature it in the magazine. For all its diversity, the old *Southern Review* had been a lily-white magazine, which mentioned race only in the context of defending the Old South against the attacks of polemicists such as Van Wyck Brooks. (The closest thing to a black presence at the 1935 conference was the patronizing dialect writer Rorark Bradford.) Ernest J. Gaines and Gloria Naylor gave readings in 1985, and Naylor joined with Houston Baker, Henry Louis Gates, and Daniel Littlefield in a panel discussion on the Afro-American Writer and the South. Only Baker used his position at the conference to attack the Fugitive-Agrarians. At one point, he referred to Allen Tate as a "son of a bitch." Later, he quoted out of context the line "Nigger, your breed ain't metaphysical" from Warren's poem "Pondy Woods."[4] This cheap shot so incensed Cleanth that he later pointed out to the conference that Baker had quoted a dramatic speech by a imaginary character (in this case a buzzard) rather than the literal opinion of Robert Penn Warren.

Other participants in the conference included Lewis P. Simpson (who was primarily responsible for organizing the affair), Bob Heilman, Thomas W. Cutrer, Charles East, James W. Applewhite, Walter Sullivan, Elizabeth Spencer, William C. Havard, Louis D. Rubin, Jr., L. E. Phillabaum, George Core, Ronald Schuchard, Denis Donoghue, and Walker Percy. No international figure of the stature of Ford Madox Ford was present, although Mrs. T. S. Eliot had been listed on the program before canceling out. One virtually unknown participant was the young filmmaker Ken Burns, who recreated the ambience of 1935 with a documentary film on Huey Long. A few years later, Burns produced an extraordinarily popular documentary on the Civil War for PBS—a project suggested by Red Warren, who had been featured prominently in the Huey Long film.

Only Red's family and closest friends realized what an ordeal the trip to Baton Rouge had been for him; he had been in failing health and showed every one of his eighty years. (In contrast, Cleanth possessed the energy of a man half his age.) As the conference wore on, Red spent more and more time in his room at the faculty club, drinking bourbon and swapping stories with Cleanth, Tinkum, and Eudora Welty. His single public performance (a poetry reading) was interrupted by a fit of coughing so serious that James Olney had to finish for him. The one question that cast a shadow over the festivities was whether Red was simply under the weather or seriously ill. His prolific output of poetry caused many to assume that he was ageless. But he was making many fewer public appearances and even canceling invitations he had accepted. His brogue seemed to grow thicker, so that his comments in radio and television interviews were frequently indecipherable. Then, in the summer of 1985, he was diagnosed with inoperable bone cancer. Walter Sullivan recalls asking the Brookses what was wrong with Red that final night in Baton Rouge. Ever the diplomat, Cleanth said: "He's not feeling well." The more plainspoken Tinkum replied: "He's doomed."[5]

II

One day in May 1986, Tinkum Brooks awoke from her afternoon nap to discover strange shapes and figures dancing in front of her eyes. Cleanth was so alarmed by his wife's condition that he insisted she go to the emergency room of the New Haven Hospital as soon as she could see well enough to drive. After a long and stressful wait, an internist performed a CAT scan. As suspected, there was a tumor on Tinkum's optic nerve. The situation could probably be corrected by surgery if the tumor had not started elsewhere and simply metastasized in the brain. The doctor suggested that Tinkum have her regular physician take X-rays. The results proved devastating. In addition to a brain tumor, she had inoperable lung cancer. When the doctor entered the room where Tinkum, Cleanth, and Carver Blanchard were awaiting his verdict, he simply said that he knew Tinkum had always lived a life of the mind and he would do nothing to take that away from her in her remaining months. Tinkum, Cleanth, and Carver left the hospital to eat lunch at the Graduate Club, each trying to put a brave face on the inevitable. When Carver's sister called later that day to inquire about her aunt's condition, Tinkum announced in her matter-of-fact way: "I have the summer to tie things up."[6]

Although news of Tinkum's illness spread, only close friends and family realized that the end was near. On May 9, which was before Tinkum's first seizure, Cleanth wrote to Harriet Owsley about a book she was preparing on her late husband, Frank. He said that he hoped that he and Tinkum would see her at a literary conference in Tennessee that October. Then, on May 18, he wrote to apologize for not having retrieved the manuscript of her book from Red Warren as quickly as he had expected. "I had to give up driving (on account of my eyes) some several years ago," he writes, "and Tinkum, our only driver, will be going into the hospital very soon—for tests that may lead to an operation. The operation if deemed necessary is not, we are assured, life-threatening, but it may be serious enough to cause real concern." Later in the letter, he says of the literary conference, "I still hope to come and, long before October, I trust that Tinkum will be quite able to come along with me." On June 21, however, he wrote to Harriet to say that he would not be coming to Tennessee in the fall. Tinkum "has for some weeks had a difficult time," he writes. "But the side effects and the after effects of her treatment seem to me to be wearing off and I do think that she is returning to something like her former feelings."[7]

Even as Tinkum's health deteriorated, Cleanth was slowly going blind. A combination of cataracts and glaucoma made it difficult for him to read or write without the aid of a special magnifying device that projected the enlarged image of a page on a screen as the book was moved back and forth under a special light. (Cleanth remained such a consummate professional that he used this cumbersome machine to reread *All the King's Men*, a novel he practically knew by heart, for a talk he had agreed to give.) For years now, Tinkum had read to Cleanth, and she continued to do so as he attended to the demands of her final illness. They faced the end of life as they had faced their previous fifty-two years together—with a quiet stoicism and an abiding love. The stress was such that Cleanth lost a good deal of weight that summer. By the fall, Tinkum herself was down to eighty pounds.[8]

Realizing his aunt's condition, Carver agreed to spend the summer at Ogden Street, helping in any way he could. He recalls that Tinkum's attitude toward death was the same as her attitude toward every other experience in life—it was something to be done right and with the least possible fuss and trouble for others. She began sorting through her belongings, assigning those parts of her that were assignable. Some mementos (such as first prize in an essay contest at Sophie Newcomb College) were only of sentimental value, but collectively they told the story of a remarkable life.

Although her physical energies waned toward the end, Tinkum remained surprisingly lucid and in command. She went wig shopping with Margaret Wimsatt in anticipation of losing her hair through chemotherapy, but she never wore the wig. One suspects that the shopping trip was motivated more by a desire for companionship than by personal vanity. Before long, she was unable even to leave the house and the source of oxygen that sustained what little life she had left. (When the hose to her oxygen supply allowed her to move only so far about the room, she would laugh and say that now she was indeed at the end of her tether.)[9] Walker Percy discovered Tinkum's immobility when he wrote to Cleanth to suggest that he come up from Louisiana and drive the Brookses around to the historic New England inns. At this point, Percy was waging his own losing battle with cancer, but his first thought was to be near friends who might need him. Cleanth was touched by the gesture, even though it was impossible to accept.[10]

One can only speculate on the role that religious faith played in sustaining Cleanth and Tinkum during her final illness. Tinkum's religious development had been different from her husband's. Unlike Cleanth, she had not been brought up in a churchgoing family. In a letter to Rosanna Warren dated June 9, 1988, Cleanth wrote: "Her mother had very little use for Christianity. Her mother was a strenuous woman who did a lot of good works and had great virtues, but her experiences with Christianity had been unfortunate and she was no believer. I could not, and certainly would not, for every reason, have tried to force Tinkum into my way and I did not. Graciously, she came along and I think got much further on the pilgrimage than I did." After Tinkum's death, Cleanth derived a measure of consolation from reading C. S. Lewis's *A Grief Observed*.[11]

A month or so before she died, Tinkum and her doctor both expected her to be gone within a week. Ever practical, she announced that the people at the funeral parlor would need a complete set of clothes, including underwear, and told Cleanth and Carver where they were to be found. On her final night, she awoke at least twice in her hospital bed to comment on the unfairness of death in taking so long to claim her. She was ready to go, and the seemingly pointless delay offended her sense of order. The only regrets she articulated were for those she was leaving behind. Three months before her departure, she had written to Bob Heilman, who had recently lost his wife of many years. In the letter "she reported the medical diagnosis that had been made, and she treated it as if it were a surprising, but not quite fitting, jest. Her central concern was for her husband, and that concern, too, was put humorously: 'Poor Cleanth is going to have to get to work' " (Heilman, 102–103).

Shortly after Tinkum's death on October 1, 1986, the family gathered for a private funeral in a chapel on Orange Street in New Haven. This was followed by a flight to Baton Rouge to lay her mortal remains to rest. The plane was delayed on the ground in New York for two hours, while Cleanth, along with Paul and Carver Blanchard, felt like long-distance runners straining to break the tape. When they finally arrived in Louisiana, the weather was unseasonably hot. There was only a small group around the open grave—Cleanth and Carver, Carver's sister, Catherine, and brother, Paul, and Tinkum's sister, Eleanor. They were joined by Tommy and Josie Kirby, who were now Cleanth's oldest friends in Baton Rouge. It had been a year to the month since the Brookses had made their triumphant return to celebrate the *Southern Review*. Many people urged them at that time to come back to the South to live. With the job of dying complete, Tinkum was home to stay.[12]

III

Because Cleanth and Tinkum had been so much a part of each other's life for more than fifty years, friends wondered how her death would affect his daily routine. The depth of his grief and loneliness was taken for granted. What they did not know was whether he would be able to function without her. To the surprise of many, he did. (As Carver bluntly put it, he chose to live.) Because of his advancing age and weak eyesight, Cleanth took in a succession of graduate student boarders to help him with his domestic chores. In the years after Tinkum's death, he had two married couples and several single men living for various periods on Ogden Street. They drove him different places, kept his larder full, fetched the cleaning lady once a week, and generally were on call in case of emergency.

During the summer of 1989, Cleanth's housemate was a young Yale librarian named Alphonse Vinh. Vinh's father, who had been head of the

South Vietnamese Air Force, settled in Virginia after the fall of the Diem
government. Deprived of his own homeland, Alphonse passionately em-
braced the cause of the American South and soon became fast friends with
Cleanth. Returning home from a conference on the 4th of July holiday,
Cleanth discovered Alphonse in a cold sweat and running a high fever.
After being repeatedly misdiagnosed by the Yale Health Service, he was
found to be suffering from a near-fatal case of double pneumonia. When
Cleanth called for an ambulance, he was told that fallen trees from a recent hurricane made the route to Ogden Street impassable. Undaunted,
Cleanth called a venturesome teenager who lived in the neighborhood.
The lad managed to navigate enough backstreets to get Alphonse to the
hospital, where he recovered over a period of five weeks. As Cleanth visited Alphonse daily, he must have been filled with painful memories of a
similar pilgrimage three years earlier. Vinh was not only in the same hospital but the same room and the very bed where Tinkum had died.[13]

If anything, Cleanth became more independent in his final years. Because of a spectacularly successful operation for cataracts, he went from
near blindness to near normality; with the aid of glasses, he could get
around on his own and read without depending on his magnifying machine. The improvement was so pronounced that he seemed to many
friends to have rolled back the calendar by ten to fifteen years. Necessity
and advances in medical science had allowed him to see again. Whenever
he said that we must be concerned with ends as well as means, Cleanth
was always quick to add that he owed his life and much of his well being
to the wonders of medical technology.

After Tinkum's death, Cleanth became more concerned than ever with
reestablishing relations with the nieces and nephews on his own side of
the family. Because these people had generally lived blue-collar lives, they
were not compatible with the sophisticated ambience of Yale. Nevertheless, Cleanth accepted his kin for what they were with no hint of condescension. During the last few years of his life, he maintained a close correspondence with Patricia Brooks Pratt, the daughter of his brother Bill.
Patty was a bright and resourceful survivor who had lived the sort of star-
crossed life chronicled in hundreds of country songs. Her letters to
Cleanth describe her unsuccessful efforts to collect thousands of dollars in
unpaid child support from one of her ex-husbands. She also writes of attending a self-help group at a local church and hoping to go back to school
so that she can land a better job when her disability payment runs out. For

Christmas, she always sent Uncle Cleanth a subscription to *Reader's Digest* to thank him for his thoughtful letters and the generous checks that usually accompanied them.

Not long after his career as a guest professor in the South ended, Cleanth turned his attention to a project that would encourage the literary creativity of his native region. In the spring of 1987, Cleanth and twenty-five compatriots met in Chattanooga to found the Fellowship of Southern Writers. Although the twenty-six original members included critics and editors, the organization was intended primarily to consist of poets, dramatists, and fiction writers. Cleanth did not want this simply to be another academic society. Neither was it a secessionist group—most of its members already belonged to such national organizations as the American Academy of Arts and Letters and had no intention of withdrawing into a sectionalist enclave. They simply thought that it was high time to recognize and promote the considerable amount of good writing being done in the post-Renascence South. To this end, the fellowship secured corporate backing for six annual awards: the Hanes Prize for Poetry, the Hillsdale Prize for Fiction, the Byran Family Foundation Award for Playwriting, the Fellowship's Non-Fiction Prize, the Chubb LifeAmerica Award in honor of Robert Penn Warren, and the Cleanth Brooks Medal for Distinguished Achievement in Southern Letters.

Although the formation of the Fellowship of Southern Writers was one of Cleanth's proudest accomplishments, it came during a difficult time in his life. Because his acceptance of Tinkum's death had been so stoic, his deep grief was almost completely internalized. He would dream of her at night and then worry during the day that he was being morbidly subjective.[14] Also, during the first two years of the fellowship's existence, Cleanth's eyesight was at its worst. Friends remember him walking into walls and having to be helped on and off planes. He even had to put up a fight to be allowed to go to a public bathroom by himself. Along with the other members of the group, Cleanth realized that the glory days of southern literature were gone (Andrew Lytle was convinced that the fellowship had been formed too late), and he was having doubts about his own standing in the literary world. When the other fellows insisted on electing him the group's first chancellor, he said: "You're making a mistake. Everywhere, my name is mud."[15]

Nevertheless, the fellowship survived and flourished. In addition to Cleanth, the group's original driving forces were Louis Rubin, George Core, and the novelist George Garrett. As of 1993, there were twenty-eight other living members—A. R. Ammons, Wendell Berry, Fred Chappell, James Dickey, Ellen Douglas, Ralph Ellison, Horton Foote, Shelby Foote, John Hope Franklin, Ernest J. Gaines, Blyden Jackson, Madison Jones, C. Eric Lincoln, Romulus Linney, Andrew Lytle, Reynolds Price, Mary Lee Settle, Lewis P. Simpson, Lee Smith, Monroe K. Spears, Elizabeth Spencer, William Styron, Walter Sullivan, Peter Taylor, Eudora Welty, C. Vann Woodward, and Charles Wright. Within three years of its founding, two of the fellowship's most distinguished original members were dead. Walker Percy succumbed to cancer in April 1990; Red Warren had been claimed by the same disease the previous September.

On September 16, 1983, nearly two years before the discovery of his terminal illness, Red had written to Cleanth about what their friendship meant to his work:

> You can't imagine how much I owe you about poetry—on two counts.
> Our long collaborations always brought something new and eye-opening
> to me, seminal notions for me, often couched in some seemingly incidental
> or casual remark. One of the happiest recollections I have is that of the
> long sessions of work on UP [*Understanding Poetry*]—not to mention ear-
> lier and later conversations. The other count has to do with the confidence
> you gave me about my own efforts. I'm sure that you were over-generous,
> but even allowing for that, it still meant something fundamental to me. I
> have often wanted to say something like this to you, but I know that you'd
> give me an embarrassed shrug and disclaimer. Anyway I can say it now
> without your interruption.

During the four years that it took for Red to die, he continued to be lionized by a public unaware of his illness. (As George Garrett has noted, Warren received so many honorary degrees and medals "that some anonymous wag called him the General Pinochet of American Literature in honor not of his politics at all, but rather the top-heavy tinkling appearance of over-decorated Latin American leaders"; Garrett 50–51.) In the spring of 1986, Congress found a new way to honor the country's greatest living poet by naming him America's first poet laureate. The job was actually that of poetry consultant to the Library of Congress (a position that Red had held more than forty years earlier), but the title was new and impressive. It came perilously close to being a posthumous honor.

During the last year of his life, Red was virtually unable to speak. Toward the end, Albert Erskine told Rosanna to read her father one of his oldest poems, "Bearded Oaks." Upon hearing the poem's final lines—"We live in time so little time / And we learn all so painfully, / That we may spare this hour's term / To practice for eternity"—Red gave a smile of recognition and, with difficulty, spoke the name "Albert."[16] He slipped back into a coma and never uttered another word. On September 15, 1989, he was gone. His burial near the family's summer home in West Wardsboro, Vermont, seemed to come right out of a movie script. Although it was still fairly early in the fall, there was already snow and sleet on the ground. The funeral procession made its way from an old church down a long gravel path to the graveyard. As he had done at his aunt's graveside nearly three years before, Carver sang that wonderful old Scottish hymn "Abide with Me." When Red was laid to rest, it was the first time in a hundred years that this old Vermont burying ground had been disturbed. Pondering the final ritual, Lewis P. Simpson writes: "We may fancy that this act expressed the last vision of a place to come to by a poet for whom the mystery of his identity was deeply fused with the mystery of place; for a poet who was an unmovable nonbeliever but who said repeatedly that he yet yearned to believe; for a poet who was southern to the bone—knew that he could never be at home save in the South—and yet knew as deeply that, because of his very nature as a southerner, he was an exile who could never come home again" (Simpson, "Warren and the South," 11).

It remained only for Vanderbilt to pay its last respects to its most distinguished graduate. A memorial service was held on campus in November, as the friends and admirers of Red Warren gathered to measure the extent of their loss, while cherishing all that was vouchsafed them in art and memory. The note of premature nostalgia that Cleanth had struck in his class poem over sixty-one years before now seemed to ring true:

> But we shall merely wink our eyes and turn,
> And close the ledger, put back in the file
> The folded paper there, and so dismiss
> The picture with some casual inward smile
> At our own sentiment, to be so stirred
> At some vague phrase or some chance spoken word . . .

After the public speeches in the Vanderbilt chapel, a few of Red's family members and closest friends gathered in a private dining room in the administration building, Kirkland Hall. After dinner, they swapped stories and reminiscences about the man they had known (Andrew Lytle was in typically fine form). When it came Cleanth's turn, he spoke of Red's love of popular music and his amusement whenever he heard the inimitable

Brooks rendition of one of America's great folk songs. Pretty soon, the entire table was urging a reluctant Cleanth to perform as he had at Oxford half a century earlier. Finally, Eleanor said: "Do it for Red." Cleanth pushed his chair back from the table and sat straight, without even touching his back to the back of the chair. He then began to sing in the most proper angelic voice: "Frankie and Johnny were lovers . . ." [17]

IV

Late in his career, Brooks returned to a topic that had interested him at least since his days as a graduate student at Tulane—the relationship between historical evidence and literary criticism. Although myopic pedants from Douglas Bush to Hershel Parker had attacked the new critics for an indifference to history, such a charge has always rung hollow when leveled at Cleanth Brooks. In 1991 Brooks made yet another effort to set the record straight by publishing a book called *Historical Evidence and the Reading of Seventeenth-Century Poetry*. The case that this book makes for its author's interest in history is neither new nor revisionary. John Walsh's bibliography of Brooks's prose writings indicates that only two of the nine essays in this volume had not been previously published in some form. Included are three essays we have already examined—those on "The Faeryes Farewell," "To a Grasse-Hopper," and Marvell's "Horatian Ode." One comes away from this book convinced that Cleanth Brooks is an adept historical sleuth but that he is correct in believing that the real business of criticism lies elsewhere.

Although one of the first lessons we are supposed to learn as readers of literature is to differentiate between the author and the protagonist of a work, the temptation to confuse the two is sometimes very strong. In the case of Henry King's "Exequy," for example, we have a husband's grief-stricken lament for his late wife. At least two impressions come across very clearly—the present sorrow of the speaker and his resolution to remain faithful to his wife's memory until the day they are reunited in the Resurrection. Because the biographical information indicates that King was writing about his own wife, we are naturally curious to know if he lived up to the promises made in the poem. Historical evidence suggests that he did not.

Several years after "The Exequy," King wrote a poem entitled "The Anniverse," which is another elegy on the death of his wife Anne. After a "sorrowfully affectionate opening," the speaker declares himself bound alive to a corpse. By now, his devotion is obviously beginning to wear thin. A third poem, "The Short Wooing," proposes marriage while arguing wittily against a long courtship. "The Legacy," which is another undated poem, offers a "reasoned justification for second marriages." And, Brooks argues, a final undated poem, "St. Valentine's Day," makes sense "only as a poem written by a widower who is proposing marriage to a prospective second wife" (*Historical Evidence*, 19). Although there is no external record of King having married a second time, his "most thorough and conscientious biographer," Lawrence Mason, concludes from these poems that he probably did (*Historical Evidence*, 18).

Naive readers might well regard Brooks as a mean-spirited investigative reporter out to convict Henry King of gross hypocrisy. Brooks's point, however, is that our appreciation of "The Exequy," or any other poem is hopelessly superficial if it is based on something as sentimental as a belief in the poet's sincerity. "A truly good poem," Brooks writes, "is not tarnished by the fact that its author wrote a bad poem or even two dozen of them, or even lived a bad life. For authentic poems are not inextricably attached to their authors so as to be affected by the author's subsequent actions" (21). If anything, a knowledge of literary biography shows us how often banal and even loathsome human beings can transcend their personal limitations within the alchemy of art. We might feel like ringing up the author on the telephone after finishing a good book, but in most cases we would find the book to have been better than the conversation.

In "Men of Blood and State," no detective work is required. The historical dimension lies in a comparison of typical poems on the same theme from three different centuries. The representative seventeenth-century poem is a lyric on death from James Shirley's *The Contention of Ajax and Ulysses*. Brooks explicates this poem and then places it in its historical context. The message that it conveys is that death is the great leveler. Although the references in the poem are all to members of the nobility who risk their lives in battle (*men of blood* in two senses of the term), the relevance to those lower on the social scale is unmistakably implied. The consolation offered them after death is that the actions of the just shall smell sweet even when their remains are in the dust.

By the time we get to Gray's "Elegy" in the eighteenth century, the reward for dying a lowly death is the realization that one did not put his faith in earthly glory. Hardy's thoroughly modern poem "In the Time of the Breaking of Nations" takes us another step farther from the seventeenth century. Its focus is entirely on the peasantry, a farmer in his field and a young couple in the midst of courtship, while the presence of the nobility is implied only by the admission that "Dynasties pass." Although Hardy was a patriotic Englishman who believed in his country's war effort in 1915 (the year the poem was written), he was also philosophical enough to take the long view. Brooks explains: "War and dynastic glory are ultimately irrelevant to the human enterprise. The old man preparing the field for planting and the youth and maiden plighting their troth are things that must go on as long as this globe is to be inhabited by human beings" (*Historical Evidence*, 51). The fact that one could not have conceived of the sentiments of Hardy's poem (and perhaps not even those of Gray's elegy) being expressed in the age of Shirley's lyric tells us something of great historical interest. What it does not do is provide us with a *literary* basis for judging the poems in question.

The following essay, which discusses the minor poet Aurelian Townshend, sheds little light on the relationship between historical research and literary criticism. Brooks begins by introducing us to three different poems by Townshend—a witty love lyric addressed to the Countess of Salisbury, an example of vers de société that employs the myth of Medea and Aeson, and an allegorical dialogue between "Time" and a "Pilgrime." The impression we are to derive from the second and third of these poems is of the ease with which the court poets of the seventeenth century alluded to classical myth. Townshend's work helps Brooks to make this point precisely because of its status as minor verse. As he asserts in the introduction to *Historical Evidence*, "minor poets are less likely than their great contemporaries to go beyond, or deviate from, a period style" (20).

In discussing Sir Richard Fanshawe's poem "The Fall," Brooks again faces a task of historical investigation. In his *Oxford Book of Seventeenth-Century Verse*, H. J. C. Grierson erroneously identifies the grisly beheading depicted in this poem as that of Charles I. By dating the poem, Brooks demonstrates the unlikelihood of that surmise. A knowledge of Fanshawe's biography, coupled with internal evidence from the poem, seems to indicate that the bloody and headless trunk described in "The Fall" almost certainly belonged to Thomas Wentworth, Earl of Strafford. An adviser to Charles I, Strafford excited such jealousy among his political rivals that he was eventually framed, indicted, and executed in what most historians regard as a judicial lynching. At the most universal level, Fanshawe's poem is a meditation on the caprice of fate. A reader can understand and appreciate what he has to say on that issue without identifying the protagonist of the poem. For that matter, it would make little difference if the protagonist were a fictional character. As a literary critic, Brooks realizes this, but, as a reader with normal human curiosity, he wants to know all he can about the background of the poem.

When we consider Fanshawe's personal closeness to Strafford, we can better appreciate the extent to which he has controlled the tone of his poem. One might have expected a cry of anguish or a protest against injustice rather than this calm meditation. By demonstrating that the poem is not about Charles I, Brooks prevents us from interpreting "The Fall" in light of our preconceptions about Charles. Because it is an earl rather than a king who has fallen, the wheel of fortune has not had to take quite so wide a turn. Still, the injustice is probably greater. Even the most committed Royalist would have to admit that Strafford was a more impressive figure than Charles and that Charles revealed a lamentable weakness of character in assenting to the execution of the innocent Strafford. The external evidence we call "history" can thus give us a better understanding and a higher regard for Fanshawe's poem. But that is not where the relationship ends. The poem itself is a historical document and, as such, sheds light on the historical question of whether Strafford was ever buried (in whole or in part) in a marked grave. Unfortunately, so little other information exists that the small light of Fanshawe's poem has finally led researchers nowhere. Nevertheless, Brooks has established that the connection between history and literature is sometimes symbiotic.

After examining the verse of Lord Herbert of Cherbury Brooks discusses two important works by Andrew Marvell, the only major poet considered in this book. The principal historical question here is biographical—how could the same sensibility have produced poems with such apparently different views of the world as "To His Coy Mistress" and "The Garden"? It is one thing to expect a reader to appreciate poems that make contradictory truth claims, quite another to explain how the same writer could produce two such poems. In light of Marvell's known Puritan leanings, the spiritual pleasures he extols in "The Garden" would seem to be more congenial to his true feelings. This is not to say that "To His Coy Mistress" is insincere, only that it expresses a mood less characteristic of its author. Another possibility is to identify an underlying unity that transcends differences in mood and emphasis. Brooks argues that such unity can be found in the concern with time and eternity shared by both poems. Even when assuming the libertine persona of the lover wooing his coy mistress, Marvell comes across more as a lapsed Puritan than an antinomian lecher. Although he does not cite his own essay on Milton's twin poems, Brooks does suggest that we read "To His Coy Mistress" and "The Garden" as if they were meant to appeal to different aspects of the same personality.

Historical Evidence and the Reading of Seventeenth-Century Poetry concludes with the discussion of Richard Lovelace's "To a Grasse-Hopper" that Brooks had originally published in 1962 and with his earlier and better known analysis of Marvell's "Horatian Ode." Although that last essay makes the most cogent case imaginable for the virtues and limits of both history and criticism, Brooks feels compelled to argue that case once again in a personal epilogue. If the canard that he was indifferent to history got started with *The Well Wrought Urn*, he finds it more than a little ironic that the year before that book appeared, he had published his edition of the Percy-Farmer correspondence. (*Historical Evidence* is itself dedicated to the "memory of David Nichol Smith.") Not only do scholarship and criticism have their place within the realm of literary study, both skills can be practiced by a single individual. At a time when the humanities were under attack both inside and outside the academy, Brooks must have felt that old historians and new critics had better things to do than refight ancient wars with each other.

V

Even as various literary theories have come in and out of vogue, the new criticism has reigned supreme as a pedagogical method. Although *Understanding Poetry* has waned in popularity, other textbooks have carried on the tradition of the new criticism. In a letter to me dated December 6, 1993, the poet and critic Dana Gioia writes: "The three best selling college poetry textbooks of the past thirty years were probably *How Does a Poem Mean?* by John Ciardi, *Sound and Sense* by Laurence Perrine, and (probably the best selling of all) *An Introduction to Poetry* by X. J. Kennedy. All three are strictly New Critical as are the legions of their imitators. These are the books that are used by millions of students and tens of thousands of teachers in the classroom. New Criticism, even if it doesn't go by that name, remains virtually unchallenged as the method of choice in college classrooms." [18]

If one had to pick a single year in which the tide of professional discourse in the humanities began to turn back toward traditional values, it would be 1987—the year that Allan Bloom's *The Closing of the American Mind* and E. D. (Donald) Hirsch's *Cultural Literacy* became two of the top nonfiction best-sellers of the decade. A philosophy professor at the University of Chicago, Bloom argued that a pervasive relativism was ruining higher education in America. A mind that is forced to see all values as equal is not open but closed, because it is prevented on principle from making judgments. Hirsch's book pursued the classic liberal agenda of universal education. Cultural literacy was broadly defined as those things one ought to know to be a fully functioning citizen in our democratic society. As secretary of education, Cleanth's old friend Bill Bennett so effectively reiterated some of these same themes that there was talk of his possibly running for president.

Finally, in the summer of 1987, the Belgian scholar Ortwin de Graef discovered that during the Second World War Paul de Man had published at least ninety-two articles in the pro-Nazi newspaper *Le Soir*. He had also abandoned his original wife and family before coming to the United States and claiming to have been an heroic member of the anti-Nazi underground. Strictly speaking, the despicable nature of de Man's personal life should not have discredited his literary theory. Nevertheless, that theory seemed eerily self-serving in light of de Man's recently uncovered hypocrisy. "The scandal had to do with words and with silence," David Lehman notes, "with what de Man wrote in Belgium and what he didn't say in America. Perhaps it wasn't coincidental that de Man's own critical practice dealt on an abstract plane with words and with silence—and that there had long been those who felt that de Man's theory had the effect of silencing language" (Lehman, 158).[19]

By 1993, one could see signs that recent literary fads had begun to run their course. One example was Stanley Fish's essay "Why Literary Criticism is Like Virtue," published in the June 10, 1993, issue of the *London Review of Books*. Fish began by saying: "There is a great difference between trying to figure out what a poem means and trying to figure out which interpretation of a poem will contribute to the toppling of patriarchy or to the war effort. Until recently the assertion of this difference would have been superfluous, but in many circles it has come to be an article of faith that the idea of a distinctively literary system of facts and values is at best an illusion and at worst an imposition by the powers that be of an orthodoxy designed to suppress dissent" (Fish, "Why Literary Criticism," 11). Many informed readers were surprised to see such a statement coming from Stanley Fish, who had generally been associated with the movement to transform literary criticism into a more politically engaged form of discourse. Should there be any mistake about which side of

this controversy he was now endorsing, Fish recalled the old debate between Cleanth Brooks and Douglas Bush regarding the meaning of Marvell's "Horatian Ode." Surprisingly, he agreed with Brooks in arguing that
history can be of only preliminary and ancillary benefit in interpreting a
literary text.

Had Stanley Fish, with his legendary knack for knowing which way the
wind was blowing, come full circle to a position suspiciously like that of
the old new criticism? The conclusion of his article would suggest that that
was what had happened:

> If you ask me why it is a good thing to explicate *Paradise Lost*, I can do
> nothing better or more persuasive than do it, spinning it out in directions
> at once familiar and surprising, ringing the changes, sounding the notes in
> the hope that the song is one you know or that it will be infectious enough
> to start you singing. Literary interpretation, someone has recently said, has
> no purpose external to the arena of its practice; it is the "constant unfold-
> ing" to ourselves "of who we are" as practitioners. The only "value of the
> conversation is the conversation itself." That's all there is, even when we
> try to enlarge it by finding in it large-scale political and cultural implica-
> tions. I say again, that's all there is, but it's enough for those who long ago
> ceased to be able to imagine themselves living any other life. (Fish, "Why
> Literary Criticism," 16)

CHAPTER TWENTY-TWO

April Is the Cruellest Month

On October 16, 1992, Cleanth Brooks turned eighty-six years old. When he was not traveling (which he continued to do at a pace that would exhaust much younger men), his life fell into a daily routine. He would wake up around six or six-thirty in the morning. The newspaper and CNN kept him abreast of what was happening in the world as he ate a light breakfast of juice, coffee, and cold cereal. (On one occasion when I was staying with him, the business reporter on CNN announced that the real estate industry had indeed found April to be the cruellest month.) Cleanth's morning hours were often spent preparing lectures or writing articles he had promised. (Keeping up with a far-flung correspondence, reading the many periodicals to which he subscribed, and entertaining visitors from around the world took up much of his remaining time.) As the noon hour approached, he would catch the Yale shuttle bus into New Haven and eat lunch at either Mory's or the Graduate Club. After spending the early afternoon hours in town running errands and seeing friends, he would catch the shuttle bus home and take a late afternoon nap. Unless he had been invited to a dinner party, he would eat a light supper, sip some bourbon, and read until it was time to go to bed—usually around ten o'clock.

Cleanth had long since adjusted to the winter weather and was gradually coming to terms with the human hazards of living in New Haven. Because there is no real line of demarcation between the campus and the city, it is impossible to shield oneself from urban blight. In negotiating the five-minute walk from the Beinecke Library to Mory's, one is accosted by an underclass of winos, panhandlers, and madmen. In broad daylight, they inspire little more than irritation and occasional pity. After dark, however, they rule the streets. In his later years, Cleanth carried two wallets with cash and different credit cards, along with a separate supply of traveler's checks. The idea was that, if he were assaulted, he could give the thief some money, while still having a few dollars hidden with which to rescue himself and seek medical attention.[1] After his house on Ogden Street was burglarized, he installed an alarm system. Upon entering the house, one had to punch a certain combination of numbers to deactivate the alarm. Although Cleanth kept a flashlight near by so that he could see the numbers, he sometimes failed to punch them in in time. After the police had answered a few false alarms, he became wary about turning the system on at all.

Cleanth went back to LSU one last time a week after his eighty-sixth birthday. A group of conservative intellectuals called the Intercollegiate Studies Institute was sponsoring a conference on the Agrarians and Distributists and had asked him to speak on his recollections of the *Southern Review*. The trip gave him a chance to see old friends from Baton Rouge and elsewhere. Lewis Simpson was there, now several years retired. Mel Bradford and Russell Kirk—two friends who were elder statesmen in the American conservative movement—were on the program. And Tommy and Josie Kirby were living in a rest home not far from campus. The visit got off to an unusual start when David Madden, a novelist and professor in the English department, summoned Cleanth to campus on the morning before the conference began. A crowd was gathered outside the English department in Allen Hall. By searching through old departmental files, Madden thought that he had located the office that Cleanth and Red had once shared, and he had ordered a plaque to mark the spot. The only problem was that Madden had identified the wrong office. When Cleanth informed him that the office had actually been at the other end of the hall, David led a procession to the right spot—or to the nearest approximation Cleanth could recall. So much had changed in half a century. And even in the seven years since the great celebration of 1985. Tinkum and Red were dead. And Eudora was a virtual recluse in her house in Jackson, too crippled with rheumatism to write, and keeping literary sleuths at bay with a "No Trespassing" sign.

From the LSU conference, Cleanth rode out to Texas with Bedford Clark (a longtime friend who taught at Texas A&M) to visit Tinkum's sister and brother-in-law. By the end of the week, he was back east in Tennessee to help Andrew Lytle celebrate his ninetieth birthday two and a half months early. George Core had decided that this festivity should coincide with a program honoring the centennial of the *Sewanee Review*, which had been founded by William P. Trent ten years before Lytle's birth.

In a fundamental sense, the magazine had been reborn when Lytle and Allen Tate took it over in the mid-1940s. Although Cleanth had twice rejected the opportunity to become editor of the magazine, he had appeared frequently in its pages. He enjoyed visiting Sewanee and had even received an honorary degree from the University of the South. Also, seeing Andrew was a way of keeping the torch aflame now that all the other Fugitive-Agrarians were gone.

The following weekend, Cleanth was in Knoxville for SAMLA. Having taught twice as a guest professor at the University of Tennessee, he knew several of the permanent faculty there. By far his oldest acquaintance was a native of Ripley, Tennessee, named Robert Drake. Drake's parents had been married by Cleanth, Sr., in 1922, and Bob himself would surely have been baptized by Brother Brooks had he not waited until 1930 to be born. When Bessie Lee Brooks moved back to west Tennessee after her husband's death, she became reacquainted with the Drake family. Because of these old regional ties, Cleanth had helped Bob get into the Ph.D. program at Yale, where he became one of many fathers Drake adopted in his quest to become a southern writer. Because none of the usual Friday night dinner group were there (as they usually weren't when the conference was held outside of Atlanta), Cleanth was largely at the mercy of casual acquaintances who, having met him once years earlier, were now claiming an unwarranted intimacy. Nevertheless, he found time to visit the book exhibit, where Andrew Lytle, over from Sewanee for the day, held court one afternoon. The University of Missouri Press had just published Lytle's critical study of *Kristin Lavransdatter*, by Sigrid Undset, the Nobel Prize winner from Norway, whose submission to the *Southern Review* Cleanth and Red had turned down so many years ago.

The literary climate in America had changed sufficiently that, after several years absence, Cleanth attended the MLA Convention once again in December 1992. With Tinkum gone, the Christmas season was a particularly lonely time. The MLA always met between Christmas and New Year's, and this time the convention was just down the road in New York City. Since Red's death, a Robert Penn Warren Circle had been formed to encourage Warren scholarship, and the group had asked Cleanth to speak at its meeting during the convention. The political battles were not nearly as strident as in years past (perhaps because the radicals had won everything they wanted), and deconstruction now seemed less the wave of the future than one of many competing theories. Stanley Fish and Gerald

Graff greeted Cleanth warmly, and the MLA itself featured his picture on the front page of its next newsletter. Live long enough, Cleanth later reflected, and eventually things start coming back your way.

As 1993 dawned, Cleanth remained active and in good health for a man of his age. Still, he realized that his prospects for survival diminished with each passing year. In addition to leaving money for his family and for Tinkum's, he wanted to provide a legacy for humanistic study at Yale. The *Yale Weekly Bulletin and Calendar* for January 18–25, 1993, announced that he had provided a gift to fund up to four graduate fellowships a year in the humanities. Although no figure was announced, the gift was large enough to support the fellowships from interest income alone. (Cleanth's executor, Paul Blanchard, believes that the bequest was around $500,000.) In announcing the gift, the *Bulletin* quoted Cleanth as saying: "We live today in a highly technocratic society. . . . Our machinery is at once the most delicate and the most powerful that the world has ever seen. All honor to our study of processes and techniques; but we need all the more a concern for the humanities. We cannot live by means alone. Means without good ends are dangerous. The humanities need now all the help that can be given to them" (*Yale Weekly Bulletin*, "Gift," 1). For Cleanth, one of the pleasures of giving such a generous donation to Yale was seeing the university administrators baffled by how a college professor got so much money.

In March, Cleanth visited England with John Michael Walsh, the literary biographer Virginia Spencer Carr, and Virginia's colleague Mary Robbins. When he had been in London as cultural attaché nearly thirty years before, Cleanth had already developed the paunch that often comes to sedentary men in their late middle years. But diet had long since taken that off; he now seemed delicate and wraithlike. For that reason, his reserves of energy were all the more remarkable. After two weeks abroad, he flew to Atlanta and was driven up to Chattanooga just in time for the biannual meeting of the Fellowship of Southern Writers. Even though he was in much better shape physically than when the organization had been formed six years earlier, friends noticed that his absentmindedness was starting to carry over from mundane to academic matters. (In May, he would deliver a talk before the Katherine Anne Porter Society, only after being reminded at the last minute of a commitment he had made months earlier.) At the Fellowship meeting, his sole responsibility was to make some perfunctory introductions. Louis Rubin had to write out the relevant information three times, as Cleanth kept losing the script almost as soon as Louis would give it to him. It was an uncharacteristic performance, but perhaps jet lag was to blame.

Tommy Kirby did not make it through the winter, and even Mel Bradford (nearly thirty years Cleanth's junior) failed to survive heart surgery in March. Then, in the late spring, Albert Erskine died. He had had a satisfying career at Random House and a good life at home in the Connecticut countryside. After his disastrous union with Katherine Anne Porter and a failed second marriage, he enjoyed a long period of domestic happiness with his third wife, Marissa. But, in recent years, Albert had fought a protracted battle with oral cancer and was having a difficult time eating and talking. When the cancer recurred in 1993, he decided not to fight it anymore and refused surgery. The golden boy of Baton Rouge told his friends and family that he wanted to die. The circle of friends in New Haven, whose presence had persuaded Cleanth and Tinkum to remain in Connecticut after retirement, was gradually diminishing. In June of 1993, I asked Cleanth if he ever thought about moving south. "I just might," he said, "if any more of my friends around here die."

Even those friends who remained alive were frequently in failing health. René Wellek, whom Cleanth regarded as one of the most learned men he ever knew, had suffered a stroke and was confined to a nursing home. It was there, under straitened circumstances, that he summoned the fortitude to complete his multivolume history of modern criticism. Knowing that Wellek had been a longtime friend of Cleanth and a charter member of the Boys Friendly, I sought to interview him when I was in New Haven in June of 1993. Wellek's wife, Nonna, drove Cleanth and me out to see her husband on a Saturday afternoon. The three of us seemed to be the only ones who were not either in bathrobes or hospital garb. Wellek was sitting up in bed, where he could read and receive visitors. We could only guess what thoughts were locked in his head, because sustained communication was next to impossible. He recognized Cleanth but forgot that he had ever seen books that he had read and discussed just a few years earlier. None of my questions about Yale in the 1940s seemed to make any sense to him, and his responses were indecipherable. Even though his wife kept urging him to "e-nun-ciate, René, enunciate," his efforts to do so were largely fruitless. One couldn't help thinking that this was how Cleanth's father must have spent his final years.

The last time I saw Cleanth was in August of 1993 at the annual meeting of the St. George Tucker Society. This organization had been founded the year before as an interdisciplinary fellowship of scholars working in various aspects of southern culture. The eclecticism of the group was due at least in part to its original driving forces, the Marxist historian Eugene Genovese and the Agrarian literary critic Mel Bradford. Cleanth's role on the program was to introduce George Garrett, who delivered the keynote address on the state of southern letters. Perhaps because he had flown in from New Haven rather than London, Cleanth seemed more rested and in better command of himself than he had in Chattanooga in March. Also, unlike the typical celebrity scholar, he actually *participated* in the conference—attending sessions and commenting on papers. The presentation that disturbed him most was an analysis of Faulkner's novels offered by two economists, who were trying to determine the verisimilitude of Faulkner's world by comparing the average height of his characters with the available historical records. During the question-and-answer period, Cleanth stood up and said: "For over sixty years now, I've tried to teach people how to read literature. After hearing this paper, I'm about ready to give up."

I

Cleanth made his final visit to England in the late winter of 1994, leaving on February 22 and returning on March 4. In a letter to Louis Rubin, dated March 16, he writes:

> The trip to England—ten days of it—was pleasant enough. England was a little chilly and cloudy but we had sunshine a good deal of the time and I was treated very handsomely, it seemed to me, by the Institute of United States Studies, one of the many institutes formed by the University of London. I was put up in a tiny, but beautifully accommodated little flat, everything with everything, clean and tidy. I was taken to lunch and dinner at a dozen or so interesting restaurants and though I'm having to watch my food intake these days, I did enjoy the meal-taking. But I also found that though with a little alcohol and some lively talk, I could liven up and do a lot of talking myself—probably too much talking—I also, once I was alone by myself, got terribly quiet and tired and had to do a lot of napping and sleeping.[2]

The purpose of Cleanth's trip was to deliver a lecture on American innocence in James, Fitzgerald, and Faulkner. Although this was actually a reworking of a talk given at Stanford University thirty years earlier and published in *A Shaping Joy*, his British hosts were less interested in breaking new ground than in seeing the lone surviving monument of a great age of criticism. For Cleanth, the trip meant a chance to talk before an appreciative audience and to see England again. He even made a side trip to Oxford, where he was reunited with one of his old rugby teammates and ate at the high table in Exeter College. That his doctors allowed him to go at all seemed a confirmation that he still had a few good years left in him. Cleanth clung to this hope, because late in 1993 he had learned that he had terminal cancer.

Cleanth took the news of his condition with a characteristic stoicism. When he asked how long he had left, he was told that in cases like his the prognosis was anywhere from six months to five years. As the cancer began to work away at his esophagus, he found eating to be more and more difficult. He was finally reduced to drinking cans of liquid nutriment to keep his weight from plummeting any farther or faster than it already had. At the same time, another cancer was attacking his liver. Because his condition was incurable, friends hoped that the relatively painless liver cancer would kill him before the agony in his throat became unendurable. In his letter to Louis Rubin, he tried to strike a philosophical tone. "I am not feeling particularly depressed," he wrote. "I'm eighty-seven and had hardly expected to make it to ninety, surely not above ninety, so I'm not unduly worried about the state of affairs, but I do have a lot of things to clear up and clean up before I say farewell."

Less than two years before, Cleanth had made a memorable trip to Great Britain with Rubin and his wife, Eva. In the summer of 1992, they toured the Scottish Highlands, retracing the famous journey that Boswell and Johnson had taken through the Hebrides in 1773. As Rubin recalls that trip, they left Boston on a late evening Northwest Air Lines flight that arrived in Glasgow six hours later. Because of his slight stature, Cleanth curled up and slept for most of the flight, a luxury the heftier Rubins were unable to enjoy. Because the disorganization at the Glasgow airport was of Third World proportions, the party did not board the train for Edinburgh until the morning was almost over. Fresh from his night's sleep, Cleanth began chattering about Scottish place names, while Louis and Eva, who had now been awake for twenty-two hours, could hardly keep their eyes open.

For the next twelve days, Cleanth and the Rubins toured the Highlands with Boswell's account in one hand and the *Blue Guide* in the other. "Cleanth was eighty-five at the time," Rubin recalls, "but each morning he was first down to breakfast, and he outwalked us throughout the

Hebrides. . . . I think of it now as a lost opportunity. If only I'd brought along a cassette recorder or taken notes I might have produced a travel book of my own, entitled *A Journey Through the Western Isles of Scotland with Cleanth Brooks, B.A., B.Litt. (Oxon), Litt.D*" (Rubin, "Cleanth Brooks," 265–66).

Despite the discovery of oil in the North Sea, Scotland was much the same as it had been when Cleanth walked the stark beauty of the Highlands sixty years before. It was the rest of the world that had changed. Nazism and Communism had come and gone, Great Britain itself had ceased to be a world power, and a southern Rhodes Scholar not even born until after World War II was running for President of the United States. The once apt analogy between Scotland and the American South seemed no longer to apply. Southern aristocrats no longer read Sir Walter Scott, and their Snopesean cousins who still burned the fiery cross of the clans had probably never heard of his name. One night on his 1992 Scottish tour, Cleanth returned to his hotel in Tobermory on the Isle of Mull to find his room decorated with stuffed cats in honor of the town's most famous namesake, a talking feline in a popular story by Saki.

The day after he returned from his 1994 trip to England, Cleanth began radiation therapy. After ten days, it had become apparent that the treatments were robbing him of what little energy he had left without halting the advance of the cancer. On March 15, Cleanth's doctor, James D. Kenney, discontinued the therapy and advised his patient to get his affairs in order. This meant not only providing for the disposition of his property and his papers but also doing what he could to advance several projects that he hoped would see the light of day after he was gone. Beverly Jarrett, director of the University of Missouri Press, had commissioned a selection of his recent essays. Alphonse Vinh was working on an edition of Cleanth's correspondence with Allen Tate, and Jewell Brooker was editing the letters of Tinkum and Katherine Anne Porter. Finally, Cleanth remained committed to seeing my account of his life brought to fruition. On the same day that he wrote to Louis Rubin, he wrote to me to say "I do hope to get time to send you soon a good deal of fresh material on these last chapters. . . . If we do need to get together and you find it too difficult to get to me here, maybe I can find it possible to come see you." [3]

By now, Cleanth was beginning to suspect that, even if he were to live for another five years, his normal activities would soon be cut short. But he tried to make as much of his remaining time as his waning energy would allow. He particularly looked forward to a reunion of Rhodes

Scholars to be held at the United Nations not long after his return from England. Originally, Cleanth had planned to attend the entire two-day function and even had a reservation to spend the night at the Waldorf Astoria. As the day grew closer, however, his health had deteriorated to the point where Carver Blanchard suggested that he simply go in and out of the city in a single day. This would allow Cleanth an hour at the stand-up cocktail party that he most wanted to attend. By the time the train pulled into Grand Central Station, the city was wet and icy from a spring snowstorm. After negotiating the slippery plaza in front of the UN build-ing and following a confused set of directions, Cleanth arrived at the party in a state of near collapse. He and Carver were back at Ogden Street by nine o'clock that night. He never ventured from New Haven after that.[4]

Had it been physically possible, Cleanth would have liked to have gone to Ralph Ellison's funeral in late April. Ellison was a member of the Fel-lowship of Southern Writers, but Cleanth had known him for many years before that organization was even formed. Albert Erskine had been Elli-son's editor at Random House, and Red Warren had been a particularly close friend. Cleanth respected Ellison as a serious artist who never played the race card. As they grew older, their shared southern heritage began to mean more to both men. At the memorial service that Yale held for Red Warren, Ellison told Cleanth that he had dreamed of Red the night before. In the dream, Red was swimming out to sea. As he got closer to an island barely visible from shore, he turned around and waved to Ralph. Like so many of Cleanth's friends, Ralph Ellison had now reached that faraway island.[5]

Before his illness became common knowledge, Cleanth was selected to receive the Mory's Cup for 1994. This award was given each year to an individual who had made a significant contribution to the life of Yale. Having been part of the Yale community for most of his adult life, Cleanth was particularly touched by this award—probably more so than by any of the honorary degrees he had received. Although the presentation of the cup was scheduled for May 5, it became doubtful by late March that Cleanth would live that long. But to move the presentation up would have seemed too much like an abandonment of hope. So the official ceremony remained scheduled for May 5, with Cleanth actually receiving the cup at home several weeks earlier.

As late as May 2, Cleanth was in Mory's for a meeting of the Boys Friendly. By then, he had been off of solid food for well over a month and was taking his cans of chocolate nutriment with him to restaurants so that he could enjoy the company of friends. Knowing that the end was near, he began saying good-bye to those who had been closest to him. This meant a general parting with the Monday luncheon group. But as the meal wore on, he began directing his attention more and more to Maynard Mack. They had known each other since 1940 and had joined forces in numerous professional battles. Maynard was also the man most responsible for bringing both Cleanth and the new criticism to Yale. It had been a good life, Cleanth told his friend, but now he was ready for it to be over.[6]

As much as he wanted to attend the Mory's Cup ceremony three days later, Cleanth was now scarcely able to get out of bed under his own power. So he had Carver put on a tuxedo and accept the award in his behalf. The entire ceremony, including Carver's rendition of some bawdy Renaissance songs, was videotaped so that Cleanth could enjoy it in the comfort of his home. When he took a drink of bourbon from the actual cup a few weeks before, it seemed to have a tonic effect on him. Visitors were officially discouraged because of the demands their presence made on Cleanth's strength and attention. But he always seemed to get a rush of adrenaline when he was able to hold court, even if it was only in his living room. No one will ever know whether winning the Mory's Cup added a few days, or even a few weeks, to Cleanth's life, but it certainly enhanced the quality of what life he had left.

Early on the morning of May 6, Randy Anderson, the graduate student who was then living at Ogden Street, heard faint calls for help. Summoning Carver, who was also staying at the house, he discovered that Cleanth had fallen some time during the night and was unable to get up. Without having to be told, everyone now knew that the end was near. This fact was confirmed by Dr. Kenney, who was summoned the next day. The blood work indicated that Cleanth would probably not last another week. The only question was where he would spend his final days. Because it was possible to get hospice care at home, he decided that that was where he wanted to remain. From the time that decision was made on Friday May 6 until the hospice people arrived in the middle of the afternoon on May 8, Paul Blanchard and Alphonse Vinh were Cleanth's primary caregivers. (Carver, who had been on call for weeks, was making a much-delayed trip to New Orleans.) Between them, they stayed with Cleanth and made phone calls to friends and family who needed to be informed of the situation.

A few friends from New Haven came by personally to show their love and concern. Alphonse Vinh has particularly vivid memories of Vann Woodward arriving on Sunday afternoon. Less than a year earlier, Woodward had told me that he admired the stoicism with which Cleanth faced old age and its inevitable conclusion.[7] Like Cleanth, Woodward had lost his wife and many of his closest friends. To see another of those friends go simply confirmed the sad fact of mortality. The previous Monday, Vann had had a long and animated conversation with Cleanth, in which they read one of their favorite poems—Marvell's "To His Coy Mistress." This time, Vann expected to stay about twenty minutes. After three minutes, he came back down the stairs, his eyes filled with tears. "What happened?" Alphonse asked. "We said hello," Vann replied. "We shook hands. And then we said good-bye."[8]

Later that night, Cleanth recovered enough lucidity to tell Alphonse that he wanted to give two last gifts to Yale—the keys to Guthrie and Murray, Kentucky. He had been given the key to Guthrie in honor of Red Warren. The key to Murray was a memento of his last visit to that town a little over a year earlier. When the Kentucky Philological Association held its twentieth annual meeting at Murray in March of 1993, it invited the native son home as its honored guest. (The account of his speech occupied more space in the local paper than stories about the bombing of the World Trade Center and the beginning of a siege against religious separatists in Waco, Texas.) Reversing the path of his earlier life, Cleanth flew to Nashville, and rode up to Murray by car. A retired judge and local antiquarian obligingly drove him around the county and even located the probable site of the old Methodist parsonage where he was born. It had long since been torn down to make way for a British Petroleum gasoline station.

At seven o'clock Tuesday morning, May 10, the attending nurse came downstairs at Ogden Street and advised Alphonse to come to Cleanth's bedside (Paul, who was staying upstairs, was already there). Now unconscious, Cleanth was lying on his side and breathing with great difficulty. Even though he was not aware of them, Paul and Alphonse felt that it was important for them to be present at the end. They sat on either side of his bed, immobile and silent. The arrangements for the funeral had already been made. (Cleanth wanted to be buried in his best British suit.) The ordeal of selling the house and disposing of the many items of personal property not specified in Cleanth's will remained ahead of them. An even more imminent task was taking the body to Baton Rouge for burial alongside Cleanth's parents and Tinkum. The period immediately preceding and following death is a busy time for the living, but the actual moment of dying is a time of unearthly stillness. For Cleanth, it came in the course of half an hour. By seven-thirty he was gone.

II

On May 11, Louis Rubin was attending a literary luncheon in Charleston, South Carolina. This was the city where the Civil War had started with the firing on Fort Sumter. Charleston still retained some vestiges of the Old South, even if these were largely exploited for commercial purposes. It was the one city for which Cleanth would have left New Haven—if any more of his friends at Yale had died. At the luncheon, Rubin sat next to a southern writer named Louise Shivers. Published in 1983, her best-known novel, *Here to Get My Baby Out of Jail*, had earned her a solid regional reputation. (If there are fewer great southern writers today than in the age of Faulkner, there may be more good ones.) The literary culture that produced such writers as Louise Shivers would not have been possible without the efforts of Cleanth Brooks. Shivers told Rubin that the book that influenced her the most was something called *Understanding Fiction*. Sensing that she had not read the morning papers, Rubin said, "The man who wrote that book died yesterday."[9]

Cleanth's funeral was held on Thursday, May 12, at St. John's Episcopal Church in New Haven. Claude Rawson recalls being surprised by the number of different people from various walks of life who were there—everyone from the Boys Friendly to Vasily Rudich, a Russian expatriate who taught in the Classics department at Yale.[10] As Cleanth had requested, Father Peter Rodgers used the rite of the 1928 *Book of Common Prayer*. Because not everyone in attendance was a Christian, there was no celebration of the Eucharist. The pall bearers were Paul and Carver Blanchard, Jonathan Leff, Alphonse Vinh, Claude Rawson, and Cleanth's lawyer, David Totman.

The burial was scheduled for May 17 at Greenlawn Cemetery in Baton Rouge, but a torrential rainstorm had softened the earth to the point where it was impossible to dig a proper grave. Despite the weather, nearly fifty people showed up at the cemetery that morning. They were greeted at the gate by Paul Blanchard, who told them that the service had been moved from the graveside to a mausoleum on the grounds. Because of the number of people in attendance, most were forced to stand. They heard Carver's twin sister, Catherine Blanchard, read a poem in which

Cleanth had found unexpected subtlety and depth—Tennyson's "Tears, Idle Tears." After a short time, the umbrellas went back up and the mourners returned to the routine of their daily lives. The casket with Cleanth's body was loaded back into the hearse and returned to the funeral home.

On Friday, May 20, Lewis Simpson checked his answering machine after returning home from a brief trip. He had a message from Carver Blanchard saying: "Be at the cemetery at ten tomorrow morning and we'll sure enough bury Cleanth." In contrast to the funeral in New Haven and the rain-drenched ceremony in Baton Rouge earlier that week, the actual burial was a small and private affair. The only persons in attendance were Lewis and Mimi Simpson, Carver and Catherine Blanchard, the New Orleans poets Amy Baskin and Mark McKutcheon, and McKutcheon's wife, Carmen Chancellor. As he had done for Tinkum and Red Warren and, more recently, Albert Erskine, Carver sang that great nineteenth-century hymn "Abide with Me." It was a beautiful spring morning in Louisiana, and the ground was now dry enough to receive the casket bearing Cleanth's mortal remains. "Abide with me; fast falls the eventide," Carver sang. ". . . Earth's joys grow dim; its glories pass away; / Change and decay in all around I see; / O thou who changest not, abide with me." Each of the people at the graveside threw a clod of earth on the casket as they passed by. Even as the mourners were leaving, the groundskeepers began filling in the grave. "Well," Catherine Blanchard remarked, "There's reality for you." [11]

On April 14, 1994, less than a month before his death, Cleanth had made final revisions in his will. Specific bequests of one thousand dollars each were made to his cleaning lady, Jeannette Desarbo, his namesake, Cleanth Brooks Toledano, his nephews, Murray Brooks and John Brooks Bryant, and his nieces, Betty Lee Bryant Wiggington and Mary Jo Bryant Gould. The bulk of his estate was divided equally between the Brooks and Blanchard sides of the family. Paul, Carver, and Catherine each received three-tenths of one-half of the estate, while two of Tinkum's nieces in Texas each got one-twentieth of that half. James Brooks, son of Cleanth's half-brother Jack, received one-quarter of what was left, with the remaining three-quarters going to Patricia Brooks Pratt. [12] Certain personal items of no great monetary value were distributed at the discretion of Paul and Carver Blanchard. Among these was a varsity letter from the McTyeire School, class of 1924.

The last time Cleanth had been to the site of the McTyeire School was in June of 1992. No one had attended the school in over sixty years, and the building in which it was housed was now a parking lot for the local Methodist Church. Nevertheless, the Methodists thought enough of what the school had been to place a marker there and to invite all living graduates back for one final reunion. Cleanth had come by airport limousine from New Haven to New York, flown to Chicago, then to Memphis, and on to Jackson. In Jackson, a car met him to travel the remaining few miles to McKenzie, Tennessee, a town that was no longer known even as a railroad crossing. Most of Puss Puryear's boys were too feeble or too far away to attend; many were no longer alive. Those who came were the remnant of another era, before hard drugs, metal detectors, and widespread illegitimacy had invaded the halls of learning. It had been a long time since anyone had entertained the idea of teaching Latin and Greek to adolescents from the farms and small towns of west Tennessee and north Mississippi. The aging graduates gathered in the Methodist parking lot that afternoon in June would probably have said, "more's the pity." In the distance, one could almost see Mr. Jim coming up the road, field glasses in hand, and hear the cry of "Fourth year Latin's up, Fourth year Latin's up" from the boys he helped turn into men.

NOTES

WORKS CITED

INDEX

NOTES

CHAPTER ONE: The Road to Nashville

1. In that essay, published in 1920, Mencken said of the South of his time: "In all that gargantuan paradise of the fourth-rate there is not a single picture gallery worth going into, or a single orchestra capable of playing the nine symphonies of Beethoven, or a single opera house, or a single theater devoted to decent plays" (Mencken, 138).

CHAPTER TWO: The Campfire Still Glowing

1. Brooks used the campfire metaphor at the 1956 Fugitive Reunion. See Purdy, 220.

2. Interview with Walter Sullivan, June 4, 1991.

3. Representative issues of the *Masquerader* can be found in Special Collections at the Jean and Alexander Heard Library, Vanderbilt University.

4. Brooks's letters to Fannie Neel are part of the Cheney papers in Special Collections at the Heard Library, Vanderbilt.

5. Interview with Jane Sullivan, July 6, 1991.

6. Kipling's "The Man Who Would Be King" is one of the stories included in Brooks and Warren's *Understanding Fiction*, a book that is dedicated to Davidson.

CHAPTER THREE: Tinkum

1. Letter from Jane Ann Klock, July 25, 1991.

2. The letters from Brooks to Davidson cited in this chapter are part of the Donald Davidson papers in Special Collections at the Heard Library, Vanderbilt.

3. This and the preceding quotation are from Harold McSween's work in progress, *Roosevelt, Huey Long, and Robert Penn Warren*, the first installment in a projected eight-volume history of Louisiana politics during the Long era.

4. Interview with Carver Blanchard, June 19, 1993.

5. Letter from Mrs. Merrill Moore, February 28, 1995.

6. The letters between Cleanth and Tinkum cited throughout this book are part of the private papers left by Cleanth Brooks at the time of his death and are quoted by permission of his executor, Paul Blanchard.

7. The original text of Hodding Carter's letter to Brooks is in the Beinecke Rare Book and Manuscript Library at Yale University. It is quoted by permission of Hodding Carter III.

CHAPTER FOUR: A Reb at Oxford

1. This letter is part of the Donald Davidson papers in Special Collections at the Heard Library, Vanderbilt. Although no year is indicated on the letter, internal evidence would place it in 1931.

2. See Henry Hazlitt, "So Did King Canute," *Nation*, January 14, 1931: 48–49.

3. The reference is probably to H. L. Mencken, "Uprising in the Confederacy," *American Mercury* 22 (March 1931): 379–81.

4. "Reconstructed but Unregenerate." Unless otherwise noted, the essays cited in this letter are from Twelve Southerners, *I'll Take My Stand*.

5. "A Mirror for Artists."

6. The Neo-Humanist critic Irving Babbitt.

7. T. S. Eliot was a student of Babbitt at Harvard, although he believed that his old professor was fundamentally mistaken in trying to base morality on secular humanist principles.

8. "The Hind Tit." In this essay Lytle strongly advocates the subsistence farm and the yeoman farmer.

9. "A Critique of the Philosophy of Progress."

10. "The Irrepressible Conflict." This essay was an extremely polemical attack on the North for its continual exploitation of the South.

11. "Remarks on the Southern Religion."

12. This book, which is subtitled "An Unorthodox Defense of Orthodoxy," maintains that the South ought to hold on to a fundamentalist supernatural religion for the sake of the aesthetic coherence it can give to life. In terms of substantive belief, however, Ransom was a skeptic and a near-positivist.

13. Because Ransom did not save letters that were sent to him, this one has not been preserved.

14. "Education, Past and Present."

15. *The Tall Men* was a book-length poem Davidson published in 1927.

16. Mencken gave Warren's *John Brown* a favorable notice in his review-essay "American Worthies," *American Mercury* 19 (January 1930): 122–25. "It is a capital piece of work," Mencken writes, "careful, thorough and judicious—and its merits are not diminished by the somewhat surprising fact that its author is but twenty-five years old" (125).

CHAPTER FIVE: Baton Rouge

1. Interview with C. Vann Woodward, June 17, 1993.

2. Interview with Lewis P. Simpson, August 16, 1994.

3. Interview with Robert B. Heilman, August 28, 1992.

4. The original text of this letter is in the Beinecke Library at Yale.

5. The original text of this letter (dated June 8, 1933) is among the *Southwest Review* papers at Southern Methodist University in Dallas.

CHAPTER SIX: The Left Bank of the Mississippi

1. The original text of Cleanth's letter is contained in the Allen Tate papers at the Princeton University Library.

2. This observation was made by John Palmer in an interview on June 21, 1993.

3. The original text of Fletcher's letter is in the Beinecke Library at Yale. It is quoted by permission of Fletcher's nephew, William L. Terry.

4. For evidence of Shakespeare's popularity on the southern stage, see Philip C. Kolin, *Shakespeare in the South: Essays in Performance* (Jackson: Univ. Press of Mississippi, 1983). For a discussion of Shakespeare's influence on southern literature, see Kolin's *Shakespeare and Southern Writers: A Study in Influence* (Jackson: Univ. Press of Mississippi, 1985).

5. Brooks and Warren later included "The Face" in *Understanding Fiction*.

6. Three years later, *Partisan Review* did carry an article denouncing Schuman, calling his article in the *Southern Review* "a new low in American scholarship." See Frank N. Trager, "F. L. Schuman: A Case History," *Partisan Review* 7 (Spring 1940): 143–51.

CHAPTER SEVEN: The Confederacy of Letters

1. This information was gleaned from the personnel files in the English department at Louisiana State University.

2. In addition to the students mentioned here and the even more famous ones discussed in chapter 12, the graduate English program at LSU produced such future luminaries as John Edward Hardy, Aubrey Williams, Walton Patrick, Melvin Watson, Arthur H. Scouten, Ernest Clifton, Patrick Quinn, and David Malone.

3. Interview with Paul Blanchard, September 9, 1994.

4. The original text of Cleanth's letter is contained in the Allen Tate papers at the Princeton University Library.

5. The original text of Cleanth's letter to Red is in the Beinecke Library at Yale.

6. The *State-Times* clipping is part of Special Collections of the Hill Memorial Library at Louisiana State University.

7. This was Cleanth Brooks's surmise when he recalled the incident to me during a series of interviews in June 1992.

CHAPTER EIGHT: An Extended Family

1. Unless otherwise noted, the original texts of the letters cited in this chapter are in the Beinecke Library at Yale. The unpublished letters of Allen Tate cited in this book are quoted by permission of his widow, Helen Tate.

2. The original text of Cleanth's letter is contained in the Allen Tate papers at the Princeton University Library.

3. Interview with Robert B. Heilman, August 28, 1992.

4. Brooks himself believed that his acknowledgment of Kendall's genius was responsible for their friendship. The other observations about Kendall in this paragraph are from my interview with Heilman on August 28, 1992.

5. The feminist critic Elaine Showalter has tried to use this telegram as evidence that Cleanth, along with Cal Lowell and Stafford's father, constituted a patriarchal troika that hampered Jean's literary ambitions. At the end of a review of two recent Stafford biographies, Showalter writes: "Stafford may have mutilated herself to get back at [Lowell] or at her father or at Cleanth Brooks for that matter" (15). See Elaine Showalter, "I wish she'd been a dog," *London Review of Books* 7 February 1991: 14–15.

6. In another letter to Hightower, Stafford describes office procedures at the *Southern Review*: "Letters from contributors are rec'd with shrieks of laughter, mss. are sneered at, rejection slips go out furiously. [In comparison,] The Atlantic Monthly looks like a bunch of kind old ladies" (see Roberts, 189).

7. Although the bulk of Stafford's papers are at the University of Colorado, these letters are contained in the Beinecke Library at Yale. The unpublished letters of Jean Stafford cited in this chapter are quoted by permission of Russell and Volkening Literary Agency.

8. The Catholic Worker movement was a group of Catholic social activists who lived and worked among the poor in the slums of New York City. Their isolationism, mentioned by Stafford later in the letter, was due to categorical pacifism rather than any pro-Nazi sympathies.

9. Interview with Andrew Lytle, April 22, 1992.

10. Consider, for example, a story that Porter told to the notoriously gullible interviewer Enrique Hank Lopez. In the summer of 1947, Porter claims, she was reading about the Civil War and had come across "a genuinely heartrending passage about the fall of Richmond": "Quite suddenly I felt myself cornered inside that lovely besieged city and actually imagined the walls crumbling around me as the huge guns of the Union Army shelled everything in sight, and I felt all the anguish and frustration of its loyal defenders as their women and children fled in terror. The tears welled in my eyes and deep sighs wracked my body. Finally I threw myself on the bed and delivered myself to the full luxury of my grief. I was still lying there in the half-light of the gradual sundown, gently crying, when my husband came home and called to me from the patio. Getting no response, he searched for me in the kitchen and then the living room, and finally realized I was in the bedroom. As he entered the shadowy room I rose to one elbow and cried (perhaps merely whimpered), 'Oh, Albert, Richmond has fallen!' I was absolutely heartsick" (see Lopez, 9).

The only problem with this story is that by 1947, Albert and Katherine Anne were no longer married and had not lived together for seven years.

11. This, of course, is Katherine Anne Porter's side of the story and should be read with her general reputation for veracity in mind. Being a southern gentleman, Albert Erskine never commented publicly on his marriage to Porter.

12. In a letter to Cleanth dated February 17, 1939, Young continues the game by referring to "the young man who had the grip and whose name I never heard

that evening, only his first name. I was delighted that he and his wife were there. She doubtless does not know, and is not deeply concerned, with the extent to which I have felt and appreciated her extraordinary quality."

CHAPTER NINE: What Is Poetry?

1. William Terry Couch, director of the University of North Carolina Press.

2. Unless otherwise noted, the original texts of letters cited in this chapter are contained in the Beinecke Library at Yale.

3. In his review of Fogle's *Imagery of Keats and Shelley*, Brooks replies: "In the first two instances, I do agree; and I am more nearly in agreement on the third—if I understand what Mr. Fogle means—than he is aware" (114).

4. Ransom's private reaction to *Modern Poetry and the Tradition* (which he read in typescript) was contained in a letter he sent to Brooks on August 22, 1938. He expresses his genuine admiration for the book, calling it "the most unified of all the fine critical books of our day, with the possible exception of Empson, coming to a fine climax with the chapter on reform of literary history." But Ransom also observes: "You never discuss any *limit* to complication, and you tend to think that *any* complication in a modern is logical or functional complication, whereas poor Burns' *my luve's like a red, red rose* is not functional or logical. To most readers it will seem that *Waste Land* is excessive complication and no unit[ary] poem at all, after reading your exposition" (Ransom, *Letters*, 247).

5. In a letter to Donald Davidson, dated May 29, 1940, Brooks comments on Ransom's review of *Modern Poetry and the Tradition*: "I felt that John said so many flattering things about me and the book in his review, and that it was so obvious he was trying to do the handsome thing throughout, that I couldn't but feel very well satisfied with the review as a whole. But I agree thoroughly with you that John is out on a limb in his emphasis on 'logic.' I am glad to have your confirmation on this point."

CHAPTER TEN: The Man Who Knew MacArthur

1. Betty Carter made this comment in a documentary film on Huey Long shown for the first time at a conference commemorating the fiftieth anniversary of the *Southern Review* at Baton Rouge, Louisiana, in October 1985. See *Huey Long*, dir. Ken Burns (Florentine, 1985).

2. The original text of Cleanth's letter to Tommy Kirby is contained in special collections of the Hill Memorial Library at Louisiana State University.

3. The original text of Cleanth's letter to Donald Davidson is contained in Special Collections of the Heard Library at Vanderbilt.

4. The original text of this and the remaining letters cited in this chapter are contained in the Beinecke Library at Yale.

5. Although the Yeats symposium was wide-ranging, one of the recurring questions concerned the extent to which Yeats could be regarded as a Romantic. Mizener argues, for example, that Yeats never abandoned Romanticism but simply got better at it in his later poetry. (Does not Yeats himself declare, "We were the

last romantics?") He is frankly amused by the attempts of critics such as Brooks to turn Yeats into a neometaphysical poet and to impose a syllogistic structure on poems such as "Sailing to Byzantium." "We are today almost pathologically sensitive about our romanticism," Mizener writes, "as up-to-date critics must, in Wordsworth's day, have been about their neoclassicism" (614). See Arthur Mizener, "The Romanticism of W. B. Yeats," *Southern Review* 7 (Winter 1942): 601–23.

CHAPTER ELEVEN: The Mating Dance

1. Unless otherwise noted, the original texts of letters cited in this chapter are contained in the Beinecke Library at Yale. The unpublished letters of Robert Penn Warren cited in this books are quoted by permission of his literary executor, John Burt. The unpublished letters of Marshall McLuhan are quoted by permission of his widow, Corinne McLuhan.

2. A copy of Tommy Kirby's letter to Roosevelt is contained in Brooks's personnel file in the English department at Louisiana State University.

3. This letter from his father was found among Cleanth Brooks's private papers at the time of his death and is quoted by permission of his executor, Paul Blanchard.

4. Cleanth told this story to Jonathan Leff, who related it to me in an interview conducted on September 10, 1994.

5. When Hutchins inquired about the reasons for Brooks's departure, Cleanth advised him to call Marshall McLuhan in to explain the deficiencies in the Chicago program.

6. As Robert Penn Warren has observed, the greatest scientists of the modern era possess a sensibility not unlike that of the greatest poets. As a case in point, he cites Kekulé's attempt to find a formula for the benzene ring. One night while trying to solve the problem intellectually, the chemist fell asleep and had a nightmare about snakes biting each other. He woke up with this image in his mind and spent the rest of the night working out the formula suggested by it. See Floyd C. Watkins and John T. Hiers, eds., *Robert Penn Warren Talking: Interviews, 1950–1978* (New York: Random House, 1980), 143.

7. One of the best descriptions of how to tell stories on the motion picture screen can be found in the third chapter of F. Scott Fitzgerald's unfinished novel *The Last Tycoon.* Here the producer Monroe Stahr (loosely based on Irving Thalberg) delivers a lecture on the practical aesthetic of filmmaking to the British writer George Boxley (modeled on Aldous Huxley). Like Fitzgerald himself, Boxley tended to write movie scripts that relied either on too much dialogue or on visual effects that were laughably melodramatic. Stahr improvises a scene in which a stenographer inexplicably burns several personal items in an office stove. In the course of her labors, she is interrupted by a telephone caller to whom she denies ever having owned a pair of black gloves (one of the items she has just burned) and by the realization that she is being watched by a man in the office. Whereas Boxley's screenwriting is numbingly predictable, Stahr's scene possesses the aura of mystery. As he tells Boxley, it is "something that isn't either bad dialogue or jump-

ing down a well." See F. Scott Fitzgerald, *The Last Tycoon*, ed. Edmund Wilson (1941) in *Three Novels of F. Scott Fitzgerald* (New York: Scribner's, 1953), 32.

8. Cleanth's letter to Tommy Kirby and the following one from William A. Read are contained in the Special Collections of the Hill Memorial Library at Louisiana State University.

CHAPTER TWELVE: The Interior Life of the Poem

1. For a dissenting view, see Oscar James Campbell, "Shakespeare and the New Critics," in *Joseph Quincy Adams Memorial Studies*, ed. James G. McManaway et al. (Washington, D.C.: Folger Library, 1948), 81–96.

2. Empson glosses the stanza as follows: "What this means, as the context makes clear, is that eighteenth-century England had no scholarship system or *Carrière ouverte aux talents*. This is stated as pathetic, but the reader is put into a mood in which one would not try to alter it. . . . By comparing the social arrangement to Nature he makes it seem inevitable, which it was not, and gives it a dignity which was undeserved. Furthermore, a gem does not mind being in a cave and a flower prefers not to be picked; we feel that the man is like the flower, as short-lived, natural, and valuable, and this tricks us into feeling that he is better off without opportunities" (see Brooks, *Urn*, 102–3).

3. As Maynard Mack pointed out to me in a letter dated July 21, 1995, "this [new] spectrum of qualities *will* cover Homer, Dante, Chaucer, and the *Dunciad*— and indeed the entire canon. *But* this a sweeping change from the *old* touchstone."

CHAPTER THIRTEEN: A Connecticut Yankee

1. Unless otherwise indicated, the original texts of letters cited in this chapter are contained in the Beinecke Library at Yale.

2. Ten of these residential colleges were established in the 1930s; Ezra Stiles and Morse were added later.

3. For an account of Thomas's own response to Johnnie Ray, see Brinnin, 217–18.

4. By 1939, Hitler's rise to power in Germany had given the mystique of the strong leader a bad name throughout most of the civilized world. Martz made these observations to me in an interview on June 21, 1993.

5. While at Iowa in 1949, Wellek collaborated with Austin Warren on *The Theory of Literature*, a volume that would become the standard new critical textbook in introductory level graduate courses for a generation or more.

6. The story about Short was told to me by Louis Martz on June 21, 1993.

7. Cleanth Brooks has made this observation to me in several conversations.

CHAPTER FOURTEEN: The Backlash

1. Although Brooks's discussion of the Horatian Ode has been published several times, most recently in *Historical Evidence and the Reading of Seventeenth-Century Poetry* (1991), my citations of this essay, of Bush's rejoinder, and of

Brooks's subsequent reply will be from the single volume that contains all three—William R. Keast's *Seventeenth-Century English Poetry: Modern Essays in Criticism.*

2. Surely, Bush's silliest charge is that Brooks is trying "to turn a seventeenth-century liberal into a modern one" (see Keast, 351). As Brooks hastens to point out, "the title *liberal* . . . is one I am scarcely entitled to claim: I am more often called a reactionary, and I have been called a proto-fascist . . . [for having] taught at a university closely related to the late Huey Long" (see Keast, 354).

3. For a satirical response to Van Wyck Brooks's book, see Robert Penn Warren, "Homage to Oliver Allston," *Kenyon Review* 4 (Spring 1942): 259–63.

4. This information is contained in a letter Brooks wrote to Tate on December 20, 1941.

5. The Bollingen Prize is always awarded for a work produced during the previous year.

6. "Over the last two decades, in the journals of the new Criticism," Davis writes, "*authority, hierarchy, catholicism, aristocracy, tradition, absolutes, dogma, truths* became related terms of honor, and *liberalism, naturalism, scientism, individualism, equalitarianism, progress, protestantism, pragmatism,* and *personality* became related terms of rejection and contempt" (10). See Robert Gorham Davis, "The New Criticism and the Democratic Tradition," *American Scholar* 19 (Winter 1949–50): 9–19.

7. Because Fiedler's concept of the signature contains communal as well as personal elements, it can be seen as involving more than an event in the poet's psyche; the archetype is defined broadly enough not to be as privileged a poetic subject matter as Brooks suggests. But Brooks is certainly correct in noting that all of Fiedler's impressive theorizing fails to produce a standard for *evaluating* the literature produced by the interplay of archetype and signature.

CHAPTER FIFTEEN: The Squire of Northford

1. The Fugitive alumni who participated in the 1956 reunion were Donald Davidson, William Y. Elliott, Sidney Hirsch, Merrill Moore, John Crowe Ranson, Alfred Starr, Alec B. Stevenson, Allen Tate, Robert Penn Warren, and Jesse Wills. The non-Fugitive participants were Richmond Croom Beatty, Dorothy Bethurum, Cleanth Brooks, William Cobb, Louise Cowan, Robert Jacobs, Andrew Lytle, Frank Owsley, Louis D. Rubin, Jr., and Willard Thorp.

2. McLuhan's title may well be a veiled allusion to the Brooks and Warren textbooks.

3. Unless otherwise noted, the original texts of the letters cited in this chapter are contained in the Beinecke Library at Yale.

4. Interview with Carver Blanchard, June 19, 1993.

5. Interview with Rosanna Warren, June 16, 1993.

6. Interview with Louis D. Rubin, Jr., September 24, 1994.

7. The original text of Cleanth's letter to Davidson is contained in the Heard Library at Vanderbilt.

8. For a discussion of the influence of Brooks and Warren on Woodward's approach to history, see Roper, 202–208.

9. Interview with Reid Buckley, May 12, 1994.

10. Interview with Paul Blanchard, September 9, 1994.

11. Interview with Hugh Kenner, February 12, 1994. Maynard Mack and other longtime members of the Yale community regard this story as pure caricature.

12. Brooks is taking a more severe view of Richards's position on this issue than he had in his letter to Tate discussed in chapter 7.

13. In a letter dated November 20, 1963, Cleanth wrote to Andrew Lytle disclaiming any interest in the chairmanship of the Vanderbilt English department should it be offered: "The reason is simply that conditions would have to be so special for me at this time to pull up stakes that I think the whole matter is remote and improbable." The original text of this letter is contained in the Heard Library at Vanderbilt.

14. When Vanderbilt was again looking for a chairman of the English department, Cleanth wrote a "personal" letter on the matter to Chancellor Alexander Heard on August 7, 1967. The letter reads in part as follows: "I am unhappy about what happened last time. I had then the feeling that my advice was not wanted, and later, when it was asked for, that it was completely misunderstood. Very early in the proceedings I did get a 'feeler' as to whether I would myself consider taking the chairmanship. But the inquiry was so diffident—even coy— that I could not determine whether it was simply the gesture of a friend concerning himself with me as a friend or whether the Vanderbilt administration was actually interested. Later, when the department was undergoing a process of 'self-examination'—nearly always a waste of time since any intelligent person can usually see at once what is at fault—various friends of mine from all over the country were summoned to Vanderbilt to give their advice, but nobody at Vanderbilt asked mine. Very late in the day, when I was in Nashville on another mission, I was asked to make suggestions and did so. Among other things, I pointed out that I thought it useless to ask a certain type of man, however excellent, on the grounds (1) that in the present competition his own university would happily make up any money difference and (2) that unless there were something more than money involved— unless there was some kind of tie with Vanderbilt or the South—such a man would not want to give up his last ten or fifteen productive years to the painful task of building up a department to which he had no emotional attachment. In order to make my point, I named a brilliant member of the profession at Cornell [M. H. Abrams] as an example of a person who couldn't possibly be got. Imagine my consternation to learn later that an offer was promptly made to him, an offer which he immediately turned down."

The original text of this letter is contained in the Heard Library at Vanderbilt.

15. Although Vanderbilt had never given Cleanth an honorary degree, he was sent the appropriate gown and hood so that he could represent his alma mater when Yale installed Richard C. Levin as its president in 1993. He was also instructed to return the robes as soon as the ceremony was over. This story was told to me by Jonathan Leff on September 10, 1994.

CHAPTER SIXTEEN: A Postage Stamp of Soil

1. The original text of Cleanth's letter to Red Warren is contained in the Beinecke Library at Yale.

2. For Brooks's unenthusiastic response to Harry M. Campbell and Ruel E. Foster, *William Faulkner: A Critical Appraisal* (Norman: Univ. of Oklahoma Press, 1951), see "Primitivism in *The Sound and the Fury*."

3. The lone exception is the protagonist of "Pantaloon in Black," who simply lives on land rented from Roth Edmonds, the McCaslin heir.

4. This woman's name is spelled "Molly" in "The Fire and the Hearth" but "Mollie" in "Go Down, Moses." This is just another example of inconsistency of detail in the Yoknapatawpha saga.

CHAPTER SEVENTEEN: Albion Revisited

1. These observations come from a letter Tinkum Brooks wrote to her family on February 5, 1965. The original texts of the letters from Mrs. Brooks to her family were in the possession of Cleanth Brooks at the time of his death and are quoted with his permission.

2. "Spike" is ecclesiastical slang for an ultra–High Churchman; the joke here is that Eliot was himself widely regarded as the ultimate spike.

3. See "A. E. Housman" in *Shaping Joy*, 291–313.

CHAPTER EIGHTEEN: The Attack on Tory Formalism

1. The original text of Cleanth's letter to Tommy Kirby is contained in the Hill Memorial Library at Louisiana State University.

2. The original text of Cleanth's letter to Bob Heilman is contained in the Beinecke Library at Yale.

3. The argument against ordaining women to the priesthood lies in the fact that Christianity is both a patriarchal and sacramental religion. The visible symbols of the faith do matter. One might derive as much nutrition from celebrating Holy Communion with pizza and Coke as with bread and wine, but the sacrament simply would not be the same. Women priests would be appropriate for a religion with a matriarchal or androgynous deity but not for one that worships the incarnate Jesus. Although feminists remain unconvinced, this argument is not the same as saying that women are morally or intellectually unfit for the Christian ministry.

4. If any evidence were needed that the SPBCP was not slavishly devoted to the 1928 prayer book, two of the society's directors, Walter Sullivan and Harold Weatherby, belonged to a parish that used the English missal for Sunday worship. Although based on the structure and language of the 1928 book, this liturgy incorporates changes that make the Episcopal Mass much more Catholic or High Church.

5. For several particularly egregious examples, see Margaret A. Doody, "How Shall We Sing the Lord's Song upon an Alien Soil?: The New Episcopalian Liturgy," in *The State of Language*, ed. Leonard Michaels and Christopher Ricks (Berkeley: Univ. of California Press, 1950), 108–24.

6. Lewis notes that Brooks and Warren had broken with their own earlier practice by addressing a single "Letter to the Reader" rather than separate ones to student and teacher.

7. David H. Hirsch makes this same pairing of Donald Hirsch and Stanley Fish in the first chapter of his book *The Deconstruction of Literature*.

8. When interpretive communities begin to exert power, the result can be either implicit or explicit censorship. Such tendencies, when emanating in recent years from the Left, have been labeled "political correctness."

9. By the sixties, the intellectual climate was once again safe for Marxism. Beginning in the late seventies, this once discredited ideology began to make great inroads in the academy. Probably the most notable Marxist attack on the new criticism is John Fekete's *The Critical Twilight: Explorations in the Ideology of Anglo-American Literary Theory from Eliot to McLuhan* (London: Routledge and Kegan Paul, 1977).

10. See, for example, Eugene D. Genovese, *The Southern Tradition: The Achievement and Limitations of an American Conservatism* (Cambridge: Harvard Univ. Press, 1994); and Mark Jancovich, *The Cultural Politics of the New Criticism* (Cambridge: Cambridge Univ. Press, 1993).

11. As we have seen, Brooks's work on Faulkner can be regarded as an example of socially engaged Agrarian criticism.

12. Interview with Judith and George Farr, May 15, 1994.

13. Interview with Walter Sullivan, April 21, 1992.

14. Interview with Rosanna Warren, June 16, 1993.

CHAPTER NINETEEN: A Place to Come To

1. Tinkum's letter to her mother was found among Cleanth Brooks's papers at the time of his death and is quoted by permission of his executor, Paul Blanchard.

2. Interview with Eugene Waith, September 9, 1994.

3. Interview with Claude Rawson, September 16, 1994.

4. Letters from the McCelos family to the Brookses were found among Cleanth Brooks's papers at the time of his death and are quoted by permission of his executor, Paul Blanchard.

5. Interview with Carver Blanchard, September 11, 1994.

6. Interview with Jonathan Leff, September 10, 1994.

7. In addition to *William Faulkner: The Yoknapatawpha Country* and *To Yoknapatawpha and Beyond*, Brooks published *William Faulkner: First Encounters* in 1983 and *On the Prejudices, Predilections, and Firm Beliefs of William Faulkner* in 1987. The latter two books contain simplified essays and lectures addressed to a general audience. Although of considerable pedagogical value, they add little to what Brooks had said in his first two books on Faulkner.

8. If Crews found Brooks's work on Faulkner to be unimpressive, he was quite taken with Lawrence H. Schwartz's *Creating Faulkner's Reputation: The Politics of Literary Criticism* (Knoxville: Univ. of Tennessee Press, 1988). Schwartz argues that the rise in Faulkner's stock after World War II had less to do with the discovery—or rediscovery—of literary genius than with Cold War politics. Ac-

cording to Schwartz's scenario (and that generally overused word fits here), re-
pentant ex-Stalinists (particularly Malcolm Cowley) joined forces with defeated
neo-Confederates (principally the Fugitive-Agrarians) to transform an apolitical
regionalist into a world literary figure.

9. Like a latter-day Quentin Compson, Fletcher became more reactionary and
more insane with each passing year. In 1950 he finally drowned himself in a cattle
pond on his farm outside Little Rock. One is reminded of Tate's jaguar leaping at
his own reflection in the jungle pool.

10. The original text of this and the remaining letters cited in this chapter
are contained in the Beinecke Library at Yale.

11. Interview with Louis D. Rubin, Jr., September 24, 1994.

12. Interview with Lewis P. Simpson, August 16, 1994.

13. Bradford had studied under Donald Davidson at Vanderbilt and saw himself as a southern conservative in the tradition of Davidson and Richard Weaver.
Despite his brilliance as a literary scholar, constitutional historian, and classical
rhetorician, Bradford was branded an extremist because he dared to criticize the
philosophical legacy of Abraham Lincoln. Bennett's supporters ruthlessly distorted Bradford's views in order to advance their own man's candidacy. This incident did much to divide the conservative coalition along regional and cultural
lines.

14. Interview with Paul Blanchard, September 9, 1994.

15. Interview with Monroe and Betty Spears, April 23, 1992.

16. Interview with John Michael Walsh, September 10, 1994.

17. Interview with Louis D. Rubin, Jr., September 24, 1994.

18. Interview with Lewis P. Simpson, August 16, 1994.

CHAPTER TWENTY: Claiming Criticism

1. Graff is a peculiarly eclectic figure. Although his defense of a Wintersian
rationalism would seem to make him something of a literary conservative, he has
long been a committed partisan of the political Left. In regard to deconstruction,
Graff has recently slid down his own slippery slope to become a champion of a
movement he once reviled.

2. For additional attacks on the new criticism by literary historians, see Brian
Higgins and Hershel Parker, "The Chaotic Legacy of the New Criticism and the
Fair Augury of the New Scholarship," in *Ruined Eden of the Present: Critical Essays in Honor of Darrel Abel*, ed. G. R. Thompson and Virgil Lokke (West Lafayette, Ind.: Purdue Univ. Press, 1981), 27–45; and Roy Harvey Pearce, "Historicism Once More," *Kenyon Review* 20 (Autumn 1958): 554–91.

3. Brooks is certain that a critical theorist as resourceful as Miller would have
an absolute field day with "Mary had a little lamb." "Consider, for example, the
number of meanings of 'lamb,' " Brooks writes, "and the number of analogies for
Mary. To a richly stored literary mind these two words offer almost infinite possibilities" (*Community*, 000). It should also be noted that in the heyday of the new
criticism, some tactless enthusiasts made a cult of "close reading," even to the

point of imposing wit, irony, and paradox on texts when those qualities were clearly absent.

4. The original text of Cleanth's letter to Murray Kreiger is contained in the Beinecke Library at Yale.

CHAPTER TWENTY-ONE: Ogden Street

1. Unless otherwise noted, the original texts of this and other letters cited in this chapter are contained in the Beinecke Library at Yale.

2. *Adventures of Huckleberry Finn* was published in England a few months prior to its first appearance in America. Plans to bring out the book in both countries simultaneously were foiled when an irate print shop employee obscenely defaced the plate for one of the illustrations in the American edition. Repairing the damage delayed the first American publication from late 1884 to early 1885.

3. Consider the example of Harold McSween. A native of Alexandria, Louisiana (who was baptized by Cleanth, Sr.), McSween took Cleanth Brooks's class in sophomore English; he later enjoyed a successful career as a lawyer, businessman, and U.S. congressman. After losing congressional races to a dying Earl Long and to Earl's cousin Gillis Long, McSween retired from politics. He has since become a widely published writer, contributing fiction, poetry, and criticism to such leading magazines as the *Sewanee, Southern*, and *Virginia Quarterly* reviews.

4. At one point in his panel discussion with Naylor, Gates, and Littlefield, Baker pointed out that Tate once refused to attend a literary symposium at Vanderbilt that included Langston Hughes. Ironically, the college English teacher who most influenced Baker was Charles Watkins, a black professor at Howard University whose own views were decidedly new critical.

5. Interview with Walter Sullivan, April 21, 1992.

6. Interview with Carver Blanchard, June 19, 1993.

7. These three of Cleanth's letters are in the private possession of Harriet Owsley and are quoted with her permission.

8. Interview with Carver Blanchard, June 19, 1993.

9. Cleanth tells this story in a letter he mailed to all those who had sent condolences on Tinkum's death.

10. Brooks mentions this in the obituary essay he wrote on Percy for the *New Criterion*. He goes on to say: "I knew that [Percy's new novel] *The Thanatos Syndrome* though it had not yet appeared, was going through the press. I told him that my wife had so much enjoyed hearing him read an excerpt from it the year before that I wondered if he had an extra proof that he could send for her to read in her hospital bed. A typed copy with corrections appeared within a few days. It proved to be my wife's last reading matter" (58). See Cleanth Brooks, "Walker Percy, 1916–1990," *New Criterion* 10 (February 1992): 58–61.

11. Cleanth's letter is in the possession of Rosanna Warren and is quoted with her permission.

12. Interview with Carver Blanchard, June 19, 1993.

13. Interview with Alphonse Vinh, June 9, 1994.

14. This information is contained in a letter from Cleanth to Rosanna Warren,

dated November 4, 1986; the letter is in Professor Warren's possession and is quoted with her permission.

15. Information in this paragraph was gleaned from interviews with the following individuals: George Garrett on August 14, 1993; Andrew Lytle on April 22, 1992; and Walter Sullivan on April 21, 1992.

16. Interview with Carver Blanchard, June 19, 1993.

17. Interview with Walter and Jane Sullivan, April 21, 1992.

18. Gioia goes on to say: "Having spent the last two years taking over [the editorship of] three of [X. J.] Kennedy's books, I have been thinking a great deal about how influential these books are and how invisible they remain in literary study. Old editions are impossible to find. Libraries don't keep them, and they were never sold by the book trade. I get letters from bibliographers all the time trying to track down information not found in the biggest research libraries in America. (I suspect in a hundred years these books will be like 18th century broadsides in their desirability to libraries.)"

19. Since the late 1980s, several books have appeared directly attacking deconstruction. These include John Ellis's *Against Deconstruction* (Princeton: Princeton Univ. Press, 1989); David Lehman's *Signs of the Times*, and David H. Hirsch's *The Deconstruction of Literature*. The backlash against political correctness in academia is even more pronounced.

CHAPTER TWENTY-TWO: April Is the Cruellest Month

1. Interview with Jonathan Leff, September 10, 1994.

2. Cleanth's letter to Louis Rubin is quoted by permission of Louis D. Rubin, Jr.

3. This letter is in my possession. The collection of essays was published by the University of Missouri Press in 1995 under the title *Community, Religion, and Literature*.

4. Interview with Carver Blanchard, September 11, 1994.

5. Interview with Alphonse Vinh, June 9, 1994.

6. Interview with Claude Rawson, September 16, 1994.

7. Interview with C. Vann Woodward, June 17, 1992.

8. Interview with Alphonse Vinh, June 9, 1994.

9. Interview with Louis D. Rubin, Jr., September 24, 1994.

10. Interview with Claude Rawson, September 16, 1994.

11. Interview with Lewis P. Simpson, August 16, 1994.

12. At the time of the memorial service for Cleanth, which was held at Yale on November 1, 1994, members of the Brooks and Blanchard families met for the first time. Carver was particularly impressed with the poise and intelligence of Patty's daughter, Rebecca Means, whom he had known previously only from the adolescent pictures she sent to Cleanth.

WORKS CITED

Primary Works

The bulk of Cleanth Brooks's papers are collected in the Beinecke Rare Book and Manuscript Library at Yale University.

BOOKS WRITTEN

Community, Religion, and Literature. Columbia: Univ. of Missouri Press, 1995.

The Hidden God: Studies in Hemingway, Faulkner, Yeats, Eliot, and Warren. New Haven: Yale Univ. Press, 1963.

Historical Evidence and the Reading of Seventeenth-Century Poetry. Columbia: Univ. of Missouri Press, 1991.

The Language of the American South. Athens: Univ. of Georgia Press, 1985.

Literary Criticism: A Short History. With W. K. Wimsatt. New York: Knopf, 1957.

Modern Poetry and the Tradition. Chapel Hill: Univ. of North Carolina Press, 1939.

On the Prejudices, Predilections, and Firm Beliefs of William Faulkner. Baton Rouge: Louisiana State Univ. Press, 1987.

The Relation of the Alabama-Georgia Dialect to the Provincial Dialects of Great Britain. Baton Rouge: Louisiana State Univ. Press, 1935.

The Rich Manifold: The Author, the Reader, the Linguistic Medium. Ed. with an interview by Joseph M. Ditta and Ronald S. Librach. Columbia: *Missouri Review*, 1983.

A Shaping Joy: Studies in the Writer's Craft. New York: Harcourt Brace, 1971.

The Well Wrought Urn: Studies in the Structure of Poetry. New York: Reynal and Hitchcock, 1947.

William Faulkner: First Encounters. New Haven: Yale Univ. Press, 1983.

William Faulkner: The Yoknapatawpha Country. New Haven: Yale Univ. Press, 1963.

William Faulkner: Toward Yoknapatawpha and Beyond. New Haven: Yale Univ. Press, 1978.

BOOKS EDITED

American Literature: The Makers and the Making. With R. W. B. Lewis and Robert Penn Warren. 2 vols. New York: St. Martin's Press 1973.

An Anthology of Stories from the Southern Review. With Robert Penn Warren. Baton Rouge: Louisiana State Univ. Press, 1953.

An Approach to Literature; A Collection of Prose and Verse with Analyses and Discussions. With Robert Penn Warren and John Thibaut Purser. Baton Rouge: Louisiana State Univ. Press, 1936. Rev. ed. New York: F. S. Crofts., 1939, 1952, 1964. Englewood Ciffs, N.J.: Prentice-Hall, 1975.

The Correspondence of Thomas Percy and Richard Farmer. Baton Rouge: Louisiana State Univ. Press, 1946.

Facets: An Anthology of Verse. With others. Nashville, Tenn.: Calumet Club of Vanderbilt, 1928.

Fundamentals of Good Writing: A Handbook of Modern Rhetoric. With Robert Penn Warren. New York: Harcourt Brace, 1950.

Modern Rhetoric: With Readings. With Robert Penn Warren. New York: Harcourt Brace, 1949. Rev. ed., 1958, 1972.

The Poems of Mr. John Milton: The 1645 Edition with Essays in Analysis. With John Edward Hardy. New York: Harcourt Brace, 1951.

Report on Academic Conditions at the Louisiana State University. Prepared by faculty members of Phi Beta Kappa.

Tragic Themes in Western Literature. New Haven: Yale Univ. Press, 1955.

Understanding Drama. With Robert B. Heilman. New York: Holt, 1945. Rev. ed., 1948.

Understanding Fiction. With Robert Penn Warren. New York: F. S. Crofts, 1943. Rev. ed., 1959. Englewood Cliffs, N.J.: Prentice-Hall, 1979.

Understanding Poetry: An Anthology for College Students. With Robert Penn Warren. New York: Holt, 1938. Rev. ed., 1950, 1960, 1976.

ESSAYS, REVIEWS, MISCELLANEOUS

"Brooks on Warren." *Four Quarters* 21 (May 1972): 19–22.

"Cantankerous and Other Critics." *Kenyon Review* 6 (Spring 1944): 282–88.

"Criticism and Literary History: Marvell's 'Horatian Ode.'" In Keast, ed., *Seventeenth-Century English Poetry,* 321–40. Reprint of *Sewanee Review* 55 (Winter 1947): 199–222.

"Editorial." With Robert Penn Warren. *Southern Review* 7 (Autumn 1941): n.p.

"Editorial." With Robert Penn Warren. *Southern Review* 7 (Winter 1941–42): n.p.

"Edna Millay's Maturity." *Southwest Review* 20 (January 1935): 1–5 of separately paged section at end of number.

"Eliot's Harvard Lectures." *Southwest Review* 19 (January 1934): 1–2 of separately paged section at end of number.

"Empson's Criticism." *Accent* 4 (Summer 1944): 208–16.

"The English Language in the South." In *A Southern Treasury of Life and Literature,* ed. Stark Young, 350–58. New York: Scribner's, 1937.

"Eudora Welty and the Southern Idiom." In *Eudora Welty: A Form of Thanks,* ed. Ann J. Abadie and Louis Dollarhide, 3–24. Jackson: Univ. Press of Mississippi, 1979.

"Forty Years of *Understanding Poetry*." *College English Association Forum* 10 (April 1980): 5–12.

"Geometry of Sunset." *Literary Digest*, November 30, 1929: 26. Poem.

"God, Gallup, and the Episcopalians." *American Scholar* 50 (Summer 1981): 313–25.

"I. A. Richards and *Practical Criticism*." In Core, ed., *The Critics Who Made Us*, 35–46.

"I. A. Richards and the Concept of Tension." In *I. A. Richards: Essays in His Honor*, ed. Reuben Brower, Helen Vendler, and John Hollander, 135–56. New York: Oxford Univ. Press, 1973.

"Irony as a Principle of Structure." In *Literary Opinion in America*, vol. 2, ed. Morton D. Zabel, 729–41. Rev. ed. New York: Harper and Row, 1962.

"The Life and Death of an Academic Journal." In *The Art of Literary Publishing: Editors on Their Craft*, ed. Bill Henderson, 88–99. Wainscott, N.Y.: Pushcart, 1980.

"List of 'Wicked Esthetes' Wanted." *Saturday Review of Literature*, October 29, 1949: 24. Letter to the editor.

"Literary Criticism: Poet, Poem, and Reader." In *Varieties of Literary Experience*, ed. Stanley Burnshaw, 95–114. New York: Columbia Univ. Press, 1962.

"Literature and the Professors: Literary History vs. Criticism." *Kenyon Review* 2 (Autumn 1940): 403–12.

"The McTyeire School." McTyeire School Reunion. McKenzie, Tenn. June 1992.

"The Maelstrom." *Sewanee Review* 54 (Winter 1946): 116–18. Poem.

"Metaphor and the Function of Criticism." In *Spiritual Problems in Contemporary Literature*, ed. Stanley Romaine Hopper, 127–37. New York: Harper and Brothers, 1952.

"Mr. Kazin's America." *Sewanee Review* 51 (Winter 1943): 52–61.

"Mrs. Cleanth Brooks [Sr.]" *Journal of the Louisiana Conference* (Methodist Episcopal Church South), 1963, 272–73.

"Mrs. Colum and Mr. Jones." *Sewanee Review* 54 (Spring 1946): 334–43.

"The New Criticism and Scholarship." In *Twentieth-Century English*, ed. W. S. Knickerbocker, 371–83. New York: Philosophical Library, 1946.

"1928 Class Poem." *Vanderbilt Alumnus* June 1928: 20.

"A Note on the Limits of 'History' and the Limits of 'Criticism.'" In Keast, ed., *Seventeenth-Century English Poetry*, 352–58. Reprint of *Sewanee Review* 61 (Winter 1953): 129–35.

"A Plea to the Protestant Churches." In *Who Owns America? A New Declaration of Independence*, ed. Herbert Agar and Allen Tate, 323–33. Boston: Houghton Mifflin, 1936.

"The Poem as Organism: Modern Critical Procedure." In *English Institute Annual 1940*, 20–41. New York: Columbia Univ. Press, 1941.

"Primitivism in *The Sound and the Fury*." In *English Institute Essays, 1952*, ed. Alice S. Downer, 5–28. New York: Columbia Univ. Press, 1954.

"The Reading of Modern Poetry." With Robert Penn Warren. *American Review* 8 (February 1937): 435–49.

"The Relative and the Absolute: An Exchange of Views." With Herbert J. Muller. *Sewanee Review* 57 (Summer 1949): 357–77.

Review of *Anatomy of Criticism*, by Northrop Frye. *Christian Scholar* 41 (1958): 169–73.

Review of *The Imagery of Keats and Shelley*, by Richard Harter Fogle. *Keats-Shelley Journal* 1 (January 1952): 113–14.

"Studies in Baroque: An Examination of the Conceit Poetry of the Elizabethan Sonnet-Sequences." M.A. Thesis. Tulane University, New Orleans, 1929.

"T. S. Eliot as Modernist Poet." In *Literary Theory and Structure: Essays Presented to William K. Wimsatt*, ed. Frank Brady et al., 353–77. New Haven: Yale Univ. Press, 1973.

"What Are English Teachers Teaching?" *CEA Critic* 33 (November 1970): 3–4.

"The Woman and Artist I Knew." In *Katherine Anne Porter and Texas: An Uneasy Relationship*, ed. Clinton Machann and William Bedford Clark, 13–24. College Station: Texas A&M Univ. Press, 1990.

Secondary Sources

Aaron, Daniel. *The Unwritten War: American Writers and the Civil War*. New York: Knopf, 1973.

Auden, W. H. "Against Romanticism." *New Republic* February 5, 1940: 187.

Batts, W. O., ed. *Private Preparatory Schools for Boys in Tennessee*. Nashville: n.p., 1957.

Bloom, Harold. "The Central Man: Emerson, Whitman, Wallace Stevens." *Massachusetts Review* 7 (Winter 1966): 23–42.

———. *Shelley's Mythmaking*. New Haven: Yale Univ. Press, 1959.

———. *The Visionary Company: The Reading of English Romantic Poetry*. 2d ed. Ithaca, N.Y.: Cornell Univ. Press, 1971.

Bloom, Harold, et al. *Deconstruction and Criticism*. New York: Seabury, 1971.

Bohner, Charles. *Robert Penn Warren*. Rev. ed. Boston: Twayne, 1981.

Brinnin, John Malcolm. *Dylan Thomas in America: An Intimate Journal*. Boston: Little, Brown, 1955.

Bronson, Betrand H. "A Sense of the Past." *Sewanee Review* 67 (Winter 1959): 145–55.

Brooks, Van Wyck. *The Opinions of Oliver Allston*. New York: Dutton, 1941.

Brown, Stuart Gerry. "Poetry and Tradition." *Sewanee Review* 48 (Fall 1940): 547–52.

Buchanan, David. *The Treasure of Auchinleck: The Story of the Boswell Papers*. New York: McGraw-Hill, 1974.

Buckley, Reid. "A Partisan Conversation: Cleanth Brooks." *Southern Partisan* 3 (Spring 1983): 22–26.

Burke, Kenneth. "The Rhetoric of Hitler's "Battle." *Southern Review* 5 (Summer 1939): 1–21.

Bush, Douglas. "Marvell's 'Horatian Ode.'" In Keast, ed., *Seventeenth-Century English Poetry*, 341–51. Reprint of *Sewanee Review* 60 (Fall 1952): 363–76.

————. "The New Criticism: Some Old-Fashioned Queries." *PMLA* 64, supp., pt. 2 (March 1949): 13–21.

Cain, William E. *The Crisis in Criticism: Theory, Literature, and Reform in English Studies.* Baltimore: Johns Hopkins Univ. Press, 1984.

————. *F. O. Matthiessen and the Politics of Criticism.* Madison: Univ. of Wisconsin Press, 1988.

Campbell, Colin. "The Tyranny of the Yale Critics." *New York Times Magazine,* February 9, 1986: 20–26, 28, 43, 47–48.

Coleridge, Samuel Taylor. *Biographia Literaria; or Biographical Sketches of My Literary Life and Opinions.* 1817. Reprint, New York: Macmillan, 1926.

Conkin, Paul K. *Gone with the Ivy: A Biography of Vanderbilt University.* With Henry Swint and Patricia S. Miletich. Knoxville: Univ. of Tennessee Press, 1985.

————. *The Southern Agrarians.* Knoxville: Univ. of Tennessee Press, 1988.

Core, George. "Agrarianism, Criticism, and the Academy." In Havard and Sullivan, eds., *A Band of Prophets,* 117–39.

————. "The *Sewanee Review* and the Editorial Performance." In *Yearbook of English Studies,* vol. 10, ed. G. K. Hunter et al., 105–15. Leeds: Modern Humanities Research Association, 1980.

————. "Vanderbilt English and the Rise of the New Criticism." In Winchell, *The Vanderbilt Traditon,* 119–35.

————, ed. *The Critics Who Made Us: Essays from the Sewanee Review.* Columbia: Univ. of Missouri Press, 1993.

Cowan, Louise. *The Fugitive Group.* Baton Rouge: Louisiana State Univ. Press, 1959.

Cowley, Malcolm, ed. *The Portable Faulkner.* New York: Viking, 1946.

Crane, R. S. "The Critical Monism of Cleanth Brooks." In *Critics and Criticism,* ed. Crane et al., 83–107. Chicago: Univ. of Chicago Press, 1952.

Crews, Frederick C. "The Strange Fate of William Faulkner." *New York Review of Books,* March 7, 1991: 47–52.

Culler, Jonathan D. *On Deconstruction: Theory and Criticism after Structuralism.* Ithaca, N.Y.: Cornell Univ. Press, 1982.

Cutrer, Thomas W. *Parnasus on the Mississippi: The Southern Review and the Baton Rouge Literary Community, 1935–1942.* Baton Rouge: Louisiana State Univ. Press, 1984.

Daily Town Talk (Alexandria, La.). "First Methodist Church Religious Building Under Construction Here." August 10, 1927: 1.

Daspit, Alex. "Dean Pipkin." *LSU Graduate Report* 21 (Spring 1976): 5.

Davidson, Donald. "A Mirror for Artists." In Twelve Southerners, *I'll Take My Stand,* 28–60.

————. *Southern Writers in the Modern World.* Athens: Univ. of Georgia Press, 1958.

Davis, Bertram H. *Thomas Percy.* Boston: Twayne, 1981.

Donald, David Herbert. *Look Homeward: A Life of Thomas Wolfe.* Boston: Little, Brown, 1987.

Duvall, John N. *Faulkner's Marginal Couple: Invisible, Outlaw, and Unspeakable Communities*. Austin: Univ. of Texas Press, 1990.

Eagleton, Terry. *Literary Theory: An Introduction*. Minneapolis: Univ. of Minnesota Press, 1983.

Eliot, T. S. *For Lancelot Andrewes: Essays on Style and Order*. London: Faber and Gwyer, 1928.

———. *Selected Essays*. New York: Harcourt Brace, 1950.

Empson, William. *Seven Types of Ambiguity*. 1930. Reprint, New York: New Directions, 1966.

Epstein, Joseph. *Once More Around the Block: Familiar Essays*. New York: Norton, 1987.

Erskine, Albert. "The Sempiternal Rose." *Southwest Review* 20 (April 1935): 21–27. Review of *So Red the Rose*, by Stark Young.

Fain, John Tyree, and Thomas Daniel Young, eds. *The Literary Correspondence of Donald Davidson and Allen Tate*. Athens: Univ. of Georgia Press, 1974.

Farr, Judith. "A Tribute." In James W. Hipp, ed., *Dictionary of Literary Biography Yearbook, 1994*, 250–51. Detroit: Gale, 1995.

Faulkner, William. *The Collected Stories of William Faulkner*. New York: Random House, 1950.

———. *Knight's Gambit and Other Stories*. New York: Random House, 1949.

Ferris, Paul. *Dylan Thomas: A Biography*. New York: Dial, 1977.

Fiedler, Leslie. *Collected Essays of Leslie Fiedler*. 2 vols. New York: Stein and Day, 1971.

Fish, Stanley. *Is There a Text in this Class? The Authority of Interpretive Communities*. Cambridge: Harvard Univ. Press, 1980.

———. *Surprised by Sin: The Reader in "Paradise Lost"*. 1967. Reprint, Berkeley: Univ. of California Press, 1971.

———. "Why Literary Criticism is Like Virtue." *London Review of Books*. 10 June 1993. 11–16.

Fogle, Richard H. *The Imagery of Keats and Shelley*. Chapel Hill: Univ. of North Carolina Press, 1949.

———. "Romantic Bards and Metaphysical Reviewers." *English Literary History* 12 (1945): 221–50.

Foote, Shelby. *Red River to Appomattox*. Vol. 3 of *The Civil War: A Narrative*. New York: Random House, 1974.

Franklin, Bruce. "The Teaching of Literature in the Highest Academies of the Empire." In Kampf and Lauter, eds., *The Politics of Literature*, 101–29.

Frye, Northrop. *Anatomy of Criticism: Four Essays*. Princeton: Princeton Univ. Press, 1957.

The Fugitive: A Journal of Poetry / Volumes 1–4 / 1922–1925. New York: Johnson Reprint, 1966.

Garrett, George. "Warren's Poetry: Some Things We Ought to Be Thinking About." *South Carolina Review* 23 (Fall 1990): 49–57.

Givner, Joan. *Katherine Anne Porter: A Life*. New York: Simon and Schuster, 1982.

Goodman, Charlotte Margolis. *Jean Stafford: The Savage Heart*. Austin: Univ. of Texas Press, 1990.

Graff, Gerald. "Fear and Trembling at Yale." *American Scholar* 46 (Autumn 1977): 467–78.

———. *Literature Against Itself: Literary Ideas in Modern Society*. Chicago: Univ. of Chicago Press, 1979.

———. *Poetic Statement and Critical Dogma*. Evanston, Ill.: Northwestern Univ. Press, 1970.

———. "New Criticism Once More." *Critical Inquiry* 5 (Spring 1979): 569–75.

———. "Statement and Poetry." *Southern Review*, n.s., 2 (Summer 1966): 499–515.

Grierson, H. J. C., ed. *Metaphysical Lyrics and Poems of the Seventeenth Century*. Oxford: Clarendon, 1921.

Griffith, Albert J. *Peter Taylor*. Rev. ed. Boston: Twayne, 1990.

Hair, William Ivy. *The Kingfish and His Realm: The Life and Times of Huey P. Long*. Baton Rouge: Louisiana State Univ. Press, 1991.

Hamilton, Ian. *Robert Lowell: A Biography*. New York: Random House, 1982.

Hartman, Geoffrey H. "Beyond Formalism." In *Beyond Formalism: Literary Essays, 1958–1970*, 42–57. New Haven: Yale Univ. Press, 1970.

Havard, William C., and Walter Sullivan, eds. *A Band of Prophets: The Vanderbilt Agrarians after Fifty Years*. Baton Rouge: Lousiana State Univ. Press, 1982.

Heilman, Robert Bechtold. *The Southern Connection*. Baton Rouge: Louisiana State Univ. Press, 1991.

Henry, Robert Selph, ed. *As They Saw Forrest: Some Recollections and Comments of Contemporaries*. Jackson, Tenn.: McCowat-Mercer, 1956.

Hirsch, David H. *The Deconstruction of Literature: Criticism after Auschwitz*. Hanover, N.H.: Univ. Press of New England, 1991.

Hirsch, E. D., Jr. *Validity in Interpretation*. New Haven: Yale Univ. Press, 1967.

Hulbert, Ann. *The Interior Castle: The Art and Life of Jean Stafford*. New York: Knopf, 1992.

Hyman, Stanley Edgar. *The Armed Vision: A Study in the Methods of Modern Literary Criticism*. Rev. ed. New York: Random House, 1955.

Idol, John L., Jr. "Wolfe in Richmond: A Great Story That Never Happened." *Thomas Wolfe Review* 10 (Fall 1986): 3–4.

Johnston, Alva. "Louisiana Revolution." *Saturday Evening Post*, May 11, 1940: 16–17, 97–98, 100, 102.

Jones, Howard Mumford. "The Limits of Contemporary Criticism." *Saturday Review of Literature* September 6, 1941: 3–4, 17.

Judis, John B. *William F. Buckley, Jr.: Patron Saint of the Conservatives*. New York: Simon and Schuster, 1988.

Justus, James H. Review of *William Faulkner: The Yoknapatawpha Country*, by Cleanth Brooks. *Modern Language Quarterly* 25 (1964): 231–33.

Kampf, Louis, and Paul Lauter, eds. *The Politics of Literature: Dissenting Essays on the Teaching of English*. New York: Pantheon Books, 1972.

Kazin, Alfred. *On Native Grounds: An Interpretation of Modern Prose Literature*. New York: Harcourt Brace, 1942.

Keast, William R., ed. *Seventeenth-Century English Poetry: Modern Essays in Criticism*. New York: Oxford Univ. Press, 1962.

Kenner, Hugh. "A Tribute." In James W. Hipp, ed., *Dictionary of Literary Biography Yearbook, 1994*, 251–52. Detroit: Gale, 1995.

Lehman, David. *Signs of the Times: Deconstruction and the Fall of Paul de Man*. New York: Simon and Schuster, 1991.

Leitch, Vincent B. *American Criticism from the Thirties to the Eighties*. New York: Columbia Univ. Press, 1988.

Lentricchia, Frank. *After the New Criticism*. Chicago: Univ. of Chicago Press, 1980.

Lewis, R. W. B. "Warren's Long Visit to American Literature." *Yale Review* 70 (July 1981): 568–91.

Littlejohn, David. "Cleanth Brooks's Faulkner. In *Interruptions*, 131–34. New York: Grossman's, 1970.

Lopez, Enrique Hank, ed. *Conversations with Katherine Anne Porter: Refugee from Indian Creek*. Boston: Little, Brown, 1981.

Lowell, Robert. *Life Studies*. New York: Farrar, Straus, and Cudahy, 1959.

Lyday, Lance. "Faulkner Criticism: Will It Ever End?" *South Carolina Review* 25 (Fall 1992): 183–92.

Lynn, Kenneth S. "F. O. Matthiessen." In *Masters: Portraits of Great Teachers*, ed. Joseph Epstein, 103–18. New York: Basic Books, 1981.

Lytle, Andrew. One of "Six Reminiscences." In *The Southern Review Original Series, 1935–1942: A Commemoration, 1980*, 14–15. Baton Rouge: Louisiana State University, 1980.

MacLeish, Archibald. *The Irresponsibles*. New York: Duell, Sloan, and Pierce, 1942.

Matthews, T. S. *Great Tom: Notes Toward the Definition of T. S. Eliot*. London: Weidenfeld and Nicholson, 1974.

Matthiessen, F. O. *The Responsibilities of the Critic: Essays and Reviews*. Selected by John Rackliffe. New York Oxford Univ. Press, 1952.

McAlexander, Hubert H., ed. *Conversations with Peter Taylor*. Jackson: Univ. Press of Mississippi, 1987.

McCallum, James Dow, ed. *The College Omnibus*. New York: Harcourt Brace, 1933.

McHaney, Thomas L. "Brooks on Faulkner: The End of the Long View." *Review* 1 (1979): 29–45.

McLuhan, Marshall. "An Ancient Quarrel in Modern America (Sophists vs. Grammarians)." In *The Interior Landscape: The Literary Criticism of Marshall McLuhan*, ed. Eugene McNamara, 223–34. New York: McGraw-Hill, 1969.

Mencken, H. L. "The Sahara of the Bozart." In *Prejudices, Second Series*, 136–54. New York: Knopf, 1920.

Memphis Conference Minutes. 1905.

Memphis Conference Minutes. 1913.

Memphis Conference Yearbook. 1919.

Miller, J. Hillis. "On Edge: The Crossways of Contemporary Criticism." In *Romanticism and Contemporary Criticism*, ed. Morris Eaves and Michael Fischer, 96–126. Ithaca, N.Y.: Cornell Univ. Press, 1986.

Mims, Edwin. *The Advancing South: Stories of Progress and Reaction.* Garden City, N.Y.: Doubleday, Page, 1926.

Mizener, Arthur. "The Desires of the Mind." *Sewanee Review* 55 (Fall 1947): 460–69.

———. "The Equality of Poetry." *Poetry* 71 (October 1947-March 1948): 318–24.

———. "The Romanticism of W. B. Yeats." *Southern Review* 7 (Winter 1942): 601–23.

Morrison, Ray. "James A. Robins (Mr. Jim)." In Batts, ed., *Private Preparatory Schools for Boys*, 20–22.

Mudrick, Marvin. "The Over-Wrought Urn." *New York Review of Books* January 9, 1964: 8.

Muller, H. J. "The Relative and the Absolute: An Exchange of Views." With Cleanth Brooks. *Sewanee Review* 57 (Summer 1949): 357–77.

O'Brien, Michael. "The Middle Years: Edwin Mims." In *Rethinking the South: Essays in Intellectual History*, 131–56. Baltimore: Johns Hopkins Univ. Press, 1988.

———, ed. "Edwin Mims and Donald Davidson: A Correspondence, 1923–1958." *Southern Review*, n.s., 10 (Autumn 1974): 904–22.

Ohmann, Richard. "Teaching and Studying Literature at the End of Ideology." In Kampf and Lauter, eds., *The Politics of Literature*, 130–59.

Paschall, Douglas. "English Origins of Southern Accents: An Interview with Cleanth Brooks." *Touchstone* 13 (1988): 3–6.

Porter, Katherine Anne. *Letters of Katherine Anne Porter.* Ed. Isabel Bayley. New York: Atlantic Monthly Press, 1990.

———. "Old Mortality." In Brooks and Warren, eds., *Stories from the Southern Review*, 144–92.

Price-Stephens, Gordon. "The British Reception of Faulkner." *Mississippi Quarterly* 18 (Summer 1965). Special issue.

Purdy, Rob Roy, ed. *Fugitives' Reunion: Conversations at Vanderbilt, May 3–5, 1956.* Nashville: Vanderbilt Univ. Press, 1959.

Rackliffe, John. "Notes for a Character Study." In *F. O. Matthiessen: A Collective Portrait*, ed. Paul M. Sweezy and Leo Huberman, 76–92. New York: Henry Schuman, 1950.

Ranson, John Crowe. "Apologia for Modernism." *Kenyon Review* 2 (Spring 1940): 247–51.

———. *The New Criticism.* New York: New Directions, 1941.

———. *Selected Essays of John Crowe Ransom.* Ed. Thomas Daniel Young and John Hindle. Baton Rouge: Louisiana State Univ. Press, 1984.

———. *Selected Letters of John Crowe Ransom.* Ed. Thomas Daniel Young and George Core. Baton Rouge: Louisiana State Univ. Press, 1985.

———. "The Teaching of Poetry." *Kenyon Review.* 1 (1939): 81–83.

Richards, I. A. *Practical Criticism: A Study of Literary Judgment.* New York: Harcourt Brace, 1929.

———. *Selected Letters of I. A. Richards, CH* Ed. John Constable. Oxford: Clarendon, 1990.

Roberts, David. *Jean Stafford: A Biography.* Boston: Little, Brown, 1988.

Rollin, Roger. "Apologia Pro Vita Literaria." Review of *Historical Evidence and the Reading of Seventeenth-Century Poetry,* by Cleanth Brooks. *South Carolina Review* 27 (1994-95): 374–75.

Roper, John Herbert. *C. Vann Woodward, Southerner.* Athens: Univ. of Georgia Press, 1987.

Rubin, Louis D., Jr. "Cleanth Brooks: A Memory." *Sewanee Review* 103 (Spring 1995): 265–80.

———. "The Gathering of the Fugitives: A Recollection." *Southern Review,* n.s., 30 (Autumn 1994): 658–73.

———. "RPW, 1905–1989." In *The Mockingbird in the Gum Tree: A Literary Gallimaufry,* 137–45. Baton Rouge: Louisiana State Univ. Press, 1991.

———. *The Wary Fugitives: Four Poets and the South.* Baton Rouge: Louisiana State Univ. Press, 1978.

Russo, John Paul. *I. A. Richards: His Life and Work.* Baltimore: Johns Hopkins Univ. Press, 1989.

Said, Edward W. "Two Without a Context." *New York Times Book Review,* December 10, 1972: 4–5, 12.

Schuman, Frederick L. "Leon Trotsky: Martyr or Renegade?" *Southern Review* 3 (Summer 1937): 51–74.

Shapiro, Edward S. "American Conservative Intellectuals, the 1930's, and the Crisis of Ideology." *Modern Age* 23 (Fall 1979): 370–80.

Shils, Edward. "Robert Maynard Hutchins." *American Scholar* 59 (Spring 1990): 211–35.

Simpson, Lewis P. "A Certain Continuity." In Simpson et al., eds., *The Southern Review and Modern Literature,* 1–18.

———. "Robert Penn Warren and the South." *Southern Review,* n.s., 26 (Winter 1990): 7–12.

———, ed. *The Possibilities of Order: Cleanth Brooks and His Work.* Baton Rouge: Louisiana State Univ. Press, 1976.

Simpson, Lewis P., et al., eds. *The Southern Review and Modern Literature: 1935–1985.* Baton Rouge. Louisiana State Univ. Press, 1988.

Smith, Henry Nash. "The Dilemma of Agrarianism." *Southwest Review* 19 (April 1934): 215–32.

Spears, Monroe K. *American Ambitions: Selected Essays on Literary and Cultural Themes.* Baltimore: Johns Hopkins Univ. Press, 1987.

———. *Countries of the Mind: Literary Explorations.* Columbia: Univ. of Missouri Press, 1992.

———. "The Mysterious Urn." *Western Review* 12 (Autumn 1947): 54–58.

———. "The *Sewanee Review* and the Southern Renascence." *South Carolina Review* 25 (Fall 1992): 7–11.

Stafford, Jean. "Some Letters to Peter and Eleanor Taylor." *Shenandoah* 30 (Spring 1979): 27–55.

Stevens, Wallace. *Letters.* Ed. Holly Stevens. New York: Knopf, 1966.

Sullivan, Walter. *Allen Tate: A Recollection.* Baton Rouge: Louisiana State Univ. Press, 1988.

———. *In Praise of Blood Sports and Other Essays.* Baton Rouge: Louisiana State Univ. Press, 1990.

Sutton, Walter. *Modern American Criticism.* Westport, Conn.: Greenwood, 1977.

Tassin, Anthony G. "The Phoenix and the Urn: The Literary Theory and Criticism of Cleanth Brooks." Ph.D. diss. Louisiana State University, Baton Rouge, 1966.

Tate, Allen. "The Function of the Critical Quarterly." In *Essays of Four Decades,* 45–55. Chicago: Swallow, 1968.

———. "Hardy's Philosophical Metaphors." In *Essays of Four Decades,* 329–40.

———. "Peter Taylor." *Shenandoah* 28 (Winter 1977): 10.

———. "What I Owe to Cleanth Brooks." In Simpson, ed., *The Possibilities of Order,* 125–27.

Time. "The Curse and the Hope." July 17, 1964: 44–48.

———. "Wessex and Louisiana." June 10, 1940: 92, 94.

Trice, W. E. "Rev. Cleanth Brooks." *Annual of the Louisiana Conference* (Methodist Episcopal Church South), 1943, 81.

Trillin, Calvin. *Remembering Denny.* New York: Farrar, Straus, and Giroux, 1993.

Trowbridge, Hoyt. "Aristotle and the 'New Criticism.'" *Sewanee Review* 52 (Fall 1944): 537–55.

Tuve, Rosemund. Review of *Modern Poetry and the Tradition,* by Cleanth Brooks. *Modern Language Quarterly* 2 (March 1941): 147–50.

Twelve Southerners. *I'll Take My Stand: The South and the Agrarian Tradition.* 1930. Reprint, New York: Harper and Row, 1962.

Voegelin, Eric. *Autobiographical Reflections.* Ed. Ellis Sandoz. Baton Rouge: Louisiana State Univ. Press, 1989.

Wade, John Donald. "Prodigal." *Southern Review* 1 (Summer 1935): 192–98.

———. "Sweet Are the Uses of Degeneracy." *Southern Review* 1 (Winter 1936): 449–66.

Waldron, Ann. *Close Connections: Caroline Gordon and the Southern Renaissance.* New York: Putnam: 1987.

———. *Hodding Carter: The Reconstruction of a Racist.* Chapel Hill, N.C.: Algonquin, 1993.

Walsh, John Michael. *Cleanth Brooks: An Annotated Bibliography.* New York: Garland, 1990.

Warren, Robert Penn. *All the King's Men.* New York: Harcourt Brace, 1946.

———. "*All the King's Men*: The Matrix of Experience." *Yale Review* 53 (Winter 1964): 161–67.

———. "Brooks and Warren." *Humanities,* April 1985: 1–3.

———. "A Conversation with Cleanth Brooks." In Simpson, ed., *The Possibilities of Order,* 1–124.

————. "A Reminiscence." In *Nashville: The Faces of Two Centuries,1780–1980*, ed. John Edgerton, 205–20. Nashville, Tenn.: PlusMedia, 1979.

————. *Segregation: The Inner Conflict in the South*. New York: Random House, 1956.

————. *Selected Essays*. 1958. Reprint, New York: Vintage, 1966.

Watkins, Floyd C. "Thomas Wolfe and the Nashville Agrarians." *Georgia Review* 7 (Winter 1953): 410–23.

Watkins, Floyd C., and John T. Hiers, eds. *Robert Penn Warren Talking: Interviews, 1950–1978*. New York: Random House, 1980.

Webb, Max. "Ford Madox Ford and the Baton Rouge Writer's Conference." *Southern Review* 10 (Fall 1974): 892–903.

Wellek, René. *A History of Modern Criticism, 1750–1950*. Vol. 6, *American Criticism, 1900–1950*. New Haven: Yale Univ. Press, 1986.

Wiencek, Henry. *The Smithsonian Guide to Historic America: Southern New England*. New York: Stewart, Tabori, and Chang, 1989.

Wills, Garry, *Confessions of a Conservative*. Garden City, N.Y.: Doubleday, 1979.

Wimsatt, W. K. "Northrop Frye: Criticism as Myth." In *Northrop Frye in Modern Criticism: Selected Papers from the English Institute*, ed. Murray Krieger, 75–107. New York: Columbia Univ. Press, 1966.

————. *The Verbal Icon: Studies in the Meaning of Poetry*. With Monroe C. Beardsley. Lexington: Univ. of Kentucky Press, 1954.

Winchell, Mark Royden. "Cleanth Brooks." In James W. Hipp, ed., *Dictionary of Literary Biography Yearbook, 1994*, 236–49. Detroit: Gale, 1995.

————. *The Vanderbilt Tradition: Essays in Honor of Thomas Daniel Young*. Baton Rouge: Louisiana State Univ. Press, 1991.

Witherspoon, William. "As I Remembered It." In Henry, ed. *As They Saw Forrest*, 66–136.

Wolfe, Thomas. *The Web and the Rock*. New York: Harper, 1939.

Wolseley, Garnet. "General Viscount Wolseley on Forrest." In Henry, ed., *As They Saw Forrest*, 17–53.

Wood, Sally, ed. *The Southern Mandarins: Letters of Caroline Gordon to Sally Wood, 1924–1937*. Baton Rouge: Louisiana State Univ. Press, 1984.

Wortman, Marc. "Shattering the Urn." *Yale Alumni Magazine* December 1990: 32, 34–35, 38–39.

Yale Weekly Bulletin and Calendar. "Gift to support graduate fellowships in humanities." January 18–25, 1993: 1–2.

Young, Stark. *So Red the Rose*. New York: Scribner's, 1934.

Young, Thomas Daniel. *Gentleman in a Dustcoat: A Biography of John Crowe Ransom*. Baton Rouge: Louisiana State Univ. Press, 1976.

————. *Waking Their Neighbors Up: The Nashville Agrarians Rediscovered*. Athens: Univ. of Georgia Press, 1982.

Young, Thomas Daniel, and Elizabeth Sarcone, eds. *The Lytle-Tate Letters: The Correspondence of Andrew Lytle and Allen Tate*. Jackson: Univ. Press of Mississippi, 1987.

INDEX